CONVEYANCING

CONVEYANCING

FOURTH EDITION

By

GEORGE L. GRETTON, W.S.
Lord President Reid Professor of Law,
University of Edinburgh

and

KENNETH G.C. REID, W.S.
Professor of Scots Law, University of Edinburgh

W. GREEN  THOMSON REUTERS

Published in 2011
3rd edition published 2004

Published in 2011 by W. Green, 21 Alva Street,
Edinburgh EH2 4PS
Part of Thomson Reuters (Professional) UK Limited
(Registered in England & Wales, Company No 1679046. Registered
Office and address for service: Aldgate House, 33 Aldgate High Street,
London EC3N 1DL)

Typeset by LBJ Typesetting Ltd of Kingsclere
Printed in Great Britain by TJ International Ltd, Padstow, Cornwall

No natural forests were destroyed to make this product; only
farmed timber was used and replanted.

A CIP catalogue record for this title is available from the British Library

ISBN 978-0-414-01761-0

Thomson Reuters and the Thomson Reuters Logo
are trademarks of Thomson Reuters.

For AAG and GCR

FOREWORD

This book seeks to be of use both to the practitioner and to the student. Much of the material which will be of use to the latter will, of course, be familiar to the former. The focus is on residential conveyancing, and other topics, such as leases, are not covered. As this is a text on conveyancing, there is little coverage of property law as such. However, we see property law and conveyancing as being two sides of the same coin, and we hope, and believe, that that outlook informs the book.

The last edition was prepared in 2004, just as land law and conveyancing were about to change for ever with the abolition of the feudal system, and major new legislation on title conditions and the law of the tenement. Seven years' later these reforms have bedded in, and it has become clearer which aspects are of continuing importance and which of minor or transitional interest. One response, in this book, is the addition of three new chapters—on the default rules which govern tenements and other communities (Ch.14); on the methods by which those default rules can be altered in the titles, either by community burdens or through the Development Management Scheme, which became available in 2009 (Ch.15); and on the way in which the Lands Tribunal has approached its reformulated powers for the variation and discharge of title conditions (Ch.16).

Much else has changed since the last edition in 2004. A dozen or more statutes bearing, directly or indirectly, on conveyancing, have been enacted by the Scottish Parliament. There have been more than 500 cases, many routine but some ground-breaking or startling, covering topics such as descriptions of common areas, conclusion of missives by fax or email, the use of A-to-A dispositions for prescription, and the enforcement of standard securities. And there have been important changes in practice: against the background of the worst downturn in the housing market that anyone can remember, the profession has engaged with home reports, with standard-form "regional" missives, and with automated registration of title to land ("ARTL"). There is no reason to suppose that the pace of change will slacken. As we lay down our pens, there are rumours that a Land Registration Bill, based on the work of the Scottish Law Commission, will be in Parliament in the autumn. If that turns out to be correct, it will not be long before our pens are taken up once more.

We give our thanks to those who have contributed, directly or indirectly, to this edition, and in particular to Alan Barr, for reading Ch.18, and to Graeme Reid, for commenting on Ch.2 and for patiently answering an unending stream of questions on current practice.

We have attempted to state the law as at May 31, 2011. Website URLs are correct as at the same date.

CONTENTS

ABBREVIATIONS

ARTL	Automated registration of title to land
Gordon (2nd edn)	William M. Gordon, *Scottish Land Law*, 2nd edn (1999)
Gordon and Wortley (3rd edn)	William M. Gordon and Scott Wortley, *Scottish Land Law*, 3rd edn (2009), Vol.1
Halliday	J.M. Halliday, *Conveyancing Law and Practice*, 2nd edn (edited by Iain J.S. Talman, two volumes, 1996 and 1997)
Reid, *Property*	Kenneth G.C. Reid, *The Law of Property in Scotland* (1996), with contributions by George L. Gretton, A.G.M. Duncan, William M. Gordon, and Alan J. Gamble (being a revised reprint of the first part of Vol.18 of *The Laws of Scotland: Stair Memorial Encyclopaedia*)
Reid and Gretton, *Conveyancing*	An annual series of update volumes by the present authors, beginning in 1999, and differentiated by year, e.g. Reid and Gretton, *Conveyancing 2009*.
CML	Council of Mortgage Lenders
CMS	Community Management Scheme
DMS	Development Management Scheme
FSA	Financial Services Authority
GRS	General Register of Sasines
HMRC	HM Revenue & Customs
NSEA	Non-solicitor estate agent
PEC	Property enquiry certificate
Personal Register	The Register of Inhibitions and Adjudications
Property Registers	The Land Register and the General Register of Sasines
ROTB	Ian Davis and Alistair Rennie (eds), *Registration of Title Practice Book*, 2nd edn (2000); available both in print and at *http://www.ros.gov.uk*
SDLT	Stamp duty land tax
SEA	Solicitor estate agent
TMS	Tenement Management Scheme

TABLE OF CASES

TABLE OF STATUTES

TABLE OF STATUTORY INSTRUMENTS

TABLE OF EUROPEAN LEGISLATION

CHAPTER 1

ABOUT CONVEYANCING

Who can do conveyancing?

Whereas estate agency work can be done by anyone,[1] conveyancing is restricted to solicitors and advocates,[2] and to licensed conveyancers.[3] In practice advocates do not do conveyancing, and the number of licensed conveyancers is tiny.[4] More precisely, the rule is that only such persons may do conveyancing for reward, except that an unqualified person can do conveyancing within a law firm or "legal service provider" licensed under the Legal Services (Scotland) Act 2010.[5] Anyone can do conveyancing on an unpaid basis, whether for themselves or for others. So do-it-yourself conveyancing is possible, though rare. The restriction is confined to conveyancing in the narrow sense and does not extend to conclusion of missives.[6]

The Law Society of Scotland recommends caution when an offer is received from a unqualified person.[7] In any event it is necessary to check the identity of the agents for the other party.[8]

For whom can conveyancing be done?

The question of capacity belongs to the law of persons. A full treatment would therefore be out of place here: a few words must suffice. First, natural persons.

1-01

1-02

---

[1] Subject to the Estate Agents Act 1979. This Act applies only to non-solicitor estate agents. It has a "negative licensing" system whereby persons can be banned by the Office of Fair Trading. As now amended by the Consumers, Estate Agents and Redress Act 2007, the Act requires estate agents to belong to a redress scheme and to keep proper records. See the Estate Agents (Redress Scheme) Order 2008 (SI 2008/1712). A helpful discussion can be found in the OFT's *Home Buying and Selling: A Market Study* (2010), esp. paras 5.18 et seq. For marketing of property, see below, para.1–22.

[2] Solicitors (Scotland) Act 1980 s.32. See *Council of the Law Society of Scotland v Express Mortgages (Scotland) Ltd*, 1994 G.W.D. 14-906.

[3] Law Reform (Miscellaneous Provisions) (Scotland) Act 1990 s.17.

[4] The licensed conveyancers' professional body, the Scottish Conveyancing and Executry Services Board, was abolished by the Public Appointments and Public Bodies etc. (Scotland) Act 2003, and its functions were transferred to the Law Society of Scotland.

[5] Such providers of "Tesco-law" need not be fully owned by solicitors although, by s.47(2), they must include at least one solicitor with an unrestricted practising certificate. At the time of writing the relevant provisions were not fully in force. A legal service provider is not subject to the prohibition on carrying on conveyancing for reward: see Solicitors (Scotland) Act 1980 s.32(2)(ea).

[6] Solicitors (Scotland) Act 1980 s.32(3)(b).

[7] (2004) 49 J.L.S.S. January/41.

[8] The CML *Lenders' Handbook for Scotland*, para.3.2 says that "if you are not familiar with the seller's solicitors or independent qualified conveyancers, you must verify that they appear in a legal directory or they are currently on record with the Law Society of Scotland . . . as practising at the address shown on their note paper". Para.3.3 adds: "If the seller does not have legal representation you should check part 2 to see whether or not we need to be notified so that a decision can be made as to whether or not we are prepared to proceed". Whilst this is explicitly required only when acting for a CML lender, it is probably an implied duty in every case.

Those under 16 have capacity to own land, but juridical acts, such as entering into missives and signing dispositions, must be done on their behalf by their parents or guardians.[9] Where a child acquires land this may be through a legacy. Such a legacy may necessitate the involvement of the Accountant of Court.[10] Those aged 16 or above have full capacity, but juridical acts done by those aged 16 and 17 may be voidable if they are "prejudicial".[11] Someone dealing with such a person may therefore wish to insure against a subsequent challenge.

If an adult's capacity is impaired, for instance by senility, it may be that he or she can no longer act, in which case juridical acts, if they are to be valid, must be done by someone else on the adult's behalf. This can happen in more than one way.[12] One possibility is a continuing power of attorney,[13] whuch must be registered with the Public Guardian,[14] and should also be registered in the Books of Council and Session. Powers of attorney must be scrutinised carefully since they are traditionally construed in a restrictive way.[15] The holder of the power is under a fiduciary duty to act in the best interests of the principal. That will normally exclude, for instance, any power to donate. Another possibility is an intervention order or a guardianship order by the court.[16] This must be registered in the Land Register or the General Register of Sasines ("GRS").[17] Whether there exists power to buy or sell, or otherwise deal with heritable property, depends on the terms of the order and whether consent has been given by the Public Guardian.

The capacity of juristic persons, such as companies, depends on the terms of the legislation under which they are established. Juridical acts outwith their powers (*ultra vires*) are always unlawful and may, depending on the type of juristic person, be voidable or even void. The position of partnerships, limited liability partnerships and—the common type of juristic person in practice— companies is considered elsewhere.[18] There exist certain entities, notably trusts and trade unions, which are not juristic persons but which are subject to special rules and which function very nearly as juristic persons.[19] Trustees have power to buy or sell heritable property, and to grant leases and standard securities, unless this is contrary to the terms or purposes of the trust.[20] Finally, there exists a multitude of clubs, associations and businesses whose legal status may be obscure and which must be clarified at the outset.[21]

---

[9] Age of Legal Capacity (Scotland) Act 1991. See generally A.B. Wilkinson and Kenneth Norrie, *Law Relating to Parent and Child*, 2nd edn (1999); J.M. Thomson, *Family Law in Scotland*, 6th edn (2011).

[10] Children (Scotland) Act 1995 s.9, though the meaning is obscure: see Gretton, (1997) 42 J.L.S.S. 308.

[11] Age of Legal Capacity (Scotland) Act 1991 s.3.

[12] See generally Adrian D. Ward, *Adult Incapacity* (2003).

[13] An ordinary power of attorney is of no use for this purpose since (unless executed before April 2, 2001) it will lapse when the principal becomes *incapax*. For powers of attorney, see below, para.17–14.

[14] Adults with Incapacity (Scotland) Act 2000 s.19.

[15] Halliday, para.13–03.

[16] The guardian replaced the *curator bonis* of the common law.

[17] Adults with Incapacity (Scotland) Act 2000 ss.19, 56 and 61.

[18] See below, Chs 27 and 28.

[19] For trusts see below, Ch.25.

[20] Trusts (Scotland) Act 1921 s.4(1).

[21] For unincorporated associations, see Scottish Law Commission, Report on *Unincorporated Associations* (Scot. Law Com. No.217, 2009). For a case where the body ("the Members of the 227

Taking instructions

Solicitors are often called law agents. The term is useful because it focuses the 1–03 fact that the solicitor is an agent and the client is the principal. Obvious though this is, it can too easily be overlooked in practice. Solicitors must ensure that they have been duly appointed by the principal. If someone telephones to say that her aged mother wants to sell her house, that is not enough: instructions must be obtained from the aged mother. The matter is put succinctly in the Standards of Conduct laid down by the Law Society of Scotland: "Solicitors are agents of their clients, and must have the authority of their clients for their actings".[22] The person who has telephoned may or may not be a client of the firm but for this sale she is not the client. Again, if a client says that he and his wife wish to buy or sell a house, instructions must also be obtained from the wife.[23] If he says he wants to sell his house and says that "I just put it in my wife's name for tax purposes" that makes no difference. She owns the house. After all, had ownership not been transferred to her the very purpose of the transfer would have failed. Instructions to sell must, therefore, come from her. Families often act as a single entity, and treating the members as separate clients may seem artificial and awkward. But it has to be done.[24] Separate instructions must be obtained from each member of the family, and any important letters should be sent under separate cover to each member.[25] If there is a family company, that is an additional party.[26] Where a company is a client, the instructions must come from someone with authority to give them on behalf of the company.

A "terms of engagement" letter must be sent at the outset.[27] Rule 3 of the Solicitors (Scotland) (Client Communication) Practice Rules 2005 provides that "a solicitor shall . . . at the earliest practical opportunity upon receiving instructions to undertake any work on behalf of a client, provide the following information to the client in writing . . .". The required information includes

---

Syndicate") turned out not to exist, see *Halifax Life Ltd v DLA Piper Scotland LLP* [2009] CSOH 74; 2009 G.W.D. 19-306.

[22] Solicitors (Scotland) (Standards of Conduct) Practice Rules 2008 r.4(1).

[23] See generally *Hopkinson v Williams*, 1993 S.L.T. 907; *MacDougall v Akram*, 1993 G.W.D. 33-2142; *Safdar v Devlin*, 1994 G.W.D. 17-1085; *Glasper v Rodger*, 1996 S.L.T. 44; *Merrick Homes Ltd v Duff*, 1996 S.C. 497; *Brady v Neilsons*, 1999 G.W.D. 4-209. Robert Rennie, *Solicitors' Negligence* (1997), para.6.15 suggests that each spouse can be presumed to be the agent of the other for conveyancing purposes, but we would respectfully dissent. See further *Suleman v Shahsavari* [1989] 2 All E.R. 460; *Penn v Bristol & West Building Society* [1997] 1 W.L.R. 1356.

[24] In *Broadway v Clydesdale Bank*, 2000 G.W.D. 19-763 and 2001 G.W.D. 14-552 the law firm addressed its letters to "the Broadway Family" and opened with the words "Dear All". This sort of thing can be sensible, but it also has its dangers. For an account of this case see Reid and Gretton, *Conveyancing 2000*, p.87 and Reid and Gretton, *Conveyancing 2001*, p.92. See also *Brady v Neilsons*, 1999 G.W.D. 4-209.

[25] It also must be borne in mind that family members may have interests that conflict, and in that case the same solicitor must decline to act for one or more: see below, para.1–10.

[26] See for example *Thomson v Royal Bank of Scotland Plc*, 2003 S.C.L.R. 964, where a man ran a company. He and his wife granted security for its debts. One and the same solicitor acted both for the lender and for the company. Whether he was also acting for either or both the spouses was unclear. It should not have been unclear.

[27] The Law Society's Professional Practice Committee has waived the requirement to provide such a letter to mortgage lenders in domestic conveyancing transactions where solicitors are acting for both lender and borrower. See (2005) 50 J.L.S.S. Nov./38.

details of the work involved and the person or persons by whom it will mainly be done, and an estimate of the fee and outlays.[28]

To give proper instructions the clients need to understand what is going on: this is the idea of informed consent. Usually there is no problem. But sometimes there is. A donation, particularly by an elderly client, needs to be handled carefully: does the client truly understand what is proposed and truly wish it? Another problem area is where the client does not speak English well and the solicitors find that the actual communications are coming from another member of the family whose grasp of the language is better. There are dangers of miscommunication or even of fraud. If clients need to sign a deed, and there is doubt as to whether they understand it, it is wise to have someone who understands the language in question to swear an affidavit, deponing that he or she knows both the English and Ruritanian languages, and has explained the meaning of the deed to the client in question. An area that has sometimes caused great difficulty is where a deed is to be signed that may involve the grantor in liability for someone else's debts.[29]

Checking identity

1-04   If the clients are new, the solicitors must satisfy themselves as to their identity.[30] This is a measure of self protection, for obvious reasons, but there is also a professional duty involved: other law firms are entitled to assume that when a solicitor claims to represent a person, the solicitor knows who that person is. Since the arrival of legislation on money laundering (see below), verification of identity has been taken more seriously. Nowadays it is normal for a new client to be asked to produce a passport, and for a photocopy of this to be put in the file. Obviously, the stated date of birth should be reasonably consistent with the client's appearance.

If the client is a company, or other body corporate, it is important to verify that it is duly incorporated. If it is not a Scottish company this may involve obtaining a formal letter from a lawyer in the place where the company is incorporated confirming due incorporation.[31] The fact that the person who claims to speak on behalf of the company is authorised to do so should be checked. A company search will give a list of current directors. In some cases it is wise to obtain a copy of the minutes of the board meeting authorising the transaction to proceed.[32] There may also be questions as to whether the company is acting within its corporate powers, especially for entities other than UK companies.

A solicitor who enters into missives on behalf of a non-existent principal is personally liable to the counterparty.[33]

---

[28] For the view that the letter should say whether ARTL is to be used and if not why not, see Robert Rennie and Stewart Brymer, *Conveyancing in the Electronic Age* (2008), para.9–02. In residential conveyancing it may be prudent to state that environmental matters do not form part of the solicitor's remit: see below, para.4–39.

[29] See below, para.1–11.

[30] For the dangers of identity theft, see (2011) 56 J.L.S.S. March/42.

[31] For a style see below, para.28–12.

[32] Arguably this should be done in all cases, but in practice it is done only selectively.

[33] See also below, para.3–03. In *City of Glasgow Council v Peart*, 1999 Hous. L.R. 117 missives were purportedly concluded on behalf of someone who was dead. But compare *Frank Houlgate Investment Co Ltd v Biggart Baillie LLP* [2009] CSOH 165; 2010 S.L.T. 527 in which solicitors were held not to be liable where they acted for a person who had the same name as the person who was owner of the property but was not that person.

The secured lender as client

If, as is often the case, solicitors are also acting for a secured lender, that lender 1–05
is also a client. It is easy, psychologically, to overlook this, because the lender
will be merely a one-off client who comes into the picture as an adjunct to the
"real" client. But law firms have sometimes come to grief because they have
forgotten that, as a matter of law, the lender is as much a client as the "real"
client. Solicitors must always be mindful of lenders' standard-form instructions and in particular of the detailed requirements contained in Pt 1 of the
Lenders Handbook for Scotland issued by the Council of Mortgage Lenders.

Some consequences of the agency relationship

Solicitors are agents and so should do what the clients tell them, provided that 1–06
this is legal, ethical and practicable. Decisions are for the clients to make. If a
problem arises in the course of a transaction, it is for the clients to decide what
to do. For instance, if on examining the title the purchasing solicitors find that
there is a defect, it is for the clients to decide whether to refuse to settle,[34] not
for their solicitors, though the latter's advice is obviously important. Of course,
the clients do not want to be bothered by technical details. Deciding what
needs to be referred to the clients and what does not can be difficult, and solicitors have often got into trouble by deciding something themselves which
should have been referred. If in doubt, it is necessary to refer to the clients. The
clients must always be kept informed, for instance by copying the missives to
them, so that if anything worries them they can make their views known.

Clients have an understandable expectation that their solicitors will, like a
fairy godmother, bring about a happy ending, and the higher the fee being
charged the stronger that expectation is likely to be. But solicitors cannot guarantee happy endings. If the clients are told what is happening, when it is
happening, they will be aware of any emerging difficulties, and if problems
become serious the task of explaining those problems is then less difficult. This
is a matter of prudence from the standpoint of the solicitors. All legal practice
has to be defensive legal practice. Every client is a potential negligence
claimant. But it is not only prudence for the benefit of the solicitors. It is something that clients are reasonably entitled to. Physicians no longer administer
unnamed medicines, nor do they conceal the diagnosis when the malady is
serious. Nor should solicitors do the equivalent.

Finally, just as solicitors are law *agents*, so also they are *law* agents. What
they have is a professional knowledge of the laws of their country. They are
not plumbers, surveyors, town planners, electricians, accountants, civil engi-
neers or architects.[35] They should not give the impression that they have
any expertise in such fields.

Law Society of Scotland

The Law Society of Scotland has power to promulgate rules that are legally 1–07
binding on solicitors. The Society also issues guidelines, which do not have
legal force but which represent good professional practice, and which may be

---

[34] The lender, if there is one, will also have a right of veto.

[35] cf. *Wylie v Jefrey Aitken*, 2002 G.W.D. 40-1360 on which see Reid and Gretton, *Conveyancing
2002*, p.70. In this case a client sued a law firm for allegedly having given wrong advice as to
whether a drainage system was sufficient.

regarded by a court as relevant in determining whether conduct was or was not reasonable. These rules and guidelines are available in Division F of the Parliament House Book.[36] They vary greatly in length and in importance. But none of them can be ignored. At the time of preparing this edition, rules of particular importance to conveyancers included:

- The Solicitors (Scotland) Practice Rules 1986[37];
- The Solicitors (Scotland) Accounts, Accounts Certificate, Professional Practice and Guarantee Fund Rules 2001[38];
- The Solicitors (Scotland) Professional Indemnity Insurance Rules 2005;
- The Solicitors (Scotland) (Client Communication) Practice Rules 2005.

It is expected that all practice rules, including those listed above, will be combined and rationalised in a single set of consolidated rules, which is likely to be in operation by the end of 2011.

Guidelines of importance to conveyancers include:

- Guidelines on Acting for Separated Spouses/Civil Partners and Cohabiting Couples 2006;
- Guidelines on Avoidance of Delay in Concluding Missives 1998;
- Guidelines on Common Repairs 1999;
- Guidelines on Deeds of Conditions in Housing Estates 1999;
- Guidance Notes on Coal Mining Reports 2006;
- Guidelines on Electronic Transfer of Funds 1999;
- Guidelines on Exhibition of Title Deeds 1996;
- Guidelines on Faxed and Email Documents 1998;
- Guidelines on Fixed Price Offers 1998;
- Gazumping, Gazundering and Closing Dates 2005;
- Guidelines on Letters of Obligation in Land Registration Cases 1997;
- Guidelines on Postal Settlements 2001;
- Guidelines on Property Schedules and Mortgage Advice Service 2006;
- Guidelines on Retention of Funds 1998;
- Guidelines on Settlement Cheques Sent to be Held as Undelivered 1998;
- Guildelines on Settlement by Cheque, Loan Redemption and Remit of the Free Proceeds of Sale 2008;
- Guidelines on Conflict of Interest 2009;
- Guidelines on Conflict of Interest between Borrower and Spouse 1998;
- Guidelines on Conflict of Interest in Commercial Security Transactions 1994;
- Guidelines on Conflict of Interest and Ranking Agreements 1998;
- Guide to the Solicitors (Scotland) Accounts, Accounts Certificate, Professional Practice and Guarantee Fund Rules 2001 and Solicitors (Scotland) Accounts etc. (Amendment) Rules 2004.

---

[36] Also published separately as *Greens Solicitors Professional Handbook*. The Law Society's website, *http://www.lawscot.org.uk/*, is another source but is incomplete. Another source is Janice H. Webster, *Professional Ethics and Practice for Scottish Solicitors*, 4th edn (2004).

[37] Commonly known as the Conflict of Interest Rules.

[38] Commonly known as the Accounts Rules.

Money laundering[39]

Criminals, like other people, need to move funds, and a fashionable tool for 1–08
fighting crime is to make it harder for them to do so, and also to confiscate the
profits made from their crimes. The legislation is European[40] and in the United
Kingdom is implemented by the Money Laundering Regulations 2007.[41] These
Regulations require "independent legal professionals" (i.e. solicitors) who
engage in conveyancing and estate agency work[42] to set up certain procedures
for verifying the identity of clients, for careful record keeping, and so forth.
Verifying identity must be done *before* a business relationship is established
with a client or work carried out and requires the use of "documents, data or
information obtained from a reliable and independent source".[43] In addition,
s.330 of the (incomprehensible) Proceeds of Crime Act 2002 requires solicitors to tell the Serious Organised Crime Agency[44] if they have reason to suspect
the laundering of money from criminal sources.[45] This will apply mainly to the
solicitors acting for buyers, if they have suspicions about where the purchase
price has come from, but if the sellers' solicitors have the same suspicions then
they come under the same duties. Moreover the property being sold might
itself represent the proceeds of crime. All this is perhaps overkill, but criminals
do use law firms for their wicked purposes.

There are many telltale signs which will raise suspicions in the mind of the
experienced conveyancer. Examples include payment in cash, payment from a
third party, vague or improbable statements as to source of funds, last-minute
changes to the source of funds, and obscurity as to the client's permanent
address.

Other fraud

As well as keeping an eye out for money laundering, the solicitor must beware 1–09
of other kinds of fraud. Being a solicitor does not confer immunity from
naivety.[46] The solicitor must have a suspicious mind.[47] Clients may be misrep-
resenting their financial circumstances to the lenders. Or they may claim that
they will be living in the property but in fact intend to let it out. That would
contravene the terms of the security[48] and is likely also to be a tax fraud, in that

---

[39] See further Alastair N. Brown, *Money Laundering* (2009); Robin Booth et al., *Money
Laundering Law and Regulation: A Practical Guide* (2011).

[40] Directive 2005/60, the Third Money Laundering Directive.

[41] Money Laundering Regulations 2007 (SI 2007/2157). Further provision is made by the
Solicitors (Scotland) Accounts, Accounts Certificate, Professional Practice and Guarantee Fund
Rules 2001.

[42] Drafted in that profoundly unionist spirit which has been so manifest in UK legislation ever
since 1707, reg.3(9) refers to "participating in . . . real property transactions".

[43] Money Laundering Regulations 2007 regs 5(a) and 9(2). For this purpose it is permissible to
rely on certain professionals including those in other jurisdictions (reg.17).

[44] *http://www.soca.gov.uk/*.

[45] There are some exceptions. See further Alastair N. Brown, *Money Laundering* (2009), Ch.4.
This is a case where breach of client confidentiality is permitted: see Law Society of Scotland,
Guidance Notes on Confidentiality 2009, para.7.

[46] Even worse than naivety is active participation. In *Di Ciacca v Normand*, 1995 S.L.T. 482,
£18,000 of the price of land was paid in cash, and the price stated in the deed was reduced by that
amount, to evade tax. A solicitor was prosecuted and convicted for his involvement.

[47] For 10 sets of circumstances where a solicitor should be wary, see Scott, (2009) 54 J.L.S.S.
Jan./58.

[48] Conveyancing and Feudal Reform (Scotland) Act 1970 Sch.3 s.c.6.

the clients may intend to claim capital gains tax relief on the footing that the property will be their main residence. Again, there are ingenious ways for buyer and seller to collude for fraudulent purposes. For example, Adam owns a property worth £250,000. Beatrice agrees with him that she will buy it at a notional price of £300,000. Missives are concluded at that price. Beatrice persuades a bank that the property is worth £300,000 and on that basis borrows £275,000. The transaction settles at £300,000, with Beatrice paying £25,000 of her own money. The settlement is done between the two law firms.[49] Immediately thereafter Adam repays Beatrice £40,000 (keeping £10,000 for himself as his share of the scam) and Beatrice promptly vanishes into thin air. Her profit is £15,000. The bank loses £25,000, being the difference between what the property is worth and the amount of the loan.[50] There are many variants on this basic idea.

Conflict of interest[51]

1–10 Conflict of interest primarily means the situation which arises when two clients of the same law firm have interests opposed to each other.[52] In general, solicitors should avoid that situation, and, if it occurs, should cease to act for one of the clients. The reason is that, while they are bound to advance the interests of clients, here they cannot advance the interests of one without detriment to the interests of the other. That is common law. More importantly, it is common sense. But the scope of the common law principle is rather vague. For instance, it is obvious that the same firm should not act for both pursuer and defender, but it is not so obvious that the same firm should not act for both buyer and seller: in some cases the conflict is more pronounced than in others.[53] Because of this uncertainty, the principle has been focused and developed by rules and guidelines from the Law Society. The rules are the Solicitors (Scotland) Practice Rules 1986 (commonly called the Conflict of Interest Rules), and they should be read in conjunction with the *Guidelines on Conflict of Interest in Commercial Security Transactions 1994* and the *Guidelines on Conflict of Interest 2009*.[54]

A firm must not act for both seller and buyer, or for both lender and borrower, or for both tenant and landlord. But there are certain exceptions.[55] One of the most important is that a solicitor can act for both lender and borrower if the loan is a secured one whose terms have been agreed before the solicitor has been instructed by the lender. This exception covers most home loans.[56]

---

[49] The fraud is easier if the settlement can be done direct between buyer and seller. It is always a matter for inquiry if that happens.

[50] And will consider suing the law firm.

[51] See generally Janice H. Webster, *Professional Ethics and Practice for Scottish Solicitors*, 4th edn (2004).

[52] A secondary meaning is where the interests of the law firm become opposed to those of the client, for instance where the client accuses the firm of negligence. In this case also it is in general necessary for the law firm to advise the client to seek separate representation. But judging when that time has finally arrived can be difficult, and experience is required.

[53] Another difficult area in the common law is the question of clients waiving their rights to object to the conflict.

[54] For conflict of interest in security transactions see also (2003) 48 J.L.S.S. Oct./45 for a statement by the Professional Practice Committee. For discussion see D. J. Cusine and Robert Rennie, *Standard Securities*, 2nd edn (2002), Ch.2. See also (2003) 48 J.L.S.S. March/9.

[55] Solicitors (Scotland) Practice Rules 1986 r.5(1).

[56] But note an important exception to the exception: a law firm cannot act for a lender if the borrower is a partner, spouse of a partner, etc. See the Solicitors (Scotland) Accounts, Accounts Certificate, Professional Practice and Guarantee Fund Rules 2001 r.22.

Another exception is where the parties are related by blood, adoption, marriage or civil partnership. A third is where both parties are established clients. These rather wide exceptions have been criticised,[57] but in any event are confined to cases where "no dispute arises or might reasonably be expected to arise". Examples of disputes include title problems, unauthorised alterations and problems with the purchaser's funding.[58] In some of the exceptions (but not the mortgage one) the solicitor must send to the clients a "rule 5(2) letter"[59] setting forth the position and telling them that if a dispute does arise then separate legal representation will be necessary. This letter must be sent at the outset, not merely when the dispute arises.

Where co-owners sell there is not normally a problem. But they may be at loggerheads: the classic case is where a couple are splitting up in bitterness and the matrimonial home is to be sold. They may agree on the sale but on little else.[60] For instance they may disagree on whether the proceeds should be divided equally and they may disagree as to whether any unsecured debts should be paid from the proceeds.[61] Such cases are death traps for the law firms involved, and the advice of the Law Society is that a different firm should be instructed for the sale unless the parties have entered into a written agreement with each other as to how the proceeds are to be divided.[62]

Finally, disgruntled clients sometimes allege conflict of interest, and on that basis claim damages. But even if conflict does exist, that does not of itself give rise to any claim by a client for compensation unless the conflict caused a loss.

Cautionary wives

It sometimes happens that solicitors must advise someone who is thinking of signing a deed that may involve her in liability for someone else's debts. We say "her" because this area, though ostensibly gender neutral, is in substance highly gendered. The cases, which are numerous,[63] all concern a wife incurring liability for the debts of her husband's business.[64] This can happen in more than one way. One variant is the nature of the husband's business: (a) he may be a sole trader; (b) he may be a partner in a firm with unlimited liability; (c) he may control a company (e.g. sole director and main shareholder) and the debts are in fact those of the company. Another variant is the deed to be signed by the wife: (d) it may be a straightforward cautionary obligation, without any standard security; (e) there may be both a cautionary obligation and a standard security securing that obligation granted over property of which she is the sole

1–11

---

[57] Ferguson, (2011) 79 *Scottish Law Gazette* 7.

[58] Law Society of Scotland, *Guidance Notes on Conflict of Interest 2009.* See the English case of *Hilton v Barker Booth & Eastwood* [2005] UKHL 8; [2005] 1 W.L.R. 567 where solicitors acting for both buyer and seller failed to disclose to the seller that the buyer had a criminal record for fraud.

[59] The reference is to r.5(2) of the Solicitors (Scotland) Practice Rules 1986.

[60] One other thing they are likely to concur in is the correct evaluation of the other's character and reliability.

[61] See below, para.10–16.

[62] Law Society of Scotland, *Guidelines on Acting for Separated Spouses/Civil Partners and Cohabiting Couples 2006*, para.2.

[63] See generally Eden, (2003) 7 Edin. L.R. 107; and (2004) 8 Edin. L.R. 276. In recent years the cases have rather dried up.

[64] But in principle the issues are general ones, and might involve, for example, parent and child, or two companies in the same group, or a business person and the company through which he or she does business.

owner or co-owner; (f) there may be no cautionary obligation at all, but a standard security granted directly for her husband's business debts[65]; (g) it may be a standard security for an ordinary home loan, granted jointly by herself and her husband, without any idea that the deed might relate to any other debts, but which in fact is so worded that other debts may be covered by it. In all these cases except the last there is a potential conflict of interest between husband and wife,[66] and the same solicitors should not act for both.[67]

There is a danger that if, later, things go wrong and the wife suffers loss she will say that she was not properly advised. The unanswerable logic is that had she been properly advised she never would have signed. This line of argument may in the first instance be used as a shield against the bank,[68] but if that fails it may be used as a sword against the solicitors who advised her—or failed to advise her properly. The advising solicitor must ensure that the wife fully understands the meaning and effect of the document, and should keep evidence of this. It is a good idea to send a letter explaining it and asking her to acknowledge that she has read and understood the letter. Naturally solicitors always have a duty to be reasonably satisfied that the client's consent is genuine and informed. But in some cases special care is advisable. Law firms may be reluctant to advise the cautionary wife, especially because of English case law imposing on solicitors impossibly onerous duties in such cases.[69]

Where the standard security is for an ordinary home loan,[70] and no business borrowing appears to be in contemplation, there is probably no conflict of interest as between husband and wife. But the solicitor must read the bank's standard style carefully, and if there is any possibility that the deed might cover future debts due by just one of the parties, that must be explained to the clients. It will be wise to record that advice in an outgoing letter.[71]

Confidentiality

1–12   A client's affairs are confidential: the solicitor must not divulge them except with the client's permission. This obligation of confidentiality does not, however, apply to information which is in any case in the public domain, for instance an entry in a public register. Solicitors are also not bound by

---

[65] In this case she has no personal liability. Suppose that the debts were £300,000 and the property worth £100,000. She could lose the property but could not be liable for the balance due to the bank.

[66] There may in fact be three (or even more) parties: husband, husband's company, and wife.

[67] So advised by the Law Society of Scotland's Professional Practice Committee and the Conveyancing Committee in (2003) 48 J.L.S.S. Oct./46.

[68] The leading case is *Smith v Bank of Scotland*, 1997 S.C. 111. Consent improperly obtained by the husband can be pled in some cases by the wife against the bank. See further below, para.22–04.

[69] The high-water mark was the decision of the Court of Appeal in *Royal Bank of Scotland Plc v Etridge (No.2)* [1998] 4 All E.R. 705, on which see Gretton, 1999 S.L.T. (News) 53. When the case went to the House of Lords a slightly more moderate line was taken: [2002] 2 A.C. 773. The Scottish courts have declined to follow this case (see in particular *Royal Bank of Scotland Plc v Wilson*, 2004 S.C. 153, discussed in Reid and Gretton, *Conveyancing 2003*, pp.73–82), but the reported cases have not so far involved actions by the cautionary wife (after her husband's business has failed) against the solicitors who advised her, and so the law remains somewhat unclear. Reluctance to advise the cautionary wife is fully understandable. See further D.J. Cusine and Robert Rennie, *Standard Securities,* 2nd edn (2002), paras 2.03 and 2.04. The latter paragraph is headed "Impossible burden for solicitors".

[70] Case (g) above.

[71] For a style, see (2003) 48 J.L.S.S. Oct./38.

confidentiality where they have reason to believe that the client plans to commit a crime. In such a case they may inform the appropriate authority,[72] and indeed are probably under a professional obligation to do so if the intention seems serious and the proposed crime is not of a minor nature.

Where possible past crime is involved, the Law Society has issued the following advice:

> "If you are asked to give a statement to the Police or the Procurator Fiscal in relation to a matter where the information sought is not already in the public domain (for instance having been disclosed in open court, or published in a public register) but is actually confidential, the Professional Practice Committee view is that you should offer to be precognosced on oath before the sheriff. If you answer a question on the direction of the court you would not be subject to a complaint of breach of confidentiality."[73]

The Accounts Rules

The current Account Rules, in place since 2001,[74] were under review at the time of writing and seemed likely to be replaced in the course of 2011. Accounts Rules have a fearsome reputation, but the basics are not especially complex. Indeed, to a large extent they are simple common sense. A law firm must segregate moneys which it holds for clients from its own funds.[75] At any one time a law firm will hold some money on behalf of clients.[76] Usually such moneys are held only for a short time, perhaps only a few days, but at any given moment the total of such moneys may be substantial in amount. One example would be money received from the sale of property. Another would be money received from a client with which to settle a purchase, which has not yet taken place. A third example would be money ingathered in the course of executry administration. The law firm must hold a client account with a recognised bank, into which such moneys are paid, and from which they are withdrawn as and when needed. This account is in the name of the firm, but is expressly designated as the client account.[77] A fundamental principle is that the amount held in the client account must never—not for a single day—be less than the total amount held by the firm on behalf of clients.[78] If that principle is honoured, the objective of segregation has been achieved. Breaches of this principle occur

1–13

---

[72] The Procurator Fiscal, the Lord Advocate, the Chief Constable, or the Serious Organised Crime Agency.

[73] Law Society of Scotland, *Guidance Notes on Confidentiality 2009*.

[74] The Solicitors (Scotland) Accounts, Accounts Certificate, Professional Practice and Guarantee Fund Rules 2001. See further Janice H. Webster, *Professional Ethics and Practice for Scottish Solicitors*, 4th edn (2004), para.2.25.

[75] Though the legislation does not expressly say that the client funds are held in trust, that is the view taken by the courts: *Council of the Law Society of Scotland v McKinnie*, 1991 S.C. 355.

[76] This is a major practical difference between advocates and solicitors. It should be mentioned however that a few law firms do not hold such funds to any significant degree, such as firms dealing only in criminal work.

[77] A firm may hold more than one client account, and indeed in theory could hold as many client accounts as it has clients.

[78] Account Rules r.4(1): "Every solicitor shall–(a) ensure that at all times the sum at the credit of the client account, or where there are more such accounts than one, the total of the sums at the credit of those accounts, shall not be less than the total of the clients' money held by the solicitor . . .".

too often. It is a sensible precaution for the firm to keep a float in the client account so that inadvertent errors will (it may be hoped) not cause a breach of the rules.[79]

It should be noted that the principle implies that withdrawals from the client account can be made only where a disbursement is being made on behalf of a client, and out of funds which the client has on deposit with the firm. For example, suppose that a firm issues a fee note and withdraws the amount of the fee from the client account, paying it into the firm's ordinary account. That will be lawful if the client has on deposit with the firm sufficient funds to cover the fee.[80] But otherwise there will have been a breach of the Accounts Rules. (In effect, the firm will have been paying itself the fee out of funds held for *other* clients.)

Another way in which the rules may be breached is if a disbursement is made on behalf of a client out of the client account without the client having first deposited funds to cover that disbursement. If such a disbursement is to be made without such a previous deposit it will have to be made out of the firm's own funds, and the moneys recovered from the client thereafter.

From the external standpoint the moneys held by the firm are held in a bank account, the client account. But internally, the rules also require that the firm keep proper records and accounts. That means that each client has an account with the firm, on which all financial transactions are recorded, including moneys received from the client, from third parties for the client,[81] payments to the client, or to third parties for the client,[82] fees deducted, and so on. The total amount held for clients on all these various internal accounts should, at any moment in time, be not less than the total held on the external client account.

Interest earned on the client account is subject to two rules. If more than £500 is held for a client for more than two months, the client should normally be credited with the interest, but in other cases the firm may keep such interest for itself.[83]

Every firm must have a "designated cash room partner" who is the compliance officer for the purposes of the rules. That partner, together with one other partner, must send to the Law Society, every six months, a certificate that the rules have been complied with. The Law Society has powers to audit the accounts to verify compliance.

The buying client's expectations

1–14 Once upon a time, solicitors were employed to get a good title. That was, and remains, an important task. Today, however, clients expect more. One of the problems of modern practice is that there can be a mismatch of expectations between clients and solicitors. It can be hard to know what clients can reasonably expect of their solicitors, and in any event reasonable expectations change over time.

Clients may well not understand the difference between open missives and concluded missives. The distinction must be explained. Furthermore, clients

---

[79] This goes against the principle of segregation but is permitted by r.5.
[80] But even then it is permissible only if the fee has been rendered to the client. See r.6.
[81] For instance, the client is selling, and money is received from the buyer's solicitors.
[82] For instance, moneys paid to a lender to pay off a loan.
[83] Account Rules r.11(2).

tend to assume that if rights are created by missives then they will be enforceable. That is not always so: the counterparties may have disappeared, for example, or become insolvent.

One problem area concerns the physical condition of the house. It must be explained to purchasers that sellers of heritable property (unlike sellers of moveables) do not normally warrant the condition of the property.[84] In most cases the property is not a new one,[85] and clients need to understand that they are buying something that is second-hand, or indeed twentieth-hand, and must adjust their expectations accordingly. If the house collapses the day after entry, the sellers are unlikely to have contractual liability. They warranted the title, and the purchasers' title to the shattered bricks and splintered beams is indeed good. Buying a second-hand house is like buying anything second-hand. There is always a risk. Even the best surveyor may overlook some defect, such as deeply hidden wood rot. It must be explained that the home report can have shortcomings which sometimes makes it advisable for clients to have their own survey. It should also be explained what clauses will be put in the offer, and their limitations.[86] As a checklist, the following are common physical problems: timber (wet rot, dry rot and woodworm), subsidence, roofing, electrics (wiring and appliances), gas (piping and appliances), central heating, drains, plumbing, and damp (rising, penetrating and condensing).[87]

Another problem area is that, while solicitors acting in a purchase will check the planning situation for the property itself, they will not necessarily do so for adjacent properties.[88] It is true that sellers must disclose, in the (mandatory) property questionnaire,[89] whether they have been notified of a neighbour's planning application, but sellers can be forgetful or even dishonest. The consequences are easy to imagine. Reassured that all is well, the buyer moves in and one month later finds that the charming field next door, over which she has views to the sea and the hills, is being converted into an all-year, open-air, 50-metre high, pop concert venue. The buyer's musical tastes go no later than Brahms, and she has three children under five. Why wasn't she told? Her solicitors didn't tell her because they didn't know, and they didn't know because they didn't ask the Council. Why not, the client asks? Her husband has had a nervous breakdown and her house is unsellable. Here there has been a mismatch of expectations. Clarity at the outset is the aim.

A problem in modern practice is that many houses have been altered without planning permission or building consent from the local authority. The subject is covered in the missives, with a typical clause requiring the seller to deliver all necessary consents for alterations carried out within some period such as 20 years. But as buyers are unlikely to know what alterations were carried out (although the survey and property questionnaire[90] may help), the clause is

---

[84] This is, at least, the conventional view, but it can be challenged: see below, para.4–22.

[85] For new properties see below, Ch.30.

[86] See below, para.4–22.

[87] There is fashion in all things. Once upon a time, what everyone worried about was drains. When the authors did their apprenticeships, no one cared much about drains, and the fashionable worries were damp and subsidence. But damp and subsidence have gone the way of drains. The fashion for some years now has been to worry about unauthorised alterations.

[88] See below, para.4–33.

[89] There is usually a similar warranty in the missives.

[90] Question 6 of the property questionnaire (included as part of the home report) requires sellers to declare any alterations made during their period of ownership.

difficult to police. And if it turns out, later, that the clause was breached, there is the usual problem that suing a seller is unsatisfactory at best and that at worst the seller may be unsueable. Any consents produced should be checked against the works which have actually been done, for it is not safe to suppose that if (a) works have been done, and (b) building consent exists, then (c) the works conform to the consent.

Another point which needs to be explained is that in a typical conveyancing transaction the buyers' solicitors will not visit the property. They are too busy and the fee chargeable does not cover time spent on a site visit, which in most cases would be pointless anyway. But occasionally this can cause problems. The unauthorised new garage, a problem of access rights, a boundary problem, which cause such trouble later, might all have been spotted in time if the buyers' solicitors had visited the property. But most firms will only make a site visit if the clients will pay for it. However, if at any stage it becomes clear that a site visit is advisable, then obviously it must be made. There is always the danger that if a law firm is sued for having missed something that a site visit would have revealed, a court might be unsympathetic to the plea that conveyancing fees do not justify such visits.

Another source of dispute concerns the proposed use of the property. The buyers' solicitors need to check what their clients' plans are. The real burdens may for instance forbid commercial use. If the clients wish to convert the property into a hotel, their solicitors will need to know this before the clients are committed to the purchase. So the clients must be asked. And as soon as the burdens writs have been seen, the clients must be informed of their provisions, as part of the report on title that should be given.[91] Unfortunately this does not always happen, at any stage, let alone before conclusion of missives.[92] Proposed usage also has implications for planning permission and various types of licence. Such issues are, however, more likely to arise in commercial than in residential conveyancing.

However careful one is, the fact is that for many or most clients, lawyers are part of "the law" and it is the job of "the law" to ensure that their transaction proceeds reasonably smoothly, and unreasonably cheaply. For example, the typical purchasing clients regard closed missives as inviolable, so that settlement will take place when they want it even if the seller has died, been sequestrated, gone mad, run off with the barmaid/barman, or been abducted by aliens.[93] The typical client does not understand the distinction between contract and conveyance—between personal rights and real rights. Most clients do not expect there to be risks in conveyancing. The conveyancer knows that such risks exist, and that although steps can be taken to reduce them, they cannot be eliminated. In a survey of solicitors conducted in 2007, the two most common causes of problems for clients were found to be late or incomplete

---

[91] Even such an apparently minor condition as on the keeping of cats can cause major problems: see e.g. (1992) 37 J.L.S.S. 118.

[92] According to the Scottish Consumer Council, *Home Truths: A Report on Research into the Experiences of Recent House Buyers in Scotland* (2000), only 54 per cent of buyers questioned said that they had been given information on the burdens affecting their property; and in the case of tenements only 55 per cent said that the arrangements for common repairs had been explained. Broadly similar findings are contained in a survey carried out for the Scottish Law Commission, and reproduced at the end of the Commission's Report on *Real Burdens* (Scot. Law Com. No.181, 2000).

[93] Clients may also expect the other side to be bound by open missives, though themselves free to repudiate them.

loan instructions and unauthorised alterations.[94] As a matter of fact the attitude of the typical client is not wholly unreasonable.[95] The conveyancer needs to be able to look at matters from the client's standpoint, so as to be able to explain the risks. Happily, there are some clients who will understand.

Getting information from the selling client

When clients decide to sell, various questions need to be asked of them. For example: 1–15

(1) Whether there have been any alterations in the property which would require planning or building consent.
(2) Whether the property has wet or dry rot or woodworm, whether any eradication work has been done for these recently, whether the central heating is in working order, and any other similar matters which are likely to be raised in an offer to purchase.
(3) Whether any statutory repairs notice has been received.
(4) Whether the client has received any "neighbour notification" for any planning applications for nearby property.
(5) Whether the client has received any court writs. The classic example would be an inhibition, which would prevent any sale, but there are other possibilities such as a sequestration or an action by a neighbour about, for instance, a boundary dispute.
(6) What debts are secured over the property, since all secured debts will have to be paid off at sale. Typically there will be a bank or building society mortgage and the client should know roughly what is due. The lender normally sends an annual statement. The exact amount can be found out from the lender in due course. The great danger is that there is also a second security which the clients have granted. They may not reveal this unless asked.
(7) What moveables, if any, are included in the sale.

Many of the answers will be found in the property questionnaire which the client must complete and sign before the property is marketed. Others are relevant to the conclusion of missives, or are simply to alert the solicitors to potential problems.

On the importance of record-keeping

As in all legal business good records should be kept. Partly this is for one's own convenience (memory is fallible) and partly in case someone else in the firm has to take over the transaction. But it also important as a defence against a later claim for negligence. When there is such a claim there is often a difference in the clients' account of events and that of the solicitor. 1–16

> "The solicitor is unlikely to recall after a period of several years what advice he gave to the client on a routine matter. The best that he can do is to describe his usual advice in the particular circumstances or to speculate

---

[94] (2007) 52 J.L.S.S. May/51.
[95] As to what the "system" should ideally deliver to them. What is obviously unreasonable is the desire to get a professional service at bucket-shop prices.

as to what he 'must' have said, which is unlikely to carry as much weight as the recollection of the claimant."[96]

That is common sense and it is the way the courts tend to look at the matter.[97] So the file should contain not only all incoming and outgoing correspondence, but also a note of every significant telephone conversation and meeting, and such a note should usually be backed up by an outgoing letter or email.[98] Significant documents should be photocopied, or digitally scanned, before being posted out.

When the transaction is finished, a client may ask for the file. For fraudulent clients this is a means of destroying the evidence. When a paper file is given up a copy should be retained.[99]

Negligence: delict

1–17 Negligence actions against solicitors are commoner today than they used to be. Possibly this is because standards have declined,[100] but the major reason is probably that clients expect more. Little will be said about negligence here,[101] but it should be noted that a conveyancer is not liable merely because something goes wrong and a client loses money—though clients are likely to think otherwise.

The delictual standard of care of solicitors is generally accepted as being the same as that laid down in one of the leading cases on medical negligence, *Hunter v Hanley*.[102] There Lord President Clyde said:

> "To establish liability by a doctor where deviation from normal practice is alleged, three facts require to be established. First of all it must be proved that there is a usual and normal practice; secondly it must be proved that the defender has not adopted that practice; and thirdly ... it must be established that the course the doctor adopted is one which no professional man of ordinary skill would have taken if he had been acting with ordinary care."

That is an undemanding standard of expertise that makes no reference to best practice. The test is readily satisfied if the solicitor can lead evidence from an independent expert to the effect that the actings would have been be regarded as proper by a responsible body of professional opinion. It is, however, subject to the qualification, as stated in the English case of *Bolitho v City and Hackney*

---

[96] R.M. Jackson, *Jackson & Powell on Professional Negligence*, 6th edn (2007), para.11–175.

[97] But the absence of proper records does not raise any actual presumption in favour of the clients: see *Wylie v Jeffrey Aitken*, 2002 G.W.D. 40-1360; Reid and Gretton, *Conveyancing 2002*, p.70.

[98] For a horror story see *Cheltenham & Gloucester Plc v Sun Alliance & London Insurance Plc (No.2)*, 2002 G.W.D. 18-605, with details in Reid and Gretton, *Conveyancing 2002*, p.68.

[99] The CML *Lenders' Handbook for Scotland*, para.14.3.1 requires files to be kept for six years.

[100] In the 1990s there was strong downward pressure on conveyancing fees, and it may be that there was a resulting downward pressure on standards. But the whole subject is controversial.

[101] See Robert Rennie, *Solicitors' Negligence* (1997); and Robert Rennie, *Opinions on Professional Negligence in Conveyancing* (2004). English law is highly relevant in this area. See John Powell, Roger Stewart and R.M. Jackson, *Jackson & Powell on Professional Negligence*, 6th edn with 4th supplement (2010); Hugh Evans, *Lawyers' Liabilities*, 2nd edn (2002).

[102] *Hunter v Hanley*, 1955 S.C. 200.

Health Authority,[103] that such normal practice must be capable of rational analysis. An expert opinion may be rejected as the benchmark in the rare circumstances where it cannot logically be supported.[104]

Of course the solicitor cannot trust his or her luck too far. It must be borne in mind that what was acceptable conveyancing practice at one period may not be so at a later period. For instance, in acting for a buyer, a solicitor who agrees to open-ended liability for interest in the event of failure to pay the purchase price falls short of the required standard even though, until relatively recently, such liability was routinely accepted.[105] Thus changing practice itself changes the level of ordinary competence. One moral is that conveyancers must keep abreast of new developments, whether legislation, case law or simply new standard practices. Conveyancers must therefore, if only for their own protection, keep an eye on the law reports and legal journals and attend appropriate CPD events.[106]

It must also be borne in mind that conveyancers often have to act under pressure. In a negligence action, counsel for the pursuer may ask the solicitors why they drafted some clause as they did. With hindsight it may seem indefensible, and in law it may indeed be indefensible. What the solicitors know, and what other conveyancers know, but what the counsel and the judge and the (former) client may not understand, is the pressure of chamber practice, when a clause must be drafted immediately, the drafting being interrupted several times by the ringing of the telephone and the consumption of aspirins, all in pursuit of a fee which, though no client ever believes it, may not do much more than cover overheads. At times like this solicitors rue the day when they filled in "law" on the UCAS form.

Negligence: contract

Hunter v Hanley was a delict case, and in practice actions against solicitors 1–18 tend to be based on a delictual standard of care. But in the vast majority of cases the pursuer has a contract with the defending law firm,[107] and in principle there is no reason why the contractual standard of care should be the same as that in *Hunter v Hanley*. This is an area which has not been properly developed in our law,[108] but the possibilities are clear. For instance, suppose that buyers' solicitors fail to spot a serious discrepancy between the boundaries in the title and the boundaries on the ground. Had they visited the property they would have seen the problem. Are they liable? Perhaps not under *Hunter v Hanley*. But a court might possibly accept an argument that the solicitors were in breach of an implied term of the client–agent contract. Moreover, one need not invoke

---

[103] *Bolitho v City and Hackney Health Authority* [1998] A.C. 232. For discussion of *Bolitho* in relation to Scots cases see M. Earle and N.R. Whitty, "Medical Law", *Stair Memorial Encyclopaedia Reissue* (2006), para.172; *Honisz v Lothian Health Board* [2006] CSOH 24; 2008 S.C. 235.

[104] *Bolitho*, per Lord Browne-Wilkinson at 243D–E.

[105] See below, para.5–18.

[106] The *Journal of the Law Society of Scotland* has a regular feature called "Risk Management" (previously "Caveat"). According to the column at (1992) 37 J.L.S.S. 156, 47 per cent of claims arise in respect of conveyancing. The column is useful reading for any conveyancer, as are, unfortunately, the reports of the discipline tribunal. For a collection of these, see Ian S. Smith and John M. Barton, *Procedures and Decisions of the Scottish Solicitors' Discipline Tribunal* (2000).

[107] In some unusual types of case a solicitor can be professionally liable to a non-client, in which case contractual liability will not normally be possible. For a discussion, see Sheriff Principal Risk in *Tait v Brown & McRae*, 1997 S.L.T. (Sh. Ct) 63.

[108] An example is *Haberstich v McCormick & Nicholson*, 1975 S.C. 1.

implied terms to go beyond *Hunter v Hanley*. If the solicitors have not carried out express instructions, there will be *prima facie* liability, regardless of the practices of "ordinarily competent conveyancers". In residential conveyancing, buyers usually do not issue much in the way of express instructions (except as to such obvious matters as price, date of entry, etc.), but commercial clients are often more insistent. Banks, when taking security, often have extremely detailed and highly demanding requirements which the solicitors are expected to agree to in writing. In such a case a defence based on the *Hunter v Hanley* standard of care is unlikely to succeed. Indeed, claims by banks for faulty security work constitute one of the most active areas of professional negligence today.

Negligence: insurance

1–19   Solicitors are insured against their own negligence: such insurance is in fact compulsory.[109] However, the Master Policy has certain qualifications, one of which is that the solicitor must have acted honestly and in good faith. Where that condition is not met, the insurance cover is void.[110]

Negligence: some examples of claims

1–20   There are, alas, many reported cases. Here is a selection: negligence was not established in all of them, and the facts given below are as averred by the pursuers and not necessarily as proved[111]:

- A house was resold within three years of having been purchased from the local authority, thus inadvertently triggering liability for repayment of discount.[112] The solicitors were sued for having failed to advise on the timing of the sale.[113]
- A client sued the law firm for having failed to ensure that the property had the appropriate planning permission, building consents and fire certificate.[114]
- A client sued the law firm for having failed to ensure that the property was properly served by servitudes of access and cabling.[115]
- In selling land, no servitude right of access in favour of the retained land was reserved.[116]
- Money was to be borrowed against a standard security. The lender transferred the money to the law firm which it was using. The latter handed the money over to the borrower's solicitors, who in turn handed

---

[109] Solicitors (Scotland) Professional Indemnity Insurance Rules 2005.

[110] For a remarkable example, see *Cheltenham & Gloucester v Sun Alliance and London Insurance Plc*, 2001 S.L.T. 347 (discussed in Reid and Gretton, *Conveyancing* 2000, pp.116–17) rev. 2001 S.L.T. 1151 (discussed in Reid and Gretton, *Conveyancing 2001*, pp.30–32); and *Cheltenham & Gloucester Plc v Sun Alliance & London Insurance Plc (No.2)*, 2002 G.W.D. 18-605 (discussed in Reid and Gretton, *Conveyancing 2002*, pp.68–70).

[111] The examples given are Scottish. In England there is a rich harvest of such cases, and the law of professional negligence is in many ways similar on the two sides of the border.

[112] For which see below, para.30–10.

[113] *Higginbotham v Paul Gebal & Co*, 1993 G.W.D. 3-221.

[114] *Paterson v Sturrock & Armstrong*, 1993 G.W.D. 27-1706.

[115] *Watson v Gillespie Macandrew*, 1995 G.W.D. 13-750.

[116] *Moffat v Milne*, 1993 G.W.D. 8-572. But the position may sometimes be rescued by the doctrine of access as a right inherent in ownership: see below, para.13–27.

it over to the borrower, who "dissipated" it.[117] All this was done without the standard security having been put in place. The lenders sued both law firms.[118]

- Land was sold in a way that was not tax efficient. The seller sued his solicitors for not having advised him about the tax aspects.[119]
- Solicitors faxed an offer to the wrong number with the result that the client lost the opportunity to buy the property.[120]
- A title was bad. In the first place, the seller was an undischarged bankrupt. In the second place, the property turned out not to be belong to the seller at all, but to a company. In the third place, that company did not in fact exist, and never had existed.[121] (Is this the worst title in the history of Scots law?)

Negligence: claims by lenders

In *National Home Loans Corp v Giffen Couch & Archer*[122] Peter Gibson L.J. **1–21** remarked that increasing competition between lenders had resulted in more speculative lending with a consequent higher level of defaults, and "this has led mortgage lenders to seek ways to recover their losses from others, and actions in negligence against their professional advisers have become only too common". In that case the court held that the solicitors were not liable merely because they had not told the lenders that the borrowers had a rocky financial record. That may seem like simple commonsense, but it came just after *Mortgage Express Ltd v Bowerman & Partners*,[123] a decision that frightened every conveyancer in the United Kingdom, and which has not been overruled, even though some later cases have happily been able to distinguish it. In *Mortgage Express* the defendants were instructed by a Mr Hadi to buy a house for £220,000. They also acted for the mortgage lenders, the plaintiffs. The loan was for £180,000. The property had been valued at £198,000. The defendants became aware that the seller, a Mr Arrach, had just bought the property from a Mr Khedair for only £150,000, but they did not tell the plaintiffs. After borrowing and buying, Mr Hadi promptly defaulted. The plaintiffs sold the property but it fetched only £96,000. The plaintiffs were professional money-lenders, capable of forming their own assessment of Mr Hadi's creditworthiness. They had had the property valued by professional valuers. The defendants were not professional moneylenders and they were not professional valuers. All the decisions were taken by the plaintiffs, and the role of the defendants was merely to put in place a registered mortgage. This they did. When it turned out that the plaintiffs had made a bad lending decision, instead of accepting the loss they took the view that they should be compensated by the defendants. The basis of the claim was that the defendants should have told them that the property might be worth less than valuation, because it had recently

---

[117] "Dissipation" may well describe precisely what happened.
[118] *The Mortgage Corp v Mitchells Roberton*, 1997 S.L.T. 1305.
[119] *Smith v Gordon & Smyth*, 2001 G.W.D. 26-1066. See Reid and Gretton, *Conveyancing 2001*, p.104.
[120] *Watts v Bell & Scott WS* [2007] CSOH 108; 2007 S.L.T. 665. See Reid and Gretton, *Conveyancing 2007*, pp.143–44.
[121] *Di Ciacca v Archibald Sharp & Sons*, 1995 S.L.T. 380.
[122] *National Home Loans Corp v Giffen Couch & Archer* [1997] 3 All E.R. 808.
[123] *Mortgage Express Ltd v Bowerman & Partners* [1996] 2 All E.R. 836.

been sold for less than valuation. Alarmingly, the Court of Appeal held the defendants to be liable. Although *Mortgage Express* is an English case and thus of no more than persuasive authority, the standard of care applied in professional negligence cases is little different as between Scots and English law.[124]

Lenders, unlike private clients, have their own pre-printed instructions which are normally non-negotiable, detailed and onerous. The result is often that the obligations owed are stricter than those owed to a purchaser. Obviously there are dangers here, and in practice solicitors will often be wise to qualify their reports on title, especially since some of the demands may be unreasonable or of uncertain meaning.

Marketing of property

1–22 Traditionally, property marketing was done mainly by law firms, but in the 1960s estate agents in the English style began to establish themselves.[125] Such estate agents are sometimes called non-solicitor estate agents ("NSEAs") to distinguish them from solicitor estate agents ("SEAs"). Law firms responded to the challenge by improving their marketing services, especially by establishing Solicitors Property Centres ("SPCs"). Today there are 11 such SPCs, the oldest (Aberdeen) dating from 1969.[126] The original Glasgow SPC failed, and for many years NSEAs dominated the Glasgow market, but a new Glasgow SPC was founded in 1993 and made rapid progress. SPCs have offices, where the public are welcome to browse, looking for suitable properties. In addition, SPCs publish magazines, and have websites, listing the properties on offer: these magazines (which also carry advertising) are issued free and have a wide circulation. By the 1990s the success of SPCs was such that there were complaints by NSEAs and the Scottish Consumer Council that they were monopolistic. But action by the Office of Fair Trading under the Restrictive Trade Practices Act 1976 failed,[127] and a subsequent investigation by the Monopolies and Mergers Commission, in 1997, concluded that SPCs were not operating unfairly.[128]

Today the picture has changed yet again. The online property portals offered by national or multi-national bodies such as Rightmove and Globrix, and used by NSEAs and SEAs alike, perform much the same function as SPCs and

---

[124] For English law, see Willis and Bending, (2008) 158 N.L.J. 83. Scottish negligence claims by lenders against solicitors include *Bristol & West Building Society v Rollo Steven & Bond*, 1998 S.L.T. 9; *Midland Bank v Cameron Thom Peterkins & Duncan*, 1988 S.L.T. 611 (an important pre-*Mortgage Express* decision); *Royal Bank of Scotland Plc v Harper Macleod*, 1999 G.W.D. 16-733; *Bristol & West Building Society v Aitken Nairn*, 1999 S.C. 678 (on which see Reid and Gretton, *Conveyancing 1999*, p.72); *Leeds & Holbeck Building Society v Alex Morison & Co*, 2001 S.C.L.R. 41 (on which see Reid and Gretton, *Conveyancing 2000*, p.114); *Cheltenham & Gloucester Building Society v Royal & Sun Alliance Insurance*, 2001 S.L.T. 347; *Newcastle Building Society v Paterson Robertson & Graham*, 2001 S.C. 734 (on which see Reid and Gretton, *Conveyancing 2001*, p.29); *Preferred Mortgages Ltd v Shanks* [2008] CSOH 23; [2008] P.N.L.R. 20.

[125] See John H. Sinclair and Euan Sinclair, *Handbook of Conveyancing Practice in Scotland*, 5th edn (2006), para.1.14.

[126] For links to the various SPCs see *http://www.sspc.co.uk/*. Some SPC websites have extensive information for the public: see e.g. *http://www.espc.com/*.

[127] *Aberdeen SPC Ltd v Director General for Fair Trading*, 1996 S.L.T. 523.

[128] *Solicitors Estate Agency Services in Scotland* (Cm. 3699, August 1997). This is a mine of information about the housing market in the mid-1990s.

provide a notable challenge to them. At present, market share is thought to be split roughly equally between the two types of estate agent, with NSEAs dominant in Glasgow and west-central Scotland and SEAs in Edinburgh, Aberdeen and Tayside. In a study of *Home Buying and Selling* published in 2010, the Office of Fair Trading reported that, "anecdotally", NSEAs appear to be gaining in market share.[129]

Both SEAs and NSEAs charge much the same by way of sale commission— around 1.1 per cent[130]—and there is a certain amount of sniping between them as to which provides the better service to the public or the better value for money. The agency contracts which clients are asked to sign with NSEAs are sometimes draconian in their terms, and actions by NSEAs to compel payment of commission are common.[131] SEAs seldom contract on such terms and actions by them to compel commission are almost unknown.

Some figures about the housing market

The OFT study mentioned above has much useful information on the property market.[132] Scotland has 2.3 million households, 29 per cent of which are located in Glasgow, Edinburgh, Dundee and Aberdeen. The number of houses which are owner-occupied has almost doubled since public-sector tenants were first given the right to buy their homes in 1980 but has remained steady, at around 65 per cent, for several years now.[133] The volume of residential property transactions peaked in 2007 at 148,000, with a total value of £24.5 billion. With the recession, there was then a steep decline to 99,000 transactions in 2008 and 74,000 in 2009. Average house prices rose rapidly from not much more than £100,000 in 2004 to £150,000 only four years later, in 2008, but have since fallen back to around £140,000.[134]

1–23

The future

Conveyancing has for decades been in a state of change, both as to law and as to practice.[135] Changes since the first edition of this book in 1993 have been vast. Here are just some of the statutes relevant to the conveyancer passed

1–24

---

[129] Office of Fair Trading, *Home Buying and Selling: A Market Study* (2010, available at *http://. oft.gov.uk/shared_oft/reports/property/OFT1186.pdf*), paras 8.29 and 8.47.

[130] Office of Fair Trading, *Home Buying and Selling: A Market Study* (2010), para.8.41. This figure relates to the first half of 2009. To this fee must be added advertising costs.

[131] See e.g. *Chris Hart (Business Sales) Ltd v Cunie*, 1992 S.L.T. 544; *Chris Hart (Business Sales) Ltd v Niven*, 1992 S.C.L.R. 534; *Chris Hart (Business Sales) Ltd v Duncan*, 1994 S.C.L.R. 104; *Stuart Wyse Ogilvie Estates Ltd v Bryant*, 1995 G.W.D. 27-1429; *Chris Hart (Business Sales) Ltd v Mitchell*, 1996 S.L.T. (Sh. Ct) 132; *Robert Bany & Co v Doyle*, 1998 S.L.T. 1238; *Christie Owen & Davis Plc v King*, 1998 S.C.L.R. 786; *G & S Properties Ltd v Henderson*, 1999 G.W.D. 6-282; *G & S Properties v Francis*, 2001 S.L.T. 934; *Countryside North Ltd v GWM Developments Ltd* [2007] CSOH 60.

[132] Although it is a UK-wide study, Ch.8 is devoted to Scotland. For the figures that follow, see in particular paras 8.3–8.6.

[133] For the steep decline in the sales of council housing in recent years, see below, para.30–06. In England and Wales, owner-occupation is rather higher, at 73 per cent.

[134] Office of Fair Trading, *Home Buying and Selling: A Market Study*, chart 3.2. For more figures about the housing market see below, Ch.21.

[135] It was not always thus. The third edition of *Conveyancing Practice* by John Burns appeared in 1926. The fourth edition, by Farquhar MacRitchie, which appeared in 1957, was remarkably little changed from the previous edition. Nowadays much more changes in a decade than it did in the 31 years from 1926 to 1957.

since the previous (third) edition in 2004: the Tenements (Scotland) Act 2004, the Antisocial Behaviour etc. (Scotland) Act 2004,[136] the Nature Conservation (Scotland) Act 2004, the Licensing (Scotland) Act 2005, the Housing (Scotland) Act 2006, the Planning etc. (Scotland) Act 2006, the Bankruptcy and Diligence (Scotland) Act 2007, the Crofting Reform etc. (Scotland) Act 2007, the Climate Change (Scotland) Act 2009,[137] the Home Owner and Debtor Protection (Scotland) Act 2010, the Crofting Reform (Scotland) Act 2010, the Housing (Scotland) Act 2010, the Private Rented Housing (Scotland) Act 2011, the Wildlife and Natural Environment (Scotland) Act 2011, and the Property Factors (Scotland) Act 2011. At the time of writing a new Land Registration Bill, based on the work of the Scottish Law Commission[138] and replacing the 1979 Act in its entirety, appeared to be imminent, while a Bill providing for the conversion of ultra-long leases into ownership, the Long Leases (Scotland) Bill, which failed to make the statute book before the Scottish Parliamentary elections in May 2011, seemed likely to be reintroduced. The Scottish Law Commission is starting work on the reform of standard securities,[139] and major legislation on that topic seems likely in due course.

Meanwhile, the cyber-revolution carries on apace. Communications are increasingly by email. Digital files are replacing those kept on paper. Since 2008 e-deeds and e-registration have been available under the system known as automated registration of title to land ("ARTL").[140] And the proposed Land Registration Bill offers the heady prospect of full e-conveyancing, including e-missives.[141]

---

[136] Part 8 provides for the registration of private landlords.

[137] Which, among other things, introduced a new type of personal real burden, the climate change burden: see below, para.13–20.

[138] Scottish Law Commission, Report on *Land Registration* (Scot. Law Com. No.222, 2010). See below, para.8–25.

[139] Scottish Law Commission, *Eighth Programme of Law Reform* (Scot. Law Com. No.220, 2010), paras 2.27–2.33.

[140] See below, para.8–23.

[141] See below, para.8–24.

CHAPTER 2

THE CONVEYANCING TRANSACTION

Introduction

In a typical conveyancing transaction each client is simultaneously a buyer 2–01 (of the new house) and a seller[1] (of the old one), and also a borrower (in respect of the secured loan on the new house). The conveyancer thus has to handle all three aspects at the same time. It is like learning to drive a car: to change gear one must manipulate the accelerator, the clutch and the gearstick. It is tricky at first but gets easier with practice. Technology can assist here, and it is becoming more common for firms to use electronic case-management systems.

The object of this chapter is to give an overview of the whole process of buying and selling a house, with details to follow in later chapters.

Contract and conveyance

The sale of property has two main elements: contract and conveyance. The 2–02 contract usually takes the form of missives: a missive of offer to buy, generally followed by further missives adjusting terms, and finalised by a missive of acceptance. "Missive" means a letter, especially a letter intended to have legal effect. In modern usage it means an offer or an acceptance. "The missives" as a collective term means the contract as constituted by the letters. There is no reason why a contract for the sale of heritable property should not be entered into without missives. In that case there is a single document setting out the agreement, which both parties sign. This is uncommon in practice, though it is always adopted in sales by roup.[2] In such cases the seller pre-signs a document called the articles of roup,[3] and at the end of the roup the successful bidder signs too. The contract of sale itself, as created by the missives letters (or otherwise), is in practice sometimes called "the bargain". Thus "the bargain was concluded on April 12" means that the contract of sale came into existence at that date.

A contract for the sale of land must be in writing and subscribed.[4] Witnessing is not necessary but is common in practice.[5] The missives can be direct between

---

[1] The English term "vendor" is also in use, especially in commercial transactions, where English influence is always strong. In addition, the Inland Revenue insists that this term be used for stamp duty land tax ("SDLT") purposes.

[2] Auction.

[3] Despite the plural form, articles of roup are a single document.

[4] Requirements of Writing (Scotland) Act 1995 s.1(2)(a)(i).

[5] Before the 1995 Act missives letters had to be either witnessed or adopted as holograph. In practice the latter method was almost always used. The 1995 Act relaxed the law so that simple signature now suffices. That the response of solicitors to this change was to make witnessing virtually compulsory is curious.

the parties, but normally are between their solicitors on their behalves. By the missives the sellers bind themselves to convey and the buyers bind themselves to pay. The contract is then performed by delivery of the disposition and payment of the price. This is called "settlement",[6] and traditionally used to happen at a meeting between the two solicitors, but now usually happens by DX or Legal Post. In a simple case there will be just two missives, the offer and the acceptance, but in most cases there will be several missives, adjusting terms. When the last missive is sent, unconditionally accepting the terms which have been negotiated, the missives are said to be "concluded".[7] Traditionally, when missives were short, they could usually be concluded within a week of the offer. During the 1970s that period began to lengthen, but matters have improved recently with the widespread use of standard-form offers. The period from the original offer until settlement will vary according to circumstances (and the date of settlement will be stipulated in the missives themselves) but is typically two months or so, and is seldom less than one month. After settlement, the disposition is registered by the buyer in the Land Register. It is at the moment of registration that ownership passes to the buyer,[8] though the right to take possession will usually have been given at settlement.

Co-ordinating the purchase and the sale

2–03   People need a roof over their heads. So clients do not wish to sell until they have another house to go to. But equally they do not want to buy another house until they have sold the old one because otherwise they would be faced with financing the loans on two houses, which may be ruinously expensive. On one side there is the abyss of two houses, and on the other the abyss of no house at all. The ideal, of course, is for the two transactions to be perfectly co-ordinated, but this is often not possible in practice. Even if the entry dates can be lined up in the missives, for one reason or another they may not line up in reality. Clients need to be asked at an early stage which they would prefer, if the choice has to be made: a period with two houses, and two loans, or a period with no loans, and no house.

In Scotland the problem is handled in a way different from in England. Indeed, Scottish conveyancing is very different from English conveyancing. In England the usual practice is to have a gentleman's agreement to sell (called a sale "subject to contract"), which may last for a considerable period, often several months. This is mainly to enable the buyers to sell their existing property. That sale will also be "subject to contract" for the same reason. Hence what the English call a chain develops. This may include a dozen persons or more. Each will know only two others: the prospective buyer and prospective seller. During this period either side can walk away from the agreement. Finally something happens to switch the system on, for example at one end of the chain there appears someone who can make a cash purchase. Then the contract is made ("exchanging contracts"),[9] and the transaction is finally settled ("completed") one month later.

---

[6] In commercial conveyancing, the English term "completion" is often used.
[7] Until then the missives are said to be "open". Open missives are not binding.
[8] Abolition of Feudal Tenure etc. (Scotland) Act 2000 s.4.
[9] Usually the documents are posted, to be held as undelivered, and "exchange of contracts" then happens by agreement over the telephone.

What happens in Scotland varies to some extent from case to case. Chains are unusual although by no means unknown.[10] Traditionally, if the housing market is good, and if they are rather choosey in what they want to buy, clients might decide to buy first and then sell. They look for a new house and then bid for it. If successful, they then put the old house on the market, and a purchaser is found. They typically have to pay for the new house rather sooner than they are paid for the old house, and the gap is covered by bridging, which means a short-term loan from a bank.

However, it is risky to buy first because the old house may stick on the market, and in the current recession it is hardly ever done. Apart from anything else, open-ended bridging is hard to obtain, is subject to periodic review, and involves a large arrangement fee. So at present almost everyone sells first and then buys. The clients put their old house on the market. When they find a buyer they bid for a new house. If the market is bad there will, they hope, be plenty of houses to bid for.[11] Bridging may again be necessary. In both cases careful consideration needs to be given to the entry date stated in the missives. It may be possible to achieve perfect co-ordination, but often the clients will find themselves, temporarily, either with two houses or no house. In either case the period needs to be kept as short as possible.

Can one rely on "open" missives (i.e. missives which are lacking a final acceptance)?[12] Suppose—as is usual—that the clients decide to sell first. They find a buyer in July and there are open missives for settlement on September 30. On August 1 they find the new house of their dreams. Should they offer for it? To do so is to assume that the open missives for the sale of the old house will mature into a sale. That is risky. They may decide to offer, but to try to keep the missives on the new house open for some time. But that too has its risks. For instance, the seller of the new house may get fed up with the non-conclusion of the missives and sell to someone else. There are no magic answers. The experienced solicitor gets used to the juggling, but must explain everything to the clients and, ultimately, it is the clients who must decide what risks to take.

The secured loan

The buyer will normally need a loan, usually from a bank or building society, and this will be secured over the property by a standard security (i.e. what in England is called a mortgage), which will become a real right upon its registration. The property being sold will also usually have a standard security over it and the debt secured will be paid off out of the proceeds of sale, with the lender granting a discharge which will then be registered. Thus typically a sale involves three registrations: the discharge of the seller's security, the buyer's security, and the disposition itself.

2–04

---

[10] Usually this involves the use of open missives. In its study of *Home Buying and Selling* (2010), para.8.26, the Office of Fair Trading found that 21 per cent of sellers in Scotland said they were in a chain (as compared to 46 per cent in England), but the Scottish sample was too small to be reliable.

[11] But one obvious drawback about selling first is that it means that the time available to find a new house is limited, and the house actually bought may prove not to be the ideal choice.

[12] There is even some risk in relying on concluded missives. A seller may turn out to be unable to grant a good title. A more common risk is that purchasers simply find themselves unable to come up with the money.

Fixed price sales and upset sales

2–05 A property may be offered at a fixed price, or by the upset system.[13] In the first, the sellers are announcing that they will accept the first offer at that price, though they are not legally bound to do so.[14] Fixed price sales are less usual, though they become more common in property slumps, and of course builders tend to offer new houses and flats at fixed prices.[15] In the upset system, the advertisement solicits offers over a stated figure. The upset is generally lower than the price the seller expects to receive, although the introduction of home reports (containing a professional valuation) in 2008 has checked a tendency to fix an artificially low figure in the hope of stimulating interest.[16] Unlike a fixed price property, this does not mean that the sellers will accept an offer at that price but it does suggest that they would accept an offer of not much over that price. A variant which is growing in use is to invite offers "around" or "in the region of" a certain price. Parties are then invited to bid, and the sellers normally accept the highest offer. If more than one potential buyer is interested, it is usual to set a "closing date". This means that the interested parties are told that written offers must be received by a certain time, when they will be opened by the sellers. The bidding is "blind" in the sense that no one knows how much a competitor will offer.

ACTING FOR THE SELLER

Initiating the sale

2–06 The estate agency side of a sale is the advising on a sale price, advertising the property, and generally trying to find a buyer.[17] Most law firms offer this service, and many have special estate agency departments. If the client goes to a non-solicitor estate agent ("NSEA") then the first the solicitors learn of the sale may be when the NSEA sends them an offer with instructions to accept.

As soon as the selling solicitors are instructed, they need to obtain the deeds, and the best advice is to check them before the property is advertised.[18] The traditional term is "title deeds", abbreviated to "the deeds" or "the titles". For properties in the General Register of Sasines ("GRS") title flows from the recorded deeds, but for properties in the Land Register title flows from the register itself, evidenced by the land certificate, a document which may or may not, according to taste, be called a title deed. We use the term "deeds" broadly, as including the deeds in the narrow sense, the land and charge certificate, and anything else relevant to the title, such as affidavits. If there is a secured loan,

---

[13] A third possibility is roup (auction), though this is uncommon. A fourth possibility, also uncommon, is that the seller will find a buyer privately, without ever actually marketing the property.

[14] See the Law Society's *Guidelines on Fixed Price Offers 1998*, published at (1998) 43 J.L.S.S. June/42.

[15] In England fixed price sales are almost invariably used, but the seller expects the buyer to negotiate downwards from that price.

[16] For home reports, see below, para.2–07.

[17] See John H. Sinclair and Euan Sinclair, *Handbook of Conveyancing Practice in Scotland*, 5th edn (2006), Ch.3.

[18] Though this is not always done. But if there is a title problem, the sooner it is discovered the better, and above all before missives.

which is usually the case, the deeds will often be held by the lender, in which case a letter needs to be sent asking to borrow them. If the selling solicitors are also acting as estate agents, there should be time enough to obtain them, though some lenders are slow. But if the seller is using a NSEA, there may be a problem, because the agents will not usually have done anything about the deeds, so that one may be confronted by an offer to purchase without having the deeds to hand. In that case there are various possibilities, one of which is to accept on the basis that the purchasers may withdraw if the deeds, when available, reveal anything unsatisfactory.

If the sale will switch the property from the GRS to the Land Register it is usually necessary, at the time of marketing the property, to obtain a form 10 report (a pre-registration report on title) and, in most cases, a form P16 (comparison of the title boundary with the Ordnance map).

If the selling solicitors are acting as estate agents, then someone from the firm will visit the property. In that case, an eye must be kept open for problems. Some examples are: (1) The property has a shared private access road. There may be problems about servitudes and maintenance. (2) The property's physical boundaries are indeterminate or do not tally with the boundaries in the title. (3) The house has recent alterations. Have both planning permission and building consent been obtained? (4) The property is tenanted. Will a purchaser be able to obtain vacant possession?

The selling solicitors draw up a "schedule of particulars" which describes the property in attractive, but truthful, terms, gives the price (whether upset, guidance or fixed), and so on. These schedules are given out to anyone interested, and (in most cases) can also be obtained through the solicitors property centre ("SPC").

Home report[19]

Since December 1, 2008 all houses put on the market (other than new ones[20]) have needed a home report, which must be supplied on request to potential buyers.[21] In practice they are usually viewed online. The home report[22] comprises three elements: 2–07

- The *survey report* (generally referred to as "the single survey").[23] As well as describing the condition of the property, this identifies problems and classifies them on a scale of 1–3 (3 being "urgent"), gives a valuation and also the estimated reinstatement cost for insurance purposes, and provides an accessibility audit covering matters such as parking, lifts, whether all door openings are greater than 75 mm, and whether there is a toilet on the same level as a bedroom. The survey must follow a prescribed form.

---

[19] Helpful information can be found at *http://www.scotland.gov.uk/Topics/Built-Environment/Housing/BuyingSelling/Home-Report*.

[20] This and a small number of other exceptions appear in regs 7–14 of the Housing (Scotland) Act 2006 (Prescribed Documents) Regulations 2008 (SSI 2008/76).

[21] Housing (Scotland) Act 2006 Pt 3.

[22] The form is prescribed by the Housing (Scotland) Act 2006 (Prescribed Documents) Regulations 2008 (SSI 2008/76).

[23] The Royal Institution of Chartered Surveyors ("RICS") regards this as equivalent to the scheme 2 survey (often known as the Home Buyer's Survey and Valuation), which is the type of survey most often instructed by purchasers who wish a survey of their own.

- The *energy report*, comprising (i) the energy performance certificate ("EPC") which, since January 4, 2009, has been needed for all buildings (including non-residential buildings) which are to be sold or leased[24]; and (ii) certain additional information. An EPC expresses the "asset rating" of a building[25] by means of columns headed "Energy Efficiency Rating" and "Environmental Impact Rating", each graded on a scale of A–G (A being best). Victorian houses, much prized on the property market, usually score particularly badly on these measures. In addition, an EPC looks to the future by including "cost effective recommendations for improving the energy performance of the building" (e.g. cavity wall insulation or draught-proof windows).
- The *property questionnaire*. As its name suggests, this comprises a series of questions on the property, designed to provide information on a whole range of topics such as council tax, alterations to the building, the heating system, services, the extent of responsibility for shared maintenance, access rights and boundaries, and specialist treatments for dry rot, etc.

The survey and the energy report must be prepared by a surveyor registered with or authorised to practise by the Royal Institution of Chartered Surveyors; the property questionnaire is answered and signed by the seller or by a person authorised to act on the seller's behalf.[26] The Law Society's view is that the questionnaire is a matter for the client and not for the solicitor and that there is no obligation on solicitors to verify the answers.[27]

A number of providers are in the market for home reports, including surveyors' organisations,[28] the Law Society, and SPCs.[29] The cost is around £400 for a property worth up to £100,000 and rises in increments of about £100 for every £100,000 of value thereafter.[30] Some providers, however, are cheaper and discounts may be available through selling agents as an inducement to use their services.

A home report must not be more than 12 weeks' old at the time when the house is put on the market,[31] and should be as up-to-date as possible. That means that if a house proves hard to sell, the seller may need to update the report. If the buyer is obtaining a loan and the lender accepts the home report, the report requires to be not more than 12 weeks' old, but a cash purchaser may sometimes be more indulgent. The Law Society's guidance, however, is that home reports should not be relied upon by buyers if more than 12 weeks' old.[32]

---

[24] Energy Performance of Buildings (Scotland) Regulations 2008 (SSI 2008/309), transposing, in part, the Energy Performance of Buildings Directive (Directive 2002/91).

[25] Defined (in reg.2(1)) as "a numerical indicator of the estimated amount of (a) energy consumed and (b) carbon dioxide emitted, to meet the different needs associated with a standardised use of the building".

[26] 2008 Regulations reg.5.

[27] *Guidance on Home Reports 2008*, paras 5–7.

[28] Such as Survey Scotland Ltd: see *http://www.surveyscotland.com/why-us.php?gclid=CIOj3s 7G4KgCFQkLfAodYC7mrQ*.

[29] See e.g. *http://www.espc.co.uk/HRHowCanWeHelp.html*.

[30] Tribal in association with George Street Research and Optimal Economics, *Interim Review of the Home Report* (2010, available at *http://www.scotland.gov.uk/Resource/Doc/325815/0105025. pdf*), p.2.

[31] 2008 Regulations reg.6(1).

[32] *Guidance on Home Reports 2008*, para.1.

Although the survey is instructed by the seller, the legislation provides that a negligent survey can give rise to liability to a buyer who has relied on it.[33] There is, however, no liability to a lender (i.e. to the buyer's bank), and lenders continue to instruct their own mortgage valuations, in principle at the buyer's expense. In practice lenders are often willing to instruct the surveyor who prepared the single survey, in which case the cost of producing a separate report in the lender's format is absorbed into the cost of the single survey. But lenders will insist on an independent survey if, for example, the original surveyor is not on their panel, or the single survey is more than 12 weeks' old.

Unluckily, the introduction of home reports coincided with a severe downturn in the property market. For that and other reasons it was deeply controversial, with conveyancers in particular often being hostile to the idea.[34] To some extent the controversy remains, especially in respect of the single survey. On one view, it increases consumer knowledge and choice, so that prospective buyers have more and better information at an earlier stage, and do not waste time, money and emotional energy pursuing properties which, for one reason or another, are unsuitable for them. Upset prices have become more realistic as a result, and it is now possible to offer for a property without incurring the expense—wasted if the offer is unsuccessful—of obtaining a survey of one's own.[35] On another view, the single survey imposes a significant, and in some cases unaffordable, burden on sellers without necessarily relieving buyers of the need to obtain a survey of their own—either because they want a report which is independent, up-to-date and can be discussed with a surveyor or because their lender requires such a survey. An interim review commissioned by the Scottish Government and published in 2010 concluded that it was too early to draw firm conclusions as to the effectivenenss of home reports.[36] In England and Wales, home information packs—the equivalent of the home report but without a survey—were withdrawn in 2010. In Scotland, all the signs are that the home report is here to stay.

Misdescriptions

If the solicitors are marketing the property they must ensure that they do not   2–08
mislead prospective purchasers, whether in the sales particulars or otherwise. To do so is unprofessional and might also lead to a claim by the buyers against

---

[33] Housing (Scotland) Act 2006 (Consequential Provisions) Order 2008 (SI 2008/1889). For claims against surveyors see e.g. *Martin v Bell-Ingram*, 1986 S.L.T. 575; *Robbie v Graham & Sibbald*, 1989 S.L.T. 870; *Hunter v J&E Shepherd*, 1992 S.L.T 1095; *Melrose v Davidson & Robertson*, 1993 S.L.T. 611; *Leeds Permanent Building Society v Walker Fraser & Steele*, 1995 S.L.T. (Sh. Ct) 72; *Mortgage Express Ltd v Dunsmore Reid & Smith*, 1996 G.W.D. 40-2295; *Lawson v McHugh*, 1998 G.W.D. 31-1618; *Stewart v Ryden Residential Ltd*, 1999 G.W.D. 12-576; *Purdie v Dryburgh*, 2000 S.C. 497; *Douglas v Stuart Wise Ogilvie Estates Ltd*, 2001 S.L.T. 689; *Howes v Crombie*, 2001 S.C.L.R. 921; *Harrison v DM Hall*, 2001 G.W.D. 33-1314; *Beechwood Development Co (Scotland) Ltd v Stuart Mitchell*, 2001 S.L.T. 1214; *Bank of Scotland v Fuller Peiser*, 2001 S.L.T. 574; *Murray v J&E Shepherd*, 2007 G.W.D. 7-108.

[34] On the day of introduction, Ian Ferguson, speaking on behalf of the Scottish Law Agents Society, offered the thought that: "Today is Black Monday. It's the birth of Home Reports but, quite possibly, the death of the Scottish property market. I predict that Home Report costs will become as despised as the Poll Tax."

[35] Latterly, however, this was often avoided by putting in offers "subject to survey".

[36] Tribal in association with George Street Research and Optimal Economics, *Interim Review of the Home Report* (2010).

the sellers for misrepresentation.[37] Moreover, to mislead prospective purchasers is an offence. Under the Property Misdescriptions Act 1991 it is an offence to make "in the course of an estate agency business" any statement which is "false or misleading".[38] These words are open-ended. In *Enfield LBC v Castles Estate Agents Ltd*[39] a property was advertised as a "bungalow", and the agents were prosecuted because the building, which was 30 years old, did not have planning permission and therefore could not fairly be called a bungalow. The prosecution failed, but (amazingly) only because it was found in fact that the agents reasonably believed planning permission to exist. However, case law on the Act is sparse.[40]

On receipt of the successful offer

2–09   If there is more than one offer, the selling solicitors will discuss with the clients which to accept. They then send a copy of that offer to the clients by email or first class post, raising certain points or asking them to get in touch to go over the offer clause by clause. Typical clauses which may require discussion are those concerning the physical condition of the property and the existence of planning and building consents for alterations. It is wise to follow discussion by an email or letter confirming the points discussed and the instructions given. After this the solicitor sends off the qualified acceptance, copying this to the clients. At about this time a request should be sent for the property enquiry certificates ("PECs"). These are issued by the local authority, and can also be obtained from independent firms working from local authority records, and cover such matters as planning, roads, statutory repairs notices and so on.[41]

What should be sent?

2–10   At an early stage in the transaction the selling solicitors send to the purchasing solicitors various items. What is sent depends on whether the property is in the GRS or Land Register. If the sale will switch the property from the GRS to the Land Register, there should be sent (a) the title deeds; (b) the form 10 report; (c) if applicable, the form P16 report[42]; and (d) a draft form 11. These reports can be obtained from the Keeper or from independent searchers. If the property is already in the Land Register, there should be sent (a) the land certificate[43], (b) the form 12 report, and (c) the draft form 13 report.[44] A draft letter of obli-

---

[37] In *Stambovsky v Ackley*, 169 A.D. 2d. 254, 572 N.Y.S. 2d 672 (1991) the seller did not disclose that the house was haunted. It was held by the Supreme Court of the State of New York that this amounted to misrepresentation by non-disclosure. (For a photograph of the house, but not, alas, of the ghost, see Jesse Dukeminier and James Krier, *Property*, 4th edn (1998), p.581.)

[38] Property Misdescriptions Act 1991 s.1(1). As to whether the seller of a haunted house might commit an offence for non-disclosure (because the buyer might object to a haunted house), or equally an offence for disclosure (because the buyer might be disappointed if the ghost did not manifest itself), see John Sinclair, *Handbook of Conveyancing Practice in Scotland*, 4th edn (2002), p.43. Haunting is a sadly neglected branch of the law.

[39] [1996] 36 E.G. 145; [1996] 12 E.G.L.R. 21; 73 P. & C.R. 343.

[40] The only reported Scottish case is *George Wimpey UK Ltd v Brown*, 2003 S.L.T. 659.

[41] See below, para.4–25.

[42] This states whether the boundaries as set forth in the title correspond with the physical boundaries as shown on the Ordnance Survey map. See below, para.12–12.

[43] If available. In first registrations there may be a long delay. It can easily happen that the buyer wishes to sell again before the land certificate is available.

[44] For form 12/13 reports, see below, para.9–07.

gation[45] and a draft discharge of the existing standard security (if there is one) should also be sent. The various drafts are sometimes referred to collectively as the "seller's drafts".

The purchasing solicitors may come back with queries about the title or other matters.[46] With luck the selling solicitors' answers will satisfy them. They will also send to the selling solicitors a draft disposition, usually by email, which the latter approve, with any suggested changes, and send back.[47] The traditional practice is that a conveyancing deed is drafted by the solicitors for the grantee, and then revised by the grantor's solicitors. But there are some exceptions, notably leases, which are usually drafted by the solicitor for the grantor, and then revised by the solicitor for the grantee.

The purchasing solicitors will also return the draft form 11 or 13, having added the name of their client for the purpose of a personal search. After a while the selling solicitors receive the "engrossment" (i.e. final version) of the disposition from the purchasing solicitors. The selling solicitors have their clients execute it, also completing the "signing schedule" which gives details of the date and place of signing and the name and address of the witness. This schedule is for the benefit of the purchasing solicitors, who will use it after settlement to complete the testing clause.[48] The selling solicitors now sit back doing the crossword, until the settlement date arrives.

In ARTL transactions, the purchasing solicitors input into the system the information needed to generate a disposition and this is checked and signed digitally by the selling solicitors on the basis of a written mandate from their clients.[49]

Settlement

Settlement traditionally took place at the office of the selling solicitors but nowadays it is usually done through DX, Legal Post or courier. In a typical case the selling solicitors send:

    2–11

  (a) the executed disposition, with the signing schedule;

  (b) the land certificate and charge certificate, or, in a first registration, the GRS deeds;

  (c) the executed letter of obligation, with the draft for comparison;

  (d) the form 13 report (form 11 report for a first registration);

  (e) the executed discharge of the existing standard security;

  (f) any necessary documentation in respect of occupancy rights[50];

  (g) the keys, unless this is being dealt with separately by the clients themselves; and

  (h) any other relevant documents, such as PECs, building warrants, etc.

---

[45] For letters of obligation, see below, para.9–25; for discharges, see below, para.2–13.

[46] Alas, observations on title are sometimes aggressive in tone. Having identified what is or may be a problem, there is a sort of psychological compulsion to shout about it. "A letter raising observations on title should always be courteously phrased whatever you may think of the quality of the conveyancing offered": David A. Brand, Andrew J.M. Steven and Scott Wortley, *Professor McDonald's Conveyancing Manual*, 7th edn (2004), p.726.

[47] See below, para.11–25.

[48] See also below, para.17–07.

[49] See below, para.8–23.

[50] See below, Ch.10 and esp. para.10–14.

In return, the selling solicitors receive the price. In an ARTL transaction, the disposition is delivered electronically by being returned to the control of the buyers' solicitors.[51]

Payment is still usually by a cheque from the buyers' solicitors, but payment by electronic transfer (which conveyancers commonly call "telegraphic transfer") is increasingly common, especially for more expensive properties, and in commercial cases. It is of course perfectly lawful for the clients to settle between themselves, but it is rare for this to happen, and when it does the solicitors should be aware of the possibility of a fraud of some sort. Settlement between the solicitors also avoids the problem as to whether the buyers' cheque might bounce.

The price is payable in exchange for the disposition, and both are sent on the basis that each is to be held as undelivered pending receipt of the other.[52] If either party fails to perform, the other party can require the return of the price or, as the case may be, the disposition (and other items such as the title deeds). The Law Society's view is that "in extreme circumstances" the selling solicitor can stop the cheque, although what these circumstances might be is not explained.[53]

Following settlement, the selling solicitors pay the (old) lender the amount outstanding on the existing secured loan (on all of them, if more than one), put through a fee note, and send an account to the clients. Later on, and assuming, as is generally the case, that the letter of obligation will have been satisfied by the issue by the Keeper of a land certificate in satisfactory terms, the purchasing solicitors will return the letter, marked as implemented. The titles—the land and charge certificates and any other relevant documents—are then sent by the purchasing solicitors to the (new) lender. At this stage it should be possible to close the file.

Council Tax

2–12   A notification of change of ownership is sent by the selling solicitors to the local authority, which will then apportion council tax as between the buyer and seller. Local authorities have standard forms for such notices.

Discharging the old standard security

2–13   At the same time as carrying out the conveyancing for the sale itself, the selling solicitors will be arranging for the discharge of any standard security over the property.[54] They ask the lender for a redemption statement, i.e. a note of exactly how much will be outstanding at settlement. The draft discharge of security, once approved by the purchasing solicitors, is immediately engrossed and sent to the lender for execution and return. In ARTL transactions this is done electronically.[55] Ideally the signed discharge should be obtained before settlement and held for the lender as undelivered, but some lenders[56] will not release the discharge until the loan is repaid. At settlement the usual practice is to give the

---

[51] See below, para.8–23.

[52] See further (1998) 43 J.L.S.S. Oct./47.

[53] *Guidelines on Settlement by Cheque, Loan Redemption and the Remit of the Free Proceeds of Sale 2008* (reproduced at (2008) 53 J.L.S.S. Nov./31).

[54] See further the Council of Mortgage Lenders ("CML") *Lenders' Handbook for Scotland*, para.17. (For the CML see below, Ch.21.)

[55] See below, para.8–23.

[56] Such as the Lloyds Banking Group.

executed discharge to the purchasing solicitors who will then arrange for its registration. This is permissible only if the amount outstanding is repaid (by the selling solicitors out of funds in their hands) on the same day. If the discharge is not available, an obligation to deliver it, normally within 21 days, is included in the letter of obligation.

If the existing secured loan is an endowment mortgage, the selling solicitors may also have to arrange for the retrocession of the life policy, but nowadays lenders often do not require such policies to be assigned in the first place. Again the lender will execute this in advance, and after settlement the selling solicitors intimate the retrocession to the life assurance company. The life policy has nothing to do with the title to the house, so the purchasing solicitors are not interested in its retrocession and there will be no communication about this between the solicitors.

Insurance

After settlement the sellers' house insurance policy should be cancelled, while 2–14 the purchasing solicitors need to ensure that there is insurance cover from the moment when risk passes, which in current practice is normally at settlement.[57] Whilst the purchasing solicitors need to check the point, it is left to the clients to effect the insurance, which in a majority of cases they will do through their lenders, who will normally insist on insurance[58] and who will typically decline to release the loan funds unless insurance cover is in operation.

ACTING FOR THE BUYER

Taking instructions in a purchase

Most buyers are also sellers, and vice versa, but for convenience of exposition 2–15 the two sides are treated separately here. Sometimes purchasing clients contact their solicitors only when they are ready to bid for a house. If, however, they make contact sooner, their solicitors have the chance to discuss with them the sort of property they want, current market prices for that sort of property, their finances, the sale of their present house, if any, the type of loan they need, and so on. It is not usual to charge for such advice, but as well as being useful to the clients it also helps the solicitors to keep close contact with them, which is a key element in retaining client loyalty. One thing that should be explained at the first meeting is the general outline of a purchase transaction, including the likely timetable. If there are two (or more) buyers then instructions must be taken from both and reporting must be to both.

A survivorship destination must not be inserted in the disposition without the informed consent of the clients.[59] Co-owners may later become estranged and there may be disputes as to who contributed what and whether the proceeds

---

[57] The default rule is that risk passes when missives are concluded (*Sloans Dairies v Glasgow Corp*, 1977 S.C. 23) but missives usually provide that it will pass at settlement. See below, paras 4–16 to 4–20.

[58] Where there is a standard security there is an implied obligation to insure: Conveyancing and Feudal Reform (Scotland) Act 1970 Sch.3 standard condition 5. A tenement flat must also be insured: see Tenements (Scotland) Act 2004 s.18.

[59] For survivorship clauses, see below, Ch.26.

of eventual sale should be divided equally or unequally.[60] It should be explained that equal *pro indiviso* shares will mean an equal division of proceeds. If something different is desired then unequal shares may be the answer, while if one party regards himself or herself as lending part of the down payment to the other then it may be that that should be formally documented as a loan.[61] When cohabitants split up, if one of them contributed disproportionately to paying the bills connected with the house, such as the home loan, that party may demand a compensating payment from the other on the basis that no donation was intended, and so it may be wise to have a formal agreement to cover such matters in advance, although this is seldom done in practice.

Finances of buying

2–16 Some clients have the finances of buying and selling at their finger tips, and hardly need advice, while others are vague, and some unrealistic. It is good practice to make reasonably sure (a) that the clients will be able to come up with the purchase price at settlement date and (b) that they will be able to keep up with the monthly loan payments thereafter. The first of these is particularly important when the clients are new ones about whom the solicitor knows little. In Scotland (unlike England) it is not normal practice for sellers to demand a deposit.[62] The main reason for this is that it is assumed that the solicitors acting for buyers will have done at least a preliminary check on their clients' finances.

In the typical case the finances are simple. The purchasers will have the proceeds of the sale of their old house (which are known or can be estimated) less the outstanding loan (which can be checked), less costs (which can be estimated), plus the loan which will be obtained for the new house (which can be estimated).[63] The solicitors must stress that cleared funds be in the firm's hands by a stated date in good time for settlement. If the solicitors have real doubts about whether this will happen, they should consider declining to act. Of course, the danger that purchasers will fail to come up with the price can never be wholly eliminated. But solicitors are under a professional responsibility to make reasonably sure that they will be able to do so before they submit any offer on their behalf.

Making the offer

2–17 When the clients have identified a house for which they wish to offer, the first step is to "note interest" to the selling solicitors. A phone call suffices. The effect of noting interest has traditionally been considered as being that the sellers will not sell without first giving to the person who has noted interest a chance to bid. If there is more than one noted interest, a closing date is normally set by which all offers must be received.[64]

The next step is to discuss with the client any issues that are thrown up by the home report. Sometimes the advice may be to instruct an independent survey, or a specialist survey in respect of matters such as the roof or subsid-

---

[60] See for instance *Grieve v Morrison*, 1993 S.L.T. 852. And see also below, para.10–17.
[61] cf. Rennie, 2004 S.L.T. (News) 33.
[62] In residential conveyancing. In commercial conveyancing a deposit of, say, 10 per cent on conclusion of missives is common.
[63] For charges payable on obtaining a loan, see below, para.21–51.
[64] See below, para.3–07.

ence or rot. If the survey in the home report is not acceptable to the lender, a further survey is always necessary.[65] Surveys quite often note that there have been alterations, in which case—if the purchase goes ahead—the sellers' solicitors will need to be asked for the appropriate public law consents.[66]

A further discussion with the clients is what figure to offer.[67] The solicitors' own knowledge of the market will help here (and the clients may to some extent be relying on that knowledge), and it is wise to check the computer record of recent sales in the area kept at the local SPC. Registers of Scotland also has an online search facility for house prices which is open to be public and free of charge.[68] Another obvious factor is the valuation put on the property by the home report or other survey.

It is likely that there will be other points to be discussed such as what moveables (if any) in the property are to be included in the purchase. The purchasing solicitors should have in front of them, when preparing the offer, the schedule of particulars issued by the seller, and indeed it is not uncommon for this to be docqueted as part of the offer.

At some stage the clients will have to submit the application form for the new loan. The solicitors should check that this is done. In modern practice this is usually done after a successful offer has been made. In theory this exposes the clients to the risk that the lender might not agree to lend, but in practice the loan will have been informally agreed with the lender before submission of the offer, and the lender is unlikely to back off unless the application form discloses something unexpected.

Examining title

At an early stage in the transaction, the selling solicitors will send the deeds   2–18 and seller's drafts to the purchasing solicitors, as outlined above.[69] The latter then examine the title,[70] and check, as far as possible, other matters such as statutory notices and planning and building consents, and raise any queries with the selling solicitors. They will also send to their clients a report on title, with a plan, a note of rights and burdens, and a summary of the PECs. The purchasing solicitors then draft the disposition and send it to the selling solicitors for revision, together with a draft of the registration forms (form 1 or 2 plus form 4).[71] At the same time they revise and return the seller's drafts, and return the title deeds.

As settlement approaches, the purchasing solicitors must make sure that they will have sufficient funds on the day to cover not only the price but other items such as stamp duty land tax ("SDLT")[72] and the registration fee. Often this will involve the clients obtaining a bridging loan until the proceeds of the sale of their old house are available. Settlement itself was outlined above.[73] At settlement the purchasing solicitors should check that the terms of the letter of

---

[65] On home reports generally, see above, para.2–07.

[66] See below, paras 4–33 to 4–39.

[67] See also below, para.3–09.

[68] *http://ros.gov.uk.*

[69] See above, para.2–10.

[70] For examination of title, see below, Ch.7.

[71] If the transaction proceeds under ARTL, this is done electronically. For the application forms, see below, para.8–20.

[72] For SDLT, see below, Ch.18.

[73] See above, para.2–11.

obligation conform to the draft, and that all the relevant deeds have been properly executed. In return they release the purchase price.[74]

The keys

2–19   One essential thing at settlement is to obtain the keys from the selling solicitors, unless this is being arranged directly between the clients. The novice conveyancer, trying desperately to keep on top of the legal procedures, can forget that for the purchasers the main point of the whole business is to get the keys. If the purchasers are standing outside the house with a laden removal truck plus hungry family at 6pm on Friday with no keys, with the seller uncontactable and their own solicitors' switchboard shut till 9am on Monday, they will have some choice remarks to make when they phone their solicitors from the hotel where they spent the weekend.

After settlement

2–20   After settlement the purchasing solicitors add the testing clause to the disposition, submit the land transaction return for SDLT, usually online, and pay the tax due.[75] They then send the disposition, with other documents, to the Land Register. What is sent typically are (i) the disposition, (ii) the discharge of the old standard security, (iii) the new standard security being granted by the buyers, and (iv) the SDLT certificate. If this is a first registration it will also be necessary to send (v) a prescriptive progress of GRS deeds.[76] Then there are the various Land Register forms.[77] These will be (vi) form 2—or a form 1 if this is a first registration—in respect of the disposition. The terms of these forms will have been adjusted between the solicitors in advance. Next, (vii) form 2 (registration of a dealing, in this case the new standard security), and (viii) form 4 (inventory of the deeds being sent).

For ARTL transactions, all of the above is carried out electronically, the relevant forms being completed online.[78] ARTL cannot be used for first registrations.

The new home loan

2–21   Acting for both borrower and lender is potentially to be subject to a conflict of interest.[79] But in residential conveyancing, matters are usually routine and uncontroversial and so it is generally permissible, and also common, to act for both parties. However, this is only possible if the law firm is on the "conveyancing panel" for the lender in question.[80] For the client there is the benefit that it is quicker and cheaper for the same solicitor to be used for both the purchase

---

[74] Except on the clear, and well-documented, instructions of the clients, the purchasing solicitors should not pay except in exchange for the disposition, clear reports and so on. *Mason v A&R. Robertson & Black*, 1993 S.L.T. 773 illustrates some of the risks of pre-payment.
[75] For payment of SDLT, see below, para.18–12.
[76] For details, see below, para.8–22.
[77] For details, see below, para.8–20.
[78] See below, para.8–23.
[79] See above, para.1–10.
[80] In 2010 Lloyds Banking Group introduced new criteria for solicitors to remain on its panel based on the number of transactions carried out, and numerous, mainly smaller, firms were discarded as a result.

and the security.[81] In commercial cases the danger of conflict of interest is more serious and accordingly separate solicitors must act for the parties, except in low-value cases. Even in residential cases it can occasionally happen that a conflict of interest emerges, and in that case the solicitors must cease to act for one side or the other. Where the same firm acts for both borrower and lender, it must not be overlooked that the solicitors have in law two clients, the borrower/buyer and the lender.

Once the home loan has been agreed, the lender will send to the solicitors a formal letter of instruction, and this will typically include standard-form documents which are to be used.[82] Solicitors must also have regard to the detailed rules set out in the Council of Mortgage Lenders ("CML") *Lenders Handbook for Scotland*. The standard security is drafted and engrossed, and sent for signature to the clients (i.e. the borrowers) in advance of settlement. In ARTL transactions the standard security is an electronic deed signed on behalf of the borrowers by their solicitors by means of an electronic signature.[83] If a client is taking title to the property in his or her sole name, it will also be necessary to prepare and have signed appropriate documentation in respect of occupancy rights.[84]

After the title has been examined a report on title, also called a certificate of title, is sent to the lender. Shortly before settlement the solicitors "requisition" the loan. The funds are then paid by direct transfer into the client account of the purchasing solicitors. If there is any significant delay in settlement the loan funds must be returned to the lender and requisitioned a second time when the problems have been resolved.[85] Following settlement the security is registered at once, for until registration the lender is unsecured.

Closing the file

The purchasing solicitors then put through a fee note and send an account to their clients. Some time later they will receive back from the Keeper the land certificate, plus a charge certificate for the standard security. These will come fairly quickly if the property was already in the Land Register, but if the transaction triggered a first registration, the certificates are likely to take many months and quite easily more than a year.   2–22

In the case of first registrations in particular, it is important to read the land certificate from cover to cover, checking, among other things, that the plan is accurate, that the clients are correctly named, that the sellers' security does not appear in the charges section, that the real burdens and servitudes are as expected, that there is the appropriate clause about occupancy rights,[86] and, vitally, that there is no exclusion of indemnity. The land certificate and charge certificate are then sent to the lender for safekeeping (if the lender wants them), and the selling solicitor's letter of obligation returned, marked as implemented. The Keeper will return the disposition and any other deeds submitted to him. Any of particular importance should be retained. Some solicitors simply

---

[81] In a secured loan it is almost invariable for the lender to require the borrowers to pay its legal fees.

[82] For fuller details on the procedure to be followed in respect of the loan, see below, para.22–06.

[83] See below, para.8–23.

[84] See below, para.10–14.

[85] CML *Lenders' Handbook for Scotland*, paras 10.6–10.8.

[86] See below, para.10–14.

discard the disposition. (An electronic copy is retained by the Keeper.) After
the successful completion of a first registration, the GRS deeds are sometimes
thrown out and sometimes sent to the clients to do with as they like.

MISCELLANEOUS

Fees, outlays and getting paid

2–23   The solicitors need to be paid two things: fees and the outlays. The latter are
moneys paid out for the benefit of clients, such as advertising charges, search fees,
registration dues, SDLT and so on. Some firms require clients to pay disbursements as they are made or in advance, thus giving credit only for the fees. On
being presented with the final account, clients often look only at the bottom line,
and complain about how much it is all costing. The distinction between fees and
outlays should therefore be explained. There was once a Law Society scale of fees
for conveyancing, but this disappeared in 1984, since when charging has been
unregulated. "Feeing up" a transaction is thus no longer the mechanical process it
once was. The basis of charge will have been agreed with the clients at the outset.[87]
It needs to be borne in mind that the amount of work is not the only factor. For
instance, the conveyancing on an expensive property may involve no more work
than for a cheap one, but the fee will be higher, because the financial consequences
of a mistake are greater. Part of the fee is thus, in a sense, an insurance premium.

Sometimes at the end of the transaction the solicitors will be holding funds
for their clients, and so the payment of the fee is relatively painless, being
simply a deduction. The clients are sent two bits of paper, namely the fee note
and an account showing all the receipts and disbursements and the fee. It is
important not to forget anything. There is nothing worse than having to contact
clients six months after the transaction to say that one had overlooked some
outlay and please could they send a cheque.

Fee levels

2–24   The old scale kept fees high, so the effect of deregulation has been that fee
levels have fallen.[88] Client loyalty has been eroded and it is increasingly
common for people to shop around seeking quotations. Moreover, NSEAs
often do deals with law firms (typically small outfits) whereby the former feed
them clients and the latter do the legal work for astonishingly low rates. This is
a matter which has been troubling the profession greatly in recent years. There
have been accusations that such clients do not always receive a proper professional service, that time-bomb negligence claims are accumulating, that some
firms are operating below real cost levels and so are running the risk of eventual insolvency, and so on. In this book we offer no views.

An example

2–25   The following is an example which is not untypical, but it should be borne in
mind that individual cases vary enormously. In the example below the SDLT

---

[87] See above, para.1–03.
[88] Overall conveyancing fee levels are, in broad terms, similar as between Scotland and England.
In most of Europe costs are far higher, partly because of higher stamp duty, or equivalent.

payable by the purchaser is £2,000, but for a more expensive property the cost will rise rapidly: thus for a property costing twice as much (£400,000) the SDLT payable would be six times as much (£12,000). If a property disconforms to building regulations there may be costs to the sellers, if only a comfort letter from the local authority at, say, £150. And so on. Obviously the clients will incur expenditure of other kinds as well.

(1) Purchase of property for £200,000 with £130,000 secured loan

(a)	SDLT	£2,000[89]
(b)	Registration dues	£420[90]
(c)	Solicitor's fee	£800
(d)	VAT thereon	£160
TOTAL		**£3,380**

(2) Sale of property for £200,000 with discharge of £130,000 secured loan

(a)	Press advertising	£400
(b)	SPC advertising	£145
(c)	Home report	£500
(d)	PEC	£60
(e)	Registration dues for discharge of standard security	£60[91]
(f)	form 12 and form 13 reports	£51
(g)	Commission on sale	£2,000
(h)	VAT thereon	£400
(i)	Solicitor's fee	£800
(j)	VAT thereon	£160
TOTAL		**£4,576**

Non-standard transactions

By definition, non-standard transactions defy classification. There is the cash 2–26 buyer, who does not need a loan. There is the first-time buyer, who will not have a house to sell. There is the last-time seller, such as a widow who is selling her house and will move into protected accommodation for elderly people. There is the purchase by a tenant from the landlord. A variant of this is the council house purchase, where the tenant is purchasing at a discount under the right-to-buy legislation.[92] There is the sale where an owner has defaulted on a secured loan and the sale is by the lender.[93] There is the executry sale, where the sale is by the executor of the deceased owner.[94] There is the insolvency sale, where the owner has become insolvent and the property is being sold by the trustee in sequestration or liquidator.[95] And there is the new house,

---

[89] See below, para.18–03.

[90] £360 for the disposition and £60 for the standard security: see below, para.8–06. If the transaction had proceeded under ARTL, the total fee would have been £100 less.

[91] £50 if ARTL is used.

[92] See below, paras 30–6 to 30–11.

[93] See below, paras 22–31 et seq.

[94] See below, para.25–13.

[95] See below, Ch.29.

where the client is buying from a builder.[96] Some of these are mentioned again later, but a detailed account of non-standard transactions is beyond the scope of this book.

The course of a typical transaction

2–27 What follows is a simplified version of a typical transaction. Naturally, individual transactions vary widely. The middle column shows the direction of communication between the solicitors. The outside columns show communications with parties other than the solicitors, such as the clients. Communication can be by email, letter, telephone or face-to-face. This is a conventional, paper-based transaction: if ARTL is used—which, at the time of writing, it hardly ever was—the preparation, signing and registration of the deeds take place electronically.

	BUYER'S SOLICITORS		SELLER'S SOLICITORS	
→	Take instructions. Verify client's identity. If a business, check that the contact has authority. Agree terms of business. Send out "terms engagement" of letter.[97]		Take instructions. Verify client's identity. If a business, check that the contact has authority. Agree terms of business. Send out "terms of engagement" letter.[98]	←
			Instruct home report.	→
			Advertise.	→
←	Check that client will have funds.		Order deeds[99] from lender. Check them.	→
			Instruct form 10 or 12 reports and (if first registration) P16 report.	→
			Request PEC.	→
	Note interest.	→		

---

[96] See below, paras 30–01 to 30–05.

[97] See above, para.1–03.

[98] See above, para.1–03.

[99] The "deeds" might be simply the land certificate. But there may be more, and if the property is still in the GRS the deeds are likely to be a substantial bundle.

		←	Set closing date.	
	Submit offer.	→		
			Examine offers with client.	→ ←
		←	Send qualified acceptance plus deeds plus form 10 or 12 report plus (for first registration) P16 report plus PEC.	
	Examine title for any matter on which "the buyers must satisfy themselves".			
→ ←	Report to client on title as soon as possible and obtain confirmation that boundaries and conditions are acceptable.			
←	Ensure client has applied for loan and knows that in principle it will be offered.			
	Further missives until bargain concluded, checking with client that terms are acceptable.[100]	→ ←	Further missives until bargain concluded, checking with client that terms are acceptable.	
		←	Draft and send "seller's drafts": (1) letter of obligation; (2) discharge of standard security; (3) form 11/13.	

---

[100] If missives take some time to conclude, the conveyancing steps below must be progressed in the mean time.

	BUYER'S SOLICITORS		SELLER'S SOLICITORS	
	Examine title.			
	Resolve any issues arising out of the examination of title.	→ ←	Resolve any issues arising out of the examination of title.	
	Draft disposition.		Draft any necessary documentation in respect of occupancy rights.[101]	
	Return deeds and revised seller's drafts. Send draft disposition plus draft forms 1 (or 2) and 4.	→		
		←	Revise buyer's drafts and return.	
			Engross seller's drafts.	
	Engross disposition and send.	→		
	Draft and engross standard security,[102] and any necessary documentation in respect of occupancy rights.[103]			
→ ←	Have client sign the above.		Send discharge to lender for signature.	→ ←

---

[101] If the seller is sole owner the disposition will need to be backed up by appropriate documentation: see below, para.10–14.

[102] The standard security will normally be a printed form sent by the lender.

[103] If there is a sole buyer the standard security will need to be backed up by appropriate documentation: see below, para.10–14.

			Have disposition, and documentation in respect of occupancy rights (if any), signed.	→ ←
			Instruct form 11 or 13 report.	→
			Receive form 11 or 13 report.	←
		←	Send form 11 or 13 report.	
→ ←	Prepare and send draft SDLT return and have client sign a declaration.[104]			
←	Send report on title and requisition loan from lenders.			
→ ←	Ensure that full price and outlays are available in cleared funds.			
	SETTLEMENT Money	→ ←	**SETTLEMENT** Keys, letter of obligation, disposition with signing schedule, deeds, documentation in respect of occupancy rights, form 13 or 11 report, discharge, signed form 2 for discharge.	
→ ←	Submit SDLT return online and receive SDLT certificate.		Pay off loan.	→

---

[104] See below, para.18–12.

	BUYER'S SOLICITORS		SELLER'S SOLICITORS	
	Add testing clause to disposition.		Intimate to local authority forthcoming change of ownership.	→
	Send to Land Register: (1) disposition; (2) standard security; (3) discharge of old security; (4) SDLT certificate; (5) deeds (for first registrations); (6) forms 1 or 2 for the disposition[105]; (7) form 2 for the standard security; (8) form 4.		Bill client for fees and outlays and pay any balance.	→
←	Bill client for fees and outlays.			
→	Receive land certificate and charge certificate and check carefully.			
←	Send deeds to lender.[106]			
	Return letter of obligation marked as implemented.	→		

---

[105] Depending on whether this is a first registration or not.

[106] If the lender does not want the deeds, they should be returned to the client or stored on his or her behalf.

CHAPTER 3

MISSIVES I: MAKING THE CONTRACT

A unitary law of sale

There is no special law of sale for land and buildings. Rather there is a general 3–01
law of sale which applies to land as it applies to property of other kinds—to
property which is heritable or moveable, corporeal or incorporeal. The law of
sale deals with matters such as formation of contract, implied obligations of seller
and buyer, warrandice, and the passing of risk.[1] Admittedly, the law of sale of
goods was detached from the rest of the law of sale and remodelled on English
lines by the Sale of Goods Act 1893 (now 1979). Admittedly too, much of
the (copious) nineteenth-century case law on sale is about moveable property[2]
and can involve issues which have no application to land.[3] Nonetheless, in
considering the topic of this and the next two chapters, it is important to remember
that missives are simply a species of the genus, contract of sale, and that they
are subject to a series of rules which are by no means confined to heritable
property.[4]

The rise and rise of missives

Once upon a time conveyancing, in the narrow sense, was complex, but 3–02
missives were simple. Here is a style offer from 1881:

> "On behalf of . . . I hereby offer to purchase from you the house no . . .
> Street Edinburgh at the price of £ . . . sterling. Entry to take place at the
> term of Whitsunday next, when the price will be payable, you relieving
> me of any casualty which may be due at the date of entry. This offer shall
> be binding for . . . days from this date."

---

[1] The only book devoted to the common law of sale is Mungo Brown's comprehensive but aged
Treatise on the Law of Sale (1821) which owes most of its organisation and some of its content to
Robert-Joseph Pothier's celebrated *Traité du contrat de vente* (1762). Other significant literature
includes Kenneth Reid and Reinhard Zimmermann (eds), *A History of Private Law in Scotland*
(2000), Vol.2, Ch.12 (W.M. Gordon); Reinhard Zimmermann, Daniel Visser and Kenneth Reid
(eds), *Mixed Legal Systems in Comparative Perspective: Property and Obligations in Scotland
and South Africa* (2004), Ch.10 (Robin Evans-Jones and Alastair Smith). The whole subject is in
need of further research.

[2] Horses were a popular topic. For a glimpse into a vanished world, see D. Ross Stewart, *The
Law of Horses* (1892), published on the eve of the Sale of Goods Act.

[3] And, following the passing of the Sale of Goods Act, no application to moveable property
either.

[4] And which for that reason are sometimes overlooked.

This offer was met by an unqualified one-sentence acceptance.[5] To modern eyes, that offer comes from a golden age of innocence. Offers today can run for pages and are met by, sometimes lengthy, qualified acceptances. While conveyancing in the narrow sense has become simpler than it was in 1881, missives have become more complex. As the years go by they have become longer, with new clauses being added. Sometimes the new clauses result from legislation. Sometimes they result from new case law. Sometimes they result from problems which have arisen in the practice of the law firm concerned, and sometimes from problems highlighted in the legal press. But one way or another the clauses accumulate, and few are ever removed.[6] Only recently has the tendency been checked, to some extent, by the use of regional missives for residential conveyancing.

FORMATION

Instructions

3–03   Throughout the transaction the solicitors act as agent for their clients. Therefore the solicitors must make sure that they have authority to act.[7] If solicitors purport to conclude missives on behalf of clients and it turns out that no proper agency had been constituted, there is no contract, but the solicitors may be personally liable to the other would-be party to the contract for breach of an implied warranty that they had authority to act.[8] Solicitors will usually accept oral instructions, but this involves an element of risk, in that the client may subsequently deny the instructions, or admit the instructions but deny an important detail, such as the price. Once appointed, the solicitors have authority to conclude the contract (in consultation with the clients) and to carry out the usual steps in a conveyancing transaction.[9]

Formal writing

3–04   The letters making up missives of sale must be in formal writing.[10] They can be signed by the parties themselves, but in practice they run in the name of the law firm as agents for their clients.[11] If the firm is a limited liability partnership, the signature must be that of a "member"[12]; for ordinary partnerships, any authorised person can sign but a signature by a partner is normal. Missives are normally done in probative form, i.e. witnessed, usually by someone within the

---

[5] From *A Complete System of Conveyancing* (commonly called *Juridical Styles*), 5th edn (1881), Vol.1. For a set of missives from 1948 see *Anderson v Lambie*, 1953 S.C. (HL) 43. These missives are longer than the 1881 missives but still slight by modern standards, and were concluded quickly: the offer was dated December 15, the qualified acceptance was dated December 16 and the third missive, concluding the bargain, was dated December 17.

[6] See further Rennie, 2000 S.L.T. (News) 65, near the end of which can be found the best missive clause in recorded history.

[7] See generally above, para.1–03.

[8] *Scott v JB Livingston & Nicol*, 1990 S.L.T. 305; *MacDougall v Akram*, 1993 G.W.D. 33-2142; *Halifax Life Ltd v DLA Piper Scotland LLP* [2009] CSOH 74; 2009 G.W.D. 19-306.

[9] *Heron v Thomson*, 1989 G.W.D. 11-469.

[10] Requirements of Writing (Scotland) Act 1995 s.1(2)(a)(i). See further below, Ch.17.

[11] A traditional opening is: "On behalf of and as instructed by our clients . . . we hereby offer . . .".

[12] 1995 Act Sch.2 paras 2(1) and 3A(1).

firm, although it is difficult to see any good reason for this practice.[13] Since a purchaser does not normally sign either the missives or the disposition, it is possible for a person to buy heritable property without ever signing anything at all.[14] It is curious that the age-old rule requiring subscribed writing before a person can be bound to a contract for the purchase or sale of heritable property has been construed in this way. The key point is that the missives can be signed by the solicitors, and that their authority can be granted orally.[15] This seems unsatisfactory as a matter of policy, and is contrary to the system adopted by many other countries.

Missives by pdf or fax?

Documents must be delivered as well as signed,[16] and in the case of missives 3–05 letters the practice is for them to be transmitted by pdf attachment to an email or by fax, and thereafter by post or messenger. Is a missives letter binding after it is emailed or faxed but before the original arrives? The answer, of course, will rarely matter, but in *Park Ptrs (No.2)*,[17] where it did, it was held that transmission by fax was not sufficient to conclude the contract. But while email or fax is not of itself a form of delivery, it may be possible to achieve constructive delivery where the parties agree that a letter is to be held by the sending solicitors on behalf of the receiving solicitors.[18]

E-missives?

"Electronic" missives can mean two things. It can mean missives that use 3–06 conventional, wet-signed sheets of paper, images of which are sent as a pdf or by fax in the manner considered in the previous paragraph. In that case, there still needs to be paper and there still needs to be ink. Or it can mean "pure" e-missives, i.e. missives that need no paper and ink. In pure e-missives what happens is simply that the missive is sent as an email, with an electronic

---

[13] The practice developed when the 1995 Act was passed. But the Act did not require missives to be probative, and before the Act missives were normally improbative.

[14] There may be a cheque to be signed, and if, as is usual, there is a loan, the loan documentation will have to be signed.

[15] Presumably the person orally authorised need not be a solicitor. Presumably, too, oral authority to sign a disposition would be possible. Neither is attempted in practice, and one might question the law which would allow such things. The law as summarised in the text was the law before the Requirements of Writing (Scotland) Act 1995, and those responsible for that Act did not intend to change the law in this respect: see the Scottish Law Commission's *Consultative Memorandum* No.66 (1985), para.8.4. But there might be an argument that the law was in fact changed by the 1995 Act. Section 2(1) says that signature must be by the grantor. Section 12(2) allows signature on behalf of the grantor by a person holding a "power of attorney". The 1995 Act does not require powers of attorney to be in writing (see s.1), but the expression "power of attorney" is generally understood to involve a written document, and it is noteworthy that s.12(2) avoids the general terms "agency" and "mandate". If there is a difficulty here, however, it is ignored in practice.

[16] See e.g. *Stamfield's Creditors v Scot* (1696) IV Br. Supp. 344 where Sir James Stamfield signed a document and told the other party it was ready to be uplifted: immediately thereafter he was murdered. It was held that the document was ineffective.

[17] *Park Ptrs (No.2)* [2009] CSOH 122; 2009 S.L.T. 871. See Anderson, 2010 S.L.T. (News) 67 and 73. A different view had been reached by the sheriff in *McIntosh v Alam*, 1998 S.L.T. (Sh. Ct) 19; cf. *Merrick Homes Ltd v Duff*, 1996 S.C. 497.

[18] This was the suggestion of the Temporary Judge (M.G. Thomson QC) in *Park Ptrs* at para.23. For possible difficulties, see Gretton, (2010) 14 Edin. L.R. 280.

signature. Not competent under the current law, e-missives are expected to be allowed under the proposed new legislation on land registration.[19]

Noting interest and closing dates[20]

3–07 The proper way of expressing interest in buying a house is to "note interest" with the solicitors (or estate agents) representing the seller. This can be done by a phone call. Noting interest is an indication that the interested party is likely to put in an offer.[21] Moreover, the convention is that sellers who have received notes of interest will not sell without giving those who have noted interest a chance to offer. This, however, is not a rule of law and it is permissible, if regrettable, for the sellers to negotiate only with one potential purchaser.[22]

Normally, all interested parties are given the chance to offer for the property. This is done by setting a closing date, i.e. a day and time by which all offers must be received, and intimating this date (through their solicitors) to those who noted interest. Once the closing date arrives, the sellers' solicitors must go over the offers carefully, and discuss them with the clients. If there is more than one offer a decision must be made as to which one to accept (usually the highest, but where there is not much between the first two offers there may be other reasons, e.g. better date of entry or personal reasons, for preferring the second-highest). Once the sellers have made their decision, their solicitor should at once telephone the firms which submitted offers to tell them the outcome.

Gazumping and gazundering

3–08 Sellers are not bound to accept the highest offer, and indeed they can reject all offers. Unless and until missives have been concluded, sellers are legally free to accept an offer which comes in after the closing date. They may also accept an increased offer from one of the unsuccessful bidders.[23] This is called gazumping, and the bidder who was at first successful but later unsuccessful will be understandably incensed. There is normally no legal redress, but there is a question as to whether co-operation in gazumping is unprofessional.[24] Law Society Guidelines say that a later offer is (from a professional standpoint) acceptable only if negotiations on the originally successful offer have "fallen through".[25]

Gazundering is the converse: it is where a buyer opts out of a purchase which is not yet binding so as to persuade the seller to sell for a lower figure. Unless there is a cogent reason for the re-negotiation (such as the discovery of

---

[19] The Scottish Law Commission has so recommended: see Report on *Land Registration* (Scot. Law Com. No.222, 2010), Pt 34. On one view, allowing e-missives is a requirement of the E-Commerce Directive 2000/31 art.9, which had to be transposed by Member States by January 17, 2002.

[20] See generally Janice H. Webster, *Professional Ethics and Practice for Scottish Solicitors*, 4th edn (2004), para.4.05.

[21] In theory, missives could equally well be initiated by an offer to sell made by the seller. Occasionally this is seen. But in the normal case the missives begin with an offer to buy.

[22] And for their solicitors to continue to act. See the Law Society's *Guidelines on Gazumping, Gazundering and Closing Dates 2005*.

[23] Or threaten to do so in order to persuade the successful bidders to up their price.

[24] For a case involving a late offer see *Morston Assets Ltd v City of Edinburgh Council*, 2001 S.L.T. 613.

[25] *Guidelines on Gazumping, Gazundering and Closing Dates 2005*. Otherwise the solicitor should decline to act for the client in concluding a contract with a different party.

a title defect), the Law Society regards this is as professionally unacceptable and advises that the solicitor should cease to act.[26]

Gazumping tends to happen in rising markets and gazundering in falling ones. Gazumping and gazundering used to be regarded as English diseases, back in the days when missives were concluded promptly. Nowadays, when missives tend to remain open for rather longer, the disease exists in Scotland too, though it is not so widespread as in England.[27]

How much?

In a buoyant housing market a seller will hope to collect a number of noted   3–09
interests. But once the first note of interest has come in there is immediate pressure to set a closing date: potential buyers will be looking at other houses as well, and they will not want to wait indefinitely for this one. Normally a closing date follows within a week to 10 days. It is usually at noon, and often on a Friday.

The offerors are bidding blind. They have the valuation figure provided by the home report and may have a second figure from a survey of their own. They will also usually know, through the local solicitors property centre, the recent selling prices of comparable properties. And they may know how many other people are bidding against them. If advising offerors, the trick is to offer enough to get the property but not so much that they pay more than absolutely necessary. But in practice there is a lot of luck involved and it is difficult to fix on the right figure. The clients may be up against another offeror who has just lost seven houses in a row, and is willing to offer an absurd figure to secure this one. If the market is weak there may be no noted interests at all. In that case offers can sometimes be enticed by making the house available at a fixed price: in principle the first person to submit an offer at that price is then the person to whom the property will be sold, although it does not always work out like that, partly because two offers may be submitted at about the same time.

Standard missives

In the case of residential property, at least, there is broad agreement within the   3–10
legal profession as to what provisions should and should not be part of the contract. Yet the tradition was for each law firm to have its own style of offer, with its own peculiarities, and usually weighted down by a number of pro-buyer provisions which the law firm fully expected to be challenged by the solicitors acting for the sellers. And while most concluded contracts were largely similar in content and consisted of clauses which were largely uncontroversial, it could take a great deal of time and effort for the terms to be finally agreed. That this was time and effort poorly spent, and not properly remunerated, was obvious to anyone who thought about it. Nonetheless, law firms proved curiously reluctant to abandon their own way of doing things, and a rather misjudged attempt by

---

[26] *Guidelines on Gazumping, Gazundering and Closing Dates 2005.* For criticism, see McCormick, (2005) 50 J.L.S.S. April/10, who comments that: "These Guidelines are presumably designed to impose a moral sanction on wayward punters. With one or two exceptions the reaction will be that they will just go to another solicitor who will earn his/her crust from a client's immorality while denying the previous solicitor his/her fee."

[27] It is a problem which exists in many other countries too.

the Law Society in the early 1990s to introduce a set of standard clauses for residential transactions[28] was quick to end in failure.[29]

In the last few years, the position has changed beyond recognition with the flourishing of locally-agreed standard clauses for offers in respect of residential property. The Law Society website discloses ten different sets of "regional" missives which, taken together, cover most of Scotland.[30] As well as avoiding the chaos of a multitude of individually-drafted offers, the standard clauses are also designed to produce an offer which is even-handed as between buyer and seller and can be accepted by the latter's solicitors with a minimum of qualification. The idea is to reduce unproductive work and to speed up the conclusion of missives, to the benefit of both solicitors and clients alike.[31]

In 2009, the previously separate clauses for Glasgow and Edinburgh were combined into a single set of "Combined Standard Clauses", and it may be that this will set the pattern for further combinations in the future. If so, an all-Scotland set of clauses will no longer be as unthinkable as once it seemed. Meanwhile, a group based on four commercial law firms—the Property Standardisation Group—has produced a series of styles of offer to sell in respect of commercial property.[32]

Bargaining

3–11 Even with standard missives, it is seldom possible to meet an offer with a *de plano* (i.e. unqualified) acceptance, and with non-standard offers—as occur sometimes in residential conveyancing and much more often in commercial conveyancing—the need for qualification is much the greater. Indeed, so rare are *de plano* acceptances that the receipt of one may induce panic in the recipient. Why must the buyers' offer be qualified by the sellers? One reason is that, with non-standard offers at least, the terms of the offer are likely to be unfairly loaded in favour of the buyers, so that it is necessary to redress the balance. Indeed the temptation is to load it down the other way. Another is that the property may not satisfy all the conditions laid down in the offer. In order to judge to what extent the terms of the offer can be accepted, the sellers' solicitors must consult with their clients and also have at least a nodding acquaintance with the title. (The sellers' solicitors should have the deeds and the property enquiry certificates ["PECs"] to hand before any offer is received, although for one reason or another it is not always possible to manage this.) A third reason for a qualified acceptance is that it may be necessary to alter, say, the date of entry, or the list of extras to be included in the price. Where possible, such qualifications should be agreed with the other side by telephone at the time when they are told that the offer is to be accepted. Not only does this cut down on work later but there is always the chance that in the immediate euphoria of success

---

[28] A first version was registered in the Books of Council and Session on August 9, 1991 and a second on April 3, 1992.

[29] The clauses were withdrawn by the Law Society in 1995: see (1995) 40 J.L.S.S. 326. One problem was that there had been no consultation with the profession as a whole. Another was that the first of the three parts was declared unalterable—an unenforceable but irksome attempt to limit freedom of contract.

[30] *http://www.lawscot.org.uk/*. Standard missives exist for Aberdeen, Ayr, Borders, Dumfries and Galloway, Dundee and Tayside, Edinburgh and Glasgow, Highland, Inverclyde, Moray, and Paisley.

[31] For a sceptical view of their value, see Smith, (2009) 54 J.L.S.S. Dec./54.

[32] *http://www.psglegal.co.uk/*.

the buyers will be more accommodating than on the morning after. What is to be avoided is qualification for its own sake and where there are no real issues between the parties. Some firms cannot resist the temptation of trying to slip something past the other side. Sometimes indeed precisely this happens. But unless one is transacting with Rip van Winkle, W.S., the final contract is likely to be much the same no matter how long is spent on negotiations. Meanwhile, as the days lengthen into weeks without the contract being concluded, the clients are being exposed to the risk that the other party may (for some quite unconnected reason) decide to withdraw. The solicitors involved will then have difficulty in justifying their tactics to their own clients.

The drafting of a qualified acceptance is difficult and should be done with care. Unlike with offers, there is no style to follow. Though there is pressure of time, it is vital to get the acceptance right: the clients will be bound and errors can be costly. It should be borne in mind that certain obligations, most notably the obligation to provide a good and marketable title, are implied by law. So in such cases it is not enough to delete the obligation as stated in the offer: the common law obligation is only excluded if the qualified acceptance expressly states that the clients will not, for instance, guarantee the absence of unduly onerous burdens.[33]

Finally, practical problems can arise where there are several missives letters. An offer met by a qualification met by a final acceptance makes three letters. That is reasonable, in the sense that working out the final terms of the contract is not too difficult. But the more letters there are, the harder it is to work out which terms have been deleted, which reinstated, which modified, and so on. Trying to see whether the seller has or has not agreed to warrant the condition of the central heating becomes a brainteaser taking several minutes. Moreover, the client may be unimpressed by all this clutter. There has been judicial criticism. One judge commented that the set of papers before him was "a poor advertisement for the traditional process of developing the definition of the rights and obligations of the parties through qualification and counter-qualification".[34] At worst, it may lead to real uncertainty as to the terms which have actually been agreed.[35] One possible response to the problem is to use draft missives, whereby an offer is adjusted between the agents until it is mutually satisfactory. It can then be sent as a formal offer and met by a *de plano* acceptance. This is quite often done in commercial conveyancing, and should be adopted into residential conveyancing, at least where the number of missives letters starts to become substantial.

Delay in concluding missives

Traditionally missives were concluded within a few days. Quick contracts 3–12 were a matter of national pride: in England there was envy and admiration of what was called "the Scottish system". During the 1970s the period began to

---

[33] See e.g. *Baird v Drumpellier & Mount Venon Estates Ltd*, 2000 S.C. 103; and for the implied obligation of good and marketable title, see below, Ch.6.

[34] *Evans v Argus Healthcare (Glenesk) Ltd*, 2001 S.C.L.R. 117, per Lord Macfadyen.

[35] As in *Middlebank Ltd v University of Dundee* [2006] CSOH 202, where the the final qualified acceptance read, in part: "we . . . offer to amend the terms of our formal letter, dated 17 February 2004, relative to your formal letter, dated 9 February 2004 . . . relative to our formal letter, dated 3 February 2004, relative to your formal letter, dated 27 January 2004, being a qualified acceptance of our offer, dated 21 January 2004 . . and make the following further qualifications . . .".

lengthen until it became common for missives to remain open until the eve of settlement. A study in 2009 found that the average period between making an offer and concluding the contract was seven weeks.[36] Since that time there is likely to have been some improvement due to the growing use of standard missives.

The reasons for these developments are not wholly certain. To some extent it is due to the increasing complexity of offers. To some extent it is due to delay by lenders.[37] To some extent it is because some clients are deliberately keeping missives open so as to keep their options open. To some extent it is because some solicitors seem no longer to feel much urgency about concluding missives. And there may be other reasons. Open missives are not binding, a fact which may or may not be satisfactory to the parties, or which may be satisfactory to one but not to the other. Even the party who is content for missives to be open may suddenly be of a different opinion. Clara is buying from Donald and is keeping the missives unconcluded until she has sold her old house. Donald may get fed up and resile, leaving Clara less than happy. She wanted to have it both ways, but what is sauce for the Clara-goose is also sauce for the Donald-gander. Fortunately, however, cases in which one party resiles from open missives are not common. The Law Society's *Guidelines on Avoidance of Delay in Concluding Missives* (1998) narrate, all too truly, that "it is increasingly common for missives to be in an unconcluded state until shortly before – or even at – the date of entry". They go on to state that there is a "professional duty to conclude missives without undue delay". If the client instructs delay, then the professional duty is to disclose the circumstances to the other side. These *Guidelines* seem not to have made much impact.[38]

One consequence of the change in practice is that, whereas it used to be the norm for missives to be concluded before the agents for the buyers had had the opportunity to examine the title, nowadays the buyers' agents often examine title before conclusion of missives. The report on title can thus be sent to the buyers before, rather than after, the contract is made. In the old days, if there was something in the title which was unsatisfactory to the buyers, they would have to argue that there was a breach of the terms of the missives. By contrast, nowadays the missives will often still be open when the difficulty comes to light, and in that case the buyers can simply choose not to conclude the missives. The current practice thus does have certain advantages to offset the drawbacks.

Offer and acceptance

3–13 Unlike many contracts, missives fit neatly into the textbook category of offer and acceptance. Once an offer has been made, it presumptively remains available for acceptance for a "reasonable time". The same is true of qualified acceptances, which in law are considered as new offers. In practice the initial offer will almost invariably contain an express, and short, time limit by which acceptance must be made. In reality, though, time limits often matter little, because most offers are met by qualified acceptances, and a qualified

---

[36] Office of Fair Trading, *Home Buying and Selling: A Market Study* (2010, available at *http://www.oft.gov.uk/shared_oft/reports/property/OFT1186.pdf*), para.8.25. This figure was based on responses from only 80 buyers and sellers and so its accuracy may be open to question.

[37] All conveyancers have a rich store of horror stories about institutional lenders.

[38] For interesting discussion see a letter by Jenny H. Clark at (1999) 44 J.L.S.S. July/15.

acceptance is regarded as an entirely new offer, which therefore need not adhere to the time limit in the previous missive. It is only where a missive constitutes a final acceptance that it has to meet the time limit in the immediately previous missive. In practice, however, each missive usually has a clause expressly deleting the time limit stated in the previous missive.

Can a party withdraw an offer? The rules are as follows. (i) In general a party is free to withdraw at any time before acceptance. (ii) But if the offer is stated to be open for acceptance until a stated time, it cannot be unilaterally withdrawn before that time has arrived. (iii) A distinction exists between a clause saying that an offer will lapse by a certain date, if not accepted, and a clause which says that an offer is open for acceptance until a certain date. Only the latter falls under rule (ii).[39] The exact wording is therefore important. (iv) If the offer provides that it can be withdrawn, then withdrawal is competent notwithstanding rule (ii). In order to ensure that the right to withdraw exists, it is advisable, and normal, to make use of this rule. For instance: "This offer, unless previously withdrawn, is open for acceptance until . . .". (v) Withdrawal is never competent if the offer has already been accepted.[40] Assuming the withdrawal to be competent, it need not be in formal writing, and indeed may be oral,[41] though of course from a practical point of view a formal written withdrawal is advisable.

On receipt of an offer two choices are in theory open: to accept or to reject. In practice a successful offer is usually met by a qualified acceptance, and a qualified acceptance is deemed to be both (a) a rejection and (b) a new offer.[42] It is easy to overlook (a). Once a qualified acceptance is sent the original offer is rejected once and for all and cannot be revived by withdrawing the qualified acceptance.[43] The only effect of withdrawing a qualified acceptance is that there is now no live offer available for the other party to accept. The earlier offer does not revive. Care should be taken with the use of qualified acceptances, particularly at a late stage in the negotiations where the qualification may concern a trivial point. For as soon as a qualified acceptance is sent the ball is back in the other party's court and the chance to bring about a concluded contract is lost until the ball is returned. It may not be returned.

The postal rule

Details of the "postal rule" can be found in the standard texts on contract law.[44] 3–14
Its effect is that an acceptance may be deemed delivered at the time when it is posted, even though the offeror has so far received nothing back. Thus an offer to buy is posted on April 1 and the withdrawal posted on April 3. If the seller posts the acceptance on April 2, reaching the offeror on April 4, the law says that there is a binding contract. The rule does not apply to qualified acceptances because

---

[39] See William W. McBryde, *The Law of Contract in Scotland*, 3rd edn (2007), para.6–57.

[40] That is to say, genuinely accepted, as opposed to being met by a qualified acceptance.

[41] *McMillan v Caldwell*, 1991 S.L.T. 325.

[42] The term "qualified acceptance" is thus in a sense a misleading one, because in law it is not an acceptance at all. Indeed, each and every new missive is a rejection of what has gone before and is a new offer which incorporates parts of what has gone before. The exception is the final missive, which accepts the immediately previous one. This final missive is the only one which is truly an "acceptance".

[43] *Rutterford v Allied Breweries*, 1990 S.L.T. 249; and cf. *Findlater v Maan*, 1990 S.L.T. 465.

[44] See e.g. William W. McBryde, *The Law of Contract in Scotland*, 3rd edn (2007), paras 6–114 et seq.

these are regarded as fresh offers.[45] Most missives letters nowadays are sent by DX or Legal Post, and whether the postal rule applies to such forms of communication is uncertain.[46] The postal rule has many obscure aspects. It is generally regarded as a nuisance, but happily it can be excluded if the offer expressly states that the acceptance is to "reach this office" by the stated deadline.

Personal bar

3–15 Contracts for the sale of heritage must be constituted in formal writing. But where formal writing has not been used a contract may still be set up by the operation of the doctrine of personal bar. This used to be governed by common law but is now statutory. If there is an informal contract for the sale of heritable property, and one party "has acted or refrained from acting in reliance on the contract . . . with the knowledge or acquiescence of the other party" then the other party "shall not be entitled to withdraw from the contract".[47] The conduct in question must be of some significance.[48] In one case taken at common law the purchaser had done no more than draft a disposition and prepare a few other forms and this was held not to justify a plea of personal bar.[49]

Before this provision can apply there must be a contract, that is to say, an agreement which would have been legally binding had it not been for the absence (partial or total) of formal writing. And it seems that the agreement must be evidenced by something other than the actings relied on for the purpose of establishing personal bar.[50]

Defects of consent

3–16 Like other contracts, missives may be affected by defects of consent such as essential error or undue influence. This subject, which belongs to the general law of contract, will not be dealt with here, except for a few words about error. In the typical case, error is both unilateral and also uninduced. Thus it gives rise to no remedy. A standard example is where the buyers think that they are getting a larger piece of land than turns out to be the case.[51] Unilateral error may, however, be relevant where the error was known to, and taken advantage of by, the other party to the contract.[52] Where the missives misdescribe the property, or misstate some other matter, so that they fail to represent the common

---

[45] It also does not apply to other forms of communication such as the exercise of an option. See *Carmarthen Developments Ltd v Pennington* [2008] CSOH 139; 2008 G.W.D. 33-494 at para.14, per Lord Hodge.

[46] See William W. McBryde, *The Law of Contract in Scotland*, 3rd edn (2007), para.6–118 for general discussion, though DX or Legal Post are not specifically dealt with.

[47] Requirements of Writing (Scotland) Act 1995 s.1(3). For analysis, see Elspeth C. Reid and John W.G. Blackie, *Personal Bar* (2006), paras 7–07 to 7–34; Robert Rennie and Stewart Brymer, *Conveyancing in the Electronic Age* (2008), Ch.3.

[48] *Mitchell v Caversham Management Ltd* [2009] CSOH 26; 2009 G.W.D. 29-465.

[49] *Rutterford v Allied Breweries*, 1990 S.L.T. 249.

[50] *Stratton (Trade Sales) Ltd v MCS (Scotland) Ltd*, Unreported March 24, 2005, Glasgow Sheriff Court, discussed in Reid and Gretton, *Conveyancing 2005*, pp.130–32. The previous law seems to have been different: see *Errol v Walker*, 1966 S.C. 93.

[51] As in *Oliver v Gaughan*, 1990 G.W.D. 22-1247.

[52] This is the doctrine of "taking unfair advantage" of error. Compare *Spook Erection (Northern) Ltd v Kaye*, 1990 S.L.T. 676 with *Angus v Bryden*, 1992 S.L.T. 884; and see also *Parvaiz v Thresher Wines Acquisitions Ltd* [2008] CSOH 160; 2009 S.C. 151; discussed by Hogg, (2009) 13 Edin. L.R. 286. See further Thomson, 1992 S.L.T. (News) 215 and William W. McBryde, *The Law of Contract in Scotland*, 3rd edn (2007), paras 15–30 to 15–33.

intention of the parties, judicial rectification may be available.[53] In practice, parties may be in dispute as to whether the error is unilateral (for which there is, in general, no remedy) or whether the error is in expression, misstating a prior common intention (for which rectification is competent). Unilateral error will found reduction where it has been induced by the other party to the contract; and damages are also due if the misrepresentation was either fraudulent or negligent.[54]

If there is misrepresentation in a conveyancing transaction, it is almost always by the seller. The representation may be oral, or it may be in the property questionnaire or the printed sale particulars; in the last case the effect is negatived, as far as private law is concerned,[55] by the more or less standard disclaimer that their accuracy is not guaranteed. Some contracts circumvent this disclaimer by express incorporation of the sale particulars. Typical misrepresentations by the seller are that the roof is in good condition, that the central heating system was recently overhauled, or that the next-door neighbours are aged, friendly and quiet. In *Smith v Paterson*[56] reduction was granted where the seller had, by deliberately careless words, misrepresented the extent of the front garden. But, as *Smith* itself shows, it is difficult to prove oral representations.

Promises and options

It is competent to make a gratuitous promise to transfer ownership of land. The promise must be in formal writing.[57] Naturally such promises are rare in practice. More important is the option.[58] In an option, the owners undertake to sell[59] land on certain terms at a certain price, but the potential purchasers are not bound to buy. They may buy or not as they see fit. The option will be open for a stated period, such as a year, and if the option-holders choose not to exercise their option in that time, the option lapses.[60] Options are occasionally granted gratuitously but normally are onerous, i.e. the owner sells the option. If the option is exercised, the price for the land will be in addition to the price paid for the option itself. In commercial conveyancing, options are quite common,[61] but in residential conveyancing they are rarely encountered.

An option, like missives, must be sufficiently definite as to parties, property and price.[62] It must be exercised in the form and within the timescale laid down

3–17

---

[53] Under s.8 of the Law Reform (Miscellaneous Provisions) (Scotland) Act 1985. See below, Ch.20.

[54] Law Reform (Miscellaneous Provisions) (Scotland) Act 1985 s.10. See e.g. *Palmer v Beck*, 1993 S.L.T. 485; *McNally v Worrell*, 2006 G.W.D. 37-741.

[55] False sales particulars may amount to an offence under the Property Misdescriptions Act 1991. See above, para.2–08.

[56] *Smith v Paterson*, Unreported February 18, 1986 OH.

[57] Requirements of Writing (Scotland) Act 1995 s.1(2)(a)(i).

[58] On the troublesome subject of the legal characterisation of an option, see *Carmarthern Developments Ltd v Pennington* [2008] CSOH 139; 2008 G.W.D. 33-494 at para.15, per Lord Hodge.

[59] Options can in fact either be options to buy ("call" options) or options to sell ("put" options). So an owner might buy a put option. But this is rare for heritable property.

[60] There may sometimes be disputes as to whether the time limit has been complied with: see *Fortune Engineering Ltd v Precision Components (Scotland) Ltd*, 1993 G.W.D. 1-49.

[61] They can provide commercial flexibility and can save capital gains tax. See Halliday, para.30–164.

[62] *Bogie v Forestry Commission*, 2001 G.W.D. 38-1432. For a marginal case see *Miller Homes Ltd v Frame*, 2001 S.L.T. 459. For the corresponding rules for missives, see below, para.4–03.

in the initial grant of the option.[63] But unless the grant specifies otherwise, an option need not be exercised in formal writing or indeed in any writing at all, though the original option itself must have been in formal writing.[64] An option is not exercised by an offer to buy, for an offer to buy may be rejected, or accepted only conditionally, whereas an owner is immediately and completely bound by the valid exercise of an option. In other words, an option is not given effect to by later missives, unless both parties so wish. In practice, options do not usually contain the multifarious terms and conditions found in missives, but to some extent these will be implied.[65]

Finally, missives subject to a suspensive condition can in practice work very like an option in favour of the buyers, and, moreover, an option for which they do not have to pay.[66] To this subject we may now turn.

SUSPENSIVE CONDITIONS

Introduction

3–18 Suspensive conditions are quite common, particularly in commercial conveyancing.[67] These are conditions in a contract which are suspensive of performance. In other words there is a concluded contract between the parties—each is bound to the other—but neither can be made to perform unless or until the condition is purified, so that if the condition is not purified within the time limit set for that purpose both parties are freed from its terms. For as long as the suspensive condition remains unpurified, the contract is in suspense. Its activation depends on the purification of the condition. No obligation arises under the suspensive condition itself. Indeed, typically its purification is out of the control of both parties. If the condition is not met no damages are due; the contract simply falls away. However, in practice missives often provide that the buyers shall use their best endeavours to bring about the purification of the condition. The typical example is planning permission, with the purchasers being bound to pursue the planning application with reasonable diligence and so on.

Identifying suspensive conditions

3–19 It is not always easy to say whether a particular contractual term is an ordinary condition or a suspensive condition.[68] A well-drafted term should leave no doubt on the matter, but not all terms are well-drafted. The standard way of

---

[63] See e.g. *Hallam Land Management Ltd v Perratt*, 2005 S.C.L.R. 230; *Simmers v Innes* [2008] UKHL 24; 2008 S.C. (HL) 137.

[64] 1995 Act s.1(2); and see *Stone v MacDonald*, 1979 S.C. 363; and *Mitchell v Caversham Management Ltd* [2009] CSOH 26; 2009 G.W.D. 29-465 at paras 41 and 42, per Lord Bracadale.

[65] *Zani v Martone*, 1997 S.L.T. 1269; *McCall's Entertainments (Ayr) Ltd v South Ayrshire Council*, 1998 S.L.T. 1403 and 1421.

[66] See below, para.3–22.

[67] See generally Thomson, in A.J. Gamble (ed.), *Obligations in Context: Essays in Honour of Professor D.M. Walker* (1990); and William W. McBryde, *The Law of Contract in Scotland*, 3rd edn (2007), paras 5.35–5.40.

[68] Or a resolutive condition. In this latter case the formula is generally that if a certain condition is not met, either party may resile without liability to either side. For an example see *Ford Sellar Morris Properties Plc v EW Hutchison Ltd*, 1990 S.C. 34.

introducing a suspensive condition is with the words "this contract is conditional on" or "this contract is subject to" (e.g. the obtaining of planning permission). Clauses which begin this way are usually suspensive. But less will do. In *Zebmoon Ltd v Akinbrook Investment Developments Ltd*[69] a clause which began with the words "it is an essential condition of this offer" was held to be suspensive even though these words are often found introducing non-suspensive conditions as well.

Sometimes conditions are apparently suspensive but are coupled with an express right for the purchasers to rescind if the condition is not purified. This is a natural attempt by the draftsman to protect the clients. Yet if the condition is truly suspensive such a provision is unnecessary, for in the absence of purification the contract automatically falls. Indeed, such a provision may be the basis for an argument that the clause is in fact an ordinary, non-suspensive, condition.[70] A possible alternative interpretation of such a clause is as a suspensive condition but with a right in the purchasers to waive purification; for if they have an express right to resile they also appear to have an implied right not to resile.

Time limit for purification

From the sellers' point of view it is most important that a time limit for purifi-   3–20 cation be stipulated. Otherwise they may be left in the situation where they do not know whether the sale will proceed (and do not know when they will know) but yet cannot lawfully withdraw and remarket the property. If purification requires one of the parties to do something (such as to apply for planning permission), an alternative approach is to set out a timetable, in which case time should be made of the essence or, which comes to the same thing, a right of immediate rescission reserved in the event of non-compliance.[71] A right of rescission need not be exercised immediately, and can still be exercised if the condition was purified but out of time.[72]

If no date is given, the condition must be fulfilled within a reasonable time.[73] But where missives have a date of entry which is fixed independently of the suspensive condition,[74] the condition must be fulfilled by that date.

Can the purchasers waive a suspensive condition?

If a suspensive condition is not purified, the purchasers will usually wish to with-   3–21 draw from the purchase and, generally speaking, the effect of non-purification is for the contract to fall. Sometimes, though, the purchasers may wish to proceed

---

[69] *Zebmoon Ltd v Akinbrook Investment Developments Ltd*, 1987 S.C. 252. Compare *Khazaka v Drysdale*, 1995 S.L.T. 1108.

[70] See *Tarditi v Drummond*, 1989 S.L.T. 554 at 557–558. But no objection was raised on this account in *Zebmoon Ltd v Akinbrook Investment Developments Ltd*, 1987 S.C. 252.

[71] In the absence of such a provision, an ultimatum must first be sent giving a "reasonable time" for performance: see below, para.5-08; and *Miller Group Ltd v Park's of Hamilton (Holdings) Ltd*, 2003 G.W.D. 8-225.

[72] *Ford Sellar Morris Properties Plc v EW Hutchison Ltd*, 1990 S.C. 34; *Bluestone Estates Ltd v Fitness First Clubs Ltd*, 2003 G.W.D. 27-768. A long delay will give rise to arguments of personal bar.

[73] See *T Boland & Co v Dundas's Trustees*, 1975 S.L.T. (Notes) 80, per Lord Keith.

[74] As opposed, for example, to a clause which provides that the date of entry is one week after the grant of a liquor licence. Such clauses tying entry to purification are common.

after all, and the question then arises as to whether they are entitled to waive the suspensive condition. It seems that such waiver is allowed in two circumstances only. The first is where there is an express right to do so.[75] The second is where the condition was inserted solely in the purchasers' interests and it is severable from the rest of the contract.

The second set of circumstances is not easily established. In only one reported case has the purchaser succeeded on this ground,[76] and that decision has been questioned in subsequent cases.[77] In these later cases the purchaser's argument was unsuccessful either because the seller had an express right to resile in the event of non-purification (which negatived the idea of the condition being for the sole benefit of the purchaser) or because the date of entry was tied to the date of purification (which prevented it from being severable). These were perhaps fairly straightforward cases. In *Imry Property Holdings Ltd v Glasgow YMCA*[78] Lord Dunpark said that the mere fact there was nothing in the missives to show that the seller had an interest was not enough, and that the missives must give positive evidence that the suspensive condition was conceived in favour of the purchaser only. But the later cases suggest that the rule may be less strict than this.

This rule restricting waiver applies to suspensive conditions only. A party is always free to waive the performance of ordinary contractual obligations incumbent on the other party to the contract. For instance, the fact that the sellers cannot produce a flawless title does not prevent the purchasers from proceeding with the contract if they wish to do so.

Suspensive conditions as quasi-options

3–22   Missives which are subject to a suspensive condition can sometimes function as quasi-options in favour of the purchasers, and furthermore this can happen without any payment for the option. Thus developers may conclude missives to purchase subject to a suspensive condition about planning. Such missives lock the sellers in (subject to the time limit) but they leave the purchasers with a free hand. If they decide that they do not wish to proceed, they back-pedal on the planning application. In effect the developers have an option to purchase at any time within the time limit, but, cunningly, have not paid an option price.[79] For this reason it is usual for the missives to require the purchasers to use their best endeavours to achieve the purification of the condition.[80] However, it is in practice difficult to prove breach of such a term. In such cases sellers would sometimes be wiser to sell an option rather than to agree to suspended missives.

---

[75] Which is a wise precaution as far as the buyers are concerned.

[76] *Dewar and Finlay Ltd v Blackwood*, 1968 S.L.T. 196. The soundness of this decision may be doubted: see *Manheath Ltd v HJ Banks & Co Ltd*, 1996 S.C. 42.

[77] *Ellis and Sons Second Amalgamated Properties Ltd v Pringle*, 1974 S.C. 200; *Imry Property Holdings Ltd v Glasgow YMCA*, 1979 S.L.T. 261; *Zebmoon Ltd v Akinbrook Investment Developments Ltd*, 1987 S.C. 252; *Manheath Ltd v HJ Banks & Co Ltd*, 1996 S.C. 42.

[78] *Imry Property Holdings Ltd v Glasgow YMCA*, 1979 S.L.T. 261. This case also holds that the buyer cannot circumvent the rule simply by announcing that the condition has been purified, a point confirmed by *Manheath Ltd v HJ Banks & Co Ltd*, 1996 S.C. 42.

[79] Though they are likely to have invested money in professional fees.

[80] For the meaning of phrases such as "best endeavours", see below, para.3–23(6).

DRAFTING

Offers

Drafting offers is a difficult and skilled business. Admittedly, the availability 3–23
of standard-form offers has simplified the conveyancer's task. But as well as
being of variable quality, these offers are suitable only for standard transactions and will have to be altered, supplemented or even discarded where the
transaction is complex or unusual. Drafting can only be learned by practice,
but here are some thoughts:

(1) It is helpful to define the principal terms, e.g. seller, buyer and property. At all events consistency is desirable. The buyer should not be
referred to as "the buyer" on one page and "our client" on the next.

(2) The introductory formula "it is understood that" should be avoided.
Understood by whom? What if it is a misunderstanding? Usually
intended as a preliminary clearing of the throat, the formula may have
the effect of reducing what was usually intended as a direct obligation
to a mere expression of the parties' understanding, with potentially
serious implications for its enforceability.[81]

(3) Other introductory formulae, "it is condition that" and "it is an essential condition that", should be used with care. These suggest that the
clause has some special status, but without making clear what that
status is supposed to be. There seem to be three possibilities. The first
is that the clause is a suspensive condition. The second is that it is a
term whose breach will constitute material breach. The third possibility is that the draftsperson simply felt that the clause was dealing
with a particularly important matter. One may suspect that this is in
fact the commonest meaning, in which case the formula is legally
meaningless.

(4) If the intention is that breach of some provision will entitle the innocent party to rescind, that should be stated expressly, and it should be
stated whether the option to rescind is to emerge immediately on
breach or only after a defined period. For example, it is common for
missives to provide that if the buyer fails to pay within a defined
period (such as 14 days) after the due date then the seller has the
option to rescind.

(5) Most positive obligations in missives (i.e. obligations to do something) are on the seller. Indeed, in residential conveyancing often the
only obligation on the purchaser is to pay the price. But whichever
party is subject to obligations it is important to stipulate the date by
which the obligation in question must be performed. Normally obligations need to be performed by the date of entry. But there is a potential ambiguity here. If the transaction actually settles on the contractual
date of entry, well and good. But sometimes transactions do not settle
then, in which case there are two dates of entry, namely (a) the
contractual date of entry and (b) the date on which entry is actually

---

[81] *Wood v Edwards*, 1988 S.L.T. (Sh. Ct) 17, per Sheriff R.J.D. Scott at 21. But compare *Neilson
v Barratt*, 1987 G.W.D. 13-467.

taken.[82] It is wise to anticipate this difficulty by providing in missives for two defined dates, namely the "date of entry" and the "date of settlement", the latter being the date on which entry is actually taken. For each obligation it should be made clear which of the two dates is the relevant one.

(6) Suspensive conditions are often accompanied by an obligation on one of the parties—usually the purchasers—to use "reasonable endeavours" or "best endeavours" to procure something, such as planning consent. In drafting such clauses, it is important to be aware that the courts regard "all reasonable endeavours" as imposing a more exacting standard than "reasonable endeavours", with "best endeavours" meaning much the same as "all reasonable endeavours" or perhaps something more exacting still.[83] In assessing whether "all reasonable endeavours" have been used, it is necessary, according to one case:

> "to consider whether there were reasonable steps which could have been taken but were not taken. The party on whom the obligation is placed will be expected to explore all avenues reasonably open to him, and to explore them all to the extent reasonable. But unless the contract otherwise stipulates, he is not required to act against his own commercial interests."[84]

(7) To lay down some provision and then to add "or otherwise as may be mutually agreed" (for instance as to the date of entry) does not help matters since the parties are in any event free to renegotiate terms. Moreover such a clause does not make it clear whether it is intended to make possible oral variations of the contract. Clauses of this sort are better avoided.

(8) As far as possible each clause should deal with just one item. If the item is complex it should be split into sub-clauses. It makes the offer easier to understand. Moreover, when the other side prepare the qualified acceptance, they can deal with the whole of a clause or sub-clause, and are not forced to say something like: "With reference to your fourth schedule clause, the words from 'and if' to 'penalty' are deleted and the following words are substituted." That is messy and, with drafting being done at speed, can cause errors.

(9) Finally, before an offer is sent, it should be checked for errors, bearing in mind that there is usually no remedy for a unilateral error. An offer to purchase which states the price at £275,000, being a typing error for £257,000, is likely to be binding.[85]

---

[82] For discussion see Reid, (1988) 33 J.L.S.S. 431; Gretton, (1989) 34 J.L.S.S. 175. See further *Spence v W&R Murray (Alford) Ltd*, 2002 S.C. 615; and Reid and Gretton, *Conveyancing 2002*, pp.55–57.

[83] *Mactaggart & Mickel Homes Ltd v Hunter* [2010] CSOH 130; 2010 G.W.D. 33-683 at para.63, per Lord Hodge.

[84] *EDI Central Ltd v National Car Parks Ltd* [2010] CSOH 141; 2011 S.L.T. 75 at para.20, per Lord Glennie.

[85] *See Steel v Bradley (Scotland) Homes Ltd*, 1974 S.L.T. 133. However, the doctrine of "unfair advantage" may apply: see above, para.3–16.

Qualified acceptances

The offer must be gone through carefully with the clients. Are the facts as   3–24
stated correct? Are the clients really willing to throw in the dining room carpet
and the tumble dryer? Is the date of entry suitable or should the purchasers be
pushed on this? Any meeting or telephone conversation with the clients should
be documented by letter or email confirming the information and instructions
received.

If the offer incorporates a schedule of conditions, it should be made clear
whether the clause being qualified is a clause of the letter or a clause of the
schedule. Wherever possible amendments should be done by outright deletion
(e.g. "Clause 6 of your Schedule is deleted" or "The second sentence of clause
3 of your letter is deleted"). This is better than leaving the clause undeleted
while adding complex amendments to it, resulting in a dog's breakfast. Thus in
Hood v Clarkson[86] the offer had a clause about the planning situation. The
qualification did not delete this clause or any part of it, but delivered a counter
salvo, couched in different words, about local authority PECs and the right to
resile. In the result it was wholly unclear whether a major road proposal which
came to light was or was not covered by the clause.

The number of qualifications should not be excessive, lest this delay conclusion of missives unnecessarily. The sellers' solicitors should have the titles and
the PECs and so should be in a position to deal intelligently with the contents
of the offer. But even without the titles or PECs, the wording of standard-form
offers will often avoid the need for qualification by providing that the only
remedy of the buyers in respect, for example, of onerous title conditions or
some prejudicial disclosure in the PECs is to rescind within a limited period
(such as ten working days) of receipt of the documentation—a compromise
position which is likely to be acceptable to both parties.[87]

"Working days"

Disputes sometimes arise as to how periods such as "five working days" are to   3–25
be calculated.[88] The law is probably as follows. Suppose the documents are
sent by DX on Friday, April 10. They are received on Monday, April 13. This
is day zero. Tuesday, April 14 is day one. Friday, April 17 is day four. Saturday,
April 18 is probably not a "working day" in modern practice. So day five will
be Monday, April 20. If, therefore, the buyers' solicitors have "five working
days" in which to resile, they have until close of business on the Monday to do
so. "Five" days have thus become 10. The resiling communication must, it is
thought, be actually received by the sellers' solicitors by close of business on
April 20: it is not sufficient to put it into the Monday night post.[89] Scottish bank
holidays are presumably not "working days" though in practice law offices
sometimes open on some bank holidays. Many areas also have non-statutory
local holidays when local law offices are usually shut. Again, these are probably not "working days" where the holiday is in the area of the buyers' law
office. Hence "five" will sometimes work out as being more than even 10 days.

---

[86] *Hood v Clarkson*, 1995 S.L.T. 98.
[87] See below, para.6–06.
[88] See David C. Coull, "Time", in *The Laws of Scotland: Stair Memorial Encyclopaedia* (1987),
Vol.23.
[89] *Carmarthern Developments Ltd v Pennington* [2008] CSOH 139; 2008 G.W.D. 33-494.

INTERPRETATION

Effect of a prior deletion

3–26 If something is deleted, the fact of deletion is itself not normally relevant to the interpretation of the contract. Thus in *Baird v Drumpellier & Mount Venon Estates Ltd*[90] a provision about good title was deleted. The sellers later argued that the deletion indicated that they were not binding themselves to guarantee title. This argument was rejected. The missives, as concluded, contained nothing to oust the common law rule that the seller presumptively guarantees that the title is good.[91]

No favour to either party

3–27 In missives both parties have usually been professionally advised and in the interpretation of the contract no favour is shown to either side.[92]

Reasonableness

3–28 A term is sometimes implied in missives that parties will act reasonably. So in *Gordon District Council v Wimpey Homes Holdings Ltd*,[93] where missives were subject to a suspensive condition that planning permission would be granted "to the satisfaction of the purchaser" and the permission ultimately granted was fenced in with conditions, Lord Clyde rejected the purchaser's argument that what was to his "satisfaction" was a matter for him alone and not subject to challenge, and took the view that "each party must have intended that the other would act reasonably".[94] Presumably it would be open to the parties to contract so as to exclude this "reasonable" criterion.

Extrinsic evidence

3–29 At common law there was a rule that if a contract was embodied in writing, evidence from outside that document,[95] whether written or oral, was not admissible to prove that the terms of the contract were actually other than those set forth in the document.[96] The Contract (Scotland) Act 1997[97] rationalised the rule by changing it into a simple presumption: "Where a document appears . . . to comprise all the express terms of a contract . . . it shall be presumed . . . that

---

[90] *Baird v Drumpellier & Mount Venon Estates Ltd*, 2000 S.C. 103.

[91] For the common law rule, see below, Ch.6.

[92] See *GA Estates Ltd v Caviapen Trs Ltd*, 1993 S.L.T. 1051; *Park v Morrison Developments Ltd*, 1993 G.W.D. 8–571.

[93] *Gordon District Council v Wimpey Homes Holdings Ltd*, 1989 S.L.T. 141.

[94] *Gordon District Council v Wimpey Homes Holdings Ltd*, 1989 S.L.T. 141 at 142. In the event the court held that the purchaser had acted reasonably. See also *John H Wyllie v Ryan Industrial Fuels Ltd*, 1989 S.L.T. 302; *Rockclife Estates Plc v Co-operative Wholesale Society Ltd*, 1994 S.L.T. 592; *Hutton v Barrett*, 1994 G.W.D. 37-2188; *Palmer v Forsyth*, 1999 S.L.T. (Sh. Ct) 93. On this last case see Reid and Gretton, *Conveyancing 1999*, p.40. Reading these cases together, it may be regarded as doubtful whether there exists any settled doctrine in this area.

[95] Or set of documents, as in the case of missives.

[96] Though of course a contract could be altered, or even wholly novated, by a later contract. Moreover, whilst extrinsic evidence was (in principle) not allowed to contradict a written contract, it was admissible to explain points which were obscure.

[97] For background, see the Scottish Law Commission, Report on *Three Bad Rules in Contract Law* (Scot. Law Com. No.152, 1996). The rule applied to evidence of terms agreed at an earlier stage. The rule did not prevent contracts from being varied by subsequent agreement.

the document does . . . comprise all the express terms".[98] However, the rules about the need for formal writing remain intact.[99] In practice, missives sometimes contain "entire agreement" clauses in order to exclude prior communings and undertakings.

The 1997 Act deals with evidence of terms which are inconsistent with the terms of the written contract. It does not deal with extrinsic evidence for the purpose of interpreting the terms themselves. On that topic the law cannot be regarded as entirely settled, but the general approach is to interpret the words used in the light of the surrounding circumstances—the so-called "factual matrix"[100]—at the time when the parties entered into the contract.[101] Such extrinsic evidence is available even though the words used are not ambiguous in themselves.[102] But it is not usually relevant to consider pre-contractual negotiations or post-contractual performance.[103]

VARIATION AND WAIVER

Variation

The terms of missives can be varied by subsequent agreement, and indeed this 3–30 is not uncommon, but, except in cases involving personal bar, it requires the consent of both parties expressed in formal writing.[104] Oral variation is ineffectual.[105]

Missives commonly contain a clause on the following lines: "Entry and vacant possession will be given on February 14, 2012 or on such other date as may be mutually agreed". Do these last words authorise an informal (unsubscribed) fixing of a fresh date of entry? Sometimes the clause goes on to stipulate for writing, but where it does not, the position seems uncertain.[106] The safe course is that if the date of entry is changed by mutual agreement, there should

---

[98] Contract (Scotland) Act 1997 s.1(1).

[99] Contract (Scotland) Act 1997 s.1(4). There is room for argument about how the law outlined in the text fits in with s.8 of the Law Reform (Miscellaneous Provisions) (Scotland) Act 1985, discussed below in Ch.20.

[100] Or "matrix of facts": see *Prenn v Simmonds* [1971] 1 W.L.R. 1381 at 1384, per Lord Wilberforce.

[101] An authoritative review of the current position can be found in Ch. 5 of the Scottish Law Commission's Discussion Paper on *Interpretation of Contract* (Scot. Law Com. D.P. No.147, 2011). Among the leading cases are *Bank of Scotland v Dunedin Property Investment Co Ltd*, 1998 S.C. 657; and *Multi-Link Leisure Developments Ltd v North Lanarkshire Council* [2010] UKSC 47; 2011 S.L.T. 184. Cases involving missives include *Glasgow City Council v Caststop Ltd*, 2003 S.L.T. 626; *Connell v Hart* [2008] CSIH 67; 2009 G.W.D. 1-12; *Aberdeen City Council v Stewart Milne Group Ltd* [2010] CSIH 81; 2010 G.W.D. 37-755. Scots law does not, so far at least, embrace the use of extrinsic evidence with quite the enthusiasm shown by Lord Hoffmann in the English case of *Investors Compensation Scheme Ltd v West Bromwich Building Society* [1998] 1 W.L.R. 896 esp. at 912–13.

[102] *Luminar Lava Ignite Ltd v Mama Group Plc and Mean Fiddler Holdings Ltd* [2010] CSIH 1; 2010 S.C. 310 at para.38, per Lord Hodge.

[103] Scottish Law Commission, Discussion Paper on *Interpretation of Contract*, para.5.28.

[104] Requirements of Writing (Scotland) Act 1995 s.1(3)–(6). For personal bar, see above, para.3–15.

[105] *Aitken v Hyslop*, 1977 S.L.T. (Notes) 50; *Inglis v Lownie*, 1990 S.L.T. (Sh. Ct) 60. These cases predate the Requirements of Writing (Scotland) Act 1995 and the Contract (Scotland) Act 1997 but it is thought that the outcome would be the same under current law.

[106] Contrast *Imry Property Holdings Ltd v Glasgow YMCA*, 1979 S.L.T. 261 with *Jaynor Ltd v Allander Holdings Ltd*, 1990 G.W.D. 30-1717.

be two letters, both subscribed, one setting forth the new date and the other, from the other side, confirming it.

Waiver

3–31 Similar in effect to variation is waiver.[107] Apart from the special case of suspensive conditions, it is always open to parties unilaterally to waive one or more of their rights under the contract. Waiver may be express, or be implied by actings, and in practice the latter is more common. But arguments based on implied waiver often fail. In order to succeed it is necessary to show, first, that one side to the contract has acted in such a way as to indicate clearly that they will not found on a particular contractual right, and secondly that now to allow the right to be enforced would be, in some broad sense, unfair.[108]

---

[107] See Elspeth C. Reid and John W.G. Blackie, *Personal Bar* (2006), paras 3–08 et seq., and esp. paras 3–18 to 3–21. For waiver of the right to rescind, see below, para.5–04.

[108] See e.g. *James Howden & Co Ltd v Taylor Woodrow Property Co Ltd*, 1998 S.C. 853. Implied waiver is part of the law of personal bar and can only be established if both constituent elements of bar—inconsistent conduct by one party and unfairness to the other—are present. But with implied waiver the unfairness is unlikely to be that the counter-party relied on the right not being enforced. See Reid and Blackie, *Personal Bar*, paras 2–03, 2–52 and 2–53.

CHAPTER 4

MISSIVES II: CONTENT

Introductory

This chapter is divided into four parts: terms about the title, terms about price 4–01
and settlement, terms about physical condition (including questions of risk)
and, lastly, terms about public law, such as planning and building control. The
division is, however, not always perfectly precise.

Essential terms

A contract for the sale of land requires, as a minimum, express agreement as to 4–02
the "three Ps"—the parties to the transaction, the property being sold, and the
price. Without such agreement there is no contract.[1] At one time express agreement as to date of entry was also thought essential, but it now seems that an
appropriate date of entry will, if necessary, be read into the contract.[2]

More is said later about the property and the price.[3] As to the parties, offers
sometimes do not identify the seller but just say "your client". That is less than
ideal, but is understandable in the context of busy practice and lower-value
transactions. In such cases the qualified acceptance should identify the seller.
If missives are concluded without clear identification of the parties, the contract
is valid provided that the undisclosed principals are capable of eventual identification; but obviously it is poor practice to conclude missives on this basis.
If a law firm concludes missives on behalf of a non-existent principal the
missives are void, and the law firm is itself liable for breach of warranty of
authority.[4] Examples include companies that have never been incorporated,
companies that were incorporated but have been dissolved, and clients who
have died.[5] A purported principal who exists but who has not authorised the
missives is also a non-existent principal for these purposes.[6]

---

[1] As in *NJ&J Macfarlane (Developments) Ltd v MacSween's Trustees*, 1999 S.L.T. 619. The
fact that without the three Ps there is no contract does not mean that if the three Ps are present then
there is a contract: this is a common misconception.

[2] See below, para.4–14.

[3] Respectively below, paras 4–03 and 4–04, and paras 4–12 and 4–13.

[4] See above, paras 1–04 and 3–03.

[5] *City of Glasgow Council v Peart*, 1999 Hous. L.R. 117.

[6] These remarks are subject to the law about ostensible authority.

TERMS ABOUT THE TITLE

Property

4–03 The parties must agree on what is being sold. Therefore the missives must contain an adequate description. But only rarely is a full conveyancing description given in missives. For houses just a postal address is common. In commercial conveyancing the offer usually has a plan, which will have been made available to bidders by the seller, and plans are also needed in a first break-off (i.e. if the property has not previously been owned as a separate unit).

It is no objection to a description that it needs to be supplemented by extrinsic evidence.[7] Thus, in the event of a dispute, it is competent to bring evidence as to which property is known, for example, as "4 High Street". But the extrinsic evidence cannot be made to do the work of the written description, and if the description itself is hopelessly vague there is no place for extrinsic evidence. *Grant v Peter G Gauld & Co*[8] provides a cautionary tale. The missives began with the words:

> "We hereby offer to purchase from you the ground presently being quarried by our client and the surroundings thereto extending to twelve acres . . . and that on the following terms and conditions, namely: 1. The actual boundaries will be agreed between you and our client . . ."

Since clause 1 amounted to a direct admission that no agreement as to the property had been reached, it was held that there was no contract. But the court indicated that even without clause 1 the result might have been the same, on the basis that the expression "the surroundings thereto extending to twelve acres" was too vague to allow extrinsic evidence. Another description found to be too vague was: "a part of Druim Na Pairc Buildings, comprising of two workshop units and garage unit amounting to 6140 sq. feet approx., together with adjoining land comprising of yard of approx. 1 acre and approx. 8½ acres of rough undeveloped land lying to the East of the above property".[9]

In practice, disputes about the definition of the property are uncommon. But where a dispute does arise extrinsic evidence can be used. Roughly speaking, extrinsic evidence can be of two kinds, objective and subjective. Objective evidence answers the question: what is the property known as 4 High Street? The kinds of evidence which are relevant here are the boundaries as stated in the seller's title, physical features such as hedges or fences, and the position as understood by neighbours. Subjective evidence[10] answers the question: what is the property that was agreed between the parties in the course of negotiations? In *Merrick Homes Ltd v Duff*[11] the contract was for the sale of "three separate areas of land . . . agreed between [the parties] which have been shown by [the seller] to [the purchasers]". The court considered this sufficient.[12]

---

[7] See above, para.3–29.

[8] *Grant v Peter G Gauld & Co*, 1985 S.C. 251.

[9] In *NJ&J Macfarlane (Developments) Ltd v MacSween's Trustees*, 1999 S.L.T. 619.

[10] In this sense. We are not here concerned with the subjective intentions of individual parties to the contract.

[11] *Merrick Homes Ltd v Duff*, 1996 S.C. 497.

[12] See also two cases involving options: *Miller Homes Ltd v Frame*, 2001 S.L.T. 459; *Bogie v Forestry Commission*, 2001 G.W.D. 38-1432.

Often there is only objective evidence, or if subjective evidence exists it is consistent with the objective evidence. But if the two are not the same a choice has to be made, and while each case will turn on its own facts, a major consideration seems to be whether the sellers are selling all or only part of what they own.[13] In the former case, the property will usually be construed as that described in the title (i.e. objective evidence). Even if the sellers in fact indicated a larger area to the purchasers (i.e. subjective evidence) the case will be analysed as (1) a contract for the smaller area as per the title, but (2) one which is voidable at the instance of the purchasers for misrepresentation.[14] Conversely, where the sellers are selling part only of what they own there is less scope for objective evidence, and subjective evidence will often be conclusive.[15]

Since sellers are more likely to overstate than understate the extent of the property, subjective evidence usually favours the purchaser. One method commonly used to ensure that full weight is given to evidence of this kind is to incorporate it expressly into the offer to buy, typically by adding to the brief description of the property the words "all as advertised by you and as seen by the purchaser". And if necessary the sellers' schedule of particulars can be annexed to, and adopted as part of, the offer.

Effect of error about the property

Where parties are in dispute as to the property, one of them is presumptively in error. Thus the sellers think they sold plot A while the buyers think they bought plot B (which includes but extends beyond plot A). Since the error will have been unilateral it gives rise to no remedy against the other party, unless it has been induced, or unless, while uninduced, the other party took unfair advantage of it.[16] But occasionally it is impossible to reach a concluded view as to who is right. The evidence is consistent with plot A or with plot B—or very likely with plot C as well—and in that case there is mutual error[17] and so no contract at all, because there is no consensus. **4–04**

Fixtures and fittings

The term "fixtures" means things which were originally moveable but which have acceded to the property and thus become part of it,[18] and so are now heritable, while the term "fittings" means things which have not acceded and have retained their moveable nature.[19] If the contract is silent, a purchaser is entitled to fixtures (since they are part of the land) but not fittings. But usually certain fittings, e.g. curtains and carpets, are in fact included in the sale. And it is not **4–05**

---

[13] In a sense, of course, this line of approach may beg the question, for the sellers' position may precisely be that they were not selling all they owned.

[14] *Smith v Paterson*, Unreported February 18, 1986 OH. In this case reduction was granted where the seller had, by deliberately careless words, misrepresented the extent of the garden.

[15] *Houldsworth v Gordon Cumming*, 1910 S.C. (HL) 49 (especially per Lord Shaw); *Angus v Bryden*, 1992 S.L.T. 884; *Barratt Scotland Ltd v Keith*, 1993 S.C. 142; *Martone v Zani*, 1992 G.W.D. 32-1903.

[16] For the doctrine of unfair advantage, see above, para.3–16.

[17] In the sense that the parties are at cross-purposes (rather than that they both share the same mistake). See William W. McBryde, *The Law of Contract in Scotland*, 3rd edn (2007), paras 15–34 to 15–37.

[18] Such as doors.

[19] Such as carpets. The expression "heritable fittings" is sometimes encountered, but for obvious reasons is unsatisfactory.

always clear whether certain other items are fixtures or fittings. The only way to avoid disputes later is to give a full list in the offer of the fittings, etc. which the purchasers expect to receive. Standard-form offers usually list the most common items. For example, the Combined Standard Clauses provide that the property is sold with:

> "the following items insofar as any were in the Property when viewed by the Purchaser: garden shed or hut, greenhouse, summerhouse; all growing plants, shrubs, trees (except those in plant pots); all types of blinds, pelmets, curtain rails and runners, curtain poles and rings thereon; all carpets and floorcoverings (but excluding loose rugs), stair carpet fixings; fitted bedroom furniture; all bathroom and cloakroom mirrors, bathroom and toilet fittings; kitchen units; all cookers, hobs, ovens, washing machines, dishwashers, fridges and freezers if integral to or encased within matching units; extractor hoods, extractor fans, electric storage heaters, electric fires, electric light fittings (including all fluorescent lighting, external lighting, wall lights, dimmer switches and bulbs and bulb holders but not shades); television aerials and associated cables and sockets, satellite dishes; loft ladders; rotary clothes driers; burglar alarm, other security systems and associated equipment; secondary glazing; shelving, fireplace surround units, fire grates, fenders and associated ironmongery."[20]

Many of these are fixtures but some are of uncertain status and others are plainly fittings. Obviously the purchasers' solicitors must ask their clients whether there are other items which need to be mentioned. The sellers' schedule of particulars will usually form the basis of any list of extras.

The sale of moveables is governed by the Sale of Goods Act 1979, and accordingly ownership passes in accordance with ss.17 and 18 of that Act and not by virtue of the disposition. It may be that the sellers do not actually own all the moveables included in the sale, but hold them on leasing or hire-purchase arrangements. In such cases the buyers will not normally be able to obtain a good title,[21] but will need to consider whether they wish to approach the supplier to take over the contracts. This issue is more likely to arise in commercial conveyancing where the moveables may constitute a substantial part of the total value. For instance, a hotel may be sold with the room furnishings, kitchen and dining goods, wetstock and so on, while a factory may be sold with machinery. In such cases considerable attention has to be paid to questions of valuation and inventorying.[22]

Coal and other minerals[23]

4–06 Unlike legal separate tenements such as salmon fishings, the missives include the minerals unless they are expressly excluded.[24] So an offer for "4 High Street" includes the minerals unless otherwise stated. If it then turns out that the sellers have no title to the minerals (and often they were long ago reserved by the owner

---

[20] Combined Standard Clauses (2009) cl.1(d).

[21] In certain cases good title can be obtained by virtue of s.25 of the Sale of Goods Act 1979.

[22] In important cases the inventory may be photographic as well as verbal.

[23] For the law of minerals, see Robert Rennie, *Minerals and the Law of Scotland* (2001); Gordon and Wortley (3rd edn), Ch.5.

[24] This is because they are "conventional separate tenements". See Reid, *Property*, para.209.

of the landed estate out of which the plot was originally carved), they are in breach of contract and the purchasers can rescind.[25] At one time this rule could be used by a purchaser as a handy method of escaping from a contract where it was unsatisfactory for other reasons, but nowadays offers almost always provide that the minerals are included in the sale only insofar as the sellers have right to them. If, therefore, the sellers do own the minerals, they will pass to the purchasers, but if they do not own them, the purchasers cannot complain. This is an example of a clause which, although appearing in the purchasers' offer, is solely for the sellers' benefit. But the sellers' solicitors must check the point, in case the standard clause is not in fact included in the offer.

The purchaser of a house is seldom interested in the mineral rights.[26] But there is a danger that the minerals may be worked in the future—or, more usually nowadays, that they have been worked in the past—and while the withdrawal of support causing subsidence is a delict of strict liability, clauses of reservation of minerals sometimes vary the common law by excluding liability for subsidence. Hence it is wise for an offer to stipulate that any third party's right to the minerals must be subject to satisfactory compensation provisions and must not include any right to enter upon or change the level of the surface.[27] In the case of subsidence caused by coal mining, there is a statutory compensation scheme.[28] If the property is in a coal-mining area, it is usually necessary to obtain a coal mining report from the Coal Authority which will give such information as is contained in the Authority's records[29]; an online search by postcode will indicate whether such a report is needed.[30]

Good and marketable title

It is provided in missives (and if it were not so provided, it would anyway 4–07
be implied) that the seller must exhibit or deliver a good and marketable title to the property sold. The meaning of this important provision is considered in Ch.6.

Burdens

It is important for the buyers' solicitors to find out what their clients plan to use 4–08
the property for. For example, real burdens often forbid commercial use. If the buyers' solicitors wrongly assume that their clients intend to use the property as a dwellinghouse, and accept the burdens accordingly, they may find themselves being sued for negligence. If the buyers do not have plans for change of

---

[25] *Campbell v McCutcheon*, 1963 S.C. 505. On this issue as applied to tenement properties, see C. Waelde (ed.), *Professor McDonald's Conveyancing Opinions* (1998), p.238.

[26] Obviously in commercial and agricultural conveyancing the mineral rights may be of more importance.

[27] For a valuable discussion of the way minerals rights should be handled in missives, see D.J. Cusine and R. Rennie, *Missives*, 2nd edn (1999), para.4.73. As to the marketability of a title which is not protected by a right to compensation, see D.J. Cusine (ed.), *The Conveyancing Opinions of J.M. Halliday* (1992), pp.437–39.

[28] Coal Mining Subsidence Act 1991. For the law of support to land see Robert Rennie, *Minerals and the Law of Scotland* (2001); Gordon and Wortley (3rd edn), paras 5–80 et seq.; Reid, *Property*, paras 252 et seq.

[29] Coal searches are usually done online: *http://www.coalminingreports.co.uk/*. See further (2003) 48 J.L.S.S. Sept./56.

[30] See further the Law Society's *Guidance Notes on Coal Mining Reports 2006*, and also para.5.3.3 of CML's *Lenders Handbook for Scotland*.

use, the general clause that the property is subject to no "unusual or unduly onerous burdens" will normally suffice.[31] But otherwise the offer should specify the proposed use and stipulate that the title contains nothing that would prevent it. The sellers' response is likely to be to send the titles while either deleting the clause or qualifying it by requiring the buyers to satisfy themselves as to the position within a stipulated number of days.[32]

Occupancy rights

4–09 The provisions in missives about occupancy rights of non-entitled spouses and civil partners are considered elswhere, as are property transfer orders.[33]

Content of disposition

4–10 In general, a seller is only bound to grant, and a purchaser is only bound to accept, a disposition drawn up in the "usual" form.[34] Therefore, if either party wishes the disposition to contain something extra, this must be stipulated for expressly in the missives.

Offers sometimes contain a clause to the effect that, if the tranaction is ARTL-compatible, then it is to proceed under ARTL.[35] First registrations and split-offs are not ARTL-compatible, and even those transactions which are ARTL-compatible tend not, at the moment, to proceed under ARTL.

Supersession clause

4–11 Missives normally contain a clause providing that they will remain in force (except insofar as implemented) for a certain period, usually two years, after which they will expire and can no longer be founded on. Such a "supersession" clause is always found in standard-form offers, but in other cases is likely to have to be added by the sellers (for whose benefit it mainly is) in the qualified acceptance. This subject is further discussed in Ch.19.[36]

TERMS ABOUT PRICE AND SETTLEMENT

Price

4–12 Mungo Brown states the rule in this way: "The price must be *certain*, i.e. it must be absolutely fixed, or it must be capable of being ascertained".[37] Thus the contract must either state the price or give some method by which the price can be determined. As Brown goes on to note, "the price is sufficiently certain

---

[31] For the meaning of this general clause, see below, paras 6–04 to 6–07.

[32] See below, para.6–06.

[33] See below, paras 10–15 and 10–16.

[34] See *Corbett v Robertson* (1872) 10 M. 329. The point seems to have been overlooked in *Morris v Ritchie*, 1991 G.W.D. 12-712.

[35] Robert Rennie and Stewart Brymer, *Conveyancing in the Electronic Age* (2008), para.9–03. For ARTL transactions, see below, para.8–23.

[36] See below, paras 19–02 and 19–03.

[37] Mungo P. Brown, *A Treatise on the Law of Sale* (1821) § 201, citing Justinian, *Institutes*, III, xxiv, 1.

for the support of the contract, if it is referred to a third party".[38] But it must not depend on future agreement being reached by the parties.[39]

Payment of deposit

In some countries, such as England, payment of a deposit (e.g. 10 per cent of 4–13 the price) is usually required. In Scottish practice such deposits are almost unknown, except in some commercial cases or, with new houses, as a reservation fee.[40] The law about deposits in sale contracts is in some respects unclear. The problems tend to arise where the sale aborts because of the buyer's fault. The authorities seem to say that a deposit is presumptively not merely a partial payment but a security for performance, and that if the buyer fails to settle the deposit is forfeited.[41] But the logic here is obscure, since the law of rights in security has a well-known principle—so strong that it defeats even stipulations to the contrary—that a security is enforceable only to the extent of the obligation secured. Hence to classify a deposit as a security would lead to the conclusion that if the buyer defaults then the deposit is lost only to the extent of the loss to the seller. If a deposit is wholly forfeited that is presumably because it is to be regarded not as a security but as a pre-payment that is subject to an express or implied right to the seller to take it by way of liquidated damages. But we must repeat that the law on deposits is obscure.[42]

Date of entry

The offer should state the date of entry. It is common, though not invariable, to 4–14 state the hour as well as the date. If no hour is agreed then noon seems to be implied by law.

It was finally settled in *Gordon DC v Wimpey Homes Holdings Ltd*[43] that it is not fatal for their validity if missives fail to state an entry date. But a practical problem remains, because if there is no date of entry, the parties' obligations will never become due and missives can never be enforced. This problem has yet to be faced up to directly by the courts. But it appears that the law is more accurately stated as being, not that a date of entry is not required, but that an express date of entry is not required. So if no express date is given the court will assume that the parties, being agreed on so much else, must be agreed that the obligations will at some stage become prestable, and an appropriate date will be read into the contract. In *Gordon* it was suggested that, where the contract depends on a suspensive condition being purified, the date of entry should be the date of purification. Otherwise, presumably, entry will be at a reasonable time after conclusion of missives, what is "reasonable" depending

---

[38] Mungo P. Brown, *A Treatise on the Law of Sale* (1821) § 201. Brown goes on to consider whether it is competent for one of the parties to be given the right to fix the price, and whether, if the price is to be fixed by a third party, that person's figure is binding even if manifestly unjust.

[39] For a case in which there was no agreed price and hence no contract see *MacLeod's Exr v Barr's Trustees*, 1989 S.L.T. 392. And see *NJ&J Macfarlane (Developments) Ltd v MacSween's Trustees*, 1999 S.L.T. 619.

[40] See below, para.30–01.

[41] See *Zemhunt (Holdings) Ltd v Control Securities Ltd*, 1992 S.L.T. 151.

[42] For further discussion see William W. McBryde, *The Law of Contract in Scotland*, 3rd edn (2007) paras 22–163 to 22–165.

[43] *Gordon DC v Wimpey Homes Holdings Ltd*, 1988 S.L.T. 481.

on the facts and circumstances of the case. It is in practice almost unknown for missives to omit a date of entry.

Delay in settlement

4-15 Missives invariably make provision for what is to happen if the buyers do not come up with the money when settlement is due. This is because the common law rules in this area are opaque or inadequate. It is normal to provide that, if the delay persists beyond a certain defined period, such as 14 days, the sellers may rescind the contract. Furthermore, at least in residential conveyancing, sellers are normally given a choice between claiming ordinary damages or, alternatively, interest, at a defined rate,[44] for the period ending when either payment is made, the property is resold following rescission, or a fixed term (such as a year) has elapsed since the original date of entry. This whole topic is explored elsewhere.[45]

PHYSICAL CONDITION AND RISK

Risk: general

4-16 Risk concerns liability for accidental damage to the property in the interval between conclusion of the contract (for pre-contractual damage, see below[46]) and the transfer of ownership.[47] By "accidental" damage is meant damage which is not the fault of either party to the contract. For heritable property the common law rule is that risk passes from the sellers to the buyers when the contract of sale is concluded, except where there is a suspensive condition, when, it seems, risk does not pass until its purification.[48] But this rule may be altered by agreement, and this almost always happens in practice, so that risk does not usually pass until the date of settlement. There are thus two possibilities, namely that the risk remains with the sellers until settlement, and that it passes to the buyers on conclusion of the contract.

If risk remains with the sellers

4-17 As already mentioned, the current practice is almost always that risk stays with the sellers. What happens then if the house is accidentally damaged after the conclusion of missives but before settlement? The buyers could probably rescind if the damage is major, though the law is not quite clear, so that it is common for the point to be covered specifically in the missives.[49] Usually the sellers are also given a right to rescind, without penalty. Where they are not, the buyers would have the alternative remedy of enforcing the contract by insisting that the sellers repair the damage (the expense of which will typically be paid by the sellers' insurance company).

---

[44] Such as four percentage points above the base rate of a named bank.
[45] See below, paras 5–17 to 5–20.
[46] See below, para.4–21.
[47] For a discussion, see Forte, (1984) 19 Irish Jurist 1. Reform has been recommended by the Scottish Law Commission: Report on the *Passing of Risk in Contracts for the Sale of Heritable Property* (Scot. Law Com. No.127, 1990), but the proposals seem likely to remain unimplemented.
[48] *Sloans Dairies Ltd v Glasgow Corp*, 1977 S.C. 223.
[49] Care must be taken with the drafting: see *Hall v McWilliam*, 1993 G.W.D. 23-1457.

If risk passes to the buyers

Occasionally, the common law position is not altered and risk passes to the 4–18 buyers as soon as the contract is concluded. This means that they might have to buy charred remains. The fact that risk has passed does not relieve the sellers from a duty to take reasonable care of the property. Risk concerns accidental destruction only: if the sellers are at fault, they must pay.[50]

Insurance

As soon as risk passes, the buyers should have insurance cover. If they are 4–19 obtaining a loan, the lenders will normally arrange cover. Otherwise, the buyers' solicitors must ensure that this is done. Temporary cover can be obtained by phoning an insurance broker, and thereafter the clients will have to complete a proposal form.

Moveables

A typical house purchase will include some moveables, such as carpets, and 4–20 here the legal presumption as to risk is different, risk normally not passing until the passing of ownership.[51] There may be difficulty in establishing when ownership of the moveables passes.[52] With new houses and in other cases where the sellers act in the course of business, the rule is different and risk does not pass until delivery.[53] These rules can be contracted out of,[54] and missives clauses which provide that risk passes at settlement are often so worded as to cover moveables.

Pre-contractual damage

Damage prior to conclusion of the contract is not governed by risk. But such 4–21 damage occurs more often than might be thought. Thus, suppose that after viewing a house the clients make an offer for it. The offer is accepted in principle but it takes three weeks for missives to be concluded, during which time (unknown to the buyers) the house is damaged by fire. What then is the position? The answer seems to be that, unless the contract provides otherwise, the buyers have no remedy and must accept the house in its damaged state. Until the contract is concluded, the sellers have no duty of care to the buyers; and the buyers' error as to the physical state of the house is unilateral and uninduced. Missives sometimes have a clause stipulating that the property must be in substantially the same state at settlement as at conclusion of missives,[55] but

---

[50] This rule was applied in *Meehan v Silver*, 1972 S.L.T. (Sh. Ct) 70 even though settlement had been delayed and the damage happened after the contractual date of entry. But a different view was expressed, without reference to *Meehan*, in *Chapman's Trustees v Anglo Scottish Group Services Ltd*, 1980 S.L.T. (Sh. Ct) 27 at 28.

[51] Sale of Goods Act 1979 s.20(1).

[52] On one view, if the missives make no special provision as to passing of the ownership of the moveables, ownership will pass at missives: Sale of Goods Act 1979 s.18 r.1. As against this, it could be argued that ownership passes at settlement since this is presumably the intention of the parties: s.17(1).

[53] Sale of Goods Act 1979 s.20(4) applying to "a consumer contract in which the buyer acts as a consumer". The definition of "consumer contract" in s.25(1) of the Unfair Contract Terms Act 1977 is imported by s.61(1) of the Sale of Goods Act.

[54] Sale of Goods Act 1979 s.20(1).

[55] *Hall v McWilliam*, 1993 G.W.D. 23-1457.

this will be of no help, since the damage was already in place at conclusion of missives. One way of dealing with the danger is to use such a clause but making the date of the original offer the reference date for the condition of the property.

Warranties of quality

4–22 The sellers warrant the title but, at least on the traditional view of the law, they do not warrant the physical state of the property.[56] Instead the default rule is said to be *caveat emptor*: it is for the buyers to have the property surveyed.

The parties are, of course, free to insert into the missives warranties as to physical quality. This was seldom done until the late 1970s, but since then such contractual warranties have become normal in respect of some or all of the following appliances: central heating, water, drainage, electricity and gas. Typically, the warranty is subject to a "commensurate with age" qualification, and the buyers are only allowed a short period after settlement to intimate defects.[57] This is a compromise between the interests of buyers and sellers which is usually found in regional missives; in other cases, the sellers' solicitors should take care to qualify any open-ended guarantee which may appear in the offer. A common problem with these clauses is that the sellers may have lived happily with their central heating for years, regarding it as being in reasonably good working order, while the purchasers see all sorts of defects. A further warranty sometimes found in offers, but which should usually be resisted, is that the gas and electricity systems comply with applicable regulations. This may sound innocuous, but the regulations change constantly, so that a system which is in perfect working order, and which complies fully with the regulations applicable at the time of installation, may not comply with whatever the current regulations may happen to be.

There is no perfect way of drafting clauses of this kind. What is vital is that both clients be aware of the position. Thus, if the missives are silent as to the plumbing, the buyers must know this, so that if they find the plumbing to be defective, they cannot complain. In general, a buyer of a second-hand house is in the same position as the buyer of anything else second-hand, such as a car. There is always the risk of defects. To the extent that buyers wish to take no risks, they must have surveys done. If they are worried about, say, the plumbing, they may need to have a plumber visit the property before missives are concluded.

Infestation

4–23 An offer will typically require the sellers to warrant that, as far as they know, the property is not affected by infestations such as wet rot, dry rot, damp[58] or

---

[56] That view can, however, be challenged on the basis (i) that, as noted above in para.3–01, the sale of land is simply part of the general law of sale, and (ii) that under that general law, the physical state of the property may be warranted. For discussion, see Black, 1982 J.R. 31; Halliday, 1983 J.R. 1; Cusine, (1983) 28 J.L.S.S. 228; Reid, in D.J. Cusine (ed.), *A Scots Conveyancing Miscellany: Essays in Honour of Professor J. M. Halliday* (1987), p.152. This area of law is in need of thorough investigation. Assuming the traditional view to be correct, there can nonetheless be exceptions, e.g. where the seller is a builder: see *Owen v Fotheringham*, 1997 S.L.T. (Sh. Ct) 28.

[57] See *Williams v Mutter*, 2002 S.C.L.R. 1127 for difficulties in phrasing and interpreting a clause of this sort.

[58] Damp may be rising damp (from the ground), or penetrating damp (rain or snow meltwater coming through the roof, walls, etc.) or condensing damp (water vapour bedewing surfaces).

woodworm, and that, if eradication work has been been carried out in the past, there is a valid guarantee which will be transferred to the buyers. The value of such clauses is usually slight, for the obvious reason that it is difficult or impossible to establish what the seller really knew or did not know. And the latter part is odd in as much as a seller who never obtained a guarantee is in a better position, in this respect, than one who did.

Access

Before settlement the buyers have no right to visit the property, or have anyone 4–24 visit the property on their behalf to inspect it, except by the permission of the sellers. This fact can be unsatisfactory and hence it is common for the missives to make provision for such access.

PUBLIC LAW AND PUBLIC SERVICES[59]

Property enquiry certificates ("PECs")

The solicitors buying a house for clients are concerned with a number of 4–25 matters which come under the control of local authorities. The main ones are planning law, building control law, the provision of certain services, and statutory notices requiring the building to be repaired or, worse, demolished.

On payment of a fee, local authorities will issue standard-form certificates, called property enquiry certificates ("PECs"), giving certain information in relation to the property. PECs are also issued by independent firms, working from local authority records. Without these certificates the sellers' solicitors would be unable to respond properly to the clauses in the offer dealing with such matters, and indeed regional missives usually require that PECs be furnished to the buyers, who are then allowed to resile within a period such as ten working days in the event that the PECs disclose something untoward.[60] Applications for PECs can usually be made online. It is important to identify the property adequately. A postal address is generally sufficient, but sometimes more precision is needed, especially in rural areas or for urban development sites. In some cases a plan may need to be sent.

The information provided by PECs is reasonably comprehensive.[61] For example, those issued by the City of Edinburgh Council cover[62]:

---

[59] The subject is a large one and the following treatment is selective and brief, especially since much public law about land and buildings is aimed at commercial property whereas this book is mainly about residential property. Whether any particular point about public law or services needs to be dealt with in the missives depends on the circumstances of the case.

[60] The test is often that the thing disclosed is "materially prejudicial": see e.g. *Smith v Jack*, 2005 G.W.D. 1-14. Clause 19(c) of the Combined Standard Clauses (2009) provides, for the avoidance of doubt, that this does not include the property being sited within a conservation area, being a listed building, being subject to the local authority windows policy or an art.4 direction, or being affected by a tree preservation order. That view was reached on general principles by *McPhee v Black*, Unreported June 20, 2008 Glasgow Sheriff Court.

[61] The CML *Lenders' Handbook for Scotland*, para.5.3.6 requires that the PECs deal with certain matters relating to contaminated land.

[62] *http://www.edinburgh.gov.uk/info/180/planning-applications_warrants_and_certificates/ 1031/property_enquiry_certificates_pecs/1.*

Subject	What is covered
Planning	Planning applications for the property since October 1990, whether it is a Listed Building, in a Conservation Area, affected by an art.4 Direction, or subject to an enforcement notice.
Building warrant	Recent decisions on applications for the property.
Roads information	Whether the road access is adopted by the Council for maintenance purposes and if the property is affected by any transport proposals.
Statutory notices	Served under the Civic Government legislation or the Edinburgh District Council Order Confirmation Act for repairs to the property.
Statutory notices	Served under housing, environmental protection and health and safety legislation.
Water and drainage	Information from Scottish Water, (optional).
Contaminated land	Information on whether land is in the Contaminated Land register.

But there are also things that are not covered. For instances, PECs will not normally show whether there have been any breaches of planning or building law. Nor does it follow from the absence of statutory notices in the certificates that the house is actually in a good state of repair. The technical services departments of local councils do not maintain a large and vigilant band of inspectors who ceaselessly patrol the streets looking for cracks in the stonework. Moreover, PECs may not disclose older statutory notices, even if the notice has not been obtempered.

The buyers' solicitors must check the certificates carefully.[63] PECs are seldom wrong, but if they are, and if loss results, the issuer may be liable in damages.[64] One practical problem is that by the time of settlement the certificate may be some months old and the purchaser may naturally be unhappy with this. Offers often insist that the certificate be dated not more than a certain period prior to settlement, and the Council of Mortgage Lenders *Lenders' Handbook for Scotland* stipulates for three months.[65]

---

[63] For a cautionary tale see (1992) 37 J.L.S.S. 408.

[64] *Runciman v Borders Regional Council*, 1988 S.L.T. 135; *National Children's Home and Orphanage Trustees v Stirrat Park Hogg (SPH)*, 2001 S.L.T. 469; *Maypark Properties Ltd v Stirrat (SPH)*, 2001 S.L.T. (Sh. Ct) 171; *Anderson v Perth & Kinross Council*, 2000 S.C.L.R. 987.

[65] CML *Lenders' Handbook for Scotland*, para.5.3.2.

Roads[66]

The buyers will be concerned about the road outside their new house in two 4–26
respects. They wish to be sure that they have a right of access, and they will not
wish to have to maintain the road at their own expense. Both are likely to be
stipulated for in the offer.[67]

Roads can be divided into those which are maintained at public expense and
those which are not. The Roads (Scotland) Act 1984 calls the former "public"
and the latter "private".[68] It is the "roads authority" which is responsible for the
upkeep of public roads. For most roads this is the local council, but Scottish
Ministers are the roads authority for "trunk" roads. "Public" and "private" can
also be used in a different sense to indicate the road's status as to use. Although
there is no necessary connection, a road which is public as to maintenance is,
almost always,[69] public as to use, and purchasing solicitors in practice look no
further if the PECs show that the road outside (*ex adverso*) is publicly maintained.[70] Even where a road is privately maintained it may still be subject to
public use if a public right of way has been constituted by prescriptive use for
20 years; otherwise it can only be used by those who own the road or have a
servitude right of way over it. Obviously, purchasing solicitors must take care
in such cases that their clients will acquire a sufficient right of access, including,
if appropriate, a right of access by vehicle.

If the road is private as to maintenance, the client must be warned of the
potential cost of upkeep. Further, assuming it is public in the sense of being
subject to a public right of way, the council can require the buyer, as a "front-
ager", to maintain both the road and the pavement.[71]

Where a road is constructed by a roads authority, the land on which it is built
will first have been acquired by the authority either by agreement or by compulsory purchase. Such roads are public as to maintenance from their birth. But many
roads are built by private builders in the course of developing a housing estate.
These begin life as private roads, but the idea is that, by the time the development
is completed, the roads authority will have taken them over. By s.16 of the 1984
Act, a roads authority must "adopt" a road provided it has been constructed to a
sufficient standard. It used to be a worry, in buying a new house, that the builder
might become insolvent before completing the development, so that the bill for
making up the road would have to be picked up by the house owners. To meet this
risk builders commonly obtained a commercial guarantee (called a road bond) to
cover the costs of completing the roads. Nowadays the problem has been more or
less solved by s.17 of the 1984 Act and regulations made thereunder[72] which

---

[66] See Ann Faulds, Trudi Craggs and John Saunders, *Scottish Roads Law*, 2nd edn (2008).

[67] A common formulation is to provide that there is direct access to the property from a road
which has been adopted for maintenance by the local authority. This does not quite hit the mark
because, as explained below, a road which is public in respect of maintenance is not necessarily
public in respect of use.

[68] Roads (Scotland) Act 1984 s.151(1) (definitions of "public road" and "private road").

[69] For a celebrated case where it was not, see *Hamilton v Dumfries and Galloway Council
(No.2)* [2009] CSIH 13; 2009 S.C. 277. For a discussion of what is now the leading case in this
whole area, see Reid and Gretton, *Conveyancing 2009*, pp.156–63.

[70] If a road is public both as to use and as to maintenance, the right of use extends over the whole
road, including its verge: see *Hamilton v Nairn* [2010] CSIH 77; 2010 S.L.T. 1155.

[71] Roads (Scotland) Act 1984 s.13.

[72] Security for Private Road Works (Scotland) Regulations 1985 (SI 1985/2080) as amended by
the Security for Private Road Works (Scotland) Amendment Regulations 1998 (SI 1998/3220).

provide that no building work can begin until the developer grants a road bond in favour of the local authority.[73] But some developers flout the law and fail to obtain a road bond, and it is precisely this type of developer that is most likely to become insolvent, at which point the absence of a road bond becomes a disaster. So an offer for a house being built should still stipulate that a road bond exists and must be exhibited.[74]

Who owns the solum beneath the road? There are three main possibilities. (1) It may belong to the roads authority. This will usually be the case with major roads. (2) It may belong to the frontagers, in sections. When houses are built on both sides of a road—or plots sold for building—the boundaries between individual properties are often the centre line of the road. And this ownership is not affected by the road subsequently being taken over by the local authority for maintenance. (3) It may belong to the original developers or their successors, simply because on conveying the houses they never parted with ownership of the solum. Often it can be difficult to find out who owns the solum. Ownership is seldom of much practical significance except when a road is "stopped up" by the roads authority so that the former road becomes available for other purposes. By s.115 of the 1984 Act, ownership of a stopped up road vests in the frontagers "subject to the prior claim of any person by reason of title".[75]

Sewerage

4–27   The purchaser will normally expect public sewerage[76] provision and indeed public water, electricity and gas. In towns this may usually be taken for granted (except for gas), but in the countryside there may be no public supply and each public utility has its own rules about entitlement. Where public provision is made, the rule is usually that the local authority (or other utility) will bring the resource in question up to the property but the cost of making and maintaining connections remains with the owner.

Sewerage is governed by the Sewerage (Scotland) Act 1968, as amended. As sewerage authority, Scottish Water has a statutory duty to construct adequate sewers, subject to the proviso that nothing need be done "which is not practicable at a reasonable cost".[77] So in many rural areas there is no public system, and the outflow drains into a septic tank.[78] If the tank is located in a neighbouring property, which it sometimes is, a servitude of drainage is necessary.[79] Septic tanks require to be registered with the Scottish Environmental

---

[73] Section 17 applies to (a) the erection of private dwelling-houses and (b) the conversion of an existing building which is not a private dwelling-house for use as such a dwelling-house.

[74] A road bond is required by the CML *Lenders' Handbook for Scotland*, para.6.8.1.

[75] Presumably this is to cover the case where ownership is vested in another party such as the original developers or their successors—case (3) in the text. But the provision is odd, because if the frontagers own it already, it is superfluous, while if they do not, it is inoperative (because if they do not own it already, somebody else must do so, and that person's title is declared to prevail).

[76] Sewerage is the system. Sewage is what passes through the system.

[77] Sewerage (Scotland) Act 1968 s.1(1), (3). If impatient developers construct the sewers themselves, they cannot recover the cost under the law of recompense: see *Varney (Scotland) Ltd v Burgh of Lanark*, 1974 S.C. 245.

[78] On septic tanks, see Macrae, (2001) 46 J.L.S.S. March/48.

[79] The relevant servitude is that sometimes called "sinks" or "outfall" which is the servitude right to discharge foul water into a neighbouring property. See e.g. *Cochrane v Ewart* (1861) 4 Macq. 117. See generally D.J. Cusine and R.R.M. Paisley, *Servitudes and Rights of Way* (1998), paras 3.80 et seq.

Protection Agency ("SEPA"),[80] and this can be done online.[81] Standard-form offers tend to provide that the property is connected to mains drainage, meaning that the offer will have to be qualified if there is a septic tank.[82]

Water

Public water supplies are provided by Scottish Water.[83] The law relating to   4–28
supply is contained in the Water (Scotland) Act 1980, as amended, s.6 of which imposes a general duty (but subject to a reasonable cost proviso) to supply "wholesome" water for domestic purposes. As with sewerage, in some rural areas there will be no public supply, with the owner taking water from a well. And, at least in rural areas, offers tend to provide that, in the absence of a mains water supply, the private supply is established by the appropriate servitudes,[84] and is sufficient in quantity for normal domestic purposes. Private water supplies are required to be wholesome.[85]

Statutory notices: general

Local authorities have wide-ranging powers to require the repair or demolition   4–29
of buildings although, for reasons of cost, they may often be reluctant to exercise them. There are a number of different statutory provisions, mainly found in the Building (Scotland) Act 2003 and the Housing (Scotland) Act 2006, but most work in much the same way.[86] First, the council is alerted to a defective building either by its own inspectors or, very often in the case of tenement property, by a telephone call from a proprietor who cannot persuade the other owners to carry out repairs. The council serves on the proprietor or proprietors of the building a formal statutory notice which requires specified works to be carried out within a specified (and usually short) time. The notice must sufficiently describe the works in question.[87] In the case of tenements, councils often serve a notice on all the proprietors in the building, even for repairs which concern only one or more individual flats.[88] There is a right of appeal against the notice, usually to the sheriff, but the right must be exercised within the statutory time limit which, typically, is

---

[80] Regardless of whether the septic tank discharges to land via full soakaway or to a watercourse or loch. See Water Environment (Controlled Activities) (Scotland) Regulations 2005 (SSI 2005/348). There is an exception for septic tanks which were previously authorised under the Control of Pollution Act 1974.

[81] *http://www.sepa.org.uk/*.

[82] See also para.6.8.2 of the CML *Lenders' Handbook for Scotland*, which reads: "The property must be served by a public sewer or by private sewerage arrangements which have the necessary approvals from the sewerage authority or you must report to us".

[83] Water Industry (Scotland) Act 2002. Unlike in England, water supply is not privatised.

[84] Aquaehaustus (the right to water from a source in another property) and aquaeductus, also called watergang (the right to pipe water across or underneath another's land).

[85] See in particular the Water (Scotland) Act 1980 ss.76G and 76H as read with s.76HA, and the Private Water Supplies (Scotland) Regulations 2006 (SSI 2006/209).

[86] See further Gordon and Wortley (3rd edn), paras 15–159 et seq.

[87] In practice, the specification is sometimes vague. It is, however, unusual for the notice to be challenged. For an example of a successful challenge see *Gardner v City of Edinburgh DC*, 1992 S.L.T. 1149.

[88] They are entitled to do this: *University of Edinburgh v City of Edinburgh DC*, 1987 S.L.T. (Sh. Ct) 103; *City of Edinburgh DC v Gardner*, 1990 S.L.T. 600. See, further, Reid, (1990) 35 J.L.S.S. 368.

21 days.[89] Once a notice is served the proprietors must carry out the work. If they fail to do so the council may and often does instruct contractors to do the necessary work,[90] recovering the cost from the proprietors. The amount then due to the council can be secured by a charging order (a statutory heritable security) on the building.[91] It is always more expensive in the end if the council has to carry out the work but, particularly in a tenement, the proprietors may be unable to reach agreement on carrying out the work themselves.[92]

Where the PECs show the property as being subject to a statutory notice, the purchasers' solicitors must find out more details. If the notice has been complied with, well and good. If the notice is about to be complied with, that is also acceptable provided that there is clear agreement that the sellers are to pay the costs. The main problem which arises is where the notice has not been complied with and the council has, or is about to, carry out the work itself. Thereafter the council is entitled to recover the cost from the new owner,[93] and there seems to be no satisfactory right of relief under the general law.[94]

Offers vary as to how they handle the possibility of statutory notices. One approach is for the sellers to be asked to warrant that there are no such notices at the time of missives. If a notice turns out to exist, the selling solicitors will so state in the qualified acceptance, and this may then lead to an agreement that the sellers will be responsible for the costs. Another approach, often favoured in standard-form offers, is to fix liability on the sellers for any pre-missives notices (if such exist) and to provide for a retention from the purchase price of the estimated cost of the sellers' likely contribution plus an extra 25 per cent (for luck). This sum is kept in an interest-bearing account of the purchasers' solicitors, or on deposit receipt in the joint names of both sets of solicitors; once the repairs are completed and paid for, the sum is released to the sellers.[95] A simpler version of the same is to agree to reduce the purchase price by the amount of the estimated costs, which will then be the responsibility of the purchasers.[96] Whatever provision is made in missives, it is important that it is exempted from the two-year supersession clause which applies to the rest of the contract,[97] for in practice repairs can easily run on for more than two years.[98]

The main statutory notices concern dangerous buildings, buildings not of a tolerable standard, and buildings in disrepair.

---

[89] On rights of appeal, see *Norcross v Kirkcaldy DC*, 1993 G.W.D. 3-146; *Lindsay v City of Glasgow DC*, 1998 Hous. L.R. 4; *Boutineau v City of Glasgow DC*, 1998 Hous. L.R. 121.

[90] *Crawford v City of Edinburgh DC*, 1994 S.L.T. 23. In practice, however, councils often delay taking this step for long periods.

[91] See e.g. Housing (Scotland) Act 2006 s.172, and the Housing (Scotland) Act 2006 (Repayment Charge and Discharge) Order 2007 (SSI 2007/419).

[92] For statutory notices in tenements, see below, para.14–13.

[93] *Purves v City of Edinburgh DC*, 1987 S.L.T. 366; *Pegg v City of Glasgow DC*, 1988 S.L.T. (Sh. Ct) 49. But there are limits: see *Smith v Renfrew DC*, 1997 S.C.L.R. 354.

[94] See the discussion of the obligation of relief clause below in para.11–20.

[95] If, however, the work is not done the purchaser will wish to obtain the contents of the deposit receipt and this can cause technical difficulties. See *Hamilton v Rodwell*, 1998 S.C.L.R. 418.

[96] Logically, the purchase price offered should already have taken account of the state of the building. A building in poor repair will attract lower bids than a building in good repair. In practice, however, purchasers usually take into account only imminent repair bills in making their bids.

[97] See above, para.4–11.

[98] For an example of what can go wrong, see *Hamilton v Rodwell*, 1998 S.C.L.R. 418; and *Hamilton v Rodwell (No.2)*, 1999 G.W.D. 35-1706.

Statutory notices: dangerous buildings

If a building is actually dangerous, whether to its occupants or to the public 4–30
at large, the council can serve a notice under s.30 of the Building (Scotland)
Act 2003 requiring the owner either to demolish the building or to secure and
repair it.

Statutory notices: buildings not of tolerable standard

"Tolerable standard" is concerned less with structural stability than with the 4–31
provision of basic facilities.[99] Where a house falls below the tolerable standard
the council has a choice of courses of action.[100] (1) It may serve a work notice
requiring the owner to carry out certain works.[101] (2) It may serve a demolition
order.[102] (3) Where a demolition order would be appropriate but for the fact
that the house forms part of a larger building in which the other houses are
satisfactory, it may serve a closing order which prevents the house being used
for human habitation.[103] Closing and demolition orders can be revoked or
suspended, at the council's discretion, where either the house is brought up to
the tolerable standard or where the owner plausibly undertakes to do so.[104]
Where a number of houses in the same area are sub-standard the council can
declare a housing renewal area, which allows it to make an "action plan" for
the area, and which removes the need for individual statutory notices.[105]

Statutory notices: buildings in disrepair

These are the commonest in modern practice, especially in tenement property. 4–32
Councils have a choice between defective building notices under s.28 of the
Building (Scotland) Act 2003 and work notices under s.30 of the Housing
(Scotland) Act 2006. In addition, notices are sometimes served under local
statutes.[106]

Planning permission

Planning law is a large subject in its own right[107] and the treatment here is 4–33
necessarily brief. Planning permission is required for any significant building
work and for certain changes of use. The purchasers' agents will have four
main concerns. The first is whether planning permission has been obtained for
the present buildings, and for their present use. The PECs will very probably
not disclose the answers to these questions, except in the unusual situation of
an enforcement notice having been served. For the purposes of planning law,
there are various defined types of use, called Use Classes, and a change of use

---

[99] Housing (Scotland) Act 1987 s.86.
[100] Housing (Scotland) Act 2007 s.85(1).
[101] Housing (Scotland) Act 2006 s.30.
[102] Housing (Scotland) Act 1987 s.115.
[103] Housing (Scotland) Act 1987 s.114.
[104] Housing (Scotland) Act 1987 ss.116 and 117.
[105] Housing (Scotland) Act 2006 ss.1–9.
[106] Such as the City of Edinburgh District Council Confirmation Order Act 1991 Pt VI.
[107] Jeremy Rowan-Robinson, Eric Young, Michael Purdue and Elaine Farquharson-Black, *Scottish Planning Law and Procedure* (2001); Neil Collar, *Planning*, 3rd edn (2010); Ray McMaster, Alan Prior and John Watchman, *Scottish Planning Law*, 3rd edn (2011).

within a Use Class does not require planning permission.[108] For instance an office used by an accountancy firm could be taken over by a law firm without need for planning permission.

The second concern is whether any conditions are attached to the grant of planning permission and, if so, whether they have been observed. In commercial developments there may also be s.75 obligations[109] or good neighbour agreements.[110]

The third concern is whether the building is listed, or in a conservation area.[111] The PECs usually reveal this. One of the many consequences of being in a conservation area is that demolition requires permission.[112] Outwith such areas an owner is generally free to demolish without permission, except where the property is listed,[113] or is an ancient monument.[114]

The fourth concern is whether the property is affected, directly or indirectly, by planning applications for neighbouring property. For instance the next door neighbours may have applied for, or even obtained, planning permission to build 10 flats in their garden, overlooking the house being purchased. The PECs will not normally disclose this. If the purchasers wish this checked, it will have to be done as an extra request to the council.[115] Apart from that, the missives will normally require the sellers to warrant that they have received no notification of any planning application for neighbouring property.[116]

The local authority's right to object to breaches of planning law prescribes after either 4 or 10 years, depending on the nature of the breach.[117]

Finally, it is important to grasp that the fact that something has planning permission does not mean that it is therefore lawful from the standpoint of public law. Other consents may be required. The most obvious one, which will be relevant in the case of most new buildings, is building consent (discussed below). Many particular activities also require particular consents. For instance, use of land as a caravan site requires special permission.[118]

---

[108] Currently regulated by the Town and Country Planning (Use Classes) (Scotland) Order 1997 (SI 1997/3061) (as amended), commonly called the Use Classes Order.

[109] Which can be either unilateral, by the owner, or entered into by way of agreement with the planning authority: see Town and Country Planning (Scotland) Act 1997 s.75, as substituted by the Planning etc. (Scotland) Act 2006 s.23.

[110] Entered into with a community body: see Town and Country Planning (Scotland) Act 1997 s.75D, inserted by the Planning etc. (Scotland) Act 2006 s.24.

[111] Currently regulated by the Planning (Listed Buildings and Conservation Areas) (Scotland) Act 1997, as amended especially by the Historic Environment (Amendment) Scotland) Act 2011. They are very common. Within the boundaries of the City of Edinburgh alone there are 36 such areas.

[112] Planning (Listed Buildings and Conservation Areas) (Scotland) Act 1997 s.66. This Act does not contain all the law on conservation areas: trees in such areas are covered by the Town and Country Planning (Scotland) Act 1997 s.172.

[113] Planning (Listed Buildings and Conservation Areas) (Scotland) Act 1997 s.6.

[114] Currently regulated by the Ancient Monuments and Archaeological Areas Act 1979, as amended especially by the Historic Environment (Amendment) Scotland) Act 2011.

[115] For example, the City of Edinburgh Council offers an "area search service", which provides a check of the neighbourhood surrounding a property to find out what planning applications have been approved or refused. It provides current and historic planning application information going back six years for an area up to 250 metres around a chosen property.

[116] For an action of damages on the basis of such a warranty, see *Hendry v Egan*, 2010 G.W.D. 36-737. And for neighbour notification, see Town and Country Planning (Development Management Procedure) (Scotland) Regulations 2008 (SSI 2008/432) reg.18.

[117] Town and Country Planning (Scotland) Act 1997 s.124.

[118] Caravan Sites and Control of Development Act 1960.

Building consent

Building consent is concerned with the practicalities of building and not with 4–34
aesthetics or community amenity.[119] The governing legislation is the Building
(Scotland) Act 2003, and building regulations are promulgated to provide
functional standards for the construction of new buildings and for alterations to
existing buildings. The current version is the Building (Scotland) Regulations
2004.[120] Where the building regulations apply, a building warrant from a
"verifier"—which, under present rules, means the relevant local authority[121]—
is needed before work begins, and will not be granted unless the work appears
to comply with the regulations.[122] On completion, a completion certificate
is submited to the verifier certifying that the work was carried out in accordance with the building warrant and the building regulations. If satisfied
"after reasonable inquiry" that all is in order, the verifier formally accepts the
certificate.[123]

From a purchaser's point of view, an accepted completion certificate should
not be regarded as a guarantee that all is well. There will be much that the verifier's inspector has been unable to see and this is so even where, as with the
construction of a new house, several visits are made during the course of
building. If the inspection has been negligent, a purchaser relying on the
completion certificate cannot normally hold the verifier liable in damages.[124]

It is an offence to carry out work without a warrant, and it is also an offence
to occupy or use the building without an accepted completion certificate.[125]
Even if the local authority does not take enforcement action,[126] as is often the
case, problems may still arise, partly because the unauthorised work may be
unsound and eventually have to be repaired, altered or demolished, and partly
because, when the owners come to sell, they may find that prospective
purchasers object to the lack of building consent. This issue is not merely of
theoretical interest for, while warrants are usually obtained for major works
(e.g. the construction of a new house or major alterations to an existing house),
they are often not obtained for minor alterations. One reason for this was and
is ignorance: most people do not realise that a warrant is needed. Tradesmen do
not always know either, and if they do they may not tell their customer. A
second reason is that, even where people are aware in general terms about
building warrants, they may be uncertain as to precisely what does and what
does not require a warrant. Thirdly, councils in practice seldom enforce the law
in relation to minor alterations. Fourthly, no special simplified procedure exists
for where the work is minor, so that the applicant who wishes to move a sink a
metre must submit much the same forms and drawings as the applicant who

---

[119] Not much is written on this important subject.

[120] Building (Scotland) Regulations 2004 (SSI 2004/406), as amended.

[121] Although private verifiers are permitted under s.7 of the Act, none has so far been appointed,
although at the time of writing the matter was under consideration. The need for detailed scrutiny
by the verifier is avoided if the work is certified by a suitably qualified professional with the status
of "certifier": see ss.7, 11 and 19.

[122] Building (Scotland) Act 2003 ss.8 and 9.

[123] 2003 Act ss.17 and 18.

[124] *Taylor v City of Glasgow DC*, 1997 S.C. 183. But cf. *Perth & Kinross Council*, 1998 Hous.
L.R. 78.

[125] Building (Scotland) Act 2003 ss.8 and 21. However, prosecutions seem to be almost
unknown in practice.

[126] 2003 Act s.27.

wishes to build an entire house.[127] In practice, it is difficult to get a warrant without professional help in preparing the application, preferably from an architect. This is expensive, so that for minor works the expense of the application may exceed the cost of the work itself. No one knows what proportion of the housing stock has alterations that are unauthorised, in the sense that no warrant was issued, or, if it was issued, was not followed up by a completion certificate. But the proportion is certainly substantial: probably more than 25 per cent. One reason that no one knows is that minor alterations are often invisible.

Unauthorised alterations: practice

4–35 Once upon a time, solicitors acting for purchasers checked building consents for major works, but seldom bothered about minor works. Practice began to change about 1990. The main reason was a change in the attitude of surveyors. As a result of negligence claims, surveyors became more cautious, and began to comment on evidence they detected of recent works which might have required building consent. Of course, they could and can only mention what they notice, and minor alterations are often invisible. Surveyors do not have time machines by means of which the present state of the building can be compared with earlier states. One practical way of identifying possible problems is to ask the local authority for a building standards assessment, to determine whether the building is or is not in breach of building regulations.[128]

Typically the existence of unauthorised alterations will come to light in the home report or other survey, and hence before missives are concluded, in which case the matter can be dealt with in the missives themselves.[129] Precisely what the missives will say varies from case to case. Usually the offer will have a clause saying something like: "All necessary consents including planning permissions, building warrants and completion certificates have been obtained and satisfactory evidence to this effect will be exhibited at or before settlement." The sellers may, in the qualified acceptance, simply delete the whole clause, or limit it to a period such as the past ten years, or add a qualification about specified alterations. As with other missives provisions, some arm-wrestling may ensue. The outcome depends on the circumstances. During this process both solicitors have some knowledge of the premises and what alterations there seem to have been, and what documentation is available.

One possible approach is for the sellers to try to put matters right. There are three ways in which this might be done. One is to seek retrospective consents from the council.[130] But although the costs will not be too high unless the council insists on remedial work being done, the whole process is likely to take months rather than weeks. A further difficulty is that the work may have complied with earlier versions of the building regulations but not with the current version. A second option is to apply for a relaxation of the building

---

[127] See the Building (Procedure) (Scotland) Regulations 2004 (SSI 2004/428), as amended especially by the Building (Procedure) (Scotland) Amendment Regulations 2007 (SSI 2007/167).

[128] Although this practice long pre-dates the Building (Scotland) Act 2003, it is provided for by s. 6 of that Act (not yet in force).

[129] See e.g. a letter at (1999) 44 J.L.S.S. Feb./12.

[130] Building (Scotland) Act 2003 s.15.

regulations in relation to the alterations in question.[131] This is not likely to be an attractive solution unless expensive remedial work would otherwise be required to comply with the regulations. Finally, it is possible to seek a "letter of comfort" from the council, i.e. a letter stating that enforcement proceedings will not be taken. This is the normal solution, as well as the cheapest, although in some cases it may still be necessary to employ an architect to make representations to the council. Regional missives sometimes expressly allow this as an alternative to a building warrant and completion certificate[132]; otherwise purchasers are not bound to accept such a letter, but can insist that the full terms of the missives be honoured.[133] If the sellers know that there are unauthorised alterations, it often makes sense to obtain a comfort letter in advance and then to make it clear in the missives that this is all that the purchasers can require. Inevitably, different local authorities have different policies as to letters of comfort.

How far back need one go?

The solicitors for the purchasers will need to see both building warrant and 4–36 (accepted) completion certificate[134]—or at least a letter of comfort—for all works which require them. But for how long? For works in the last 10 years? Or 20 years? Or 50 years? Or 100 years? This question is not easily answered for, unlike planning permission, the legislation does not impose a cut-off period for enforcement by the local authority. Some help may be had from long negative prescription: it is arguable that the obligation to obtain a building warrant or completion certificate prescribes after 20 years.[135] Some local authorities have a policy of not enforcing the requirements after a certain number of years. But it must be borne in mind that, whether or not warrant and certificate were obtained, s.25 of the 2003 Act gives the council power, in certain circumstances, to require buildings to conform to current building regulations.

There are practical difficulties about going back too far. Although councils maintain registers of building warrants and completion certificates, and although such registers are put on a statutory footing by the 2003 Act (as "building standards registers") and are often searchable online,[136] the longer ago the alteration, the greater the possibility that the records cannot be located. Not many councils have proper records for building warrants and completion certificates before the reorganisation of local government in 1975.

Since there is no clear legal cut-off period, there is no logically defensible place to stop, so that in the purchase of a flat in Edinburgh's New Town one might in theory need to see the original Dean of Guild consents for its construction in 1788, plus consents for all subsequent alterations.[137] But this would be

---

[131] 2003 Act s.3.

[132] See e.g. Combined Standard Clauses (2009) cl.7(a).

[133] See *Hawke v Mathers*, 1995 S.C.L.R. 1004.

[134] Under the former law, which applied until May 1, 2005, the council issued completion certificates rather than accepting them.

[135] Prescription and Limitation (Scotland) Act 1973 s.7.

[136] Building (Scotland) Act 2003 s.24.

[137] For although the current law is regulated by the Building (Scotland) Act 2003, the need for building consent has existed for hundreds of years. Before 1975 consents were given (in burghs) by the Dean of Guild Court. Such consent originally bore the curious name of the "jedge and warrant of the Dean of Guild".

absurd.[138] Missives in practice vary considerably on this point. Some have no cut-off period. Some have a 20-year cut-off, and others a 10-year period. Others again cover the period in which the building has been in the ownership of the present sellers. The agent for the sellers should certainly resist an unlimited period. As the law stands there is no correct solution. There is also the obvious practical difficulty of showing that an alteration (for which no documentation exists) was indeed done outwith the defined period.

Trees

4–37 There is a great deal of legislation about trees. Residential conveyancers probably need to know (and tell their clients) only that cutting down a tree in a conservation area normally requires permission, and that even outside such areas a tree preservation order can be made having the same effect.[139]

Fire prevention and employee safety

4–38 In the case of buildings in public or commercial use, such as factories, hotels and shops, the occupiers must take such fire safety measures as are reasonable to ensure the safety of persons lawfully on the premises, and must carry out assessments to identify risks to safety in respect of harm caused by fire.[140] Such buildings must also meet a minimum standard for the health and safety of employees, for instance in such matters as heating, toilet facilities and so on.[141] The cost of adapting a building so as to meet such requirements can be high.

Contaminated land

4–39 Environmental law is a large subject in its own right.[142] Numerous statutes regulate it, and more than one public agency may be involved, especially the Scottish Environment Protection Agency ("SEPA"). For conveyancers the most important legislative provisions are in Pt IIA ("Contaminated Land") of the Environmental Protection Act 1990. If a client plans any activity with a possibly negative environmental impact, it may turn out to be lawful, or unlawful, or lawful with the requisite permissions, and the client must be advised accordingly. Missives may need to stipulate that any necessary consents already exist.

The main worry in most cases, however, is not so much what the buyer can do but whether the land is already contaminated. Contamination may be obvious but may also be hard to detect. PECs give certain basic information,

---

[138] No cut-off point, however, is suggested in the CML *Lenders' Handbook for Scotland*, para.5.4.1.

[139] Town and Country Planning (Scotland) Act 1997 ss.159 et seq.

[140] Fire (Scotland) Act 2005 Pt 3; Fire Safety (Scotland) Regulations 2006 (SSI 2006/456). See further P.N. McDonald, "Fire and Rescue Services", in *The Laws of Scotland: Stair Memorial Encyclopaedia Reissue* (2009), paras 66–97.

[141] See e.g. Mines and Quarries Act 1954; Mines and Quarries (Tips) Act 1969; Offices, Shops and Railway Premises Act 1963; Health and Safety at Work etc. Act 1974, plus numerous statutory instruments.

[142] The literature is vast. See e.g. Vincent Brown, *Environmental Pollution Law and Commercial Transactions* (2003); Francis McManus (ed.), *Environmental Law in Scotland* (2007); Mark Poustie, "Environment", in *The Laws of Scotland: Stair Memorial Encyclopaedia Reissue* (2007), esp. paras 642 et seq. on contaminated land; Andrew Waite et al., *Environmental Law in Property Transactions*, 3rd edn (2009).

such as whether the land is on the contaminated land register maintained by the local authority, but a negative return should not be taken as indicating that the land is uncontaminated. In some cases (especially commercial purchases) the buyers may wish to know something of the environmental history of the site and its immediate surroundings beyond what is disclosed in the PECs. Such reports are commercially available. They can be either "desktop" searches, in which the provider gathers data from old local maps, old planning permissions and so on, or there can be a more expensive "environmental audit" in which environmental experts make a site visit and may take and test samples, make trial bores, and so on.

In commercial conveyancing, contamination is likely to be dealt with extensively in missives, which should make clear whether liabilities are to lie with the sellers or the buyers.[143] In residential conveyancing, the Law Society's view is that conveyancing practitioners are not qualified to give advice on environmental matters and should include a clause in their standard terms of business indicating that environmental matters do not form part of their remit.[144]

Access rights in favour of the public

It may be that the property is subject to a public right of way. The existence of 4–40 such a right will in most cases be fairly obvious. As a result of the Land Reform (Scotland) Act 2003 the general public has access rights to the whole of Scotland, subject to a variety of exceptions.[145] For instance, the access right does not include access to buildings, nor does it extend to "sufficient adjacent land" to allow occupiers a reasonable amount of privacy.[146] Thus gardens are generally exempted as well as houses.

Liability to compulsory purchase

All land is potentially liable to be compulsorily purchased for public 4–41 purposes.[147] This is a risk that a buyer has to take, like the risk of taxation. In addition, in certain cases local community organisations may have a right of compulsory purchase under the Land Reform (Scotland) Act 2003. This Act creates two sorts of purchase right.[148] One is the "community right to buy" which is a pre-emption right, that is to say a right that can be exercised only if the owner puts the property up for sale. It exists only where an appropriate community body has registered its interest in the Register of Community

---

[143] See e.g. the style offers to sell available at *http://www.psglegal.co.uk/*.

[144] (2009) 54 J.L.S.S. Dec./57. See also Reid and Gretton, *Conveyancing 2010*, pp.79–80. For terms of business letters, see above, para.1–03.

[145] See Guthrie, in Robert Rennie (ed.), *The Promised Land: Property Law Reform* (2008), Ch.5.

[146] Land Reform (Scotland) Act 2003 s.6(1). See *Gloag v Perth & Kinross Council*, 2007 S.C.L.R. 530; *Snowie v Stirling Council*, 2008 S.L.T. (Sh. Ct) 61. And see also Reid and Gretton, *Conveyancing 2007*, pp.127–35, and *Conveyancing 2008*, pp.112–14; Combe, (2008) 12 Edin. L.R. 463.

[147] See Jeremy Rowan-Robinson, *Compulsory Purchase and Compensation*, 3rd edn (2009). For a useful summary of the law see David A. Brand, Andrew J.M. Steven and Scott Wortley, *Professor McDonald's Conveyancing Manual*, 7th edn (2004), paras 29.19–29.23.

[148] In, respectively, Pts 2 and 3 of the Act. For an overview, see Reid and Gretton, *Conveyancing 2003*, pp.135–41 (Andrew J.M. Steven and Alan Barr); Combe, 2006 J.R. 195.

Interests in Land.[149] The other is the "crofting community right to buy". This is geographically much more restricted, but is a stronger right, since it can be exercised at any time, and not merely if the owner happens to put the property up for sale. These rights tend to apply to larger rural estates rather than to residential or commercial property.

---

[149] Land Reform (Scotland) Act 2003 ss.36–46. See *Holmehill Ltd v The Scottish Ministers*, 2006 S.L.T. (Sh. Ct) 79, discussed by Combe, (2007) 11 Edin. L.R. 109.

CHAPTER 5

MISSIVES III: BREACH OF CONTRACT

Introduction

Where transactions go wrong, the outcome depends on the stage that has been 5–01
reached. For as long as missives remain open, either party can walk away
without financial penalty.[1] And as buyers usually have an early opportunity to
look at the titles, many title problems are disposed of in this way. But once the
parties are locked into concluded missives, the position is governed by a
combination of the missives and the common law of contract. The most
common default at this stage is in payment of the price (which, in residential
conveyancing, is often the only obligation on the buyers). Finally, after the
transaction is settled and the disposition delivered, claims must be made under
the warrandice clause of the disposition, except for an initial period of two
years during which the missives too are usually still in force.[2] As by this stage
the buyers are likely to have paid the price, any outstanding claims are usually
against the sellers. Post-settlement claims are the subject of Ch.19, below; in
this chapter we are concerned only with claims under concluded missives.

Breach, or alleged breach, of missives may lead to litigation, and litigation
is something that both the loser and the winner will in all probability end up
regretting. As well as the stress and worry, and as well as the time consumed,
even the winner is likely to end up out of pocket. The best advice is to avoid
litigation if at all possible. Clients usually underestimate the human and financial costs of litigation and overestimate their chances of success, and are often
more legalistic than lawyers.[3] But sometimes the combativeness comes from
the solicitors themselves, who should know better, but who rush into head-on
conflict on behalf of their unfortunate clients.

DECIDING WHAT TO DO

A menu of choices

If one party defaults on an obligation under missives—if, for example, the 5–02
buyers fail to pay, or the sellers to give vacant possession or a flawless title—
the wronged party is likely to have a choice of remedy. Often it will be possible
to bring the contract to an end by rescission. But, at least at first, parties may

---

[1] By and large, Scots law does not allow recovery of (wasted) pre-contractual expenditure.
Compare the "Melville Monument" liability case of *Walker v Milne* (1823) 2 S. 379 with *Khaliq v
Londis Holdings Ltd* [2010] CSIH 13; 2010 S.C. 432, discussed by Hogg and MacQueen, (2010)
14 Edin. L.R. 451.

[2] See above, para.4–11.

[3] An insightful observation of Professor Roddy Paisley's.

draw back from so drastic a solution, for a number of reasons. Buyers may be so in love with the house that they will be reluctant to give up the bargain. Sellers may fear a return to the market in case it does not produce so high a price, or perhaps any sale at all. There may be reasonable prospects that, given time, the other party will be able to perform. Or the breach may be minor and one that the innocent party might, in the end, be willing to live with. Of course sometimes it is obvious from the beginning that the contract will not be performed. The buyers, unable to sell their existing house, may have no real prospect of raising the funds to pay for a new one; or the sellers' title may be irremediably bad. Immediate rescission is then the only viable option. Or again a party may repudiate the contract by announcing that he or she cannot or will not perform—although, even in the face of repudiation, it is still permissible, if hardly wise, for the other party to insist on performance.[4] These are clear cases. All too often, however, the position is not especially clear, and the innocent party is willing to let matters run on for a while and see what happens. Decision time can be postponed, at least for the moment. Meanwhile the day fixed for settlement arrives and is gone, and the transaction is becalmed.

In favour of delay: the mutuality principle

5–03   Letting things run on would hardly be an attractive option were it not for the mutuality principle.[5] This holds that, for as long as one party to a contract is in breach, that party cannot insist on performance by the counter-party. So for example in *Bowie v Semple's Exrs*[6] the buyer was held entitled to withhold payment where the seller, an executor, had still not obtained confirmation.

Only counterpart obligations are suspended in this way. But, as Lord Hope has emphasised:

> "The guiding principle is that the unity of the overall transaction should be respected. The analysis should start from the position that all the obligations that it embraces are to be regarded as counterparts of each other unless there is a clear indication to the contrary."[7]

As applied to conveyancing, this suggests that a party can refuse to settle a transaction unless the other party is able to perform in full. So the buyers must be able to pay the price, and the sellers to give possession, to deliver a valid disposition and good and marketable title, and to comply with warranties in relation to matters such as building and planning consents or ongoing repairs.

---

[4]   *White & Carter (Councils) Ltd v McGregor*, 1962 S.C. (HL) 1. The abolition of this rule has been recommended, 1999: Scottish Law Commission, Report on *Remedies for Breach of Contract* (Scot. Law. Com. No.174, 1999). On repudiation, see Hector L. MacQueen and Joe Thomson, *Contract Law in Scotland*, 2nd edn (2007), paras 5.27–5.33. If repudiation occurs before the date on which performance is due (which is typically the date of entry), the contract-breaker's breach is said to be "anticipatory".

[5]   Or, in the language of the *ius commune*, the *exceptio non adimpleti contractus*. On the mutuality principle, see William W. McBryde, *The Law of Contract in Scotland*, 3rd edn (2007), paras 20–44 to 20–61; Hector L. MacQueen and Joe Thomson, *Contract Law in Scotland*, 2nd edn (2007), paras 5.8–5.15.

[6]   *Bowie v Semple's Exrs*, 1978 S.L.T. (Sh. Ct) 9. Compare *Moor v Atwal*, 1995 S.C.L.R. 1119.

[7]   *Inveresk Plc v Tullis Russell Papermakers Ltd* [2010] UKSC 19; 2010 S.C. (UKSC) 106 at para.42. For commentary on this case, see Godfrey, (2011) 15 Edin. L.R. 115.

Only the most trivial obligation might be argued to fall outside the bonds of mutuality.[8]

Against delay: implied waiver

If, however, things run on for too long, the innocent party may be faced with an argument, based on personal bar, that the right to rescind has been lost by implied waiver.[9] In fact mere delay by itself (unless very lengthy) is no bar to rescission.[10] Nor is taking entry a bar, although rescission may then be prevented on the different ground that *restitutio in integrum* is not possible.[11] Nor does it make any difference that the contract itself contains a fixed date after which rescission is expressly permitted and the date is allowed to pass.[12] Nonetheless, waiver can sometimes occur. A rare example is *Macdonald v Newall*[13] where the buyer, having examined title and taken no objection to it (except on another unrelated point), took entry and did not then raise her objection until some further months had passed.[14]   5–04

Decision time

With luck a period of delay allows the problem to be sorted out. Given time, the buyers may come up with the money, or the sellers with the missing title deed or letter of comfort. The transaction can then settle, and the only remaining issue is whether damages might be due.[15] But quite frequently matters do not work out so well. Days ripen into weeks, or even weeks into months, and still one of the parties remains in default. Sometimes, of course, this suits the counter-party, who may be in no hurry to acquire the house (not having managed to sell the old one) or, as the case may be, to sell the house (not having managed to buy a new one). But even in cases such as this, the time will come when a decision has to be made. At this point the innocent party has three choices. One is to pull out of the transaction.[16] Another is to proceed with it, even, it may be, in the face of imperfect performance.[17] The third is to settle the transaction on the basis of some temporary accommodation such as placing the   5–05

---

[8] William W. McBryde, *The Law of Contract in Scotland*, 3rd edn (2007), para.20–60. In offers, a traditional formula was to say that "in exchange for the price" the sellers will provide certain things, such as a good and marketable title, a valid disposition, and so on, and this survives in some of the regional missives. See e.g. Combined Standard Clauses (2009) cl.16. The danger of this way of expressing things is that it might seem to exclude from the mutuality principle any obligation of the sellers which is not included in the list.

[9] See Elspeth C. Reid and John W.G. Blackie, *Personal Bar* (2006), paras 3–08 et seq., and especially paras 3–18 to 3–21.

[10] See *Park Lane Developments (Glasgow Harbour) Ltd v Jesner*, Unreported May 3, 2006 Glasgow Sheriff Court, where the buyer objected to a disposition before settlement but six months after his agents had first seen a draft. It was held that the right to rescind had not been waived. For a discussion, see Reid, (2006) 10 Edin. L.R. 437 at 440–41.

[11] See *Armia v Daejan Developments Ltd*, 1979 S.C. (HL) 56.

[12] *Lousada & Co Ltd v JE Lesser (Properties) Ltd*, 1990 S.C. 178; *Elwood v Ravenseft Properties Ltd*, 1991 S.L.T. 44; *Atlas Assurance Co Ltd v Dollar Land Holdings Plc*, 1993 S.L.T. 892.

[13] *Macdonald v Newall* (1898) 1 F. 68.

[14] *Mowbray v Mathieson*, 1989 G.W.D. 6-267 is another example.

[15] For which see below, para.5–20.

[16] See below, paras 5–06 to 5–18.

[17] See below, paras 5–19 to 5–21.

price on joint deposit receipt.[18] These options are the subject matter of the rest of the chapter.

PULLING OUT

Terminology: rescinding and resiling

5–06 Some contract lawyers argue that one "resiles" when one withdraws from an agreement which is not yet legally binding (e.g. open missives), and that the term "rescind" should be used where one party withdraws from a binding contract because of breach by the other party. This terminological approach has some judicial support.[19] There are other possibilities as well, such as withdrawing on the basis of an express contractual right to do so in certain circumstances, or, again, withdrawing on the ground that the contract is void-able. For all such possibilities conveyancers tend, rightly or wrongly, to use the word "resile". In this book we have preferred "rescind" to "resile" for cases where a person pulls out of a contract on the ground of the other party's breach.

With rescission, two questions of importance arise. One is whether, and if so when, the innocent party is entitled to rescind. And the other is what damages, if any, might be due.

Right to rescind: positive obligations and warranties

5–07 Missives comprise a mixture of positive obligations and warranties. Examples of the former are the sellers' obligation to deliver a disposition or a good and marketable title, or the buyers' obligation to pay; among the warranties are provisions that all necessary consents have been obtained for alterations or that there are no unusual or unduly onerous burdens. The difference is important for present purposes because the rules as to right to rescind are not the same.[20]

Positive obligations: time not of the essence

5–08 Unless the defaulting party repudiates the contract, the mere fact that he or she has failed to perform a positive obligation does not normally amount to mate-rial breach, entitling the innocent party to rescind. For, subject to the excep-tions mentioned below—exceptions which in fact usually apply in modern practice—time is not "of the essence" in a contract of sale, meaning that the defaulting party must be given a reasonable time to perform that which he or she has undertaken.[21] Only after the expiry of a "reasonable time" does the breach become material, permitting rescission. The fact that "time is not of the

---

[18] See below, paras 5–22 to 5–24.

[19] *Zemhunt (Holdings) Ltd v Control Securities Ltd*, 1992 S.L.T. 151; *Lloyds Bank Plc v Bamberger*, 1993 S.C. 570. For discussion of terminology see William W. McBryde, *The Law of Contract in Scotland*, 3rd edn (2007), paras 20–02 to 20–06.

[20] There can also be suspensive conditions (see above, paras 3–18 to 3–22), where non-purifica-tion by the agreed date means that the contract falls at once: *T Boland & Co Ltd v Dundas's Trustees*, 1975 S.L.T. (Notes) 80.

[21] See generally McBryde, (1996) 1 Edin. L.R. 43 at 58–60. The rule is in some ways a curious one. If the innocent party can be compensated by damages the rule is, on the whole, not unfair. But it seems to be applied in other situations: see e.g. *Khazaka v Drysdale*, 1995 S.L.T. 1108. Perhaps the correctness of that decision could be doubted.

essence" does not mean that delay is not breach. It is breach, and thus will presumptively give rise to a claim for damages. The issue being considered here is whether it is a breach that will justify the other party in rescinding.

The normal way to deal with the "reasonable time" requirement is to use the ultimatum procedure laid down in *Rodger (Builders) Ltd v Fawdry*.[22] The chronology of this procedure is as follows:

(a) the date for performance of the obligation passes without performance being tendered;
(b) the defaulting party is then allowed a "reasonable time" to perform;
(c) after expiry of the "reasonable time" the aggrieved party serves an ultimatum, demanding performance within a further "reasonable time";
(d) if performance is still not tendered the aggrieved party may rescind.

Whether stages (b) and (c) are independently necessary is very doubtful, but in practice it is safer to assume that they are.[23] How long is "reasonable" will depend on the facts and circumstances of the individual case. In one case[24] the following timescale was approved by the court for failure to pay the price: the contractual date of entry, at which the price was due, was December 15; the ultimatum was sent on January 13; the expiry date of the ultimatum was January 31. However, a longer period may be necessary for other types of failure, or where, as in *Rodger (Builders) Ltd v Fawdry* itself,[25] eventual performance is likely. So where a seller has applied for, say, confirmation as executor or for a local authority completion certificate, "reasonable time" probably means the time that it usually takes to obtain a document of the kind in question.[26] There may, of course, be difficult cases and it is always open to a party to seek a declarator[27] that the contract has been validly rescinded.

When immediate rescission is possible: (i) where the law implies such a right

Rescission is permitted as soon as the contractual settlement date arrives if 5–09 the sellers turn out to have no title whatsoever to all or part of the property. If the sellers cannot produce a title by the date of entry they are not entitled to further time in which to acquire one.[28] Further, it has been held in the Outer House that immediate rescission may be available in a second situation, namely where the sale is primarily of a business. In the case in question the business was conducted from premises which were held on lease, and the breach was a failure to obtain the landlord's consent to the assignation by the date of entry.[29]

---

[22] *Rodger (Builders) Ltd v Fawdry*, 1950 S.C. 483. See William W. McBryde, *The Law of Contract in Scotland*, 3rd edn (2007), paras 20–128 to 12–131.
[23] cf. *George Packman & Sons v Dunbar's Trustees*, 1977 S.L.T. 140, per Lord Stott.
[24] *Lloyds Bank Ltd v Bauld*, 1976 S.L.T. (Notes) 53.
[25] *Rodger (Builders) Ltd v Fawdry*, 1950 S.C. 483.
[26] *McLennan v Warner & Co*, 1996 S.L.T. 1349.
[27] As in *Lloyds Bank Ltd v Bauld*, 1976 S.L.T. (Notes) 53.
[28] *Campbell v McCutcheon*, 1963 S.C. 505.
[29] *Ahmed v Akhtar*, 1997 S.L.T. 218.

When immediate rescission is possible: (ii) express agreement

5–10 Not having the option of immediate rescission is often unsatisfactory, especially if there is reason to believe that the other party will never perform. The difficulty is avoided by an express provision in the missives. This is invariably done in respect of payment of the price, but only selectively in respect of the sellers' obligations. Express clauses can be drafted in either of two ways. One is for the missives to state that timeous performance is "of the essence", thereby implying that breach will constitute material breach, so that the other party will be able to rescind immediately.[30] An alternative is to provide that, if the performance is not made by a defined date, the other party may rescind.[31] If the defined date is the contractual date of settlement, the two possibilities come to the same thing. But missives usually provide that the right to rescind emerges not immediately on default but after a defined period, such as 14 or 21 days. Clauses of this sort provide a fair balance between the interests of the two parties.

Such time-is-of-the-essence or right-to-resile clauses commonly state that rescission is available only where the fault is exclusively on one side. This is a rule which would almost certainly be implied even though not expressed.[32]

Care must be taken in the wording. In one case[33] sellers found themselves having to persuade the court that the phrase "the sellers have the option immediately thereafter [i.e. on non-payment] to resile" meant, not that the option must be exercised immediately (which it had not been), but merely that it arose immediately and could be exercised at any time.

Rescission before the date of entry?

5–11 Could a party rescind before the contractual date of entry? The answer is that this is not normally possible, but there are two, or perhaps three, exceptions. The first is where the missives confer such a right. The second is where the other party repudiates the contract. A third, and doubtful, case is where the sellers have no title to all or part of the property. As mentioned earlier, this fact will justify rescission at the settlement date,[34] but in *Campbell v McCutcheon*[35] it was held that rescission before the settlement date was valid. This is, however, contrary to the general principle of contract law that a party need not be in a position to perform at the time of the contract, but only at the time when performance is due. Sellers might have no title when missives are concluded but still be confident that they can obtain such a title in time for settlement. *Campbell* may create an exception, but it is arguable that the approval of pre-settlement rescission was *obiter* or, if not *obiter*, simply wrong.

---

[30] Sometimes the formula is that that timeous payment is an "essential condition" or "material condition". This is an ambiguous expression, for it can indicate that the condition is a suspensive one, but as applied to timeous payment the meaning is presumably that breach will constitute material breach.

[31] Sometimes both forms are used in the same clause, making it unclear whether the innocent party can rescind at once or only after 14 days. Probably the latter is what is intended. See *McPhee v Black*, Unreported July 31, 2006 Ayr Sheriff Court, and the comments by Sheriff Principal James A. Taylor at para.8 (quoted in Reid and Gretton, *Conveyancing 2006*, pp.89–90). Regional missives now usually avoid this puzzling formula.

[32] See *Davidson v Tilburg Ltd*, 1991 G.W.D. 18-1109.

[33] *Toynar Ltd v R&A Properties (Fife) Ltd*, 1989 G.W.D. 2-82. The sellers were successful.

[34] See above, para.5–09.

[35] *Campbell v McCutcheon*, 1963 S.C. 505.

Rescission: warranties

Apart from positive obligations, missives may also include warranties.[36] If 5–12
properly drawn, they will state the date at which the particular thing is guaranteed (generally the date of conclusion of missives or date of entry). It seems
that breach of a warranty, provided it is material, gives entitlement to immediate rescission.[37] For the warranty is either satisfied or it is not, and if it is not,
the seller is in immediate and conclusive breach. There seems no place here for
the ultimatum procedure because, unlike a positive obligation, there is nothing
for the seller still to do. If this is correct, then, at least in this respect, a warranty
is superior to a positive obligation. Missives often lay down a time period
(such as 14 days after receipt of the appropriate documentation) within which
rescission for warranties must be pursued. In practice, warranties often concern
relatively minor matters and often the buyer will not wish to rescind.

Rescission: the risk of getting it wrong

Rescission can be a wise decision, but it carries a risk: unjustified rescission is 5–13
itself a breach of contract. Suppose that Jack is selling to Jill. Missives have
been concluded and the settlement day has been and gone, but Jill has not
settled because of problems raising the money. Jack is fed up and rescinds. If
he rescinds prematurely, he is in breach. If, as is usually the case, the missives
provide for a deadline—for instance that if Jill fails to pay within three weeks
of the due date then Jack may rescind—it is important not to send the letter of
rescission too soon.[38] Moreover, if Jack unlawfully rescinds and resells the
property to Jenny, Jill may even be able to reduce the resale, whether she can
or not depending on the state of Jenny's knowledge.[39]

Method of rescission

A contract is rescinded by giving notice to the other side, whether in writing, 5–14
by oral communication, or even by actions.[40] But if the missives have a
provision as to the form of notice, that form needs to be observed. Such provisions seem best avoided. One which used to be common in missives and
can still be found is for rescission to require the giving of a "prior written
notice". The word "prior", however, invites the question: prior to what? A
possible reading is that rescission cannot be immediate but that there must
instead be a two-stage process: first, the sending of the notice, and then, after
the elapse of a reasonable time, the actual act of rescission. Yet this is presumably not what is intended. Fortunately, the courts have taken the indulgent

---

[36] For the distinction, see above, para.5–07.

[37] It seems that the point has never been expressly decided. See, however, *Morris v Ritchie*,
1992 G.W.D. 33-1950. In any case the buyers can achieve virtual rescission simply by refusing to
settle. Under the mutuality principle (above, para.5–03), they cannot be required to settle while the
counterparty (here the sellers) persists in breach (unless the breach is trivial). If the sellers cannot
purge their breach, they can never require the buyers to settle.

[38] This, however, was thought not to invalidate the notice in *Miller v Maguire*, Unreported
August 10, 2005 Glasgow Sheriff Court.

[39] This is the "offside goals rule" as to which see *Rodger (Builders) Ltd v Fawdry*, 1950 S.C.
483; Reid, *Property*, paras 695 et seq.; David A. Brand, Andrew J.M. Steven and Scott Wortley,
Professor McDonald's Conveyancing Manual, 7th edn (2004), paras 32.52 et seq.

[40] William W. McBryde, *The Law of Contract in Scotland*, 3rd edn (2007), para.20–107.

view that "prior" is mere surplusage and that the notice itself can effect rescission.[41]

In practice, missives are always rescinded in writing, and it is also the practice to state the reason for it. It has been held that rescission can be effectual even if the wrong reason is given, provided of course that a good ground for rescission does actually exist.[42] If that is so, then presumably it also follows that it is not necessary to give the reason in the first place.

Damages

5–15   Quite often, warranties are expressed as being on a take-it-or-leave-it basis, so that a buyer who is dissatisfied with, say, the title conditions can rescind the contract, usually within a limited time frame, but is prevented from seeking damages.[43] But, that case apart, rescission is usually accompanied by a claim for damages. This subject is simply part of general contract law.

Before looking at that law as applied to the sale of heritable property, two general remarks are worth making. The first is that the ascertainment of damages is not an exact science. The second is that the innocent party must mitigate, or minimise, his or her loss. However, the duty[44] to minimise does not begin until the contract comes to an end, e.g. by formal rescission, which may be some time after the contractual date of entry.[45] Under what heads can damages be recovered? There is surprisingly little case law on this important subject, and what follows is only an educated guess.

Damages: (i) sellers in default

5–16   Buyers who rescind following the sellers' failure to produce a good title, or other material default, will have to begin all over again finding a house. The expenses incurred on the abortive purchase will have been wasted. The only reported case dealing with damages in this situation is *Fielding v Newell*.[46] Unfortunately, the report is not very full and gives only the heads of damage which were disputed. These were: (a) legal fees for the unsuccessful contract; (b) survey fee; (c) travel and accommodation costs to inspect the property; (d) cost of telephone calls to solicitor and surveyor. The reason for the dispute was that all these expenses were incurred prior to the contract being concluded. No final view was reached by the court, which instead allowed proof before answer. Damages of this kind protect what is sometimes known as the "reliance interest"

---

[41] *Charisma Properties Ltd v Grayling (1994) Ltd*, 1996 S.C. 556.

[42] *Owen v Fotheringham*, 1997 S.L.T. (Sh. Ct) 28.

[43] Clause 15 of the Combined Standard Clauses (2009) is typical in this regard. After reciting warranties in relation to title conditions, the clause continues: "If the title deeds disclose a position other than as stated above, the Purchaser (regardless of his previous state of knowledge) will be entitled to resile from the Missives without penalty to either party but only provided (i) the Purchaser intimates his intention to exercise this right within ten working days of receipt of the Seller's titles; and (ii) such matters intimated as prejudicial are not rectified or clarified to the Purchaser's satisfaction (acting reasonably) by the Date of Entry or within 6 weeks from the date of such intimation whichever is earlier. The Purchaser's right to resile shall be his sole option in terms of the Missives."

[44] Strictly speaking, there is no "duty". Rather, the rule is that if the injured party does not mitigate, the damages are calculated as if he or she had done so. See William W. McBryde, *The Law of Contract in Scotland*, 3rd edn (2007) para.22–37.

[45] *Johnstone's Exrs v Harris*, 1977 S.C. 365.

[46] *Fielding v Newell*, 1987 S.L.T. 530.

by compensating for wasted expenditure and so putting the buyer in the same financial position as if no contract had ever been entered into.[47]

Damages: (ii) buyers in default

If the buyers fail to pay, the sellers will normally re-market the house. Often 5–17 they will have bought another house in reliance on the sale and so may be faced with interest payments on two loans. Fortunately there is more authority here.[48] The subject may be divided into six parts:

(a) The sellers are entitled to the difference (if negative) between the price in the first, abortive, sale and the price in the second, successful sale.[49] If there is no re-sale, the value of the property is assessed as at the date when the contract was rescinded. Where the difference turns out to be positive not negative (i.e. the price in the second sale is higher than the price in the first, abortive, sale), then there is a profit to the sellers which must be set off against other heads of loss. The consequence may be that no damages are due.[50]

(b) The sellers are entitled to the legal, advertising and other expenses of one of the sales but (as they were going to sell anyway) not of the other.[51] Authority is divided as to whether the expenses properly due are those of the first (abortive) sale or the second (successful) one.[52] There is sometimes a missives provision on this issue.

(c) If the house is no longer being used (the sellers having moved into their new house), the sellers are entitled to the cost of running the house from the abortive date of entry until entry is taken on the second sale. This includes insurance and routine maintenance. In one case the cost of employing a caretaker was not allowed as being too remote.[53]

(d) A difficult issue is whether the sellers can recover the cost of servicing a loan. The fact that payment was not tendered on the date of entry may place the sellers in financial difficulties, and this is especially so where they have bought a new house in reliance on the sale of the old one. In this situation the sellers will be financing two loans: on the one hand they typically will still be paying the loan on the old house, and on the other hand (the sale price not having materialised) they may be paying bridging finance on the full purchase price of the new house. This can be ruinously expensive. And it is no fault of the sellers. Can the sellers recover the cost of servicing one of these loans

---

[47] Hector L. MacQueen and Joe Thomson, *Contract Law in Scotland*, 2nd edn (2007), para.6.27. For the reliance interest, see the classic article by Fuller and Purdue, (1936) 46 Yale L.J. 52.

[48] *Grant v Ullah*, 1987 S.L.T. 639; *Voeten v Campbell Brook & Myles*, 1987 G.W.D. 26-1009; *Hopkinson v Williams*, 1993 S.L.T. 907; *Field v Dickinson*, 1995 S.C.L.R. 1146.

[49] *King v Moore*, 1993 S.L.T. 1117. This is on the assumption that the seller has taken proper steps to obtain a good price. If not, that means that the seller has failed to mitigate, and the first buyer can use this fact as a defence.

[50] See William W. McBryde, *The Law of Contract in Scotland*, 3rd edn (2007), para.22–51.

[51] See e.g. *Kerr v McCormack*, Unreported January 12, 2005 Glasgow Sheriff Court, discussed in Reid and Gretton, *Conveyancing 2005*, pp.59–62.

[52] Compare *Johnstone's Exrs v Harris*, 1977 S.C. 365 with *Grant v Ullah*, 1987 S.L.T. 639. And see also the comments of Sheriff Principal E.F. Bowen QC in *Black v McGregor*, 2006 G.W.D. 17-351 at para.15.

[53] *Chapman's Trs v Anglo Scottish Group Services Ltd*, 1980 S.L.T. (Sh. Ct) 27.

from the buyers?[54] In *Tiffney v Bachurzewski*[55] a claim in respect of a
bridging loan failed because the possibility of the seller having to
bridge was said not to be within the reasonable contemplation of the
parties at the date of the contract and so not allowable under the
second rule in *Hadley v Baxendale*.[56] Not many conveyancers or
indeed housebuyers would accept this conclusion. The difficulty is
commonly avoided by a provision in missives allowing recovery of
the cost of a new loan.[57]

(e) If, as occasionally happens, the buyers have paid a deposit, the sellers
may be able to keep it.[58]

(f) A claim for general inconvenience, but not for solatium, may also be
possible.[59]

Liquidated damages

5–18 One way of avoiding uncertainties and disputes in quantifying a claim in
damages is for the parties to pre-estimate the loss in the form of a clause of
liquidated damages.[60] This type of clause has a long history in residential
conveyancing[61] in the context of non-payment of the price, and has undergone
a number of convulsions along the way.[62] Initially it was part of the standard
provision included in missives to ensure that a buyer who pays late must also
pay interest.[63] When, however, in 1993 the courts refused to apply such a
clause to a case of rescission—that is to say, to a case of non-payment as
opposed to late payment—the clause was modified accordingly.[64] In its new
form it provided for payment of interest from the date of entry until the date
when, following rescission, the price was received following a resale. This too
proved to be unsatisfactory, partly because the seller might not want, or be
able, to resell,[65] and partly because, if resale was too long delayed, the resulting
bill for the original buyer was unacceptably high. The latest change dates
from around 2007. The clause currently found in most regional missives gives

---

[54] They cannot recover both, and it is not wholly clear which is appropriate.

[55] *Tiffney v Bachurzewski*, 1985 S.L.T. 165. The sale eventually proceeded to settlement, but the
principles are the same. See also *Hopkinson v Williams*, 1993 S.L.T. 907; *Rapide Enterprises v
Midgley*, 1998 S.L.T. 504. Oddly, the position seems to be different where it is the seller who is in
default and the buyer who incurs interest charges. See *Caledonian Property Group Ltd v
Queensferry Property Group Ltd*, 1992 S.L.T. 738.

[56] *Hadley v Baxendale* (1854) 9 Ex. 341.

[57] See *Grant v Ullah*, 1987 S.L.T. 639; Nicholas J.S. Lockhart, "Interest", in *The Laws of
Scotland: Stair Memorial Encyclopaedia*, Vol.12 (1992), paras 1009 et seq.

[58] *Zemhunt (Holdings) Ltd v Control Securities Plc*, 1992 S.L.T. 151.

[59] *Mills v Findlay*, 1994 S.C.L.R. 397.

[60] For the view that the common law is generally to be preferred to attempts to draft round it, see
McBryde, (2007) 11 Edin. L.R. 242.

[61] The position in commercial conveyancing is different, and parties are more inclined to rely on
the common law of damages.

[62] For a full account, and an analysis of the difficulties of such clauses, see Reid and Gretton,
Conveyancing 2006, pp.85–97. For their "outing" as clauses of liquidated damages, see *Black v
McGregor* [2006] CSIH 45; 2007 S.C. 69 at para.11, per Lord Philip.

[63] See below, para.5–20.

[64] *Lloyds Bank Plc v Bamberger*, 1993 S.C. 570.

[65] In which case the clause would not apply and no interest would be due: see *Black v McGregor*
[2006] CSIH 45; 2007 S.C. 69; and *Wipfel Ltd v Auchlochan Developments Ltd* [2006] CSOH 183;
2006 G.W.D. 39-763.

sellers a choice. They can claim common law damages, as described above,[66] or they can claim a sum by way of liquidated damages. What they cannot do is to claim both. Although not interest as such,[67] liquidated damages are calculated as the amount of interest which would have run on the price, at the rate of 4 per cent[68] above the base rate of a nominated bank, from the original date of entry to the date of entry under any contract of resale or, if earlier, some fixed date—a year is typical—after the original date of entry. Thus the longest that "interest" can run is one year.

Even in its current, modified form, this clause is not perfect. With its rigid formula for payment, there is not much sign of a genuine attempt to pre-estimate the sellers' loss.[69] And in cases where interest has to be paid for a full year, the result is likely to be highly favourable to the sellers and so highly unfavourable to the buyers. Viewed in this light the provision must be at some risk of being struck down as a penalty clause.

KEEPING GOING

Introduction

Often the parties will try to keep the contract going. Where they succeed there   5–19
are two possible outcomes. One is that the defaulting party ultimately performs in full. The other is that the defaulting party does not. In the second case damages are due for non-performance. In the first case damages may be due for late performance.

Late (but complete) performance

Performance may be satisfactory but late, as where the buyers pay the price   5–20
two weeks after the date of entry, or the sellers need an extra month to obtain confirmation of executors or a building warrant. Once performance is made, albeit late, rescission probably ceases to be available,[70] and the only question is whether there has been consequential loss which is recoverable in damages.[71] The possible heads of damage are the same as those, described above, which arise on rescission.[72]

Where the delay is in payment of the price, no interest is due under the general law unless the buyers are allowed to take entry, which in practice almost never happens.[73] But missives invariably contain a provision allowing

---

[66] See above, para.5–17.

[67] For there cannot be interest on a sum which, following rescission, is no longer due.

[68] Or it can be higher.

[69] Although in some versions the sellers must deduct any profit they made on the resale.

[70] *Cumming v Brown*, 1993 S.C.L.R. 707; *Grovebury Management Ltd v McLaren*, 1997 S.L.T. 1083. But compare *Ford Sellar Morris Properties Plc v EW Hutchison Ltd*, 1990 S.C. 34, and McBryde, (1996) 1 Edin. L.R. 43 at 60–62. The rule may be different for suspensive conditions: see *Bluestone Estates Ltd v Fitness First Clubs Ltd*, 2003 G.W.D. 27-768.

[71] Notwithstanding the statement to the contrary by Lord Hunter in *Tiffney v Bachurzewski*, 1985 S.L.T. 165.

[72] See above, paras 5–16 and 5–17.

[73] Erskine III, iii, 79. This is because the "fruits" of the price (i.e. interest) are treated as the equivalent of the "fruits" of the land (i.e. possession). But if an action for payment is raised, interest will then run from the date of citation: see *Tiffney v Bachurzewski*, 1985 S.L.T. 165 at 168; and 1988 G.W.D. 37-1530; but compare *Thomson v Vernon*, 1983 S.L.T. (Sh. Ct) 17. The Scottish

interest to run at a fixed percentage above base rate, and in residential conveyancing the clause is often worded in such a way that the sellers must choose
between interest and damages, and cannot have both.[74]

Occasionally, the defaulting party requires the stimulus of an action of
specific implement in order to perform. Where the problem is that the sellers
refuse to sign the disposition, the court can order its execution by the Deputy
Principal Clerk of Session.[75] But four points should be borne in mind in relation to actions for implement. First, implement is not available for warranties,
for there the sellers are under no positive obligation.[76] Secondly, implement
will be refused if performance is impossible (e.g. defaulting sellers with no
title cannot be ordered to acquire one). Thirdly, by virtue of the mutuality principle, implement will not be granted if the pursuers are also in breach of
contract. Finally, implement of the obligation to pay the price is not straightforward. A simple action for payment requires a debt which is due and so, in the
context of missives, means that the sellers must already have delivered the
disposition and given entry—something which they are hardly likely to do.[77]
The other option is an action for implement of the contract by payment within
a specified period of time in exchange for entry and a valid disposition, with an
alternative crave for damages in the event of non-payment.[78] Overall, an action
of implement is usually unwise. If the counter-party simply will not settle, it is
almost always better to rescind and then claim any damages which may be due.

Incomplete performance

5–21   If there is incomplete performance in residential conveyancing it is normally
by the sellers. Typical problems are an outstanding building warrant or some
minor blemish in the title. In this situation the buyers will usually wish to
proceed with the sale—assuming that the lender (if there is one) will let them—
but may also claim damages. The issue can arise in either of two ways. The
problem may arise before settlement, in which case the buyers may wish to
go ahead, but against a reduction of the price. Or it may emerge after settlement, in which case the buyers want to get part of the price back again, by
way of damages.[79] The method of calculating quantum is not free from doubt.
The usual approach is to take the difference in value between the promised
and the actual performance. But there is nothing in principle to prevent the

---

Law Commissiion has recommended legislation providing for interest on unpaid debts, including
the unpaid price in the sale of heritable property: see Report on *Interest on Debt and Damages*
(Scot. Law Com. No.203, 2006), para.3.20.

[74] This seems to be a carry-over from the way clauses are framed in respect of liquidated
damages (for which see above, para.5–18).

[75] *Mackay v Campbell*, 1966 S.C. 237; *Boag, Ptr*, 1967 S.L.T. 275; *Hoey v Butler*, 1975 S.C. 87.
For the sheriff court see the Sheriff Courts (Scotland) Act 1907 s.5A as inserted by the Law Reform
(Miscellaneous Provisions) (Scotland) Act 1985 s.17.

[76] For the distinction between warranties and positive obligations, see above, para.5–07.

[77] *AMA (New Town) Ltd v McKenna*, 2011 S.L.T. (Sh. Ct) 73.

[78] *Newcastle Building Society v White*, 1987 S.L.T. (Sh. Ct) 81; *AMA (New Town) Ltd v
McKenna*, 2011 S.L.T. (Sh. Ct) 73 at para.18, per Sheriff Principal E.F. Bowen QC.

[79] The remedy of claiming damages while continuing with the transaction is sometimes classi-
fied as the Roman law remedy of the *actio quanti minoris*, and was not available at common law.
See *Fortune v Fraser*, 1995 S.C. 186, and, for a detailed discussion of this complex subject,
Stewart, (1966) 11 J.L.S.S. 124; Reid, (1988) 33 J.L.S.S. 285; Evans-Jones, 1991 J.R. 190; Evans-
Jones, (1992) 37 J.L.S.S. 274. The remedy is now allowed by s.3 of the Contract (Scotland)
Act 1997.

adoption of a "cost of cure" approach if that provides a more accurate measure of the loss.[80]

SETTLEMENT BY SPECIAL ARRANGEMENT

Introduction

Although the party not in breach cannot be forced to settle (because of the mutuality principle[81]), he or she may often wish to do so. In that case there can be settlement by special agreement. The form that the agreement takes depends on which party is in default.

 5–22

If the buyers are in default (i.e. the price is not paid), it is unlikely that settlement will proceed. This is because, so long as they are protected by an interest clause, the sellers have nothing to gain by permitting entry and indeed have something to lose, because the buyers may never come up with the money and, once in the property, may be difficult to dislodge.

If the sellers are in default this is usually because they have failed to come up with a sufficient title or other documentation by the contractual date of settlement. Almost invariably, the sellers will be keen to settle, because, being themselves in default, they cannot claim interest on the price, and will lose heavily if settlement is delayed. The buyers may be less keen. Their attitude will depend partly on the seriousness of the default and partly on whether they have sold their own house. Buyers who have sold will have nowhere to live and so will be keen to settle; buyers who have not sold may welcome an excuse to delay settlement.

Possible arrangements

Buyers are not, of course, bound to settle where the sellers are in default; but if they agree to settle, the agreement usually takes one of the following forms (sometimes in combination).

 5–23

In the first place, if the default is minor, settlement might take place on the basis of a letter of obligation granted by the sellers' solicitors and undertaking to deliver the missing document. Payment is then made in full, except that there is sometimes a small retention (e.g. £1,000) if the thing missing involves the expenditure of money. Note, however, that the sellers' solicitors are likely to be unwilling to grant a letter of obligation in such terms, even if they are reasonably consident that the document is one that can be obtained.[82] Apart from anything else, a default would not be covered by professional indemnity insurance.[83] Sometimes a buyer may be willing to do without a letter of obligation, on the basis that the sellers are already bound to perform in terms of the missives.

---

[80] *Tainsh v McLaughlin*, 1990 S.L.T. (Sh. Ct) 102; *Hardwick v Gebbie*, 1991 S.L.T. 258; Fraser Davidson, "Substitutionary Redress", in *The Laws of Scotland: Stair Memorial Encyclopaedia*, Vol.15 (1996), para.911. For the difficulties of this approach see *Ruxley Electronics and Construction Ltd v Forsyth* [1996] 1 A.C. 344 and, more generally, Hector L. MacQueen and Joe Thomson, *Contract Law in Scotland*, 2nd edn (2007), paras 6.20 and 6.21.

[81] See above, para.5–03.

[82] There may, however, be strong pressure from the client, and this pressure may be hard to resist if the firm feels in some way responsible for the problem. Giving in to the pressure leads to instant relief and to non-instant problems and costs.

[83] This will be a "non-classic" letter of obligation and therefore the undertaking will not be covered by the master policy. See para.9–26.

In the second place, if the default is more serious, the buyers may not be willing to hand over the money. Indeed, it may be impossible for them to do so, at least without bridging, because the lender (if there is one) may not be willing to release the loan until the default is put right. The buyers' solicitors, who may also be acting for the lender, must not let their sympathy for the buyers interfere with their professional duty to the lender. As a general rule, buyers should never hand over the price if a valid disposition cannot be produced in exchange. The main, but not only, danger here is the risk of supervening insolvency.[84] And even for less serious defaults the buyers may not be willing to pay the sellers. But it may be possible for settlement to take place without the sellers actually being paid. What happens is that the purchase price is placed ("consigned") on deposit receipt (or equivalent) with a bank in the joint names of the solicitors for the sellers and the buyers.

A third method of settlement sometimes found is where the buyers take entry on the basis of a deposit, which is either paid over to the sellers or put on joint deposit receipt. This will be attractive to buyers where the loan has been withheld, so that they could not pay the full amount without bridging. Obviously, it is less attractive to the sellers. Whether the sellers are also due interest on the unpaid balance is a matter for negotiation. If nothing is said, interest is due because the buyers have possession.[85]

A note on D/R settlements

5–24   The precise legal effects of consignations on deposit receipt are surprisingly obscure. One possibility is that a trust is created, with the two law firms being joint trustees.[86] But this view does not have support in the case law, and it might perhaps be better to regard the arrangement as a four-handed contract. In one case, where settlement proved impossible, the buyer was held entitled to the money on the basis of the doctrine of *causa data causa non secuta*.[87] An alternative basis for the decision would have been implied contractual terms. In addition to the theoretical problems as to the nature of the arrangement, there are two other problems. One is that the two law firms will have different loyalties, and will find it almost impossible to agree as to what is to happen to the money if their clients cannot so agree. Indeed, there are difficulties as to whether a firm will agree to the uplift of the deposit receipt without the instructions of its clients.[88] The other is that "D/R settlements", as they are sometimes called, are often made at the last minute, often on the telephone, in a desperate attempt to get a quick solution, so that written evidence of what was agreed is slight or even absent.

The money cannot be released from D/R without the consent of both firms, and in practice this often puts the buyers in a strong position, for they have

---

[84] *Gibson v Hunter Home Designs Ltd*, 1976 S.C. 23; *Burnett's Trustee v Grainger* [2004] UKHL 8; 2004 S.C. (HL) 19.

[85] See above, para.5–20.

[86] This view was adopted in the first edition of this book, but we now incline to think it incorrect. It would, however, be possible for an express trust to be created, with the money constituting the trust fund. Invoking trust law is not necessary in order for the arrangement to survive the insolvency of one of the parties: cf. *Craiglaw Developments Ltd v Wilson*, 1998 S.L.T. 1046.

[87] *Singh v Cross Entertainments*, 1990 S.L.T. 77.

[88] Logically, if the terms of the settlement are clear, the firm should release the D/R when certain conditions are satisfied, whether or not its client so agrees. But in practice no firm wishes to act without instructions, and, moreover, the terms of the settlement are often unclear.

what they want, namely possession, and there is no reason why they should agree to release the money until the sellers have met their obligations in full. However, if time goes by and the problem in respect of which consignation was made fails to be resolved, the buyers may wish to take the consigned sum as compensation. But it can be unclear as to whether they are so entitled. Even if they are so entitled, getting both firms to agree can be highly problematic. Moreover, in practice the missives may have lapsed by this time as a result of a supersession clause.[89] Finally, if litigation is necessary, the existence of up to five parties[90] can cause great difficulty. All this is not to say that D/R settlements should never be used. They can be extremely convenient. But they should be used sparingly, with an awareness of the potential problems, and with the fullest documentation of the agreed basis.

---

[89] *Hamilton v Rodwell*, 1998 S.C.L.R. 418; *Hamilton v Rodwell (No.2)*, 1999 G.W.D. 35-1706. These two connected decisions seem to mean that, under these circumstances, neither party is entitled to the money. If that is so, that is good news for banks. But it cannot be so.

[90] The sellers, their solicitors, the buyers, their solicitors, and the bank itself.

CHAPTER 6

GOOD AND MARKETABLE TITLE

MEANING OF GOOD TITLE

Introduction

6–01 In a contract for the sale of land the sellers normally give an absolute guarantee of title.[1] This is implied by law,[2] but in practice an express clause is included in the missives.[3] Naturally the parties are free to modify the obligation to give a good title, and sometimes they do so. The importance of the idea of "good and marketable title" has declined somewhat over the past 30 years or so. The older practice was, in the typical case, to conclude missives within a few days. Thus at the time of conclusion of missives the buyers' agents had not usually had the opportunity to investigate the title. The provision in the missives—and a provision implied by law—that the title had to be good and marketable was thus of great importance. If the title fell short of the required standard, the buyers would found on their contractual rights. But nowadays it is usual for the agents for the buyers to have had the opportunity to examine the title before missives are concluded. If a problem comes to light the buyers do not need to found on their right to a good and marketable title. (Indeed, they have no such right, since as yet there is no contract.) Instead, they can protect their interests simply by declining to conclude missives. Nevertheless, the concept of good and marketable title is still of considerable importance, especially in respect of problems which, for one reason or another, come to light after missives have been concluded.[4]

The idea of a good title involves two essential elements. First, the buyers are to be made the owners.[5] Second, after acquiring ownership, they will not be subject to any third party rights,[6] with the exception of title conditions of an ordinary nature, and with the possible exception of leases.

Ownership

6–02 The sellers must offer a title to the whole of the property described in the missives. But while on general principles of landownership that necessarily includes a title to the minerals, this is usually negatived by a clause to the effect that the minerals are included only insofar as the sellers have right thereto.

---

[1] This obligation can be characterised as warrandice, and it covers much the same ground as the obligation of warrandice normally contained in a disposition. See Reid, *Property*, paras 702–714.

[2] cf. *Baird v Drumpellier & Mount Vernon Estates Ltd*, 2000 S.C. 103.

[3] See e.g. cll.15 and 16 of the Combined Standard Clauses (2009).

[4] See e.g. *Snowie v Museum Hall LLP* [2010] CSOH 107; 2010 S.L.T. 971.

[5] In the normal case. If what is being sold is a lease, then obviously the buyers are to become the new lessees of the property, not the owners of it.

[6] As far as private law is concerned. The buyers may be subject to various rights under public law.

Third party rights

The third party rights may be subordinate real rights. In practice the most likely 6–03
such right is a heritable security. But there exist other third party rights which
may prevent the title from being a good one. One example would be occupancy
rights of a non-entitled spouse or civil partner.[7] Another would be where the
buyer's title is voidable at the instance of a third party. In such cases the Keeper
would register the title with an exclusion of indemnity in relation to the right of
challenge. Hence the obligation to give a good title is roughly speaking an obligation to give a title that the Keeper will neither (a) reject nor (b) accept with
exclusion of indemnity. But the identity of good title with (a) and (b) is not a
complete one, as two examples will show. In the first place, suppose that Jack
sells land to Jill. The property is subject to an undischarged standard security.
The Keeper will register Jill as owner with no exclusion of indemnity, though
the security will still appear in Section C. But unless Jill was happy about taking
a title subject to a security, Jack has not complied with his obligation to give a
good title. In the second place, suppose that the Keeper registers Jill as owner
but excludes indemnity in relation to part of the property because he thinks that
Jack's title was of uncertain validity. In fact the Keeper has misread the relevant
deeds and Jack's title was a perfect one. Here Jack has complied with his
common law obligation to give a good title. He may, however, still be in breach
of his obligations under the missives, because missives usually state that the
buyer will be registered as owner without exclusion of indemnity.[8]

Title conditions

Title conditions[9] such as servitudes and real burdens are a partial exception to 6–04
the common law rule that a good title is a title that is not subject to third party
rights.

Most properties are subject to title conditions of one kind or another. Thus,
there may be real burdens regulating use and apportioning maintenance costs,
or there may be servitudes. Buyers (or at least their solicitors) know about
these things. They are expected. In themselves they give no ground for
complaint: a title subject to title conditions is in most cases still a good title.[10]
This is common sense, for otherwise, as Lord Young observed:

> "[I]t would generally be impossible to make an effective sale of a house
> in town without a very minute and ponderous written contract specifying
> all restrictions and conditions, however usual, that applied to it. If a man
> simply buys a house he must be taken to buy it as the seller has it, on a
> good title, of course, but subject to such restrictions as may exist if of an
> ordinary character, and such as the buyer may reasonably be supposed to
> have contemplated as at least not improbable."[11]

---

[7] For which see below, Ch.10.
[8] Though since the Register can be rectified so as to remove the exclusion of indemnity, it may
be that the quantum of Jack's liability is zero.
[9] For title conditions generally, see below, Ch.13.
[10] *Urquhart v Halden* (1835) 13 S. 844; *Whyte v Lee* (1879) 6 R. 699; *Smith v Soeder* (1895) 23
R. 60; *McConnell v Chassels* (1903) 10 S.L.T. 790.
[11] *Whyte v Lee* (1879) 6 R. 699 at 701.

As Lord Young indicates, however, not absolutely all title conditions are acceptable. Some may amount to a breach of the sellers' obligation to provide a good title. This is a difficult and uncertain area, both in theory and in practice. It is necessary to distinguish (1) the obligation implied by law; (2) the standard express obligation; and (3) special express obligations.

The implied obligation about title conditions

6–05 The obligation implied by law sets three criteria which must be met before a condition of title can be objected to by the buyers. These are: (i) that the condition must be unknown to the buyers at the date of conclusion of missives; (ii) that it must be unusual or unduly onerous[12]; and (iii) that it must materially diminish the value of the property. In practice the second criterion is the most difficult to apply. A condition is unusual in the sense of criterion (ii) if it is unusual in relation to the type and location of the property in question. But how unusual does it have to be? The question is important because a wide interpretation would open up an all-too-convenient escape route from missives.

Unfortunately, the case law is insufficiently developed to provide a clear answer. The leading case is *Armia v Daejan Developments Ltd*,[13] in which a property in Kirkcaldy High Street bought for redevelopment was found to be subject to a wide servitude right of access affecting the frontage with the street. Although, as will be explained later, the case was actually decided on the basis of a special clause in the missives, the House of Lords indicated that even without such a clause the servitude would have constituted a breach of the seller's obligation to furnish a good title. But it is difficult to generalise from this. Would it have made any difference if the servitude had not prejudiced the redevelopment? Is the position for rural properties different? A servitude of way in itself is presumably not "unusual".[14] The test is whether it is "unusual" for a property of a particular type.

As for criterion (iii), burdens do commonly diminish the market value of a property. For example, a tenement flat may be burdened with a larger share of the upkeep of the roof and common parts than would be the case under the Tenement Management Scheme.[15] But buyers can object to a burden only if all three criteria are met. A burden of the type mentioned is not unusual, and so the buyers must accept it, unless the missives provide otherwise. Likewise, a burden on a house forbidding commercial use is common and so cannot be objected to.[16] More problematic is the situation where a burden is common in the particular locality but not elsewhere. Thus, in some urban areas burdens forbidding the sale of alcohol are common. Such a burden is usual for that area, but arguably unusual in the broader context. The law here seems unclear.

The standard express obligation about title conditions

6–06 It is normal practice for the obligation about unusual conditions to be made express in the offer, often with slight variations; for example: "There are no

---

[12] "Unusual" and "unduly onerous" probably mean the same in this context. In *Umar v Murtaza*, 1983 S.L.T. (Sh. Ct) 79 this criterion was overlooked.

[13] *Armia v Daejan Developments Ltd*, 1978 S.C. 152, reversed 1979 S.C. (HL) 56.

[14] *Morris v Ritchie*, 1991 G.W.D. 12-712; 1992 G.W.D. 33-1950.

[15] The Tenement Management Scheme contains default provisions which can be overridden by the titles: see further below, paras 14–08 and 14–09.

[16] *Snowie v Museum Hall LLP* [2010] CSOH 107; 2010 S.L.T. 971.

servitudes or other third party rights and no unusual or unduly onerous real conditions which materially and adversely affect the property".[17] Such clauses typically differ from the implied obligation in making no mention of the state of the buyers' knowledge.[18] But while this opens up the argument that buyers could rescind even though they knew of the title condition before entering missives, it is thought that the argument would not succeed. Often the clause restricts the buyers' remedy to rescission and gives a limited period after the condition's disclosure, such as 10 working days, in which it can be exercised.[19] Where this is not done, it is common for the entire clause about burdens to be deleted by the sellers' solicitors in exchange for an opportunity to inspect the deeds. This has the merit of avoiding disputes as to what is or is not unusual or unduly onerous. The buyers can see what they are getting before becoming contractually committed to proceed. In particular, they can verify that the use they propose to make of the property is not excluded by the terms of the titles. In return the sellers have the reassurance of knowing that the buyers will not start making difficulties on the eve of settlement on some merely technical point about the state of the burdens.

Special express obligations

The standard obligation, whether in its express or its implied form, may not 6–07 always give the buyers sufficient protection. Consider the following example. Suppose that the purpose behind a particular purchase is to rent the property to students. And suppose further, which is not improbable, that the titles contain a real burden limiting the use of the subjects to occupation by "one family only". The buyers have a problem. The standard obligation will probably not help them. The restriction is a fairly common one, and so is probably not "unusual". Consequently, the title is probably good and marketable. Unless the discovery is made before the conclusion of missives, the buyers must proceed. The lesson to be drawn here is, of course, simple. Where buyers intend to use the property other than simply to live in (or, in commercial properties, to work in), or where their purpose is otherwise esoteric, they should include a special clause in the missives to the effect that the proposed use is not excluded by the terms of the title.

This is what was done in the leading case of *Armia v Daejan Developments Ltd*,[20] though ironically litigation nevertheless ensued. The buyer, intending to redevelop the land, included the following clause in his offer: "There is nothing in the titles of the said subjects which will prevent demolition and redevelopment". It was held by the First Division that this clause replaced the obligation implied by law against unusual burdens, and that since the burden in question (the servitude) could not be said actually to prevent demolition and redevelopment, the buyer must proceed with the purchase. This was a harsh and, with respect, implausible construction. Fortunately, it did not survive the appeal to

---

[17] Highland Standard Clauses (2007) cl.11.1.8.

[18] i.e. criterion (i) above.

[19] See e.g. *McPhee v Black*, Unreported June 20, 2008 Glasgow Sheriff Court, discussed in Reid and Gretton, *Conveyancing 2009*, pp.90–92. Clause 8 of the Borders Standard Clauses (2007) extends this to all of the sellers' obligations in respect of title, but that seems hardly acceptable: if buyers must pay the price, or be liable for damages if in default, sellers should be under a corresponding obligation in respect of the title.

[20] *Armia v Daejan Developments Ltd*, 1978 S.C. 152, reversed 1979 S.C. (HL) 56.

the House of Lords, where it was decided that the special clause must be read as adding to and not as replacing the implied obligation. Further, the seller was found to be in breach of the special clause, giving the buyer the right to rescind. The interpretation adopted by the First Division was criticised as placing the buyer at a disadvantage in consequence of a clause which had clearly been intended to strengthen his position.[21]

Leases

6–08 It is not clear whether the existence of a lease, at least where the duration and rent are reasonable, prevents a title from being a good one.[22] In practice, therefore, both the missives and the disposition will normally stipulate for "actual occupation" or "vacant possession". In the disposition this is coupled with the clause of entry, which will typically read: "With entry and actual occupation (or 'vacant possession') as at the . . . day of . . . two thousand and . . .". If the buyers are acquiring leased property, typically as an investment, the missives and disposition will omit any reference to vacant possession, or actual occupation, and indeed will normally refer to the existing lease.

Pertinents

6–09 In some cases the full use of a property may require rights over neighbouring property, and in particular servitudes. Whether, in such cases, the absence of such rights would mean that the title was not a good and marketable one is uncertain, but probably they would not be regarded as prejudicing the title.[23] Hence where they are required they ought to be stipulated for in the missives.[24]

EVIDENCE OF GOOD TITLE

Sellers must produce evidence

6–10 It is not sufficient for the sellers to have a good title. They must also be in a position to demonstrate that fact to the buyers.[25] If they cannot do so, then, even if their title is in fact good, they have failed in their obligation and the buyers need not proceed with the purchase.

What needs to be produced (Land Register properties)?

6–11 If the property is in the Land Register, the sellers can be expected to appear as proprietors in the land certificate. Assuming that there is no exclusion of indemnity, all that is required is that the certificate be updated through form 12

---

[21] The view that special clauses generally augment rather than replace the implied obligation has since been given effect to in *Umar v Murtaza*, 1983 S.L.T. (Sh. Ct) 79.

[22] *Lothian and Borders Farmers Ltd v McCutchion*, 1952 S.L.T. 450 (which was decided on the warrandice clause in a disposition).

[23] It is to be noted that the law will often allow at least some form of access rights: *Bowers v Kennedy*, 2000 S.C. 555, discussed below in para.13–27. Other rights, such as drainage, may turn out to be constituted as implied servitudes, although buyers are naturally reluctant to accept a right which is not vouched for by either writing or registration.

[24] As is usually the case in standard missives. See e.g. Aberdeen Standard Clauses (2007) cl.14(e).

[25] See also below, Ch.7.

and 13 reports. If for some reason the sellers do not appear as proprietors it is necessary to produce writs (e.g. confirmation as executor) showing why the sellers have the right to deal with the property. Where, however, the Keeper's powers of rectification[26] are unrestricted—which will normally occur only if indemnity has been excluded—it will be necessary to go behind the land certificate in much the same way as if the title had not been registered.

Even without exclusion of indemnity the buyers may in theory be vulnerable to judicial rectification of the deed on which the sellers' title is based,[27] and may be vulnerable in certain other circumstances also.[28]

What needs to be produced (GRS properties)?

For properties that are still in the General Register of Sasines—meaning that the   6–12 current sale will trigger the switch into the Land Register—the rule is, in the words of Hume,[29] that the sellers must "furnish him [the buyer] with a sufficient progress of titles to the subject such a progress (for aught that can be seen) as shall maintain his right against all pretenders". The sellers' obligation ends with *prima facie* validity (Hume's "for aught that can be seen"). They need not prove that each individual writ actually is good and unchallengeable. That would be impossible. It is enough to produce writs that appear to be valid and it is then for the buyers, if they can, to show that a particular writ is bad. This rule was settled by the leading case of *Sibbald's Heirs v Harris*.[30] There the buyer refused to accept a prescriptive progress containing a decree of general service on the basis that such a decree was vulnerable to future reduction, for example by the emergence of a closer heir. But this objection was rejected by the court. A decree of special service was *prima facie* valid. It was no more vulnerable to reduction than any other writ. Unless, therefore, the buyer had concrete grounds for fearing reduction, and he had not, the title was one which he was bound to accept.

What writs must the sellers actually produce? They must produce a good prescriptive progress (including any midcouples), together with a search going back to the foundation writ, which in practice will be a standard form 10 report. If the foundation writ is less than 40 years old, as is usually the case, there is a view that buyers are entitled to a 40-year search, and such a search often forms part of the prior titles in any event. The sellers must also produce all writs referred to for burdens and descriptions. The deeds must actually be produced: it is not sufficient to invite the buyers to inspect them themselves on the register.[31] It is arguable, although undecided, that all deeds within the prescriptive progress must be probative. What has been described so far is the rule implied by law, but it would be a very unusual contract which did not attempt to spell out what the sellers must produce.[32]

---

[26] Land Registration (Scotland) Act 1979 s.9.

[27] Law Reform (Miscellaneous Provisions) (Scotland) Act 1985 s.8. See below, Ch.20.

[28] *Short's Trustees v Chung (No.2)*, 1998 S.C. 105, affirmed 1999 S.C. 471, in which the proprietor in possession was ordered to convey the property to the person challenging the title.

[29] *Lectures*, ii, 38.

[30] *Sibbald's Heirs v Harris*, 1947 S.C. 601. There is some tension between this decision and *Duke of Devonshire v Fletcher* (1874) 1 R. 1056; and *Bruce v Stewart* (1900) 2 F. 948. However, it is difficult to state a confident view on this question.

[31] *Sutherland v Garrity*, 1941 S.C. 196.

[32] See e.g. Combined Standard Clauses (2009) cl.16(a).

Personal and company searches

6–13   With both registered and unregistered land it is necessary to produce a search
in the Personal Register and, where the sellers are a company, in the Companies
Register also. In view of the strict rule about clear searches (see below) the
sellers should take care that the list of persons to be searched against is not
longer than is absolutely necessary. Searches are considered elsewhere.[33]

Occupancy rights

6–14   Though there is no authority, the general view is that if a property is or may be
affected by the occupancy rights of spouses or civil partners, then it is necessary, for the title to be good and marketable, for the sellers to produce the
written declarations or consents or renunciations contemplated by the relevant
legislation.[34]

Is the history of possession relevant?

6–15   For property in the Land Register, the history of possession is seldom of relevance, since title flows from the Register itself, not from prescriptive possession. However, if the title contains a restriction of indemnity, possession may
become more important.

        If the property is still in the GRS, then title rests on positive prescription.
Positive prescription in turn presupposes possession for the requisite period,
currently 10 years. Do the sellers have to offer to prove this? In practice, the
answer is no, the buyers taking the fact of possession on faith. This is generally
safe enough. But take this case: Donald records in the GRS an *a non domino*
disposition in 2001, and in 2011 offers to sell the land to Elaine. Donald can
give a good title if, but only if, he has had 10 years of possession.

Disputes as to sufficiency of title

6–16   Inevitably, buyers and sellers do not always agree as to the sufficiency of the
title offered, though such disagreements are more common for GRS titles than
for Land Register ones. The reason is evident: if the Land Register shows the
sellers to be registered as owners, without exclusion of indemnity, someone
taking title from them will almost invariably acquire ownership without fear of
challenge. However, even with properties in the Land Register there is still
some scope for dispute. For instance, the sellers might not be registered, but be
selling under a power of sale, for instance as judicial factors, or executors, or
heritable creditors and so on. Or there may be a question as to whether the title
the sellers have meets what the missives require. If the title is still in the GRS
there is evidently even more scope for disagreement.

        In the event of disagreement, there are various possibilities short of litiga-
tion. Thus, the parties may accept the opinion of a third party. This is quite
common, and while occasionally done as a formal arbitration is more usually
done informally. Or the sellers may be prepared to give, and the buyers to
accept, a title insurance policy. Or again one of the parties may yield. But if
both parties remain entrenched in their respective positions, litigation may be
unavoidable. It may take a number of forms: for example, an action by the

---

[33] See below, Ch.9.
[34] As to which see below, Ch.10.

sellers to enforce the contract, or an action by the buyers for declarator of entitlement to rescind, or a special case brought by both parties. But whatever form
it takes the sellers are at a disadvantage. In order to succeed they must satisfy
the court that the title tendered is good beyond "rational doubt"[35]; and that high
standard is not attained unless the only step asked of the court is to apply
clearly settled law to the facts of the instant case.[36] If the law itself is in doubt
the court will not normally resolve that doubt in an action between buyers and
sellers because the "proper contradictors" (i.e. the parties entitled to found on
the alleged defect) are absent. Hence, the title will not be forced on reluctant
buyers unless it is clearly a good one. As Lord Deas put it in *Duke of Devonshire
v Fletcher*: "No buyer is obliged to take the risk of law suits. If, as the sellers
say, the adjudications[37] are nullities, they are such nullities as I should be sorry
to have anything to do with".[38]

It is always open to the sellers to avoid the difficulty of no "proper contradictors" by an action of declarator against the appropriate parties to have the
alleged defect found ineffective. Precisely this had been done in the *Duke of
Devonshire* case. But it was held that because the action of declarator had been
undefended, there was the theoretical danger, however slight, that it might one
day be reduced. Hence this case is authority that a title based on a decree in
absence is unmarketable,[39] until the possibility of such a reduction has been
removed by prescription, or, of course, by registration without exclusion of
indemnity. There are a number of reasons for doubting the correctness of this
view, and in practice decrees in absence are generally regarded as sufficient.

As has already been said, disputes about whether a title is good and marketable are rarer in Land Register cases, and the facts of *Duke of Devonshire*
illustrate why. If those facts happened today, and if the sellers could have
persuaded the Keeper that the adjudications were null, the Keeper would have
deleted them from the title sheet, and the buyers could have relied on that deletion. But the effect is often simply to shift the forum of the dispute, so that
instead of being a dispute between the buyers and the sellers it becomes a
dispute between the owner and the Keeper.

Title insurance

In practice, disputes are often settled by the sellers obtaining, at their expense, 6–17
a policy of title insurance, though buyers cannot be compelled to accept this
(unless the missives so provide). If the sellers are a major corporation of
undoubted financial standing a policy is arguably pointless. The sellers are
usually bound in absolute warrandice in any event, and the danger that the
major corporation would not be able to pay up on a warrandice claim is as
small, or perhaps smaller, than the danger that the title insurance company
would be unable to pay up on a title policy.

Where a policy is obtained, a one-off premium is paid. The premium is
calculated according to the value of the property, the risk involved, and so
forth. The cover should last until the problem will have been removed by

---

[35] *Brown v Cheyne* (1833) 12 S. 176, per Lord Meadowbank. See also *Dunlop v Crawford*
(1849) 11 D. 1062.

[36] See *Lamb's Trustees v Reid* (1883) 11 R. 76.

[37] Which were the defects in title that the buyer was objecting to.

[38] *Duke of Devonshire v Fletcher* (1874) 1 R. 1056.

[39] *Bruce v Stewart* (1900) 2 F. 948 is to the same effect.

prescription. The amount of the cover should not be the present value of the property but its expected maximum value during the cover period. Thus, if a house is bought for £300,000, and seven years later the owners are evicted due to a defect in the title, their loss will probably be more than that sum, because the house will probably be worth more at that stage. There is obviously no way of predicting the future value. But a commonly used method is to calculate the future value on the assumption that the movement of property prices in recent years will continue into the future. If a percentage figure is used that must be projected into the future on a compound basis.

Title insurance policies are less likely to be needed for property in the Land Register. The need may arise, however, where there is an exclusion of indemnity. Suppose that Shona buys 50 hectares from Tom. The Keeper issues a land certificate, but in respect of half a hectare indemnity is excluded. Title insurance may be advisable for the half hectare until the exclusion of indemnity is deleted, after 10 years' possession. Whether it is Tom or Shona who pays the premium depends on the circumstances. If the missives are unqualified, Tom will be in breach of his obligations, and the quantum of loss to Shona is the cost of a policy, so Tom will have to reimburse her for this. If the problem comes to light before missives, then it is a matter for negotiation. In general, if the price is a full price, Tom should pay, but if the price reflects the title problem, Tom should not pay, since effectively he is already paying through the lower price.

CLEAR SEARCH

General

6–18 "Search" is the traditional term though, strictly, it is not used for the Land Register, where the official term is "report". On a first registration the seller will produce form 10/11 reports, and on a subsequent sale form 12/13 reports. In form 10/11 reports, the search is in the Personal Register and the GRS, plus a search of the Land Register to check that the property has not in fact already been registered there. In form 12/13 reports, the search is in the Personal Register and the Land Register. Where a company has been involved it will also be necessary to produce a search in the Companies Register.

The obligation to demonstrate a good title includes an obligation to produce a search: that the search so produced be clear is, however, a separate and distinct obligation. It is probably implied by law, but in any event it is always expressly stipulated for, both in missives and also in the letter of obligation subsequently granted by the selling solicitors. Today the word "clear" is no longer used. The usual provision now is that the form 10/11 or form 12/13 reports will "show no entries adverse to the seller's interest" and that the land certificate will "disclose no entry deed or diligence prejudicial to the purchaser's interest other than such as are created by or against the purchaser".[40]

This obligation is, of course, closely related to the wider obligation to demonstrate a good title. Usually an unclear search indicates a bad title and the former obligation becomes subsumed in the latter. But it can occasionally happen that a title is good when the search is not clear. For example, a search may disclose a standard security for a fixed sum of £40,000, which has, in fact,

---

[40] See *Registration of Title Practice Book*, paras 8.9 and 8.37.

been repaid, though no formal discharge has been registered. Since there is no debt the security is implicitly discharged. So the title is good. But nonetheless the search is not clear as it discloses an apparently undischarged security. It is only in odd cases of this kind that the separate obligation to provide a clear search is of importance. In other words, a title may be good, but the search not clear, if the title looks bad from what appears in the public registers, but is in truth good because of off-register facts.

When is a search clear?

The question of whether a search is clear arises less often as a result of registra-   6–19
tion of title. The reason is that if the Keeper thinks that something does not affect a title he has the ability simply to omit it from the land certificate.[41] Nevertheless the basic issues remain the same.

According to Burns's *Conveyancing Practice* "[if] deeds or diligences appear on record[42] the search is not clear till they are disposed of, though it is doubtful whether they really affect the buyer's title, or even, it may be, though the contrary is true in law".[43] The final words of Burns's definition rest on certain remarks in *Dryburgh v Gordon*.[44] In *Dryburgh* the search disclosed two inhibitions predating the sale. Such inhibitions would in the normal course of events strike at the sale, but the seller's agents, whose letter of obligation was the subject of the action, argued that their client's title[45] was in its nature incapable of being affected by these inhibitions. It was held that the search was not clear. Whatever the merits of the case against the inhibitions, on which the court expressed no decided view, there was an apparent encumbrance on the face of the search which the buyer was entitled to have discharged.

It is suggested that this case is less far-reaching than Burns seems to have feared. The point about the inhibitions in *Dryburgh* is that no one could say for certain whether or not they affected the sale, in the absence of litigation involving the inhibitors themselves. The issue was not, or at any rate was not perceived to be, one of settled law.[46] In short, the title was not good and marketable, and the remarks of the court must be read against this background. The rule, therefore, is not, as Burns appears to contemplate, that any apparent encumbrance prevents a search from being clear. The facts are subject to the law. And where the encumbrance is one which, as a matter of settled law, could not possibly affect the sale, the search is clear.[47] A search is only not clear, therefore, where either the title is actually affected by the encumbrance or where, as in *Dryburgh*, the law, or the application of the law, is in doubt.

This view appears to be confirmed by *Newcastle Building Society v White*,[48] seemingly the only reported case on the point since *Dryburgh*. There, security subjects were sold by a heritable creditor on the default of the debtor. The

---

[41] For instance, suppose a seller is inhibited after missives but before settlement. In such a case the Keeper will, if satisfied of the facts, issue an unqualified land certificate: ROTPB, para.6.19. In the equivalent situation in old GRS conveyancing the search was not clear.

[42] That is, in a public register.

[43] J.Burns, *Conveyancing Practice*, 4th edn (1957), p.303.

[44] *Dryburgh v Gordon* (1896) 24 R. 1.

[45] A reversionary right under an *ex facie* absolute disposition.

[46] In fact, the inhibitions probably did strike at the sale: G.L. Gretton, *The Law of Inhibition and Adjudication*, 2nd edn (1996), p.190.

[47] *Cameron v Williamson* (1895) 22 R. 293.

[48] *Newcastle Building Society v White*, 1987 S.L.T. (Sh. Ct) 81.

interim report on the search disclosed an inhibition against the debtor which postdated the granting of the standard security in favour of the creditor. A dispute arose as to whether the search was clear. It was held that it was. In terms of s.26(1) of the Conveyancing and Feudal Reform (Scotland) Act 1970 the recording of a disposition in such circumstances disburdened the security subjects of all diligences ranking *pari passu* with or postponed to the security. "Accordingly merely by applying the law any future buyer can establish *ex facie* of the records and without reference to extrinsic material that the inhibition no longer has any relevance to the property."[49]

In evaluating the form 10/11 reports, the form 12/13 reports and the land certificate (or the interim and final searches in an old GRS transaction) it is therefore necessary to apply the relevant law to the relevant facts. But while the only limitation as to the law is that it should be certain, there is an important limitation as to the facts to which that law may be applied. Were this not so, the obligation to deliver a clear search would collapse into the more general obligation to demonstrate a good title. The limitation, in the words already quoted of the Sheriff Principal in *Newcastle Building Society v White*, is that the facts must be "*ex facie* of the records". Off-register information is irrelevant—not irrelevant in a broader sense, but irrelevant for present purposes. This rule, which is now well established, seems first to have been laid down in *Cargill v Craigie*.[50] The search in that case disclosed three inhibitions against the seller. These had in fact been discharged, but the discharges had not been registered. Thus, the title was good, but the buyer was held entitled by the House of Lords (reversing the Court of Session) to have the record cleared.[51]

The rule against extrinsic material must be set in the broader context of the need for such evidence of title as will satisfy buyers without at the same time placing an unfair burden on sellers. For the most part the rule seems to draw the line in the right place. Thus, it is not unreasonable that buyers faced with an apparent standard security or, as in *Cargill v Craigie*, with an apparent inhibition, should be entitled to more than informal evidence that the debt to which they relate has been repaid. If the debt really has been repaid the sellers can readily enough obtain and register a discharge. It seems just that they should be made to do so.

---

[49] *Newcastle Building Society v White*, 1987 S.L.T. (Sh. Ct) 81 at 85. In fact, at common law also the inhibition could not strike at the sale.

[50] *Cargill v Craigie* (1822) 1 Shaw App. 134.

[51] In such cases, where the title is good, but appears from the searches not to be good, the title is sometimes said to be "good" but not "marketable". But this distinction between good and marketable is not universally adopted. The point is purely semantic.

CHAPTER 7

EXAMINATION OF TITLE

INTRODUCTORY

Introduction

This chapter deals with examination of title, both for property in the Land 7–01
Register and for property still in the General Register of Sasines ("GRS").[1] The
latter is more complex, and so more space is devoted to it. A complete account
of examination of title is impossible, since examination of title potentially
involves the whole of property law and conveyancing. In this chapter it is
assumed that title is being examined by solicitors for a buyer, but the same
principles will in general apply in relation to a heritable creditor.

Procedure

A report on title must be sent to the clients. This will include a copy of the plan, 7–02
a statement of any relevant pertinents (such as servitudes in favour of the property), title conditions to which the property is subject, information in the property enquiry certificates ("PECs") and anything else of relevance. The clients
should be asked for any comments, and in particular should be asked to confirm
that the plan correctly shows what they think they are buying. But it needs to
be borne in mind that the clients will perhaps only have visited the property a
couple of times, for a total of perhaps an hour, and they may be fuzzy about the
boundaries. The plan will in most cases use colour, and in that case the clients
must receive a coloured plan. If the office photocopier is monochrome that
means hand-colouring.

Once examination of title is complete the deeds are returned to the sellers'
solicitors, with the disposition drafted by the purchasers' solicitors, and with any
observations arising out of the examination. A photocopy of the land certificate,
or of the key deeds if the title is still in the GRS, should be retained on file.

Tenement titles

Tenement titles pose special difficulties, and these difficulties can exist not 7–03
only for GRS titles but also for titles in the Land Register. The title may be
unclear as to which parts of the building are included, and as to the rights to the
attached ground. It occasionally happens that title is taken to the first floor

---

[1] On examination of title see further Halliday, Ch.36; John H. Sinclair and Euan Sinclair,
Handbook of Conveyancing Practice in Scotland, 5th edn (2006), Ch.8; David A. Brand, Andrew
J.M. Steven and Scott Wortley, *Professor McDonald's Conveyancing Manual*, 7th edn (2004),
Ch.32.

south when the clients think they are buying the first floor north.[2] Compass directions sometimes turn out to be approximate only, and there is sometimes confusion as to the floors. Take, for instance, a tenement with a half-sunk basement. Is that the "first" floor? Or perhaps the floor above is the first floor? Or perhaps the latter is the "ground" floor so that the third[3] storey is the "first"?

Feudalism

7–04   Feudal law was gradually sliced away by legislation stretching over many centuries. What remained was abolished by the Abolition of Feudal Tenure etc. (Scotland) Act 2000 (with effect from November 28, 2004).[4] No account of the subject will be given here. But although feudalism is abolished, conveyancers will need to know something of it for many years to come, since references to feudal writs (notably feu dispositions, feu charters, feu contracts, charters of novodamus and blench dispositions) litter existing titles.[5]

What is being looked for?

7–05   In examining a title the purchasers' solicitors seek the answers to the following (not exhaustive) list of questions: (a) Do the sellers have power to convey the property? (b) What are the title conditions and are they acceptable? (c) Are there any securities?[6] (d) Are the searches clear? (e) Are there any occupancy rights of a spouse or civil partner? (f) Have the necessary planning and building consents been obtained? This chapter deals with the first three questions.[7]

LAND REGISTER TITLES[8]

The land certificate

7–06   Whereas GRS titles depend on a mass of recorded deeds, to be read in the light of the complex statutory and common law rules, and with positive prescription playing a large role, where the title is in the Land Register, there is a land certificate and little else. Under the 1979 Act the role of prescription is slight.[9]

---

[2] In such cases the sellers will also typically have been under the same error, and possess the "wrong" flat which the buyers then blithely move into. It will be found that the descriptions were muddled up when the individual flats were first sold off.

[3] This word begs the question, of course.

[4] Implementing Scottish Law Commission, Report on *Abolition of the Feudal System* (Scot. Law Com. No.168, 1999). For a detailed account of the legislation, see K.G.C. Reid, *The Abolition of Feudal Tenure in Scotland* (2003).

[5] There are many sources on feudal tenure. See e.g. Reid, *Property*, paras 41–113; Gordon, Ch.2; K.G.C. Reid, *The Abolition of Feudal Tenure in Scotland* (2003), Ch.1. See also Ch.23 of the 2nd edition of the present book.

[6] Until recently it was also important to check whether the feuduty had been redeemed, but all remaining feuduty has now disappeared as a result of the 2000 Act s.7. Any compensatory payment due under the Act but still unpaid is a personal debt of the person who was owner on November 28, 2004 (the day on which the feudal system was abolished), and does not transmit to purchasers: see s.8.

[7] For the others, see Chs 9, 10 and 4 respectively.

[8] For the Land Register more generally, see below, paras 8–08 et seq.

[9] In the event that the Scottish Law Commission's reforms are implemented, prescription will become fully available: see Report on *Land Registration* (Scot. Law Com. No.222, 2010), para.35.3.

Reading the certificate takes a matter of minutes. At a glance it is possible to see the boundaries of the property, the name of the current owner, and the securities and real burdens which affect the property. Further, there is little in the way of evaluation to be done. Most of the information in the land certificate is correct as a matter of law—even in the rare cases where it should not have been entered in the first place.[10] Although the position will change if the Scottish Law Commission's proposals for reform are implemented,[11] the current rule is that title flows from the Register and not from the deed which gave rise to the entry. So if the land certificate shows the sellers as owners of the property, then they are indeed the owners, and the purchasers' solicitors need look no further. Naturally, the land certificate will be examined in conjunction with the form 12 and 13 reports which bring it up to date. Although land certificates enable the title to be reviewed quickly and with confidence, they are not necessarily perfect. Indeed, errors or obscurities of one sort or another are unfortunately quite common. Many are trivial, but not all. For example whilst the Land Register is map-based, there is also a verbal description, and in some titles the verbal description is obscure.

Do the sellers have power to convey the property?

Nemo plus juris ad alium transferre potest quam ipse haberet.[12] Buyers will   7–07
receive a good title only if the sellers (or consenters, if any) own the property, and are not limited in their power of disposition by some factor such as sequestration, inhibition or mental incapacity. Alternatively, buyers will receive a good title if the sellers, though not themselves the owners, have power of sale. For example, the seller might be a judicial factor, or an executor, or a heritable creditor enforcing a security, or a trustee in sequestration. In all such cases it will be necessary to check that the seller does indeed have power to convey; the rules can be found elsewhere in this book.[13] So the first task is to check the sellers' title, including, of course, the boundaries.

In a land certificate the boundaries are usually defined with a fairly high degree of precision. The main exception is tenemental property, where the land certificate will show the footprint of the building and the ground attached, but it may not indicate what parts of the building are included in the title, and there may be imprecision as to what rights exist in the ground attached.[14] But whether the land certificate is precise or not, it should be borne in mind that the task is not only to determine what the sellers own, but also to determine whether that corresponds with what the buyers think they are buying. In this connection it must be borne in mind that the missives will seldom be plan-based so that there may be a question of interpreting them. A copy of the land certificate must be sent to the clients as soon as possible with a request for comments

---

[10] 1979 Act s.3(1). This of course assumes that the land certificate is an accurate copy of the title sheet.

[11] For those proposals, see below, para.8–25.

[12] Or, in a briefer version, *nemo dat quod non habet*: no one can transfer greater rights to another than he has himself.

[13] For the particular issues which arise in buying in such cases, see below, Chs 22, 25 and 29.

[14] See e.g. *North Atlantic Salmon Conservation Organisation v Au Bar Pub*, 2009 G.W.D. 14-222, where it was held that in a standard description of a flat ("subjects within the land edged red on the Title Plan"), "within" did not mean "comprised", so that the red boundary was likely to be over-inclusive. For discussion, see Reid and Gretton, *Conveyancing 2009*, pp.173–76.

A problem affecting housing estates and other developments was high-lighted by *PMP Plus Ltd v Keeper of the Registers of Scotland*.[15] While gener-ally clear in their description of individual houses, developers have often been lax in respect of the common areas. In *PMP Plus* it was held that an attempt to describe the common areas by reference to what would ultimately be left after the individual houses were sold could not be accepted as a sufficient descrip-tion of the areas in question. This was because no one could tell, at the time of the granting of the split-off dispositions of individual houses, what those areas comprised. Accordingly, the inclusion of a right in common to those areas in the split-off dispositions was void and ineffective, with the unwelcome conse-quence that they continued to belong to the developer. In guidance issued after the *PMP Plus* decision, the Keeper distinguished between "old" developments (i.e. those where the first split-off disposition was registered before August 3, 2009) and "new" developments.[16] For the latter, common areas must be clearly identified, and in a way which does not depend on a future uncertain event (such as what ground is left after everything else has been sold). If this standard is not met, no title to the common areas will be accepted for registration.[17] For the former, the Keeper will continue the previous practice of registering a title to the common areas even where the description is deficient. As the decision in *PMP Plus* shows, however, the mere fact of registration will not confer owner-ship if the areas in question cannot be identified. But once a development is complete and the boundaries of the common areas settled, it is arguable, though not certain, that the registration of *subsequent* dispositions will confer a title by operation of the Keeper's Midas touch.[18] If that is correct, buyers can take a relaxed view of the issue, in respect of "old" developments, provided that the development is now completed.

What are the title conditions and are they acceptable?

7–08   Title conditions (real burdens and servitudes) are considered in a separate chapter[19] and only a few remarks will be made here, beginning with real burdens. Almost all property is subject to real burdens of one kind or another. Old burdens writs, although often long and sometimes irrelevant, have usually been transcribed faithfully into the D (burdens) section of the title sheet. The purchasers' solicitors must wade through them in case something important to the clients is lurking there.

The clients are going to have to live with such burdens as have continuing force.[20] So they need to be told what they are. If possible this should be done before conclusion of missives, so that if the burdens are unacceptable the remedy is simply not to conclude missives. If that is not possible the clients must at all events be told what the burdens are before settlement. The missives will typically stipulate that the burdens shall not be "unusual or unduly

---

[15] *PMP Plus Ltd v Keeper of the Registers of Scotland*, 2009 S.L.T. (Lands Tr.) 2. See further Reid and Gretton, *Conveyancing 2008*, pp.133–49.

[16] *Update* 27. For a full discussion, see Reid and Gretton, *Conveyancing 2009*, pp.123–26.

[17] For possible reform, see below, para.12–25.

[18] Reid and Gretton, *Conveyancing 2008*, pp.145–46. The "Midas touch" is the Keeper's ability to cure all title defects by the mere act of registration. See below, para.8–07.

[19] See below, Ch.13.

[20] Typically these control either maintenance or use. Many burdens, particularly in older deeds, impose one-off obligations (e.g. to build a house) and can be disregarded.

onerous", an expression the meaning of which was discussed in the previous chapter. Most burdens are neither. If the buyers want to develop the property it is therefore particularly risky to conclude missives without having seen the land certificate. One possible approach in that case is for the buyers to insert in the missives a provision that, for instance, "there is nothing in the title of the property which will prevent demolition and redevelopment".[21]

Whilst a real burden, to be valid, must enter the Register, there is no corresponding rule that all burdens on the Register are valid. A burden which has been properly registered might still fail because of the nature of its terms, or because it is too vague, or because there is no one with title and interest to enforce. In fact a significant number of burdens which appear on land certificates—how many is hard to say—are invalid and unenforceable, not least because of the abolition of the feudal system.[22] Here the solicitors' skill continues to be necessary. A real burden which can be shown to be invalid can be removed by an application for rectification,[23] although this is rare in practice, while valid burdens must be evaluated, in the usual way, against the sellers' obligation to produce a good title.[24] A burden which is valid but awkward can often be removed by application to the Lands Tribunal,[25] or, if more than 100 years' old, by service and registration of a notice of termination.[26]

For servitudes burdening the property, much the same considerations apply as for continuing real burdens. But there are certain differences. Servitudes, unlike real burdens, can be constituted by prescription and also by implication. If created by grant before the 2003 Act, they need not be registered (though in practice they usually are). Hence, it may be that the purchasers' solicitors cannot discover their existence. Servitudes created in writing after the 2003 Act must be registered against both the dominant and servient properties.[27]

Two other points may conveniently be mentioned here, even though they do not involve real burdens or servitudes. The first is that the land certificate should contain a statement, in the proprietorship section, that there are no subsisting occupancy rights of a spouse or civil partner of a previous owner.[28] Further, it may be necessary to make inquiries in respect of possible occupancy rights affecting the current seller. This rather complex subject is discussed elsewhere.[29] The second is that the land certificate should show any entry in the Personal Register which is adverse to the title. Thus if the sellers have been inhibited, the inhibition will be mentioned.[30]

---

[21] These words are from the missives in *Armia Ltd v Daejan Developments* Ltd, 1979 S.C. (HL) 56. See above, para.6–07.

[22] See below, para.13–18. It is for this reason that no indemnity is payable for loss arising from inability to enforce a real burden, unless (which seems unknown) the Keeper expressly assumes responsibility for its enforceability. See 1979 Act s.12(3)(g).

[23] *Brookfield Developments Ltd v Keeper of the Registers of Scotland*, 1989 S.L.T. (Lands Tr) 105.

[24] Usually the sellers warrant in the missives that there are no unusual or unduly onerous burdens. See above, para.6–06.

[25] See below, Ch.16.

[26] See below, para.13–24.

[27] Title Conditions (Scotland) Act 2003 s.75, but subject to the qualifications in s.75(3).

[28] Land Registration (Scotland) Rules 2006 r.5(j).

[29] See below Ch.10 and in particular para.10–14.

[30] 1979 Act s.6(1)(c). For some of the difficulties with this provision, see G.L. Gretton, *The Law of Inhibition and Adjudication*, 2nd edn (1996), pp.39–43; Scottish Law Commission, Discussion Paper on *Diligence against Land* (Scot. Law Com. D.P. No.107, 1998), paras 3.97–3.111.

Are there any securities?

7–09 Heritable securities, as subordinate real rights, are unaffected by a change of ownership of the encumbered land. So if a security affects the property in the hands of the sellers it will continue to affect the property in the hands of the buyers, unless it has been discharged. An undischarged security would be a breach of the sellers' obligation to produce a good and marketable title.[31] That obligation can be changed by agreement, but that is rare in practice. It is thus the duty of the buyers' solicitors to ensure that all securities have been or will be discharged.

If the seller is a company (or a limited liability partnership) there may be a floating charge, but since a floating charge is not, until crystallisation ("attachment"), a real right it will not run with the property and no discharge is necessary, though it is normal to require a certificate of non-crystallisation from the chargeholder.[32] Floating charges will not be discovered from the land certificate, or form 12/13 reports, but from a search of the Companies Register.

Other documentation

7–10 The information on the land certificate is correct only at its date, which, typically, is the date on which the sellers acquired. In order to find out what, if anything, has happened since it is necessary to see a form 12 report, updating the land certificate. The report also includes a search in the Personal Register against anyone listed in the initial form 12 application, typically the sellers and the purchasers. If necessary, the form 12 report can itself be updated by a form 13 report.[33]

Not everything will appear on the land certificate. The property may be affected by overriding interests, which is to say rights affecting the property even though not appearing on the Register. Some overriding interests will in fact appear if the Keeper knows about them, servitudes being one example, but others, such as short leases, cannot appear on the land certificate. And the purchasers will still require to pay attention to matters such as planning permission and building consents, in the usual way.[34]

Looking behind the land certificate

7–11 A difficult question is whether it is ever necessary to go behind the land certificate and examine the deed or deeds which led to the sellers being entered as owners.[35] The orthodox view is that this is unnecessary, unless indemnity has been excluded. Exclusion of indemnity not only indicates that the Keeper is unhappy with the title, but also makes rectification relatively easy in the event of a future challenge. This is the only case in Land Register titles where positive prescription is allowed to run.[36] In effect, the title must be treated almost

---

[31] See above, para.6–03.
[32] See below, para.28–29.
[33] See generally on forms 12 and 13 reports, *Registration of Title Practice Book* ("ROTPB"), Ch.3.
[34] See below, Ch.4.
[35] The principle that one should not have to go behind the Register is sometimes referred to as the "curtain principle".
[36] 1973 Act s.1(1).

like a GRS one. Since in such cases the Register can readily be rectified it is necessary to examine the underlying deeds; and since prescription runs, the examination should encompass the normal prescriptive period.[37]

Whilst this orthodox view is generally correct, case law shows that certain exceptions may exist.[38] In *Kaur v Singh*[39] the defender became registered owner on the basis of a disposition purportedly granted by the pursuer and her husband. The pursuer, alleging that her signature had been forged, sought reduction of the disposition and rectification of the Register. As matters initially stood it was plain that the pursuer could not succeed. For even if the disposition were reduced, the Register could not be rectified to the prejudice of the defender, who was a proprietor in possession and who had not been fraudulent or careless. (Since the alleged defect in the disposition was latent, there had of course been no exclusion of indemnity.) The pursuer responded by forcing the door, changing the locks and resuming possession. The defender, stripped of his possession, could no longer resist rectification. So he responded in kind and resumed possession in turn. These events suggest shortcomings in the legislation.[40] Protection depends on possession, but possession is easily lost. Purchasers who lose possession face the prospect of rectification on the basis of any defects contained in the underlying deeds.

Another case illustrating the limits of the orthodox view is *Short's Trustee v Chung (No.2)*.[41] This was the last in a protracted series of litigations arising out of a gratuitous alienation by Mr Short in 1986. Short's trustee in sequestration reduced the offending disposition[42] but could not rectify the Register because Mrs Chung was a proprietor in possession.[43] So instead he sought a fresh court order ordaining Mrs Chung to grant a disposition in his favour. Such a disposition could enter the Land Register by registration, thus circumventing the rules that make rectification so difficult. The trustee was successful.

A non domino conveyances

A non domino conveyances,[44] important under the GRS system, continue to play a role in registration of title.[45] Suppose that there is a conveyance from Adam to Beth, and Beth applies for registration, but the Keeper considers that

7–12

---

[37] For examination of title by reference to positive prescription, see below, paras 7–18 et seq.

[38] For a discussion, see Steven, 1999 S.L.T. (News) 163.

[39] *Kaur v Singh*, 1999 S.C. 180. See also below, para.8–15.

[40] A cynic might add, unkindly, that it seems to revive the priority system of the Stone Age, though perhaps that is unfair to our ancestors. For another case where matters degenerated into an unseemly struggle for possession, this time benefiting local divers rather than locksmiths, see *Safeway Stores Plc v Tesco Stores Ltd*, 2004 S.C. 29. For discussion, see Reid and Gretton, *Conveyancing 2003*, pp.91–96. It may be that some cases of short-term dispossession will be disregarded: see *Burr v Keeper of the Registers of Scotland*, Unreported November 12, 2010, Lands Tribunal, discussed in Reid and Gretton, *Conveyancing 2010*, pp.159–62.

[41] *Short's Trustee v Chung (No.2)*, 1998 S.C. 105; affirmed 1999 S.C. 471. For an overall account of this saga see Reid and Gretton, *Conveyancing 1999*, pp.69–71. See also below, para.8–17.

[42] *Short's Trustee v Chung*, 1991 S.L.T. 472; affirmed 1991 S.L.T. 751.

[43] We should be relieved that he did not try to deprive her of possession. An earlier attempt to register the extract decree of reduction had failed: see *Short's Trustee v Keeper of the Registers of Scotland*, 1996 S.C. (HL) 14.

[44] i.e. a conveyance by a person who does not own the property in question.

[45] ROTPB, para.6.4. For *a non domino* conveyances in the GRS system, and generally, see below, para.7–25. For proposals for reform, see below, para.8–25.

Adam had no right to grant the deed. The Keeper then has two choices. The first is to reject the application.[46] The second is to accept it, but with exclusion of indemnity.[47] If the second course is adopted, Beth is now the owner, but the effect of exclusion of indemnity is that if Caroline (the rightful owner)[48] turns up within 10 years and objects, Beth's name can be deleted,[49] and she will have no claim for compensation.

In certain cases it is the Keeper's practice to enter both names on the title sheet, i.e. both Beth's and Caroline's.[50] If the latter applies for rectification, Beth's name is deleted. Otherwise, after 10 years' prescriptive possession Beth can apply for Caroline's name to be deleted. It is, however, open to serious question whether this double entry, whereby two persons can be simultaneously on the register as owners (other than co-owners or joint owners), is a competent procedure.[51] There is nothing in the legislation which warrants an entry of this sort. Indeed, to the contrary, it is suggested that the legislation actually excludes any such possibility. Section 3 of the 1979 Act roundly declares that registration vests the interest (here, ownership) in the person registered; and it is simply not possible for two different persons both to be owners at one and the same time.[52] The word "rank" which the Keeper uses[53] betrays the truth. For ranking is possible only between compatible rights. For instance, two standard securities have a mutual ranking, precisely because one property can be subject to two standard securities. But two ownerships cannot rank with each other. If one ownership is superior to the other, the other is not merely postponed: it is null. The same problem arises when there is a boundary problem and the Keeper decides to register both parties as owners of the disputed area.[54]

GRS TITLES[55]

Introduction

7–13   The General Register of Sasines ("GRS") dates from 1617 and is in the process of being replaced by a new property register, the Land Register. The transition,

---

[46] Traditionally the Keeper based the rejection on s.4(2)(c) of the 1979 Act (frivolous and vexatious) but this was said to be incorrect in *Mackay v Keeper of the Registers of Scotland*, Unreported February 1, 2006 Lands Tribunal. A more plausible basis is the Keeper's general right to reject under s.4(1).

[47] In certain exceptional cases, the Keeper may choose not to exclude indemnity.

[48] She will not be the actual owner, who at this stage is Beth. Rather, she is the person entitled to ownership.

[49] In other words, the Register can be rectified under s.9(3)(a)(iv) of the 1979 Act.

[50] For example, in *BG Hamilton v Ready Mixed Concrete (Scotland) Ltd*, 1999 S.L.T. 524 one party was registered as owner in 1985 and then another party was registered in 1990 in pursuance of an *a non domino disposition*. The latter received a land certificate with the following exclusion on it: "Indemnity is excluded in terms of s.12(2) of the Land Registration (Scotland) Act 1979 in respect (1) that a Disposition to the Proprietors in Entry 1, of inter alia the subjects in this Title was registered on Jan. 19, 1985 and ranks prior to the Disposition to the Proprietors in Entry 2, registered 26 Nov. 1990 on which their entitlement was founded and also (2) that no evidence of Title prior to said Disposition to the Proprietors in Entry 2 has been produced to the Keeper".

[51] See Reid, 1991 J.R. 79.

[52] Other than as co-owners.

[53] See above, fn.50.

[54] For an example see *Safeway Stores Plc v Tesco Stores Ltd*, 2004 S.C. 29. See Reid and Gretton, *Conveyancing 2003*, pp.95–96.

[55] For the GRS more generally, see below, paras 8–26 et seq.

however, is a gradual one so that for many years to come both registers will remain in operation. A title which is in the Land Register consists, usually, of a single document, the land certificate. Examination of Land Register titles is thus usually a relatively straightforward task. A GRS title, by contrast, comprises a bundle of deeds, often numerous and usually uninviting. Reading and evaluating such a title is difficult.

If the property is still in the GRS, a sale will trigger a change of registers.[56] The current transaction, in other words, will be a "first registration" in the Land Register. Thus the examination of title in a transaction where the property is in the GRS and will stay in the GRS seldom happens. Examples are gratuitous transfers, either by way of donation or by way of succession. Since one does not look a gift horse in the mouth, in such cases examination of title may be cursory or non-existent. However, there is still one major type of case where property may stay in the GRS (for the time being) and where examination of title is important. That is where a standard security is being granted.

From the point of view of examination of title there is little difference between (a) the case where the property is in the GRS and will remain there (for the time being) and (b) the case of first registration in the Land Register. In both cases what is being examined is a GRS title. But on a first registration there is the stimulus of knowing that the title will be immediately re-examined by the Keeper, and that if the Keeper is not satisfied she is entitled either to refuse registration, or to allow registration only on the basis of exclusion of indemnity.[57]

Which deeds?

A GRS title comprises an unappetising bundle of deeds, many of which are 7–14 likely to be irrelevant. Conveyancers traditionally never throw anything away. The size of the bundle depends on the length of time the property has existed as a separate entity. A late eighteenth-century villa will have a large number of titles. A recently-built house will have few, and it may be necessary to borrow the prior titles (which will deal with the whole development from which the house has been split off) from the builders' solicitors. It is rash to assume that the buyers' solicitors will be given all the titles that they need. What they need, and what therefore they are entitled to receive,[58] are the following. (a) A prescriptive progress of titles, i.e. the foundation writ for the purposes of positive prescription, plus all subsequent conveyances. (b) All security deeds and discharges of security deeds of the recent past—in practice 40 years is usually regarded as sufficient and people sometimes make do with less. (c) All deeds which impose real burdens and servitudes. (d) The principal deed, or deeds, describing the property, if not already included under (a) or (c) above. (Usually they are included.) (e) Searches in the GRS, the Personal Register, and, where applicable, the Companies Register. In the case of a first registration, these are supplemented by a form 10 report. Searches are considered further below in Ch.9. (f) Miscellaneous other documents. In first registrations there is usually

---

[56] 1979 Act s.2(1)(a)(ii).
[57] 1979 Act ss.4(1) and 12(2). Both are rare, especially the former.
[58] As part of the obligation for good and marketable title, for which see above, Ch.6

a form P16 report, indicating whether the boundaries in the title coincide with those on the Ordnance Survey.[59]

If any of the above items are missing the buyers' solicitors should ask for them. For deeds within the prescriptive progress the sellers should produce either the originals or extracts (the validity of which is guaranteed by the 1970 Act s.45). Quick copies (i.e. ordinary photocopies) are acceptable for burdens writs. To what extent sellers are bound at common law to deliver the deeds (principals or extracts) and to what extent they are bound merely to exhibit them, is not wholly clear. In the absence of special agreement, the matter is now regulated by statute, obliging the sellers to deliver all deeds and searches relating exclusively to the land conveyed.[60]

How exacting?

7–15 The buyers' solicitors must examine the title carefully. This is one of the main things they are being paid for. It is obviously better to discover a title defect before, rather than after, settlement. The buyers can refuse to settle (or conclude missives), as opposed to trying later to pursue the sellers for damages. In practice, most GRS titles contain something or other which is not quite perfect. How exacting should the buyers' solicitors be? Three types of defect may be distinguished. There is the obviously trivial, for instance an alteration of an inessential word in one of the deeds which has not been declared in the testing clause. Such defects can be ignored. Next there is the obviously fatal defect. For instance, one of the deeds has not been signed, or the seller turns out just to have been sequestrated. In that case the title must be rejected. Third, there is the intermediate defect. Many defects are sufficient to put the sellers in breach of their obligation to produce a good title, without being particularly serious. They are technical defects only. Something has not been done completely correctly. The title may be satisfactory, but it is impossible to be absolutely sure. In other words, there is "rational doubt".[61] Usually there is no real danger of the defect coming home to roost. Even if there is some third party out there who might, in theory, be able to found on the apparent defect, this will almost certainly never happen in practice. The buyers' solicitors know that. So do the sellers' solicitors. Nonetheless, the buyers' solicitors may well object to the title and insist on remedial measures. Traditionally the main reason for this was that they were worried that when their clients came to resell the property, the solicitors acting for the then buyers would be less accommodating, with the result that the sale would fall through. Nowadays the worry is more likely to be that the Keeper may take a strict line and exclude indemnity from the title (which would itself make the title unmarketable). And in either case since there has been no judicial eviction there will then be no remedy against the original sellers under the warrandice clause in the disposition. So the buyers' solicitors will be reluctant to take any risk. Risk-averseness is understandable but it does not make for speedy (or harmonious) conveyancing.

Examination of title is a skilled task. Possible defects can arise in many different, and unexpected, ways and it is impossible to examine title properly

---

[59] ROTPB, Ch.4.

[60] 1979 Act s.16(1)(a)(i). The word "all" here is odd. Why should some trivial deed, 50 or 150 years old, perhaps long since lost, have to be delivered?

[61] The phrase of Lord Meadowbank in *Brown v Cheyne* (1833) 12 S. 176. See above, para.6–16.

without a good working knowledge of the whole of conveyancing law. It is important not only to spot defects but to classify them properly. Minor errors should not be confused with more serious ones. The most irritating person to do business with is the smart Alec who reads conveyancing books (such as this one) on the bus on the way to work and who sees it as his duty to give free conveyancing lessons to the solicitor acting for the other party. If a defect is trivial, it should be ignored. There is no need to point it out to the other side. That merely wastes time, a point all the more worth remembering today when conveyancing fees have become so unremunerative. The conveyancer must know when to speak up and when to shut up.

Notes on title

In examining a GRS title, the buyers' solicitors traditionally made an elaborate 7–16 summary of the various deeds. This summary was called notes on title.[62] Such notes had two main purposes. In the first place, before photocopiers came into use, the notes would provide a substitute for the deeds themselves, which might well leave the law office quickly, for instance to go to secured lenders. The law firm could thus answer questions about the title without having to call up the deeds. In the second place the making of the notes was a useful discipline, whereby the conveyancer forced him/herself to check everything systematically. Any points arising that needed to be pursued—for instance deeds not seen—would be marked prominently, for instance in red ink. In recent years notes on title have tended to become less elaborate, and if the title is in the Land Register the buying solicitor is unlikely to write anything that a traditional solicitor would recognise as notes on title.

Do the sellers have power to convey the property?

The basic issues here are the same as for a property in the Land Register but the 7–17 way of establishing the seller's right is very different. Suppose that the client, Ian, is buying a house from Harriet. Ian will receive a good title only if (i) Harriet is the owner (or has power to convey as, for instance, executor or judicial factor or heritable creditor, etc.) and (ii) the disposition by Harriet to Ian is valid (i.e. properly executed and so on). Point (ii) is easily checked. But what of point (i), namely, whether Harriet was owner, or at least had power to convey? The answer is: as for Ian, so for Harriet. Harriet owned the property if, and only if, (i) the person from whom she acquired (George) owned the property, or at least had power to convey, and (ii) the disposition from George to Harriet was valid. So one must consider George's title, and then Frank's title (George's author)[63] and then Emma's title (Frank's author), and so on. The problem is that title is derivative. Harriet has a good title only if George had a good title, whose title in turn depends on Frank and on Emma. Where does it all stop? Is it necessary to go right back to the original Crown grant by Alexander III or by God to Adam and Eve? The answer is no, because of the doctrine of positive prescription.

---

[62] For an example see J.H. Sinclair, *Handbook of Conveyancing Practice in Scotland*, 3rd edn (1995), p.262. It is a sign of the times that the later editions omit this section.

[63] By "author in title" conveyancers mean the person from whom the property was acquired.

Positive prescription[64]

7–18 The basis of positive prescription is s.1 of the Prescription and Limitation (Scotland) Act 1973.[65] Its importance in conveyancing law and practice for GRS titles cannot be overstated: its role in the Land Register is different and much less important. Positive prescription is the acquisition of real rights in land by possession or use for a certain period of time.[66] The chief real rights in land are: (a) ownership; (b) heritable security; (c) lease: (d) proper liferent; (e) servitude; and (f) real burden. However, real burdens cannot be acquired by prescription,[67] while special provision is made for servitudes in s.3. Also excluded are short leases, i.e. leases of 20 years or less, as s.1 covers only real rights that can be registered, and short leases cannot be registered.[68] This chapter is concerned only with ownership, but the same rules apply to other real rights in land, and indeed must be applied in, for instance, the purchase of a leasehold title, the latter being common in commercial conveyancing. In practice, prescription is almost never encountered with reference to the remaining real rights in land, i.e. security and proper liferent.

There are two main requirements if prescription is to operate. First, there must be an appropriate deed which has been recorded in the GRS (called the foundation writ or the prescriptive writ). Secondly, the land must be possessed for 10 years.

Identifying the foundation writ

7–19 Examination of title begins with a bundle of deeds, sometimes a large one, tied up with red tape.[69] Which is the foundation writ? The rule for prescription is that the 10 years of possession must follow and be founded on (hence "foundation" writ) the recording of the deed. So the foundation writ is the first property writ recorded more than 10 years before the current transaction. By "property writ" is meant a deed which conveys the property: usually this will be a disposition or feu disposition, but it may also be a notice of title or a judicial decree having the effect of a conveyance.[70] Thus, if it is now 2012, and Sarah is selling to Thomas, and Sarah acquired the property in 2008 from Rona, and Rona acquired the property in 2004 from Paul, and Paul acquired the property in 1996 from Norah, the foundation writ is the disposition of 1996.[71] (If there is a qualifying writ

---

[64] On prescription generally see David Johnston, *Prescription and Limitation* (1999); and D. M. Walker, *The Law of Prescription and Limitation of Actions in Scotland*, 6th edn (2002).

[65] As amended by the Abolition of Feudal Tenure etc. (Scotland) Act 2000 s.76(1) and Sch.12 para.33(2).

[66] David Johnston, *Prescription and Limitation* (1999), para.14.04 says that positive prescription does not result in acquisition, but we would respectfully disagree. If the Scottish Law Commission's reforms on land registration are implemented, the 1973 Act will be amended to make clear that acquisition occurs: see Report on *Land Registration* (Scot. Law Com. No.222) paras 35.5–35.9.

[67] 1973 Act s.1(3).

[68] However, it must not be supposed that only long leases can be real rights. Short leases generally are real rights too, by virtue of the Leases Act 1449.

[69] It is one of the mysteries of existence that red tape is pink. And one of the skills to be learned by the novice, apart from trying to find out how the dictaphone works, and where the loo is, is how to tie the writs up again so that they won't promptly spill out all over the floor. (The secret is to tie the tape as tight as possible, leaving one deed out, and then slide that one in.)

[70] See 1973 Act s.5(1).

[71] The foundation writ can sometimes be very old. One of the authors once acted in the purchase of property from a corporation which had bought it in 1646 and was now selling for the first time. The 1646 deed in favour of the corporation was thus the foundation writ.

which is not quite 10 years old this can be treated as the foundation writ provided that the 10-year period will have expired by the time the clients' disposition is recorded.)

Once the foundation writ has been identified, it must be read to ensure that it complies with s.1. For this purpose only the deed itself should be considered[72] and extrinsic evidence is disregarded. This is less straightforward than it sounds. By the deed itself is meant (a) the actual words of the deed including schedules, plans and other annexations[73] and (b) any other words which are formally imported by reference, typically descriptions and real burdens. Other deeds which are referred to but are not formally imported are not part of the foundation writ and fall to be disregarded for this purpose. This includes any midcouples (also called links in title) mentioned in the foundation writ for the purposes of deduction of title.[74]

"Sufficient in respect of its terms"

In the words of s.1(1), the foundation writ must be sufficient in respect of its 7–20 terms to constitute a real right in the land or to land of a description *habile* to include the particular land.[75] To test this, the description given in the dispositive clause must be examined. All that is required is that the words of description are capable of including the land in question, even if this is not the only, or even the most natural, interpretation of the words.[76] For instance, it is common to find that the description is little more than a glorified postal address. In that case, the property actually possessed for the prescriptive period will be owned. By contrast, if the description states a boundary line, and the successive owners have in fact possessed beyond that line, there will be no ownership of the extra land, no matter how long the possession has endured.[77] Where a description contains contradictory elements, so that the land possessed is included by one element (for example a plan) but excluded by another (for example, a verbal account of a boundary), it is capable of founding prescription.[78]

Not *ex facie* invalid or forged

The foundation writ must not be invalid *ex facie* or forged.[79] If a deed is forged 7–21 it is not a good foundation writ. But this case aside, defects which are not apparent from a visual inspection of the deed do not matter. The concern is only with *ex facie* validity and, as explained earlier, extrinsic evidence is irrelevant. Thus, so long as the deed looks correct, it does not matter (for the purpose of qualifying as a foundation writ) if it is actually fundamentally defective, e.g. if it was granted by a non-owner, or if an inspection of the

---

[72] 1973 Act s.1(1)(a): "Sufficient in respect of its terms".

[73] The schedules, plans and annexations must, however, be incorporated into the deed in conformity with s.8 of the 1995 Act (discussed in para.17–08).

[74] See Halliday, para.36–07.

[75] 1973 Act s.1(1)(a). For descriptions in general, see below, Ch.12.

[76] *Auld v Hay* (1880) 7 R. 663; *Suttie v Baird*, 1992 S.L.T. 133; *Rutco Inc v Jamieson*, 2004 G.W.D. 30-620. For a qualification of the doctrine see *Michael v Carruthers*, 1998 S.L.T. 1179.

[77] The rule is the same even where it is argued that the land is possessed as a part and pertinent: see *Cooper's Trustees v Stark's Trustees* (1898) 25 R. 1160.

[78] *Nisbet v Hogg*, 1950 S.L.T. 289; compare *Compugraphics International Ltd v Nikolic* [2011] CSIH 34.

[79] 1973 Act s.1(2).

midcouples listed in the deduction of title clause would reveal that they are inept or even non-existent. Nor does it matter that such defects are actually known about. The law is concerned only with the appearance of the foundation writ. Good faith is irrelevant in positive prescription. The test is whether, if there were no extrinsic defects, the deed would be sufficient to confer the right in question. If the answer is yes, the deed is good as a foundation writ. In marginal cases the test may be difficult to apply, but it appears that doubts should be resolved in favour of validity. Only a deed bearing clear evidence of its own invalidity fails to make the grade.[80]

The requirement of possession

7–22 Possession must follow the recording of the foundation writ. The period is 10 years.[81] The possession must be continuous, by which is meant, not that the possessors must be there all that time, but that they must not have yielded possession to anyone else (e.g. a squatter) who does not recognise their title. Possession may be civil, for example through a tenant.[82] Section 1(1) of the 1973 Act says that possession may be "by any person and his successors". So the fact that the property has changed hands does not matter, so long as the new proprietor or proprietors also took possession. Section 1(1) provides that the possession must be exercised "openly" (i.e. not just when the neighbour is out shopping), "peaceably" and "without any judicial interruption". Possession must be founded on the foundation writ, by which is meant that the possession must be "adverse" (i.e. attributable to the foundation writ) and not of consent (i.e. attributable merely to the consent of the true owner).

Both a foundation writ and 10 years' possession are required for prescription. But while foundation writs are anxiously examined and argued about by solicitors, possession is usually taken for granted and no evidence is required. Whether this is entirely wise seems open to question. But, of course, verifying past possession is difficult. What in practice usually happens is that the purchasers' agent checks the search for the past 40 years. If there is a competing title, this will be shown up by the search, and in that case it may be necessary to investigate the history of the possession. There is no magic about the figure of 40 years. It is a practical point. Thus, suppose the foundation writ is 12 years old, and in fact was invalid at the time, someone else owning the property. A 40-year search will, in practice, reveal this fact, in which case it would be necessary to verify that the sellers, or their predecessors, have had 10 years of possession. Conversely, if a 40-year search throws up no competing title, almost certainly there is no competing title.[83]

Effect of prescription

7–23 According to s.1(1) of the 1973 Act, the effect of prescription is that "the validity of the title . . . shall be exempt from challenge". This means that even if the foundation writ was voidable or, worse, void, this no longer matters, and

---

[80] The wording of s.1(2) of the 1973 Act suggests as much. See further John Burns, *Conveyancing Practice*, 4th edn by F. MacRitchie (1957), p.201.

[81] In certain questions with the Crown, the period is 20 years: s.1(5). Generally, on the calculation of time, see s.14.

[82] 1973 Act s.15(1).

[83] For the potential risks in taking possession for granted, see *Hamilton v McIntosh Donald Ltd*, 1994 S.C. 304. For discussion see Rennie, 1994 S.L.T. (News) 261.

the title based on that deed can no longer be challenged. Of course, in practice, most foundation writs are perfectly good anyway; but the value of prescription is that it is not necessary to prove that this is so. It no longer matters whether it was good or not. Take the example given earlier, where it is now 2012, and Sarah is selling to Thomas, and Sarah acquired the property in 2008 from Rona, and Rona acquired the property in 2004 from Paul, and Paul acquired the property in 1996 from Nora. The foundation writ is the disposition of 1996. The title is now good, provided that there has been possession, even if Nora had no title, so that the 1996 deed was void. Prescription cuts off any right to reduce the title. But it will not cut off other rights. For instance, the ordinary running of positive prescription will not cut out real burdens or servitudes or heritable securities.[84] (If it did, then anyone with a mortgage more than 10 years old would be happy.)

A quirk: prescriptive reacquisition

There is a curious quirk which arises from the law of prescription. Suppose that 7–24 in 2002 Alan disponed 50 hectares to Beth, who recorded her disposition in the GRS. Beth took possession, but due to a misunderstanding about boundaries only took possession of 49 hectares, Alan remaining in possession of the extra hectare. In 2012 Alan would have reacquired, by prescription, title to that hectare. For Alan would have had 10 years of possession and this would be attributable to the deed by which he had (sometime before 2002) acquired the property. Correspondingly, in 2012 Beth's ownership of that hectare would cease.[85]

A note on the disposition *a non domino*

It sometimes happens that someone notices that a piece of ground is unoccu- 7–25 pied and apparently abandoned. Using prescription, it is possible to acquire ownership. What happens is that the person gets a friend to grant to him a gratuitous disposition of the land, and the disposition is recorded.[86] This is called a disposition *a non domino*, i.e. "by a non-owner". The disponee takes possession, and 10 years later will become the owner. The disposition must be granted by someone other than the disponee: a disposition by a person to herself does not bear to be a transfer and so cannot found prescription.[87] Acquisition on the basis of an *a non domino* disposition may seem like theft, but good faith is not a requirement of positive prescription.[88] Moreover, the true owner has 10 years to reclaim the property, and the policy of the law is that an owner who abandons property cannot expect indefinite protection. A challenge to the equivalent doctrine in English law before the European Court of Human Rights was initially successful but was ultimately rejected by the

---

[84] Such rights may be extinguishable by negative prescription, but not merely by possession for 10 years.

[85] See Hume, *Lectures*, iv, 549; *Wallace v University of St Andrews* (1904) 6 F. 1093; *Love-Lee v Cameron of Lochiel*, 1991 S.C.L.R. 61.

[86] Who should, of course, exclude warrandice.

[87] *Board of Management of Aberdeen College v Youngson* [2005] CSOH 31; 2005 S.C. 335. The decision, anticipated in previous editions of this book, caused some dismay: for a discussion, see Reid and Gretton, *Conveyancing 2005*, pp.63–65. The restriction does not apply where either disponer or disponee was acting in some special capacity, e.g. where A as executor grants a disposition to A as an individual.

[88] And as far as the criminal law is concerned, heritable property cannot be stolen.

Grand Chamber.[89] When purchasing from someone who purports to have acquired ownership in this manner, it is obviously wise to verify that there has been 10 years of possession, unless the acquisition took place long ago, such as more than 40 years ago.

A disposition *a non domino* must not reveal that the disponer is not the owner, or it will lose its potential status as a foundation writ.[90] Here candour does not pay. So a deed which admitted, in the narrative clause, that "we have occupied the subjects hereinafter disponed continuously since 1955, openly, peaceably and without any judicial interruption, but without a title" was held to fail as a foundation writ.[91] However, the cautious words "only so far as I have right thereto" do not amount to a denial of title and do not prevent the running of prescription.[92]

Traditionally the Keeper would accept dispositions *a non domino* without querying them. However, practice changed in 1996, and she will now accept them, for either register, only in certain types of case, though what those types of case are is not wholly clear.[93]

As well as unoccupied property, the *a non domino* disposition will sometimes be encountered where a person has long been in possession of land but without a good title. One example would be a company which possesses land under a 999-year lease granted in the eighteenth century. No rent has been paid for many decades and indeed the lessee does not even know who the landlord is. The lessee registers an *a non domino* disposition in its favour. After 10 years it will have a good title. One problem, in cases of this sort, is that it could be argued that the possession for 10 years is referable to the lease rather than to the disposition, in which case it would not be "adverse" and the title would not be good. The position probably depends on whether rent is being paid.[94] If it is, the possession is referable to the lease. If not, possession is capable of being founded on the disposition.[95]

Writs subsequent to the foundation writ

7–26   Assuming a good foundation writ followed by 10 years' possession, the title 10 years ago today can be treated as having been good. The important date is 10 years' ago today and not the date of the foundation writ (which may be much earlier). What has happened since? The owner may have been inhibited, or sequestrated, or have died, or have disponed the property to someone else. The task of the buyers' solicitor is to connect the current sellers with the good title of 10 years ago. If the property has not changed hands during that period, the sellers will have been the grantees of the foundation writ, and there is nothing

---

[89] *JA Pye Ltd v United Kingdom* (2008) 46 E.H.R.R. 45. See Gretton, (2008) 12 Edin. L.R. 109; McCarthy, 2008 S.L.T. (News) 15.

[90] This is because it would be invalid *ex facie*.

[91] *Watson v Shields*, 1994 S.C.L.R. 819; affirmed 1996 S.C.L.R. 81.

[92] *Landward Securities (Edinburgh) Ltd v Inhouse (Edinburgh) Ltd*, 1996 G.W.D. 16-962.

[93] See ROTPB, para.6.4. There may be room for doubt as to whether the Keeper has the right to reject which she asserts, as far as the GRS is concerned. She does of course have that right in respect of the Land Register. For discussion and proposals for reform, see Scottish Law Commission, Report on *Land Registration* (Scot. Law Com. No.222, 2010) Pt 16, and see also below, para.8–25.

[94] *Houstoun v Barr*, 1911 S.C. 134; *BG Hamilton v Ready Mix Concrete (Scotland) Ltd*, 1999 S.L.T. 524.

[95] *Grant v Grant* (1677) Mor. 10876; David Johnston, *Prescription and Limitation* (1999), para.16.27.

further to be checked in this respect. But in some cases the property will have changed hands. If so, the dispositions or other writs connecting the current sellers to the good title of 10 years before must be examined. Such writs must be absolutely, and not merely *ex facie*, valid, for prescription has not yet operated on them. So extrinsic defects matter as much as intrinsic defects, although in practice it may not always be possible to find out about such extrinsic defects. Each title is different and an exhaustive list of things to look out for cannot be given, but some of the more important points are given below.

Each consecutive deed must follow on from its predecessor. This means either that the granter of deed 4 was the grantee of deed 3, or that, the grantee of deed 3 having died or been sequestrated, etc. without having conveyed the property, the property has passed to the granter of deed 4 in some other way, e.g. as a result of a grant of confirmation of executors or act and warrant in favour of a trustee in sequestration or the calling up of a loan by a heritable creditor. In such cases the authority to sell must, of course, be carefully checked. Another example is the special destination. For instance, a house is conveyed to Alan and Beth and the survivor of them. Alan dies, and the next deed is a disposition by Beth alone. All these issues are considered elsewhere in this book.[96]

Each deed must be checked for errors, such as the designations of the parties, the description of the property, and the mode of execution.[97] In principle, the warrants of registration should be checked, as should the stamp duty, though in practice it is most unlikely that the Keeper would have accepted a deed with errors of these kinds. Warants of registration ceased to be needed on or after November 28, 2004.[98] The conveyancer should consider whether there is anything in a deed which raises reasonable suspicions and suggests that further evidence is needed. It must be remembered that the deeds after the foundation writ must be absolutely (and not merely *ex facie*) valid. A party who signs as "Postman Pat" is probably under age and unable to convey property. Further inquiries must be made of the sellers' solicitors.

There is also the possibility that a deed, while not void, might be voidable. Examples of potentially voidable deeds include: (i) deeds by persons aged 16 or 17 which are "prejudicial"[99]; (ii) gratuitous alienations and unfair preferences granted by persons when insolvent; (iii) deeds by a party who has been inhibited; (iv) disposals by a spouse within five years prior to a claim by the other spouse for aliment or financial provision.[100]

Voidable titles and good faith

Where a deed within the prescriptive progress is voidable (not void), there are 7–27 two possibilities. The first is that the purchasers do not know about the problem and have no reasonable means of knowing about it, for example because it appears neither from the deed itself nor from the search. In such a case they are protected, because voidability does not affect a subsequent purchaser in

---

[96] See below, Chs 22, 25, 26 and 29.

[97] This can require historical knowledge of the law. For instance, the current rules on execution of deeds only go back to August 1, 1995, when the 1995 Act came into force. See further below, Ch.14.

[98] Abolition of Feudal Tenure etc. (Scotland) Act 2000 s.5.

[99] Age of Legal Capacity (Scotland) Act 1991 s.3.

[100] Family Law (Scotland) Act 1985 s.18.

good faith.[101] Unless the deed is reduced, and the extract decree recorded before the purchasers record their own disposition, there is no danger from a subsequent reduction.[102] The right to reduce is a personal right which does not transmit against successors in good faith. The other possibility is that the purchasers do know, or ought to know, that the deed is voidable. In that case, the right to reduce will normally transmit against them, with the result that the sellers are not offering a good and marketable title and must take steps to buy off the party with the right to reduce.

Gratuitous alienations[103]

7–28 A "gratuitous alienation" means any act (or, in some cases, omission) whereby the value of the debtor's patrimony is diminished. The main example is a donation—i.e. a gratuitous transfer. Gratuitous alienations are normally valid, and are common between family members. But persons who are insolvent are forbidden to give away property, and if they do so, the donation is voidable at the instance of the creditors. However, since the donation is voidable only and not void, a third party acquiring for value and in good faith has nothing to fear.[104] Thus suppose Mark gratuitously transfers title to his house to his wife, Nicole. He is insolvent, and a year later is sequestrated. In the meantime, Nicole has sold the property to Oliver. If Oliver was in good faith, his title cannot be reduced by Mark's trustee in sequestration, who in that case can do no more than sue Nicole for the value of the property. The trouble is that if the fact that Nicole's acquisition was gratuitous appears from the face of the title, which in a GRS case it usually does, Oliver is probably barred from pleading good faith.[105] So Oliver is at risk, at least in theory. In practice, of course, most gifts are not made by insolvent donors. The law is probably that unless there is some particular ground for suspecting voidability, or unless there is some special clause in the missives, a purchaser cannot object to a title which includes a gratuitous transfer.[106] The creditors' right to reduce depends on the donor being sequestrated or granting a protected trust deed within five years.[107] Hence, provided that the personal search is clear, there is no reason to worry about a donation which is more than five years old.

Identification of property

7–29 It is pointless establishing that the sellers have a good title, unless it is a good title to the property which the purchasers have contracted to buy. But in practice checking this is easier said than done, not least because missives are themselves often dangerously vague in describing the property. In a GRS title all deeds within the prescriptive period will usually contain the same description, which will normally consist of (a) a general description and (b) a particular description

---

[101] Stair, IV, xl, 21; Erskine, III, v, 10; Hume, *Lectures*, iii, 236–238. See, further, Reid, *Property*, para.692.

[102] Conveyancing (Scotland) Act 1924 s.46(1).

[103] Bankruptcy (Scotland) Act 1985 s.34. And see William W. McBryde, *Bankruptcy*, 2nd edn (1995).

[104] Bankruptcy (Scotland) Act 1985 s.34(4), proviso.

[105] *Hay v Jamieson* (1672) Mor. 1009; Erskine, IV, i, 36; Bell, *Comm.*, ii, 183.

[106] cf. *Sibbald's Heirs v Harris*, 1947 S.C. 601, discussed above in para.6–12.

[107] Bankruptcy (Scotland) Act 1985 s.34(3). The period is only two years if the alienation is not to an "associate" (defined in s.74 to include close relative, business partner, employer, and employee).

imported by reference from the break-off writ.[108] The general description may not take matters very far. But unless there is a good plan, the particular description may also be of limited help. Old particular descriptions are often vague. They may refer to boundary features which no longer exist. In *Anderson v Lambie*[109] Lord Reid remarked that "the lands were described as 'parts of the twenty-six shilling and eightpenny land of old extent[110] of Blairmackhill' and otherwise were only identified as having been possessed by persons long since forgotten or bounded by other lands apparently now unidentifiable".

Although a plan-based title is in general preferable, for obvious reasons, planless ones are often fine, while plans often turn out to be inadequate. Some employ the dreaded "floating rectangle",[111] i.e. a plan showing a plot of ground apparently in the middle of nowhere and which is not anchored to any recognisable and permanent landmark such as a public road. Even if the plan shows a road, this may not be sufficient. Thus, the plan may show the property next to "the public road from Drumbeg to Balnacraig" with no indication of where on that road (which is 5 kilometres long) the property actually lies. Some plans lack a north sign,[112] and some lack measurements. It is common to see plans which can only be understood on the basis of colouring: for instance, the property is defined as the area coloured red. But if the principal deed is lost, the plan may prove uninterpretable, since in the GRS everything is in monochrome. Even if the deed is not lost, a deed whose terms do not appear in its recorded version is unsatisfactory. If there is no plan, or if the plan is inadequate, then a new plan will be required, assuming that the transaction is a first registration. As already mentioned, descriptions of common areas in developments are often particularly badly done, with potentially serious consequences.[113]

In some cases the plan or other description looks first class but in truth does not correspond to the property as actually possessed. Assuming that the transaction is a first registration this problem will normally be brought to light by a P16 report.[114]

What are the title conditions and are they acceptable?

The issues here are substantially the same as for properties in the Land Register, 7–30 already discussed.[115] The main difference is that whereas in a land certificate all the real burdens are set out in type in the D section, in a GRS title the burdens may be scattered among numerous different deeds. Older ones will be handwritten and perhaps barely legible.

---

[108] In other words, the successive deeds will not normally contain the full description, but refer to an earlier deed by A to B. (Clients are often puzzled why the deed in their favour should refer to other people.) For descriptions, generally, see below, Ch.12.

[109] *Anderson v Lambie*, 1954 S.C. (HL) 43.

[110] *Anderson v Lambie* was more than half a century ago but even now there are some GRS titles that are defined by reference to the "old extent". The old extent was an official land survey made in the 13th century. It was the subject of a classic work of Scottish legal historiography: *Memorial on Old Extent* (1816) by Thomas Thomson, published as vol.10 of the Stair Society series (1946).

[111] Occasionally also called the "floating shape" because of course it may not be an actual rectangle.

[112] Some helpfully include a north sign which in fact points south.

[113] *PMP Plus Ltd v Keeper of the Registers of Scotland*, 2009 S.L.T. (Lands Tr) 2. See above, para.7–07.

[114] For P16 reports see below, para.12–12.

[115] See above, para.7–08.

Are there any securities?

7–31   The issues here are substantially the same as for properties in the Land
       Register.[116] One difference is that if the property is in the Land Register,
       discharged heritable securities will simply be invisible. They will be omitted
       from the land certificate. But in a GRS title the conveyancer must examine the
       discharges to check that they are valid.[117] In the case of discharges more than
       five years old the rule is that a defect not discoverable from the face of the deed
       will not affect purchasers unless they know about it.[118] So only *ex facie* validity
       matters. This rule does not apply to discharges within the last five years, but at
       common law a *bona fide* purchaser is only affected by defects sufficiently
       serious to make the deed void (as opposed to voidable), and such defects are
       usually discoverable from an examination of the deed itself.

---

[116] See above, para.7–09.
[117] See Halliday, para.36–60.
[118] Conveyancing and Feudal Reform (Scotland) Act 1970 s.41.

CHAPTER 8

REGISTRATION

INTRODUCTION

General

The Land Register and the General Register of Sasines ("GRS") are often 8–01
referred to as the "property registers", and registration in the property registers
is described as registration for "publication",[1] as opposed to registration for
"preservation" (or for "execution") in the Books of Council and Session.[2] Like
other registers, the property registers are open to the public. Both are divided
into 33 registration areas, corresponding to the traditional counties, except that
Glasgow is a separate registration area. Despite being so divided, both the
Land Register and the GRS are registers for the whole of Scotland, and are
based in Edinburgh.[3] Unlike many countries, property registration in Scotland
is done on a national rather than a local basis.[4]

The Land Registration (Scotland) Act 1979, which is the basis of the Land
Register, is unsatisfactory in a number of respects, and the Scottish Law
Commission has recommended that it be replaced.[5] At the time of writing there
seemed good prospects that a new Land Registration Bill, based on the Law
Commission's work, would shortly be introduced in the Scottish Parliament.
Further details are given later in the chapter.[6]

---

[1] The reason being that real rights must be made public: this is the publicity principle.

[2] This is the register of the Court of Session. But it is administered by the Keeper rather than by
the Court. Typically this register is used for the safekeeping ("preservation") of deeds which
cannot be registered in the property registers (e.g. deeds of trust or powers of attorney). But since
any probative deed can be registered, it is competent to register deeds such as dispositions,
standard securities and so on. As well as preservation, registration is useful as proving conclu-
sively that the deed existed not later than the date of registration. The register is public, and anyone
can obtain an extract. The register has other functions too. In particular, a probative document of
debt, with a consent clause, can be registered for "execution", allowing the creditor to do summary
diligence. The Sheriff Courts have similar registers, called the Sheriff Court Books.

[3] These registers are based at Meadowbank House, 153 London Road, Edinburgh, EH8 7AU.
The website is *http://www.ros.gov.uk/*. This is full of valuable information and advice.
Administratively the body in charge is the "Registers of Scotland Executive Agency" but in law,
and in conveyancing parlance, everything is done by "the Keeper" (i.e. the registrar), more properly "the Keeper of the Registers of Scotland".

[4] There used to be a system of local Registers of Sasines, with both county registers (called the
"particular" registers) and burgh registers. People had the option to use the local register or to use
the GRS. These local registers were gradually phased out, under the Land Registers (Scotland) Act
1868 and the Burgh Registers (Scotland) Act 1926. The last to close was the Dingwall Burgh
Register of Sasines, on June 30, 1963.

[5] Scottish Law Commission, Report on *Land Registration* (Scot. Law Com. No.222, 2010).

[6] See below, para.8–25.

Introduction of the new register

8–02　The GRS, which was established in 1617,[7] is being phased out, with properties being gradually transferred to the Land Register. There are roughly two million title units in Scotland, and at the time of this edition around 55 per cent of individual titles, relating to about 20 per cent of the land mass, appeared on the Land Register, increasing at 2–3 per cent a year.

The new register was brought into operation county by county. The first county to become "operational" was Renfrewshire, on April 6, 1981. The original plan was to have all 33 counties operational by 1992, but in fact the process took until 2003 to complete. The 33 counties are listed below, with the date when they became operational in the new register.

Aberdeen[8]	April 1, 1996	Kirkcudbright[9]	April 1, 1997
Angus[10]	April 1, 1999	Lanark	January 3, 1984
Argyll	April 1, 2000	Midlothian[11]	April 1, 2001
Ayr	April 1, 1997	Moray	April 1, 2003
Banff	April 1, 2003	Nairn	April 1, 2002
Berwick	October 1, 1999	Orkney & Shetland[12]	April 1, 2003
Bute	April 1, 2000	Peebles	October 1, 1999
Caithness	April 1, 2003	Perth	April 1, 1999
Clackmannan	October 1, 1992	Renfrew	April 6, 1981
Dumfries	April 1, 1997	Ross & Cromarty[13]	April 1, 2003
Dunbarton	October 4, 1982	Roxburgh	October 1, 1999
East Lothian[14]	October 1, 1999	Selkirk	October 1, 1999
Fife	April 1, 1995	Stirling	April 1, 1993
Glasgow[15]	September 30, 1985	Sutherland	April 1, 2003
Inverness	April 1, 2002	West Lothian[16]	October 1, 1993
Kincardine	April 1, 1996	Wigtown	April 1, 1997
Kinross	April 1, 1999		

---

[7] Registration Act 1617.
[8] The practice of conveyancers is to refer to the "County of Aberdeen" rather than "Aberdeenshire", and likewise for the other counties.
[9] Stewartry of Kirkcudbright.
[10] At one time called the County of Forfar.
[11] At one time called the County of Edinburgh.
[12] Orkney and Shetland form a single area.
[13] Ross and Cromarty form a single area.
[14] At one time called the County of Haddington.
[15] Barony and Regality of Glasgow.
[16] At one time called the County of Linlithgow.

Transfers into the new register

When each county became operational, that did not mean that all the properties   8–03
in that county promptly switched into the new register. Individual properties
remain in the GRS until they are individually transferred to the new register,
which may not happen for years or decades. The basic idea, explained further
in the next paragraph, is that when a property is sold it switches to the new
register but until that happens it stays in the GRS. That not only means that
properties remain in the GRS while they continue in the hands of the owner at
the time the county became operational, but they will even stay in the GRS if
the property is transferred for reasons other than sale, such as a disposition by
an executor to a beneficiary, or a disposition in implement of a donation.[17]
So not only are many properties still in the GRS, but registrations of deeds in
the GRS are still taking place. Since sometimes the same property stays in the
hands of the same family for generations, with transfers from one family
member to another happening on the basis of donation or inheritance rather
than sale, there might still be deeds being recorded in the GRS for many
decades to come. To address this issue the Scottish Law Commission has
recommended not only that all dispositions should trigger a switch of
registers but that the Keeper should have power to enter properties on the Land
Register even without the owner's consent, subject to certain safeguards and to
remission of fees.[18] Voluntary registration in the Land Register is possible
under the current system, at the Keeper's discretion, and the present policy is
to encourage it.[19]

Primary and secondary rights

For the purposes of land registration a distinction can be made between primary   8–04
and secondary real rights in land. The Act itself does not express matters thus,[20]
but the distinction is implicit. The primary real rights are ownership[21] and long
lease, which is to say a lease for more than 20 years. All other real rights in land
are secondary. The sale of a primary real right triggers a compulsory switch to
the new register.[22]

This means that the first time a property is sold after the county became
operational there is a first registration in the Land Register. The same is true for
the first transfer of an existing long lease. Similarly, if a primary real right is
still in the GRS but another primary real right is carved out of it, the new
primary real right goes into the new register while the balance of the existing
primary real right remains, for the time being, in the old register.[23] This happens

---

[17] But, of course, once a property has been switched into the Land Register, non-sale dispositions will enter the Land Register, not the GRS.

[18] Scottish Law Commission, Report on *Land Registration* (Scot. Law Com. No.222, 2010)
paras 33.16 to 33.66.

[19] 1979 Act s.2(1)(b). 1,200 such applications were accepted in 2009/10: see Registers of
Scotland, *Annual Report and Accounts 2009–2010*, p.14.

[20] And indeed shows its origins in, still feudal, times by the use of "interest in land" instead of
the more precise "real right in land" found in modern statutes.

[21] Before the abolition of feudalism, there was *dominium utile* (which is now simple ownership)
and also various levels of superiority, all of which were primary real rights for the purposes of land
registration.

[22] 1979 Act s.2(1)(a)(ii). However, the assignation of a lease triggers a switch even without
payment of consideration: see s.2(1)(a)(v).

[23] 1979 Act s.2(1)(a)(i).

when a long lease is granted. The ownership retained by the landlord remains, for the time being, in the old register, while the newly created long lease enters the new register. It is also possible for a lease to be in the old register while the property is in the new one. This would happen if the lease was granted before the county became operational, and thereafter the property was sold, while the lease remained in the hands of the original lessee.

The rule for secondary real rights is different. The rule is that a newly created secondary real right is entered in the same register as the primary real right to which it relates.[24] For example, if a standard security is granted over land which is still in the old register, the security is also entered in the old register. But a standard security over land which is in the new register will itself enter the new register.

The switch operates in one direction only. Once a title is registered in the Land Register, all subsequent rights are registered there also.[25] To the GRS there is no return.

How soon should the grantee register?

8–05   There is no time limit for registration in either the Land Register or the GRS. The grantee can rush or dawdle to Register House. The disposition (or other deed) remains valid indefinitely.[26] However, the grantee, if a natural person, must still be alive at the time of registration.[27] If the grantee has died, the disposition does not cease to be valid, and the executor can complete title using the disposition and the confirmation as the midcouples.[28] If the grantee is a company, or other juristic person, it must still exist at the time of registration. But although there is no time limit for registration, in practice it should be done as soon as possible. One reason is to protect the grantee against the possible insolvency of the granter.[29] The standard letter of obligation stipulates for registration within 14 days.[30] Unless the application is later rejected or withdrawn, the date of receipt is the date of registration. Two deeds arriving on the same day rank equally.[31]

Registration dues

8–06   The idea is that the registers should be self-financing. Registration costs money, and has become more expensive since the introduction of registration of title. The fees for registration in the two property registers are the same; but since running the Land Register is more expensive, fees paid for the GRS subsidise the Land Register. The fee levels bear some relation to the financial position of Registers of Scotland. Thus in 2006, when times were good and a handsome surplus had accrued, it was possible to make significant

---

[24] 1979 Act s.2(3).

[25] 1979 Act s.2(3), (4).

[26] By law. Occasionally (and this was especially the case in feu dispositions) one sees an express time limit of, say, six months.

[27] Titles to Land Consolidation (Scotland) Act 1868 s.142.

[28] In a GRS case where the grantee has died without recording there will normally have to be a notice of title in favour of the executor. See further below, Ch.25.

[29] *Burnett's Trustee v Grainger* [2004] UKHL 8; 2004 S.C. (HL) 19.

[30] For letters of obligation, see below, Ch.9.

[31] Titles to Land Consolidation (Scotland) Act 1868 s.142; 1979 Act ss.4(3) and 7. Before the 1979 Act, deeds ranked not only by date but by hour of registration.

reductions.[32] But the current fees, effective from January 10, 2011, reflect the decline in income caused by the recession and introduce some significant increases over previous levels.[33] The fee is due when the application is made and is paid by (variable) direct debit arrangements made by law firms.[34]

For dispositions the fee is based on the price paid, or, where there is no price, on the value of the property. Conventional paper-based transactions are more expensive than electronic transactions made under the automated registration of title to land ("ARTL") system.[35] For ordinary dispositions the fee is as follows:

	Consideration/value	Paper fee	ARTL fee
Not exceeding	£50,000	£60	£50
Not exceeding	£100,000	£120	£90
Not exceeding	£150,000	£240	£180
Not exceeding	£200,000	£360	£270
Not exceeding	£300,000	£480	£360
Not exceeding	£500,000	£600	£450
Not exceeding	£700,000	£720	£540
Not exceeding	£1,000,000	£840	£660
Not exceeding	£2,000,000	£1,000	£800
Not exceeding	£3,000,000	£3,000	£2,500
Not exceeding	£5,000,000	£5,000	£4,500
Exceeding	£5,000,000	£7,500	£7,000

A disposition which creates real burdens or servitudes will need to be registered against two or more title sheets,[36] with a fee of £60 for each title sheet after the first. Registration of a standard security attracts a flat fee of £60 for paper transactions and £50 for those using ARTL. So where a house is bought for £360,000 with the help of a bank loan, the total fee is £660 or £500 depending on whether ARTL is used.

For registrations in the Land Register part of the fee is a premium for title insurance. It is thus curious that the same fee is payable even if such insurance is refused (by exclusion of indemnity). It is equally curious that the fee is the same in the GRS, where no title insurance is obtained.

The Land Register and the GRS compared

The Land Register and the GRS work in different ways. The GRS is a register 8–07
of deeds. It consists of copies of countless deeds stretching back to the

---

[32] Fees in the Registers of Scotland (Amendment) Order 2006 (SSI 2006/600).
[33] Fees in the Registers of Scotland Amendment Order 2010 (SSI 2010/404).
[34] Land Registers (Scotland) Act 1995.
[35] For ARTL, see below, para.8–23.
[36] See below, paras 13–12 and 13–26.

establishment of the register in 1617. These are divided by county, but apart from that there is no arrangement, except chronological. The deeds affecting a given plot are thus scattered in an unconnected way over vast numbers of record volumes. They are traceable by the indexes and by the search sheets. The GRS is not a register of title, as such. Nowhere in the register is there anything which gathers together the real rights in a plot of land and states authoritatively who holds them. Moreover, although, subject to minor qualifications, registration in the GRS is a necessary condition of obtaining a real right, it is not a sufficient condition, for a deed in the GRS may be void. Suppose that Rachel dispones her farm to Tara. A small strip of land which is included in the disposition, and which is possessed as part of the farm, actually belongs to a neighbour. Despite the recording of the disposition, Tara does not acquire ownership of that strip. *Nemo plus juris ad alium transferre potest quam ipse haberet*. The disposition would be ineffectual to that extent and the neighbour would still be the owner. Thus, the fact that there exists in the GRS a deed ostensibly passing ownership to X does not necessarily mean that X thereby became the owner. Hence, the task of ascertaining from the GRS what are the real rights in a plot of land or a house, and in whom such rights are vested, is not a straightforward one. It is a task for a trained conveyancer.[37]

The Land Register employs a different system, which is used in a number of other countries, called registration of title. In registration of title the register maps the boundaries of each plot, or title unit, and says who has what real rights in it. The Land Register, as well as being divided into counties, is divided into title units, one for each primary real right which exists in each separate property, and each unit has its own title sheet, identified by letters (indicating the county) and numbers, such as REN123456. So if a property is subject to a long lease, there will be two title sheets for that property, one for the right of ownership and the other for the lease. To change the real rights the same deeds are used as in the GRS system—dispositions, standard securities, and so forth—although under ARTL the deeds are virtual rather than actual. Instead of being recorded,[38] however, such deeds are used by the Keeper as the basis for altering the title sheet. Registration (i.e. alteration of the title sheet) is necessary, in the sense that, subject to minor qualifications, there can be no real right without registration. But the system goes further than this. In registration of title, there is, again subject to minor qualifications, no such thing as a void registration.[39] Registration is, thus, not only necessary to obtain a real right, but it is also sufficient.[40] Whereas in the GRS the role of the Keeper is limited and passive, in registration of title the Keeper's role is extensive and active. The Scottish Law Commission has referred to the "Midas touch"—to the idea that, whatever the Keeper touches turns, not to gold as in the legend, but to good.[41] If the Keeper registers a right, it immediately becomes valid, whatever the status of the deed underlying the entry. This Midas touch has been subject to

---

[37] See above, paras 7–13 et seq.

[38] Though the Keeper does retain a copy of all such deeds.

[39] One possible exception would be where a registration was made in the name of a non-existent person. Another would be where the land was insufficiently identified at the time of registration for ownership to be conferred: see *PMP Plus v Keeper of the Registers of Scotland*, 2009 S.L.T. (Lands Tr) 2, discussed above at para.7–07.

[40] 1979 Act s.3(1).

[41] Scottish Law Commission, Report on *Land Registration* (Scot. Law Com. No.222, 2010), para.13.9.

severe criticism by the Law Commission,[42] which recommends its replacement by a rule of *bona fide* acquisition.[43] While it works well enough in some
cases, in others it produces results which are hardly acceptable; for the trouble
with the Midas touch is that it is indiscriminate, affecting all rights equally and
without any regard to their merit.[44]

In the GRS system, title—good, bad or indifferent—flows from the recorded
deed. In the Land Register, by contrast, title does not flow from the deed, but
from the Register. Strictly, the deed is not registered. Its function is, so to
speak, to persuade the Keeper to make an entry in the Register. This principle
has many consequences. For instance, whereas in the GRS system a void deed
will mean a void title, in the Land Register if the Keeper makes an entry on the
basis of a void deed, the entry is not void and so the title is not void. Again, if
a deed that is not void but is voidable is reduced, the consequences in the GRS
system are dramatic, for the effect of the reduction is that the deed becomes
void, and as a result the title becomes void. But in the Land Register the reduction of a voidable deed has, in itself, no real effect. Title does not flow from
the deed, so its reduction does not alter the title. It will merely make the title
inaccurate, and hence subject to the possibility of rectification.

From what has just been said it will be seen that the Land Register cannot
normally be wrong. Nonetheless, "inaccuracy" can still occur.[45] But here again
the users of the system are protected, for a person who suffers as a result of an
inaccuracy is normally entitled either to demand "rectification" of the Register,
or, in the alternative, "indemnity", i.e. compensation from the Keeper. If rectification is granted, then the person who loses the property normally gets
compensation. So whether rectification is allowed or refused the Keeper will
usually end up paying compensation. As between two competitors for title, one
gets the "mud" (i.e. the property), and the other the money.[46] That is a great
advantage of the system over the GRS, where it is possible (if unusual) to end
up with neither the mud nor the money. However, one advantage of the GRS is
that once one does have the mud one is absolutely secure. By contrast, a Land
Register title is always slightly precarious. The fact that title flows from the
Register makes it certain that one gets the mud in the first place—but also
means that one can lose it, if the Register proves fickle in its affections and
allows someone else to be registered in one's place.[47] "Easy come" leads
inexorably to "easy go".[48]

With the GRS the question "who is the owner?" can be difficult to answer.
With the Land Register it is almost always easy to answer. But it must not be
supposed that in consequence the Land Register is always plain sailing. Once
the easy question of ownership has been answered, there occasionally remain

---

[42] Report on *Land Registration*, paras 13.11–13.28.

[43] Report on *Land Registration*, Pt 21.

[44] Thus in the legend, King Midas touches, and so turns to gold, not only ordinary household
items but also his own daughter. Under the 1979 Act system the Keeper frequently does the equivalent of turning her daughter into gold.

[45] See below, para.8–13.

[46] This turn of phrase comes from T.W. Mapp, *Torrens' Elusive Title* (1978), para.4.24. "Torrens"
systems of land registration are common round the world. The 1979 Act system has important
affinities with the Torrens family.

[47] *Willemse v French* [2011] CSOH 51; 2011 G.W.D. 12-282 especially at paras 7 and 22, per
Lord Tyre.

[48] This phrase too is that of the perceptive Mapp: see *Torrens' Elusive Title*, paras 3.13 and 4.26.

difficult questions, notably: (i) is the Register inaccurate? (ii) if so is it rectifiable? and (iii) is indemnity payable, and if so to whom? Similar remarks can be made about subordinate real rights such as standard securities.

THE LAND REGISTER

Primary and secondary real rights

8–08   An indispensable if now rather elderly guide to the Land Register is the second edition of Registers of Scotland's *Registration of Title Practice Book* ("ROTPB"), which dates from 2000 and is available both in hard copy and online.[49] A revision is promised. In addition, a great deal of useful information can be found in the *Legal Manual*, available online only.[50] Written for the guidance of staff at Registers of Scotland, and up to date, this gives the official line on a large number of topics. Finally, there is much of interest on the Registers of Scotland website.[51]

As mentioned above,[52] the 1979 Act divides real rights into two classes, primary and secondary. There are two kinds of primary real right, namely ownership and long lease (i.e. a lease of over 20 years).[53] Other rights are secondary. Examples are standard securities, real burdens, and servitudes. Primary real rights have their own title sheet. Secondary real rights do not, and are registered on the title sheet of the primary real right to which they relate.[54]

The title sheet

8–09   The title sheet is part of the Register: the Register is composed of title sheets. The Register is kept in digital form and can be examined online, for a fee, using the Registers Direct service.[55] The title sheet is divided into four parts.[56] (a) The property section defines the property. There is a verbal description, typically little more than the postal address, coupled with a detailed plan, based on the Ordnance Survey map.[57] Pertinents such as servitudes may also be included. (b) The proprietorship section names the person who owns the property. (c) The charges section lists any heritable securities which affect the property. (d) The burdens section lists the real burdens and, sometimes, servitudes. Only those real rights (burdens, securities, etc.) listed in the title sheet affect a proprietor, except for overriding interests.[58] The title sheet thus gives an almost complete picture of the state of the title. Any educated person can understand it.

---

[49] *http://www.ros.gov.uk/rotbook/index.html.*
[50] *http://www.ros.gov.uk/foi/legal/Frame~Home.htm.*
[51] *http://www.ros.gov.uk.*
[52] See above, para.8–04.
[53] Before the entry into force of the 2000 Act there were three kinds of primary real right, namely *dominium utile, dominium directum* and long lease.
[54] 1979 Act s.5(1).
[55] *www.ros.gov.uk/registersdirect/index.html.*
[56] Land Registration (Scotland) Rules 2006 (SSI 2006/485) Pt II.
[57] For descriptions see below, Ch.12.
[58] 1979 Act s.3(1)(a). For overriding interests, see below.

Certificates of title (i): the land certificate

There are two kinds of "certificate of title", namely the land certificate and 8–10 the charge certificate. The land certificate is a certified paper or electronic ("dematerialised") copy of the title sheet. This is what the owner will receive.[59] A land certificate is thus an extract from the register. At one time it was different from the ordinary or "office" copy of the title sheet which anyone can obtain,[60] but today it has lost its distinctive status and, since 2006, has no longer had to accompany applications for registration. The Scottish Law Commission has recommended the abolition of both types of certificate of title.[61]

Certificates of title (ii): the charge certificate

A standard security is not a primary real right and so does not attract its own 8–11 title sheet. Instead it is registered in the charges section of the title sheet to which it relates. However, the Keeper issues to the creditor a document in paper or electronic form called a charge certificate which contains the security deed itself, with certification that it has been entered on the title sheet.[62] As with a land certificate, the role of this type of certificate is purely evidential. The security exists as a real right by virtue of its entry in the title sheet.

Overriding interests

The principle of registration of title is that all real rights affecting a property 8–12 are entered in the title sheet, and that, consequently, any right not so entered has no real effect. But this ideal is not fully realisable in practice.[63] Hence, there exists a category of rights called overriding interests[64] whose validity is unaffected if they are omitted from the title sheet. Servitudes are one example, the reason for this being that a servitude can be created by implication or prescription and until 2004 could be created by unregistered deed,[65] so that the Keeper can never be certain that she knows of all servitudes. Other important examples are short leases, floating charges, and the occupancy rights of spouses and civil partners. Even here the ideal is for overriding interests to be noted in the title sheet, and (with some exceptions) the Keeper may note them if she knows of their existence.[66]

Inaccuracy

The 1979 Act makes certain provisions for the situation where the Register is 8–13 "inaccurate". At first sight it might seem impossible that the Register could ever be inaccurate. It is not as if real rights existed independently of the Register, so that the Register could somehow fail to reflect their existence or

---

[59] 1979 Act s.5(2); Land Registration (Scotland) Rules 2006 r.15 and form 6. A long lease has its own title sheet and there will be a separate land certificate.

[60] 1979 Act s.6(5). An office copy is also a form 15 report since it is requested on a form 15.

[61] Report on *Land Registration* (Scot. Law Com. No.222, 2010), para.37.10.

[62] 1979 Act s.5(3); Land Registration (Scotland) Rules 2006 r.16 and form 7.

[63] Any more than it is realisable under the GRS system, which has an almost identical class of overriding interests (not so-called).

[64] Defined in the 1979 Act s.28(1). Not all overriding interests are real rights.

[65] See below, paras 13–26 and 13–27.

[66] 1979 Act s.6(4)(b). In certain situations the Keeper is actually obliged to note them if she knows of them: s.6(4)(a). The exceptions are short leases and occupancy rights.

nature.[67] To say that the Register is wrong is thus rather like saying that a passage in Hamlet is a misquotation from Shakespeare. Suppose that Oliver owns land, and Charles forges Oliver's signature on a disposition in favour of Barry. Barry applies for registration, and is successful. Barry is now owner. He is owner because the Register says so, the Midas touch having operated; and the Register cannot be wrong.[68] That being the case, what is "inaccuracy" and how is inaccuracy possible?

While no definition is given in the 1979 Act, it seems to be that an entry on the Register is inaccurate if it was not justified, or is no longer justified, by the deed which induced it. An entry can thus be inaccurate in two ways. Either it can be inaccurate from the beginning, as in the example just given; or it can start life as an accurate entry but become inaccurate as a result of events. For instance, suppose that Oliver is owner, and then Charles, by fraud, induces Oliver to dispone to him. Charles is registered as owner. The disposition, though good (for the moment), is voidable by reason of the fraud. Oliver reduces it. At this stage, but only at this stage, the Register becomes inaccurate.

An entry does not cease to be effective just because it is, or has become, inaccurate. Inaccuracy may not matter at all. Whether or not it matters depends on whether rectification[69] is possible. Sometimes it is, and sometimes it is not.

Inaccuracies can arise for a variety of reasons, not least the fault of the applicant. One source is error at Register House, especially on first registration. The Law Society of Scotland's Conveyancing Committee has noted the following as being complained about by solicitors: (i) An incorrect postcode or address. (ii) The title number is not consistent throughout the document. (iii) The plan does not show the boundaries correctly. (iv) The proprietorship section does not contain the correct details and designations. (v) All prior heritable securities have not been discharged or ranking agreements have been incorrectly shown. (vi) Real burdens are not correctly stated or irrelevant burdens have not been excluded. (vii) There are grammatical or spelling errors.[70]

Rectification

8–14 In principle an inaccuracy on the Land Register can be rectified by the Keeper, whether on request,[71] on her own initiative, or on being ordered by the court.[72] Rectification, if allowed, does not have retrospective effect: the past cannot be altered.[73] Rectification cannot normally proceed if it would prejudice a proprietor in possession.[74] Sometimes, of course, rectification is to the benefit of such a proprietor, for example the removal of real burdens or other encumbrances.[75]

---

[67] Overriding interests, however, exist independently of the Register, and are not made any more real merely by being noted there.

[68] It is otherwise for the GRS, where the disposition, though recorded, would still be void, and since title flows from recorded deeds, the title would likewise be void.

[69] Rectification within the meaning of the 1979 Act is not to be confused with judicial rectification in the sense of s.8 of the Law Reform (Miscellaneous Provisions) (Scotland) Act 1985, on which see below, Ch.20.

[70] (2003) 48 J.L.S.S. Nov./61.

[71] An application for rectification is made on form 9.

[72] 1979 Act s.9(1). The court includes the Lands Tribunal.

[73] *Stevenson-Hamilton's Exrs v McStay*, 1999 S.L.T. 1175; *Keeper of the Registers of Scotland v MRS Hamilton Ltd*, 2000 S.C. 271.

[74] See below, paras 8–15 and 8–16.

[75] An example is *Brookfield Developments Ltd v Keeper of the Registers of Scotland*, 1989 S.L.T. (Lands Tr) 105.

More usually it is not. If rectification is competent, it is unclear whether it could still be refused on a discretionary basis, with indemnity being paid instead. It depends on what "may" means in s.9(1). In one case it has been interpreted as conferring not only a power but also a discretion.[76] If an application for rectification is successful, any party prejudiced will normally be entitled to compensation ("indemnity") from the Keeper.[77]

Proprietor in possession: general

Perhaps surprisingly in view of its importance, the term "proprietor in posses- 8–15 sion" is not defined in the legislation. For example it is not stated whether the "possession" can be civil (indirect) as well as natural (direct) possession. The meaning of the expression was considered in *Kaur v Singh*.[78] There the First Division, having decided that a heritable creditor was not a proprietor in possession, inclined to limit "proprietor" to the holder of a primary real right. "Possession", however, was thought to include civil possession, so that owners who let their houses would still be proprietors in possession. Courts have been unable to agree as to whether there can be a proprietor in possession in relation to a servitude.[79] The relevant date for possession is also not given in the legislation but appears to be the date on which the application for rectification is made or, perhaps, the date on which the Keeper issues her decision.[80]

The criterion is perhaps a crude one.[81] If a disposition erroneously conveys part of a neighbouring property, the neighbour is expropriated,[82] and if the disponee has taken possession of the extra area the neighbour cannot normally get title back, but is limited to claiming compensation. Compensation may be sufficient, but often is not. Cases of this sort have happened and have led to much criticism of the 1979 Act. The rule about possession also encourages self-help as between parties, with results that may be unacceptable or absurd.[83]

When being a proprietor in possession is no defence

Even a proprietor in possession is not always secure against rectification. The 8–16 legislation provides five situations where rectification remains possible.[84] The first is where the purpose of rectification is to note or correct an overriding interest. The second is where all parties having an interest agree in writing.

---

[76] *Kaur v Singh*, 1998 S.C. 233, per Lord Hamilton. With respect we have reservations about this interpretation.

[77] See below, para.8.19.

[78] *Kaur v Singh*, 1999 S.C. 180. For commentary, with some facts not in the reports, see 1997 S.C.L.R. 1075 and 1998 S.C.L.R. 862. This litigation is of considerable significance for registration of title. For the sequel see *Kaur v Singh (No.2)*, 2000 S.L.T. 1323, dealing with the quantum of the Keeper's liability. See also above, para.7–11.

[79] Compare *Griffiths v Keeper of the Registers of Scotland*, Unreported December 20, 2002 Lands Tribunal with *Yaxley v Glen* [2007] CSOH 90; 2007 S.L.T. 756 and *Orkney Housing Association Ltd v Atkinson*, Unreported July 14, 2011, Kirkwall Sheriff Court. See Reid and Gretton, *Conveyancing 2007*, pp.124–26.

[80] *Burr v Keeper of the Registers of Scotland*, Unreported November 12, 2010 Lands Tribunal, discussed in Reid and Gretton, *Conveyancing 2010*, pp.159–62.

[81] Scottish Law Commission, Report on *Land Registration* (Scot. Law Com. No.222, 2010), paras 21.22–21.25.

[82] Due to the Midas touch, discussed above at para.8–07.

[83] See above, para.7–11.

[84] 1979 Act s.9(3).

The third is where the inaccuracy has been caused by the "fraud or careless-ness" of the proprietor. Carelessness requires reasonable foresight of the inac-curacy and therefore a degree of knowledge on the part of the proprietor.[85] Carelessness of the proprietor's solicitor is attributed to the proprietor.[86] Causation is required as well as fraud or carelessness. So if the Keeper knows of a defect but proceeds to register regardless, it seems that the resulting inac-curacy is caused by the Keeper and not by the proprietor in possession. The same is likely to be true if both proprietor in possession and Keeper were care-less but the carelessness of the latter greatly exceeded that of the former.[87]

In order for a proprietor in possession to "cause" an inaccuracy, the careless-ness must be present at or before the time of registration. The evidence is often the application form for registration. If the statements on the form turn out to have been incorrect the Keeper has the possibility of arguing that the proprietor was careless (or even fraudulent) and so not protected against rectification.[88] Needless to say, the Keeper retains the application forms for future scrutiny. One might say, with only a small degree of exaggeration, that a registered title is only as good as its underlying application form.[89] In this connection, it should be noted that the application forms, as well as containing a battery of particular questions, have a catch-all question asking whether there are "any facts and circumstances material to the right or title of the applicant which have not already been disclosed in this application or its accompanying documents".[90] In practice, purchasers are most at risk in first registrations, where a new title sheet is made up partly in reliance on the statements in the forms. In subsequent transactions, purchasers are entitled to rely on the Register, and are not careless merely because they happen to know that the Register is in fact inaccurate.[91]

The fourth case is where the point is one about which indemnity has been excluded. For example, Sandra applies for the first registration of a plot of land. The Keeper checks her (GRS) title and finds that, although good for the most part, there is doubt about its validity in respect of a small area. She regis-ters Sandra as owner of the whole, but in respect of the small area she excludes indemnity. A neighbour, Nigel, now points out that he was[92] the owner of this area and asks for rectification in his favour. Since indemnity had been excluded, rectification is possible. It will be observed that exclusion of indemnity has a double consequence, both as to indemnity and as to rectifiability. Conversely, if indemnity is not excluded the proprietor has a double protection: normally the title will not be subject to rectification, and, if for some reason it is never-theless rectified, he or she should be protected by indemnity.

---

[85] *Dougbar Properties Ltd v Keeper of the Registers of Scotland*, 1999 S.C. 513.

[86] e.g. *McCoach v Keeper of the Registers of Scotland*, Unreported December 19, 2008, Lands Tr, discussed in Reid and Gretton, *Conveyancing 2008*, pp.121–33.

[87] *McCoach v Keeper of the Registers of Scotland*, Unreported December 19, 2008, Lands Tr.

[88] e.g. *Stevenson-Hamilton's Executors v McStay (No.2)*, 2001 S.L.T. 694. Fraud/carelessness has a double effect: it opens the door to the possibility of rectification, even against a proprietor in possession, and it cancels or restricts the Keeper's indemnity. For the latter see ss.12(3)(n) and 13(4).

[89] For the application forms, see below, para.8–20. There is an obvious analogy here with insur-ance law. The proposal form becomes the basis of the contract of insurance, and a misstatement in it may vitiate the contract.

[90] Question 14 in form 1 and question 10 in form 2.

[91] *Dougbar Properties Ltd v Keeper of the Registers of Scotland*, 1999 S.C. 513.

[92] "Was" not "is" because the registration in favour of Sandra, albeit wrong, made her the owner.

The fifth case is where rectification is consequential on the judicial rectification of the underlying deed. This topic is explored further below, in Ch.20.[93]

Reduction

Reduction of a disposition[94] has, of itself, no effect on a registered title, because 8–17 title flows from the Register and not directly from the deed. The deed is important, but only indirectly, as being the justification for what the Register says. So how can the reduction of the deed be given effect to? Normally there are just two ways in which the Register can be changed: by registration and by rectification.[95] In GRS titles the extract decree of reduction is registered. But protracted litigation has established that this cannot be done in the Land Register. If a decree of reduction is to enter the Land Register, this can only be by rectification and not by registration as such.[96] But even rectification may not be possible to give effect to a decree of reduction.[97] If rectification turns out to be barred (typically because there is a proprietor in possession, who has not been guilty of "fraud or carelessness", and there is no exclusion of indemnity) then the reduction cannot be given effect to at all, in which case the deed is void but the title based on the deed is unaffected. However, in such a situation pursuers can in some cases achieve their objective by another route, namely an action against the owner compelling the grant of a disposition.[98] The disposition could then be registered as of right.[99]

Rectification: further restrictions

The legislation says that the Keeper must rectify when so ordered by the court, 8–18 but may also rectify by her own administrative act. This can lead to problems. It can be argued that a person adversely affected by the rectification is deprived of property without due process of law, in a manner inconsistent with the European Convention on Human Rights.[100] As a public official, the Keeper is bound to respect the Convention. If the argument is correct, it may suggest that

---

[93] See below, para. 20–11.

[94] Reduction is aimed at the deed, not at the title. The title is affected only in so far as the deed is affected.

[95] One of a number of conceptual difficulties with the 1979 Act is a failure to distinguish adequately between the two.

[96] *Short's Trustee v Keeper of the Registers of Scotland*, 1996 S.C. (HL) 14. See Reid, (1996) 1 S.L.P.Q. 265. This litigation, the costs of which doubtless exceeded the value of the property many times over, well illustrates the shortcomings of the legislation.

[97] Procedurally the simplest course is often to have conclusions for (a) reduction of the deed and (b) rectification of the Register. See e.g. *Stevenson-Hamilton's Exrs v McStay (No.2)*, 2001 S.L.T. 694. The Scottish Law Commission has suggested that registration should be allowed in respect of the reduction of voidable deeds: see Report on *Land Registration* (Scot. Law Com. No.222, 20104), Pt 28.

[98] *Short's Trustee v Chung*, 1998 S.C. 105; affirmed 1999 S.C. 471. This was the third and last stage of an astonishing saga. For the first two stages see *Short's Trustee v Chung*, 1991 S.L.T. 472; and *Short's Trustee v Keeper of the Registers of Scotland*, 1996 S.C. (HL) 14. For discussion see Reid and Gretton, *Conveyancing 1999*, pp.68–71. Another possible route, reduction of the entry in the Register, was rejected in *Foster v Keeper of the Registers of Scotland* [2006] CSOH 65; 2006 S.L.T. 513.

[99] The protection of the proprietor in possession is confined to rectification and has no application to registration.

[100] Specifically art.6 read with art.1 of the First Protocol. A comparable argument could be made in respect of registration in a case where the applicant was not entitled to the property, but this was rejected in *Foster v Keeper of the Registers of Scotland* [2006] CSOH 65; 2006 S.L.T. 513.

the Keeper should not rectify unless those involved have consented or the court has so ordered.[101]

Even without the human rights dimension, the Keeper has no power to rectify (except with the consent of those involved) where the alleged inaccuracy derives from a deed which, though voidable,[102] stands unreduced. The reason is simple: until such reduction has happened, the Register is accurate.[103] A voidable deed remains valid unless or until it is reduced, and in practice voidable deeds are often never reduced at all, for a variety of reasons.

Indemnity

8-19   The Keeper is obliged to indemnify, i.e. to pay compensation to, certain persons who suffer loss.[104] She may be liable not only for loss caused by her fault, but also for loss arising without any fault on her part. Compensation payments are funded by the fees charged for registration. In effect it is a compulsory title insurance scheme.[105] Indemnity is normally due when loss is caused by an inaccuracy in the Register, and is payable to the person who suffers that loss. Who suffers the loss depends on whether the inaccuracy, on being discovered, is rectified or not. There are thus two possibilities. The first is that the Register is rectified, in which case the person who suffers loss is the person against whom the rectification is made.[106] The second is that the Register is not rectified, in which case the person who suffers loss is the person who suffers by the fact that the inaccuracy stands uncorrected.[107] For example, suppose that there are two neighbouring plots of land, owned by Alan and Beatrice respectively, and by some error the Register has the boundary wrong, giving Alan a strip of what should be Beatrice's land. The Register is inaccurate. If it is rectified, Alan loses ownership of the strip, and so he is presumptively entitled to be compensated by the Keeper. If the Register is not rectified, Beatrice fails to recover what should be hers, and she is therefore presumptively entitled to be compensated by the Keeper. In short, if the Register is inaccurate, then indemnity is presumptively payable whether it is rectified or not, but to different persons in each case: indemnity for rectification, and indemnity for non-rectification.[108] Some rectifications involve relatively trivial matters and do not change the legal rights of parties, in which case no indemnity is due.[109]

---

[101] For fuller discussion see Gretton, in Alan Boyle, Chris Himsworth, Andrea Loux and Hector MacQueen (eds), *Human Rights and Scots Law* (2002).

[102] If the deed is void then the issues are not quite the same, but whether a deed is voidable or void itself may need judicial determination.

[103] See further Reid and Gretton, *Conveyancing 2000*, p.110. *Higgins v North Lanarkshire Council*, 2001 S.L.T. (Lands Tr) 2 is a valuable case in many respects but may be criticised on the various grounds mentioned above.

[104] See McDonald, (2001) 55 Prop. L.B. 3 and (2002) 56 Prop. L.B. 1.

[105] 1979 Act s.24.

[106] 1979 Act s.12(1)(a).

[107] 1979 Act s.12(1)(b). Section 12(1) also imposes liability on the Keeper in two other cases, namely if she loses a document and if she issues a land certificate with an error. On the latter provision, see *Keeper of the Registers of Scotland v MRS Hamilton Ltd*, 2000 S.C. 271.

[108] Because of the way the 1979 Act is framed, it is sometimes said that "whoever wins, the Keeper loses". This is not entirely true, but there is much truth in it.

[109] These are "actual" inaccuracies as opposed to "bijural" inaccuracies. For this terminology, see Scottish Law Commission, Report on *Land Registration* (Scot. Law Com. No.222, 2010), paras 17.6–17.11.

Even in cases of loss, indemnity is not always due. Exclusions of indemnity may be either express or implied. At the time of registration the Keeper can expressly exclude indemnity either for the whole title, or in respect of particular aspects only,[110] although this is uncommon. Any exclusion of indemnity will be stated on the land certificate and so will be obvious to purchasers. In addition, there are implied exclusions of indemnity. Section 12(3) of the 1979 Act contains a long and miscellaneous list of exclusions which apply to all titles. These include: reductions under the Bankruptcy (Scotland) Act 1985 and certain other statutes[111]; minor inaccuracies in boundaries[112]; inability to enforce real burdens; matters concerning overriding interests; and fraud or carelessness on the part of the claimant.[113] The precise meaning of many of these exclusions is unclear. The last is of particular importance, because it means any inaccuracy or omission in the form 1 or form 3 has the potential to count as carelessness, with consequences that may be serious: this is very like the rule in insurance law that the proposal form is the "basis of the contract" and that the proposer must disclose everything material.[114]

The amount paid out by way of indemnity is surprisingly small. In 2009/10, for example, the Keeper paid out £444,600 in respect of 102 cases, representing 0.04 per cent of the total number of Land Register cases despatched during the year. The single largest category of error was mapping.[115]

As well as liability for indemnity under the legislation, the Keeper is presumably subject to the normal law of negligence and might incur liability on that ground also. This might be a useful alternative to a claimant in circumstances where the amount payable under the legislation does not adequately reflect his or her loss.[116]

Application forms

The procedure for registration depends on whether the application is made on 8–20 paper, as it usually is, or made electronically under the ARTL system. A discussion of ARTL can be postponed until later[117]; for the moment we are concerned only with traditional paper applications.

---

[110] 1979 Act s.12(2). Just as the Act gives little guidance as to when the Keeper should accept or reject an application, so it gives little guidance as to when, on accepting an application, he should grant or withhold indemnity.

[111] For a strained and unsatisfactory interpretation of this provision, see *Short's Trustee v Keeper of the Registers of Scotland*, 1996 S.C. (HL) 14.

[112] Section 12(3)(d) provides that "there shall be no entitlement to indemnity in respect of loss where . . . the loss arises as a result of any inaccuracy in the delineation of boundaries shown in a title sheet, being an inaccuracy which could not have been rectified by reference to the Ordnance Map . . .". The ROTPB, para.4.26 says this is "to cover the limitations in scaling". That interpretation may be right, but we confess to finding s.12(3)(d) hard to understand.

[113] For the fraud and carelessness exclusion, see e.g. *Dougbar Properties Ltd v Keeper of the Registers of Scotland*, 1999 S.C. 513; and *Stevenson-Hamilton's Executors v McStay (No.2)*, 2001 S.L.T. 694.

[114] The same point arises in respect of rectification against a proprietor in possession on the ground of fraud or carelessness: see above, para.8–16.

[115] *Registers of Scotland Annual Report and Accounts 2009–2010*, p.26.

[116] *Braes v Keeper of the Registers of Scotland* [2009] CSOH 176; 2010 S.L.T. 689 is the only attempt so far to rely on the common law of negligence. In the event, the factual basis of the pursuer's claim could not be established. See Reid and Gretton, *Conveyancing 2009*, pp.128–30.

[117] See below, para.8–23.

A paper application for registration in the Land Register must be made on the appropriate form. There are three.[118] Form 1 is used for a first registration, i.e. for the disposition or other deed which triggers the switch from the GRS to the Land Register. Form 2 is the standard form for other cases. However, where part only of registered land is being transferred, form 3 should be used. The forms contain a number of questions not all of which can be answered by the grantees' solicitor, and the normal practice is for the form to be completed in draft and then revised by the solicitor for the granters. The questions must be taken seriously: by asking certain key questions, for example as to the state of possession, or occupancy rights,[119] or whether a company is in liquidation, the Keeper is passing the responsibility for verifying the position to the applicant's solicitor—a practice known jauntily as "tell me, don't show me". If the answers turn out to be incorrect, this may form the basis for a later rectification of the Register on the ground of carelessness (or even fraud).[120] Because of the form's importance a copy should be retained. Application forms are signed by the grantees or (as usually in practice) by their solicitors. As circumstances can change quickly, it is important that the forms are as up to date as possible. If there is a significant gap between the date on which a form is certified and the date of its receipt at the registers (more than five to ten working days, depending on the type of transaction), the Keeper may return the form and ask for its content to be re-certified.[121]

Since November 2008 all application forms and accompanying deeds have been scanned and are held by the Keeper in electronic form.[122] To assist scanning, forms must be typed in block capitals using only prescribed fonts and taking care to keep within the text boxes.[123] Alternatively, and preferably, the forms can be completed online using Register of Scotland's eForms service.[124]

A separate form is required for each deed, and all deeds submitted at the same time are listed in a single inventory, known as form 4. Thus, buyers of land already registered in the Land Register who are also taking out a loan must complete form 2 in respect of each of the disposition, standard security, and discharge of the existing security (if there is one).[125] A form 4 is also completed listing the three deeds. Receipt is acknowledged by email or letter.[126] In appropriate cases an application must be accompanied by an SDLT certificate.[127]

---

[118] Land Registration (Scotland) Rules 2006 (SSI 2006/485) r.9(1). For practical guidance, see ROTPB, Ch.5. Appendix A of David A. Brand, Andrew J.M. Steven and Scott Wortley, *Professor McDonald's Conveyancing Manual*, 7th edn (2004) contains useful examples of completed application forms.

[119] See below, para.10–14.

[120] 1979 Act s.9(3)(a)(iii). See above, para.8–16.

[121] *Practice Note*, December 4, 2008.

[122] Registers of Scotland, *Update 24* (2009).

[123] Registers of Scotland, *Update 29* (2010). £ signs and commas must not be used in monetary fields. The prescribed fonts are: OCR-B 9pt; Courier 12pt; and Arial 10pt.

[124] Available at *http://www.ros.gov.uk/eforms/index.html*.

[125] The introduction of scanning has led the Keeper to abandon the previous practice whereby a form 2 was not required for discharges.

[126] Formerly this was done by returning a copy of the form 4. There has been unhappiness in the legal profession that the acknowledgement no longer gives details of the deeds submitted: see (2009) 54 J.L.S.S. May/8/.

[127] See para.18–12.

The registration process

We begin with a historical analogy. Before 1858 conveyances could not be 8–21
recorded in the GRS. Subject to certain exceptions, notarial instruments of
sasine were recorded. The actual conveyances were mere midcouples or links
in title, the deeds that underlay and justified the notarial instrument. After 1858
conveyances could be directly recorded.[128] The Land Register reverts, in this
respect, to the pre-1858 position. The form 1 or 2 is like a notarial instrument
of sasine. The role of the actual deed of conveyance is reduced to that of a
midcouple or link in title that underlies and justifies the entry in the Land
Register, in that it connects the current applicant with the existing registered
proprietor.

The Keeper can refuse an application if it is not accompanied by the appropriate deeds and other documentation.[129] So, for example, an *a non domino*
disposition can be refused on the ground that there are no supporting deeds to
vouch for the granter's ownership.[130] Further, the legislation requires the
Keeper to refuse an application in cases where (a) the land is not sufficiently
described; (b) it relates to a right abolished by the Abolition of Feudal Tenure
etc. (Scotland) Act 2000[131]; (c) the land is a souvenir plot; (d) the application
is frivolous or vexatious; (e) (except in first registrations) the deed does not
refer to the title number; and (f) the registration fee is not tendered.[132] Unless
an application is refused or withdrawn, the date of registration is the date on
which the application is received.[133] The date of registration is the relevant date
for the creation of any real right which flows from registration.[134] Ranking is
by day and not by time within a particular day, so that two applications received
at different times on the same day carry the same date of registration and, in a
competition between them, rank equally.[135]

It sometimes happens that the documentation submitted with an application is
insufficient for the Keeper to make an informed decision. In that case she can
formally request that the applicant submit the missing documentation within a
stated period which cannot be less than 60 days and in practice is not usually
more.[136] Meanwhile the application goes into "standover". In 2009 36 per cent of
first registration applications and 16 per cent of "dealings" (i.e. transactions
involving land already on the Land Register) went into standover. No reminder
is sent when the 60-day period has elapsed,[137] and if the applicant has failed to
respond, or has responded in a manner which is judged unsatisfactory, the Keeper
will either reject the application or accept it subject to exclusion of indemnity.
Applications are no longer put into standover if the discharge of a security is

---

[128] Except for general conveyances, for which see below, Ch.24.

[129] 1979 Act s.4(1).

[130] For *a non domino* dispositions, see above, para.7–12.

[131] A provision designed to prevent applications in respect of superiorities, or of the superiority
element of a mixed estate (i.e. a title which comprises a mixture of superiority and *dominium
utile*).

[132] 1979 Act s.4(2).

[133] 1979 Act s.4(3).

[134] 1979 Act s.3(4).

[135] 1979 Act s.7(2), (4). Ranking in this sense is only really appropriate for standard securities.
If two applications for ownership are accepted, only one can confer ownership. Here s.3(1) appears
to turn the normal rules on their head by preferring the later application: see Reid, *Property*,
para.685.

[136] Land Registration (Scotland) Rules 2006 rr.12 and 13.

[137] Registers of Scotland, *Update 28* (2010).

delayed and marked as "to follow". Instead the application will be processed at once and, if completed before the discharge is presented for registration, the land certificate will show the undischarged security.[138]

Typically, around 10 per cent of applications for registration are rejected, in the process attracting a fee of £30. Among the common grounds for rejection are a failure to supply the correct application forms or to complete them correctly, the omission of the deed that is to be registered, or the SDLT certificate, and not having paid the correct fee.[139]

In the Land Register what is registered is the grantee's title and not the deed evidencing that title, though a copy of that deed will in fact be kept, together with the application form. In first registrations the Keeper must convert the GRS title into a Land Register title by making up a new title sheet.[140] Otherwise, her task is to make the necessary alteration to an existing title sheet.[141] So if William is acquiring registered land from Margaret, and at the same time granting a standard security, the Keeper will substitute "William" for "Margaret" in the proprietorship section, and add the standard security to the charges section. If registered land is to be divided, a new title sheet is opened up for the property being split off, and corresponding adjustments are made to the parent title sheet.

Registration of a primary real right is followed by the issue to the new registered proprietor of the land certificate, which is an authenticated copy of the title sheet.[142] There is no equivalent certificate for secondary real rights except in the case of heritable securities, where a charge certificate is issued.[143] The land certificate should be carefully checked by the grantees' solicitors, particularly in a first registration. The land certificate replaces the old GRS deeds which, in theory at least, cease to be relevant, except where indemnity has been excluded.

The Keeper also returns the deed which induced the registration, and this should be kept with the land certificate. While in practice copies of all deeds submitted are retained by the Register, only those referred to in the land certificate are available for inspection under the 1979 Act,[144] although a wider right of access is conferred by the Freedom of Information (Scotland) Act 2002.[145]

First registration: what must be sent

8–22   In a first registration the Keeper must carry out a full examination of the GRS title, with the result that the process is more complicated.[146] If problems are anticipated the Keeper should be contacted in advance: at the Registers of Scotland there is a Department of Pre-Registration Enquiries. Enquiries must be made in writing and will normally be responded to within five days of receipt. A fee of £50 is payable.[147]

---

[138] Registers of Scotland, *Update 28* (2010).

[139] Registers of Scotland, *Update 33* (2010).

[140] 1979 Act s.5(1)(a)(i).

[141] 1979 Act s.5(1)(a)(ii), (b).

[142] 1979 Act s.5(2). See above, para.8–10. By s.5(4) a land certificate is "accepted for all purposes as sufficient evidence of the contents of the title sheet of which the land certificate is a copy".

[143] 1979 Act s.5(3), (4). See above, para.8–11.

[144] 1979 Act s.6(5).

[145] Subject to exceptions, any Scottish public authority (such as the Keeper: Sch.1 para.11) must make available any information which it holds: see s.1(1).

[146] See generally above, paras 7–13 to 7–31.

[147] See generally, Registers of Scotland, *Update 31* (2010).

The following must be sent to the Keeper with the application:

(i)   the disposition;
(ii)   the new standard security (if there is one);
(iii)   the discharge of the old standard security (if there was one);
(iv)   the deeds comprising the GRS title;
(v)   any other relevant documents such as death certificates (originals only);
(vi)   form 1, in respect of the disposition;
(vii)   form 2, in respect of the standard security;
(viii) form 2, in respect of the discharge;
(ix)   form 4, listing the writs being submitted and any other deeds referred to but not submitted.

The disposition will trigger first registration, and thereafter the standard security will be in respect of an interest which has already (by a single moment) become a registered interest. However, the title number cannot be inserted because at this stage it has not been allocated. If the standard security is submitted later, the title number, which by this stage will be known, can simply be written in at the top of the first page: a new deed is not required.

Form 1 is similar to forms 2 and 3 and is fairly self-explanatory. The section headed "schedule of heritable securities, etc." is for existing, undischarged securities, including those to be discharged as part of the application, but not including the new security being granted by the purchasers. The section headed "schedule of burdens" should simply list the burdens writs by reference to the form 4. The "FAS" number is the Keeper's account number for the law firm submitting the application.

Under head (iv) above (GRS title) only the relevant deeds need to accompany the application, i.e. chiefly the foundation writ, the deeds since then, the burdens deeds, and the deeds referred to for descriptions. A specimen list is given at para.5.5 of the ROTPB. Thus, many of the deeds handed over at settlement need not, and should not, be forwarded to the Keeper.

ARTL

Registration can also take place electronically under the system known as   8–23
automated registration of title to land ("ARTL") which was introduced, in its
full form, on March 1, 2008.[148] ARTL can be used for straightforward dealings,
such as for dispositions, assignations of long leases, and standard securities
and their discharge or assignation. It cannot be used for first registrations, or
for split-off dispositions, deeds which create real burdens, or any other deed
the registration of which would require alteration of either the A or the D
sections of the title sheet.

ARTL does not govern the whole of a conveyancing transaction. Missives,
for example, continue to be concluded in paper form in the usual way.
Examination of title is still necessary. Various documents are still provided on
paper, for example declarations in relation to occupancy rights or letters of

---

[148] Keeper's Direction No.1 of 2008. There is useful material on ARTL on the websites of Registers of Scotland (*http://www.ros.gov.uk*) and of the Law Society of Scotland (*http://www. lawscot.co.uk*).

obligation, and a brand new one is even added, the client's mandate to sign. But ARTL allows the completion online of the conveyancing deed or deeds, the land transaction return for SDLT, and the equivalent of form 2. Except where the same solicitor is acting for both parties, as with some kinds of security work, two solicitors will be involved in the transaction and both must be eligible for and willing to use ARTL. Law firms (and lenders) are eligible if they have become "licensees" by entering into an agreement with the Keeper. Whether they are then willing to use ARTL is a different matter.

As deeds under ARTL are electronic, they are signed using a digital signature and without a witness.[149] Among other qualities the signature must be uniquely linked to the signatory and capable of identifying him or her,[150] and be incorporated into or logically associated with the electronic document.[151] In addition, it must be attested by a digital certificate, vouching for its authenticity,[152] and complying with exacting but, to the uninitiated, incomprehensible specifications.[153] While, however, the legislation is framed in general terms, ARTL, for the moment at least, is a closed system which only recognises signatures and certificates deriving from the certification service established by the Keeper. Each system user with signing capacity is issued with a smartcard which contains within it a unique digital certificate and is protected by a Personal Identification Number ("PIN"). An electronic signature is made by using the smartcard in association with a smartcard reader, which provides the interface from smartcard to computer.

The ARTL elements of a transaction are intended to be reassuringly familiar to those schooled in traditional conveyancing.[154] In response to prompts, the buyers' solicitor (or some other member of staff)[155] inputs information into the system from which a disposition or other deed is generated in standard form.[156] In the case of a disposition, this is then transferred to the control of the sellers' solicitor who checks it and then signs using a digital signature.[157] As only solicitors have digital signatures recognised under ARTL—and most clients would not in any event hold a digital signature of any kind—clients do not sign

---

[149] Requirements of Writing (Scotland) Act 1995 s.2A. By s.3A such deeds are probative. See generally, Robert Rennie and Stewart Brymer, *Conveyancing in the Electronic Age* (2008), paras 8–01 to 8–04.

[150] 1995 Act s.12(1) (definition of "digital signature"). The definition corresponds to the "advanced" electronic signature (as opposed to the ordinary electronic signature) of the Electronic Signatures Regulations 2002 (SI 2002/318).

[151] 1995 Act s.2A(2)(a). A signature is "logically associated" with an electronic document if there is a link or connection between the data which comprise the document and the data which comprise the signature (in the same way as, to take a familiar example, between an email and one of its attachments).

[152] 1995 Act s.2A(2)(d), (3). Subsection (3) derives from s.7(3) of the Electronic Communications Act 2000 and is expressed in technology-neutral terms.

[153] Keeper's Direction No.1 of 2007, made under the powers in the 1995 Act s.2A(2)(d)(ii). For example, the digital certificate must be issued by a certification service based on a public key infrastructure and compliant with the X.509 international technical standard.

[154] See generally, Robert Rennie and Stewart Brymer, *Conveyancing in the Electronic Age*, Ch.9.

[155] Within each law firm, access to ARTL is controlled by a "practice administrator" who must determine what level of permission different users should have. Only the grantee of the mandate can add the digital signature. See Robert Rennie and Stewart Brymer, *Conveyancing in the Electronic Age*, paras 9–26 to 9–35.

[156] For the required information, see Land Registration (Scotland) Rules 2006 r.10 and Sch.2 Pt A.

[157] "Digital signature" is defined in s.15(1) of the 1995 Act.

deeds themselves but must give written authority to sign to their solicitor by means of a mandate, in a form laid down by the Law Society of Scotland.[158] Without a mandate the deed would be void; in view of its importance, solicitors are required to send it to the Keeper for digital archiving not later than 14 days after applying for registration.[159] If the buyers are taking out a loan, the standard security is generated electronically and signed by their solicitor, again by virtue of a mandate. The (electronic) discharge of any existing security is signed either by the lender—for banks are generally licensees for the purposes of ARTL—or by the solicitor who acts for the sellers and lender.

Settlement proceeds along much the same lines as usual except that the disposition is delivered electronically, by being returned to the control of the buyers' solicitor.[160] Registration of all the deeds—disposition, standard security, and discharge—then takes place electronically, an equivalent of form 2 being completed online.[161] This is entirely within the solicitors' control and no input is needed from Registers of Scotland. In practice it takes up to 24 hours for the Land Register to be altered, during which time there will be an automatic search in the Register of Inhibitions as well as certain security checks for rogue transactions. SDLT is collected by the Keeper on behalf of HM Revenue and Customs,[162] and this together with the registration dues is paid by direct debit by the buyers' solicitors.

So far the take-up of ARTL has been unexpectedly low. Although around 40,000 applications were submitted during the first three years of operation, all but a handful involved securities, where only a single solicitor acted, and there was no sign that ARTL was likely to be used extensively in the ordinary transfer of property. One reason for this user resistance is no doubt the conservatism of the legal profession. Another is the perception, whether justified or not, that the ARTL software is "clunky", poorly designed, and even insecure.[163] Increasingly, though, banks are requiring panel solicitors to use ARTL and it remains to be seen whether this usage will extend beyond the security element of the transaction.

After ARTL: from electronic registration to electronic conveyancing

Although a valuable step forward, ARTL is by no means a complete package for electronic conveyancing. First, it does not allow for electronic deeds in the Land Register unless they are being used in an ARTL transaction. Secondly, ARTL can only be used for certain types of deed. Thirdly, documents that are not registered in the Land Register cannot be in electronic form. Examples include missives and non-registrable leases. Finally, the Register of Sasines cannot take electronic deeds, and the Books of Council and Session, equally, is open only to paper deeds. In its Report on *Land Registration*, discussed more fully in the

8–24

---

[158] See also 1995 Act s.12(3).

[159] Solicitors (Scotland) (ARTL Mandates) Rules 2006 r.4(1). The Keeper does not check the mandate: her only role is to preserve a copy. For mandates generally, see Robert Rennie and Stewart Brymer, *Conveyancing in the Electronic Age*, paras 8–05 to 8–15, who argue that mandates should be granted to individuals and not to law firms.

[160] On digital delivery, see Robert Rennie and Stewart Brymer, *Conveyancing in the Electronic Age*, paras 6–07 to 6–10.

[161] Land Registration (Scotland) Rules 2006 r.10 and Sch.2 Pt B.

[162] Stamp Duty Land Tax (Electronic Communications) (Amendment) Regulations 2006 (SI 2006/3427).

[163] See the views summarised in Reid and Gretton, *Conveyancing 2010*, p.73.

next section, the Scottish Law Commission recommends that all conveyancing documents should be capable of being in electronic form.[164] This will require extensive amendments to the Requirements of Writing (Scotland) Act 1995. One unresolved question is who would fulfil the role played by the Keeper for ARTL and be the issuing authority in respect of electronic signatures.

Reform

8–25   The Scottish Law Commission's Report on *Land Registration*, complete with draft bill, was published in 2010,[165] and there are indications that legislation may follow sooner rather than later. The Law Commission recommends the complete repeal of the Land Registration (Scotland) Act 1979 and its replacement with a new statute. That, however, is less dramatic than it sounds. The central functional features of the current system would remain. There would continue to be a map-based Land Register. Existing registered titles would carry on. Title sheets would retain their familiar four sections. Titles would continue to be guaranteed by the Keeper, though, as now, there would be certain exceptions and qualifications. Whilst the 1979 Act has its faults, it was also a progressive measure, and the new legislation would build on its successes. The watchword of the Commission's Report is evolution, not revolution. Throughout the process the Commission was aware of the importance of not causing unnecessary inconvenience to conveyancers.

A persistent criticism of the 1979 Act is that its rules about inaccuracy, rectification, and indemnity are highly complex and, moreover, too often fail to deliver reasonable solutions when problems arise. The Commission agreed with that criticism, and recommends a complete overhaul of the rules. Section 9 of the 1979 Act says that in many cases the Land Register must remain inaccurate.[166] Anyone who has tried explaining that to a non-lawyer will have found the task difficult, if not impossible. The Commission recommends that inaccuracies should be rectifiable in all cases, but that in some types of case what was at first an inaccuracy should be capable of becoming an accuracy— i.e. that in some types of case the rights of the parties should be "realigned" with what the Register says they are.[167] The details cannot be gone into here, but in summary, if the Register is inaccurate but, before it can be rectified, there is a disposition by a seller in possession to a buyer who acts in good faith, the inaccuracy would be washed out. Meanwhile, the system of title guarantee would continue but with changes of detail. A title guarantee can take two forms. (i) If the grantee's title turns out to be defective, the grantee is compensated by the Keeper. In other words, the grantee takes the "money" but does not keep the "mud". (ii) If the grantee's title turns out to be defective, it is protected from challenge. Accordingly, there is no need to compensate the grantee who, having received the mud, has no need of the money. But the Keeper must then compensate the other party whose rights are thereby infringed. The 1979 Act has a mix of the two forms of guarantee.[168] The Law Commission recommends that there should continue to be a mix in the future but with a shift somewhat

---

[164] Report, Pt 34.
[165] Scottish Law Commission, Report on *Land Registration* (Scot. Law Com. No.222, available at *http://www.scotlawcom.gov.uk*).
[166] Owing to the protection given to a proprietor in possession: see above, paras 8–15 and 8–16.
[167] Report, Pts 20–23.
[168] See above, para.8–07.

towards (i) and away from (ii). In other words, it would become more common for the grantee to receive the money and for the "true owner" to retain the mud.

Many countries have a system whereby an advance notice of a transaction can be noted on the register. Then, as and when the transaction is registered, it will take priority over any other entry that may have been made in the intervening period. Take an example from England. X is selling to Y. A priority entry is made in HM Land Registry on May 1. On May 10 a mortgage by X to Z is registered. On May 12 the conveyance by X to Y is submitted for registration. The conveyance has priority over the mortgage. The Law Commission recommends that a comparable scheme be adopted in Scotland. The details are based in part on the English system but also in part on the system that exists in Germany. The scheme has been designed to ensure that in ordinary transactions letters of obligation would become unnecessary. Although advance notices would be optional, the possibility exists that the Council of Mortgage Lenders might require their use.

To what extent those involved in land registration transactions owe a duty of care to the Keeper is uncertain. The Report recommends that there should be such a duty of care, but limited to what is reasonable in the circumstances. Thus a conveyancer who acts to the standard of an ordinarily competent conveyancer would have nothing to fear. The effect of the reform may be that application forms can be simplified, for the duty of care would mean a duty to disclose to the Keeper any problems.

Under current law no rules exist as to whether (if at all) the Keeper should accept applications based on *a non domino* deeds.[169] In the early years of registration of title, the Keeper had a virtually open-door policy. Around the mid-1990s the door was nearly, but not quite, closed, and that remains the position to this day. It is unsatisfactory that such an important issue should rest on practice, not law, and the Law Commission recommends a set of rules as to when applications based on *a non domino* deeds should be accepted and when they should be rejected. In summary, such an application should be accepted if both (i) the true owner has not been in possession for seven years, and (ii) the applicant (or the applicant's predecessor) has been in possession for at least one year. If either condition is not satisfied, the application should be rejected. These periods are separate from the 10 years needed for a prescriptive title, for the prescriptive clock starts to tick only once there has been registration.

Some other aspects of what is a very detailed Report are mentioned elsewhere in this book.

THE GENERAL REGISTER OF SASINES

Structure and contents

The General Register of Sasines ("GRS") was established by the Registration 8–26 Act 1617[170] and is now regulated chiefly by the Land Registers (Scotland) Act 1868.[171] At first dispositions, and other conveyancing deeds, were not recorded

---

[169] See above, para.7–12.

[170] Still in force. For the history, see L. Ockrent, *Land Rights: An Enquiry into the History of Registration for Publication in Scotland* (1942).

[171] See also the Register of Sasines (Scotland) Act 1987 which authorises the keeping of the Register otherwise than in paper form. See, further, a note from the Keeper at (1989) 34 J.L.S.S. 235.

directly. What was recorded was the instrument of sasine, which was a notarial deed that followed on from the conveyancing deed itself, and which would reflect its substantive provisions. But since the Titles to Land (Scotland) Act 1858 conveyancing deeds can themselves be recorded. Not far short of half of all title units are still in the GRS. Moreover, deeds are still being recorded[172] there, in cases where the property in question is still in the GRS and the deed is not one that triggers the change to the new Register, such as a standard security, or a disposition by way of donation.

Unlike the Land Register, the GRS is a register of deeds not of rights, though of course rights flow from the deeds. Physically the Register is nothing but a massive collection—one might liken it to a warehouse, not in physical terms but in functional terms—of copy deeds, stretching back hundreds of years.[173] Originally the copies were made by hand, by clerks with quills and ink. Early in the 20th century photocopying was introduced, then, in the 1980s, copying on microfilm. Since April 30, 2006 deeds have been captured electronically.[174] The original, full-sized paper copies are bound up into large and heavy record volumes. There is no arrangement by property, and the only division is by county. Thus for, say, East Lothian one deed might be a disposition of a house in North Berwick, the next a standard security over a shop in Haddington, and the third a servitude over a farm near Tranent. The next deed affecting the farm might be thousands or tens of thousands of pages later. And in all this mass of paper, microfilm, and electronic data there is nothing which actually states, in an authoritative manner, who has right to what. Of course, if there is a recorded disposition by Jack to Jill then Jill is probably the owner, but it is possible for deeds in the GRS to be voidable or actually void.[175] Deeds of every kind, it is true, can be voidable or void, and not just deeds in the GRS, but in the GRS title rests on the recorded deed, so voidability or nullity of the deed will result in voidability or nullity in the real right itself.[176] By contrast, real rights in the Land Register are rather more insulated (but not wholly insulated) from the deeds on which they are based.

Indexes and search sheets

8–27   The GRS is indexed both by person and by property.[177] Most important of all are the search sheets.[178] For any given property a separate sheet is maintained for all the primary real rights therein, that is to say for ownership, and any

---

[172] Although one can speak of "registration" in the GRS, the word traditionally favoured by conveyancers (and in legislation) is "recording".

[173] Herein lies one of the many differences between the GRS and the Land Register. The GRS offers a complete history of the title of a property going back centuries. The Land Register is non-historical, and one knows nothing of the past history of the property. There is nothing but a memory-less moving present. This aspect of the Land Register has a number of unsatisfactory consequences.

[174] Register of Sasines (Methods of Operating) (Scotland) Regulations 2006 (SSI 2006/164).

[175] This presents obvious difficulties for examination of title, discussed above in Ch.7.

[176] This statement is a little oversimplified. In particular, prescription may cure defects.

[177] For examples of the persons index and property index see G.L. Gretton, *Guide to Searches* (1991), pp.6 and 8.

[178] For an example of a search sheet, see G.L. Gretton, *Guide to Searches*, p.12. Search sheets have no statutory basis, though without them modern conveyancing would be impossible. They were introduced in 1871. Hence it can be difficult to trace pre-1871 deeds in the Register unless one knows the date of registration.

recorded leases and sub-leases.[179] Whenever a deed is recorded, a brief summary is prepared and entered into the appropriate search sheet. The summary also states the place in the register itself where the deed can be found. The search sheet system is powerful and efficient. It enables the state of the title to virtually any plot of land still in the GRS to be investigated quickly and easily. An example will give the idea. Mary owns Whiteacre. There is a search sheet for the ownership, and the disposition in favour of Mary (from Louis) is mentioned there, as are previous dispositions of the property (Kate to Louis, Ian to Kate and so on) as far back as the property has been a separate unit—or back to the start of the search sheet system in the 1870s. Also listed will be other relevant deeds such as standard securities. Suppose that, before the county became operational for the Land Register, Mary granted a 25-year lease to Nigel. This would be noted on the search sheet, but at the same time a new search sheet for the leasehold interest would be created.

Warrants of registration

Until November 28, 2004 all deeds presented for registration had to contain a warrant of registration.[180] Broadly speaking, the warrant replaced the instrument of sasine, which was mandatory until 1858.[181] The warrant was a request by the grantees (or in practice their solicitors) to record the deed. There was a statutory form.[182] The warrant could appear anywhere on the deed but in practice was usually placed at the foot of the last page.   8–28

The registration process

The deed is accompanied by an application form.[183] The same form is used for any deed and can be completed online.[184] The deed must be accompanied by the appropriate SDLT certificate.[185] The extent of the Keeper's power to reject deeds for the GRS is uncertain. Probably it is not very extensive, although there are remarks in *Macdonald v Keeper of the Registers*[186] which might suggest otherwise. Since 1996 the Keeper has begun to reject *a non domino* dispositions, except in certain circumstances,[187] but her right to do so has not been judicially tested. Three clear reasons exist for refusal to register: (a) no SDLT certificate; (b) insufficient identification of the property (the situation in *Macdonald*); (c) deed not properly executed. Much more common than unilateral rejection is an invitation by the Register to withdraw a deed. It then becomes necessary to weigh up the seriousness, or otherwise, of the error in question. It may be so minor that withdrawal is unnecessary; and occasionally the "error" turns out to be no such thing.   8–29

---

[179] This is the same as in the Land Register, with title sheets.

[180] Titles to Land Consolidation (Scotland) Act 1868 ss.15 and 141. Abolition was by s.5(1) of the Abolition of Feudal Tenure etc. (Scotland) Act 2000.

[181] Titles to Land (Scotland) Act 1858.

[182] Conveyancing (Scotland) Act 1924 s.10(1), (3) and Sch.F.

[183] Register of Sasines (Application Procedure) Rules 2004 (SSI 2004/318), as amended by the Register of Sasines (Application Procedure) Amendment Rules 2006 (SSI 2006/568).

[184] *http://www.ros.gov.uk/eforms/index.html*.

[185] For SDLT certificates, see below, para.18–12

[186] *Macdonald v Keeper of the Registers*, 1914 S.C. 854.

[187] See above, para.7–25.

Once a deed has been accepted for recording it goes through various registration processes.[188] The Presentment Book,[189] which is used as a receipt book for all writs, and which gives the date of presentment, the name of the writ, and the parties, has been computerised since April 1, 1992. The Keeper makes an electronic copy of the deed and returns the original to the grantee. A certificate of registration is stamped on the original of the deed and gives details of (a) the date of recording and (b) the sequential number (previously book and folio number[190] and then, until 2006, fiche and frame number) of the copy preserved in the Register.

Since all recorded deeds are preserved, in copy, anyone can obtain copies of such copies. Copies come in two varieties. First there is the so-called quick copy, which is a simple photocopy. Then there is an extract,[191] which is also a photocopy, but which comes complete with a backing and a certificate that it is a true copy. By s.45 of the 1970 Act an extract copy is as good as the original deed.[192]

---

[188] See John H. Sinclair, "Conveyancing", in *The Laws of Scotland: Stair Memorial Encyclopaedia*, Vol.6 (1988), paras 452 et seq. This topic is not included in the reissue title on Conveyancing.

[189] For an example of the Presentment Book in its traditional (pre-computerisation) form, see G.L. Gretton, *Guide to Searches*, p.2.

[190] The "folio" is the page.

[191] An extract of a document is not a short version of it but a full official authenticated copy.

[192] Quick copies and extracts can be obtained direct from the Keeper, or can be obtained through firms of searchers.

CHAPTER 9

SEARCHES, REPORTS, AND LETTERS OF OBLIGATION

PRELIMINARY

Introduction

To "search" the registers is simply to look to see what they say. The registers 9–01
that are most important for the conveyancers, and the ones covered in this
chapter, are the Land Register, the General Register of Sasines ("GRS"), and
the Personal Register (i.e. the Register of Inhibitions and Adjudications). The
word "search" is sometimes also used to mean the report on what was discovered by the search, but the tendency nowadays is to use the word "report" if
that is what is meant.

If the sellers' title is in the Land Register there will be a land certificate. But
a land certificate merely copies the title sheet as at the date that the land certificate was issued. The sellers may assert that nothing has changed in the title
sheet since the certificate was issued, but the buyers would be unwise to rely
on such assurances. In substance the same is true for property still in the GRS.
The sellers will hold the deeds, including the disposition in their favour, and
they may say that the deeds produced are all the relevant deeds. But there is no
way to verify that without checking the GRS itself. The risk is less in the case
of Land Register titles, for changes in the title sheet will normally be accompanied by an updating of the land certificate. But even with the Land Register
there is some element of risk.

In this chapter it is assumed that separate solicitors act for the granters and
the grantees. However, where there is a secured loan the same solicitors will
usually act for both parties.[1] Moreover, in remortgages it is common for the
borrower to be unrepresented.

Who searches?

In some countries, the registers are only semi-public, being open to lawyers 9–02
and to those able to show a legitimate interest. But in Scotland the registers are
fully public and so anyone can search them for any reason or none. In sales the
search is in practice instructed by the sellers' solicitors, and the reports are then
forwarded by them to the buyers' solicitors.[2] Production of search reports
being the sellers' responsibility, the cost falls on them, unless otherwise agreed.

---

[1] Assuming that the loan is an ordinary home loan: see above, para.1–10.
[2] See above, para.2–10.

In practice, searches are usually carried out either by the Keeper of the Registers of Scotland[3] or by firms of professional searchers. The Land Registration (Scotland) Rules 1980 (now 2006) seem to assume that searching is the Keeper's monopoly, for they prescribe forms for "an application to the Keeper for a report".[4] But there is nothing in the Land Registration (Scotland) Act 1979 to support that view of matters, and, when the dust had settled, independent searchers were providing searches as well as the Keeper. Independent searchers are normally instructed on forms substantially the same as those prescribed by the Rules for use by the Keeper. But they are free in principle to offer any kind of search, whereas the Keeper can offer only searches of the kinds prescribed by the Rules.

Liability for mistakes

9–03 A searcher is liable for loss caused by an inaccurate search. This liability is statutory in the case of the Keeper, and would seem to give rights of recovery not only to the person who instructed the search but also to third parties who have relied on it.[5] Independent searchers are liable in contract to those who have instructed them. Whether they are liable to third parties who rely on the search seems not to have been tested but, on the general principles of the law of delict, it would seem that such liability does exist.

When searches are and are not made

9–04 Searches are made before money changes hands, whether the payment of a price or the release of a loan to be secured on heritable property, and are mainly for the benefit of buyers and lenders. As well as sales and secured loans, there may be other circumstances in which a search may be made. A person acquiring a subordinate real right, such as lease or servitude, will usually wish to check the granter's title. When someone dies the executor may check the deceased's title even if no sale is being contemplated. And a person may simply be curious to know who has what rights in a particular building or plot of land.

An obligation is probably implied by law that sellers should exhibit or deliver clear searches,[6] but missives almost always make express provision. If, as occasionally happens, missives say that the sellers will neither exhibit nor deliver a search, that does not free them from an obligation to grant a valid title[7] but merely shifts the onus on to the purchasers to make the necessary searches themselves. The granter of a non-onerous deed does not need to show good title (you don't look a gift horse in the mouth) and hence need not exhibit searches. Examples are donations *inter vivos* and conveyances by an executor in implement of a legacy.

---

[3] In practice, of course, by the Keeper's staff. The Keeper offers searches in the Land Register, the GRS, and the Register of Inhibitions and Adjudications except in the unusual case where the property is in the GRS and is, for the time being, staying there. Searches can be instructed and transmitted digitally through the Keeper's eForms system on *http://www.ros.gov.uk/*. Searches in the Companies Register cannot be obtained from the Keeper.

[4] Land Registration (Scotland) Rules 2006 (SSI 2006/485) r.21.

[5] Land Registration (Scotland) Act 1979 s.12(1)(d).

[6] See above, para.6–18.

[7] For which see above, paras 6–01 et seq.

Some other registers

As already mentioned, the registers that are most important to conveyancers 9–05
are the Land Register, the GRS, and the Register of Inhibitions and
Adjudications.[8] But there exist many other registers, which may be of relevance. We shall mention a few of them. (i) One is the Companies Register.[9]
(ii) Another is the Register of Community Interests in Land,[10] which was set
up by the Land Reform (Scotland) Act 2003 and which also has a role for the
Agricultural Holdings (Scotland) Act 2003. If property is registered, then the
owner's right to sell is restricted.[11] A search in this register may be needed in
non-urban transactions. (iii) The building standards registers, maintained by
local authorities, contain information on the building law status of individual
properties.[12] (iv) Another local authority register is the planning register which
records the planning applications for particular properties.[13] (v) The Books of
Council and Session are a register too well known to require explanation:
many deeds relevant to conveyancing practice are registered there.

Registers Direct: online access

The Land Register can be accessed online, through a system called Registers 9–06
Direct. It is necessary to register as a user, but there is no subscription charge:
payment is by use. The system has not replaced searches and reports from the
Keeper and from independent firms of searchers.

LAND REGISTER[14]

Form 12/13 reports

For property already on the Land Register the usual method of search is a form 9–07
12 report, either from the Keeper or from independent searchers. This discloses
any changes in the title sheet since the date that the land certificate was issued.
In most cases there will have been no changes. If there is a significant gap
between the date of the form 12 report and settlement, it can be updated by a
form 13 report. In all cases the title number must be given to enable the search
to be effected. The form 12 should be sent to the Keeper in duplicate. The form
12 report is normally headed "12A", but for special cases the response may be
a 12B, 12C, 12D or 12E.[15]

  A form 12/13 report is double search. It searches not only the Land Register
but also the Personal Register (i.e. the Register of Inhibitions and Adjudications).
The form requesting the search needs to give the names and addresses of the
parties to be searched against. More detailed consideration of the Register of
Inhibitions will be found later in this chapter.[16]

---

[8] The first two were the subject of Ch.8.

[9] See below, para.28–01.

[10] *http://www.ros.gov.uk/rcil/*.

[11] See above, para.4–41. For a missives clause dealing with this register see Reid and Gretton,
Conveyancing 2003, p.140.

[12] See above, para.4–36.

[13] Town and Country Planning (Scotland) Act 1997 s.36.

[14] See generally above, paras 8–08 et seq. and the *Registration of Title Practice Book*
("ROTPB"), Ch.3.

[15] ROTPB, para.3.7.

[16] See below, paras 9–15 to 9–24.

Form 12/13 is drafted by the sellers' solicitors and sent with the land certifi-cate to the buyers' solicitors for revisal. If separate solicitors are acting for the buyers' lenders they too should have the opportunity to revise the draft. The form 12 report is then obtained, and exhibited to the buyers or lenders, before settlement, updated if necessary by a form 13 report. After settlement the Keeper will in due course issue a new land certificate and, in the case of a standard security, a charge certificate. These are also, in a sense, reports.

Office copy of title sheet

9–08 Another method of discovering the current state of a title is to request a copy—known as an "office copy"—of the title sheet.[17] This can be obtained either from the Keeper or from independent searchers, and it too is, in effect, a type of search. In practice, however, this facility is not much used, and a solicitor who wants to check a title is more likely to consult the Register online using Registers Direct.[18]

First registrations: form 10/11 reports

9–09 If the property is still in the GRS the present transaction will normally switch it into the Land Register, i.e. a first registration. Normally, the deeds sent to the grantee for examination will include all those which are still relevant to the title, but the buyers cannot take this on trust and need to verify the position by means of a GRS search. Where a deed is missing, this might be as a result of fraud by the sellers or, more likely, inadvertence. Here are some examples:

(i) The property being purchased is part of a large estate, from which the sellers have sold off various small parcels of land over the years. In that case, copies of the break-off deeds should have been put up with the titles. But it can happen that one or more such deeds have been overlooked, so from the deeds in the possession of the sellers it looks as if they own rather more than they actually do.

(ii) It might be that the sellers have granted a standard security without telling their solicitors. This is uncommon, but far from unknown. Far from being fraudulent in not telling their solicitors, the sellers may not realise what they have done. Such securities are commonly called "double-glazing standard securities" because they are often presented to a householder for signing for credit deals, such as for double-glazing.

(iii) There might be an adjudication against the sellers. In that case, the sellers should know of it, but a copy will not be with the title deeds, and the sellers may conveniently forget to tell their solicitors.

So in a first registration it is necessary for the GRS to be searched.[19] The Land Registration (Scotland) Rules 2006 prescribe forms to be used by the Keeper, and the forms for a first registration are forms 10 and 11. Parties are also free to instruct independent searchers. Although a form 10/11 report is primarily a

---

[17] Land Registration (Scotland) Act 1979 s.6(5). The relevant application form is form 15.

[18] For which see above, para.9–06.

[19] And also the Register of Inhibitions and, if appropriate, the Companies Register. See below and, for the Companies Register, Ch.28.

search of the GRS and the Personal Register, the Land Register will also be checked, to ensure that the property, or part of it, has not already been registered there. In practice the key to searching the GRS is the system of "search sheets". Each unit of property has its own sheet—rather like the title sheet in the Land Register—and this gives a brief summary, chronologically, of the deeds affecting that property. Copies of the actual deeds can then be found in the register itself. Form 10 was intended to be used when the property was first marketed, and form 11 was intended as an update to be used shortly before settlement. In modern practice only the form 10 is generally used, this happening shortly before settlement, and a form 11 continuation is used only if there is a delay. But an early form 10 report might be obtained for property which is part of a larger area, in order to make sure that previous break-off writs are identified.

In requesting a search the form 10 must identify the property sufficiently. This cannot be by title number since no title number yet exists. It may be that the existing GRS description is sufficient. If not, a new plan will have to be prepared, and submitted with the form 10. A copy of this plan can then be used for the disposition. In most cases the seller will, at the same time as submitting the form 10, also submit a P16.[20] Although there will almost always be an existing search report among the deeds (see below) the Keeper will not refer to it, but will search afresh.

REGISTER OF SASINES

Introduction

If the property is still in the GRS the present transaction will normally switch   9–10
it into the Land Register, i.e. a first registration (discussed above). The exceptions are (a) where the property is being transferred for a reason other than sale, such as donation or succession, and (b) where the transaction is not a transfer but the grant of a subordinate real right such as a standard security. Where one of these exceptions applies the old form of search will be required, and the following deals with that situation.

The memorandum

The purpose of a GRS search is simply to identify all deeds registered there,   9–11
affecting a defined property within a defined period.[21] Almost always there will be an existing search report among the deeds, prepared at the time of the last transaction. In that case, the practice is to send this off to the searchers with a request that they continue it to the present. This is called a "continuation of search", and the letter of request takes the form of a memorandum for continuation of search and follows a standard format. It is drafted by the granters' solicitors and sent to the grantees' solicitors for approval, revision and return. The granters' solicitors then "extend" it (i.e. make a principal version) and send it off to the searchers, who then carry out the search. The granters pay the

---

[20] See below, para.12–12.
[21] For an example of a GRS search, combined, as usual, with a search of the Personal Register, see David A. Brand, Andrew J.M. Steven and Scott Wortley, *Professor McDonald's Conveyancing Manual*, 7th edn (2004), App.A.

searchers' fee. Occasionally, there is no existing search and in that case it will be necessary to instruct a new search.

Period

9–12   How far back a search should go depends on various factors, but the general rule is that it should go back 40 years or to the date of the foundation writ, whichever is the longer. Some consider it sufficient to go back only to the foundation writ, since any prior writ will be irrelevant by reason of positive prescription. There are, however, several reasons why the standard advice is to go back 40 years. One is that there might be undischarged securities. As a rule of thumb, any security older than 40 years has probably been extinguished by payment or by the long negative prescription. A second is that positive prescription works only if there has been possession.[22] In practice, one does not normally check the fact of possession. A 40-year search is a sort of substitute, for if there were a competing title, such a search would almost certainly show it up, and in that event further inquiry could be made.

Interim reports

9–13   A GRS search report comes in two forms: interim and final. The final report will be sent by the searchers some time after settlement. Processing deeds in the GRS takes some time, so that a search carried out on a given day will not give a conclusive view of the deeds that are on the register on that day. The searchers will be asked for an interim report, shortly before settlement. This corresponds to the form 10/11, or the form 11/12 in transactions involving the Land Register. The final search report corresponds, in a sense, to the land certificate.

Start and close dates for the GRS search

9–14   The memorandum for the searchers gives both the start date and the closing date for the search. The start date will be a specific date, normally the day after the close of the existing search. The closing date will not be a specific date, but will list the deed or deeds being recorded, and the memorandum will tell the searchers to close the search as soon as this has been done. When the searchers find these deeds on the register they will then close off the search.

THE PERSONAL SEARCH

The Personal Register

9–15   The personal search is a search in the Personal Register, more properly known as the Register of Inhibitions and Adjudications, and to be renamed the Register of Inhibitions once the provision of the Bankruptcy and Diligence etc. (Scotland) Act 2007 which abolishes adjudication comes into force.[23] Though the current official name includes the word "adjudications", in fact adjudications are not normally registered here but in the Land Register or the GRS.

---

[22] See above, para.7–22.
[23] Bankruptcy and Diligence etc. (Scotland) Act 2007 ss.79 and 80.

Whereas the Land Register is a register of properties, and the GRS a register of deeds, the Personal Register is, roughly speaking, a register of names of persons against whom proceedings have begun for allegedly unpaid debts. The main entries are inhibitions and sequestrations. A person who is inhibited or sequestrated is barred from selling and from granting security.

The Personal Register is always up to date, so that a search done today will show entries made yesterday.

Types of entry in the Personal Register

Many kinds of entry may be found in the Personal Register. The following is a non-exhaustive list: 9–16

  (a) Inhibition.[24]
  (b) Notice of inhibition.[25]
  (c) Discharge, or restriction, by inhibitor.[26]
  (d) Certified copy interlocutor, or decree, of recall of inhibition.
  (e) Decree of dismissal or absolvitor where inhibition was used on dependence.
  (f) Notice of litigiosity, which may take the form either of a summons of adjudication or a summons of reduction.[27] These have an effect similar to inhibition.
  (g) Decree of adjudication. However, such decrees are not normally registered here at all, but in the Land Register or GRS as appropriate.
  (h) Notices concerning sequestration.[28]
  (i) Trust deed for behoof of creditors.[29]
  (j) Company administration petition[30] and appointment of administrator.[31]
  (k) Application for judicial rectification.[32]
  (l) English/Welsh bankruptcy order.[33]

Inhibitions[34]

Inhibition forbids the inhibited person from selling or otherwise alienating heritable property. It also strikes at a subsequent grant of heritable security, and probably a subsequent floating charge insofar as the charge affects heritage. Breaches of inhibition are not void, but are voidable at the instance of the inhibitor. This is done by an action of reduction *ex capite inhibitionis*, though   9–17

---

[24] See Bankruptcy and Diligence etc. (Scotland) Act 2007 s.148 for precisely what is registered.
[25] Titles to Land Consolidation (Scotland) Act 1868 s.155.
[26] A restriction leaves the inhibition partially in force.
[27] 1868 Act s.159.
[28] Bankruptcy (Scotland) Act 1985 s.14. See also ss.15(5) and 17(8).
[29] Bankruptcy (Scotland) Act 1985 Sch.5 para.2. Registration is non-mandatory.
[30] Insolvency (Scotland) Rules 1986 (SI 1986/1915) r.2.3(1)(g).
[31] Insolvency (Scotland) Rules 1986 r.2.19(2)(e).
[32] Under s.8 of the Law Reform (Miscellaneous Provisions) (Scotland) Act 1985. See below, Ch.20.
[33] These are registered if the English trustee so wishes but not otherwise. Their effect is uncertain.
[34] See G.L. Gretton, *Law of Inhibition and Adjudication*, 2nd edn (1996).

in certain types of case it is possible for the inhibitor to enforce without any action of reduction. An inhibition endures for five years, after which it prescribes.[35] An inhibition can be used not only in execution of a decree but also on the dependence of an action.[36] In the latter case it will become void if the pursuer fails in the action.

Inhibition may be discharged voluntarily by the inhibitor, the discharge being registered in the Personal Register. Or it may be discharged by interlocutor, this being called a "recall". Recalls likewise are registered in the Personal Register. Partial discharge and partial recall are possible, whereby the inhibition is discharged from certain property or a certain transaction, while retaining its effect as against other property and transactions. Such a partial recall is sometimes called a "restriction".

Inhibition identifies the person inhibited, without specifying any particular property, as all heritable property in Scotland is automatically affected. It is purely a negative diligence, and confers on the inhibitor no real right. A creditor who wishes to obtain a real right by diligence must use adjudication. Adjudication need not be preceded by inhibition, though in practice it usually is. A decree of adjudication, upon being registered in the Land Register (or GRS if the property is still in that register), gives the adjudger a real right, being a judicial heritable security.[37]

In principle, inhibition takes effect on the day when it is registered. But the inhibitor may register a pre-notice, called a notice of inhibition. If that happens, the inhibition takes effect when the notice is served on the inhibitee, provided that the inhibition itself is registered not more than 21 days after the registration of the notice.[38] Thus if the register shows a notice registered on June 1, and the inhibition itself is registered on June 25, the notice is irrelevant, and the inhibition takes effect from June 25. But if the inhibition itself is registered on June 15, then it *may* take effect from June 1: whether in fact it does so depends on when there was service on the inhibitee. The reason for the notice procedure is speed and surprise, because some debtors will alienate assets if they suspect that a creditor is taking action.

Inhibition affects the debtor's right to deal with property held at the time of the inhibition. Hence: (i) it does not affect the right of an inhibitee to *acquire* property, and (ii) it does not affect the right of the inhibitee to deal with property so acquired. For example, suppose that Jack is inhibited on May 1. He acquires heritable property on June 1 and also grants a standard security over it. A year later he sells that property. The acquisition, the security and the sale are all unaffected by the inhibition.[39] For this purpose property is considered as "acquired" when the deed is delivered.[40] Suppose Jill concludes missives to buy property on June 10, receives the disposition on June 15 and completes title on June 20. If she is inhibited on June 12, the property is unaffected by the inhibition. If she is inhibited on June 17 the property is affected by the inhibition.

---

[35] Conveyancing (Scotland) Act 1924 s.44.

[36] See ss.15A et seq. of the Debtors (Scotland) Act 1987.

[37] Part 4 of the Bankruptcy and Diligence etc. (Scotland) Act 2007 prospectively replaces adjudication with land attachment. But these provisions have not been brought into force.

[38] Titles to Land Consolidation (Scotland) Act 1868 s.155, as substituted by the Bankruptcy and Diligence etc. (Scotland) Act 2007 s.149.

[39] Titles to Land Consolidation (Scotland) Act 1868 s.157.

[40] Bankruptcy and Diligence etc. (Scotland) Act 2007 s.150(3).

Sequestration and trust deeds

After inhibitions, the most important entries on the Personal Register are 9–18
sequestrations.[41] An entry may mean that the person in question has been
sequestrated, but if what appears is a "warrant to cite" that simply means that
there has been a petition for sequestration. If, however, the warrant to cite is
not followed by registration of an interlocutor dismissing the petition, it is
normally a fair inference that sequestration has taken place.[42] An alternative
source of information on bankruptcies is the Register of Insolvencies.[43] On the
matters that it deals with (which do not include inhibitions) the information in
this register is more detailed than in the Personal Register.

Occasionally a seller is sequestrated so close to the time of settlement that
this is unknown to the buyer, who settles the transaction on the basis of a clear
interim report. Such sequestration may take place either just before or just after
settlement, and in either case the buyers are placed in a vulnerable position.
The issues which arise here are discussed further below in Ch.11.[44]

Instructing the personal search

A search in the Personal Register can be instructed on its own, though usually it 9–19
is instructed as part of the form 12.[45] If the transaction will switch the property
for the first time into the Land Register, it is normal to instruct the personal
search as part of the form 10.[46] In these two cases the form 10/11 report, or the
form 12/13 report, will expressly state whether there is any relevant entry in the
Personal Register. The eventual land certificate, by contrast, says nothing *unless*
there is a relevant entry.[47] Thus, if the land certificate is silent, that means that
the Personal Register was, or appeared to be, clear. If the property is, for the
time being, staying in the GRS a personal search will be instructed together with
the search in the GRS, and the same pattern of interim and final report exists.[48]

When the sellers' solicitors draft the form 10/11 or form 12/13, or the memorandum for search, they will put the sellers' names on it for the purposes of a
personal search. When the buyers' solicitors revise it they will normally add
the buyers' names. The main reason for this is that the buyers will normally be
granting a security and the lenders will want to know if the buyers are inhibited
or sequestrated.[49]

Identifying the person to be searched against

The object of the personal search is to ensure that there are no entries against 9–20
the person being searched against. The search is by name and address. A danger

---

[41] Bankruptcy (Scotland) Act 1985 s.14.

[42] The question can be settled by a search of the Register of Insolvencies.

[43] Bankruptcy (Scotland) Act 1985 s.1.

[44] See above, para.11–29.

[45] See above, para.9–07. If it is instructed on its own, that will have to be done by independent
searchers. The Keeper offers searches of the Personal Register only in conjunction with searches
of the Land Register.

[46] See above, para.9–09. The pattern thus follows the old GRS practice, whereby an instruction
for search would usually be for both the GRS and the Personal Register, and the resulting report
would include both in a single document.

[47] Land Registration (Scotland) Act 1979 s.6(1)(c).

[48] See above, paras 9–10 to 9–13.

[49] See below, para.9–23.

here is that entries, such as inhibitions, may not have quite the same name as the name stated in the search memorandum and so are not picked up by the search.[50] It is important that if the name of the person being searched against has any variants, these should also be searched against. Foreign names present a problem, partly because it may be unclear which part of the name is to be regarded as the surname and partly because there may be problems in transcribing from a non-Latin script. An inhibition against "Mao Tse Tung" would be treated in the Personal Register as an inhibition against Mr Tung, or, if the name is spelt in the Pinyin system of transcription (Mao Zedong), against Mr Zedong. This example illustrates two problems: the fact that the last name may not be the surname and the fact that different transliteration systems may exist. In Chinese usage the surname is Mao,[51] and the search instruction might have been against Mao. Hence, with such names, the search should be against all possible forms, i.e. against "Mao", "Tung" and "Zedong". Again, Saddam Hussein's surname was Saddam, not Hussein. Although such problems are especially prevalent with non-European names, European ones can also be problematic. A search against Otto von Bismarck should be against both "Bismarck" and "von Bismarck". In Spanish naming conventions there are two surnames, the father's and the mother's. The former comes first and has priority, so that Jorge Alfredo Ruiz Calderón would be Señor Ruiz not Señor Calderón, and would be indexed in a Spanish phone book under R not C.[52] Outside Spain, hyphens are sometimes used, so that in Scotland he might call himself Jorge Alfredo Ruiz-Calderón. Even our own conventions can create problems. For example, the surname of Alexander McCall Smith is not "Smith" but "McCall Smith", notwithstanding that there is no hyphen.

Another problem concerns addresses. If the name is uncommon, the searchers will report entries against it even if the address in the search instruction does not match the address in the inhibition or other entry. But if the name is common (Macdonald, Smith, Campbell, Jones, etc.) they are less likely to do this. A typical danger would be that an inhibition is made against James Campbell at his business address, but the search is instructed against James Campbell at his home address. Or the inhibition might state a previous address. The name is so common that the searchers may not report it. Their guarantee extends (or is said to extend) only to exact matches. So it is important that all addresses are stated in the memorandum, and solicitors are under a professional duty to find out from their clients all potentially relevant addresses.

A buyer (or other grantee) who "(a) is unaware of the inhibition; and (b) has taken all reasonable steps to discover the existence of an inhibition" takes free of the inhibition.[53] But there may be room for dispute as to what counts as "all reasonable steps".

Against whom, and how far back?

9–21   Against whom should personal searches be made, and for how far back? If the property is in the Land Register, only the registered owner, and the buyer,

---

[50] *Atlas Appointments v Tinsley*, 1997 S.C. 200.

[51] Though some Chinese settled in Europe adopt the Western "surname last" convention.

[52] Franco's full name was Francisco Paulino Hermenegildo Teódulo Franco y Bahamonde, son of Nicolás Franco y Salgado-Araújo and of María del Pilar Bahamonde y Pardo de Andrad.

[53] Bankruptcy and Diligence etc. (Scotland) Act 2007 s.159.

normally need to be searched against. If the property is still in the GRS, matters are more complicated. The predominant view is that there should be a personal search against every granter of every conveyance since (but not including) the foundation writ, the period of search running back for five years from the date when that conveyance was registered. In the case of the seller, that simply means searching back for five years from the present date. Thus, suppose that it is now 2011 and Adam is buying from Boris. Boris acquired from Carla in 2007, Carla acquired from Dorothy in 2002, and Dorothy acquired from Euan in 1995. The foundation writ is the 1995 disposition. Hence Boris must be searched against for the period 2006 to 2011, Carla for 2002 to 2007, and Dorothy for 1997 to 2002. Euan need not be searched against. In practice the existing search will normally show searches against these parties (except the current seller) for precisely these periods. Notwithstanding what has just been said, the form 10, used for first registrations, requests a search only for five years back from 2011. In our view this is wrong, although the missing personal searches can often be found from the full GRS search which usually forms part of the GRS titles.

If the property is in the Land Register matters are simpler: only the registered owner, and the buyer, need normally be searched against.

Sales by special parties

Where the sellers are heritable creditors exercising a power of sale, a personal search is, of course, necessary against them. It is also standard practice to search against the debtor, though in general no entry in the Personal Register against the debtor after the date of the creation of the heritable security can affect the creditors' power of sale.[54] Where the sale is by an executor, the practice is to search against both the deceased and against the executor *qua* executor. It is not necessary to search against the executor as an individual since any inhibition or sequestration against him or her in that capacity could not affect his or her powers as executor. Much the same considerations apply to sales by trustees. If the disposition contains the consent of a beneficiary, the practice is to search personally against that beneficiary as well. Indeed, in all cases where a disposition involves a consenter, the consenter should usually be searched against.[55]

If the sale is by a trustee in sequestration, a personal search is probably unnecessary. For instance, any inhibition against the bankrupt has no effect on the trustee's power of sale,[56] and it is difficult to see how a trustee in sequestration could competently be inhibited in his or her capacity as such. In practice, however, there is usually a personal search against the bankrupt. Where the sale is by a trustee acting under a trust deed for behoof of creditors, the practice is to search against both the debtor and the trustee, though the latter is probably unnecessary if the trust is "protected".

9–22

---

[54] See, for example, *Newcastle Building Society v White*, 1987 S.L.T. (Sh. Ct) 81.

[55] An exception is where the consent is by a non-entitled spouse or civil partner so as to waive occupancy rights (for which see below, para.10–10). Another exception is where A sells to B on missives and B sells to C, and the disposition is granted by A to C with B's consent. An inhibition against B will not affect C's title: Titles to Land Consolidation (Scotland) Act 1868 s.157 read with the Bankruptcy and Diligence etc. (Scotland) Act 2007 s.150(3).

[56] Bankruptcy (Scotland) Act 1985 s.31(2).

A personal search against the liquidator, receiver or administrator of a company is probably unnecessary, though it is sometimes done. A personal search against the company is normally carried out, though the seller may seek to stipulate in the missives that the purchaser cannot object to the title on the ground of any inhibition. This is probably safe for the purchaser, subject to three qualifications. First, an inhibition against a company probably, though not certainly, prevents sale by its administrator.[57] Secondly, where a company is in receivership, an inhibition against the company registered before, not merely the onset of the receivership but the original creation of the floating charge, will probably prevent sale.[58] Finally, while the liquidator in a compulsory liquidation, and in a creditors' voluntary liquidation, can sell free of any inhibition against the company, the same appears not to be true in a members' voluntary liquidation.[59] Because the law on such matters is not clear, it is useful to have clear provision in the missives.

There are also problems about how a partnership should be searched against. Practice varies, but a standard practice is to search against the firm name and against the names of the persons who hold the property for behoof of the firm.

Personal search against the buyer

9–23 An inhibition does not prevent the inhibitee from acquiring heritable property. But the practice is for the buyers to be personally searched against, as well as the sellers, at least if they are at the same time granting a heritable security to finance the purchase.[60] More serious is the possibility that a buyer might be an undischarged bankrupt, a fact which would be disclosed by the personal search.

Inhibition against the sellers after conclusion of missives

9–24 Sometimes sellers are inhibited after conclusion of missives but before the buyers' title is recorded. In that case the inhibition is ineffective because the sellers were under an obligation to sell before the inhibition was registered.[61] Nevertheless, in this situation the search is not clear because, on the face of the registers, the inhibition pre-dates the sale.[62] In this case, the general view is that the purchasers can refuse to settle. In practice, various possibilities are open. The buyers may choose to settle. Or they may agree to settle only if the sellers obtain a title insurance policy. Or they may insist that the sellers obtain a discharge or recall of the inhibition, or a consent to the sale by the inhibitor. The Keeper will register the buyers without exclusion of indemnity if satisfied as to the dates.[63]

---

[57] See below, para.29–11.

[58] See below, para.29–09.

[59] See below, para.29–07.

[60] This is required by para.5.11.1 of the CML *Lenders' Handbook for Scotland*. However, in such a case a lender is usually protected against any such inhibition. See G.L. Gretton, *Law of Inhibition and Adjudication*, 2nd edn (1996), pp.203–06.

[61] Inhibition does not strike at future voluntary acts, i.e. acts which the inhibitee was already under an obligation to perform.

[62] The missives not being on the register. See above, para.6–19.

[63] ROTPB, para.6.19.

LETTERS OF OBLIGATION

Letters of obligation: mind the gap

Letters of obligation are needed partly because the information available from 9–25 the registers may not be wholly up to date, partly because there will usually be a short delay between the receipt of the report and settlement, and partly because the buyers may not be able to complete their title instantly, so that there may be a period of a few days between the date of settlement and the date of completion of title. Thus there is a risk, albeit a very small one, that the land certificate will disclose something that was not discoverable from the form 10 or 12 report. In other words, there is a "gap" period, and the letter of obligation guarantees that no adverse entry in the registers will turn out to have appeared during this gap.

A letter of obligation is a guarantee by the sellers' solicitors that the land certificate will contain no exclusion of indemnity and show no entries prejudicial to the purchasers, and also that the answers in the form 1 or 2 remain correct as far as the sellers are concerned. The style suggested in the *Registration of Title Practice Book* has no official status but is widely used:

> "With reference to the settlement of the above transaction today we hereby (1) undertake to clear the records of any deed, decree or diligence (other than such as may be created by or against your client) which may be recorded in the Personal Register or to which effect may be given in the Land Register in the period from [*insert date of certification of form 12 report, or if a form 13 report has been instructed, the date of certification of that report*] to [*insert the date 14 days after settlement*] inclusive (or to the earlier date of registration of your client's interest in the above subjects) and which would cause the Keeper to make an entry on, or qualify her indemnity in, the land certificate to be issued in respect of that interest, and (2) confirm that, to the best of our knowledge and belief, as at this date the answers to the questions numbered 1 to 10 in the draft form 2 adjusted with you (insofar as these answers relate to our client or to our client's interest in the above subjects) are still correct."[64]

The obligation is limited to entries existing at settlement or made within 14 days[65] thereafter. But so long as the buyers register their own disposition within this period, they could not be affected by later entries which derive from the sellers.[66]

The letter of obligation takes the form of an actual letter, signed on behalf of the sellers' solicitors and addressed to the buyers' solicitors. Both the

---

[64] ROTPB, para.8.43. For the first registration style see 8.14. The wording of GRS letters of obligation was somewhat different.

[65] For some years the period was 21 days (reflecting delays in obtaining SDLT certificates), but it returned to 14 days in 2010. These periods refer to the "classic" letter of obligation, explained below. The period could be more than 14 days, but then the letter would not be "classic".

[66] Even assuming the Keeper was willing to make the entry. This is because, the sellers no longer being the owners, any later entries—e.g. a standard security by the sellers—would be invalid as granted *a non domino*.

buyers' solicitors and the buyers can enforce,[67] and liability rests with the sellers' solicitors.[68] This, indeed, is the whole point, for the sellers are liable anyway, in terms of the missives, and the buyers want something over and on top of that. In effect, the sellers' solicitors are acting as guarantors for their clients.[69]

It sometimes happens that the deed of discharge of the sellers' standard security is not yet available in time for settlement. In that case the letter of obligation will include an undertaking to deliver the deed.

Classics, non-classics, and failed classics

9-26   The professional insurers compensate solicitors for payments under letters of obligation provided that the letter of obligation is what is called a "classic" one. To be classic, a letter of obligation can cover only two matters: (i) a guarantee of the "gap" period, for a maximum of 14 days after settlement, as in the style given above, and (ii) an undertaking to deliver the deed of discharge (in the event that it is unavailable at settlement). There are four conditions for insurance cover:

> "A search must have been carried out immediately prior to the date of entry including, in Sasine cases a search in the computerised presentment book. The CML *Handbook* provides that the search in the Personal Registers be no more than three working days old but in all other cases the Conveyancing Committee ... accepts that both Property and Personal Register searches can be up to seven days old (five working days old). In calculating the number of days, the Committee considers that you should count from the settlement date back to the date to which the Search is certified as being correct (as opposed to the date on which it was issued).
>
> Proper enquiry must be made of the client as to whether or not there are any outstanding securities. Even where the client is a receiver or liquidator or other insolvency practitioner the enquiry must be made of both the insolvency practitioner and of the original owner even although no response is received.
>
> The solicitor granting the obligation must be unaware of any other security; and
>
> The solicitor granting the obligation must, in the case of an undertaking to deliver a discharge, have sufficient funds to pay off the loan(s)."[70]

A letter of obligation that guarantees anything other than the two items mentioned above is called a "non-classic" letter. An example would be an

---

[67] See *Johnston v Little*, 1960 S.L.T. 129; *Emslie v James Thomson & Sons*, noted at (1991) 36 J.L.S.S. 349; *Warners v Beveridge & Kellas*, 1994 S.L.T. (Sh. Ct) 29. See *McGillivray v Davidson*, 1993 S.L.T. 693 for the possibility of a single action against both the sellers (under the missives) and their solicitors (under the letter of obligation).

[68] But if (as occasionally happens) it is expressly granted "on behalf of our clients" then the firm itself is not bound. For an example, see *Digby Brown & Co v Lyall*, 1995 S.L.T. 932. For an unsuccessful attempt to escape liability, see *Cheval Property Finance Plc v Hill*, 2003 G.W.D. 36-999.

[69] If the solicitors are compelled to incur loss under their letter of obligation, they may be able to recover from their clients: *Marshall Wilson Dean & Turnbull v Feymac Properties Ltd*, 1996 G.W.D. 22-1247.

[70] From the Law Society of Scotland website: *http://www.lawscot.org.uk/members/member-services/a-to-z-rules–guidance/g—m/letters-of-obligations—faqs*.

undertaking to deliver building control documentation. A letter of obligation that is limited to the two items mentioned above, but which fails to satisfy any of the four conditions, is called a "failed classic".

Letters of obligation apply only in respect of the two property registers and the Personal Register. They are not normally given for the Companies Register, and indeed any such letter would be, to that extent, non-classic.

Obligation to grant?

There is no obligation to grant a letter of obligation. But it is ordinary practice 9–27 for such a letter to be granted. The Law Society says:

> "While there is no legal obligation to give a letter of obligation where missives are silent, there is a professional duty on a solicitor to grant a letter of obligation unless the solicitor advises to the contrary at the earliest possible opportunity. This expression 'at the earliest possible opportunity' does not have a particular meaning but it is interpreted as being before conclusion of missives."[71]

In sales of new properties it is common for the sellers' solicitors to refuse to grant a letter of obligation. And no letter of obligation is expected where the transaction is gratuitous.

The future of letters of obligation, and the concept of advance notices

In recent years the solicitors' profession has become increasingly unhappy 9–28 about letters of obligation, and it is said that the same is true of the professional insurers. The Scottish Law Commission has recommended a system of "advance notices" in respect of the registration of deeds, the use of which would make letters of obligation unnecessary.[72] If this recommendation is enacted, it may be that letters of obligation will disappear, except perhaps in cases where the discharge of the sellers' standard security is not available in time for settlement.

---

[71] From the Law Society of Scotland website: *http://www.lawscot.org.uk/members/member-services/a-to-z-rules–guidance/g—m/letters-of-obligations—faqs*.

[72] Scottish Law Commission, Report on *Land Registration* (Scot. Law Com. No.222, 2010), Pt 14. See above, para.8–25.

CHAPTER 10

MATRIMONIAL HOMES, FAMILY HOMES, AND HOMES IN CO-OWNERSHIP

Introduction

10–01 At common law, if the matrimonial home was owned by just one spouse, the other spouse had no rights in it, and, if the marriage broke down, the owning spouse could insist that the non-owning spouse leave. The position was not as bad as it sounds, partly because the ejected spouse could, if necessary, claim aliment to cover housing costs (and, in the event of divorce, other rights), and partly because in practice most matrimonial homes are (unless rented) owned in common by both spouses, and when two persons own in common, the common law is that neither can require the other to leave. However, the law was felt to be unsatisfactory, and the Matrimonial Homes (Family Protection) (Scotland) Act 1981 changed it, giving a set of statutory rights called "occupancy rights" to the non-owning spouse.[1] With the introduction of civil partnerships for same-sex couples by the Civil Partnership Act 2004, virtually identical rights were extended to a non-owning civil partner. The two Acts are important to conveyancers because of the need to ensure, on behalf of a grantee, that there are no outstanding occupancy rights. Fortunately, this task has been greatly eased by a series of amendments introduced in 1985 and again in 2006.[2]

As well as covering the case where the house is owned by one spouse or civil partner only, the Act also has certain provisions that apply where it is co-owned. This chapter will, in addition, consider the position where residential property is co-owned by persons who are not spouses or civil partners, such as cohabitants and siblings. In such cases the Act does not apply.[3]

The nature of occupancy rights

10–02 Occupancy rights are conferred by the Acts where title[4] is held by only one spouse or civil partner, and are conferred on the other spouse or civil partner. The Acts call the spouse or partner who holds the title the "entitled spouse" or the "entitled partner", and the other the "non-entitled spouse" or "non-entitled partner". The non-entitled spouse or partner is thus the spouse or partner who is given occupancy rights. The chief element of occupancy rights is the right to

---

[1] See generally E.M. Clive, *The Law of Husband and Wife in Scotland*, 4th edn (1997), Ch.15, although this is now somewhat out of date.

[2] Law Reform (Miscellaneous Provisions) (Scotland) Act 1985; Family Law (Scotland) Act 2006. The latter implemented, after a long delay, Pt XI of the Scottish Law Commission's Report on *Family Law* (Scot Law Com. No.135, 1992).

[3] In general. It has limited provisions about cohabitants.

[4] Occupancy rights also apply to leases.

occupy the matrimonial or family home even if the entitled party withdraws consent to such occupation.[5] In other words, if Mr and Mrs Smith live together, and title is held by Mrs Smith, she cannot throw Mr Smith out, except with the consent of the court. Indeed, he can, with the consent of the court, throw her out, for another aspect of occupancy rights is that the non-entitled party can obtain a court order excluding the entitled party from the home, this being called an "exclusion order".[6]

Matrimonial homes and family homes

The 1981 Act applies to "matrimonial homes"; the 2004 Act applies to "family homes". To all intents and purposes the definition of each is identical.[7] "Matrimonial home" is defined as: 10–03

> "Any house, caravan, houseboat or other structure which has been provided or has been made available by one or both of the spouses as, or has become, a family residence and includes any garden or other ground or building usually occupied with, or otherwise required for the amenity or convenience of, the house, caravan, houseboat or other structure but does not include a residence provided or made available by a person for one spouse for that spouse to reside in, whether with any child of the family or not, separately from the other spouse."

Three consequences of this definition are worth noting. In the first place, suppose that Mr and Mrs White live in a flat together. Mrs White then moves out, and buys a house for herself, and lives there without her husband. The new house is not a matrimonial home.[8] Mr White has no rights to it. He could not insist on moving in against her wishes. But the flat where her husband is living remains a matrimonial home.[9] She could insist on moving into that flat, against his wishes. Not only could she insist on moving in, but she could in appropriate cases compel him to move out, by means of an exclusion order. In general, once a property is a matrimonial or family home, it retains that status until something happens which takes it outwith the definition, or until something happens to bring the occupancy rights to an end—typically the dissolution of the marriage or civil partnership or a failure to occupy the home for two years.

In the second place, only something which can be lived in can be a matrimonial or family home. Thus, the Acts can be ignored in, for instance, the sale of

---

[5] Matrimonial Homes (Family Protection) Scotland) Act 1981 s.1(1); Civil Partnership Act 2004 s.101(1).

[6] 1981 Act s.4; 2004 Act s.104. There seems to be a logical problem here. Sections 4(1) and 104(1) define an exclusion order as an order "suspending the occupancy rights of the other spouse" (or civil partner). But since it is only Mr Smith who has "occupancy rights", how can he have Mrs Smith's "occupancy rights" suspended? Mrs Smith has no "occupancy rights". Her right to occupy exists, not because she has statutory "occupancy rights", but simply because she is the owner of the property. See Gretton, 1981 S.L.T. (News) 297.

[7] 1981 Act s.22(1); 2004 Act s.135(1). Simplicity of drafting is not a feature of the legislation. For discussion of this definition see D.I. Nichols and M.C. Meston, *The Matrimonial Homes (Family Protection) (Scotland) Act 1981*, 2nd edn (1986), and E.M. Clive, *The Law of Husband and Wife in Scotland*, paras 15.005 to 15.010.

[8] Hence, she could sell it, truly signing a declaration (see below) that it was not a matrimonial home.

[9] Thus, in effect he could not sell it without his wife's consent.

a factory. Or again, if Mary grants a standard security to Norah and Norah assigns this to Olga, Olga need not worry that Norah might be married or in a civil partnership, because a standard security cannot be a matrimonial or family home.[10]

In the third place, only natural persons—human beings—can be married or enter into civil partnerships. Suppose that Alan sells a house to Brian Ltd and Brian Ltd later sells it to Charles. The house cannot be a matrimonial or family home in relation to Brian Ltd, though Charles will still need to be sure that it is not a matrimonial or family home in relation to Alan.

Termination of occupancy rights

10–04   Occupancy rights are the rights of a spouse or civil partner as such, and so end when the marriage or civil partnership ends, which is either by the death of one party or by divorce or dissolution of the partnership. In addition, a person can renounce occupancy rights,[11] though this is uncommon in practice. Occupancy rights are also lost by non-exercise for a continuous period of two years[12] provided that either (i) during the two-year period there was no cohabitation with the entitled party[13] or (ii) before the period began, the entitled party had disposed of his or her interest in the home.[14] So if Mr Black walks out on Mrs Black (being the sole owner of the matrimonial home), Mr Black will lose his occupancy rights after two years. Crucially, however, occupancy rights are *not* lost merely because the entitled party sells the home or engages in some other "dealing" in respect of it. This leads on to the next topic.

Why the Act affects conveyancing

10–05   Much of the 1981 and 2004 Acts is of only limited interest to conveyancers, and occupancy rights would be of only limited interest to them as well, were it not for the fact that such rights are not merely rights by one party against the other. In certain cases they can affect third parties, such as a purchaser or heritable creditor. This is because the legislation provides that, subject to certain qualifications, a "dealing" by the entitled party does not affect the occupancy rights of the other party.[15] "Dealing" includes sale, so that if Mrs Smith sells the house, Mr Smith's occupancy rights can survive and be enforceable against the buyer. In other words, occupancy rights are not ordinary personal rights, but can behave rather like real rights. It is because occupancy rights are quasi-real that they are important in conveyancing. They are, however, not true real rights. They do not affect certain types of third party. Thus, as will be seen later, they affect some purchasers but not others, some creditors but not others, and so on. Occupancy rights are probably to be classified as personal rights

---

[10] But Olga may be affected by possible occupancy rights in the house in favour of Mary's spouse or civil partner.

[11] See below, para.10–9.

[12] For the purposes of calculating the two years no account is taken of any period during which the spouse or civil partner is attempting to assert occupancy rights in court: see 1981 Act s.9A; 2004 Act s.111A.

[13] 1981 Act s.1(7); 2004 Act s.101(6A).

[14] 1981 Act s.6(3)(f); 2004 Act s.106(3)(f).

[15] 1981 Act s.6(1); 2004 Act s.106(1).

that in some situations can bind third parties. They are overriding interests for the purposes of registration of title.[16]

If a "dealing" by Mrs Smith is subject to the occupancy rights of Mr Smith, that does not mean that the dealing is void or even voidable at Mr Smith's instance. Thus, suppose that Mrs Smith dispones to Mr Jones. Depending on the circumstances, Mr Smith's occupancy rights may survive. If so, he can stay in the house, and Mr Jones cannot move in. But nevertheless Mr Jones is the owner, and has all the rights incidental to ownership, except the right to possess.[17] That right is temporarily suspended, until, for one reason or another (e.g. the termination of the Smiths' marriage) the occupancy rights come to an end.

Two other types of right, similar to occupancy rights, deserve brief mention. The legislation gives, in certain situations, equivalent rights to cohabitants.[18] But these are of little conveyancing importance because they cannot normally affect third parties. Again, rights somewhat similar to occupancy rights are created by the Bankruptcy (Scotland) Act 1985 in favour of the family of a bankrupt.[19]

What is a dealing?

As has been seen, occupancy rights concern the conveyancer because they can   10–06 survive "dealings". What, then, is a "dealing"? It is not a term of art in Scots law, and the legislation nowhere explains it beyond saying that it "includes the grant of a heritable security and the creation of a trust but does not include a conveyance under section 80 of the Lands Clauses Consolidation (Scotland) Act 1845".[20] Sale, for example, is not mentioned, and it is only by inference that it is clear that a sale or excambion[21] is a "dealing", because provision is made for the case where "the dealing comprises a transfer for value".[22] So, apart from heritable security, trust, sale and excambion, it is a matter of speculation as to what is or is not a "dealing". The cautious view is that a "dealing" is any juridical act which might adversely affect occupancy rights. Thus, gifts, leases and servitudes are probably "dealings". With no case law, the prudent conveyancer must assume that they are.

Agreeing to the shortening of a calling-up notice for a standard security is, perhaps, not a "dealing" since there is specific provision for it in s.20 of the 1981 Act,[23] the effect of which, however, is virtually to make it a "dealing". A sale by a heritable creditor is not a "dealing" because it is not an act of a spouse. A borderline case is a further advance made by a heritable creditor. Usually there is no difficulty, as normally the spouse or civil partner will already have consented to the security. But suppose that Mr Green, a bachelor, grants a standard security to the bank, and later enters into a civil partnership. So far so good, because even though the civil partner has not consented, the

---

[16] Land Registration (Scotland) Act 1979 s.28(1).
[17] Of course, the right to possess is of great importance. But it is not everything.
[18] Including same-sex cohabitants. See 1981 Act s.18.
[19] Bankruptcy (Scotland) Act 1985 s.40. See below, para.10–17.
[20] 1981 Act s.6(2); 2004 Act s.106(2).
[21] i.e. exchange. See below, para.11–23.
[22] 1981 Act s.6(3)(e); 2004 Act s.106(3)(e).
[23] Amending s.19(10) of the 1970 Act. There is no corresponding provision in respect of civil partnerships.

security was a pre-partnership transaction and so cannot be subject to his occupancy rights. But what if Mr Green then borrows more money from the bank? This does, in a sense, put the occupancy rights of his civil partner at risk, for a larger loan must increase the danger of default. So is the further advance a "dealing"? No one knows. The prudent course is therefore to obtain appropriate documentation for a further advance.[24]

Protection of acquirers

10–07 Where occupancy rights exist, a person who buys the house, or acquires any rights in it, will normally need the consent of the non-entitled spouse or civil partner. In the absence of such consent the non-entitled party could occupy the house to the exclusion of the purchaser. That does not mean that the purchaser would not be owner, but the ownership would be subject to the occupancy rights.

If that were all, the Act would not have been such a headache for conveyancers. Purchasers would simply have checked whether the property was subject to occupancy rights, and, if so, would have asked for the consent of the person holding those rights. However, what of the case where there appear to be no such rights, typically the case where the seller is said to be unmarried and not in a civil partnership?[25] The reality might be different, for the seller might not be telling the truth. Perhaps it would have been reasonable for the legislation to have made no special provision for such a case: in this imperfect world there is always a risk that people will not tell the truth, and special legislative provisions to deal with that danger are not normally thought necessary. If special provision was thought necessary, the natural rule would have been that a purchaser in good faith would be protected. But in fact the legislation is more demanding. It gives protection to purchasers, provided that they are both in good faith and hold a signed declaration from the seller. Possibly the most sensible response of conveyancers would have been to ignore this strange and complex procedure designed to guard against remote possibilities, especially since purchasers regularly run greater risks (albeit still remote) all the time. However, since the legislation laid down this rigmarole, conveyancers felt obliged to go along with it, and, this being universal practice, a solicitor who fails to demand a declaration in such cases is likely to be guilty of negligence.

The three kinds of deed

10–08 The conveyancing side of the Act revolves around three deeds, namely (i) the renunciation (ii) the consent and (iii) the declaration. A solicitor acting for the grantee of a disposition, heritable security, or other juridical act will, wherever appropriate, seek to obtain obtain one of the three from the granter; and even if it turns out to be invalid, the legislation protects grantees in good faith in cases involving sale, excambion and heritable security.[26]

---

[24] In practice the failure to obtain documentation in relation to a standard security or further advance may not matter very much. For even if occupancy rights exist, they do not prevail in a question with a *bona fide* acquirer from a heritable creditor exercising its power of sale. See 1981 Act s.106(1A); 2004 Act s.106(1A). And see also below, para.10–14.

[25] The other main possibility is where the house is not a matrimonial or family home.

[26] 1981 Act s.6(3)(e); 2004 Act s.106(3)(e). See further para.10–14.

In the renunciation a spouse or civil partner wholly gives up occupancy rights. It can, however, only refer to "a particular property", so that a deed renouncing such rights in any future home would presumably be invalid.[27]

In the consent, also called the "consent to dealing", a person consents to a particular transaction, but does not otherwise give up occupancy rights. Thus, if the husband is sole owner, and grants a standard security, and the wife consents, her occupancy rights remain intact as against the husband himself and as against all third parties except the heritable creditor and any parties deriving right from the heritable creditor.

Lastly, there is the declaration. Whereas the renunciation and consent waive occupancy rights, either wholly or in part, the declaration has a different purpose. It is not a waiver of occupancy rights, but a statement that no such rights exist. This is typically where the owner is neither married nor in a civil partnership, but a married owner or an owner in a civil partnership can sometimes grant a declaration too, where the property is for some other reason not a matrimonial or family home. It is thus evidential rather than restrictive or extinctive. Another important difference is that, whereas a renunciation or consent is granted by the owner's spouse or civil partner, an affidavit is granted by the owner.

It seems that all three deeds can be granted by an attorney acting under an appropriately worded power of attorney.[28]

Renunciations

The renunciation has no prescribed form,[29] except that the renouncer must   10–09
swear or affirm before a notary[30] that it is made "freely and without coercion of any kind".[31] In practice, the renunciation will have three signatures, namely those of the renouncer, the notary, and a witness. The Act does not require a witness, but renunciations will normally be registered in the Books of Council and Session, and for that a witnessed deed is necessary.[32]

If made outwith Scotland a renunciation may be sworn or affirmed before "any person duly authorised by the law of the country (other than Scotland) in which the swearing or affirmation takes place to administer oaths or receive affirmations in that other country",[33] such as an English solicitor.[34] For renunciations done abroad there is the problem that there is no easy way of checking whether the person administering the oath is duly authorised. (Where can you lay your hands on the current list of notaries in Burkino Faso?[35]) The

---

[27] 1981 Act s.1(5); 2004 Act s.101(5).

[28] This is made express only in relation to declarations: see 1981 Act s.6(3)(e)(i); 2004 Act s.106(3)(e)(i). See also ROTPB, para.6.42.

[29] See Halliday, para.36–32 for a style.

[30] Thus, it seems that a justice of the peace could not do this. But an independent conveyancing practitioner can, though only in relation to the occupancy rights of spouses: Public Appointments and Public Bodies (Scotland) Act 2003 s.14. For notaries, see below, para.17–27.

[31] 1981 Act s.1(6); 2004 Act s.101(6).

[32] 1995 Act s.6.

[33] 1981 Act s.1(6); 2004 Act s.101(8).

[34] The administration of oaths is a "reserved legal activity" under s.12(1)(f) of the Legal Services Act 2007.

[35] Actually an international system exists. The old one was the so-called legalisation process. The Hague Convention of October 5, 1961 replaced this by the apostille procedure. Most but not all states are parties to the Convention (including the UK but not, it may be of help to know, Burkino Faso).

legislation helps by providing that a *bona fide* purchaser or heritable creditor will be protected if the renunciation "bears to have been properly made".[36] It should probably bear the seal of the foreign notary.[37]

Consents

10–10   For the consent, there is a prescribed style.[38] It can either be in a separate deed or be incorporated in the deed to which it consents.[39] Both are common and indeed often both are used in the same transaction, that is to say, there is a consent given at the beginning of the transaction followed by a second consent incorporated in the final deed. The prescribed style needs attestation, but does not need a notary.

The sheriff court or Court of Session can dispense with consent if the non-entitled spouse or civil partner (a) cannot be traced, (b) is incapax or (c) unreasonably withholds consent either by refusing to respond or by indicating, untruthfully, that consent would be forthcoming.[40] In practice, the consent is likely to be sought before the property is marketed, and this is allowed subject to the court fixing a minimum price and a deadline for concluding the contract.[41] In the event that the application is refused, the court can order the non-entitled party to pay rent to the owner (whether the entitled party or, following a dealing, a third party), and to comply with such other conditions in relation to occupation as the court may specify.[42]

Declarations

10–11   The declaration is the successor of the affidavit, which was in use until 2006, the difference being that while an affidavit required to be sworn or affirmed before a notary public, a declaration need only be signed in the normal way. Unlike a renunciation or consent, a declaration can cover only three types of "dealing", namely sales, excambions and securities.[43] In particular, gifts, trusts, leases and servitudes are not covered. Thus, if a married woman gives property to her daughter, the donor's husband can consent.[44] But if the woman is a widow, no documentation in respect of occupancy rights is possible in terms of the legislation. Nor is such documentation possible for the grant of a lease by a bachelor, or where a divorcee grants a trust deed for behoof of creditors. In

---

[36] 1981 Act ss.6(3)(e)(ii) and 8(2A)(b); 2004 Act ss.106(3)(e)(ii) and 108(3)(b).

[37] See Ferguson, (1992) 37 J.L.S.S. 10; Swinney, (1992) 37 J.L.S.S. 141.

[38] Matrimonial Homes (Form of Consent) (Scotland) Regulations 1982 (SI 1982/971); Civil Partnership Family Homes (Form of Consent) Regulations 2006 (SSI 2006/115). See, further, Halliday, para.36–31.

[39] For consent in a disposition or other deed, the statutory style in respect of the occupancy rights of a non-entitled spouse is: ". . . with the consent of A.B. (*designation*), the spouse of the said C.D., for the purposes of the Matrimonial Homes (Family Protection) (Scotland) Act 1981 . . .".

[40] 1981 Act s.7(1), (2); 2004 Act s.107(1), (2). An example is *East Ayrshire Council v McKnight*, 2004 Hous. L.R. 114. For procedural problems see *Longmuir v Longmuir*, 1985 S.L.T. (Sh. Ct) 33.

[41] 1981 Act s.7(1A), (1B); 2004 Act s.107(1A), (1B). This responds to the difficulty highlighted by *Fyffe v Fyffe*, 1987 S.L.T. (Sh. Ct) 38. There is an equivalent rule for the grant of a heritable security: see 1981 Act s.7(1C), (1D); 2004 Act s.107(1C), (1D).

[42] 1981 Act s.7(3A); 2004 Act s.107(3A).

[43] 1981 Act ss.6(3)(e)(i) and 8(2A)(a); 2004 Act ss.106(3)(e)(i) and 108(3)(a).

[44] Note, however, that the protection to *bona fide* third parties against the possibility of latent invalidity is also confined to sales, excambions and securities. See the 1981 Act ss.6(3)(e) and 8(2A). Thus, a forged consent produced in association with a gift would be ineffective.

all these cases the grantee must take the chance, small as it is, that there might be a spouse or civil partner with occupancy rights.

Although no style is prescribed for a declaration, the wording of the relevant statutory provision requires to be followed. Usually it will be convenient for the declaration to be included as an additional clause in the disposition or standard security, in which case it will look something like this:

> "and I declare that the subjects are neither a matrimonial home nor a family home in relation to which a spouse or civil partner of mine has occupancy rights within the meaning of the Matrimonial Homes (Family Protection) (Scotland) Act 1981 or the Civil Partnership Act 2004."

In ARTL transactions the practice is to include the declaration as part of the granter's (paper) mandate.[45] There is, of course, no objection to having the declaration on a separate piece of paper, in which case a witness, though not required, is likely to be used to make the deed probative; but a significant advantage of incorporation into a disposition, standard security, or mandate is that a scanned copy will be retained at the registers and can be consulted if the original is lost.

Co-owners

Where title is in the name of both spouses or civil partners there are no occu- 10–12
pancy rights, for there is no party who is "non-entitled". Of course, if property is co-owned, both co-owners have the right to occupy it, as a matter of common law, but that is not the same as the "occupancy rights" created by the legislation. Any deed granted by just one co-owner can have no effect on the rights of the other party, again as a matter of common law. However, the legislation does have certain provisions about co-ownership by spouses and civil partners.

Take the following case. Mr and Mrs Beige are co-owners, and become estranged, and Mr Beige leaves the house and conveys his one-half share to his brother. At common law, that could not prejudice Mrs Beige's right to possession, but the brother would also have the right to share the possession with her.[46] The legislation modifies this rule by providing that the brother has no right to occupy, except with Mrs Beige's consent.[47] Furthermore, the court is given a discretion to refuse, or postpone, decree in an action of division and sale raised by one spouse or civil partner against the other.[48] This provision is obviously of key significance, in a world where most matrimonial or family homes are co-owned.[49]

Consider, next, the case where title is held in common by two persons who are not married or in a civil partnership, at least to or with each other, and likewise the case where title is held by three persons, two of whom are spouses or

---

[45] It is included in the styles of mandate produced by the Law Society of Scotland. See further above, para.8–23. If a lender wishes the declaration to be lodged with them to avoid difficulties in the event of sale, then it can be prepared as a separate document. See Robert Rennie and Stewart Brymer, *Conveyancing in the Electronic Age* (2008), para.9–11.

[46] A potentially unworkable situation, but any co-owner can always terminate such a situation by insisting on a sale of the whole property.

[47] 1981 Act s.9; 2004 Act s.109.

[48] 1981 Act s.19; 2004 Act s.110.

[49] For cases on s.19 of the 1981 Act, see e.g. *Rae v Rae*, 1991 S.L.T. 454; *Milne v Milne*, 1994 S.L.T. (Sh. Ct) 57; *B v B*, 2010 G.W.D. 24-454.

civil partners. In such cases the legislation has virtually no conveyancing implications because of s.6(2) of the 1981 Act or the equivalent provision (s.106(2)) of the 2004 Act. The former defines "entitled spouse" for the purposes of the section thus:

> "'entitled spouse' does not include a spouse who, apart from the provisions of this Act,—
>
> (a) is permitted by a third party to occupy a matrimonial home; or
> (b) is entitled to occupy a matrimonial home along with an individual who is not the other spouse, whether or not that individual has waived his or her right of occupation in favour of the spouse so entitled."

This convoluted provision—and its equivalent in the 2004 Act—means that where there is common ownership involving a party other than the spouses or civil partners, there can be no "entitled spouse" or "entitled partner" for the purposes of s.6 or s.106, and hence a person in such a case has no protection against a dealing. In other words, in the case of common property, occupancy rights do not affect successors, and are purely personal. Thus, if two sisters own a house in common and sell it, there is no need for declarations (if they are spinsters) and no need for renunciations or consents (if they are married or in a civil partnership). However, the provision quoted is to be found only in ss.6 and 106 (protection to purchasers in, respectively, the 1981 and 2004 Acts) and not in ss.8 and 108 (protection to lenders). The practical result of the omission has been that where, in such a situation, the parties wish not to sell the property, but to grant a heritable security, occupancy rights documentation is sometimes demanded. This practice is understandable but, it is thought, not necessary. Broadly speaking, ss.6 and 106 do three things: (1) They lay down the general principle that occupancy rights are unaffected by "dealings". (2) They state exceptions to this rule, including the common ownership exception. (3) They have specific provisions for sales (and excambions). The first two of these are of general application, and are not confined to sales. Sections 8 and 108 deal with heritable securities, but their provisions correspond only to what is here called part (3) of ss.6 and 106. Parts (1) and (2) of ss.6 and 106 apply equally to heritable securities, and indeed to all "dealings".[50] Hence the conclusion, that in the common ownership situation, a heritable creditor does not need to be protected by documentation.[51] However, if a lender insists on documentation, then documentation must of course be obtained.

Guardians, trustees and executors

10–13 A dealing by a guardian is to be treated as a dealing of the incapax for whom he acts, and so, if the incapax is an entitled spouse or civil partner, as giving rise to issues as to occupancy rights. Not only does this view seem correct as a matter of legal policy—for it is not clear why a wife should cease to be protected just because her husband loses his reason—but it is also presupposed by an amendment made to the legislation in 2005 allowing declarations to be

---

[50] Here, as elsewhere in the legislation, it is difficult to admire the drafting.
[51] See also ROTPB, para.6.35.

executed by guardians.[52] So if the incapax is married or in a civil partnership, the spouse or civil partner should consent to a sale. Otherwise the guardian signs a declaration.

The legislation does not make clear how a transaction by an executor or other trustee is to be treated.[53] Clearly, no one could have occupancy rights against a trustee *qua* trustee. But might a beneficiary's spouse have occupancy rights? Under the legislation, occupancy rights arise not merely where the entitled spouse is owner but where he or she is entitled to occupy,[54] with the consequence that a right less than ownership can be a ground for occupancy rights. Thus, if a beneficiary is entitled to occupy, his spouse or civil partner might have occupancy rights. But that of itself does not prove that a purchaser, say, from the executor or other trustee, needs to obtain documentation. For the legislation says that occupancy rights will survive a "dealing" only where the "dealing" is done by the "entitled spouse" or "entitled partner".[55] It could be argued that a sale or other transaction by an executor or trustee is done only by the executor or trustee and not by the beneficiary, so that no documentation would be required, since no occupancy rights could survive the transaction. A strong example would be where a trust deed directs the property to be sold. Such a sale could hardly be a "dealing" by the beneficiary. Another strong example would be if the sale is necessary to raise funds to pay off debts: a sale by a trustee in sequestration is unlikely to be a "dealing" of the bankrupt.[56] Arguably, a transaction is never a "dealing" by the beneficiary except where his consent to it is necessary. But because of the uncertainties, the safe course, and the one generally adopted, is to obtain documentation in relation to the beneficiary, i.e. either a declaration from the beneficiary himself or a renunciation or consent from his spouse or civil partner. Thus, suppose that Kate owns a house. She dies. Her widower, Lucas, is her sole legatee and executor. He sells *qua* executor. A declaration from him *qua* beneficiary should be obtained. (He might have remarried.)

If, as often, the beneficial right is vested in more than one person, the co-ownership exception applies[57] and there is no need for documentation. But if there is any room for doubt, documentation should be obtained.

Summary: what documentation is needed?

In the end, this rather complex body of law results in some rather simple practical steps. Take the standard case of acting for the grantee of a disposition or standard security, and consider what documentation is needed in respect of occupancy rights.

In many—perhaps in most—cases no documentation is needed at all because it will be immediately obvious that no occupancy rights can exist. One such

10–14

---

[52] 1981 Act s.6(3)(e)(i); 2004 Act s.106(3)(e)(i). For a contrary view based on earlier legislation, see ROTPB, para.6.35. This dispensation does not extend to declarations in relation to grants of heritable securities.

[53] For the Keeper's view, see ROTPB, para.6.40.

[54] 1981 Act s.1(1); 2004 Act s.101(1).

[55] 1981 Act s.6(1); 2004 Act s.106(1).

[56] William W. McBryde, *Bankruptcy*, 2nd edn (1995), Ch.9. For collusive sequestrations, see Bankruptcy (Scotland) Act 1985 s.41. Section 40 of the Act imposes some restrictions on the trustee's right to sell the family home.

[57] See above, para.10–12.

case is where the property is owned in common.[58] Another is where the property is not a house. A third is where the granter is a company or other juristic person.[59] For occupancy rights are only capable of arising where a natural person is the sole owner of a house. If a sole owner is married or in a civil partnership, the documentation needed is a renunciation or, much more commonly, a consent to dealing from the spouse or civil partner.[60] Otherwise the owner must sign a declaration.[61] Whichever one of these is produced—renunciation, consent, or declaration—grantees are protected from occupancy rights provided they are in good faith.[62] So if a seller who is estranged from his wife signs a declaration to the effect that the property is not a matrimonial home in relation to which a spouse has occupancy rights, this falsehood (if it is falsehood)[63] has no effect on the buyer, who takes the property free of the wife's occupancy rights. Hence the critical importance of obtaining documentation in cases where occupancy rights might exist; whether such documentation might turn out to be latently invalid is a secondary question and not one with which, on the whole,[64] conveyancers need be concerned.

The Keeper no longer requires that the documentation be produced as part of the grantee's application for registration. Instead, where an application is made in respect of a disposition,[65] the Keeper asks in the application form whether the subjects could be a matrimonial or family home and, if so, whether "the necessary consents, renunciations, affidavits or written declarations exist confirming that the subjects will not be affected by any subsisting occupancy right".[66] Assuming the grantee answers "no" to the first question or "yes" to the second, as is invariably the case, the Keeper will issue a land certificate containing a statement in the B section to the effect that there are no subsisting occupancy rights in respect of the spouse or civil partner of a former owner.[67] Nothing is said in respect of the current owner (i.e. the grantee), for the Keeper is not in the business of predicting future domestic arrangements. In fact the Keeper's note is not conclusive as to occupancy rights. As overriding interests they either exist, or do not exist, independently of what she says. The advantage of the Keeper's statement is simply that if it turns out to be incorrect she will be liable to pay compensation (though not to a grantee who answered the question on the application form carelessly).[68] At first sight it would appear that such compensation is not in fact available, because s.12(3)(h) of the 1979 Act excludes liability where "the loss arises in respect of an error

---

[58] See above, para.10–12.

[59] See above, para.10–3.

[60] See above, paras 10–9 and 10–10. If, however, the house is not a matrimonial or family home, it would be possible instead for the seller to sign a declaration. But that might lead to disputes as to the true nature of the house, and the consent of the spouse or civil partner will always be a more attractive option.

[61] See above, para.10–11.

[62] 1981 Act s.6(3)(e); 2004 Act s.106(3)(e).

[63] There might be no occupancy rights, e.g. because they have been extinguished by two years' non-exercise and non-cohabitation: see above, para.10–4.

[64] But in the case of declarations it is necessary that the granter actually signed. So a forged declaration would not trigger the protection for grantees.

[65] But not a standard security. This is presumably because the Keeper's statement under r.4(j) (see below) relates only to *previous* owners.

[66] In form 2 this is question 4.

[67] Land Registration (Scotland) Rules 2006 (SSI 2006/485) r.5(j).

[68] Land Registration (Scotland) Act 1979 s.12(3)(n).

or omission in the noting of an overriding interest". But the view generally taken, and taken by the Keeper herself, is that the Keeper would be liable because a statement under r.5(j) is, strictly speaking, not a "noting of an overriding interest".

Thus far we have considered only the current transaction. But what of previous transactions? Must the grantee worry that there are occupancy rights held by the spouses or civil partners of those who previously owned the property? The answer is no. Unless the grantee positively knows about prior occupancy rights he is entitled, under the legislation, to assume there are none and to take free of any such rights as might have existed.[69] And even if the conditions for this immunity cannot be met, which would be highly unusual, the grantee (other than in first registrations) can rely on the Keeper's indemnified statement as to the absence of prior occupancy rights.

Missives

Strictly, it is not necessary for missives to make provision about occupancy rights or the production of documentation, for this will be covered by the general obligation to produce a good and marketable title.[70] But the usual practice is to have a clause dealing with the matter—for example: "At settlement, the Property will not be affected by any occupancy rights as defined in the Matrimonial Homes (Family Protection) (Scotland) Act 1981 as amended and the Civil Partnership Act 2004 and appropriate evidence to this effect will be delivered at settlement".[71] In addition, the issue is covered by the standard clause warranting the absence of overriding interests.[72]

10–15

Separation and divorce[73]

When a marriage or civil partnership breaks down there is often a separation agreement, and, if so, it will deal with the house. The agreement should normally contain a renunciation of all occupancy rights,[74] and a discharge of any succession rights in the house, including any right under any special destination. If the house is co-owned by Mr and Mrs Ochre with a survivorship destination and Mr Ochre is to dispone his half share to Mrs Ochre, such a disposition should be in the form of a deed by both Mr and Mrs Ochre to Mrs Ochre, so as to ensure that the destination is wholly deleted from the title.[75] The agreement should, of course, deal with any secured loan. If Mrs Ochre is to become sole owner then normally she will be assuming sole responsibility for the secured loan, but it should be recalled that as far as the bank is concerned

10–16

---

[69] 1981 Act s.6(1A); 2004 Act s.106(1A). This is one of a number of changes made to the legislation by the Family Law (Scotland) Act 2006. The immunity applies where a person acquires "the home, or an interest in it" from someone other than the entitled spouse or civil partner. The meaning of "interest" in this context is unclear. If it includes subordinate real rights like standard securities, it would have the effect of extinguishing even the occupancy rights of a spouse or civil partner of the immediate seller if the buyer was funding his purchase by a security.

[70] For which see above, Ch.6.

[71] Highland Standard Clauses (2007) cl.14.1.

[72] e.g. Highland Standard Clauses cl.10.3.5.

[73] For practicalities, see Bett, (2000) 48 Prop. L.B. 1; Bett, (2004) 68 Prop. L.B. 5. See also E.M. Clive, *The Law of Husband and Wife in Scotland*, 4th edn (1997), para.19.035.

[74] Which will in any case come to an end on the termination of the marriage by divorce or the civil partnership by dissolution. See above, para.10–4.

[75] See below, paras 26–20 and 26–21.

this is just an agreement between the Ochres, and the original loan documentation still stands, whereby Mr and Mrs Ochre will be jointly and severally liable to the bank for the whole loan. Hence Mr Ochre has the risk that Mrs Ochre might default and the bank might then claim from him. The best arrangement is to have a deed of variation signed by the bank releasing Mr Ochre from his obligation. Moreover, many banks have standard form documentation forbidding any disposition without their consent, so that the transfer of the half share to Mrs Ochre ought to be cleared with the bank. In the interval between the separation agreement and the actual conveyance Mrs Ochre's right to her husband's half share is, of course, personal, not real, and so she is exposed to an element of risk.

In an action for divorce or dissolution of a civil partnership, s.8 of the Family Law (Scotland) Act 1985 empowers the court to make an order for the transfer of property (property transfer order ("PTO")) from one spouse or civil partner to the other.[76] "Property" includes heritable property, and the order may relate to *pro indiviso* shares. A PTO is not itself a transfer: like missives, it imposes an obligation to convey. The spouse who is to acquire the property does not become owner until there has been a registered disposition in the ordinary way. The rights of heritable creditors are protected.[77]

The risk for a purchaser of a matrimonial or family home is that the court might have made such an order, which the owner is, by selling to someone else, defying. Does this matter to the buyer? The answer is that it depends. Since a PTO is not in itself a conveyance, both the purchaser and the transferee spouse are entitled to demand a disposition. Whoever registers first will become owner. But if it is the purchaser who wins, but did so in the knowledge of the prior existence of the PTO, then an "offside goal" has been scored, meaning that the title is voidable at the instance of the disappointed spouse.[78] There is little to worry about here in practice. Sales in defiance of a PTO are as rare as fraudulent double sales. No special provision is required in missives—it is covered by the good and marketable title obligation—though in practice it is quite common to put in a special clause.[79]

An estranged couple will often agree to the sale of the home. If so, well and good. But experience shows that the parties may fall out over numerous issues, and especially the question of how the proceeds are to be divided. Hence the path of wisdom is that the sale should be conducted by a firm of solicitors which acts for neither party in any other respect, and Law Society Guidelines require this unless the parties have agreed to writing on distribution of the sale proceeds.[80]

---

[76] The Act also empowers the court to make "incidental orders" in relation to matrimonial or civil partnership property, but it is difficult to see how these could affect a purchaser. For the, possibly controversial, use of a PTO as a pre-divorce incidental order under s.14, see *Adams v Adams*, 2010 S.L.T. (Sh. Ct) 2.

[77] For details see *MacNaught v MacNaught*, 1997 S.L.T. (Sh. Ct) 60.

[78] For the "offside goals rule" see Reid, *Property*, paras 695 et seq. See further Cusine, (1990) 35 J.L.S.S. 52.

[79] For example, cl.8 of the Combined Standard Clauses (2009) says, under the heading of "Family Law/Litigation", that "[t]he Seller warrants that neither the Property nor the Seller's title are affected by or are under consideration in any court proceedings or other litigation or are the subject of any dispute".

[80] See further the Law Society of Scotland's *Guidelines on Acting for Separated Spouses* (2006).

Division and sale

Where a house is co-owned, either party can insist that the property be sold,   10–17
and if necessary force matters by an action of division and sale.[81] But if the
property is a matrimonial or family home co-owned by spouses or civil partners, the court has a discretion to postpone or even refuse a sale,[82] and a similar
power exists where one of the parties is bankrupt and the action of division and
sale is raised by the trustee in sequestration.[83]

Out of the proceeds the fees and outlays in the sale must be paid, as must
debts secured on the property.[84] The net proceeds of sale fall to be divided
between the parties according to the size of their share of ownership, which in
most cases will be equal.[85] Claims which one party may have against the other
can, however, be taken into account in the division.[86] If the shares are equal but
the price was contributed wholly or mainly by one of the parties, there is
authority to support an enrichment claim by the party who overpaid.[87] The
disposition needs to be executed by both parties, but if one refuses the court
can pronounce an interlocutor authorising the clerk of court to execute it.[88]

Sometimes one party does not wish the property to be sold on the open
market, but wishes to buy the other's share at a fair price. If the other party
agrees, then there is no problem, but what if the other party refuses? Can such
an arrangement be forced through by court action? The authorities are
conflicting.[89]

---

[81] Reid, *Property*, paras 32 and 33. See e.g. *Burrows v Burrows*, 1996 S.C. 378.

[82] 1981 Act s.19; 2004 Act s.110. See e.g. *B v B*, 2010 G.W.D. 24-454.

[83] Bankruptcy (Scotland) Act 1985 s.40(2), (3). See e.g. *Accountant in Bankruptcy v Clough*,
2010 G.W.D. 35-714. See also below, para.29–03.

[84] Where shares in the house are uneven, particular care is needed in the deduction of debts and
expenses. See *Esposito v Barile*, 2011 Fam. L.R. 67, discussed in Reid and Gretton, *Conveyancing
2010*, pp.171–77.

[85] If the title is in more than one person, without specifying the size of the shares, then the shares
are equal.

[86] *Ralston v Jackson*, 1994 S.L.T. 771; *Gray v Kemer*, 1996 S.C.L.R. 331; *McMahon's Trustee
v McMahon*, 1997 S.L.T. 1090. Cf. *Johnston v Robson*, 1995 S.L.T. (Sh. Ct) 26, though that case
is odd because it is not clear what the basis of the counterclaim was. The mere fact that the defender
had made the original deposit on the house was, in itself, irrelevant (though it could have become
relevant had it been averred that it had been a loan, for instance).

[87] *McKenzie v Nutter*, 2007 S.L.T. (Sh. Ct) 17. This decision, however, seems questionable. If
two parties agree on a title share, to divide the proceeds of sale according to that title share is not,
it can be argued, unjustified enrichment: it is simply carrying out the wishes of the parties.

[88] For procedure see Lord Macphail, *Sheriff Court Practice*, 3rd edn by T. Welsh et al (2006),
paras 23.37 et seq.

[89] *Scrimgeour v Scrimgeour*, 1988 S.L.T. 590; *Berry v Berry*, 1989 S.L.T. 292; *Gray v Kerner*,
1996 S.C.L.R. 331; *Ploetner v Ploetner*, 1997 S.C.L.R. 998. And see also *Wilson v Harvey*, 2004
S.C.L.R. 313.

CHAPTER 11

DISPOSITIONS

INTRODUCTION

Deeds of constitution, deeds of transfer, and deeds of extinction

11–01 Unlike in England, "deed" in Scotland is not a technical term.[1] But lawyers know what it is and what it is not. "The significant characteristics of a deed", it has been said, "are first that it should have some degree of formality and secondly that it must demonstrate an intention to create a legal relation".[2]

Conveyancers traditionally distinguish three classes of deed: (i) deeds of constitution (also called deeds of creation), (ii) deeds of transfer, and (iii) deeds of extinction. A deed of constitution creates a new real right. Examples are leases and standard securities.[3] In such cases the granter retains a real right, but the grantee also acquires a real right of some type, newly created. A deed of transfer, or transmission, simply transfers from one person to another an existing real right. Dispositions and assignations are the sole examples for heritable property. So if Mary leases land to Nick, that is a deed of constitution, but if Nick then assigns the lease to Olga, that is a deed of transfer. A deed of extinction brings a real right to an end: it is not transferred but ceases to exist. Examples are renunciations of leases and discharges of standard securities. This chapter deals with one type of deed of transfer, the disposition. The disposition is the most important deed encountered in conveyancing.

Dispositions

11–02 A disposition is the deed used to transfer ownership[4] of land. So if Jack sells a house to Jill, the sale is effected by a disposition[5] by him in favour of her and registered in the Land Register. This is a standard disposition. What is happening is that Jack is selling what he owns. By contrast, there can also be a break-off (also called break-away or split-off) disposition, in which Jack

---

[1] *Henderson's Trustees v IRC*, 1913 S.C. 987; *Lennie v Lennie's Trustees*, 1914 1 S.L.T. 258.

[2] *Low & Bonar Plc v Mercer Ltd* [2010] CSOH 47; 2010 G.W.D. 16-321 at para.16, per Lord Drummond Young.

[3] And, before the abolition of feudal tenure, feu dispositions. Feu charters and feu contracts were in substance the same as feu dispositions.

[4] When they still existed, superiorities were also transferred by disposition.

[5] Occasionally a property is held on ultra-long lease, in which case the sale of the lease will be implemented by an assignation rather than by a disposition. For ultra-long leases, and for plans for their conversion into ownership, see Scottish Law Commission, Report on *Conversion of Long Leases* (Scot. Law Com. No.204, 2006). A Bill to implement the Law Commission's proposals— the Long Leases (Scotland) Bill—was introduced to the Scottish Parliament on November 10, 2010 but had not completed its parliamentary stages by the time of the dissolution in March 2011. It is expected to be reintroduced in the new Parliament.

conveys only a part of what he owns. Break-off dispositions have all the terms of a standard disposition but also some additional terms.

Unlike many other deeds, there is no statutory form of disposition, although certain individual clauses have prescribed statutory forms. In theory, therefore, any form can be used provided it is clear. In practice, there is a standard method of drafting a disposition which, with minor local and personal differences, is in universal use. This is not a pretty deed. It is written in the first person,[6] and, although long, is usually all one sentence, the different parts of the deed being marked off by a battery of colons, semi-colons and commas. Some of it is redundant, mere empty words of style. The language is to some extent archaic.[7] The client may not understand it, and may, not unreasonably, wish it to be explained. The deed is unilateral in form—only the granter signs[8]—but bilateral in effect: the grantee is considered bound by its terms on accepting delivery at settlement.[9] There are two forms of disposition in current use, namely dispositions of property in the Land Register and dispositions of General Register of Sasines ("GRS") land (i.e. land not yet registered in the Land Register). They are similar but not identical.

Structure of the disposition

A disposition is divided into several clauses. What, precisely, is meant by a 11–03 "clause" is perhaps not wholly determinate, but the issue is largely semantic. There can be some variation in practice, but in a typical modern disposition these are as follows:

(a) The narrative clause, also called the inductive clause, stating the parties and the cause of transfer.
(b) The dispositive clause, identifying the property and conveying it.
(c) The burdens clause, mentioning existing burdens and stating new ones, if any.[10]
(d) The entry clause, stating the date when the disponee is to take possession.
(e) The warrandice clause, whereby the granter warrants the title.
(f) Miscellaneous clauses.
(g) The testing clause, with details of how and when the deed was signed.

There is sometimes a clause declaring that there are no occupancy rights or that the granter holds in trust for the grantee, pending registration.[11] In some cases involving property still in the GRS there has to be a clause of deduction of title after the entry clause. Until 1979 there were three other clauses, namely the

---

[6] If the granter is a company or other juristic person then the deed will run in the first person plural.

[7] Conveyancing deeds often have a long history. The disposition has been evolving for more than 800 years.

[8] There is nothing to stop the grantee signing, but it is not done in practice, certain special cases apart. It might, however, be argued that the law ought to require the grantee to sign. It is curious that it is possible to acquire heritable property without ever signing anything.

[9] See e.g. *Hunter v Boog* (1834) 13 S. 205.

[10] If the property is in the Land Register it is normal to omit reference to existing burdens.

[11] See below, para.11–30.

writs clause, the rents clause and the relief clause, which came before the warrandice clause, but these are now implied[12] and are thus invariably omitted.

Two examples will be given. The first is of property that is in the Land Register. The second is of property that is still in the GRS: such a disposition will normally trigger a first registration in the Land Register but the form is the same even in the case where it will be recorded in the GRS. An alternative to the first (but not the second) would be to prepare the disposition electronically using the ARTL system, in which case little in the way of drafting skills are needed: certain basic information is fed into the system (names of the parties, price, description of the property, and so on) and the computer does the rest.[13]

Disposition of property in the Land Register

11–04　　　[*Narrative*] I, Kevin Kennedy, born on sixth May nineteen hundred and seventy,[14] residing formerly at fifty-two Cornwall Street, Aberdeen and now at fifty-five Emily Drive, Kirkcudbright, registered[15] proprietor of the subjects hereinafter disponed, in consideration of the price of two hundred thousand pounds (£200,000) paid to me by Donald Henry McQuoist, born on eleventh August nineteen hundred and seventy five, and Sara Jane Cumming or McQuoist, born on twelfth April nineteen hundred and eighty three, residing together at thirty Fairholm Drive, Paisley, of which I hereby acknowledge receipt, [*Dispositive*] do hereby dispone to the said Donald Henry McQuoist and Sara Jane Cumming or McQuoist equally between them All and Whole that area or plot of ground with the dwelling-house erected thereon and garden ground effeiring thereto known as fifty-five Emily Drive, Kirkcudbright, being the subjects registered under Title Number KRK12345: [*Entry*] With entry and actual occupation as at the fourth day of October two thousand and twelve; [*Warrandice*] and I grant warrandice; [*Occupancy rights*] and I declare that the said subjects are neither a matrimonial home nor a family home in relation to which a spouse or a civil partner of mine has occupancy rights in terms of the Matrimonial Homes (Family Protection) (Scotland) Act 1981 or the Civil Partnership Act 2004;[16] [*Trust*][17] and I declare that, until title is registered in the Land Register in pursuance of these presents, I hold the said subjects as trustee for behoof of the said Donald Henry McQuoist and Sara Jane Cumming or McQuoist: [*Testing*] In witness whereof these presents are subscribed by me at Kirkcudbright on the first day of October in the year two thousand and twelve in the presence of Arlene Duguid, trainee solicitor, fourteen Waterperry Street, Kirkcudbright.

Disposition of property in the GRS

11–05　　　[*Narrative*] I, James Jameson, born on third January nineteen hundred and sixty six,[18] residing formerly at forty-two Sauchiehall Square, Glasgow

---

[12] Land Registration (Scotland) Act 1979 s.16.
[13] See above, para.8–23.
[14] It is good but not (yet) standard practice to give dates of birth: see below, para.11–06.
[15] Or "heritable": see below, para.11–07.
[16] This is to make use of the declaration option: see above, para.10–11.
[17] Whether a trust clause ought to be inserted is arguable: see below, para.11–30.
[18] It is good but not (yet) standard practice to give dates of birth: see below, para.11–06.

and now at five Frances Street, Stornoway, heritable[19] proprietor of the subjects hereinafter disponed, in consideration of the price of two hundred thousand pounds (£200,000) paid to me by Alan Dewar Johnston, born on tenth May nineteen hundred and sixty nine, and Clare Janet Macleod or Johnston, born on tenth June nineteen hundred and seventy three, residing together at thirty-two Fairlie Drive, Dundee, of which I hereby acknowledge receipt, [*Dispositive*] do hereby dispone to the said Alan Dewar Johnston and Clare Janet Macleod or Johnston equally between them All and Whole that area or plot of ground with the dwelling-house erected thereon and garden ground effeiring thereto known as five Frances Street, Stornoway,[20] in the County of Ross and Cromarty, being the subjects described in Disposition by Fergus Chalmers Campbell in favour of Donald Macleod dated first, and recorded in the Division of the General Register of Sasines applicable to the County of Ross and Cromarty on eleventh, both days of May in the year nineteen hundred and thirty-five: together with (one) the fittings and fixtures (two) the parts and pertinents and (three) my whole right title and interest present and future [*Burdens*] But always with and under in so far as valid subsisting and applicable the burdens conditions and others specified and contained in the said Disposition by Fergus Chalmers Campbell in favour of Donald Macleod dated and recorded as aforesaid: [*Entry*] With entry and actual occupation as at the fourth day of October two thousand and twelve; [*Add deduction of title if granter's title not completed by registration*];[21] [*Warrandice*] and I grant warrandice; [*Trust*][22] and I hereby declare that, until title is registered in the Land Register in pursuance of these presents, I hold the said subjects as trustee for behoof of the said Alan Dewar Johnston and Clare Janet Macleod or Johnston: [Testing] In witness whereof these presents are subscribed by me at Stornoway on the first day of October in the year two thousand and twelve in the presence of Elspeth Marie Macdonald, trainee solicitor, fourteen Pinwherry Gardens, Stornoway.

NARRATIVE CLAUSE

Designation

The parties to a deed—granter, grantee and consenter (if any)—must be 11–06 designed (i.e. described and identified). But other people mentioned in a deed normally need not be designed.[23] Thus, when a deed refers to prior deeds for real burdens, there is no need to design the parties to those prior deeds. Where designation is required, the approved technique is to design a party on the first occasion in which he appears in the deed and thereafter to refer to him as "the said Alan Dewar Johnston".

---

[19] Or "registered": see below, para.11–07.

[20] In practice, for no good reason, the postcode is usually omitted. It is sometimes said that this is because postcodes can change. But so can street numbers and street names.

[21] See below, paras 24-11 et seq.

[22] Whether a trust clause ought to be inserted is arguable. See below, para.11–30.

[23] An exception is a clause of deduction of title. See Conveyancing (Scotland) Act 1924 Schs A and B.

The test of a successful designation is that the party in question can be identified. The normal practice is to provide the full name and address. At one time it
was common to add occupations but this has dropped out of practice although
it can still be useful where two people of the same name live at the same address
(e.g. father and son). In most legal systems a designation will state the date of
birth, and often the place of birth and nationality as well. Scotland is unusually
lax in its standard of designations in conveyancing deeds. Dates of birth ought
to be included, not as a matter of legal necessity, but as a matter of good practice. If a new Land Registration Act is passed, it is likely to include a requirement that dates of birth are given in the proprietorship section of the title sheet[24];
their inclusion in the disposition as well would be a logical consequence.

In the usual case the granters of the present disposition will be the grantees
of the immediately previous disposition of the same property (or, in the case of
Land Register titles, the person listed in the title sheet). But their address will
typically have changed. In the older disposition they will be designed as living
at their former address. It is good practice to link up the two deeds by giving
both addresses as in the style above. This demonstrates that the James Jameson
who was designed as living in Sauchiehall Square is the same James Jameson
who now lives at Frances Street.

If a married woman adopts her husband's name, her maiden name should
nevertheless be given as well. Thus if Clare Janet Macleod marries and chooses to
become Clare Janet Johnston, she should be designed as "Clare Janet Macleod or
Johnston". Where a party acts in a representative or fiduciary capacity, such as a
trustee or as a liquidator, this fact should be added to the designation, together
with details of the appointment. Thus, for an executor the designation will refer to
the confirmation, mentioning its date and the court which issued it. For a trustee
in sequestration the reference will be to the act and warrant, its date, and the court
issuing it. In the case of a trustee under a deed of trust, the deed of trust must be
identified, typically by reference to the Books of Council and Session where it
will (at least if good practice has been followed) have been registered.

Juristic persons such as companies are designed by reference to their official
address (in the case of a company this is known as the registered office) and to
the statute under which they are incorporated.[25] In the case of a company it is
nowadays invariable practice to include the company's registration number.
The reason is that it is easy for a company to change its name, and indeed a
company can have a name which was formerly held by another company. Only
the registration number is an unchangeable birthmark by which the identity
can be unambiguously determined.[26]

Bodies which are registered as charities in the Scottish Charity Register are
required to use the name as entered in the Register, and to give their registered
number, any other name by which they are commonly known, and, where the
registered name does not include the words "charity" or "charitable", to
mention that they are a charity.[27] These rules apply regardless of the form
which the body takes, which is most usually a trust or a body corporate.

---

[24] Scottish Law Commission, Report on *Land Registration* (Scot. Law Com. No.222, 2010)
paras 4.20–4.24.

[25] For where the company is insolvent, see below, para.29–14.

[26] See further below, para.28–04.

[27] Charities References in Documents (Scotland) Regulations 2007 (SSI 2007/203). No sanction
is provided for non-compliance.

Heritable proprietor and unregistered holder[28]

The traditional practice was to follow the name and designation of the granter 11–07 with either the words "heritable proprietor" or the words "uninfeft proprietor". "Heritable proprietor" meant that the granter was, or at least claimed to be, the owner of the property, implying a title completed by registration. A granter who was "uninfeft proprietor" held the property under an unregistered conveyance. To be infeft literally meant to have taken feudal entry with the superior.

Although hallowed by long usage, "uninfeft proprietor" suffered from the obvious objection that a person who was uninfeft could not be the "proprietor" of the land; and today, following feudal abolition, it is no longer possible to be either "infeft" or "uninfeft". A replacement term is needed. The Title Conditions (Scotland) Act 2003 proposes "unregistered holder".[29] "Unregistered proprietor" would be closer to the previous terminology but suffers from the objection already mentioned. "Unregistered granter" is accurate but does not fit readily into the narrative clause of the typical deed.[30] Our own preference, following the 2003 Act, is for "unregistered holder", but "unregistered proprietor" is also acceptable and is the more widely used.

The Keeper's view has been that "heritable proprietor" and "uninfeft proprietor" should not in any event be used for dispositions of properties in the Land Register.[31] But while it is true that these terms are unnecessary in such dispositions, they are unnecessary even in dispositions recorded in the GRS. Notwithstanding the Keeper's view they continue to be widely used. When it comes to tradition, the force is strong. For those who choose to continue to use these terms, we tentatively suggest the terms (a) "heritable proprietor" and (b) "unregistered holder".

Cause of granting, and consideration

Although the cause of granting is in practice always stated, in the narrative 11–08 clause, it is not a requirement of law. In most cases a disposition is in implement of a contract of sale, so the price is narrated. Where the disposition is by way of gift, the traditional style is to narrate that the deed is granted for the "love, favour and affection" borne to the grantee.[32] A disposition by an executor or trustee will usually narrate the will or deed of trust, explaining that the grantee is a beneficiary. Occasionally one sees the formula "for certain good and onerous causes and considerations". This is a legalistic way of saying that the reason for the deed is not being disclosed.

There can be many reasons, apart from sale,[33] why a disposition is granted. While silence is possible, it is normal to explain, and sometimes this becomes something of a story. Indeed, one could begin by narrating the creation of the heaven and the earth, getting on, at about page four, to the bit about Almighty

---

[28] For further details, see below, paras 24–01 to 24–10.

[29] Title Conditions (Scotland) Act 2003 s.128(1), Sch.14 para.7(3)(a), substituting "unregistered holder" for "uninfeft proprietor" in s.3(6) of the Land Registration (Scotland) Act 1979.

[30] Especially in the grant of a subordinate real right, where one can hardly be the "unregistered granter of the subjects aftermentioned".

[31] *Registration of Title Practice Book* ("ROTPB"), para.8.47.

[32] These words acquire a certain irony where the disposition arises from marital breakdown.

[33] Sale is a reason ("cause") for a conveyance, but is not a conveyance itself. This is perhaps obvious enough for heritable property, but the same is true for other property as well.

God feuing Scotland to Adam and Eve and the survivor of them.[34] It is a matter of judgment how much to include. If in doubt, include it, because the effect is to preserve evidence as to the background circumstances. Sometimes there have been conveyancing problems in the past which the present deed is intended to correct, and if so it is helpful to outline the background.

While in practice the sellers will not release the disposition until payment is made, the buyers ought nonetheless to have a formal receipt. This is achieved by including words such as "of which we acknowledge receipt". A receipt in this form raises a strong presumption that payment has been made.[35]

One reason why care needs to be taken to state the cause accurately is that inaccuracy may cause problems later. Where two people buy a house it is easy to assume that both are contributing to the price and to so state in the narrative clause.[36] But that is not always true. The potential difficulties caused by inaccuracy are all the greater because the courts have sometimes declined to allow extrinsic evidence to contradict the narrative clause.[37] However, an inaccurate narrative clause can be in principle rectified under s.8 of the Law Reform (Miscellaneous Provisions) (Scotland) Act 1985.[38]

Consenters

11–09 Where a third party has, or may have, some right in relation to the property which might prove damaging to the position of the grantee, it is wise to ensure that he or she signs the deed as a consenter. Most dispositions do not have consenters, but if there is one the relevant details are given in the narrative clause. Like the granter, a consenter needs to be designed.

Sometimes the intended effect of the consent is stated in the deed itself. A common example is where a heritable creditor consents, with the effect of discharging the security. Or again the effect may be defined by statute. An example is a consent given by the spouse or civil partner of the disponer for the purpose of discharging occupancy rights.[39] These are the simple cases. In other cases there are two, mutually exclusive, effects of signing as consenter. In the first place, if it turns out that the consenter, and not the granter, was the true owner, the fact that the consenter signed is sufficient to transfer ownership to

---

[34] In fact, we have it on the authority of no less a person than Stair that God did not convey Scotland to Adam and Eve. "In the 28th verse [of the first chapter of Genesis], God saith to Adam and Eve, 'increase and multiply, and replenish the earth, and subdue or subject the same, and have dominion over the fishes of the sea, the fowls of the heaven, and all living things which move upon the earth'. This gift, therefore, could not be to Adam and Eve, who could neither replenish the earth nor subjugate nor subdue it; but it was to mankind which then was in their persons only; and it did not import a present right of property, but only a right or power to appropriate by possession, or jus ad rem, not jus in re." Stair, II, i, 1.

[35] Erskine, II, iii, 22.

[36] As in the example above.

[37] *Gordon-Rogers v Thomson's Exrs*, 1988 S.L.T. 618; *McCafferty v McCafferty*, 2000 S.C.L.R. 256. By contrast, such evidence was held admissible in *Nottay's Trustee v Nottay*, 2001 S.L.T. 769. *Gordon-Rogers* involved a survivorship destination. Such a destination is normally non-evacuable if both parties paid the price, and the consequences of that fact can be profound. See below, para.26–16. Other examples where it was later asserted that the narrative clause was inaccurate include *Aitken's Trustee v Aitken*, 1999 G.W.D. 39-1898; and *Bank of Scotland v Reid*, 2000 G.W.D. 22-858.

[38] The subject of Ch.20.

[39] See above, para.10–10.

the grantee.[40] In the second place, if the consenter is not owner but has some other real right in the land,[41] or, alternatively, if he has only a personal right in relation to the land, he cannot[42] thereafter exercise the right to the prejudice of the grantee or the grantee's successors. A common example is where Alan sells on missives to Beth and Beth resells to Chris and the disposition is from Alan to Chris with Beth's consent. Another example is where a trustee dispones with the consent of a beneficiary.

Unless otherwise stated in the deed, the consenter corroborates only the conveyance of the land contained in the dispositive clause. The consent does not touch the other clauses, e.g. the warrandice clause.

DISPOSITIVE CLAUSE

Dispositive words

The dispositive clause is introduced by the words "do hereby dispone". 11–10 "Dispone" means "transfer",[43] so "hereby dispone to the said Alan Dewar Johnston and Clare Janet Macleod or Johnston" has the effect (upon registration) of transferring ownership of the property to the Johnstons. At common law "dispone" was a magic word, without which ownership could not pass. Synonymous terms were unavailing. By statute this rule has been abrogated,[44] and all that is now needed is some term that makes the intention plain. But in practice the word "dispone" continues to be used.

Common property or joint property

The only case where heritage can (and indeed must) be held in joint property is 11–11 where it is held by trustees. All other cases of *pro indiviso* ownership are cases of common property.[45] It should be observed, however, that ownership in common is often referred to, loosely, as ownership "in joint names". That, for example, is the terminology that clients generally use. It is not usual to specify in the disposition whether the multiple ownership being conferred is common or joint. The law is clear. But since common property, unlike joint property, can involve shares of different sizes, it is good practice to specify the size of individual shares ("to the said Alan Dewar Johnston and Clare Janet Macleod or Johnston equally between them"). If the shares are intended to be equal, which is generally the case, this is not strictly necessary, for if the size of the shares is not stated, the law will presume that equal shares are intended.

Description

The question of how the property is to be identified—the law and practice of 11–12 descriptions—is the subject of the next chapter.

---

[40] Stair II, xi, 7; *Mounsey v Maxwell* (1808) Hume 237. Erskine (II, iii, 21), however, argues that there is no transfer of ownership, although the consenter is under a personal obligation to grant a new disposition. The view of Stair is correct.

[41] e.g. a lease or a heritable security.

[42] Unless the contrary intention can be gathered.

[43] Or, more strictly, "transfer the ownership of heritable property".

[44] Conveyancing (Scotland) Act 1874 s.27.

[45] Reid, *Property*, para.34.

Burdens

11–13   The creation of new real burdens and servitudes is discussed below in Ch.13.
Here we consider the conveyancing practice where there are existing burdens,
which is usually the case.

In dispositions of property in the Land Register no reference to existing
burdens is necessary.[46] The grantee takes the property as set out in the title
sheet, and the title sheet lists the burdens.[47] What follows is therefore applicable
to dispositions of property which is still in the GRS, which is to say mainly first
registrations. Traditionally deeds imposing burdens contained a provision
requiring all future deeds to refer to the burdens. Whether such provisions were
enforceable is an open question, but at all events s.68 of the Title Conditions
(Scotland) Act 2003 now declares all such provisions unenforceable.

Nonetheless existing burdens should be referred to in the disposition. This is
partly to avoid claims in warrandice: in granting warrandice the granter guarantees the terms of the dispositive clause, and if the dispositive clause makes
no reference to burdens, the granter is taken as guaranteeing that there are
none.[48] Another reason is purely practical: when faced with a bundle of title
deeds it is difficult to know which writs contain real burdens. The list in the
disposition saves time and energy.

In practice existing burdens are almost never repeated in full. The usual
formula is: "But always with and under the burdens, conditions and others, so far
as valid, subsisting and applicable, specified in . . ." [then list the deeds in which
the burdens appear].[49] The significance of "so far as valid, subsisting and applicable" is that real burdens can become spent, and the grantee does not wish to be
committed to the proposition that all the burdens in the title remain live and
enforceable. In practice, the list is simply copied from the immediately preceding
disposition. But if a burden is obviously spent it can safely be omitted.

Typically there are two or three deeds listed. All deeds older than 1858 will
be instruments of sasine, because until that year dispositions and feu dispositions could not be registered directly and their contents were summarised in the
instrument.

Reservations

11–14   The dispositive clause also includes details of anything which is being reserved
to the granter. In most cases nothing is reserved. But in a break-off disposition
it may be that the mineral rights under the ground being disponed are reserved,
though that will be possible only if the disponer has them in the first place,
which may not be the case. In a break-off deed the disponer is likely also to
reserve real burdens and servitudes over the disponed property. Whether these
should strictly be called "reservations" is arguable, for it might be said that
only something that already exists can be reserved, and before the break-off
happens no real burdens or servitudes can exist between the two parts of the
as-yet undivided property. But at all events in practice conveyancers often

---

[46] Land Registration (Scotland) Act 1979 s.15(2).

[47] Land Registration (Scotland) Act 1979 s.3(1)(a).

[48] See below, para.19–12. However, if the grantee knows of, or is deemed to know of, the
burden, there will be no remedy in warrandice.

[49] This formula has its origins in a statutory style which has been repealed. See Conveyancing
(Scotland) Act 1874 s.32 and Sch.H, repealed by the Title Conditions (Scotland) Act 2003 s.128
and Sch.15. There is now no prescribed form of wording.

speak of "reserving" real burdens and servitudes. In a complex deed it can sometimes be unclear whether some item is being disponed or reserved, and the practice is to say something like "together with (by way of grant not exception) . . ." or vice versa.

THE IMPLIED ASSIGNATIONS

Introduction

The narrative and dispositive clauses are the two most important in a disposition. 11–15 But there are also a number of ancillary clauses. Two of these (neither usually of much importance) are the clause of assignation of writs and the clause of assignation of rents. Until the passing of the 1979 Act these clauses were set out in full.[50] But by s.16 of the Act these two clauses[51] are implied and accordingly in practice are now omitted.[52] These clauses are "assignations" since what they transfer is incorporeal, intimation being effected by registration.[53]

Assignation of writs

The assignation of writs has two effects. The first is to transfer certain personal 11–16 rights. Conveyances contain a number of contractual obligations by the granter to the grantee, the two most important being the obligation of warrandice and the obligation of relief, and therefore a number of corresponding rights of the grantee against the granter.[54] These rights can sometimes be enforced by successors of the original grantee. Suppose, for example, that Amy dispones to Beth, Beth dispones to Chris, and Chris dispones to David. In the dispositions Amy, Beth and Chris will have entered into certain obligations. But since these are personal, not real, they can, on general principles, be enforced only by Beth, Chris and David respectively. Unless, of course, they are assigned. By s.16(1) of the 1979 Act the implied assignation of writs imports "an assignation to the grantee of the title deeds and searches and all deeds not duly recorded". What this appears to mean is that some, but not all, of the granter's personal rights are assigned. In past times this was important (e.g. for unexecuted precepts of sasine, procuratories of resignation, and other antiquarian exotica). Today what it all appears to mean is that (a) rights of warrandice are assigned[55] and that (b) rights of relief are not. Why both should not be treated in the same way is a mystery.[56]

The practical effect is this. In the above example, when Amy dispones to Beth, Amy grants warrandice. So Beth has a right against Amy. When Beth dispones to Chris, Beth in turn grants warrandice to Chris. So Chris has a right of warrandice against Beth. But he also has a right of warrandice against Amy, for Amy's former right has passed to Chris by the assignation of writs.

---

[50] In the form prescribed by s.8 of and Sch.B to the Titles to Land Consolidation (Scotland) Act 1868.

[51] Together with the clause of relief, for which see below.

[52] This section applies to dispositions both of GRS property and registered property.

[53] *Paul v Boyd's Trustees* (1835) 13 S. 818; *Edmond v Magistrates of Aberdeen* (1855) 18 D. 47; (1858) 3 Macq. 116.

[54] See below, paras 11–18 et seq.

[55] Stair II, iii, 46.

[56] Similar difficulties apply to s.8 of the Titles to Land Consolidation (Scotland) Act 1868.

Likewise, when Chris dispones to David, David comes to hold three rights of warrandice, against Amy, Beth and Chris.

As well as holding personal rights against previous owners, granters of dispositions sometimes hold personal rights against the owners of different property. This issue has become important with the extinction of real burdens due to the abolition of the feudal system and other associated changes.[57] Suppose that in 2000 Gordon feued some of his land to Harry imposing certain conditions as real burdens. Later, in 2012, Gordon dispones the rest of his land to Isla. Following feudal abolition in 2004 Gordon no longer holds a real burden in respect of Harry's land.[58] But because the 2000 feu disposition was, like all conveyances, contractual in character, Gordon still has a personal right to enforce the conditions against Harry for as long as Harry continues to own the land.[59] In principle, this personal right can be assigned to Isla, but it seems unlikely that this would be achieved by the assignation of writs implied into the disposition, and an express assignation is probably required.

The second aspect of the assignation of writs concerns the delivery of the title deeds. The law here depends on whether the property is in the Land Register or not. If it is not, then s.16(1) of the 1979 Act places the granter under certain obligations as to the title deeds, including the obligation to deliver all titles relating exclusively to the land conveyed.[60] Since the title deeds are normally delivered at settlement,[61] along with the disposition, the s.16 obligation is usually fulfilled at precisely the same moment as it is incurred. If the property is in the Land Register, the obligation normally relates only to the land certificate and the charge certificate (if any). The exception is where indemnity is excluded.[62] It is common practice, upon first registration, to destroy the existing deeds, or to hand them to the purchasing clients. In the latter case they will usually cease to be available. This may occasionally cause difficulties, particularly if the title comes to be challenged by reference to an underlying deed.

Quite separately, there is a statutory right to consult title deeds for anyone who has, or is entitled to acquire, a real right in the land in question.[63] Until 1979 dispositions usually included, as an appendix, an inventory of writs listing the principal title deeds. This practice, never required by law, has now disappeared.

Assignation of rents[64]

11–17   The clause of assignation of rents, though included, by implication, in all deeds, is relevant only if the property disponed is tenanted. Its object is twofold. In the first place, it enables the disponee to draw the rents as soon as the

---

[57] See generally below, Ch.13.

[58] Abolition of Feudal Tenure etc. (Scotland) Act 2000 s.17(1). The real burden would, however, survive if Gordon had registered a notice under s.18.

[59] Abolition of Feudal Tenure etc. (Scotland) Act 2000 s.75. See Kenneth G.C. Reid, *The Abolition of Feudal Tenure in Scotland* (2003), para.1.22.

[60] Presumably one must read into the provision an implied term that the obligation relates only to deeds which the granter has or can obtain.

[61] The only common exception is in a break-off disposition, where the granter will usually retain them.

[62] Land Registration (Scotland) Act 1979 s.3(5).

[63] Abolition of Feudal Tenure etc. (Scotland) Act 2000 s.66.

[64] See Halliday, para.37–13.

disposition has been delivered and its terms intimated to the tenant. This point was important long ago when a disponee might be slow in completing title. Nowadays, when disponees almost invariably complete title at once, this aspect no longer matters. The other purpose of the clause is to arrange, as between disponer and disponee, the point in time after which the rents payable will go to the disponee. For instance, if the disposition is granted in August, and the rent is payable twice a year, at Whitsunday and Martinmas, is the disponer to keep the Whitsunday rent, and the disponee to take the Martinmas rent? Or should the rent for Whitsunday to Martinmas be split? And so on.

Before the 1979 Act, the disposition could either have a detailed clause, or could simply say "I assign the rents", the meaning of which expression was defined by statute.[65] Under s.16 of the 1979 Act the assignation of rents is implied.[66] However, the implied statutory meaning is extremely hard to understand,[67] involving as it does problems about forehand rents, backhand rents, arable farms, pastoral farms, conventional terms and legal terms.[68] Conveyancers who are unwilling to take a month or two off to investigate the law should avoid the statutory provisions by making express, detailed and clear provision as to how the rental income is to be apportioned as between disponer and disponee.

THE CONTRACTUAL OBLIGATIONS

Contractual effect of the disposition

As well as being an executory deed, conveying the land (and the writs and rents), a disposition is also a contract imposing obligations, usually on the granter but sometimes on the grantee. And whereas ownership passes to the disponee only on registration, the contractual obligations generally take effect immediately, on delivery of the disposition.[69] The contractual obligations are: (i) entry; (ii) warrandice; (iii) obligation of relief; and (iv) miscellaneous obligations.[70] Of these, warrandice may be left until later[71]; the others are discussed below.   11–18

Entry

Entry is the date at which the granter is bound to yield possession to the grantee. In a sale this will already have been contracted for in the missives. The date of   11–19

---

[65] Titles to Land Consolidation (Scotland) Act 1868 s.8.

[66] 1979 Act s.16. The meaning of this implied clause is very similar to the meaning defined in s.8 of the 1868 Act.

[67] See J. Rankine, *Law of Leases*, 3rd edn (1916); and G.C.H. Paton and J.G.S. Cameron, *The Law of Landlord and Tenant in Scotland* (1967).

[68] Not to mention quantum mechanics, special relativity theory, and the meaning of love. (Which, however, are, by comparison, easy topics.) An example will illustrate the sort of problems that can be encountered. A pastoral farm is let with the rent one term backhand. The landlord sells with entry at August 1. The rent "conventionally" payable at Martinmas is "legally" payable at the previous Whitsunday. Therefore, by the statutory provisions it goes to the disponer, even though actually paid when the disponee is already the owner.

[69] Of course, the missives will already contain contractual obligations, but we are dealing with those which derive from the disposition.

[70] Occasionally a supersession clause is also found, repeating (unnecessarily) the clause used in missives. See below, Ch.19.

[71] See below, Ch.19.

entry must be distinguished from (i) the date of the disposition and (ii) the date when the disposition is delivered.

The date of the disposition is the date of execution (signature) or, if there is more than one signature, of last execution. This date will be found from the testing clause. It has little legal significance. Usually it is before the date of entry. If it is after the date of entry (e.g. because something has gone wrong with the transaction and settlement is delayed) it is usual to add to the entry clause the words "notwithstanding the date hereof", which indicates that the unusual sequence is not just a typing error. It sometimes happens (e.g. with gifts or with sales to sitting tenants) that entry is to be on the same day as the deed is executed, and in that case the entry clause reads "with entry at the date hereof".

The date of delivery is, in a sale, the date of settlement, that is, when the disposition is handed over in exchange for the price. In a normal sale the date of entry and date of settlement are the same day. But if things go wrong (e.g. the purchasers cannot pay) the date of entry may pass without the transaction being settled. Before delivery, the disposition has no effect. After delivery, but before registration, its effect is limited, since at this stage ownership has yet to pass. But the deed still has various effects. Its contractual clauses have full effect, and the disponees, though not owners, have the status and privileges of unregistered holders.

Entry, as already mentioned, is the date at which the granter must yield possession.[72] But possession may either be natural (i.e. physically by the owner) or civil (through another person, such as a tenant) and a simple obligation in a disposition to give "entry" is satisfied by either. This means that purchasers who arrive with their removal van only to find that the property is tenanted have no redress under such a clause. Nor, probably, do they have redress under the warrandice clause.[73] The solution is to contract specifically for vacant possession, thus: "With entry and actual occupation[74] on twenty second November two thousand and twelve".[75]

The meaning of vacant possession or actual occupation has occasionally caused problems. In *Stuart v Lort-Phillips*[76] cattle belonging to a neighbour were found grazing on about one-third of the subjects of sale. The neighbour claimed he had an agricultural tenancy. Both facts were held to be a breach of the obligation to give vacant possession. This was so even although the claim to the tenancy might (and in fact did) turn out to be spurious.[77] If an express entry clause is omitted, it is implied that entry is at the next term of Whitsunday or Martinmas.[78] But in practice the clause is never omitted, except by accident.

---

[72] Until feudal abolition, "entry" also had another sense, that of entry with the superior. Until 1874 this meant obtaining a further deed, a "charter by progress". There were various forms of charter by progress. For a buyer there was a choice of two, the charter of confirmation and the charter of resignation. The former was commoner in practice. The Conveyancing (Scotland) Act 1874 Act s.4 (applied to the Land Register by s.29 of the Land Registration (Scotland) Act 1979) provided that the disponee was deemed to take entry with the superior upon registration. Entry in the feudal sense has died with feudalism itself.

[73] *Lothian & Border Farmers Ltd v McCutchion*, 1952 S.L.T. 450, though the soundness of this decision is uncertain.

[74] Or "vacant possession".

[75] The wording here can be traced back at least as far as Sch.B to the Titles to Land Consolidation (Scotland) Act 1868.

[76] *Stuart v Lort-Phillips*, 1977 S.C. 244.

[77] See also *Scottish Flavour Ltd v Watson*, 1982 S.L.T. 78 where it was held that the presence of rubbish was too trivial.

[78] Conveyancing (Scotland) Act 1874 Act s.28.

Obligation of relief

An owner of land has certain obligations *qua* owner, some of the main ones 11–20
being (a) real burdens, (b) non-domestic rates, (c) council tax and (d) statutory
notices, e.g. notices served by the local authority under s.28 of the Building
(Scotland) Act 2003 requiring the repair of buildings and empowering the
authority to carry out the work itself, if necessary, and recover the cost from the
owner. Difficult questions can arise as to when these obligations pass to the
grantees, and to what extent the grantees have relief against the granters.

For council tax[79] and rates, the grantees become liable on taking entry. For
real burdens[80] and, probably,[81] for statutory notices also, the grantees become
liable on or after accepting delivery of the disposition. Usually entry and
acceptance of the disposition occur on the same day, i.e. on settlement.

The fact that the grantees become liable does not mean that granters who
were already liable for a particular obligation, such as the payment of a sum of
money, are able to escape that liability merely by transferring the property. In
such a case both the incoming and the outgoing owners are liable, and the
former, if they pay, have, unless otherwise agreed, a right of relief against the
latter. That is so for real burdens.[82] It is also true for council tax and rates, as to
which the right of relief is based on the obligation of relief clause in the disposition. This clause, formerly express, is now implied by the 1979 Act, to the
effect of imposing on granters an obligation to relieve grantees of a variety of
burdens exigible prior to the date of entry.[83] Whether this clause includes statutory notices is uncertain,[84] but in any event the missives should, and normally
do, make provision for liability as between seller and purchaser.[85]

Miscellaneous obligations

Other provisions sometimes found in dispositions may also have contractual 11–21
effect. In particular, clauses providing for real burdens or servitudes have
contractual effect from the moment of delivery of the deed, and whereas that
effect is lost, in the case of real burdens, as soon as the burdens are constituted
by registration,[86] in the case of servitudes the contractual liability continues
alongside the real right for as long as the granter of the servitude[87] continues to
own the burdened property.

---

[79] Local Government Finance Act 1992 s.75.

[80] Title Conditions (Scotland) Act 2003 s.9 read with s.123.

[81] *Pegg v City of Glasgow DC*, 1988 S.L.T. (Sh. Ct) 49.

[82] 2003 Act s.10. Indeed, in the case of an obligation to pay for maintenance carried out before
the date of delivery of the disposition, the incoming owner has no liability at all unless a notice of
potential liability for costs had previously been registered.

[83] 1979 Act s.16(3).

[84] *McIntosh v Mitchell Thomson* (1900) 8 S.L.T. 48 suggests that it may. Where, in a tenement,
the statutory notice is not complied with and the work has to be carried out by the local authority,
the person who was owner on the date given on the statutory notice has primary liability, and while
a new owner is also liable, the new owner has a right of relief against the former owner. See
Tenements (Scotland) Act 2004 ss.11(4) and 12.

[85] See e.g. *Combined Standard Clauses* (2009) cl.5(a) fixing liability on the seller in respect of
statutory notices dated on or before the date of conclusion of missives. See para.4–29.

[86] Title Conditions (Scotland) Act 2003 s.61.

[87] Who, if the servitude is imposed on the land being disponed, is the grant*ee* of the
disposition.

Testing clause

11–22   Probative deeds finish with a testing clause giving details of execution.
Although the testing clause usually appears above the signatures, it is not
possible to complete it until the deed has been signed. When a deed is being
prepared for signature the traditional practice is to finish with the words "In
witness whereof". Granters are then asked to leave a substantial gap between
the end of the deed and their signatures so that the testing clause can be added.
Today it is also common for the testing clause to be completed before signature
except for blanks which are later filled in by hand.[88] Execution of deeds is
considered below in Ch.17.

EXCAMBIONS AND SECTION 19 AGREEMENTS

Excambions

11–23   An excambion is where A dispones land to B and B dispones other land to A.
In other words it is a swap. The deed of excambion[89] is usually called a
"contract" of excambion, a somewhat misleading term since in fact it is a
two-way disposition and will normally have been preceded by a contract, typically in the form of missives. Of course, it is possible to have two separate
dispositions instead of a deed of excambion. Excambions may be used in all
sorts of cases, but the typical one is where two adjacent landowners agree to
swap certain areas, perhaps so as to straighten out a zigzag boundary.[90]

Section 19 agreements

11–24   A deed granted under s.19 of the 1979 Act[91] is available where the title boundaries of neighbouring properties are mutually inconsistent, and the parties agree
on a solution. A deed is registered with an agreed plan, and the matter is thus
settled. The Scottish Law Commission, however, has recommended the repeal
of s.19 on the basis that it is "obscure" and that its effects can be achieved by
other means (such as an excambion).[92]

REVISIONS AND ALTERATIONS

Revisions

11–25   By convention dispositions are drafted by the solicitors for the grantees. This is
because the disposition will be the basis of the grantees' title and the grantees
have the stronger interest in ensuring that it is correct. However, in large

---

[88] See below, para.17–07.
[89] For a style see Halliday, para.37–73.
[90] In such a case a deed under s.19 of the 1979 Act is not appropriate, since that section applies
only where there is a discrepancy as between the existing title boundaries. In the typical case of
excambion, there is no such discrepancy.
[91] For a style see Halliday, para.33–91.
[92] Scottish Law Commission, Report on *Land Registration* (Scot Law Com No.222, 2010),
paras 5.31 and 5.32.

developments, such as housing estates, the granters' solicitor will usually produce a *pro forma* style of disposition to be used in all cases. Once a deed has been drafted it is sent to the solicitors acting for the other party to be revised, that is to say checked for errors, both legal and clerical. Traditionally, this was done on paper, with the revising solicitor marking "revised" in pen on the draft and adding the firm name and the date, but today a copy is usually sent by email and revised using track changes. After revision the grantees' solicitors prepare the final version, known traditionally as the "engrossment". This process is usually sufficient to eliminate both drafting and clerical errors.[93] Nonetheless it sometimes happens that even an engrossed disposition requires to be altered.

Alterations[94]

First, alterations before execution. Before execution there is no restriction on   11–26 alterations. The alteration was on the deed when executed, and so is part of the deed. At one time minor alterations were made by interlineation or marginal additions in respect of new words or by erasure in respect of existing words (known collectively as vitiations),[95] but today it is a simple matter to reprint the offending page.

Secondly, alterations after execution. Such alterations need to be re-executed by the signatories,[96] so that in practice one may as well prepare a new (and correct) deed. Apart from that, after execution a deed cannot lawfully be altered. Alteration amounts to the crime of forgery.[97] But in practice deeds are sometimes altered by one of the solicitors involved, the alteration being cheerfully and dishonestly declared in the testing clause as having been made before subscription.[98] The most brazen case of alteration is the substitution of one page for another, which is possible now that the granter does not have to sign each page.[99] Such dishonesty cannot be condoned.

INTERPRETATION

Interpretation

Each clause in a disposition has its own recognised function, and in all ques-   11–27 tions involving that function the clause is treated as the principal provision. If therefore there is a repugnancy between the principal clause and the rest of the deed the principal clause prevails. But if the principal clause itself is ambiguous, that ambiguity may be resolved by reference to the rest of the deed.[100]

---

[93] Computers have helped to eliminate clerical errors.

[94] See also below, para.17–09.

[95] As the vitiation was visibly obvious, the deed was not probative unless the testing clause declared that the alteration was already part of the deed by the time of subscription: see Requirements of Writing (Scotland) Act 1995 s.5(4), (5).

[96] 1995 Act s.5(1) and Sch.1.

[97] Hume, *Commentaries*, i, 159.

[98] The alteration is then probative (presumptively valid) but latently invalid. Sometimes (perhaps as a result of the voice of conscience) the testing clause asserts that the alteration has been made, but does not say that it was made before execution. That achieves nothing.

[99] The change was made in 1970. The current law is in ss.2 and 3 of the Requirements of Writing (Scotland) Act 1995. The wisdom of the modern law may be questioned.

[100] e.g. *Orr v Mitchell* (1893) 20 R. (HL) 27.

Certain specialities concerning the burdens clause are discussed below in Ch.13.[101]

Extrinsic evidence can be used to interpret and explain the wording of the deed, but not to modify it.[102] There are two main examples of the explanatory role of extrinsic evidence. The first is to link up words used in the deed to physical objects or people. For example to say that a property is "bounded on the south by the road known as Buchanan Street, Glasgow" might require extrinsic evidence as to the location of Buchanan Street. The second is to resolve ambiguity. If something is ambiguous, consideration of the background circumstances surrounding the granting of the deed—what is sometimes known as the factual matrix[103]—is admissible, although if the deed is elderly there may be little or nothing by way of background which is capable of discovery.[104]

DELIVERY OF THE DISPOSITION

Effect of delivery

11–28   Before delivery of the disposition, the right of the buyers is simply a personal right under the missives. The sellers have a right to be paid, and the buyers have a right to receive a valid disposition, and to obtain possession of the property. At settlement the parties perform their respective obligations, namely payment by the buyers, and delivery of the deed and transfer of possession by the sellers. But the buyers at this stage still do not have ownership. Ownership is a real right (indeed, the chief kind of real right), and a real right can be obtained only by registration in the Land Register or GRS.[105] Until the buyers register, the sellers remain owner.

Pre-registration risks

11–29   The interval between the delivery of the disposition and its registration is short—seldom more than a few days, and less than 24 hours in the case of ARTL transactions. In this period the buyer (call her Betty) is in theory at risk simply because the seller (call her Alice) is still the owner. Thus, Alice could fraudulently convey the property to someone else, say Ciaran. In that case there would be what is called a race to the register between Ciaran and Betty,

---

[101] See below, para.13–21.

[102] Except by judicial rectification, for which see below, Ch.20. The Contract (Scotland) Act 1997 s.1 (which allows the admission of additional terms in certain circumstances) applies only to contracts and promises.

[103] See in particular the speech of Lord Hoffmann in the English case of *Investors Compensation Scheme Ltd v West Bromwich Building Society* [1998] 1 W.L.R. 896 especially at 912–13. For the position in Scots law, see *Bank of Scotland v Dunedin Property Investment Co Ltd*, 1998 S.C. 657; *Multi-Link Leisure Developments Ltd v North Lanarkshire Council* [2010] UKSC 47; 2011 S.L.T. 184. An overview is given in Ch.5 of the Scottish Law Commission's Discussion Paper on *Interpretation of Contract* (Scot. Law Com. D.P. No.147, 2011). As the Scottish Law Commission acknowledges (para.6.15) "parties in general should be able to place reliance on the apparent meaning of a registered title", and accordingly conveyancing deeds cannot be interpreted with the same freedom as contracts.

[104] *Welsh v Keeper of the Registers of Scotland*, 2010 G.W.D. 23-443 is an example of the difficulties of discovery, and of the perils of relying on flimsy evidence. For a discussion, see Reid and Gretton, *Conveyancing 2010*, pp.156–59.

[105] This was always the rule and is confirmed by s.4 of the Abolition of Feudal Tenure etc. (Scotland) Act 2000.

and whoever registered first would win.[106] Much the same would apply if Alice were to be sequestrated. If Alice delivers a disposition to Betty, and Alice is then sequestrated, there is a race to the register between Betty and Alice's trustee in sequestration. Whoever wins that race takes the property, although in practice trustees in sequestration are generally so slow off the mark as to pose no danger to a buyer who registers with reasonable dispatch.[107] Just to make sure, however, an amendment to the bankruptcy legislation, in force since 2008, prevents the trustee from registering for an initial period of 28 days, beginning with the date when the notice about the sequestration first appears in the Personal Register.[108] Of course, if no disposition has been delivered then Betty is doomed to lose the race. And the position is the same where the disposition is delivered *after* sequestration, for sequestration extinguishes any power which the debtor has to deal with the property.[109] Normally, Betty would know from a search in the Personal Register that Alice had been sequestrated and would refuse to settle the transaction. But where the sequestration occurred shortly before delivery, there is a risk that it remains undiscovered; to meet this difficulty the legislation protects a *bona fide* acquirer in respect of any disposition which is delivered within seven days of the notice about sequestration first appearing in the Personal Register.[110]

There is a special rule where the seller is a company and goes into receivership after having delivered a disposition. In that case the buyer, when she registers, takes the property free from the receiver's rights. This exception derives from the controversial 1997 case of *Sharp v Thomson*.[111] At one time there was speculation that *Sharp v Thomson* had a broad *ratio* to the effect that some sort of "beneficial interest", neither a personal right nor a real right, passed to the buyer upon delivery of the disposition, but that view has not prevailed.[112]

Trust clauses

Although the buyers were eventually to triumph, when *Sharp v Thomson* was decided at first instance, in 1994, the Lord Ordinary found in favour of the   11–30

---

[106] Though Ciaran, if in bad faith, would be subject to the "offside goals rule". See further, Reid, *Property*, paras 695 et seq.

[107] For a celebrated case where the buyer was even slower than the trustee, see *Burnett's Trustee v Grainger*, 2004 S.C. (HL) 19. The same is equally true in the case of a creditor of Alice attaching the property.

[108] Bankruptcy (Scotland) Act 1985 s.31(1A). The amendment was made by s.17(1) of the Bankruptcy and Diligence etc. (Scotland) Act 2007 and implements a proposal of the Scottish Law Commission. This rule is a race-handicap rule, meaning that in the race to the register one competitor (the trustee) has a handicap which makes it virtually impossible for the trustee to win the race as against a grantee for value acting in good faith and with reasonable diligence.

[109] 1985 Act s.32(8).

[110] 1985 Act s.32(9), (9ZA). Again this is the result of an amendment made by s.17(2) of the Bankruptcy and Diligence etc. (Scotland) Act 2007.

[111] *Sharp v Thomson*, 1997 S.C. (HL) 66.

[112] *Burnett's Trustee v Grainger*, 2004 S.C. (HL) 19. See e.g. Gretton, (2004) 8 Edin. L.R. 389. For the *Sharp v Thomson* saga, see Scottish Law Commission, Report on *Sharp v Thomson* (Scot. Law Com. No.208, 2007; available at *http://www.scotlawcom.gov.uk*), which contains, at pp.44–47, an extensive bibliography on a case which has probably generated more writing than any other in Scottish legal history except *Donoghue v Stevenson*, 1932 S.C. (HL) 31. The decision in *Burnett's Trustee v Grainger* has confirmed that, although the decision of the Inner House in *Sharp v Thomson*, 1995 S.C. 455 was reversed by the House of Lords, the Inner House's exposition of Scots property law was correct and was not superseded by the decision of the House of Lords.

receiver.[113] The result was that solicitors became more conscious than before of the potential danger to buyers, and accordingly it became fairly common for dispositions to contain a clause declaring that the property would be held by the sellers in trust for the buyers until the latter registered. These trust clauses remain quite common although, perhaps just as commonly, they are omitted. They seek to take advantage of the rule that the rights of a beneficiary in a trust are protected against the insolvency of the trustee. If, therefore, sellers are transformed into trustees and the buyers into beneficiaries, then, so the argument goes, buyers are protected against the sellers' insolvency.

Because of the House of Lords' ultimate decision in *Sharp v Thomson*[114] trust clauses are not needed to protect against receivership. Whether buyers have much to fear as to the sequestration or liquidation of the sellers, or diligence against them, is doubtful, unless they are quite extraordinarily slow in registering. Hence the usefulness of a trust clause is open to question. It might also be doubted whether the trust so created is valid. If valid it gives a certain protection against unlikely possibilities, but also imposes certain duties on the sellers[115] and also creates new risks for the buyers.[116] On balance it is probably better if trust clauses are not used.[117]

---

[113] *Sharp v Thomson*, 1994 S.L.T. 1068.

[114] *Sharp v Thomson*, 2004 S.C. (HL) 19.

[115] The duties of trusteeship are potentially onerous.

[116] If there is no trust clause the buyers have some protection against a fraudulent double sale by virtue of the offside goals rule. But if there is a trust clause this protection seems to be lost on account of s.2 of the Trusts (Scotland) Act 1961.

[117] For an evaluation of the arguments, see Reid and Gretton, *Conveyancing 2004*, pp.79–85.

CHAPTER 12

DESCRIPTIONS

Introduction

The subject of descriptions[1] is divided in this chapter into seven unequal parts: 12–01

  (i)   Descriptions in the Land Register.
  (ii)   Descriptions in deeds where the property is in the Land Register.
  (iii) Descriptions in deeds triggering first registration.
  (iv)   Descriptions in General Register of Sasines ("GRS") deeds, i.e. deeds recorded, or to be recorded, in the GRS.
  (v)   Parts and pertinents.
  (vi)   Descriptions in missives.
  (vii) Final observations.

DESCRIPTIONS IN THE LAND REGISTER

General

In the Land Register each property unit is identified by a plan. The plan is part   12–02
of the title sheet itself, and hence is also contained in the land certificate, for
the land certificate is a copy of the title sheet. The plan in the title sheet is
known as the title plan, and the plan in the land certificate is known as the
certificate plan, but they are the same plan. In the early days of registration of
title, the map system was a paper one. Nowadays it is digital, though since land
certificates are in paper form the certificate plan is a paper version of the digital
original. A title plan is simply one tiny part of a single digital map—likely to
be called the Cadastral Map in the projected new legislation on land registration—which shows the title boundaries of all registered land in Scotland.[2] As
properties gradually switch from the GRS to the Land Register, this map covers
more and more of the surface of Scotland. The map is based on what the 1979
Act calls the Ordnance Map.[3] The legislation speaks of "the" Ordnance Map,
as if it were something fixed. In fact the Ordnance Survey's maps are in a state
of constant revision. New versions are sent to the Keeper on a frequent and
regular basis. The Keeper not only uses the latest map for new registrations,
but will also take "remedial action" where necessary for existing title sheets.[4]

---

[1] As to which Ch.4 of the *Registration of Title Practice Book* ("ROTPB") is essential reading.
[2] Scottish Law Commission, Report on *Land Registration* (Scot Law Com No.222, 2010),
paras 3.18, 4.10 and 4.39–4.43.
[3] See in particular the Land Registration (Scotland) Act 1979 ss.4(2)(a) and 6(1)(a), and the
Land Registration (Scotland) Rules 2006 (SSI 2006/485) r.20(a).
[4] ROTPB, para.4.26. The law hereabouts is boggy.

However, despite the constant updating, the map for a given area may, at a given time, be significantly out of date. Indeed, whilst the surveying standards of the Ordnance Survey are high, all human endeavours are fallible, so that a map may contain surveying inaccuracies, quite independently of the question of whether it is up to date. The problem of inaccurate or out of date Ordnance Survey maps is significant and perennial.

The plan in the title sheet will have a north sign, and will state the scale, but it will not usually show area measurements[5] or boundary measurements, and these have to be discovered by using the scale. If the Keeper does show these measurements she will in practice exclude indemnity as to their accuracy. The scales used by the Keeper are 1:10000, 1:2500 and 1:1250. The Keeper decides which scale to use. For urban properties she will normally use 1:1250. She can use more than one plan, with different scales. Whatever the scale, plans are limited in their accuracy. Even on the 1:1250 scale, the tiny distance of one millimetre on the plan represents 1.25 metres on the ground. The problem is worse with the other scales. The result is that descriptions in the Land Register cannot be more than approximate, and so there is scope for neighbours to war with each other.[6] A persistent criticism is that a good Sasine plan may be on a larger scale, and more accurate, than the title plan to which it is ultimately reduced.

There is also a verbal description, but in most cases this is little more than a postal address. However, the verbal description can be fuller when this is appropriate, as in tenemental property. If, due to error, the verbal description and title plan are inconsistent, it is thought that the plan would usually prevail, on the basis that registration of title is plan-based.[7] Often the mineral rights are excepted from the title. This fact will be indicated verbally. Pertinents will also be indicated verbally. The Land Registration Act[8] requires the Keeper to enter into the title sheet particulars of "any enforceable real right pertaining to the interest". Thus, if the property is the benefited (dominant) property in a servitude or real burden, this should be mentioned, if known, to the Keeper. Usually, and especially with real burdens, it is not known to the Keeper.[9] However, the position is now changing, for real burdens and servitudes granted after November 28, 2004 have to be registered in the titles of both the benefited and the burdened properties.[10]

Physical features as boundaries

12–03 Where, as often, a boundary coincides with a physical feature on the ground, such as a wall or fence, the land certificate warns that: "The physical object presently shown on the Plan may not be the one referred to in the deed. Indemnity is therefore excluded in respect of information as to the line of the

---

[5] Unless 2 hectares or more: see 1979 Act ss.6(1)(a) and 12(3)(e).

[6] *Clydeside Homes Ltd v Quay* [2009] CSOH 126; 2009 G.W.D. 31-518; *Stuart v Stuart*, Unreported July 27, 2009 Stonehaven Sheriff Court. For discussion, see Reid and Gretton, *Conveyancing 2009*, pp.176–77.

[7] Scottish Law Commission, Discussion Paper on *Land Registration:Miscellaneous Issues* (Scot. Law Com. D.P. No.130, 2005), paras 2.11–2.13, and Report on *Land Registration* (Scot Law Com. No.222, 2010), para.5.36. This is the opposite rule from the one which applies in respect of Sasine descriptions (unless the plan is declared to be taxative).

[8] Land Registration (Scotland) Act 1979 s.6(1)(e).

[9] See below, Ch.13.

[10] Title Conditions (Scotland) Act 2003 ss.4 and 75. See below, paras 13–12 and 13–26.

boundary".[11] Thus while the plan will show the feature in question, with the title boundary on it, the Keeper is not guaranteeing that the title boundary corresponds precisely to the physical line. The Keeper will sometimes, by the use of arrows or a verbal statement, indicate whether the boundary is the middle, or nearside, or farside, of a physical feature.[12]

Water boundaries, whether they are sea, lochs, rivers or burns, are not uncommon and present special problems, especially as they may shift over time.[13]

Tenements

With tenement properties the plan shows the "footprint" of the tenement, and 12–04 also the "steading", which is the footprint plus the attached land, but it does not have a "sectional" view, and so the only way the individual unit can be identified within the tenement is by the verbal description.[14] For instance, it will say something like "the eastmost house on the third or top floor" typically adding "within the land edged red on the title plan". The "land edged red" will be the steading. The word "within" is carefully chosen: while a casual look at the plan might suggest that the owner owns everything within the red line, this is not so, and indeed it is possible that land included within the steading may turn out not to be part of the tenement at all.[15] As for the back green, the rights will usually be stated verbally. If a particular part of the back green is exclusively owned, that may be indicated either verbally or by a plan.[16] In tenemental property the verbal description is, indeed, of central importance. In practice the verbal description tends to be copied more or less verbatim from the GRS title. The GRS description may well have been somewhat vague, and even sloppy, and that vagueness and sloppiness thus tend to migrate from the GRS to the Land Register. There may be no alternative in practice, but such titles hardly display the Land Register to best advantage.

Migration to Land Register of sloppy GRS descriptions

The problem of vague, obscure or sloppy verbal descriptions migrating 12–05 verbatim from the GRS to the Land Register can sometimes also arise with non-tenemental properties, especially with pertinents. The GRS title may have purported to confer on plot X rights over neighbouring plot Y, and yet the purported rights may in fact not be valid as servitudes or real burdens or indeed

[11] See 2(d) of the "General Information" printed inside every land certificate. This derives from form 6 of the Land Registration (Scotland) Rules 2006. And see also Land Registration (Scotland) Act 1979 s.12(3)(d).

[12] The arrow points to the face that is the boundary. If the arrow lies across the boundary feature, that means that the boundary is the middle line.

[13] For the common law position see *Stirling v Bartlett*, 1994 S.L.T. 763; for the Keeper's practice see ROTPB, paras 6.99–6.101, read in the light of the Keeper's statement at (2002) 47 J.L.S.S. May/11; for possible reform, see Scottish Law Commission, Report on *Land Registration* (Scot. Law Com. No.222, 2010), paras 5–33 and 5.34.

[14] Occasionally GRS titles have sectional plans, so in this respect transfer into the Land Register may cause a loss of information.

[15] *North Atlantic Salmon Conservation Organisation v Au Bar Pub Ltd*, 2009 G.W.D. 14-222. See Reid and Gretton, *Conveyancing 2009*, pp.173–76.

[16] For the Keeper's current practice in this respect see (2003) 71 Scottish Law Gazette 123–24. In cases of doubts she may require affidavits about exclusive possession, or consents from the other owners in the tenement.

anything else, for descriptions are done by fallible human beings whose knowledge of the law of Scotland is not always perfect. Yet such descriptions often migrate to the new title sheet verbatim without being seriously queried by the Keeper's staff. Sometimes matters are made worse still by mis-transcription, whether accidental or deliberate.[17] Of course, vague and sloppy conveyancing is not confined to GRS deeds. Modern deeds, and perhaps especially deeds of conditions, are often unsatisfactory, and the unsatisfactory wording will tend to end up unchanged in the title sheet.

Amenity and other common areas

12–06 Meant to be used for real burdens, deeds of conditions[18] are often also used for rights such as co-ownership of amenity areas in residential developments. In such cases the title sheet will usually follow suit, so that the Property Section will say something like "together with the rights set forth in item 4 in Section D". Traditionally, amenity areas were often vaguely described, but since 2009 the Keeper's practice has been to require a description sufficient to identify the land.[19] Indeed without such a description no rights to the amenity areas could be conveyed.[20]

Approved estate layout plans

12–07 Where a developer plans to build new houses and sell them individually, the developer can agree with the Keeper what is called an "approved estate layout plan" showing the whole proposed development with proposed boundaries. This procedure is not compulsory, but it is normal practice. It has many benefits, including avoiding muddles as to boundaries, and avoiding the need for each form 12 for each unit to have a precise description, since a plot number will suffice. The scheme is available only if the whole development site is in the Land Register, but so useful is the scheme that if the site, or a part of it, is in the GRS the Keeper will normally be happy to accept a voluntary first registration for the whole site.

DESCRIPTIONS IN DEEDS WHERE THE PROPERTY IS
IN THE LAND REGISTER

Dealings with whole: standard dispositions

12–08 The task of describing property depends fundamentally on whether what is being transferred is the whole of the granter's land, which is the normal situation, or only a part of that land with the rest being retained, for the time being at least, by the granter. The former involves a "standard" disposition, the latter a "break-off" (or "break-away" or "split-off") disposition. Standard dispositions are more straightforward and it is convenient to begin with them.[21]

---

[17] *Willemse v French* [2011] CSOH 51; 2011 G.W.D. 12-282.
[18] For which see below, para.13–11.
[19] Registers of Scotland, *Update 27* (2009).
[20] *PMP Plus Ltd v Keeper of the Registers of Scotland*, 2009 S.L.T. (Lands Tr) 2. See further above, para.7–07 and below, para.12–25.
[21] A complete standard disposition is given above in para.11–04.

If a title is in the Land Register, the description in a standard disposition is simply a reference to the title number[22] plus a brief verbal description. There is an approved statutory style: "the subjects[23] registered under Title Number . . .".[24] Thus in practice the wording would be something like "ALL and WHOLE Number Four Beech Drive, Perth being the subjects registered under Title Number PER 12345". For ARTL transactions the same information is entered into the system—and hence ultimately into the disposition itself—in response to a prompt.[25]

The postal address is an example of a "general" description—as opposed to a "particular" description, which is one in which the actual boundaries are identified.[26] General descriptions are of little importance for deeds dealing with property in the Land Register, except for tenemental property, but they are much more important for GRS deeds and are discussed later in that context.[27] The words "ALL and WHOLE . . ." (formerly "All and Haill", and before that "*Totas et Integras*") are of great antiquity and considerable theoretical obscurity. According to Craig:

> "The words 'all and whole' are exegetical and mean that the subject is conveyed as a complete unit with all its parts. In ordinary language the word 'all' is used with reference to things differing in kind, and the word 'whole' with reference to things of the same kind. Anyhow, the effect of these words is to show that the entire or universal subject is carried by the disposition. For the person who sells an estate or transfers it for some onerous cause is bound in law to hand it over complete and perfect, clear of all burdens, servitudes, and encumbrances whatsoever."[28]

But in modern practice the words have become rather like a mere punctuation mark. They are usually written in capitals, and help show at a glance where the description is starting.

Dealings with part: break-off dispositions

If a disposition or other deed[29] is a break-off deed, there is no existing title sheet, and hence no title number, which exactly corresponds to the land being disponed. Further, while a general description is likely to be included, this is

12–09

---

[22] This is required by the 1979 Act s.4(2)(d). Actually this provision is not always workable and is sometimes disregarded (e.g. an application by an unregistered proprietor based on a midcouple which contains a general description).

[23] "The subjects" is a traditional conveyancing term meaning the property in question. It can be criticised on the ground that in legal theory the term "subjects" refers to the subjects of rights, which is to say persons, in contrast to "objects" which themselves may be divided into rights and things. Land is thus an object rather than a subject.

[24] Land Registration (Scotland) Rules 2006 r.23 and Sch.3.

[25] See above, para.8–23.

[26] A general description is not to be confused with a general disposition. The former is used in a "special" disposition, i.e. the normal cases of a disposition of one or more identified properties. A "general" disposition is a disposition of all the disponer's heritable property, without description. An example of a general disposition is a trust deed for behoof of creditors, in which the granter conveys all his or her property to the trustee. See below, Ch.21.

[27] See below, para.12–15. Particular descriptions are discussed below in para.12–16.

[28] *Jus Feudale*, II, iii, 23 (translation by J.A. Clyde, 1934).

[29] Break-off writs are usually dispositions. But it is competent to have a standard security or a lease of only part of a registered title.

not sufficient by itself because it does not identify the boundaries of the property which is being broken off. For that a particular description is needed. Except in the case of a unit in a tenement such a description must be plan-based.[30] If there is in place an approved estate layout plan[31] the deed plan should normally be copied from that and should bear a docquet so stating.[32] The plan should be at one of the scales used by the Keeper, except that she will accept deeds containing 1:500 plans, and these are widely used for residential property. In some cases the deed will need a second plan, a "location" plan at a different scale, so as to anchor the first plan to surrounding features that can be identified on the Ordnance Map. Either the body of the deed or the plan itself should make clear whether the boundaries follow the middle, nearside or farside of the boundary features. Any measurements should be metric and should normally be to an accuracy of two decimal places, i.e. to an accuracy of one centimetre. The traditional detailed verbal description which used to be the norm in break-off deeds in the GRS is unnecessary and is not found in practice.[33]

In a break-off conveyance, after the description there follows a clause identifying, by reference, the larger property of which the present property was hitherto a part. The official clause is: "being part of the subjects registered under Title Number . . .".[34] In practice "part" is often expanded to "part and portion", because that is the expression traditionally used in GRS deeds. Indeed, the name of this clause, both for GRS and Land Register deeds, is the "part-and-portion" clause.[35] This is followed by the "parts-and-pertinents" clause, of particular importance in break-off deeds and discussed later in this chapter.[36]

DESCRIPTIONS IN DEEDS TRIGGERING FIRST REGISTRATION

General

12–10   The existing GRS description may well be sufficient for the purposes of a first registration disposition, bearing in mind that the Keeper must be able to plot the boundaries with reasonable precision by reference to the Ordnance Map at the appropriate scale. What is required is a particular description in the original break-off writ of the unit in question[37] which is either (a) plan-based, the plan being an adequate one, or is (b) a "full bounding description with measurements".[38] The new disposition can then simply incorporate this earlier description by reference in the usual way.[39] If neither requirement

---

[30] By contrast, in GRS deeds a particular description can be purely verbal. See below.
[31] See above, para.12–07.
[32] ROTPB, para.8.47 at p.338.
[33] For verbal particular descriptions, see below, para.12–17.
[34] Land Registration (Scotland) Rules 2006 r.23 and Sch.3.
[35] See below, para.12–20.
[36] See below, para.12–24.
[37] See below, paras 12–16 to 12–18 for particular desciptions in the GRS.
[38] Land Registration (Scotland) Rules 2006 Sch.1, form 1, Pt B, question 1. The form is prescribed by statutory instrument, and thus has legal force, but it is nevertheless curious that what is legally required can be discovered only from an application form. One would expect the requirements would be laid down directly, and that the terms of the application form would merely reflect those norms.
[39] As to which see below, para.12–19.

is met,[40] a plan will have to be drawn up, conforming to the criteria applicable to the Land Register.[41] The simplest way to do this is for the disposition to contain a new, plan-based, description, but it is also possible to submit to the Keeper a separate plan, signed by both disponer and disponee. In practice the particular description will be preceded by a brief general description, often no more than the postal address.

A break-off disposition will always need a new plan, and should also contain a part-and-portion clause. This will refer back to the descriptive deed, which is to say the earlier deed in the GRS that describes the property from which the new title unit is being broken off. This earlier descriptive deed will in the typical case itself have been a break-off disposition (or, very commonly, a break-off feu disposition, feu charter or feu contract).[42] A parts-and-pertinents clause is also likely to be needed.[43]

Tenements

There is one exception to the rule that in a first registration the title must be plan-based: this is where the property is a tenement flat.[44] However, even here a plan may be needed, for instance to identify a part of the adjacent ground that is exclusively allocated to the particular flat.[45]

12–11

P16 Report

The applicant's solicitors need to check whether the title boundaries correspond to what is actually possessed.[46] The usual way to do this is to ask the Keeper for a P16 Report, or to ask independent searchers for a P16 equivalent. Here there is a comparison of the title boundaries with the physical boundaries as shown in the Ordnance Map.[47] The usefulness of a P16 Report is that a discrepancy between the title boundaries and the physical boundaries is a warning sign that there may exist a potential boundary dispute. The fact that the applicant's alleged title boundaries exceed the physical boundaries does not necessarily mean that the Keeper will decline to register the applicant for the excess, or that she will register the applicant for the excess only with exclusion of indemnity, for it might be that the title is definitely good.[48] But, as has been said, a discrepancy is a warning sign.

12–12

---

[40] As for the nature of descriptions in GRS deeds, and some of the problems that can exist with such descriptions, see below.

[41] Land Registration (Scotland) Rules 2006 Sch.1, form 1, Pt B, question 1. See above, para.12–09 for the type of plan that is acceptable.

[42] See further below, para.12–19.

[43] See below, paras 12–22 to 12–24.

[44] Land Registration (Scotland) Rules 2006 Sch.1 form 1 Pt B question 1.

[45] ROTPB, para.4.14.

[46] Land Registration (Scotland) Rules 2006 Sch.1 form 1 Pt B question 2.

[47] ROTPB, paras 4.8–4.12.

[48] What has just been said is, we believe, the law. The Keeper's practice may not be the same. Thus para.4.16 (at p.94) of the ROTPB says that "if the extent of the property as defined in the deeds is found to be larger than the occupational extent . . . verification that the applicant is willing to accept the smaller extent must be given".

DESCRIPTIONS IN GRS DEEDS

Introduction

12–13 As the Land Register has been "operational" in all counties in Scotland since 2003, cases when a deed will be recorded in the GRS are increasingly rare. It happens when the existing title is still in the GRS, and the deed being granted is not one that triggers the switch to the new register.[49] Examples are standard securities and gratuitous dispositions, such as dispositions by executors to legatees, and dispositions for "love favour and affection". But in any event, so many titles are still GRS titles that an understanding of GRS descriptions will long remain important for the conveyancer.

The distinction between descriptions in the Land Register itself and descriptions in deeds has no counterpart for the GRS. The reason is that the GRS is in essence a warehouse of deeds, and nothing more than deeds, apart from a superb system of indexes and so on. Whereas in the Land Register map-based precision is vital, in the GRS deeds do not have to be map-based. Indeed, before 1924 deed plans could not enter the GRS at all. In principle, all that is required of a description is that it enables the property to be identified—that is to say, that it satisfies the specificity principle which applies in the creation or transfer of all real rights. Extrinsic evidence is permitted,[50] a rule which allows considerable vagueness in the description. Thus, in *Murray's Trustee v Wood*[51] the description was: "All and Whole that piece of ground fronting Baker Street of Aberdeen, in the burgh and county of Aberdeen". Since it could be established by extrinsic evidence that the granter owned only one property in Baker Street, this was held to be a sufficient description. The Keeper can reject deeds if the description is insufficient, but since for GRS deeds much latitude is allowed such rejections are rare. The only reported case is *Macdonald v Keeper of the Registers*.[52] There the Keeper was held entitled to reject a deed with the description "the house in No.140 McDonald Road, Edinburgh, the title to which is in my name" on the basis that, since No.140 was a tenement building, it was not possible to tell which flat was being conveyed. There would seem to be some tension between this decision and *Murray's Trustee v Wood*. It is generally accepted that *Macdonald v Keeper of the Registers* was correctly decided, so there seem to be two thresholds of imprecision: the lowest level, below which a description becomes meaningless and without effect, a threshold that the description in *Murray's Trustee v Wood* did not fall below, and a higher threshold, where the description, though it might be sufficient if accepted for recording, is still so vague that the Keeper is entitled (but not obliged) to reject.

---

[49] See above, para.8–03.

[50] See above, para.11–27. This is just as well, for otherwise the traditional type of estate title would be invalid.

[51] *Murray's Trustee v Wood* (1887) 14 R. 856. See also *Cattanach's Trustee v Jamieson* (1884) 11 R. 972 where the court looked for help in other parts of the deed.

[52] *Macdonald v Keeper of the Registers*, 1914 S.C. 854.

Old units of measurement

Many descriptions of property in the GRS are based on imperial units of meas-   12–14
urement, and, surprising though it may seem, some are still based on the old
Scots units.[53]

The imperial linear measures are:

> 1 mile = 8 furlongs
> 1 furlong = 10 chains
> 1 chain = 22 yards
> 1 yard = 3 feet
> 1 foot = 12 inches.

One yard = 0.9144 metres, 1 foot = 0.3048 metres and 1 inch = 25.4 millime-
tres. A shorthand is widely used for feet and inches: thus 16′7″ means 16 feet
and 7 inches.

As to imperial superficial measure,[54] 1 acre = 4840 square yards, i.e. a
furlong by a chain (0.4047 hectares). The acre is divided into 4 roods, and each
square rood into 40 square poles. A square pole is thus 30.25 square yards.[55] A
square yard is around 0.836 square metres.

The old Scottish units generally had the same names as the imperial measures, but were different in size. The fall = about 5.65 metres, and the chain = 4
falls. Forty square falls (also called simply a fall) = a square rood (also called
simply a rood), and 4 square roods = 1 acre. The Scots acre = about 1.26 imperial acres = about 0.51 hectares.[56]

General descriptions

Land may be described in a GRS deed without reference to boundaries. This is   12–15
known as a general description. Such a description may not enable the property
to be identified from the Ordnance Map on its own: local information may be
necessary.

The following are examples of general descriptions:

> "ALL and WHOLE that detached dwelling-house number twelve
> Appletree Lane, Cupar, Fife."

> "ALL and WHOLE that flatted dwelling-house[57] entering by the common
> passage and stair number fifteen Montrose Crescent, Dumfries, being the
> southmost dwelling-house on the second floor above the street or ground
> floor."

> "ALL and WHOLE the lands of Cottown of Fetterletter, Ardlogie, Little
> Gight, Blackpool, Little Milbrex, North Faddonhill, Bruckleseat, Letherty,

---

[53] Article XVII of the Treaty of Union abolished the Scots units, but this was widely ignored in
practice.

[54] "Superficial measure" refers to area, as opposed to "linear measure" which refers to length.

[55] The square pole is also called simply "the pole". Since the pole is also a linear measure of 5.5
yards, the word "pole" is ambiguous, but context generally makes it clear whether the linear or
superficial measure is meant. "Perch" means the same as pole.

[56] For old Scots units expressed as metric equivalents, see Small, 1970 S.L.T. (News) 102.

[57] "Flatted dwelling-house" is the standard expression. Not "flat" since "flat" traditionally
means "floor".

Myre of Bedlam, Moss of Blackhillock, West Auchmaliddy, Dens, Middlemuir, Belnagoak, Gowanwell, Middlethird, Backhill of Ardo, Merdrum, Cairnorrie, North Arnybogs, Auchencrieve, Auchnagatt, Skilmafilly, Mains of Inkhorn, Quilquox, Mains of Schivas, Greenness, Lethen, Mill of Crichie Den, Hornscroft, Flobbets, Milton of Fochel, and Redmoss in the County of Aberdeen."[58]

The practice is to use general descriptions in all dispositions, including those in respect of property on the Land Register.[59] As for the GRS, a break-off disposition will usually contain a particular description in addition to the general one.

Particular descriptions

12–16 A particular description (also called a bounding description) identifies the property by its boundaries, normally with measurements. When property was first conveyed as a separate unit (a split-off or break-off) it was, and remains, usual[60] to have a particular description. In some circumstances this can be done by way of exception. Thus suppose that a part of a field is split off. That deed needs a particular description. But when the remainder comes to be conveyed later on, the description of the original subjects can be repeated, "under exception of" the subjects already split off, defined by a reference to the earlier break-off deed.

A particular description can be done (a) purely verbally, or (b) purely by a plan, or (c) by both.[61] Traditionally it was done purely verbally. Sometimes a plan was attached, but there was originally no means of copying plans into the GRS, and so such plans had limited importance, and what mattered was the verbal description. Eventually, in 1924, it became competent to lodge in the GRS a duplicate copy of the deed plan,[62] and when the Keeper adopted the practice of photocopying deeds not long after, plans began to be recorded without the need for a duplicate. As a result purely verbal bounding descriptions, which are on the whole less informative than a good plan, should have been abandoned, but in practice they tended to be used in addition to the plan. It was only in the 1990s that particular descriptions without verbal bounding descriptions began to become common. A particular description using both a verbal description and a plan is given below.

Not all plans in GRS deeds were good. Indeed, the same is true today, for deeds for the Land Register, but today poor plans will usually get nowhere, because the Keeper will reject them and ask for a better one. But in the GRS

---

[58] The two previous examples are imaginary, but this is a GRS title in Aberdeenshire, with much verbiage omitted for the sake of brevity. Sir John Rankine (*Land Ownership*, 4th edn (1909), p.101), wrote disapprovingly of descriptions by "a string of uncouthly-spelt names". This was the standard form of description for estates in the old days, and is sometimes still encountered, with no plans to help. To those interested in place names or local history, these deeds are poems, and the uncouthness is a delight.

[59] See above, paras 12–08 and 12–09.

[60] But far from invariable. Descriptions of residential property were often mere postal addresses, plus words of style that meant little.

[61] It must be emphasised that this concerns the GRS. For Land Register deeds a verbal particular description in a break-off deed is not sufficient, except for tenement units. There must be a plan. See above, para.12–09.

[62] Conveyancing (Scotland) Act 1924 s.48.

the role of the Keeper was an essentially passive one, and many poor plans entered the register. Some had no north sign.[63] Others, more creatively, had a north sign pointing south, or, even east or west. Some had neither scale nor linear measurements. Some were "floating rectangles",[64] which showed only that Fergus McFeu owned 1.23 acres of a certain shape somewhere, the only definite information being that it was in Argyll. A common fault was to identify boundaries or areas by colours so that the plan became meaningless in the monochrome copy obtainable from the GRS.[65]

Verbal particular description

In a verbal particular description the conveyancer mentally stands in the middle   12–17
of the plot, and turns round clockwise, describing the boundaries and their lengths as seen from the central point. It is usual to start from the northern boundary.

Measurements are followed by the words "or thereby" since absolute accuracy is not normally attainable. It is usual to give the measurement in both figures and words. Decimals are often worded thus: "along which boundary it extends seven metres and eighty-five decimal or one-hundredth parts of a metre (7.85 m) or thereby". Or "seven metres and eight decimal or one tenth parts of a metre (7.8 m) or thereby". This is cumbersome and confusing, but is standard practice.[66] It is usual, though not invariable, practice to have a statement of area: e.g. "extending to one hectare and two hundred and twenty-five decimal or one thousandth parts of a hectare (1.225 ha) or thereby".

Where the title boundary follows a physical one, such as a road or a wall, the description ideally states whether the title boundary is the nearside or farside or middle line (*medium filum*). If the deed or plan is silent on the point,[67] the expression "bounded by" is generally construed as meaning the nearside, so that, for example, "bounded by a stone wall" excludes the wall from the property.[68] But there are exceptions, and the expression "bounded by a road" means, where the road is public, that the boundary is the *medium filum*.[69]

The following describes the property shown on the plan and is a typical example of the traditional sort of verbal bounding description:

> "ALL and WHOLE that plot of ground with the semi detached dwelling-house erected thereon known as Number Four Torduff Road, Dalry, Selkirkshire, extending to four hundred and thirty square metres or thereby, all as the said plot is shown hatched on the plan annexed and signed as relative hereto, and is bounded as follows: on or towards the north by the southern edge of Torduff Road aforesaid along which it

---

[63] For an example of the potential consequences see William Jardine Dobie, *Plain Tales from the Courts* (1957), pp.12–14.

[64] To use the common term. The shape might of course be anything at all.

[65] Of course, the title deeds would normally contain the original, coloured plan. Further, a duplicate plan could be lodged in the GRS under s.48 of the Conveyancing (Scotland) Act 1924, but such cases were rare.

[66] For criticism, see BL, 1971 S.L.T. (News) 9.

[67] See e.g. *Dalton v Turcan Connell (Trustees) Ltd*, 2005 S.C.L.R. 159.

[68] See Halliday, para.33–11; *Butt v Galloway Motor Co Ltd*, 1996 S.C. 261.

[69] *Magistrates of Ayr v Dobbie* (1898) 25 R. 1184; *Baillie v Mackay*, 1994 G.W.D. 25-1516 (reported in part, 1996 S.L.T. 507). Compare *Harris v Wishart*, 1996 S.L.T. 12. See also Gordon and Wortley (3rd edn), paras 3–35 and 3–36.

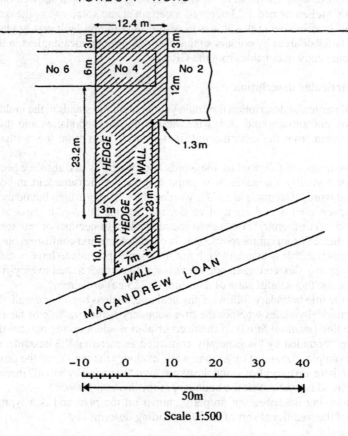

extends twelve metres and four decimal or one-tenth parts of a metre (12.4m) or thereby; on or towards the east by other subjects known as Number Two Torduff Road aforesaid, along which it extends in a southerly direction following the centre line of a brick wall three metres (3m) or thereby, again in a southerly direction following the outer or western face of the house erected on said adjacent subjects at Number Two Torduff Road aforesaid along which it extends twelve metres (12m) or thereby, then in a westerly direction following the centre line of a brick wall along which it extends one metre and three decimal or one-tenth parts of a metre (1.3m) or thereby, again in a southerly direction following the middle line of a stone wall along which it extends twenty-three metres (23m) or thereby, until it meets Macandrew Loan; on or towards the south by the outer or southern face of a stone wall separating the said plot from Macandrew Loan aforesaid along which it extends seven metres (7m) or thereby; on or towards the west by other subjects known as Number Six Torduff Road aforesaid, along which it extends in a northerly direction along the middle line of a holly hedge ten metres and one decimal or one-tenth part of a metre (10.1m) or thereby, then in a westerly direction following the middle line of said hedge along which it extends three metres (3m) or thereby, then in a northerly direction following the middle line of said hedge along which it extends twenty-three metres and two decimal or one-tenth parts of a metre (23.2m) or thereby, then in a northerly direction following the middle line of a mutual gable wall between the house erected on the plot hereby disponed and the house erected on the said adjacent subjects at Number Six Torduff Road aforesaid along which it extends six metres (6m) or thereby, then in a northerly direction following the middle line of a wooden fence along which it extends three metres (3 m) or thereby until it reaches Torduff Road aforesaid."

The deed would then normally continue with a part-and-portion clause.

Demonstrative plans and taxative plans

If a deed has both a detailed verbal description and a plan these are to be read 12–18 together. But occasionally there are irreconcilable discrepancies between them. In that case, which prevails? That depends on whether the plan is—to use the strange but time-honoured terminology—"taxative" or "demonstrative". If the deed declares the plan to be "taxative", that means that in the event of such irreconcilable inconsistency, the plan is to be deemed correct, while if the plan is stated to be "demonstrative" that means that the verbal description is to prevail.[70] The difference between a demonstrative plan and a taxative one only arises where the difference is an irreconcilable one. If it is reconcilable then there is no difference: in every case the effort has to be made to read the verbal description and the plan as two views of a single truth.

Good practice was traditionally to state that a plan was demonstrative where it was only a sketch, but if the plan was a good quality one it was better to declare it taxative. Most conveyancers, however, routinely declared a plan to be "demonstrative not taxative" as words of style. Occasionally, a deed is silent as to the point. In that case the resolution of the discrepancy can be difficult.[71] If a property is described solely by plan, without a detailed verbal description, a discrepancy cannot arise and no purpose is served by declaring the plan either taxative or demonstrative. Obvious though that fact is, such declarations were common. The taxative/demonstrative distinction remains important for interpreting existing descriptions in GRS deeds, but modern deeds do not normally have detailed verbal bounding descriptions.

Descriptions by reference, and part-and-portion clauses

Only break-off conveyances are likely to contain a particular description. 12–19 Subsequent deeds contain a general description followed by a reference to some earlier deed in the GRS where a particular description is to be found. This saves unnecessary repetition. There is a special statutory method of

---

[70] For an example see *Royal and Sun Alliance Insurance v Wyman-Gordon Ltd*, 2001 S.L.T. 1305.

[71] For the reported decisions on such cases, see Halliday, para.33–13 and Gordon and Wortley (3rd edn), para.3–08.

referring back to the earlier deed,[72] which will almost always have been a break-off disposition or a feu disposition, feu charter or feu contract. However, occasionally one finds that on account of inadequacies in the description in the existing descriptive writ, a later standard disposition contains a new particular description.

As in the Land Register,[73] a break-off disposition contains a part-and-portion clause identifying the larger property from which the property being conveyed is being broken off. The larger property will normally be identified by means of a description by reference. Thus a break-off disposition will normally contain (a) a general description, (b) a particular description, and (c) a particular description by reference in respect of the larger subjects from which the land is being broken off.

PARTS AND PERTINENTS

In general

12–20　The description is concerned with the land conveyed. But the grantee receives more than the bare land. The generic term for the extras which also pass to the grantee is "parts and pertinents". Insofar as there is any sustainable distinction between "parts" and "pertinents" it is that "parts" are those rights which are exercisable over the land itself, while "pertinents" are those rights exercised in association with the land but beyond its boundaries.[74]

Parts

12–21　Land is owned *a coelo usque ad centrum* (from the sky to the centre, i.e. of the earth). What is built on or lies underneath the land is a "part" of the land. So houses and trees and minerals are parts. But this is subject to the exception of legal separate tenements,[75] i.e. property reserved from the land by legal implication. Of these, two (gold and silver, and oil and gas) are the property of the Crown. A third, coal, was at one stage nationalised but has since been denationalised.[76] The remaining legal separate tenements are the right to fish for salmon, and the right to gather mussels and oysters.[77]

Minerals are conventional separate tenements. As such, they are not reserved by legal implication but are capable of being reserved and hence owned separately from the land. Also conventional separate tenements are the small number of sporting rights in respect of which a notice was served by superiors

---

[72] Conveyancing (Scotland) Act 1874 s.61; Conveyancing (Scotland) Act 1924 s.8 and Sch.D. Since at common law it is competent to incorporate into a deed all or part of any other deed, provided that the deed so incorporated is adequately identified, it is not clear why the special statutory provisions were thought necessary. For an example of a particular description by reference, see above, para.11–05.

[73] See above, para.12–09.

[74] Reid, *Property*, paras 199–206.

[75] *Tenementa separata*. See Reid, *Property*, paras 207–213.

[76] Coal Industry Act 1994. Nowadays coal is obtained by quarrying ("open-cast") and so the operator needs to obtain surface rights. See generally Robert Rennie, *Minerals and the Law in Scotland* (2001).

[77] Another separate tenement, teind, was abolished by s.56 of the Abolition of Feudal Tenure etc. (Scotland) Act 2000.

under s.65A of the Abolition of Feudal Tenure Act.[78] In practice, minerals were usually reserved by the superior when land was feued. Such rights were unaffected by the abolition of feudal tenure since the reserved minerals were held by the superior not as *dominium directum* but as *dominium utile*. If minerals are held by someone other than the owner of the land, then they do not pass as a part of the land. If the mineral rights have not been separated then they pass as part of the land, unless expressly reserved.

Pertinents

Pertinents form a ragbag and can be either corporeal or incorporeal. Whereas "parts" are parts by necessary implication, this is only true of pertinents in the case of tenements: in a flatted building each individual flat has, as a pertinent, rights (usually of common property) in certain other parts of the building such as the common passage and stair.[79] Otherwise a pertinent has, in practice, to be created either by express grant in a break-off conveyance or by positive prescription.[80] One common example, discussed below,[81] is shared parts in housing estates and other developments. Another is a different, and smaller, piece of property which is subordinate in some way to the principal property, for example a garage or cellar. A third, and incorporeal, example is title conditions such as servitudes and real burdens. These have the peculiarity that they cannot be severed from the property of which they are a pertinent: so if Blackmains has a servitude right over Whitemains, then that right is inseparable from Blackmains, and passes automatically in any conveyance of Blackmains.

12–22

Pertinents in standard dispositions

In an ordinary disposition the granters dispone all that they own. Nothing is retained. Accordingly, new pertinents cannot be created, for there is no retained land in respect of which a valid grant can be made. So an ordinary disposition is simply a disposition with the existing parts and pertinents, and, since parts and pertinents by definition pass with the land, no clause is actually necessary. "A grant of the lands of A . . . is as extensive as a grant of A with parts and pertinents."[82] For GRS dispositions, however, and for those triggering first registration, the practice remains to include a parts-and-pertinents clause. At one time the clause was long. Craig offers the following:

12–23

> "along with the houses, buildings, woods, plains, muirs, marshes, ways, paths, rivers, streams, lakes, meadows, pastures, and pasturages, mills, multures and the sequels thereof, fowlings, huntings, fishings, peat-mosses, turbaries, rabbits, rabbit-warrens, doves and dove-cots, gardens, orchards, smithies, malt-kilns and brewhouses, brooms, woods, forests, and coppice, timber, quarries of stone and lime, courts and their suits, herezalds,

---

[78] Where they are separate tenements, both sporting rights and minerals command their own title sheets. So do salmon fishings. See Land Registration (Scotland) Act 1979 s.5(1)(a), read with s.28(1) (definition of "incorporeal heritable right").

[79] Tenements (Scotland) Act 2004 s.3. See below, para.14–03.

[80] *Cooper's Trustees v Stark's Trustees* (1898) 25 R. 1160 is an example of the latter.

[81] See below, para.12–25.

[82] *Gordon v Grant* (1850) 13 D. 1 at 7. For Land Register titles, this is a matter of express provision: see Land Registration (Scotland) Act 1979 s.3(1)(a).

bloodwites, and merchets of women, together also with grazings, free ish
and entry, and all other liberties, conveniencies, profits, easements, and
pertinents whatsoever, named as well as unnamed, under the ground as
well as above the same, pertaining, or which may in any manner whatsoever lawfully pertain in the future, to the foresaid lands, including the
castle, mills, parts, pendicles, and pertinents thereof, freely, fully, quietly,
wholly, honourably, happily and in peace, without any impediment, revo-
cation, contradiction, or obstacle whatsoever."[83]

Modern practice is, alas, more restrained. A typical GRS clause is: "Together
with (one) the fittings[84] and fixtures (two) the parts, privileges and pertinents,
and (three) my whole right, title and interest, present and future, in and to the
subjects hereby disponed". One purpose of the reference to "whole right, title
and interest" is to cover accretion of title. If the granter does not own the property at the time of the grant but comes to own it later, ownership will accresce
automatically to the grantee. But in fact the same effect is achieved by the
clause of absolute warrandice.[85]

Legal separate tenements (such as salmon fishings) are not carried by a
disposition unless listed in the title sheet of the property in question or, in GRS
titles, expressly mentioned in the deed, this usually being done in the pertinents
clause.[86]

Pertinents in break-off dispositions

12–24   Break-off dispositions are more difficult to handle than standard dispositions.
Servitudes and real burdens may need to be granted (over the retained land), or
reserved (over the disponed land), or both.[87] Factual information will be needed
on a variety of matters such as services and access routes. In addition, and
especially in tenements or other developments, the grantee may need to be
given rights of common property in respect of certain shared parts and facilities, a subject discussed below. Rights which are conferred on the grantee—
servitudes, real burdens, and rights of common property—appear in the
parts-and-pertinents clause, or in a schedule to the disposition or a separate
deed of conditions which is then incorporated by reference into the pertinents
clause. Conversely, servitudes and real burdens conferred on the granter in
respect of the land being disponed appear, or are incorporated by reference
into, the burdens clause.

Common areas in developments

12–25   In many types of development there will be areas which will be co-owned by
the various proprietors. The break-off dispositions will need to identify these
areas in a suitable manner. A practical problem is that the development may
alter after the first break-off disposition has been granted. Indeed, developers

---

[83] *Jus Feudale*, III, iii, 30 (Clyde's translation).
[84] The reference to "fittings" is odd. In *Jamieson v Welsh* (1900) 3 F. 176 at 182 Lord Kinnear
justly commented that "a sound conveyancer in framing a disposition . . . will not think it necessary to insert a futile conveyance of the moveables which would carry nothing".
[85] Stair, III, iii, 2; Bankton, III, ii,16 and 18; Erskine, II, vii, 3. For accretion see Reid, *Property*,
para.677.
[86] *McKendrick v Wilson*, 1970 S.L.T. (Sh. Ct) 39.
[87] For servitudes and real burdens, see below, Ch.13.

often wish to reserve the right to vary their plans in response to varying commercial demands. Thus, in a residential development, instead of 20 houses the developer may wish to increase the number to 25. If that is done after the first break-off, and the first break-off granted a 1/20 share of the common parts, there is a problem. This problem is usually fudged by conveying "a right in common with the other proprietors in the said development to . . ." without specifying the proportion. It is a fudge because at the time of the first conveyance a definite share must be conveyed, and, once conveyed, cannot be changed except by corrective conveyancing.

A problem of the same sort, but more serious, is that the developer may wish to change the physical extent of the areas which are to be common parts. Once the first break-off has been granted, containing a share of those parts, any alteration becomes impossible without corrective conveyancing. Traditionally, this problem was also sometimes fudged by granting in the first disposition a right in common to common areas which were not defined in the plan but only in a vague verbal formula, the pith of which was that the common parts would be all parts of the development which are not specifically conveyed to individual purchasers. This practice was effectively ended by the decision in *PMP Plus v Keeper of the Registers of Scotland*[88] which held that no rights could be created in respect of an area which is indeterminate and potentially fluctuating and whose extent can be discovered only by future circumstances.[89] Following that decision the Keeper will only register grants in respect of common areas where the areas in question are properly described, whether by a plan or by other means.[90] Although undoubtedly correct as a matter of law, this stance is undeniably inconvenient to developers wishing to retain a degree of flexibility, and the projected legislation on land registration may allow common areas to be put into a separate title sheet where identification would not be required until after the development was complete and the extent of the common areas ascertained.[91]

MISSIVES

Missives

For missives the only requirement is that the property be described in such a   12–26
way that it can be identified. Typically the description may be no more than a
postal address, usually with the addition of some such words as "as shown to
our clients", and sometimes with the sales particulars included as part of the
missives. In commercial conveyancing, the title number may ultimately be
included where, in the course of negotiations, the buyers' agents have had a
chance to look at the land certificate. If the description is too vague the missives
will be void. Descriptions in missives are discussed further above in Ch.4.[92]

---

[88] *PMP Plus v Keeper of the Registers of Scotland*, 2009 S.L.T. (Lands Tr) 2. See Reid and Gretton, *Conveyancing 2008*, pp.133–49.

[89] This is the so-called specificity principle. The decision was anticipated in para.12–10 of the 3rd edition of this book.

[90] Registers of Scotland, *Update 27* (2009). See also above, para.7–07.

[91] Scottish Law Commission, Report on *Land Registration* (Scot. Law Com. No.222, 2010), Pt 6.

[92] See above, para.4–03.

FINAL OBSERVATIONS

Dispositions: a summary of practice for both GRS and Land Register transactions

12–27 A deed relating to property in the Land Register only needs to state the title number,[93] while for GRS dispositions (other than first registrations) a general description is sufficient.[94] But conveyancers prefer to describe property twice. So most dispositions contain both a general and also a particular description. Except with break-off deeds, the particular description will rely on an earlier description of the property and so will refer to the title number, or, if the property is not yet in the Land Register, to the original break-off disposition. A new break-off deed will contain a particular description, which will normally be plan-based, and a part-and-portion clause, identifying the larger property from which the present property is being broken off. The part-and-portion clause must refer to the title number, or, if the property is not yet in the Land Register, to the earlier break-off conveyance describing the larger propery. A parts-and-pertinents clause may be added to taste. Current practice may be summarised in the following table:

Deed	Description
Standard disposition (Land Register land)	(i) general description + (ii) particular description by title number[95]
Standard disposition (first registrations and GRS transactions)	(i) general description + (ii) particular description by reference back to the GRS descriptive deed[96]
Break-off disposition (Land Register land)	(i) general description + (ii) particular description + (iii) part-and-portion clause by title number[97]
Break-off disposition (first registrations and GRS transactions)	(i) general description + (ii) particular description + (iii) part-and-portion clause by reference back to the GRS descriptive deed[98]

[93] 1979 Act s.15(1).

[94] The sufficiency of such descriptions was discussed above at para.12–15.

[95] For instance: "ALL and WHOLE the subjects known as Two Main Street, Renfrew and registered under Title Number . . .".

[96] For instance: "ALL and WHOLE the subjects known as Two Main Street, Inverness in the County of Inverness being the subjects described in the Disposition by . . . in favour of . . . dated . . . and recorded in the Division of the General Register of Sasines for the County of Inverness on . . . together with (1) the parts and pertinents (2) the fixtures and fittings and (3) my whole right, title and interest, present and future".

[97] For instance: "ALL and WHOLE the semi-detached house number 53 William Road, Dunkeld, being the subjects delineated in red on the plan annexed and signed as relative hereto, being part and portion of ALL and WHOLE the subjects registered in the Land Register under title number PER 88888".

[98] An example would be the description of the property at 4 Torduff Road, given above in para.12–17, followed by something like: "which said subjects hereby disposed are part and portion of ALL and WHOLE the subjects described in the Disposition by . . . in favour of . . . dated . . . and recorded in the Division of the General Register of Sasines applicable to the County of Selkirk on . . .".

Different meanings of "boundary"

"Boundary" has four possible meanings in the context of land registration, and   12–28
these different meanings are easy to confuse. The four meanings of "boundary"
are (i) the title boundary, i.e. the limit of what is owned, (ii) the occupational
boundary, i.e. the limit of what is actually occupied, (iii) a physical feature
such as a wall or hedge of the sort that is typically, but not necessarily, a
boundary feature and (iv) the physical boundary feature as shown on the
Ordnance Map.

Not all four will exist in all cases: sometimes only the first two exist, there
being no physical boundary feature at all. But all four may exist, and usually
do exist. All four may coincide, but any two may differ and in theory all four
could differ. Thus a title boundary might stop a metre short of a wall, but occupation might extend five metres to the other side of the wall, while the Ordnance
Map might show the wall but in the wrong position, either because of inaccurate cartography or because the wall has been rebuilt on a different line since
the area was last surveyed.

Problems with tenements

Tenements have already been mentioned,[99] but problems are so common that   12–29
something more needs to be said. In descriptions of tenement flats, whether in
deeds or missives, there is plenty of scope for muddle. Some people call the
lowest storey the ground storey while others call it the first storey. In some
tenements the lowest storey is a basement below street level. In that case the
storey two floors up from the basement level might be called the first, or the
second, or the third storey. In GRS titles where the units have been sold off
over many years inconsistent numbering systems are sometimes encountered.
Even if the titles are consistent a flat may be marketed with a different storey
number and this is likely to be followed in the missives. Sometimes, too, there
is a muddle about compass directions. If there are two units on the second floor
and the only distinction between them is that one is east and the other west, a
muddle may cause serious problems.

In a 2004 case a bank called up a standard security over a flat in Firpark
Terrace, Dennistoun. It took possession of the wrong flat. On discovering the
mistake it took possession of a second flat in the tenement. It advertised this
second flat for sale and sold it. It was only when the owner of the second flat
turned up (it had been vacant for some weeks) that it was discovered that this
too was not the right flat, which was in fact yet another flat in the same
tenement.[100]

Because of inadequate descriptions tenements also frequently give rise to
other problems, such as title to cellars and to the back green. Obscurities in
tenemental titles often are transferred from the GRS to the Land Register.

---

[99] See above, para.12–04.
[100] *The Times* (Scottish edition), March 16, 2004, p.9 and March 17, 2004, p.7.

CHAPTER 13

TITLE CONDITIONS

INTRODUCTION

Real burdens and servitudes compared

13–01 Real burdens, servitudes, and conditions in long leases are the main examples of title conditions,[1] but, leases being beyond the scope of the present work, this chapter concerns only real burdens and servitudes. They have much in common. With one minor exception,[2] each is a right held by the owner of one parcel of land (known as the "benefited property" or "dominant tenement") in respect of another, and neighbouring, parcel of land (known as the "burdened property" or "servient tenement"). In each case the right "runs with the land", that is to say, is enforceable by the owner for the time being of the benefited property against the owner for the time being of the burdened property.[3] And each is used by conveyancers in much the same types of situation, most typically when land is being divided and split off, or for developments such as housing estates. Thus in practice real burdens and servitudes often jostle together in the same deed, usually break-off dispositions or deeds of conditions.

But there are important differences. Like so much of property law, the law of servitudes derives ultimately from the law of Rome. Real burdens, by contrast, are home-grown, dating only from the late eighteenth century. Something like one half of all real burdens originated in feudal writs and so were enforceable, at first, by feudal superiors.[4] Many of these were lost following the abolition of the feudal system although they remain as a ghostly presence on the Land Register.[5] But many also survived by being attached of new to a benefited property. The rules for such attachment were complex but transitional and are referred to in this chapter only where necessary to understand the present law.[6] As well as removing the enforcement rights of superiors, feudal abolition was also the occasion for a more general reorganisation of the law. The Title Conditions (Scotland) Act 2003, which came into force on

---

[1] Title Conditions (Scotland) Act 2003 s.122(1).

[2] Personal real burdens, discussed below in para.13–19.

[3] This over-simplifies. As will be seen below (para.13–13) title conditions are sometimes enforceable by, and against, occupiers even if they do not own.

[4] But, quite often, by neighbours ("co-feuars") as well. The enforcement rights of neighbours were unaffected by feudal abolition.

[5] Abolition of Feudal Tenure etc. (Scotland) Act 2000 ss.17(1) and 46.

[6] 2000 Act Pt 4; 2003 Act Pt 4. For a full account, see K.G.C. Reid, *The Abolition of Feudal Tenure in Scotland* (2003).

Martinmas 2004, the first post-feudal day,[7] restates the law of real burdens in statutory form but with important changes.[8] One of those is to redraw the boundary between real burdens and servitudes. Today only positive servitudes are recognised, that is to say, rights to make limited use of another's land, for example for access or the laying of a pipe. The former class of negative servitudes is now subsumed within real burdens.[9] Real burdens are of two types. An "affirmative burden" is an obligation to do something, such as to maintain a wall or pay for the cost of common services. A "negative burden" is an obligation not to do something, such as not to erect a building or not to use the burdened property for commercial purposes.[10] In creating title conditions, it is necessary to be clear what kind of condition or conditions is intended. As will be seen, the rules of creation are by no means the same.

When are title conditions needed?

There are two main occasions when title conditions are likely to be needed. One is when land is divided. The other is when land is developed, typically by a volume builder for housing. If these two situations are kept in mind, both the law and the practice are easier to understand.

13–02

The subdivision case

Suppose that Donald owns a house surrounded by a hectare of land. He sells half the land to Edmund, who wishes to build a house there. Donald might require the use of a septic tank lying in the area sold. This can be achieved by the servitude of "sinks".[11] Again, Donald may wish to continue to use a path through the land being sold, which will require a servitude of way. Donald may wish to impose an affirmative burden, for instance an obligation to contribute to the maintenance of a common boundary wall. He may also wish to impose negative burdens, to protect the amenity of his retained property. So for instance he may impose an obligation not to build more than one house, and not to use the sold property for commercial purposes. In all of these cases the burdened property is the land sold to Edmund and the benefited property the land retained by Donald. Of course, if Donald wishes to impose such

13–03

---

[7] Martinmas 2004, the "appointed day" under the Act. The term and quarter days were formerly of great importance. The term days are Whitsunday and Martinmas, and the quarter days are Candlemas and Lammas. True, i.e. ecclesiastical, Whitsunday is variable. The other true dates are February 2 (Candlemas), August 1 (Lammas) and November 11 (Martinmas). But for legal purposes the term and quarter days are now fixed as the 28th days of February, May, August and November: Term and Quarter Days (Scotland) Act 1990. So feudal abolition was on November 28, 2004.

[8] This was based on the Scottish Law Commission's Report on *Real Burdens* (Scot. Law Com. No.181, 2000; available at *http://www.scotlawcom.gov.uk*), which remains an indispensable guide to the legislation.

[9] 2003 Act ss.79 and 80. Former negative servitudes were automatically converted into (negative) real burdens.

[10] 2003 Act s.2. By s.2(3), however, a right to enter or otherwise make use of property, which must normally be a servitude, can be created as a real burden if it is for a purpose ancillary to a positive or negative burden, e.g. a right to enter in order to carry out repairs which the burdened owner has failed to make.

[11] The curiously named servitude right to discharge "foul water"—to use the polite term—into another person's land.

servitudes and burdens, he should so specify in the missives.[12] The general principle of law is that if missives do not provide for the imposition of title conditions, a purchaser can refuse to accept such imposition.[13] Equally, Edmund may wish to have burdens and servitudes imposed on the land retained by Donald, and for similar reasons.

The development case

13–04   A standard example of a development is a block of flats. When a block of flats is first built, it will be in unitary ownership—that of the developer. It may remain in unitary ownership, with the owner renting out the flats rather than selling them. But if the flats are sold off individually, either immediately after construction or at some later stage, it is normal to insert real burdens, regulating both maintenance and use. Another standard case is where a volume builder develops a housing estate. Affirmative burdens will be imposed for such things as maintenance of mutual boundary walls, and there will also be negative burdens, restricting use. One might ask why, for, once the houses are sold, the builder no longer has any commercial interest. The reason is that burdens are believed, rightly or wrongly, to increase the attractiveness of the estate to potential purchasers. Of course, as far as a purchaser's own house is concerned, he or she would prefer it to be burden-free. But a purchaser wants burdens on the other houses, to keep up the amenity of the area. The price for burdens on the other houses is to accept burdens on one's own.

Once all the flats or houses have been sold the developer can no longer enforce the burdens (having relinquished all benefited properties), and the normal arrangement is for the burdens to be mutually enforceable within the development. Thus each flat, or house, is at the same time both a burdened property and also a benefited property. It is a burdened property because, like every other flat or house, it is subject to the burdens. But it is a benefited property because the owner can enforce the burdens against any other property. In effect, the burdens form a set of local laws for the administration of the development. Burdens which are mutually enforceable in this way are referred to in the 2003 Act as "community burdens"[14] and are subject to a number of special rules, especially in relation to variation and discharge.[15] Community burdens are considered further below in Ch.15.[16] This reciprocal enforceability of community burdens may be contrasted with the typical product of subdivision, which is for burdens to affect one property (Edmund's in the example given above) but not the other (Donald's).[17] Edmund's property is a burdened property but not a benefited property. Donald's property is a benefited property but not a burdened property.

---

[12] There has been some litigation about the degree of precision needed in an obligation to create a servitude. See *Callander v Midlothian DC*, 1996 S.C.L.R. 955; *Brennan v Robertson's Exrs*, 1997 S.C. 36; *Inverness Seafield Development Co Ltd v DCS Mackintosh*, 2001 S.C. 406. For a case which failed to make clear whether successors were to be bound, see *Forbo-Nairn Ltd v Murrayfield Properties Ltd* [2009] CSIH 94.

[13] *Corbett v Robertson* (1872) 10 M. 329. cf. *Morris v Ritchie*, 1991 G.W.D. 12-712; 1992 G.W.D. 33-1950.

[14] 2003 Act s.25(1).

[15] 2003 Act Pt 2.

[16] See below, paras 15–03 to 15–07.

[17] In contrast with "community burdens" these are sometimes described as "neighbour burdens" although the term does not appear in the 2003 Act.

Real burdens and planning law

The question is sometimes asked, why negative burdens continue to be used 13–05 when modern planning law protects amenity. For example, if a neighbour in Edinburgh's Heriot Row wishes to turn the house into a nuclear reprocessing factory, there is no need to worry, because planning consent will be refused.

There are three answers to this question. The first is that negative burdens can cover points which could not be covered by planning law. The second answer is that the planning authorities often fail to enforce planning law, especially in respect of minor infringements. The third reason is that the planning authority can always grant planning consent, leaving the outraged neighbour fuming but powerless.[18] These two latter points arise from the fact that planning law is part of public law. It is enforced or waived by a public authority. Neighbours have a right to voice their objections, but the planning authority makes up its own mind. The value of real burdens is that they are part of private law, and can be enforced by the owner of the benefited property. This is true even if planning consent has been given. Thus, suppose that planning consent is given to convert a dwelling-house into a public house, but there is a real burden forbidding any "trade, business or profession", and the benefited property is the house next door. The owner of that house can interdict use as a pub, notwithstanding the grant of planning consent.[19]

Importance of use in practice

With new developments, title conditions are imposed almost as matter of 13–06 course. But with subdivisions too it should be instinctive for the conveyancer to consider the possible need for servitudes and real burdens. This applies to both parties to the deal, for it is not only the seller but also often the buyer who may need the benefit of such conditions. The clients may not have thought about this question clearly, and so an active approach is necessary. A site visit is desirable. This will, for example, reveal if there is a path to the public road from the retained subjects over the subjects to be sold. Or it will reveal problems about pipes and cables. Or it will indicate the existence of a boundary wall which will need to be kept up.[20] In addition to affirmative burdens, the clients must be asked about negative burdens which may be needed for amenity.

Occasionally, split-offs happen where the lawyers involved have failed to do these things. Such failure can cause problems to the clients in future years and may even give rise to a negligence action against the solicitors involved.[21] Sometimes, however, the position can be saved by arguing that a servitude exists by implication, or, after 20 years,[22] by prescription. However, unlike servitudes, real burdens cannot arise either by implication or by prescription.

---

[18] K. Gray and S.F. Gray, (1999) 3 Edin. L.R. 229.

[19] The fact that planning permission has been granted may, however, help the burdened owner in an application to the Lands Tribunal for variation. For the Tribunal's powers, see below, Ch.16.

[20] If there is no boundary wall there may be a need to impose a burden requiring one to be built and maintained.

[21] e.g. *Moffat v Milne*, 1993 G.W.D. 8-572.

[22] The period for the prescriptive constitution of a servitude is 20, not 10, years: 1973 Act s.3.

Permissible content

13–07   As already mentioned, a real burden must usually comprise an obligation to do
something or an obligation not to do something, while a servitude confers a
right of limited use. Since it runs with the land, a title condition must affect the
land itself and not merely the person who happens to be its owner for the
moment. And both properties must be affected: a title condition burdens one
parcel of land for the benefit of another parcel of land. It must, in other words,
be "praedial" at both ends. Thus an obligation to pay money, whether as an
ordinary debt or by way of clawback following the grant of planning permission, could not be a real burden.[23] Nor could a right to take exercise be a servitude. In practice the praedial rule is sometimes difficult to apply. For example,
if the proprietors in a housing estate are allowed to gaze at the amenity ground
they are obliged to maintain but, not being co-owners, to use it, can it be said
that the maintenance obligation "relates to" the burdened properties (i.e. the
houses), as the legislation requires?[24] More difficult in practice is the position
of the benefited property. For if a condition confers obvious benefit on a person
it may be a matter of debate as to whether it confers benefit on a property as
well. In one case, for example, it was doubted whether a prohibition on playing
tennis on a Sunday conferred more than personal benefit on the original
disponer, whose religious views, it was assumed, had led to the imposition of
the burden.[25] But it is possible to argue than even here a praedial benefit
arises,[26] for tennis can be a noisy game and hence disruptive to those living in
an, otherwise quiet, residential area. To ban it on Sundays is to preserve tran-
quility on a day when most people are at home. A right of pre-emption confers
benefit provided there is some palpable gain from the reuniting of the properties.[27] Not all pre-emptions may meet this standard.

Other restrictions apply. A title condition must not be contrary to public
policy.[28] It must not impose a periodical payment in respect of the use of land.[29]
It must not be "repugnant with ownership", that is, it must not impose an obligation so severe as to remove the normal rights of an owner.[30] Thus a real
burden cannot forbid the performance of ordinary juridical acts such as the
grant of a disposition or lease,[31] and a burden prohibiting division of the title
would be invalid.[32] On the other hand, restrictions on use are generally accept-

---

[23] *I & A Brown Ltd, Appellants*, Unreported April 28, 2010 Lands Tribunal.

[24] 2003 Act s.3(1). Section 3(2) adds that: "The relationship may be direct or indirect but shall
not merely be that the obligated person is the owner of the burdened property". The reasoning of
the Lands Tribunal in *Greenbelt Property Ltd v Riggens*, 2010 G.W.D. 28-582 suggests that a
maintenance burden of this kind may (just) qualify.

[25] *Marsden v Craighelen Lawn Tennis and Squash Club*, 1999 G.W.D. 37-1820.

[26] As the Scottish Law Commission has done: see Report on *Real Burdens* (Scot. Law Com.
No.181, 2000), para.2.13.

[27] For example commercial benefit or benefit to amenity: see *Braes v Keeper of the Registers of
Scotland* [2009] CSOH 196; 2010 S.L.T. 689 at para.66, per Temporary Judge M.G. Thomson QC.

[28] 2003 Act s.3(6).

[29] 1974 Act s.2.

[30] 2003 Act ss.3(6), 76(2). See Reid and Gretton, *Conveyancing 2010*, pp.122–24.

[31] *Moir's Trustees v McEwan* (1880) 7 R. 1141 at 1145; *Snowie v Museum Hall LLP* [2010]
CSOH 107; 2010 S.L.T. 97. As Lord Young said, "you cannot make a man proprietor and yet
prohibit him from exercising the rights of proprietorship". See also *Calder v Police Commissioners
of North Berwick* (1899) 1 F. 491 at 493.

[32] By contrast prohibitions of functional division, such as the subdivision of a house into two
units, can be valid.

able despite the fact that the permitted use may be very narrow, such as use for a swimming pool[33] or, in a sheltered housing development, for the occupation of a resident warden.[34] Servitudes too are unlikely to be repugnant with ownership even where, as with *aquaehaestus*, they may involve the maintaining of a dam and pipes on the burdened property.[35] Under the 2003 Act redemption rights are no longer valid as real burdens, but pre-emption rights remain competent and are not repugnant with ownership.[36] A real burden must not create a monopoly, for instance in relation to management of a development,[37] although the 2003 Act allows developers to reserve a power to manage, or to appoint a manager, for as long as they continue to own property in the development, but restricted to a maximum period which is normally five years.[38]

Unlike in other countries, servitudes in Scotland have traditionally been limited to a fixed list of a dozen or so "known" types, although the precise content of the list has been a matter of dispute.[39] However, the decision of the House of Lords in *Moncreiff v Jamieson* has seemed to usher in a more accommodating attitude, and, as well as a servitude of parking, recognised in *Moncrieff* itself, courts have also allowed as a servitude the right to project part of a building into the property of a neighbour.[40] The 2003 Act abolished the fixed list in the case of servitudes created by writing and registration on or after November 28, 2004,[41] but it remains in place for servitudes created by prescription or other means. For the first of these a more adventurous use of servitudes may now be anticipated.

Existing title conditions: burdened property

If the burdened property is in the Land Register, all the real burdens will be set 13–08 forth in full in the burdens section of the title sheet (and land certificate). This includes burdens which were created, prior to first registration, by a deed recorded in the General Register of Sasines ("GRS") unless they were so obviously spent that they could safely be omitted. Understandably, the Keeper's practice here is to copy the original wording, even though this may be archaic

---

[33] *Lees v North East Fife District Council*, 1987 S.L.T. 769.

[34] *Sheltered Housing Management Ltd v Bon Accord Co Ltd*, 2007 G.W.D. 32-533 (reversed on a different ground, [2010] CSIH 42; 2010 S.C. 516). In *Crampshee v North Lanarkshire Council*, 2004 G.W.D. 7-149 a right to manage a development was held not to be repugnant with ownership. No reasons were given, but a possible reason might have been that, under the 2003 Act s.63, managers can only insist on their rights for a limited period. A prohibition of any building has been recognised since Roman times as a valid servitude (now, under the 2003 Act, a real burden).

[35] *Moncrieff v Jamieson* [2007] UKHL 42; 2008 S.C. (HL) 1 especially at para.76, per Lord Rodger. The different view taken by Lady Smith in *Nationwide Building Society v Walter D Allan Ltd*, 2004 G.W.D. 25-539 (servitude of parking) cannot, it is thought, survive the decision of the House of Lords in *Moncrieff*.

[36] 2003 Act s.3(5). For pre-emptions, see below, para.13–30.

[37] 2003 Act s.3(7).

[38] This is done by a special type of real burden known as a "manager burden". See the 2003 Act s.63. The period is three years in the case of sheltered housing and 30 years in the case of council houses being sold under the right-to-buy legislation.

[39] D.J. Cusine and R.R.M. Paisley, *Servitudes and Rights of Way* (1998), Ch.3.

[40] *Compugraphics International Ltd v Nikolic* [2011] CSIH 34. For discussion of this decision at first instance, see Gordon, (2009) 13 Edin. L.R. 519; and Reid and Gretton, *Conveyancing 2009*, pp.103–05. Compare, however, *Romano v Standard Commercial Property Securities Ltd* [2008] CSOH 105; 2008 S.L.T. 859 where a servitude of signage was refused. See Gordon, (2009) 13 Edin. L.R. 139.

[41] 2003 Act s.76.

or unclear or verbose.[42] This can have a curious psychological impact. A burden which formerly existed in some nineteenth century deed, written by hand, on paper dirtied and frayed by a century and a half of use, and legible only with great effort, tends to seem unimportant. The same burden, neatly word-processed and appearing on a fresh land certificate, looks very different and rather threatening.

Servitudes can be created without registration and so are overriding interests for the purposes of registration of title.[43] They may or may not appear on the title sheet; and even if some are mentioned, there may be others which are not mentioned. Dispositions of property in the Land Register are taken to incorporate the whole terms of the title sheet and so do not list the burdens and servitudes.[44]

There is no equivalent display of title conditions for GRS property, and the practice is to list the burdens writs in each new conveyance of the burdened property[45] (including a conveyance inducing first registration). In practice, the listing is done after the description. The relevant clause begins with such words as: "But always with and under, in so far as valid subsisting and applicable, the following real burdens conditions servitudes and others namely . . .". The list then refers to the various deeds which created the burdens or servitudes.[46] It is a mere reference, not a full repetition. Those deeds, or photocopies of them, will commonly be among the titles themselves, or a copy can be obtained from the registers.

Traditionally, deeds which created real burdens imposed an obligation to make reference to the burdens in all future conveyances, but under the 2003 Act this is of no legal effect.[47]

Existing title conditions: benefited property

13–09 Title conditions are pertinents of the benefited property, and thus pass with that property by implication.[48] So they need not be mentioned in a disposition of the benefited property, although in the case of a GRS title it is helpful if this is done.[49] In a title in the Land Register real burdens and servitudes may be listed in the property section of the title sheet of the benefited property,[50] if brought to the Keeper's attention, but any list is likely to be incomplete. Since 2004 the position is gradually being transformed by the requirement that new real burdens be registered against the benefited property as well as the burdened.[51] The same rule applies to such servitudes as are created by registration,[52] but servitudes may also be created by implication or positive prescription and, if

---

[42] Land Registration (Scotland) Act 1979 s.6(2).

[43] 1979 Act s.28(1), but with the exception of those servitudes which, under the post-2004 law, require to be created by dual registration.

[44] 1979 Act s.15(2).

[45] Including notices of title (Conveyancing (Scotland) Act 1924 Sch.B) but not standard securities (1924 Act s.9(1) as applied by s.32 of the Conveyancing and Feudal Reform (Scotland) Act 1970).

[46] See further above, para.11–13.

[47] 2003 Act s.68.

[48] 1979 Act s.3(1)(a). For pertinents see above, paras 12–20 to 12–25.

[49] "Together with the servitudes and other rights created in . . .".

[50] Land Registration (Scotland) Rules 2006 (SSI 2006/485) r.4(c), (d).

[51] 2003 Act s.4(5).

[52] 2003 Act s.75. Pipeline servitudes are exempted.

so, the Keeper's practice is not now to list them unless supported by a court declarator.[53]

Even if title conditions are listed, however, their validity is not absolutely assured, for a title condition which is fundamentally bad can be removed from the property section unless—the authorities here are conflicting[54]— the benefited proprietor is capable of being regarded as a proprietor in possession and so protected against rectification.[55] In the event that rectification takes place, indemnity may be due from the Keeper but here too the law is obscure.[56]

<h2 style="text-align:center">REAL BURDENS[57]</h2>

Preparing the deed

In principle only an owner can burden land,[58] with the result that real burdens   13–10 must be created in a deed granted by the owner of the property that is to be burdened.[59] However, the holder of an uncompleted title can also burden land.[60] Any probative deed will do, but in practice real burdens are created mainly in dispositions (in the case of subdivisions) and deeds of conditions (in the case of developments).[61]

The deed must nominate and identify both the benefited property and the burdened property.[62] For the purposes of registration, a proper conveyancing description is needed, typically by reference to a plan or title number. In the case of a disposition, one of the properties (usually the burdened) will be the property that is being conveyed. The burdens themselves must be set out in full, preferably in numbered paragraphs. In the case of dispositions this is best done in a separate schedule[63]: particularly to be avoided is the traditional practice of

---

[53] *Registration of Title Practice Book* ("ROTPB"), paras 6.54–6.58.

[54] Compare *Griffiths v Keeper of the Registers of Scotland*, Unreported December 20, 2002 Lands Tribunal; with *Yaxley v Glen* [2007] CSOH 90; 2007 S.L.T. 756. See further Reid and Gretton, *Conveyancing 2007*, pp.121–27.

[55] Land Registration (Scotland) Act 1979 s.9(3)(a). See above, para.8–15.

[56] In at least some cases, payment of indemnity will be prevented by the obscurely-worded s.12(3)(g) of the 1979 Act. See further Reid and Gretton, *Conveyancing 2003*, pp.88–91. And see also Scottish Law Commission, Discussion Paper on *Land Registration: Miscellaneous Issues* (Scot. Law Com. D.P. No.130, 2005), para.5.10.

[57] A detailed study of the new law is still lacking, and the fullest treatment remains the Scottish Law Commission's Report on *Real Burdens* (Scot. Law Com. No.181, 2000; available at *http:// www.scotlawcom.gov.uk/*). A number of summary accounts can be found, for example: K.G.C. Reid, *The Abolition of Feudal Tenure in Scotland* (1993), Ch.7; Reid and Gretton, *Conveyancing 2003*, pp.106–31; D.A. Brand, A.J.M. Steven and S. Wortley, *Professor McDonald's Conveyancing Manual*, 7th edn (2004), Chs 15, 17, and 18; Robert Rennie, *Land Tenure in Scotland* (2004). Since much of the common law is re-enacted by the 2003 Act, the older texts also remain of value.

[58] However, in some cases the holder of a long lease can create conditions that bind subsequent holders. See Reid and Gretton, *Conveyancing 2003*, pp.60–63.

[59] 2003 Act s.4(2)(b).

[60] 2003 Act ss.60(1), 123(1). If the title is in the GRS a clause of deduction of title is required.

[61] For the distinction, see above, paras 13–03 and 13–04.

[62] 2003 Act s.4(2)(c). This is done straightforwardly by words such as "The benefited property is . . .", but it can also be done less directly, for example by saying that burdens are imposed on property X "for the benefit of" or "in favour of" property Y (as in the style given at the end of this chapter).

[63] As indeed recommended 40 years ago by the Halliday Report: see *Conveyancing Legislation and Practice* (1966, Cmnd. 3118), para.77

cramming burdens into the dispositive clause as part of the notionally single sentence which constitutes a disposition. It is a statutory requirement that the words "real burden" (or some permitted equivalent) be used (e.g. "but always with and under the real burdens contained in the schedule annexed and signed as relative hereto").[64] A possible style is given at the end of this chapter.[65]

The drafting of real burdens is difficult and requires close attention, particularly in view of the strict rules of interpretation (discussed below).[66] Since burdens are potentially perpetual, the wording must be intelligible not only to the parties to the deed but to successors 100 years hence. As a general rule the terms of the burden must be found within the "four corners of the deed".[67] In the leading case of *Aberdeen Varieties Ltd v James F Donald (Aberdeen Cinemas) Ltd*[68] a real burden was held invalid because it referred to an Act of Parliament and so could not be understood on its own. This is not an isolated example. Purported burdens can be found which refer to statutes such as the Town and Country Planning (Scotland) Acts,[69] while in older deeds the terms of prior articles of roup are sometimes declared to be real burdens, without, however, setting these terms out in the deed itself. Such provisions may be valid contractually between the original parties but are not valid as real burdens. There is one exception. In tenements or other developments it is common for maintenance costs to be apportioned according to some external measure such as feuduty or rateable value. This is allowed by the 2003 Act provided that, as in the examples given, the necessary information is contained in an enactment, a public register, or a record or roll to which the public readily has access.[70]

Deeds of conditions

13–11   As the name suggests, deeds of conditions are simply deeds which set out the conditions which are to affect land.[71] Servitudes are quite often included as well as real burdens. In practice, deeds of conditions are used where a disposition would not be appropriate. That might be because no disposition is in prospect, as in the case where established neighbours agree that certain matters between them should be regulated by real burdens (or servitudes). But more usually it is because, in a development, each property is to be made subject to the same burdens, and rather than repeat the burdens in every disposition it is easier to set them out in advance in a single deed which applies to the whole

---

[64] 2003 Act s.4(2)(a). As an alternative it is permissible to use the name of a type of burden (such as community burden or conservation burden) as long as it is a name provided by the Act: see s.4(3).

[65] Other styles can be found at *http://www.psglegal.co.uk*.

[66] See below, para.13–21.

[67] 2003 Act s.4(2)(a). cf. Lord Guthrie in *Anderson v Dickie*, 1914 S.C. 706 at 717: "The extent of it must be ascertained by a singular successor without travelling beyond the four corners of his titles".

[68] *Aberdeen Varieties Ltd v James F Donald (Aberdeen Cinemas) Ltd*, 1939 S.C. 788; 1940 S.C. (HL) 52.

[69] i.e. a burden providing that the owner can make no development or change of use which would require planning consent. The effect (if valid) would be that for any such development or change of use the owner would need both planning consent and the consent of the creditor in the burden.

[70] 2003 Act s.5(1)(b), (2). The provision is retrospective.

[71] Until 1874 real burdens could only be created in conveyances. Section 32 of the Conveyancing (Scotland) Act 1874 introduced the deed of conditions as a statutory facility for setting out burdens in advance of a conveyance of the land. With the repeal of s.32 by the 2003 Act Sch.15, deeds of conditions have ceased to have a specific statutory basis, but continue in use as before.

development.[72] Thus most deeds of conditions are granted and registered before any individual unit has been sold, and most create community burdens, that is, burdens which are mutually enforceable as among the individual units in the community or development. The use of deeds of conditions in the context of communities is considered further below in Ch.15.[73]

Registration

Unlike other types of real right, title conditions affect not one property but two. 13–12 Nonetheless the former law required registration of a real burden against only one of these properties, the burdened. While, therefore, an owner knew from the Register about the burdens to which the property was subject, he or she might have little or no idea as to whether that same property carried enforcement rights in respect of other burdens against other properties. The position was changed by the 2003 Act. The deed creating a real burden must now be registered against both the benefited and the burdened property.[74] If one of the properties is in the Land Register and the other in the GRS, registration in both registers is needed. In the case of a deed of conditions creating community burdens, however, there is only a single property (the community) and hence only single registration. Automated registration of title to land ("ARTL") cannot be used for deeds which create real burdens.[75]

The burdens are entered in the property section of the title sheet of the benefited property and in the burdens section of the title sheet of the burdened property, although they are set out in full only in the latter. Now that they are separated from the rest of the original deed they are sometimes hard to understand, and it is thought that it is permissible to have recourse to that deed for context where the meaning of a burden is unclear.[76]

Normally real burdens are created on registration,[77] although they do not take effect in a practical sense unless the benefited property is in separate ownership.[78] But it is possible to postpone the date of creation and this is commonly done with deeds of conditions where units in a development are being sold over a period of time.[79]

Enforcement

A real burden is enforceable by anyone with both title and interest.[80] Title is 13–13 tied to the benefited property. Its owner has title to enforce, but so too do

---

[72] An alternative way of providing for a development is to use the Development Management Scheme, introduced by Pt 6 of the 2003 Act. See below, paras 15–08 et seq. The conditions are then part of the scheme and not real burdens, although many of the same rules apply.

[73] See below, paras 15–03 et seq.

[74] 2003 Act s.4(1), (5).

[75] See above, para.8–23.

[76] *Willemse v French* [2011] CSOH 51; 2011 G.W.D. 12-282 at paras 14–17, per Lord Tyre. See also Scottish Law Commission, Discussion Paper on *Land Registration: Registration, Rectification and Indemnity* (Scot. Law Com. D.P. No.128, 2005), paras 2.42 and 2.43. Compare *Marshall v Duffy*, 2002 G.W.D. 10-318, which concerns an error in transcription rather than interpretation of an entry properly transcribed.

[77] 2003 Act s.4(1). By s.61 they cease to be binding as a matter of contract.

[78] But the burdens are in existence nonetheless. The rule for servitudes is different: see 2003 Act s.75(2).

[79] 2003 Act s.4(1). See below, para.15–06.

[80] 2003 Act s.8(1).

tenants, proper liferenters, and non-entitled spouses or civil partners with statutory occupancy rights.[81] Some of the difficulties of identifying the benefited property are explored in the next section.

Normally a person has interest to enforce only if failure to comply with the burden will, in the particular circumstances, result in material detriment to the value or enjoyment of that person's right in the benefited property.[82] Since a reduction in value may be difficult to demonstrate, the enforcer's task will often be to demonstrate material detriment to enjoyment. In that case "much will depend", it was said in *Barker v Lewis*,[83] "on the nature of its burden and its breach, the nature of the neighbourhood, including issues of proximity of burdened and benefited properties, and no doubt other circumstances particular to the case under consideration". In *Barker* itself the court reached the surprising conclusion that the owners of houses in a small development had no interest to prevent an immediate neighbour using her house for a bed-and-breakfast business notwithstanding detailed evidence as to disruption and inconvenience.[84] But if the decision may be doubted, it is certainly true that the statutory test is quite exacting, with the result that many people with title to enforce, especially in large housing estates, will lack the necessary interest in respect of the particular breach in question. It will be difficult, for example, to demonstrate interest in relation to a breach taking place several streets away, and even those who are much closer may not always have the requisite interest.

Negative burdens[85] can be enforced against any person having the use of the burdened property, including an owner, tenant, or even a squatter.[86] Otherwise real burdens could be made difficult to enforce merely by the granting of a lease. By contrast, affirmative burdens (such as obligations of maintenance) are considered too onerous for a merely temporary occupier and may only be enforced against the owner of the burdened property.[87] Sometimes leases are drawn so as to allow the owner to recover in turn from the tenant. If the property is co-owned, each owner has joint and several liability.[88] Similarly, if property is transferred at a time when an affirmative obligation remains outstanding,[89] performance may be sought from either the new owner or from the old. But in cases involving payment for maintenance or work, the new owner is liable only if a notice of potential liability for costs has been registered. A new owner who is made to pay can recover in turn from the old, unless the missives provide otherwise.[90]

---

[81] 2003 Act s.8(2). But, by s.8(4), only owners can enforce pre-emptions, redemptions and other options.

[82] 2003 Act s.8(3). But a person also has interest to enforce obligations to defray some cost (e.g. the cost of maintenance) if he or she has some proper basis for seeking payment (such as that he or she incurred the cost). For a full discussion, see Rennie, in Robert Rennie (ed.), *The Promised Land: Property Law Reform* (2008), Ch.1.

[83] *Barker v Lewis*, 2008 S.L.T. (Sh. Ct) 17 at para.27, per Sheriff Principal R.A. Dunlop QC.

[84] See Reid and Gretton, *Conveyancing 2008*, pp.92–94. For another case in which much more understandably, interest was found to be lacking, see *Clarke v Grantham*, 2009 G.W.D. 38-645. Not too much should be read into these early decisions.

[85] i.e. those which impose a restriction: see above, para.13–01.

[86] 2003 Act s.9(2).

[87] 2003 Act s.9(1).

[88] 2003 Act s.11(5).

[89] As to when an obligation is outstanding, see 2003 Act s.10(4).

[90] 2003 Act s.10.

For negative burdens the most common, and most useful, remedy is interdict. But it is necessary to act quickly, for once a breach is completed, no remedy may be available. For by then it may be too late for interdict; courts are reluctant to order the demolition of completed structures[91]; damages are available only where loss can be shown, which may be unusual; and irritancy has been abolished.[92] Moreover, even if a remedy can be found, the enforcer is likely to be met with the plea of acquiescence.[93]

Finding the benefited property: in general

The two main occasions on which the benefited property or properties must be identified are enforcement (for title to enforce is tied to the benefited property)[94] and discharge (for a real burden is discharged by the owner of the benefited property)[95]; and in practice, discharge being a great deal more common than enforcement, the search for the benefited property is normally led by the owner of a burdened property seeking to be relieved of a burden. Often the search is an arduous one. In the case of burdens created under the 2003 Act there is no difficulty, because the burdens must be registered against both properties.[96] But for burdens created before November 28, 2004 the position is a great deal more complex, for three reasons. First, there was no requirement under the former law to identify the benefited property at all, although this was sometimes done in practice. Where it was not done, benefited properties would be implied in various circumstances. The relevant rules were largely abolished by the 2003 Act and replaced by the new rules, discussed in the next paragraph.[97] Difficult as these rules are, they are simpler than those that they replaced.[98] Secondly, perhaps as many as one half of all real burdens were created in, or in association with, grants in feu. Hence they were enforceable by the feudal superior. In most cases superiors' rights were extinguished, with the feudal system, on November 28, 2004, although they were sometimes reallocated to other properties in accordance with rules set out in the 2000 and 2003 Acts. Thirdly, there is frequently more than one benefited property. The search cannot be abandoned, therefore, when the first such property is uncovered, for there may be others, and only an exhaustive investigation will reveal the true position.

13–14

Finding the benefited property: seven rules for pre-2004 burdens

How then are the benefited property or properties to be found? For burdens created before November 28, 2004[99] it is possible to reduce a complex body of law to seven main rules. As more than one rule may apply, it is necessary

13–15

---

[91] Reid, *Property*, para.423.

[92] Irritancy was the remedy of bringing the grant to an end, without payment of compensation. It was abolished by the 2000 Act s.53 and the 2003 Act s.67.

[93] See below, para.13–25.

[94] See above, para.13–13.

[95] See below, para.13–22.

[96] See above, para.13–12.

[97] 2003 Act s.49. The replacement rules are set out in ss.52–57.

[98] Insofar as they are complex this is usually because they are based on the previous rules, thus ensuring that no enforcement rights are lost as a result of the change.

[99] Usually the deed must be registered before that day, being the appointed day for the abolition of the feudal system. But in the case of rule (ii), it is sufficient if the deed imposing burdens on one of the units is registered before the appointed day: see 2003 Act s.53(1).

to consider each rule, if only briefly, in relation to each burden. It should not be supposed, however, that different rules will necessarily lead to different results, for the rules overlap both in scope and effect. The rules are as follows:

(i)   *Any express nomination of a benefited property is to be given effect.*[100] Thus if a deed of conditions provides that the burdens are to be enforceable by the owners of every unit in a development, each unit is a benefited property (and the burdens are community burdens). Or if a break-off disposition nominates land kept back by the granter as the benefited property, that nomination stands. Just occasionally it may be unclear whether an express nomination has been made or, if it has, whether the property in question has been sufficiently identified.[101]

(ii)   *Where burdens are imposed on related properties under a common scheme, each property is a benefited property.*[102] This rule, and the next—respectively s.53 and s.52 of the 2003 Act—are concerned with common schemes. A "common scheme" is where the burdens on a group of properties are the same or similar, and were imposed by the same person (or by that person and a successor). With a deed of conditions there is almost always a common scheme, for usually the whole point of such a deed is that the same burdens should be imposed on a number of different properties. Rule (ii) further requires that the properties be "related", and a non-exhaustive list of criteria is set out in the legislation.[103] For properties to be "related" there must normally be physical connection or proximity, or shared facilities or obligations. A tenement is a standard example.[104] The use of a deed of conditions is also usually sufficient indication that the properties are related,[105] as, arguably, is a building charter, i.e. a conveyance of a large area made with the idea that it be developed and broken up into smaller units.[106] Thankfully, many cases involving rule (ii) are obvious, in particular those involving development (as opposed to subdivision).[107] But while it may often be easy to say that s.53 *does* apply it is often exceedingly difficult to be sure that it *does not*. With natural caution, burdened proprietors are likely to assume the worst.[108] Thus, at least until such time as the provision is clarified by case law, the reach of rule (ii) is proving

---

[100] The legislation, in other words, leaves express nomination untouched.

[101] For examples of the latter, compare *Braes v Keeper of the Registers of Scotland* [2009] CSOH 176; 2010 S.L.T. 689 (where the identification was found to be insufficient) with *Perth and Kinross Council v Chapman*, Unreported August 13, 2009 Lands Tribunal.

[102] 2003 Act s.53. See further K.G.C. Reid, *The Abolition of Feudal Tenure in Scotland* (2003), paras 5.7–5.12; Reid, in Robert Rennie (ed.), *The Promised Land: Property Law Reform* (2008), Ch.3. The rule does not apply to rights of pre-emption, redemption or reversion, or to maintenance obligations (e.g. in respect of roads or sewers) which have been taken over by a public authority. See ss.53(3) and 122(2).

[103] 2003 Act s.53(2).

[104] 2003 Act s 53(2)(d).

[105] 2003 Act s.53(2)(c)

[106] *Brown v Richardson*, 2007 G.W.D. 28-490.

[107] See paras above, 13–02 to 13–04.

[108] As in *Smith v Prior*, 2007 G.W.D. 30-523.

to be much greater than can originally have been intended, so vindicating the stance of its critics at the time of introduction.[109] Where the rule does apply, its effect is to create community burdens, for each property, already a burdened property, is elevated into a benefited property as well. A special variant of rule (ii) applies in respect of sheltered housing.[110]

(iii)   *Where burdens are imposed on unrelated properties under a common scheme, each (or any) property is a benefited property if the deed creating the burdens for that property (a) gives notice that a common scheme exists; and (b) contains nothing to exclude mutual enforceability.*[111] This is a statutory restatement of the former law, and the previous case law will continue to be of some help.[112] A typical example of "unrelated"[113] properties is a scattering of individual plots sold by a rural estate over a number of years and made subject to the standard estate conditions. In many such cases, however, the other requirements of rule (iii) will not be met. Thus it is unusual for individual conveyances to refer, even obliquely, to a common scheme[114]; and even where this is done there may be contra-indicators which exclude mutual enforceability, such as the reservation of a right to vary or waive the burdens.[115] Unlike rule (ii), therefore, rule (iii) is not often encountered in practice.

(iv)   *In a facility burden the benefited properties are (a) the facility itself and (b) any properties which benefit (and are intended to benefit) from the facility.*[116] A "facility burden" is one which regulates the maintenance, management, reinstatement or use of facilities such as the common parts of a tenement, a common area for recreation, a private road, private sewerage, or a boundary wall.[117] In a tenement, for example, the effect of rule (iv) is that maintenance burdens are enforceable by everyone, for each flat will be a benefited property. In the case of a garden wall, a maintenance obligation would be

---

[109] Reid, in Robert Rennie (ed.), *The Promised Land: Property Law Reform*, paras 3–11 to 3–20. The rule was not included in the original draft Bill prepared by the Scottish Law Commission but was added by the Scottish Executive against the wishes and advice of Professor Reid, the Law Commissioner responsible.

[110] 2003 Act s.54. The effect is to confer the status of benefited property even on a unit which is unburdened, provided it is used in "some special way" (e.g. as accommodation for a resident warden). Many sheltered housing developments contain such a unit.

[111] 2003 Act s.52. See further K.G.C. Reid, *The Abolition of Feudal of Tenure in Scotland* (2003), paras 5.13–5.17. As with rule (ii), the rule does not apply to rights of pre-emption, redemption or reversion, or to maintenance obligations (e.g. in respect of roads or sewers) which have been taken over by a public authority. See ss.52(3) and 122(2).

[112] For which see Reid, *Property*, paras 399–401.

[113] Section 52 does not provide as such that the properties be "unrelated"; but if they are "related" the much wider s.53 applies (i.e. rule (ii)), and there is no need to consider s.52.

[114] There is sufficient notice if the burdens were imposed in a single conveyance followed by subdivision. But the fact that a single conveyance was used will often indicate that the properties are "related" and hence subject to rule (ii).

[115] Which is specially mentioned in the provision: see s.52(2).

[116] 2003 Act s.56(1)(a). See further, K.G.C. Reid, *The Abolition of Feudal Tenure in Scotland* (2003), paras 6.1–6.5. As with rules (ii) and (iii), the rule does not apply to maintenance obligations assumed by public authorities: see s.122(2). The only case on s.56 so far is hardly typical: see *Greenbelt Property Ltd v Riggens*, 2010 G.W.D. 28-586, discussed in Reid and Gretton, *Conveyancing 2010*, pp.124–26.

[117] 2003 Act s.122(1), (3).

enforceable by the owners of the land on either side. As the first example shows, rule (iv) will often overlap with rule (ii), with the same results, for many facility burdens are imposed on related properties under a common scheme. In practice, therefore, rule (iv) is of limited importance.[118]

(v) *In a service burden the benefited properties are any property to which the services are provided.*[119] A "service burden" is a burden on one property to supply services to another, for example water or electricity.[120] Such burdens are rare, and rule (v) correspondingly unimportant.

(vi) *In a (formerly) feudal burden the benefited property is any property nominated in a notice registered under s.18 of the 2000 Act.* For the final two rules it is necessary to divide burdens into "feudal" and "non-feudal". The distinction turns on provenance. The former were created in a grant in feu (such as a feu disposition) or in a deed of conditions granted in association with a grant in feu. The latter were created in a disposition or in a deed of conditions associated with a disposition. Under the old law, feudal burdens were always enforceable by the feudal superior, and were sometimes also enforceable by neighbours ("co-feuars") as a result of express provision in the deed or by legal implication. The Acts of 2000 and 2003 extinguished the rights of superiors, while at the same time amending and restating the rights of neighbours in the manner summarised as rules (i)–(v) above. But superiors could sometimes avoid the extinction by "real-lotting" the enforcement right to other land in their ownership. This was done by registering a notice under s.18 of the 2000 Act prior to November 28, 2004.[121] The result was for the nominated land to become a benefited property in the burden (and hence for the burden to survive feudal abolition). Normally, land could be nominated only if it contained a building used as place of human habitation or resort and lying within 100 metres of the feu (i.e. the burdened property).[122] In the event, only 1,960 such notices were registered, mainly at the last minute, and not all of those will be valid.[123] Rule (vi) is thus of little importance in practice.

(vii) *In a (formerly) non-feudal burden the benefited property is, transitionally, such property in the neighbourhood as was still retained by the granter at the time of creation.* This is the subdivision case. Thus

---

[118] Rule (iv) was enacted before there were any plans to have rule (ii): see Abolition of Feudal Tenure etc. (Scotland) Act 2000 s.23 (now repealed).

[119] 2003 Act s.56(1)(b).

[120] 2003 Act s.122(1).

[121] For a detailed account, see K.G.C. Reid, *The Abolition of Feudal Tenure in Scotland* (2003), Ch.3. In a few cases there was the alternative of converting the feudal burden into a personal real burden such as a conservation burden: see below, para.13–19.

[122] If the 100-metres rule could not be satisfied, the superior could attempt to reallot by agreement under s.19 of the 2000 Act, or apply to the Lands Tribunal under s.20 for the 100-metres requirement to be waived. Either case led to an entry on the property register. But there seem to have been no such cases.

[123] For a challenge, both on the grounds of the type of building (a toilet block) and the completion of the form, see *SQ1 Ltd v Earl of Hopetoun*, Unreported October 2, 2007 Lands Tribunal.

suppose, as in the example given earlier,[124] that Donald disponed half of his land to Edmund while retaining the other half. Real burdens were imposed on Edmund's land. Under rule (vii) the benefited property would be the land retained by Donald. If that land has come to be divided, each divided part is itself a benefited property.[125] Rule (vii) is not a new rule but an old one, based on case law.[126] As such, there are some limitations. Thus rule (vii) does not apply to pre-emptions,[127] or where the burden in question was imposed under a common scheme,[128] or where the deed makes express provision as to enforcement.[129] Unlike other rules derived from common law, rule (vi) is preserved by the 2003 Act but only for ten years.[130] An owner such as Donald who wishes his property to remain a benefited property must execute and register a notice in the prescribed form before November 28, 2014.[131] Otherwise the status of benefited property under rule (vii) will be lost (although it may continue by virtue of one of the other rules).

Evaluation and some examples

Although undeniably intricate, these rules are not quite as difficult to use as first impressions suggest. Rules (i) and (iii) presuppose a statement in the deed, which will in turn appear in the property register. Rule (vi) involves the registration of a separate notice, of which there are fewer than 2,000. Rules (iv) and (v) depend on a straightforward classification by type of burden. Only rules (ii) and (vii) impose serious challenges, the former involving a determination as to whether properties are "related" (whatever that may mean), the latter requiring an investigation into the landholdings of the granter at the time when the deed was first registered.[132] Fortunately, rule (vii) is temporary and its replacement, from November 28, 2014, requires the registration of a notice. From that day too the Keeper is supposed to note on the Land Register the applicability of any of rules (ii)–(v) and, where possible, identify the benefited property, but due to the difficulties created by rule (ii) in particular—the much-criticised s.53 of the 2003 Act—the legislation is likely to be altered to turn a duty into a mere power, which in practice may turn out to be used only where specifically requested.[133]

13–16

---

[124] See above, para.13–03.

[125] But if the subdivision occurs after November 28, 2004, a part which is disponed away is not a benefited property unless the disposition so provides. See below, para.13–18.

[126] It derives from *JA Mactaggart & Co v Harrower* (1906) 8 F. 1101. See Reid, *Property*, para.403. There have been few reported cases and the rule is undeveloped. A modern, and controversial, case is *Marsden v Craighelen Lawn Tennis and Squash Club*, 1999 G.W.D. 37-1 820, discussed in Reid and Gretton, *Conveyancing 1999*, pp.59–61. See also *Barr v Macrae*, Unreported November 30, 2010 Lands Tribunal.

[127] *Braes v Keeper of the Registers of Scotland* [2009] CSOH 176; 2010 S.L.T. 689 at para.67, per Temporary Judge M.G. Thomson QC.

[128] 2003 Act ss.49(2) and 50(6). But either rule (ii) or (iii) might then apply.

[129] *Braes v Keeper of the Registers of Scotland* [2009] CSOH 176; 2010 S.L.T. 689 at para.69, per Temporary Judge M.G. Thomson QC.

[130] 2003 Act s.49(2).

[131] 2003 Act s.50.

[132] A practical difficulty is that the Land Register does not disclose previous owners.

[133] 2003 Act s.58. For the proposed legislative change, see Scottish Law Commission, Report on *Land Registration* (Scot. Law Com. No.222), paras 10.19–10.30.

Some examples of how the rules operate may be of assistance:

Example 1: Deed of Conditions of 1973. Rule (ii) applies. In view of that conclusion it is unnecessary to consider whether rules (iii) or (iv) may also apply. (Rule (iii) will apply unless, as often happens, the granter has reserved a power of variation; rule (iv) will apply but only in respect of those burdens which can be classified as facility burdens.[134])

Example 2: Feu Disposition of 1934 in respect of house in a housing estate. Unless there is a common scheme, none of the rules apply, and so the burdens are not enforceable, except for any facility burdens which will be enforceable under rule (iv). But in a case like this, a search in the registers will usually reveal that such a scheme exists, i.e. that other houses in the same estate were feued subject to the same conditions. In that case rules (ii) and (iii) potentially apply. For rule (iii) it will be possible to come to a clear decision, for the criteria, if a little odd, are at least straightforward. But it will be much more difficult to decide whether the properties are "related" for the purposes of rule (ii). Are the houses similar in style? Is there any common ownership? Are there shared maintenance obligations? With inter-war housing estates the only unifying factor is often that the owners of each house must share maintenance of the boundary wall with the neighbours on the other side.[135] Is that enough to make properties "related" and, if so, is the whole estate "related" or is it rather divided into overlapping pairs of "related" houses by reference to the location of boundary walls (so houses 1 and 2; houses 2 and 3; houses 3 and 4, and so on)? In a case like this it seems unlikely that the properties actually are "related", for otherwise the mere fact of mutual maintenance of boundary walls—an obligation which is separately enforceable under rule (iv)—would have the effect of creating enforcement rights across a potentially wide area in respect of all the burdens in the deed.[136]

Example 3: Feu Disposition of 1883 in respect of three acres. This has since been subdivided into 8 plots on each of which a house is built. This is a common scheme (for eight houses are subject to the same burdens). Rule (ii) is likely to apply and, depending on the circumstances, rule (iii) also. That takes care of "internal" enforcement, i.e. enforcement among the owners of the eight houses. But in a case like this there is also the possibility of "external" enforcement, for the granter of the 1883 feu disposition may have made a number of similar grants of adjacent areas.[137] If so, the common scheme will extend beyond the initial three acres to the areas feued by the other grants. Whether there are enforcement

---

[134] In theory in this example, as in the others, rule (v) might also apply, but in practice service burdens are virtually unknown.

[135] There may also be shared obligations in relations to roads and sewers, but responsibility for these will long since have been taken over by the local authority and the burdens themselves extinguished (i.e. not preserved) due to s.122(2) of the 2003 Act.

[136] In *Smith v Prior*, 2007 G.W.D. 30-523, the Lands Tribunal thought that in a case like this there might not be a common scheme. In fact such a scheme clearly exists, and the real doubt is as to whether the properties are "related".

[137] For "internal" and "external" enforcement, see Reid, in Robert Rennie (ed.), *The Promised Land: Property Law Reform* (2008), paras 3–37 to 3–40.

rights in respect of this much larger area will again depend on whether rules (ii) or (iii) apply in respect of it. And as usual, it may difficult to exclude the possibility that the properties are "related" and that rule (ii) might apply.

Example 4: Disposition of 1951. If no land was retained by the disponer, there is no benefited property and hence the burdens are unenforceable—unless there is a common scheme, in which case rules (ii) or (iii) might apply. But if land was retained—if, in other words, the disposition was a break-off—then the retained land is the benefited property by virtue of rule (vii) (assuming that there is no common scheme). If the retained land has itself been divided up, then each separate part is a benefited property. These enforcement rights will be lost on November 28, 2014 unless preserved by registration of a notice.

Meaning to be given to "superior"

For those many pre-2004 burdens which contain the word "superior" there is statutory guidance as to how it is to be interpreted.[138] In cases where the burden is enforceable by virtue of rules (iv)–(vi), "superior" is to be read as meaning the new enforcer—the owners of the property or properties which the rule in question appoints to be benefited. Otherwise the word falls to be disregarded entirely. The result then depends on whether it is severable from the rest of the provision. Where the word "superior"—together, often, with the words which immediately surround it—can be severed without loss of meaning in the words that remain, the provision survives in its lightly mutilated form and can be enforced in the normal way.[139] But where the whole provision depends on the word "superior", the provision, inevitably, will fall. An example of the former is where some activity is forbidden except with the consent of the superiors: the consent proviso falls and the prohibition remains, now recast as an outright prohibition—enforceable, if luck is against the burdened proprietor, by the owners of the 200 other houses in the same estate.[140] An example of the latter is where there is some administrative task involving the superiors, such as notifying them in respect of a change of ownership or presenting them with data of some other kind.[141]

13–17

Unenforceable burdens[142]

The mere fact that a burden is on the Land or Sasine Register does not guarantee its validity or enforceability.[143] A surprising number of "burdens" on the registers are unenforceable, for various reasons. First, as with any other real right, there may have been an error of constitution—for example, absence of

13–18

---

[138] Abolition of Feudal Tenure etc. (Scotland) Act 2000 s.73(2), (2A).

[139] *Strathclyde Business Park (Management) Ltd v BAE Systems Pension Funds Trustee Ltd*, 2010 G.W.D. 39-791.

[140] By virtue of s.53 of the 2003 Act (i.e. rule (ii) above). Of course for many of the owners there would be no interest to enforce.

[141] The difference between the two situations is nicely captured by *At.Home Nationwide Ltd v Morris*, 2007 G.W.D. 31-535.

[142] See also Steven and Wortley, (2006) 51 J.L.S.S. June/46 and July/50.

[143] The converse proposition, however, is true: a burden which is not on the Register is invalid and unenforceable. In the case of the Land Register this rule is statutory: see 1979 Act s.3(1)(a).

title or capacity or a defect of execution. Admittedly, registration in the Land Register cures errors of this kind,[144] but many burdens originated in the GRS and are not cured merely by being listed in the Land Register following first registration.[145] Second, the burden may fail as to content.[146] Third, it may be expressed in language which is insufficiently certain.[147] Fourth, there may be no benefited property, for the application of the seven rules just described may yield a negative result, especially in relation to burdens of feudal origin. In due course it will be possible to ask for such burdens to be removed from the Land Register.[148] Finally, the burden may have been extinguished in some other way but not involving registration, for example by negative prescription or acquiescence. If a burden appearing in the title sheet turns out to be invalid, no compensation is payable by the Keeper.[149]

For the conveyancer, the possibility that a burden is unenforceable should always be borne in mind. Sometimes this can be a welcome, and cost-free, solution to an apparently intractable problem. In practice, the approach to be taken depends very much on the situation one is in. Purchasers are bound to be cautious. It is not enough that a burden is probably invalid, or, though valid, probably does not strike at the use proposed or give rise to an interest to enforce. Purchasers want certainty, or something near it. Unfortunately, s.53 (rule (ii)) in particular makes certainty difficult to obtain, and a purchaser, beset by doubt, may be driven to making a needless and time-consuming application to the Lands Tribunal.[150] By contrast, suppose that owners are using their property in a certain way, and the use is objected to. Here the law agent for the owners will be only too glad to seize upon any argument that will tend to show that the burden is invalid or is to be construed in a narrow sense. And the same, of course, applies if litigation takes place. A probable argument once accepted by a court becomes a certainty.

Division of benefited and burdened properties

13–19   Particularly in the case of older burdens, the original benefited or burdened property will often have been divided, so that one plot of land has become two or four or more, with a corresponding number of separate owners. Division of the burdened property in this way has no effect on the burdens as such, and each plot remains burdened as the undivided property was before.[151] For the benefited property, however, division results in the proliferation of enforcement rights. In place of the single owner of an undivided property there are

---

[144] 1979 Act s.3(1).

[145] Since they are not "registered" in the Land Register, s.3(1) does not apply.

[146] See above, para.13–07.

[147] See below, para.13–21.

[148] 2000 Act s.46; 2003 Act s.51. The provisions are due to come into force on November 28, 2014, 2014, but they may be overtaken by the proposed legislation on land registration under which all inaccuracies on the Register (and not merely inaccuracies as to real burdens) will, if established, require to be rectified. See Scottish Law Commission, Report on *Land Registration* (Scot. Law Com. No.222, 2010), Pt 18. Initially Registers of Scotland had intended to be pro-active in this regard (see *Update 10.6* (2005)), but difficulties in applying the background law, and especially s.53 of the 2003 Act, led to a change of heart.

[149] 1979 Act s.12(3)(g).

[150] For the Lands Tribunal, see further below, Ch.16.

[151] 2003 Act s.13. In the case of an affirmative burden, each owner is liable jointly and severally, while the owners are generally liable among themselves in proportion to the area of each plot: see 2003 Act s.11.

now as many owners, and enforcers, as there are plots. Admittedly, not all owners may have interest to enforce, for some plots may be too remote. Nonetheless the overall result is unwelcome to owners of burdened properties. Some control is now exercised by the 2003 Act.[152] Unless the disposition provides otherwise, any part of a benefited property which is split off will immediately cease to be a benefited property. Sometimes there may be good reasons for overriding this default rule and allowing the disponee the benefit of the burdens. But in the long term there will be a welcome tendency for benefited properties to shrink. The provision is not retrospective, however, and so has no effect on divisions occurring before November 28, 2004.

Personal real burdens

Some countries allow title conditions without a benefited property.[153] In Scotland this is not possible for servitudes, but a limited class of "personal real burdens" was introduced by the 2003 Act. The dissonance in the name is deliberate. The burden is "real" in the sense that all real rights are real, that is to say, as a right in a thing (the burdened property). But it is "personal" in the sense that it is held by a person without reference to a benefited property. A personal real burden is thus, in this respect, closer to a standard security or lease than to a servitude. "Personal" real burdens may be contrasted with ordinary or "praedial" real burdens—that is, real burdens *with* a benefited property.[154]

13–20

Nine types of personal real burden are listed in the 2003 Act: conservation burdens, rural housing burdens, maritime burdens, economic development burdens, health care burdens, manager burdens, personal pre-emption burdens, personal redemption burdens, and climate change burdens.[155] No others are permitted. Most of the nine are unusual and some are practically unknown. In the narrow sphere in which they operate they can be seen as a replacement for feudal burdens, allowing a person (generally a public body) to dispose of all of its land and yet still impose real burdens. Indeed any feudal burden which had the characteristics of a personal real burden could be converted into such a burden by registration of a notice prior to November 28, 2004.[156] Thus most of the first personal real burdens—943 in all[157]—came about by conversion rather than by creation of new; and two such burdens (personal pre-emption burdens and personal redemption burdens) could only be created in this way.

Personal real burdens are restricted both by content and by holder. Only two need further mention. A "conservation burden" protects the built or natural environment for the benefit of the public,[158] and may be held only by Scottish

---

[152] 2003 Act s.12.

[153] For example, South Africa and the United States of America.

[154] There is a corresponding distinction between personal and praedial servitudes, which is well known throughout the civil law world. See Stair, II, 7, pr, and Erskine II, 9, 5. "Praedial" is from the Latin word *praedium* meaning land or an estate. The only personal servitude (in this sense) recognised in Scots law is proper liferent.

[155] 2003 Act s.1(3). The last was added by the Climate Change (Scotland) Act 2009 s.68. See Leslie and Steven, (2010) 55 J.L.S.S. November/54.

[156] 2000 Act ss.18A, 18B, 18C, 27, and 27A. Maritime burdens (burdens over the foreshore or sea bed held by the Crown) did not require a notice: see s.60. For a full account, see K.G.C. Reid, *The Abolition of Feudal Tenure in Scotland* (2003), Ch.4.

[157] For the breakdown, see Reid and Gretton, *Conveyancing 2004*, pp.95–96. Most were in respect of personal pre-emption burdens and conservation burdens.

[158] 2003 Act s.38.

Ministers, by local authorities, and by certain other designated conservation bodies (mainly private trusts).[159] Thus if a conservation body restores property and sells it, conservation burdens can be included in the disposition to ensure that the historic features of the building are duly preserved. Quite different in character is the "economic development burden". As the name suggests, this has as its purpose the promotion of economic development—a rather vague notion which will no doubt be tested in the courts.[160] Such burdens can be held only by the Scottish Ministers and by local authorities, and they are the rough equivalent of the statutory agreements which were already available for Scottish Enterprise and Highlands and Islands Enterprise.[161]

For the most part, personal real burdens are governed by the same rules as praedial real burdens. In the absence of a benefited property, however, personal real burdens are transferred by assignation followed by registration.[162] But only a qualified holder can take, and some burdens (such as economic development burdens) are not assignable at all. Only the holder of a personal real burden has title to enforce, and interest is presumed.[163]

Interpretation[164]

13–21 Like other provisions in a deed, real burdens are construed in the light of the circumstances which obtained at the time they were imposed.[165] But unlike other such provisions there is a presumption for freedom. Thus if the validity of a condition is uncertain, it will generally be construed as invalid,[166] while if its scope is doubtful, it will generally be construed according to its narrowest possible meaning,[167] and the courts are reluctant to extend the scope of a burden by implication. Hence, the vital importance of accuracy when drafting new burdens. Unfortunately, a burden which looks clear, and perhaps even

---

[159] For the list of conservation bodies, see the Title Conditions (Scotland) Act 2003 (Conservation Bodies) Order 2003 (SSI 2003/453); and a series of Title Conditions (Scotland) Act 2003 (Conservation Bodies) Amendment Orders, viz. SSI 2004/400; SSI 2006/110; SSI 2006/130; SSI 2007/533; SSI 2008/217.

[160] 2003 Act s.45. The first decision takes an expansive view: see *Teague Developments Ltd v City of Edinburgh Council*, Unreported February 27, 2008 Lands Tribunal, discussed in Reid and Gretton, *Conveyancing 2008*, pp.89–92.

[161] Enterprise and New Towns (Scotland) Act 1990 s.32 (as amended by the 2003 Act s.113).

[162] 2003 Act s.39.

[163] 2003 Act s.47. In *Teague Developments Ltd v City of Edinburgh Council*, Unreported February 27, 2008 Lands Tribunal, the presumption was said to be irrebuttable, but this seems open to question. See Scottish Law Commission, Report on *Real Burdens* (Scot. Law Com. No.181, 2000), para.9.21.

[164] On interpretation, see Reid, *Property*, paras 415–422; Gordon (2nd edn), paras 22–41 to 22–50; Halliday, paras 34–31 to 34–34.

[165] *Mehrabadi v Hough*, Unreported January 11, 2010 Aberdeen Sheriff Court, discussed in Reid and Gretton, *Conveyancing 2010*, pp.93–96. For interpretation of deeds in general, see above, para.11–27.

[166] But in practice it can be difficult to predict what a court would say. Thus, in *Lothian Regional Council v Rennie*, 1991 S.L.T. 465 two judges held a burden to be ineffectual as being hopelessly imprecise in its scope, while the third judge thought that its meaning was perfectly clear. Similarly, the Lord Ordinary and the First Division took opposed views in *Grampian Joint Police Board v Pearson*, 2001 S.C. 772.

[167] For illustrative examples, in addition to the cases cited below, see *Graham v Shiels* (1901) 8 S.L.T. 368; *Shand v Brand* (1907) 14 S.L.T. 704; *The Walker Trustees v Haldane* (1902) 4 F. 594; *Heritage Fisheries Ltd v Duke of Buccleuch*, 2000 S.L.T. 800. But the court will not adopt a narrow reading unless it is a reasonable one: *Cochran v Paterson* (1882) 9 R. 634 at 638; *Frame v Cameron* (1864) 3 M. 290 at 294.

elegant, to its author may appear in a different light to a court which has the benefit of hindsight and of knowledge of events that no one may have foreseen.[168]

The case law is voluminous and, for the draftsman, disheartening. For example, an obligation to build cannot be extended to imply an obligation to maintain.[169] In one case an obligation to build a house "which may include a garage" was held not to imply a prohibition on building a second garage.[170] An obligation to supply water was held not to imply an obligation that it be of drinkable quality.[171] The terms "conventional dwelling-house"[172] and "buildings of an unseemly description"[173] have both been held to be too vague for real burdens, although it has been also held (it is submitted incorrectly) that "not of a class inferior to the houses some time ago built by" is sufficient.[174] In a remarkable series of cases an obligation that a dwelling-house must be "self-contained" has been held to refer to structure not use. Thus, such a burden does not prevent division into flats, provided that the structure remains capable of use as a single dwelling-house.[175] An obligation to erect buildings of a certain type does not imply a prohibition of additional buildings of a different type.[176] An obligation to erect houses[177] (or anything else) is invalid as a real burden if no time limit is expressed.[178] Where a burden forbids a certain use, it is presumed not to forbid such use as is merely "ancillary". For example, a prohibition of commercial use would not prevent a house being used commercially, provided that its main use continued to be that of a dwelling-house.[179] Because of this, it may be desirable when drafting a burden to add a clause expressly forbidding ancillary use, and this is sometimes done.[180]

---

[168] e.g. *Heritage Fisheries Ltd v Duke of Buccleuch*, 2000 S.L.T. 800 at 802 D–E ("language which is at once obscure and infelicitous and which seems calculated to maximise the scope for misunderstandings and disputes").

[169] *Peter Walker & Son (Edinburgh) Ltd v Church of Scotland General Trustees*, 1967 S.L.T. 297. Contrast *Clark v Glasgow Assurance Co* (1854) 1 Macq. 668. Though a House of Lords case, it is out of line with current judicial attitudes.

[170] *Carswell v Goldie*, 1967 S.L.T. 339. And see *Ross v Cuthbertson* (1854) 16 D. 732; and *Buchanan v Marr* (1883) 10 R. 936.

[171] *Anstruther's Trustees v Burgh of Pittenweem*, 1943 S.L.T. 160.

[172] *Lawson v Hay*, 1989 G.W.D. 24-1049.

[173] *Murray's Trustees v Trustees for St Margaret's Convent* (1906) 8 F. 1109; 1907 S.C. (HL) 8.

[174] *Morrison v McLay* (1874) 1 R. 1117. See also *Middleton v Leslie's Trustees* (1894) 21 R. 781.

[175] The distinction seems odd but is well supported by authority, e.g. *Moir's Trustees v McEwan* (1880) 7 R. 1141; *Buchanan v Marr* (1883) 10 R. 936; *Miller v Carmichael* (1888) 15 R. 991; *Porter v Campbell's Trustees*, 1923 S.C. (HL) 94.

[176] *Cowan v Magistrates of Edinburgh* (1887) 14 R. 682; *Fleming v Ure* (1896) 4 S.L.T. 26. For whether the burden implies a prohibition of altering the buildings see *Cochran v Paterson* (1882) 9 R. 634; *Thom v Chalmers* (1886) 13 R. 1026; *Johnston v MacRitchie* (1893) 20 R. 539.

[177] Burdens of this nature were once very common. The superior wanted to keep up the value of the land as a security for his feuduty. Clauses requiring insurance and rebuilding in the event of destruction were common for the same reason. Such clauses (except insofar as they might protect amenity) are now pointless.

[178] *Gammell's Trustees v The Land Commission*, 1970 S.L.T. 254; distinguishing *Anderson v Valentine*, 1957 S.L.T. 57.

[179] *Colquhoun's CB v Glen's Trustees*, 1920 S.C. 737; *Low v Scottish Amicable Building Society*, 1940 S.L.T. 295.

[180] Even so, in *Snowie v Museum Hall LLP* [2010] CSOH 107; 2010 S.L.T. 971 a prohibition of ancillary business use was held not to prevent such business use as did not disturb neighbours. The decision seems wrong on this ground though it could be supported on the ground of absence of interest to enforce.

The traditionally hostile approach to real burdens was due in part to the difficulty of procuring their discharge prior to the introduction of the Lands Tribunal jurisdiction in 1970. With the further reforms in the 2003 Act, discussed below in Ch.16, there is now no reason for a court to attempt discharge by means of interpretation, and indeed the 2003 Act expressly provides that "real burdens shall be construed in the same manner as other provisions of deeds which relate to land and are intended for registration".[181] As a result, it should no longer be true in the future, as it has sometimes been in the past, that real burdens are interpreted more strictly than servitudes; and some at least of the cases in the previous paragraph may no longer be good law. But even before the changes brought about by the 2003 Act the courts sometimes read deeds with a sympathetic eye. Where, for example, there was an obligation to maintain a boundary fence it was held that it could fairly be implied that the fence should be stockproof.[182] And a rather vague power for factors to act "in their sole discretion" was held enforceable, on the basis that they could not go beyond the specific obligations imposed on the owners by other clauses in the deed of conditions.[183]

It is common to find burdens which forbid "nuisances". There is only one reported case[184] where such a clause has been challenged as too vague. In that case the burden forbade: "any soap work candle work tan work slaughter house cattle mart skin work dye work oil work lime work distillery brewery or other manufacture or chemical process of any kind, nor to deposit nauseous materials thereon nor to lay any nuisance or obstructions on the roads or streets adjoining said ground nor to do any other act which may injure the amenity of the said place of the neighbourhood for private residences". The challenge failed. Clauses with this sort of wording are often to be found in older deeds.[185] The modern tendency is simply to forbid any "trade business or profession", and there can be little doubt that this expression is acceptably precise. Reference to "nuisance" as such is rare in modern burdens. One interpretative problem is that "nuisance" is a delict against neighbours in any case.[186]

Extinction: in general

13–22   Quite often owners want to do something which is prohibited by a real burden. There is then a choice. One option is to seek the agreement of those with rights to enforce, formalised in a minute of waiver. Another option is to apply to the Lands Tribunal for variation or discharge, a topic which is considered below in Ch.15. If the burden is more than 100 years old, it can often be brought to an

---

[181] 2003 Act s.14. For the ordinary rules of interpretation of deeds, see above, para.11–27. The provision applies to all burdens, whenever created: see subss.119(4), (10). For a discussion, see Scottish Law Commission, Report on *Real Burdens* (Scot. Law Com. No.181, 2000), paras 4.61–4.67. Much earlier, the Halliday Report para.81 had advocated a similar change. A post-2004 case (though not citing s.14) is *Clarke v Grantham*, 2009 G.W.D. 38-645 (holding that "temporarily" was sufficiently definite).

[182] *Church of Scotland General Trustees v Phin*, 1987 S.C.L.R. 240.

[183] *Crampshee v North Lanarkshire Council*, 2004 G.W.D. 7-149.

[184] *Mannofield Residents Property Co Ltd v Thomson*, 1983 S.L.T. (Sh. Ct) 71. See also *Meriton Ltd v Winning*, 1993 S.C.L.R. 913; 1995 S.L.T. 76.

[185] "The usual grotesque enumeration of noxious and offensive businesses and trades": Lord Shaw in *Porter v Campbell's Trustees*, 1923 S.C. (HL) 94.

[186] On nuisance as a delict, see N.R. Whitty, "Nuisance", in *Stair Memorial Encyclopaedia Reissue* (2001).

end under the "sunset rule" merely by service and registration of a notice of termination. And finally the owner can ignore the burden and do the forbidden thing anyway. Until the 2000 Act this last course was risky because the superior might have a right to irritate the feu and so reclaim the property without compensation. Today the worst that can happen is a court order to stop, or to undo, the breach. Even that is rare. In practice, burdens are not often enforced, and where they are enforced the available remedies may turn out to be unsatisfactory.[187] Indeed often the real concern is not enforcement but rather the possible reluctance of a future purchaser to accept a title where there has been a blatant breach of one of the burdens. Minutes of waiver, in particular, are often sought long after the breach has occurred, under stimulus of an anxious or demanding purchaser.

Not only does breach of a burden avoid the cost and inconvenience of a discharge, or the pain of compliance: it may also bring the burden to an end altogether, through the doctrines of acquiescence and negative prescription. This is not, of course, to advocate breach. Where possible, obligations should be complied with. But breach is common in practice, not least because the burdened owner is often quite unaware of, or indifferent to, the conditions in his or her title.

Minute of waiver

A standard method of removing or restricting real burdens is by a written minute of waiver.[188] There is no prescribed form. In practice waivers usually discharge the burden only to the extent of allowing the activity proposed by the burdened owner, so that in all other respects the burden remains in force. Although burdens can be enforced by occupiers as well as by owners, only the owner of the benefited property grants the deed. A registered title is not required of the granter provided that, in the case of GRS property, the deed includes a clause of deduction of title.[189] The burden is not varied or discharged until the deed is registered, against the burdened property. Superiors did not usually grant minutes of waiver without payment, but in the post-feudal world waivers will often be gratuitous.

It is important to identify all of the benefited properties. There is no point in obtaining a minute of waiver from the owner of one property only to find that the owner of another seeks and obtains an interdict. This obvious point was sometimes overlooked in the past, especially in respect of feudal burdens, and the register is full of minutes of waiver granted by superiors alone without regard to the, admittedly difficult, question of whether neighbours (co-feuars) had enforcement rights as well.[190] Even today the identification of benefited properties is often far from being a straightforward task[191]; and if the numbers go far into double figures there may be little prospect of persuading everyone to sign, at least within a reasonable period of time. The position is eased to some degree for community burdens: the special forms of discharge which apply there are discussed below in Ch.15.[192]

13–23

---

[187] See above, para.13–13.
[188] 2003 Act ss.15 and 48.
[189] 2003 Act s.60.
[190] D.J. Cusine and J. Egan, *Feuing Conditions in Scotland* (1995).
[191] See above, paras 13–14 and 13–15.
[192] See below, para.15–07.

Sunset rule

13–24   A minute of waiver needs the consent of the benefited owner or owners. But for burdens which are more than 100 years old the burdened owner can act alone. In terms of a procedure first introduced by the 2003 Act,[193] the owner[194] draws up a notice of termination in statutory form. A copy is sent to the owners of all benefited properties within four metres (disregarding roads), and also fixed on the burdened property and on a lamp post or lamp posts. If, after eight weeks, no application has been made to the Lands Tribunal by a benefited owner, the notice is endorsed with a certificate by the Tribunal and registered against the burdened property.[195] Registration marks the moment of extinction. The procedure is available for all real burdens other than conservation burdens, facility burdens and one or two other minor cases. Furthermore, it can be used for any number of qualifying burdens, thus allowing a title to be "cleansed" of elderly burdens in a single act. So far, however, conveyancers have been slow to make use of this new facility.

Extinction by breach: negative prescription and acquiescence

13–25   After five years of breach a real burden is extinguished by negative prescription.[196] But the burden may have been brought to an end much earlier owing to acquiescence. Specific provision for acquiescence is made in the 2003 Act.[197] The breach must involve material expenditure the benefit of which would be substantially lost if the burden were now to be enforced. Unauthorised building is the typical case. The burden is extinguished if either the owner of the benefited property or properties consented to the work, however informally, or if all those with enforcement rights (which might include tenants and other occupiers) consented or at least failed to object within the period ending 12 weeks after the work was substantially completed. The work must be sufficiently obvious that the enforcers knew of it or ought to have known. In effect, enforcers must object at once or lose their rights.

It is easy to see why these provisions are important. Suppose, for instance, that a deed of 1899 conveyed plots of ground for the erection of tenements. The deed will have imposed various real burdens. Some, such as restrictions on use, are likely still to be enforceable. But suppose that one of the burdens concerned the building line. It may, for instance, have provided that there should be no building closer than four feet from the inner line of the pavement. This is unlikely to matter today, for if the builder in fact built up to three feet from the pavement, negative prescription will long ago have barred any objection. Much the same is true even of more recent works—extensions, garages,

---

[193] 2003 Act ss.20–24.

[194] Or any other person (such as a tenant) against whom the burden is enforceable: see 2003 Act s.20(1).

[195] If, however, an application is made, then the matter has to be considered by the Lands Tribunal. See *Brown v Richardson*, 2007 G.W.D. 28-490; *Council for Music in Hospitals v Trustees for Richard Gerald Associates*, 2008 S.L.T. (Lands Tr) 17.

[196] 2003 Act s.18—on the assumption that prescription has not been interrupted. Under the previous law the period was 20 years. For transitional provisions, see s.18(5), (7).

[197] 2003 Act s.16. Specific but not exhaustive: the common law doctrine of acquiescence remains applicable insofar as not replaced by the new provision. See generally, Elspeth C. Reid and John W.G. Blackie, *Personal Bar* (2006), Ch.6; Wortley, in Robert Rennie (ed), *The Promised Land: Property Law Reform* (2008), Ch.2.

porches, greenhouses and the like. If more than five years have passed, the matter is taken care of by prescription; if less than five years, acquiescence may usually be assumed to have operated. In relation to the latter it is true that a potential purchaser cannot be sure that the unauthorised works were not objected to at the time, but there is a statutory presumption that no objections were made and hence that acquiescence operated.[198] For practical purposes this will usually be enough, even without a formal minute of waiver.

Prescription and acquiescence extinguish burdens only to the extent of the breach. So if a greenhouse is built, contrary to a general prohibition on building, the greenhouse is allowed, but in all other respects the burden remains in force and could be used to prevent further building operations.

SERVITUDES[199]

Creation by deed

A conveyancer who is instructed to create a servitude will naturally do so by 13–26 deed. And if, as typically, this affects land which is being sold, the servitude will be included in the disposition (in subdivision cases) or in the deed of conditions (in development cases).[200] In a disposition a servitude can either be reserved (in favour of any land being kept back by the granter) or granted (in favour of the land being disponed), and both are common. From time to time a servitude is also created between established neighbours, without a sale, in which case the deed used is a (freestanding) deed of servitude. In all cases the deed must be granted by the owner of the burdened property and, except where a disposition is used, the granter's title must have been completed by registration.[201] To allow registration the deed must be probative.

No particular words are necessary, although "servitude" avoids any suggestion that the right is merely contractual and should always be used.[202] For servitudes of a familiar and well-established type, not much more than the name is needed, but the new servitudes permitted by the 2003 Act[203] will require to be more closely defined.[204] In drafting it should be borne in mind that land is presumed free of burdens and that servitudes, like real burdens, are interpreted strictly.[205] Obvious errors, however, may be overlooked.[206] The basic grant of servitude is sometimes supplemented by conditions as to its exercise, and such

---

[198] 2003 Act s.16(2).

[199] The standard work is D.J. Cusine and R.R.M. Paisley, *Servitudes and Rights of Way* (1998). Useful shorter accounts can be found in works such as Gordon (2nd edn), Ch.24 and Reid, *Property*, paras 439–93 (A.G.M. Duncan).

[200] For the distinction between subdivision and development, see above, paras 13–02 to 13–04.

[201] D.J. Cusine and R.R.M. Paisley, *Servitudes and Rights of Way*, para.4.08.

[202] See e.g. *Robertson v Hossack*, 1995 S.L.T. 291; *Moss Bros Group v Scottish Mutual Assurance Plc*, 2001 S.C. 779; *Ord v Mashford*, 2006 S.L.T. (Lands Tr) 15.

[203] As to which see above, para.13–07.

[204] Sometimes, however, too much elaboration may result in a less extensive right being granted than the draftsman had intended: see e.g. *Skiggs v Adams* [2006] CSOH 73; 2006 G.W.D. 17-352 (right of access "for all necessary purposes").

[205] For real burdens, see above, para.13–21. The courts are, however, realistic as to the amount of detail that can reasonably be expected: see *Axis West Developments Ltd v Chartwell Land Investments Ltd*, 1999 S.L.T. 1416.

[206] *Chalmers Property Investment Co Ltd v Robson*, 2008 S.L.T. 1069.

conditions are in any event implied by law.[207] Ancillary rights reasonably necessary to make the servitude effective are, equally, implied provided they can be said to have been in the parties' contemplation at the time of the grant.[208] As well as giving the terms of the servitude the deed must also nominate and describe both the benefited and the burdened properties. Under the old law, there was no requirement that the deed be registered, although registration was normal in practice, but the 2003 Act requires registration against both properties.[209]

Probably the commonest servitude is that of way,[210] and as there are two main types (pedestrian and vehicular) it is important to specify which is intended. To avoid any doubt as to whether vehicular access includes pedestrian access, the phrase "pedestrian and vehicular" should be used. If the nature of the servitude has not been specified, a court will, it seems, construe the servitude on the basis of actual usage.[211]

Creation by implication or prescription

13–27   Unlike real burdens, servitudes can also be created by implication from the terms of a conveyance, and by positive prescription. The first of these is usually the mark of conveyancing negligence, for if a servitude is needed, it should be created expressly. It will not be discussed further here.[212] In *Bowers v Kennedy*[213] it was held that, for landlocked property, there is always a right of access over land of which it was formerly part, and that this is attributable, not to servitude, but to an inherent quality of ownership itself. As such it is imprescriptible and so is not lost even by long periods of non-use. The court, however, declined to be drawn on the more important question as to whether such a right arises even where there was no previous connection with the surrounding land.

Servitudes by prescription are, again, only marginally a conveyancing matter and so will not be discussed here except to say that there has been a persistent controversy as to the meaning of the possession "as of right" (or, more accurately, "as if of right") which is needed for prescriptive acquisition.[214] The relevant prescriptive period is 20 years.[215]

---

[207] For the conditions that are implied, see D.J. Cusine and R.R.M. Paisley, *Servitudes and Rights of Way*, Ch.12.

[208] *Moncrieff v Jamieson* [2007] UKHL 42; 2008 S.C. (HL) 1. See Reid and Gretton, *Conveyancing 2007*, pp.111–17. And see also *Chalmers Property Investment Co Ltd v Robson*, 2008 S.L.T. 1069; *SP Distribution Ltd v Rafique*, 2010 S.L.T. (Sh. Ct) 8.

[209] 2003 Act s.75. An exception is made for pipeline servitudes, in recognition of the fact that the sheer number of burdened properties may make registration impractical.

[210] Also called "passage", "access", "free ish and entry", etc.

[211] Authority, however, is sparse. A modern example is *Parkin v Kennedy*, Unreported March 23, 2010 Lands Tribunal, discussed in Reid and Gretton, *Conveyancing 2010*, pp.178–79.

[212] For discussion and authorities see D.J. Cusine and R.R.M. Paisley, *Servitudes and Rights of Way*, Chs 7, 8 and 9; Gordon (2nd edn), paras 24–34 to 24–41; Reid, *Property*, paras 452–457. Some important cases are *Cochrane v Ewart* (1861) 23 D. (HL) 3; *Gow's Trustees v Mealls* (1875) 2 R. 729; *Murray v Medley*, 1973 S.L.T. (Sh. Ct) 75; *King v Brodt*, 1993 G.W.D. 13-886; *McEwan's Exrs v Arnot*, Unreported September 7, 2004 Perth Sheriff Court, discussed in Reid and Gretton, *Conveyancing 2004*, pp.89–92.

[213] *Bowers v Kennedy*, 2000 S.C. 555. For commentary, see Reid and Gretton, *Conveyancing 2000*, pp.52–54; Paisley, (2002) 6 Edin. L.R. 101.

[214] The controversy is reviewed in Reid and Gretton, *Conveyancing 2008*, pp.100–07. Important modern cases include *Aberdeen City Council v Wanchoo* [2008] CSIH 6; 2008 S.C. 278; and *Neumann v Hutchison*, 2008 G.W.D. 16-297.

[215] 1973 Act s.3.

Division of the benefited property

A familiar problem is whether, on the division of the benefited property into 13–28 separate plots, a servitude enures to the benefit of all the various plots which now make up the original property. A farmer who happily granted a servitude of way for a neighbouring farmer may be less happy if he finds that, instead of the occasional tractor, countless cars drive up and down day and night because the neighbouring farm is now a housing estate. In at least some cases, such use would disturb the principle that the burden of a servitude is not to be increased; but because of uncertainties in the law, the ideal is to make clear provision on the point in the original deed, either allowing such future use or alternatively forbidding it.[216]

Extinction

A servitude is brought to an end by a formal discharge executed by the owners 13–29 of the benefited property or properties. If the servitude was entered on the Register against the burdened property, the discharge must likewise be registered against that property,[217] but otherwise registration is not required. In practice formal discharges are uncommon, and if a servitude is extinguished it is usually because it has not been exercised for the 20 years of negative prescription.[218] Extinction may also come about by acquiescence in a building project—such as a wall across a path—which is inconsistent with the future exercise of the servitude.[219] A servitude is extinguished by confusion if the benefited and burdened properties come into the ownership of the same person, but with the possibility of revival (although the law is not certain) if the properties later come to be separated.[220] Finally, and as with real burdens, a servitude may be varied or discharged by application to the Lands Tribunal.[221]

PRE-EMPTIONS, REDEMPTIONS AND REVERSIONS

Pre-emptions

Sometimes, when land is split off and sold, the seller reserves a right of first 13–30 refusal on a subsequent resale. This gives the option of buying back before the land is sold to someone else. Rights of pre-emption are common only in rural areas, and are found particularly where land is sold from a large estate. Sometimes a pre-emption is contractual in nature but more usually it is included

---

[216] Relevant cases include *Keith v Texaco Ltd*, 1977 S.L.T. (Lands Tr) 16; *Alvis v Harrison*, 1991 S.L.T. 64; and *Alba Homes Ltd v Duell*, 1993 S.L.T. (Sh. Ct) 49. For an excellent and persuasive study of the whole question see D.J. Cusine and R.R.M. Paisley, *Servitudes and Rights of Way*, Ch.14.

[217] 2003 Act s.78.

[218] Prescription and Limitation (Scotland) Act 1973 s.8. Servitudes will not, or at least not usually, fall within the exception for rights exercisable as a *res merae facultatis*: see *Peart v Legge* [2007] CSIH 70; 2008 S.C. 93.

[219] See e.g. *Millar v Christie*, 1961 S.C. 1. See further Elspeth C. Reid and John W.G. Blackie, *Personal Bar* (2006), Ch.6.

[220] D.J. Cusine and R.R.M. Paisley, *Servitudes and Rights of Way*, paras 17.22–17.31. A real burden is not extinguished by confusion: see the 2003 Act s.19.

[221] See below, Ch.16.

within a conveyance with the idea (not always successfully realised)[222] that it should be a real burden. The price is typically that which a future potential purchaser is willing to pay, although sometimes it is a fixed sum which, with inflation, will rapidly represent a bargain for the pre-emption holder.[223] It has been said that the owner must deal fairly with the pre-emption holder and so must not, for example, fix an artificially high price with the potential purchaser in order to discourage the pre-emption's exercise.[224] From an owner's point of view, a pre-emption is irksome and can delay sales and put off potential purchasers. There is also the danger that it is overlooked, at least in the initial stages of a sale.

For reasons which are largely historical, the law distinguishes between (i) real burden pre-emptions created in a grant in feu, or in a non-feudal deed executed after September 1, 1974, and (ii) real burden pre-emptions created in a non-feudal deed executed before September 1, 1974.[225] Pre-emptions of the second type are normal real burdens which run with the land and affect all future sales, thus allowing the holder to choose when to buy. Pre-emptions of the first type are, in principle, available only on the first sale. By virtue of a provision which dates from 1938 but was re-enacted in a revised form by the 2003 Act,[226] the property is offered back only on the first occasion on which it is sold. The pre-emption holder then has 21 days to accept the offer or to reject it, but in either case the pre-emption comes to an end[227]: if the holder chooses not to buy, there is no second chance. However, a proper written offer to sell must be sent to the pre-emption holder, and on terms which are both reasonable and in conformity with the clause of pre-emption. Thus it is not sufficient, under the Act, merely to write to the holder asking whether the pre-emption will be exercised (although this is commonly done in practice); and even if the answer to such a letter were to be "no", the pre-emption would live on and could be exercised on the occasion of the next sale.

In practice the requirement of a formal offer is often highly inconvenient. Since the price is generally that which a purchaser is willing to pay, no offer can be made until the property is marketed and offers from third parties received. There is then a delay while the formal offer is made to the pre-emption holder. Naturally, potential purchasers are resentful and may lose interest. For pre-emptions of the first type, however, a solution is provided by

---

[222] e.g. because there is no benefited property, as in *Macdonald-Haig v Gerlings*, Unreported December 3, 2001 Inverness Sheriff Court; discussed in Reid and Gretton, *Conveyancing 2002*, pp.63–5; or because there is no praedial benefit, as discussed by Temporary Judge M.G. Thompson QC in *Braes v Keeper of the Registers of Scotland* [2009] CSOH 176; 2010 S.L.T. 689 at para.66. Disappointments of this kind are apt to lead to actions for professional negligence against one's law agents: see *MacDonald-Haig v MacNeill & Critchley*, 2004 S.L.T. (Sh. Ct) 75.

[223] In *Macdonald-Haig v Gerlings*, Unreported December 3, 2001 Inverness Sheriff Court a low price was held not to breach art.1 of the First Protocol to the European Convention on Human Rights.

[224] *Howatson v Whyte*, Unreported July 14, 1992 Forfar Sheriff Court, discussed in Reid and Gretton, *Conveyancing 2010*, pp.166–8.

[225] 2003 Act s.82.

[226] 2003 Act s.84. The former provision was s.9 of the Conveyancing (Scotland) Act 1938.

[227] Except in the case of rural housing burdens, where the pre-emption is considered to be complied with for the current sale but is not extinguished for the future: see 2003 Act s.84(1). A rural housing burden is a right of pre-emption constituted in favour of a designated rural housing body: see 2003 Act s.43.

the 2003 Act.[228] Holders who do not want to exercise the pre-emption can make their position clear in advance by executing a pre-sale undertaking in statutory form. This lasts for a specified period and can be subject to conditions, such as that the price at which the property is sold be above a certain figure. If the property is sold during this period, a disposition duly registered, and any conditions in the undertaking complied with, the pre-emption is extinguished automatically.[229] Unsurprisingly, however, not all pre-emption holders are willing to commit themselves in advance in the manner required by the legislation.

It should not be assumed that a pre-emption is still "live" merely because it appears on the Register. Most, in fact, are not. Thus all pre-emptions in grants in feu were extinguished on November 28, 2004 except for the small numbers preserved by registration of a notice under ss.18 or 18A of the 2000 Act[230]; no pre-emption in a pre-2004 disposition is enforceable, other than between the original parties, unless a benefited property was expressly nominated, which typically it was not[231]; and, of the rest, many were extinguished on the first occasion on which the property was offered back on the basis of the rule already described. If, however, the position is in doubt, as it may be, it is wise to assume that the pre-emption remains good, and to offer the property back to the holder. A disposition granted in breach of a pre-emption is vulnerable to reduction for a period of five years.[232]

Redemptions

More onerous still are rights of redemption. These are rights of repurchase 13–31 at the option of the holder, sometimes exercisable at will and sometimes tied to the occurrence of a particular event. Importantly, it does not matter that the owner does not want to sell. Since November 28, 2004 it has no longer been competent to create redemptions as real burdens,[233] and those created on or after September 1, 1974 were restricted to 20 years.[234] Further, all redemptions created in grants in feu expired on November 28, 2004 unless preserved by registration of a notice under ss.18 or 18A of the 2000 Act. Nonetheless some elderly redemptions remain on the Register and may still be enforceable.

---

[228] 2003 Act s.83.

[229] As before, however, rural housing burdens are extinguished only in respect of the current sale: see the 2003 Act s.83(1).

[230] Section 18 provides for preservation as a praedial real burden, and s.18A as a personal pre-emption burden. See K.G.C. Reid, *The Abolition of Feudal Tenure in Scotland* (2003), paras 4.21–4.23.

[231] *Braes v Keeper of the Registers of Scotland* [2009] CSOH 176; 2010 S.L.T. 689. This is because the principle identified in *JA Mactaggart & Co v Harrower* (1906) 8 F. 1101—rule (vii) of para.13–15—does not apply to pre-emptions.

[232] *Matheson v Tinney*, 1989 S.L.T. 535; *Roebuck v Edmunds*, 1992 S.L.T. 1055. Although usually a proprietor in possession, the acquirer would have at least constructive knowledge of the pre-emption and so would probably be unprotected against rectification of the Register: see Land Registration (Scotland) Act 1979 s.9(3)(a)(iii). After five years the pre-emption is extinguished and (except in the case of rural housing burdens) cannot be exercised in respect of future sales: see the 2003 Act s.18(2), (6).

[233] 2003 Act s.3(5)(a).

[234] Land Tenure Reform (Scotland) Act 1974 s.12.

Reversions: School Sites Act 1841

13–32   A redemption is an example of a reversion.[235] The only other example of importance is reversions under the School Sites Act 1841. Here some background is necessary. The 1841 Act allowed owners to convey land (including entailed land) for the building of schools and schoolhouses. Originally these grants were to private trustees, but in due course title passed, first to education boards and ultimately to local authorities. Many of these schools and schoolhouses have now closed and the site sold by local authorities. And typically such sales disregard the third proviso to s.2 of the 1841 Act, which is to the effect that, on the land ceasing to be used for the statutory purposes, it "shall thereupon immediately revert to and become a portion of the said estate". For a long time, indeed, this proviso was forgotten about, but in recent years there has been a spate of claims by those entitled, or allegedly entitled, to the reversion. In a case where the site has been sold, this presents a threat to the title of the acquirer.

   The 2003 Act contains a provision designed to secure the acquirer's title and, more generally, to regulate the making of claims under the statutory reversion.[236] The details are complex but in essence the reverter, on the site ceasing to be used as a school, must choose between a conveyance of the site or a sum of money representing its value (although the local authority can insist on payment of money). Where the trigger event for the reversion occurred after April 4, 2003 (the date the provision came into force), the reverter is denied the benefit of improvements made to the land and, in the case of a reconveyance, must pay a sum representing their value. The provision leaves open the question of entitlement to the reversion, and here the law has yet to make a definitive choice as to whether the reversion is personal to the original granter (and so passes to the granter's heirs) or whether it is praedial (and so attaches to the estate from which the land was originally taken).[237] A practical difficulty with the second view is that the original estate may have been broken up. In England and Wales, where the 1841 Act also applied, the reversion is treated as personal.[238]

STYLE DISPOSITION WITH REAL BURDENS AND SERVITUDES

13–33   Suppose that Jack owns a house and a substantial amount of land. Jack is selling part of the land to Jill. He will want her property to be subject to certain burdens and servitudes, and likewise she will want the same, vice versa. There will thus be (a) servitudes in favour of Jack, (b) real burdens in favour of Jack, (c) servitudes in favour of Jill and (d) real burdens in favour of Jill. The disposition could be drafted in many different ways, but something on the following lines would make sense. First, there would be the two clauses following within the body of the deed:

---

[235] For classification and analysis of reversions, pre-emptions and other options to acquire land, see Scottish Law Commission, Report on *Real Burdens* (Scot. Law Com. No.181, 2000), paras 10.1 et seq.

[236] 2003 Act s.86. The only case so far on this provision is *Burgess-Lumsden v Aberdeenshire Council*, 2009 S.L.T. (Sh. Ct) 117.

[237] Scottish Law Commission, Report on *Real Burdens*, para.10.47.

[238] *Fraser v Canterbury Diocesan Board of Finance* [2000] Ch. 669; *Bath and Wells Diocesan Board of Finance v Jenkinson* [2002] 3 W.L.R. 202.

TOGETHER WITH the right to (one) the real burdens set out in part II of the schedule annexed and signed as relative hereto and (two) the servitudes set out in part III of the said schedule . . .

. . . BUT ALWAYS WITH AND UNDER (one) the real burdens set out in part IV of the said schedule, and (two) the servitudes set out in part V of the said schedule . . .

Then the schedule would be on the following lines:

SCHEDULE

Part I: Interpretation

In this Schedule—

'the retained property' means ALL and WHOLE [the property being retained by Jack];

'the disponed property' means ALL and WHOLE the subjects disponed by the foregoing Disposition by Jack . . . in favour of Jill . . .;

'the disponer' means Jack . . . and his successors as owners of the retained property; and

'the disponee' means Jill . . . and her successors as owners of the disponed property.

Part II: Real burdens affecting the retained property

The following real burdens are imposed on the retained property in favour of the disponed property [*there follow the real burdens in numbered paragraphs*]

Part III: Servitudes affecting the retained property

The following servitudes are imposed on the retained property in favour of the disponed property [*there follow the servitudes in numbered paragraphs*]

Part IV: Real burdens affecting the disponed property

The following real burdens are imposed on the disponed property in favour of the retained property [*there follow the real burdens in numbered paragraphs*]

Part V: Servitudes affecting the disponed property

The following servitudes are imposed on the disponed property in favour of the retained property [*there follow the servitudes in numbered paragraphs*]

The Schedule would be doqueted:

This is the Schedule referred to in the foregoing Disposition by Jack . . . in favour of Jill . . . dated [date of execution].

CHAPTER 14

TENEMENTS, HOUSING ESTATES, AND OTHER COMMUNITIES

TENEMENTS[1]

Meaning of "tenement"

14–01 To the ordinary person a "tenement" conjures up images of sombre stone buildings from Victorian times or earlier. But to the lawyer a "tenement" is simply any flatted building, whether new or old, purpose-built or converted, residential or commercial, and all such tenements have, since 2004, been governed by the Tenements (Scotland) Act 2004.

As the 2004 Act applies to individual tenements, it is necessary to be sure where one tenement ends and the next begins—something which can occasionally be difficult where, as traditionally, tenements are built in terraces. The problem is most likely to arise with corner buildings, or where what might be a single tenement is served by two closes. Another difficult case is the Victorian semi-detached house, where one half has been flatted and the other not: is the tenement then (i) the whole house or (ii) merely the half that has been flatted? If, as in this last example, the structure of the building does not yield a clear answer, the titles will usually make the position plain. So if maintenance of the whole building is a common responsibility, then the whole building is a tenement; but if the flatted half is treated separately from the non-flatted half, then only the former is a tenement. The Act expressly allows recourse to the titles for the purpose of identifying the tenement.[2]

Default rules and title rules

14–02 Like the common law before it, the 2004 Act sets out a default code.[3] If the titles are silent, the statutory rules will govern the tenement (including tenements built before the code was enacted). But if the titles provide, the titles prevail.[4] In practice titles are rarely silent, except in the case of the very oldest tenements, and yet are rarely comprehensive, except, sometimes, in the case of the

---

[1] See generally Gordon and Wortley, 3rd edn, paras 15–46 to 15–178, and for an account of the Tenements (Scotland) Act 2004 see: Reid and Gretton, *Conveyancing 2004*, pp.121–50; Robert Rennie, *Land Tenure in Scotland* (2004), Ch.14; Donald B. Reid, in Robert Rennie (ed.), *The Promised Land: Property Law Reform* (2008), Ch.6. The Act originated with the Scottish Law Commission's Report on the *Law of the Tenement* (Scot. Law Com. No.162, 1998; available at *http://scotlawcom.gov.uk*) and much useful information can be found there.

[2] Tenements (Scotland) Act 2004 s.26(2).

[3] There are also a number of mandatory provisions, e.g. in relation to insurance or rights to take access.

[4] 2004 Act ss.1 and 4.

very newest. The result is that most tenements are governed both by the titles and, insofar as the titles are silent, by the statutory code. In considering the rules governing a building, therefore, conveyancers must have regard to both.

Traditionally, title provision was made in the split-off (break-off) deed for each flat. The split-offs would usually be granted by the original developer as soon as the construction was complete, although sometimes the flats were let out at first and only sold gradually over a period of years. Thus, one sometimes comes across a tenement built in, say, 1890 with the break-offs being granted from, say, the 1930s onwards. In more modern developments there is usually a deed of conditions,[5] to which each break-off refers. This is obviously more convenient. It is also generally true that the more modern the development the more complex the conditions are. A split-off of a flat in 1890 may just have a few words about the roof and the back green; a modern deed may have pages of provisions.

Two main topics are covered by the statutory code, and also by the titles. One is the allocation of ownership within the building. The other is management and maintenance.

Allocation of ownership: the statutory code

On allocation of ownership, the statutory code virtually re-enacts the previous common law, while taking the opportunity to resolve doubts and fill in gaps. The rules are individualistic rather than communal, with a tenement being viewed as a group of self-contained houses built, by some odd chance, one on top of the other. Thus the proprietor of a flat owns, not only the airspace which the flat occupies in the building, but also the walls, ceilings and floors.[6] Almost nothing is shared. An outside wall is owned in its entire thickness. Each section of outer wall thus belongs to the corresponding flat, so that if one looks at the outside of a tenement with the eyes of a legal eagle there is a series of horizontal title stripes. A wall which forms a boundary with another flat is owned to the mid-line,[7] after which it is part of the adjoining flat.[8] The roof, and roof space, are part of the highest flat in the building, and the solum (i.e. the ground on which the tenement is built) and foundations are part of the lowest flat.[9]

That leaves to be accounted for only (a) the common entrance, stair and corridors (b) the garden and other ground, and (c) certain ancillary parts, and these are allocated to particular flats or groups of flats as pertinents.[10] Thus the common entrance, stair and corridors—referred to in the legislation as the "close"—are the common property in equal shares of the owners of all flats accessed by them, i.e. excluding only those main-door flats with no door to the common

14–03

---

[5] See below, paras 15–03 to 15–06. Traditionally, deeds of conditions for flats were commoner in the Glasgow area than elsewhere. For an example, see Halliday, para.34–38.

[6] 2004 Act s.2(1).

[7] Or the *medium filum*, in the Latin form beloved by conveyancers. The term is geometrically inexact since it is in truth not a line (*filum*) but a plane (*planum*). But nobody ever says *medium planum*. Conveyancers seldom perceive the beauties of mathematics, and sometimes even say "mid-point".

[8] The same is true for the boundary between the floor and the ceiling of the flat underneath.

[9] 2004 Act s.2(3), (4).

[10] For pertinents, see above, paras 12–22 to 12–25.

passage.[11] The garden is owned, in sections, by the owners of those "bottom flats most nearly adjacent".[12] And ancillary parts, such as chimney stacks, rhones, down pipes, entryphone systems and the like, are allocated according to a functional test. So a part which serves one flat only is a pertinent of that flat (only), while a part which serves two or more flats is owned in common by the owners of the flats in question.[13]

Allocation of ownership: title provisions

14–04　Titles usually vary the default rules by increasing the parts which are owned in common. The titles typically make the roof, solum, foundations, external walls and back green common property. This is not an unmitigated blessing. Common property requires agreement among owners who have been thrown together largely by chance and who may be little inclined to co-operate. And it can lead to unexpected and unwanted consequences. If, for example, external walls are common property and not, as the default rules would have it, the sole property of the owner of the flats in question, the result is that in every flat two walls (at least) are the property of everyone in the building. That includes the inside surface as well as the outside. This means that anything added to the wall— from wallpaper to an Adam fireplace—becomes, by accession, the property of everyone in the building, and that not even the wallpaper could be changed, in strict law, without their agreement.[14] As a general guide to drafting it may be said that common property is an appropriate response where the purpose is to allow everyone the *use* of something—as, for example, in the case of the back green. But it is not an appropriate response where the purpose is simply common *maintenance*. That is better achieved by maintenance burdens and without altering the rules of ownership; and, as explained below, common maintenance is usually the result of the statutory code without the need for express provision.[15]

Roof void and space above the roof

14–05　Sometimes a top owner wishes to build an upper floor in the roof void. Under the statutory code the roof void belongs to the owner of the top flat,[16] but title deeds often vary this. If they merely say that the "roof" is owned in common, without also specifying the roof void, the latter is probably not included, and so remains subject to the default rule.[17] The roof itself, however, could not then be altered without the agreement of everyone.[18] Sometimes a top proprietor has

---

[11] 2004 Act s.3(1), (2). The close includes both the roof above and the solum beneath: s.2(5). A lift is in the same position. For pends, see *Hunter v Tindale*, Unreported July 22, 2011, Edinburgh Sheriff Court.

[12] 2004 Act s.3(3). But paths are common property under s.3(4).

[13] 2004 Act s.3(4), (5). Common ownership is in equal shares except for chimney stacks where shares are allocated on the basis of number of flues.

[14] See in particular *Rafique v Amin*, 1997 S.L.T. 1385.

[15] See below, para.14–08.

[16] 2004 Act s.2(3).

[17] For a different view see C. Waelde (ed.), *Professor McDonald's Conveyancing Opinions* (1998), p.50.

[18] Reid, *Property*, para.25. For an enterprising but plainly hopeless attempt to eliminate co-owners by means of an application to the Lands Tribunal, see *Dalby v Bracken*, Unreported June 13, 2008 Lands Tribunal.

built a room in a commonly-owned roof space without obtaining dispositions from the other parties. This obviously can cause major problems and when buying a top flat for a client it is wise to check whether there has been a roof void extension and if so whether the title to the extension is good.[19] The description in the Land Register is usually too meagre to provide much assistance one way or the other.

A top owner cannot lawfully build an extra storey, for the airspace above the roof belongs to the owner of the solum[20]—who in practice is either the owner of the lowest flat (the default rule) or all the owners in the tenement (the normal variation effected by the titles). But in a case where the roof is pitched, a top owner who owns the roof also owns, and can build into, the airspace above the slope of the roof as far as the roof's highest point.[21] In this situation dormer windows are therefore unobjectionable.

Tenement Management Scheme

Under the Act every tenement is to have a management scheme, and frequent reference is made in the Act to "the management scheme which applies as respects the tenement".[22] In the absence of anything else, the management scheme which applies is the Tenement Management Scheme ("TMS"), which is set out in Sch.1 to the Act. The TMS is thus a set of default rules—just in the same way as the rules as to ownership (discussed above) are default rules. And, as with ownership, the rules are severable. Thus the TMS compromises six substantive rules (rr.2–7) and three ancillary rules (rr.1, 8 and 9) which amplify the substantive rules. It is possible for one substantive rule to apply but not another. A particular tenement, for example, may be subject to r.3 of the TMS but not to r.2. Furthermore, with the exception of r.2 (which applies either entirely or not at all) it is possible—indeed will be normal—for *parts* of a rule to apply but for *other parts* not to apply. Whether a rule or part applies will depend on whether the title makes alternative provision by "tenement burden" (i.e. by a real burden which affects the tenement).[23] If the title is silent, the relevant rule (or part rule) of the TMS applies; but if the title provides, the rule (or part rule) is superseded.[24]

It follows that the TMS does not apply at all if the title makes provision on all the matters which the TMS covers. However, very few titles achieve this, if only because the TMS deals with certain matters—such as paying for repairs in advance, or emergency repairs—which are not usually provided for in titles. Thus all, or practically all, tenements are subject to the TMS to some degree. A tenement is not, however, subject to the TMS when the opt-in management scheme, known as the Development Management Scheme ("DMS"), applies.[25] The DMS, however, is not confined to tenements and is considered further in the next chapter.[26]

14–06

---

[19] For a cautionary tale see (1991) 36 J.L.S.S. 77.
[20] 2004 Act s.2(6). In theory this could be altered by the titles but in practice it is never done.
[21] 2004 Act s.2(7).
[22] Defined in 2004 Act s.27.
[23] 2004 Act s.29(1).
[24] For further details, see 2004 Act s.4.
[25] 2004 Act s.4(2).
[26] See below, paras 15–08 to 15–14.

Management: the TMS

14–07 Virtually no provision for management and maintenance was made by the former common law.[27] In this respect the statutory code is radically different. Under the TMS, management decisions are made by a simple majority, with or without a meeting, although if no meeting is held all owners must be consulted except where it is impracticable to do so.[28] The dissenting minority and their successors as owners are bound by any such "scheme decision", subject to a right to apply to the sheriff court to have the decision annulled.[29] In calculating the majority the tenement is to be taken as it is today, so that if two formerly separate flats have been combined, the result is treated as one flat and not as two.[30]

Not everything can be the subject of a scheme decision. The owners could not decide to buy additional land or run a lottery syndicate or employ a psychiatrist or publish a lifestyle magazine. Scheme decisions may only be made in respect of certain approved topics. There are two sources of such topics. One is the titles themselves—which commonly provide for decisions in relation to matters such as maintenance or the appointment of a manager (or factor). The other is r.3 of the TMS. In principle, both sources apply to all tenements, or, in other words, r.3 supplements whatever is in the titles. If the titles already make provision on a topic covered by r.3, that part of r.3 is displaced. Otherwise r.3 applies.[31] Apart from maintenance, considered below, r.3 also allows the owners to appoint or dismiss a manager, to delegate any of their powers to the manager, such as the power to decide on repairs (perhaps subject to a financial ceiling), to arrange a policy of common insurance for the whole tenement, and to install an entry-phone system.

Traditionally, managers or factors were much more common in the west of Scotland than in the east, although the position is beginning to change, a trend which seems likely to accelerate as a result of the TMS. A study by the Office of Fair Trading in 2009 found that, while 70 per cent of those surveyed were content with their factor, a significant minority was not, especially with regard to the way in which complaints were handled.[32] Once the Property Factors (Scotland) Act 2011 is in force, managers in residential developments will require to be registered and will be subject to a Code of Conduct and to a form of alternative dispute resolution for complaints.

Maintenance: the TMS

14–08 A decision to carry out maintenance can be made by a majority under r.3 of the TMS. Improvements, however, are not covered by the TMS. "Maintenance" is defined as including:

---

[27] Except that by the doctrine of common interest, any owner could insist on the repair of any part (such as the roof) which was necessary for support or shelter, with the owner meeting the cost. Common interest disappeared with the 2004 Act but a unilateral right to insist on repairs touching on support and shelter survives: see ss.7 and 8.

[28] TMS r.2.

[29] 2004 Act s.5; TMS r.8.2.

[30] *PS Properties (2) Ltd v Callaway Homes Ltd* [2007] CSOH 162; 2007 G.W.D. 31-526.

[31] 2004 Act s.4(5).

[32] See *http://www.oft.gov.uk/shared_oft/reports/comp_policy/oft1046.pdf*.

"repairs and replacement, cleaning, painting and other routine works, gardening, the day-to-day running of a tenement and the reinstatement of a part (but not most of) the tenement building, but does not include demolition, alteration or improvement unless reasonably incidental to the maintenance."[33]

The "unless reasonably incidental" qualification will be noted. Repairs often involve a degree of betterment, as technology advances (or at least changes). That is allowed. So an old thing can be replaced by a new (and, it may be, better) thing. But what is not allowed is to add a thing which did not previously exist. So the owners can make a scheme decision to paint the close, but not to install a sauna in the cupboard under the common stair. That is a clear example, but the distinction between betterment and improvements will not always be easy to draw. This does not mean that improvements can never happen. The titles may allow improvements (with or without limits), but otherwise improvements to common property require the agreement of everyone.[34] There are special rules allowing adjustments to common parts for the benefit of disabled residents.[35]

As well as being limited to "maintenance", a decision under r.3 must relate to "scheme property". The definition, however, is wide, extending to (i) all common property, (ii) all property which is to be commonly maintained in terms of the titles, and (iii) the following key parts of the building (if not already included under (i) and (ii)): the solum, foundations, external walls, roof, and any load-bearing wall, beam or column.[36] Apart, therefore, from individual flats, most of the rest of the building is scheme property.

Once a decision on maintenance has been taken, the estimated cost can be collected in advance, thus reassuring both the owners and the contractors that the bills will be paid.[37] Liability is shared among the owners either in the manner provided in the titles[38] or, failing such provision, according to r.4 of the TMS. Under r.4, if the property in question is owned in common, liability is apportioned according to size of *pro indiviso* share (and a person who does not own has no liability).[39] Otherwise the rule is that the owner of each flat pays the same except where the flats are of unequal size, defined as occurring where the floor area of the largest flat is more than one and a half times that of the smallest, in which case liability is calculated by floor area.[40] Liability, it will be noticed, is largely separated from ownership, and a person will often be bound to contribute to the cost of maintenance of a part which he or she does not own.

---

[33] TMS r.1.5.

[34] Reid, *Property*, para.25.

[35] Equality Act 2010 s.37. At the time of writing this had not yet been brought into force.

[36] TMS r.1.2.

[37] TMS rr.3.2–3.4. A possible advantage of so doing is that, if recovery proves impossible from an owner, the local authority has power to make up the shortfall: see Housing (Scotland) Act 2006 s.50. Whether it is at all likely to do so is a different matter.

[38] See below, para.14–09.

[39] TMS r.4.2(a).

[40] TMS r.4.2(b).

Management and maintenance: title provisions

14–09 Usually there is express provision in the titles for repair of the roof and various other parts.[41] Assuming that this accounts for the full cost,[42] and is properly constituted as a real burden,[43] it prevails over the liability rules set out in the TMS and described above. Sometimes titles specify the share of liability in fractional terms (e.g. one-eighth) or percentage terms (e.g. 12.5 per cent). That is the simplest and most convenient method. But often it will be found that liability is divided either according to the ratio of the feuduty or according to the ratio of the rateable value.[44] Feuduty has disappeared and residential property is no longer subject to rates, but burdens based on the old values are still valid.[45] As they continue to age, these values may become increasingly unfair and, in the worst cases, found an application to the Lands Tribunal to have the basis of liability changed.[46] When calculating liability on the basis of feuduty it should be borne in mind that in old money the pound sterling was divided into 20 shillings, and each shilling was divided into twelve pence (and each penny was two halfpence, and each halfpenny two farthings). For example £2/12s/6d = £2.625.

Titles may also make provision for decision-making. Sometimes this is no more than a declaration that a majority can agree on repairs, but in modern developments of any size there is often provision for residents' associations, committees, managers, annual meetings, and the like. It is only where no provision is made at all that the default rule in the TMS (for decision by majority) applies.[47]

Maintenance: access

14–10 Sometimes a repair cannot be carried out without using, or taking access through, an individual flat or some other part of the tenement in single ownership. Especially if the owner in question was opposed to the repair, there may be a reluctance to grant access. Section 17 of the 2004 Act confers a general right to access for maintenance and also for certain other purposes.[48] The maintenance need not be common maintenance, following a scheme decision, but can also be private maintenance to one's own flat. Reasonable notice, in

---

[41] These are community burdens and/or facility burdens. See below, paras 15–03 to 15–07. In practice there is no sharp division between repair and improvement, and this fact can give rise to disputes. See e.g. *McLay v Bennett*, 1998 G.W.D. 16-810; *Quantum Claims Compensation Specialists v Findlay*, 2002 G.W.D. 22-733. As mentioned above in para.14–08, "maintenance" is defined for the purposes of the TMS (by r.1.5).

[42] 2004 Act s.4(6).

[43] See further above, Ch.13. Under the former law it was sometimes doubted whether an obligation to contribute to maintenance (as opposed to a direct obligation to maintain) was valid as a real burden on the ground that no actual figure was given. But these doubts have been removed, retrospectively, by the Title Conditions (Scotland) Act 2003 s.5(1).

[44] This is competent even although the relevant figures are not found in the deed (or, therefore, in the register): see the 2003 Act s.5(2), and above, para.13–10.

[45] Local Government Finance Act 1992 s.111.

[46] *Kennedy v Abbey Lane Properties*, Unreported March 19, 2010 Lands Tribunal; *Patterson v Drouet*, Unreported January 20, 2011 Lands Tribunal. See Reid and Gretton, *Conveyancing 2010*, pp.97–102. It need hardly be added that the Lands Tribunal has no jurisdiction to deal with a case where liability is determined, not by real burdens, but by shares of ownership in common property: see *Dalby v Bracken*, Unreported June 13, 2008 Lands Tribunal.

[47] 2004 Act s.4(4).

[48] A complete list is given in s.17(3).

writing,[49] must be given unless the work is urgent. A request for access can be refused only where it is unreasonable.[50] For example, it may not be reasonable to reach the ceiling void in one's own flat by breaking open the floor of the flat above.[51] Access, once granted, does not have to be taken by the owner in person but can for example be taken by a tradesman.

Insurance

Owners are required to insure their flats, and this must be for reinstatement   14–11
value and in respect of certain prescribed risks such as fire, flood and subsist-
ence.[52] But insurance is not required to the extent that it is unavailable, or only available at a cost which is unreasonably high.[53] Failure to insure is not a criminal offence, and enforcement lies in the hands of the owners.[54]

In a tenement, insurance can either be taken out for the building as a whole or, piecemeal, for individual flats. The 2004 Act makes no choice between these methods and either is allowed. However, under the TMS owners are able to make a scheme decision to move to a common policy of insurance for the whole building, and to determine on an equitable basis the liability of each owner to contribute to the premium.[55] In addition, common insurance is sometimes required by a real burden, although, at least in older tenements, the level of cover stipulated may be inadequate. Unless the burden provides otherwise, the cost of premiums in such a case is to be shared equally among the owners.[56]

Flat sold in mid-repair

As only a bare majority of owners is needed for a scheme decision, a repair can   14–12
be agreed over the opposition of an owner who is on the brink of selling and who is unlikely to support further expenditure. To avoid possible difficulties of recovery, payment of the estimated cost can be required at once, in advance of the repair.[57] And even if the money is not collected in advance, the outgoing owner remains liable for the repair costs on the basis that he or she was owner at the time the decision was taken.[58] Whether the incoming owner is also liable depends upon whether the repairs have already been carried out. Thus:

- Where the repairs have been agreed but not carried out, the buyer is jointly and severally liable with the seller for the share attributable to the flat.[59] This gives the other owners in the tenement a choice of debtor, thus facilitating repairs. But it is unwelcome to the buyer. The (not always realistic) assumption, however, is that the home report, or an

---

[49] 2004 Act s.30.

[50] 2004 Act s.17(5).

[51] The facts of *Taylor v Irvine*, 1996 S.C.L.R. 937. In the event the issue did not require to be decided.

[52] 2004 Act s.18. The risks are prescribed by the Tenements (Scotland) Act 2004 (Prescribed Risks) Order 2007 (SSI 2007/16).

[53] 2004 Act s.18(4).

[54] 2004 Act s.18(5), (6).

[55] TMS r.3.1(e).

[56] 2004 Act s.4(6); TMS r.4.4(b).

[57] TMS r.3.2(c), discussed above.

[58] 2004 Act ss.11(1), (2) and 12(1). Section 12 is a close copy of s.10 of the Title Conditions (Scotland) Act 2003, which applies to real burdens generally.

[59] 2004 Act s.12 (2). The seller is liable from the moment the decision was made, and does not lose liability by selling the flat: see ss.11(1), (2) and 12(1).

independent survey, will have alerted the buyer to the possible need for repairs. Further, even if the buyer is made to pay, he has a right of relief against the seller.[60] So in the end the liability rests with the seller.

• Where the repairs have been carried out but not paid for, the buyer has no liability unless a notice of potential liability for costs was registered against the property at least 14 days before settlement.[61] This is because repairs which have been completed might otherwise be undetectable. The owner of any flat in the building can register a notice against that or any other flat, and its effect is to make the buyer jointly and severally liable in the manner already described.[62] Such notices are being registered at a rate of about 4,000 a year and are becoming more common.[63]

Statutory notices

14–13 Statutory repairs notices were discussed in an earlier chapter.[64] In tenements they can be a convenient solution for the failure of the owners to reach agreement; and at any rate they are used much more for tenements than for property of any other type. On the other hand, local authorities are often reluctant to serve statutory notices because of the poor prospects for recovery in the event that the authority has to carry out the work itself, and there is considerable regional variation in this respect.[65]

It is common practice for the local authority to serve a notice on all the flats, even though not all are liable under the TMS, or by virtue of the titles, and even though the problem in question (e.g. wood rot in certain joists) does not affect all the flats. This blanket-bombing is lawful, and if the council does the work it will normally bill all the owners. If that happens, readjustment in terms of the titles or, if the repairs are not covered by the titles, of the TMS is usually possible,[66] but that readjustment is simply as between the parties and does not affect the council. In addition to requiring particular repairs, local authorities can also serve a maintenance order requiring the owners to make a maintenance plan to run for a fixed period not exceeding five years.[67] After approval by the owners of a majority of the flats, the plan is registered by the local authority in the Land or Sasine Register.[68]

Buying a flat

14–14 As well as the normal types of issue,[69] the purchase of a flat involves a number of specialities.[70] In the first place, the titles must be read against the

---

[60] 2004 Act s.12(5).

[61] 2004 Act s.12(3).

[62] For criticism, see Donald B. Reid, in Robert Rennie (ed.), *The Promised Land: Property Law Reform* (2008), paras 6–60 to 6–62.

[63] Reid and Gretton, *Conveyancing 2009*, p.70

[64] See above, paras 4–29 to 4–32.

[65] For example, a study in 2010 showed that, since the Building (Scotland) Act 2003 came into force, only six out of 32 local authorities have served the defective building notices and dangerous building notices which the Act permits. See Reid and Gretton, *Conveyancing 2010*, p.70.

[66] TMS r.4.1(d), which then has the effect of engaging the liability set out in r.4.2.

[67] Housing (Scotland) Act 2006 s.42.

[68] 2006 Act ss.46(3) and 61(1)(e), (3). For further details, see Gordon and Wortley (3rd edn), paras 15–149 to 15–156.

[69] See above, Ch.7.

[70] And see also above, para.14–05, discussing the problem of extensions by top floor flats into the roof void.

background of the 2004 Act and in particular of the TMS. In the absence of a title provision, the default statutory law will apply.[71]

Secondly, as a flat will almost always involve shared liability for certain parts, it is important to check both the parts and the extent of the liability. Usually, this can be ascertained from the title to the flat that is being bought and without the need to look at the titles to other flats.[72] Thus:

- If, in that title, a real burden imposes a share of the cost of maintaining a particular part, that share represents the actual liability—unless, exceptionally, the burdens in the titles of the different flats add up to less than 100 per cent of liability.[73]
- If there is no real burden but the part is common property (whether under the title or the Act), liability for maintenance is determined by the size of the purchaser's *pro indiviso* share.[74]
- If there is no real burden and the part is not common property, there is no liability for maintenance except in respect of the key parts of the building (mainly the roof and external walls).[75] Liability is then either equal or (if one flat in the tenement is more than one and a half times the size of another) by floor area.[76]

By contrast to the position before the 2004 Act, it is no longer necessary, in the purchase of a top flat, to examine the titles of the other flats in order to determine liability for roof repairs. For, as a key part of the building, the roof is automatically scheme property. This means that if the titles do not apportion liability, liability is apportioned by the TMS, and that (unless the title to the flat so provides) there is no question of the owner of the top flat being left with sole liability (as could be the position under the former common law).

A third topic is rights to the solum. One view of the old law was that it was not safe to acquire an upper flat unless it carried a right of common property in the ground itself.[77] But, whatever the merits of this view, it has no application to the law in the 2004 Act. In the event of a tenement being burnt down or demolished, any owner (including the owner of an upper flat) is entitled to have the site sold and the net proceeds divided, and no special rights attach to the person who happens to own the solum.[78] In practice, the titles often make the solum common property; but where this is not done—where, in other words, the default rule applies so that the solum goes with the lowest flat—this does not present a difficulty for the acquirer of an upper flat.

Finally, it is necessary to be alert for repairs which have already been agreed upon by the owners, for in some circumstances the purchaser will have joint and several liability for the cost with the seller.[79] It is also necessary to be alert

---

[71] See above, paras 14–02, 14–03 and 14–06 to 14–08.

[72] See above, paras 14–08 and 14–09.

[73] Real burdens prevail over the default rules in the TMS: see 2004 Act s.4(6).

[74] TMS r.4.2(a). In some cases, however, the size of a share can only be discovered by examining the titles to the other flats.

[75] Key parts are scheme property under TMS r.1.2(c).

[76] TMS r.4.2(b).

[77] Donald B. Reid, in Robert Rennie (ed.), *The Promised Land: Property Law Reform* (2008), para.6–39.

[78] 2004 Act s.22.

[79] See above, para.14–12.

for statutory notices.[80] In practice, these matters are usually the subject of express provision in the missives, for example by having the seller warrant that there are no common repair schemes or statutory notices, and by providing for a retention from the price in the event that the buyer might incur liability.[81]

HOUSING ESTATES AND OTHER COMMUNITIES

Meaning of "community"

14–15   The TMS applies only to tenements. For other types of community, the Title Conditions (Scotland) Act 2003 provides a parallel but much slighter set of default rules, which we may name the Community Management Scheme ("CMS").[82] The CMS applies only in respect of a "community", defined in the Act as "units subject to community burdens";[83] and "community burdens" are in turn defined as mutually enforceable real burdens imposed under a common scheme.[84] The relationship of the CMS with community burdens should be noted. On the one hand, the CMS comprises default rules which must give way to community burdens; but on the other hand, some community burdens at least are needed to give the CMS life, for if there are no community burdens, there can be no community.[85] A typical community is a housing estate or a commercial or mixed-use development.

Even where a "community" exists, the CMS does not apply in two cases where, self-evidently, it is not needed.[86] One is where the community is already governed by the DMS.[87] The other is in respect of a community which comprises a single tenement and so is governed by the TMS. The CMS, therefore, does not apply to single tenements. But where a community comprises two or more tenements, or a mixed development of tenements and villas, the CMS will apply to the community as a whole although it will not apply within individual tenements.

CMS: management

14–16   The CMS replicates the most important rules of the TMS in respect of management and maintenance. In relation to the former, the owners of a majority of houses or other units in a community can agree to the appointment of a manager, and to delegate to the manager certain of their powers, including the power to carry out maintenance, enforce community burdens, and vary or discharge community burdens. All must contribute equally to the manager's salary.[88] A positive decision by the owners is needed: a manager is not regarded as appointed under this provision if he was originally appointed in some other

---

[80] See above, para.14–13.

[81] See e.g. Combined Standard Clauses (2009) cl.5; Aberdeen and Aberdeenshire Standard Clauses (2007) cll.2 and 5.

[82] Title Conditions (Scotland) Act 2003 ss.28–31A.

[83] 2003 Act s.26(2). A sheltered housing development is a community even where the warden's flat and other special units are exempt from the community burdens.

[84] 2003 Act s.25. See further below, paras 15–03 to 15–07.

[85] The TMS, by contrast, applies whether there are community burdens or not.

[86] 2003 Act s.31A.

[87] For the DMS, see below, paras 15–08 to 15–14.

[88] 2003 Act s.31.

way (such as by the developer) and has simply been allowed to continue on expiry of the earlier basis with the tacit consent of the majority.[89]

A majority of owners can also dismiss a manager, regardless of how or by whom the manager was originally appointed, although the power cannot be used in respect of a manager whose appointment is attributable to a subsisting manager burden.[90] In sheltered housing developments, in particular, the power to dismiss has been used in respect of management companies inherited from a feudal past. For such developments, however, the required majority is two thirds and not a simple majority[91]; and even where the management company is dismissed, there is often the practical difficulty that the company owns the warden's flat and other parts of the development, and is unwilling to relinquish them to the new manager.[92]

Decisions taken under the CMS are binding on the owners in the community and on their successors as owners.[93]

CMS: maintenance

Where community burdens impose an obligation to maintain, a decision to   14–17
carry out the maintenance can be taken by the owners of a majority of units so bound.[94] That may or may not be the same as a majority of units in the community. So if, for example, the community comprises 100 properties but the owners of only 17 of the 100 are taken bound to maintain a particular part, then agreement must be reached by at least nine owners out of the 17. As with the TMS, the owners can further decide that the estimated cost should be collected in advance of the maintenance being instructed, and provision is made in the legislation for maintenance bank accounts and like matters.[95]

---

[89] *Peverel Scotland Ltd v Giffen*, Unreported April 2010 Elgin Sheriff Court; *Strathclyde Business Park (Management) Ltd v BAE Systems Pension Funds Trustees Ltd*, 2010 G.W.D. 39-791.

[90] 2003 Act s.28(1)(d), (4). For manager burdens, see below, para.15–05. A manager burden normally subsists for five years.

[91] 2003 Act s.54(5)(a).

[92] See *Sheltered Housing Management Ltd v Bon Accord Bonding Co Ltd* [2010] CSIH 42; 2010 S.C. 516. And see further Reid and Gretton, *Conveyancing 2010*, pp.116–21.

[93] 2003 Act s.30.

[94] 2003 Act s.29(1), (2)(a).

[95] 2003 Act s.29(2)(b), (3)–(10).

CHAPTER 15

COMMUNITY BURDENS AND THE DEVELOPMENT MANAGEMENT SCHEME

FORMS OF REGULATION

Making the choice

15–01 As explained in the previous chapter, legislation provides a system of default regulation both for individual blocks of flats ("tenements") and also for entire developments such as housing estates or groups of properties in mixed or commercial use. For the former, the default regime is the Tenement Management Scheme ("TMS"), for the latter it is a set of rules so modest in nature and scope that the legislation does not provide a name but which we may call the Community Management Scheme ("CMS").[1] These are, it should be stressed, default rules only: in building and selling off units it is a decision for the developer whether or to what extent the default rules should be left in place or should be replaced. Two mechanisms are available to modify or replace the default rules. One, familiar and long-established, is to impose real burdens— called by the 2003 Act "community burdens"[2]—in practice by use of a deed of conditions.[3] The other, available only since 2009, is to use the off-the-peg statutory scheme known as the Development Management Scheme ("DMS"), either in the version set out in the legislation or with such variations and additions as the developer chooses.[4] The conveyancing mechanism for applying the DMS is a deed of application. Although the DMS and community burdens often cover similar ground, their relationship to the default rules is different. Whereas the DMS displaces the default rules in their entirety,[5] the default rules continue to apply alongside community burdens giving way only where they are inconsistent with a rule set out in the latter. This difference in result is due to the elaborate and sophisticated nature of the DMS: when the DMS is in use, it will already cover the topics in the default rules, making a clean break possible. Thus with the DMS one can find all the rules for a development in a single place, whereas with community burdens it will usually be necessary to consult both the deed of conditions and also the relevant default rules.[6]

---

[1] For all details, see above, Ch.14.

[2] Provided (as is invariably the case) that the burdens are mutually enforceable within the community: see Title Conditions (Scotland) Act 2003 s.25.

[3] See below, paras 15–03 to 15–07.

[4] See below, paras 15–08 to 15–14. The DMS is set out in the Title Conditions (Scotland) Act 2003 (Development Management Scheme) Order 2009 (SI 2009/729).

[5] Title Conditions (Scotland) Act 2003 s.31A(2); Tenements (Scotland) Act 2004 s.4(2).

[6] Although it would be a poor deed of conditions which did not cover all the ground set out in the CMS, making recourse to those rules, at least, unnecessary.

The choices available to a developer, and the consequences of those choices, can be summarised in tabular form:

Table 1 Individual block of flats

Action	Applicable rules
Do nothing	TMS
Deed of conditions	Community burdens in the deed + TMS
Deed of application	DMS

Table 2 Entire development

Action	Applicable rules
Do nothing	TMS for blocks of flats, CMS for other properties
Deed of conditions	Community burdens in deed + TMS for blocks of flats, CMS for other properties
Deed of application	DMS

Evaluation

The course of action chosen will depend partly on the circumstances of the 15–02 case and partly on the individual preference of developers or their law agents. For a straightforward block of flats, there is quite a lot to be said for doing nothing and allowing the TMS to apply in its entirety. Admittedly, the TMS is rather basic, but it covers all the essential ground, and is well and (on the whole) clearly drafted. If a few simple rules are what is wanted, there seems little point in undertaking the labour, and risk, of preparing one's own. On the other hand, the TMS deals only with management and maintenance, so that a developer who wishes to impose use restrictions (e.g. prohibition of trade, business or profession) must augment the TMS with appropriate community burdens.

For an entire development the judgment is likely to be different. No one would peril a complex project (if it is tenement-based) on the TMS, still less (if it is not) on the minimal rules contained in the CMS. In such cases the effective choice is between community burdens and the DMS. Community burdens have the advantage to conveyancers of long familiarity, and are especially suitable for modest developments. But the larger the development, the more attractive the DMS is likely to seem. For, in the first place, the DMS is impressive as to form. It is clearly laid out, easy to read, and has been written with care by professional draftsmen. It is infinitely more attractive than the labyrinthine intricacies of many deeds of conditions. Secondly, the DMS is also impressive as to content. The development is managed through an attractive blend of democracy and autocracy: rapid day-to-day decisions by a manager with full executive power, but subject to the ultimate control of the members at a general meeting. There is provision for annual budgets, and there is the possibility of saving for major repairs by means of a reserve fund. Thirdly, the DMS achieves something which community burdens cannot: the owners' association is a juristic person. Thus the association can hold property—including heritable property such as "common" areas—in its own name,[7] and through the agency of its manager[8] it can open bank accounts, borrow money, make investments, enter into contracts and enforce obligations owed to it. Finally, there are various advantages of a technical nature. No interest to enforce is needed.[9] It is possible to make unregistered but binding rules for the use of recreational facilities.[10] And, as with tenements,[11] the sheriff court has a general supervisory jurisdiction and is empowered to resolve disputes.[12]

COMMUNITY BURDENS

Creation by deed of conditions

15–03　　Typically, community burdens are set out in a deed of conditions which is granted by the developer-owner and registered before any of the break-off dispositions are granted.[13] Yet as real burdens can be created in a deed of any kind,[14] it is also possible and, with small developments, sometimes tempting, to put the community burdens into the break-off dispositions rather than taking the trouble to use a separate deed of conditions. The temptation should be resisted.[15] To create community burdens in dispositions involves formidable difficulties with the proper nomination of benefited properties—for, with each succeeding disposition, the land held by the developer continues to shrink—and with s.12 of the 2003 Act which, unless expressly disapplied, strips land of the status of benefited property as soon as it is broken off from the parent plot.[16] Further, as progressively more units are sold, so the potential benefited properties proliferate, with a corresponding increase in the cost and complexity of "dual" registration. The firm, and surely correct, advice of Registers of Scotland is that deeds of conditions should always be used for community burdens, no matter how small the community.[17]

Drafting

15–04　　As well as the usual rules, considered elsewhere,[18] which apply in the drafting of real burdens, a number of specialities affect community burdens. First, so long as the conditions are declared "community burdens", there is no need to provide separately that they are "real burdens".[19] Secondly, a mere declaration

---

[7] The extent of the association's powers is set out in DMS rr.3.2 and 3.3. For example, while it can own any part of the development, it cannot acquire other land.

[8] DMS r.4.4.

[9] By contrast, with community burdens the requirement of interest can be a significant obstacle to enforcement: see above, para.13–13.

[10] DMS r.3.6. By r.8(g) the manager must keep a copy. The power to make unregistered rules cannot be achieved by community burdens even where, in a spirit of hopefulness, express provision for this is made, as it sometimes is. See Reid and Gretton, *Conveyancing 2002*, p.67.

[11] Tenements (Scotland) Act 2004 s.6.

[12] 2009 Order art.15.

[13] For deeds of conditions, see above, para.13–11.

[14] Title Conditions (Scotland) Act 2003 s.4(2).

[15] For a full account of the difficulties, see Reid and Gretton, *Conveyancing 2007*, pp.80–83.

[16] See above, para.13–19.

[17] Beveridge, (2008) 53 J.L.S.S. Feb./17.

[18] See above, para.13–10.

[19] 2003 Act s.4(2)(a), (3).

that the conditions are community burdens creates mutual enforceability without further provision.[20] Thirdly, provided the "community" is nominated and identified in the deed, there is no need for separate nomination and identification of the benefited and burdened properties.[21] This is because, with community burdens, the same properties are both benefited and burdened. Indeed the "community" is usually the whole development. Finally, while community burdens may ordinarily be varied or discharged by agreement of the owners of a majority of units,[22] it is competent to raise or lower this threshold in the deed of conditions, or to confer power of variation on the manager.[23] Usually the alteration will be in a downwards direction, for example to 40 per cent or 30 per cent of units, in recognition of the difficulty of obtaining large numbers of signatures. Different percentages can be provided for different classes of burden. At the same time it is competent, if desired, to exclude s.35 of the 2003 Act, which gives the alternative of variation and discharge by signature of all neighbours within four metres.[24]

Content is a matter for the developer and is limited only by the general requirements for real burdens, discussed elsewhere.[25] Helpfully, s.26(1) gives a list of possible topics in relation to management: the appointment and dismissal of a manager, and the manager's powers and duties; the nomination of the first manager; decision-making procedures and the subjects on which decisions can be made; and dispute resolution. In addition, most developers will add a number of use restrictions. Under the Act, a decision made in accordance with the procedure set out in community burdens is binding on all the owners and on their successors as owners.[26]

In drafting, the default rules should be borne in mind, for they will continue to apply except insofar as displaced by the community burdens. Admittedly, the new burdens would be remarkably unambitious if they did not displace most or all of the CMS. But, for tenemental communities it will often be the case that some at least of the TMS rules will survive. Often, the result is far from user-friendly, with owners having to have regard to both the deed of conditions and the TMS in order to work out the applicable regime. The difficulty is avoided if, in drafting the deed of conditions, one begins by writing out the TMS and then proceeds by deleting and adding to the rules as desired. The result will then be a single document, drafted in a uniform style.

As well as community burdens, deeds of conditions often contain servitudes, whether "community" servitudes, mutually enforceable within the community, or servitudes in favour of a property which lies outside the community. There is also likely to be a list of the parts of the development that are to be owned in common, e.g. parking or recreational areas.[27] However, a deed of conditions cannot actually convey the common parts: this must be done, separately, by the dispositions. Hence, it is necessary for each break-off disposition to say not only that the property is subject to the burdens in the deed of conditions, but also that it includes the appropriate share in the common areas

---

[20] 2003 Act s.27.
[21] 2003 Act s.4(2)(c), (4).
[22] See below, para.15–07.
[23] 2003 Act s.33(1)(a).
[24] 2003 Act s.35(1)(b).
[25] See above, para.13–07.
[26] 2003 Act s.30.
[27] Such areas must be properly described: see above, para.12–25.

specified in the deed of conditions. In other words, the deed of conditions needs to be referred to twice, once for the burdens and once (in the parts-and-pertinents clause) for the common parts.

Manager burdens

15–05 Often, deeds of conditions allow the developer to manage the development—or to appoint the manager—at least for as long as some units remain unsold. This is permitted under the 2003 Act, but subject to limits.[28] A burden which reserves the right to manage (or appoint the manager) is called by the Act a manager burden. This is a personal real burden, i.e. a burden held by the developer personally and not in the capacity as owner of any particular unsold unit.[29] Nonetheless such burdens are enforceable only for so long as the developer continues to own at least one unit. And in addition manager burdens have a limited life, normally of five years, but reduced to three years in the case of sheltered housing and extended to 30 years in the case of properties sold under the right-to-buy legislation.[30] Thereafter the developer can have no further say in the development.[31]

Where a manager burden is included, deeds of conditions usually make provision for how a manager is to be appointed once the burden expires. Absent such a provision, the default rule is that a manager can be appointed by the owners of a majority of units.[32] Once the Property Factors (Scotland) Act 2011 is in force, managers in residential developments will require to be registered and will be subject to a Code of Conduct.

Registration

15–06 As both benefited and burdened properties are the same in community burdens, the requirement of dual registration is satisfied by registering the deed of conditions once only, against the development or "community".[33] Normally, real burdens take effect on registration. But while developers are keen that the burdens should affect any properties which are sold, they may be less keen that they should affect such property as remains in their hands. For that would be to commit them to a building plan from which they may later wish to depart. The solution, permitted by the 2003 Act, is to postpone the date of creation; but if burdens are not to be created on registration, the deed must either specify a later fixed date or must tie creation to the registration of some other deed.[34] With deeds of conditions a common practice is to defer creation, for any individual unit, until registration of a break-off disposition into which the deed of conditions has been duly incorporated.[35] If there is then no break-off conveyance, or

---

[28] 2003 Act s.63.

[29] For personal real burdens see above, para.13–20. In theory a manager burden could also be constituted as a praedial (i.e. ordinary) real burden, but it would be difficult to know which unit to select as the benefited property, given that any unit is likely to be sold.

[30] The time periods are calculated from the date of registration of the deed of conditions: 2003 Act s.63(5), (7).

[31] 2003 Act s.3(8) prevents developers from retaining a right to release owners from having to comply with community burdens.

[32] 2003 Act s.28; TMS r.3.1(c).

[33] See above, para.13–12.

[34] 2003 Act s.4(1).

[35] In fact this was the law between 1874, when deeds of conditions were first allowed, and 1979 when, by s.17 of the Land Registration (Scotland) Act 1979, such deeds took effect immediately on registration. But the effect of s.17 could be excluded and this was commonly done.

if the conveyance does not incorporate the deed of conditions, the burdens never become live in respect of the unit in question.

Variation and discharge

The variation and discharge of real burdens was discussed in an earlier 15–07 chapter,[36] but there are some specialities which only apply to community burdens.

Normally, a minute of waiver must be signed by all of the benefited proprietors.[37] But recognising that this will rarely be achievable in a development of any size, the 2003 Act allows community burdens to be varied or discharged, in respect of all or part of the development, (i) by the owners of a majority of the units (or by the owners of such units as may be specified in the deed of conditions) or (ii) by the manager of the community, if duly authorised, whether in the deed of conditions or by the owners.[38] Any owner who did not sign must be sent a copy of the deed and a notice in prescribed form, and allowed a period of eight weeks to apply to the Lands Tribunal for preservation of the burden in its original form.[39] Assuming that no such application is made—or is made but is unsuccessful—the Tribunal endorses the minute of waiver accordingly and it can then be registered.[40] The deed takes effect on registration. Where the necessary majority cannot be assembled, it is open to one quarter of the owners to apply to the Lands Tribunal for a variation in respect of all or part of the development.[41]

An alternative method is slightly less cumbersome but can be used only to release individual properties rather than the development as a whole. This allows for the variation or discharge of a community burden (other than a facility or service burden) by a deed executed by the owners of the burdened property and of all benefited properties which lie within four metres (but disregarding roads of less than 20 metres in width).[42] The advantage, as compared to the previous method, is the relatively small number of signatories. The disadvantage is the possibility of defeat by a single unco-operative neighbour. As before, intimation must be given to the other owners, who may then make application to the Lands Tribunal, but it is sufficient intimation to fix a notice to the burdened property and to one or more lamp posts, and nothing need be sent.[43]

The scope of variation has been considered by the Inner House. While "variation" is defined in the Act as including the "imposition of a new obligation",[44] the court's view was that new burdens must have some connection with the

---

[36] See above, paras 13–22 to 13–25.

[37] 2003 Act s.15.

[38] 2003 Act s.33.

[39] 2003 Act s.34. See *Sheltered Housing Management Ltd v Jack*, 2007 G.W.D. 32-533; *Fleeman v Lyon*, 2009 G.W.D. 32-539.

[40] 2003 Act s.37(2) (as applied by s.34(4)). By s.37(4) the deed must also be endorsed with a docket, sworn before a notary public and signed by the grantee, that intimation was properly carried out

[41] 2003 Act s.91. See *Fenwick v National Trust for Scotland*, 2009 G.W.D. 32-538. For the Lands Tribunal, see below, Ch.16.

[42] 2003 Act s.35. This method is also unavailable in respect of burdens in sheltered housing developments.

[43] 2003 Act s.36. But sending is available as an alternative.

[44] 2003 Act s.122(1).

burdens that they replace, and that it is not possible to use the mechanisms just discussed for "the creation of distinct new burdens".[45]

Joining

15–08   The Development Management Scheme ("DMS") is a model statutory scheme for the management and maintenance of developments such as housing estates and blocks of flats. The text is readily accessible, and available for down-loading, in a statutory instrument.[47] Additional legislative provision is made in the 2003 Act.[48] As an opt-in scheme, the DMS only applies if it is brought into operation by registration of the appropriate deed, known as a deed of application.[49] This can apply the DMS as enacted or with such changes as seem desirable or necessary; only Pt 2, which contains mandatory provisions about the owners' association, cannot be varied.[50]

The deed of application is granted by or on behalf of the owner of the land. As with deeds of conditions, it takes effect—and so the DMS becomes live—immediately on registration unless provision is made for a later date. In theory the DMS could be used for developments which already exist and have been sold on, but this would require the agreement of all the owners. In practice, therefore, its main use is for new developments, where only a single person—the developer—has to execute the deed.

No particular form has to be used for a deed of application, but styles are available.[51] The following information must be included in order to fill certain blanks in the DMS itself: the name of the owners' association[52]; the name and address of the first person who is to manage the development; and definitions of (a) the development, (b) the scheme property, and (c) unit.[53] "The develop-ment" is the land to which the DMS is to apply,[54] while the "scheme property" is that part of the development—for example, landscaped areas, roads, and parking bays—which is to be managed and maintained under the scheme. There is thus an implicit distinction between (i) the parts of the development that are to be maintained by everyone, or at least by groups of owners, and (ii) the parts—in other words, individual properties—which are the sole responsibility of individual owners. Where the development comprises or includes flatted

---

[45] *Sheltered Housing Management Ltd v Bon Accord Bonding Co Ltd* [2010] CSIH 42; 2010 S.C. 516 at para.31.
[46] For a detailed guide, see Scottish Law Commission, Report on *Real Burdens* (Scot. Law Com. No.181, 2000), Pt 8.
[47] Title Conditions (Scotland) Act 2003 (Development Management Scheme) Order 2009 (SI 2009/729). Like all UK legislation, it is available at *http://www.legislation.gov.uk*.
[48] 2003 Act Pt 6 (ss.71–74). The reason why the scheme is severed from the Act and contained in a Westminster SI is that it provides for the owners' association to be a body corporate and is thus (on one view) not within the legislative competency of the Scottish Parliament.
[49] 2003 Act s.71(1).
[50] 2009 Order art.6.
[51] See Reid and Gretton, *Conveyancing 2009*, pp.133–34.
[52] This must take the form either of "The Owners' Association ..." or "the ... Owners' Association": see 2009 Order art.6(3). The same provision is made in s.71(2)(b) of the 2003 Act except that, oddly, the apostrophe is omitted. The apostrophe is used throughout the DMS itself.
[53] 2003 Act s.71(2).
[54] 2009 Order art.2.

property, it is necessary to include under "scheme property" those parts of the tenement building which are to be maintained in common. But in case of accidental omissions, a list of key parts—roof, external walls, foundations and the like—is automatically deemed to be scheme property.[55] This list is identical to the default meaning of "scheme property" in the TMS.[56]

The owners' association

The DMS has two principal aims. One is to provide a robust management 15–09 structure, which acknowledges that owners are often too busy or lethargic to play an active role and that professional help will often be the best solution. The other is to provide for regular maintenance and for the building up of a reserve fund to deal with major repairs.

Management is organised around an owners' association and a manager. The former is a body corporate, i.e. a juristic person, but not a company.[57] It thus has the advantages of incorporation but without the disadvantages, and so avoids the mistake made by the equivalent scheme in England and Wales ("Commonhold") where the association is a company limited by guarantee.[58] Unlike a company, an owners' association is not registered anywhere, and there are no publicity requirements. All owners of units (i.e. the individual properties) are automatically association members for as long as they remain owners.[59] The association meets once a year in an annual general meeting and can meet more often in certain circumstances.[60] The DMS makes provision in respect of the conduct of meetings and of voting.[61] The association has residual power, and can appoint or dismiss the manager and tell him or her what to do.[62] But the day-to-day running of the development is in the hands of the manager, who is thus the key figure in the DMS.[63]

The manager

The manager can be an individual or a juristic person such as a company or 15–10 partnership. Although it is possible for one of the owners to act as manager, it is envisaged that in most cases the manager will be a professional and as such will be subject to regulation under the Property Factors (Scotland) Act 2011.[64] As already mentioned, the first manager is nominated in the deed of application,[65] and serves until the first annual general meeting, when he will either be reappointed or replaced.[66] It is up to the association to determine, at a

---

[55] 2009 Order art.20(2).

[56] For which see above, para.14–08.

[57] 2009 Order art.4(2). For the powers of the association, see DMS r.3.2.

[58] Commonhold and Leasehold Reform Act 2002 s.34. This is but one aspect of the very considerable complexity of Commonhold which no doubt explains why, so far, it has been virtually unused.

[59] DMS r.2.3.

[60] DMS r.9.

[61] DMS rr.10–12.

[62] DMS rr.4.2, 4.7 and 7.2.

[63] DMS rr.4.4 and 4.5.

[64] DMS r.4.1. At the time of writing the 2011 Act had not yet been brought into force. By s.2 it applies only to those who manage the common parts of residential property in the course of business.

[65] 2003 Act s.71(2)(c).

[66] DMS r.7.1.

general meeting, for how long a manager should be appointed and on what terms.[67]

The manager's duties are listed in r.8 of the DMS, and fall into four broad categories. The first is to keep the state of the scheme property under review and carry out routine maintenance.[68] This is done without the permission of the association, but improvements or alterations require the agreement of a majority of all owners.[69] The next is to organise and attend the annual general meeting and any other general meetings which become necessary or are requisitioned by the members,[70] and to implement any decisions which a meeting makes.[71] The third is to prepare accounts for the year just ended and propose a budget for the year to come.[72] The budget, which must be approved at a general meeting,[73] sets out the annual service charge and explains how it is to be spent.[74] This can include a contribution to a reserve (or sinking) fund which accumulates money for major repairs.[75] Finally, the manager must interact with members in various ways. The manager maintains a record of names and addresses, is notified when a unit changes hands,[76] and collects the service charge in the proportions set out in the DMS,[77] where the default rule (which can and no doubt often will be varied in the deed of application) is that each owner pays the same.[78] The manager can collect up to 25 per cent more by way of service charge than was agreed in the annual budget[79]; if yet more is needed the manager must obtain approval for a supplementary budget at a general meeting.[80] The manager also has the task of enforcing the rules of the DMS against individual members.[81] Unless, however, an appropriate addition has been made to the scheme,[82] individual members cannot enforce the DMS against each other. That is an important difference from the position under a conventional deed of conditions.

The manager acts alone: the DMS is careful to avoid the inertia of management by committee. But the members at a general meeting can, if they wish, set up a committee to advise the manager.[83] The manager must listen to such advice, but does not have to take it. Only a general meeting can tell the manager what to do (or not to do).

---

[67] DMS r.7.2.
[68] DMS r.8(a), (b).
[69] DMS r.13.1.
[70] DMS rr.9.1–9.4.
[71] DMS r.8(e).
[72] DMS rr.8(d) and 18.1.
[73] If it is rejected, there is provision in rr.18.3–18.5 for a revised budget.
[74] DMS r.18.2.
[75] Use of the reserve fund for this purpose requires the approval of a majority of all owners: see r.13.1.
[76] DMS rr.4.9 and 8(h).
[77] DMS rr.19.3–19.6.
[78] DMS r.19.1.
[79] DMS rr.20.1 and 20.2.
[80] DMS r.20.3.
[81] DMS r.8(f).
[82] 2009 Order art.10(1).
[83] DMS r.15.

The Scottish Law Commission's guide

In its Report on *Real Burdens* the Scottish Law Commission included a guide, 15–11
written in non-technical language, which is intended to be given to owners
who live in developments regulated by the DMS.[84] A client-friendly way of
doing this would be to reproduce the DMS with the relevant part of the guide
after each rule. Obviously, the guide will have to be adjusted to take account of
any variations made by the developer.[85]

DMS rules as quasi community burdens

The DMS rules are not real burdens. Yet they bear a close legal and functional 15–12
resemblance to community burdens and are governed by many of the same
statutory provisions, either directly (because the relevant sections of the 2003
Act are declared to apply)[86] or indirectly (because the relevant sections are
lightly adapted and written out in the 2009 Order). So for example, DMS rules
are subject to the same or similar provisions as real burdens in relation to
content, liability, interpretation, variation or discharge by voluntary deed or by
the Lands Tribunal, and extinction by acquiescence and negative prescription.
Take the case of variation and discharge. As already seen, a community burden
can be varied or discharged for the whole community either by a deed granted
by the owners of a majority of units (or by a manager acting on behalf of that
majority) or by the Lands Tribunal on application by the owners of a quarter of
the units.[87] Comparable provisions apply to DMS rules. A deed which varies or
discharges a rule for the whole development must be approved by an absolute
majority of owners at a general meeting and then signed by the manager[88];
while the owners of a quarter of the units can make a direct application to the
Lands Tribunal.[89]

Adding amenity provisions

In practice a developer is likely to want to add amenity provisions—provisions 15–13
preventing or controlling business use, or the parking of commercial vehicles,
or the keeping of cats, dogs, dragons, etc.—to the rules on management and
maintenance already contained in the DMS. If so, the developer faces two
choices. The first is whether to constitute the provisions as community burdens
or as DMS rules. Either can readily be done. It would be an easy thing to add a
group of community burdens to the deed of application, thus resulting in what
would be in effect a combined deed of application and deed of conditions. Or
the amenity provisions could simply be added to the DMS itself in the form of
a new group of rules constituting a new part (Pt 5) of the scheme.

If the developer elects for the latter course—and this will usually be simpler
and more elegant—then there is a further choice to be made. As it stands, all
enforcement in the DMS lies in the hands of the manager, and—unlike with

---

[84] See Report, pp.438–42.
[85] The guide is in any case slightly out-of-date due to a small number of changes which were
made to the original version of the DMS produced by the Scottish Law Commission. A fully
updated version of the guide can be found in Reid and Gretton, *Conveyancing 2009*, pp.149–53.
[86] 2003 Act s.72 read with 2009 Order art.5.
[87] See above, para.15–07.
[88] 2009 Order art.8; DMS r.16.2.
[89] 2009 Order art.23.

community burdens—there can be no neighbour-to-neighbour enforcement.[90]
But neighbour enforcement rights can be added if that is what is wanted.[91]
Enforcement by the manager only may be thought to have certain advantages.
It avoids the embarrassment of suing one's neighbour; enforcement is at the
expense of the association and not of an individual owner; and—of particular
significance given the case law on this topic[92]—there is no need to show
interest to enforce. This final point requires emphasis. Many amenity provisions in a deed of conditions are not, in reality, enforceable because no owner
would ever be able to show the requisite interest. By contrast, a manager
requires no interest under the DMS and all DMS provisions are potentially
enforceable. If neighbour enforcement rights are added to the DMS, there is a
statutory requirement of interest to enforce,[93] but the rules remain enforceable
by the manager even without interest.

Leaving

15–14   Developments crumble and may eventually have to be demolished. For that
reason among others it may become necessary to bring the DMS to an end.
Leaving is much like joining: with the agreement of an absolute majority of
owners at a general meeting, the manager signs and registers a deed known as
a deed of disapplication.[94] This can be challenged within eight weeks in the
Lands Tribunal by disaffected members.[95] Otherwise the DMS comes to an
end, normally on registration of the deed, and the manager must then wind up
the owners' association and distribute any surplus funds to the members.[96] The
association itself is automatically dissolved six months after the DMS ceases
to apply.[97]

---

[90] DMS r.8(f).
[91] 2009 Order art.10(1).
[92] See above, para.13–13.
[93] 2009 Order art.10(2), (3).
[94] 2003 Act s.73; DMS r.16.2.
[95] 2003 Act ss.74, 90(1)(d).
[96] DMS rr.6.1–6.3. The default position is that each member receives the same amount: see r.17.
[97] DMS r.6.4, but subject to r.6.5.

CHAPTER 16

VARIATION AND DISCHARGE BY
THE LANDS TRIBUNAL

INTRODUCTION[1]

Jurisdiction

Since 1971 the Lands Tribunal for Scotland[2] has been able to waive or vary   16–01
title conditions, and the Tribunal's powers were refined and re-enacted by Pt 9
of the Title Conditions (Scotland) Act 2003. In addition to title conditions—
real burdens, servitudes, and, rare in practice, conditions in long leases[3]—the
Tribunal is also able vary or discharge the rules of the Development
Management Scheme as they apply to particular developments.[4] Other powers,
not considered further in this chapter, include the power to renew a real burden
which has been the subject of a notice of termination under the sunset rule,[5]
and to preserve community burdens where a minute of waiver has been
executed by a majority of owners under s.33 of the 2003 Act or by close neighbours under s.35.[6]

Usage

Conveyancers, naturally enough, are suspicious of litigation, and at one time   16–02
the Lands Tribunal tended to be under-used. But with the proliferation of
enforcement rights brought about by the 2003 Act[7]—and the consequent difficulty or impossibility of obtaining minutes of waiver—it has come to seem an
increasingly attractive option. In fact a Lands Tribunal application is often an

---

[1] For a helpful account of the Lands Tribunal's jurisdiction by a current Tribunal member, see
Wright, in Robert Rennie (ed.), *The Promised Land: Property Law Reform* (2008), Ch.7.

[2] The Lands Tribunal is not to be confused with the Land Court. The Lands Tribunal, as well as
having the jurisdiction mentioned in the text, also has an important role in hearing and determining
disputes about the "right to buy" legislation, and also disputes in relation to the Land Registration
(Scotland) Act 1979.

[3] For a rare example, see *Co-operative Group Ltd v Propinvest Asset Management*, Unreported
September 17, 2010 Lands Tribunal.

[4] See Pt 7 of the Title Conditions (Scotland) Act 2003 (Development Management Scheme)
Order 2009 (SSI 2009/729), which is a close copy of Pt 9 of the Title Conditions (Scotland) Act
2003. For the DMS generally, see above, paras 15–08 to 15–14.

[5] 2003 Act s.90(1)(b)(i). For the sunset rule, see above, para.13–24. For examples, see *Brown v
Richardson*, 2007 G.W.D. 28-490; *Council for Music in Hospitals v Trustees for Richard Gerald
Associates*, 2008 S.L.T. (Lands Tr) 17.

[6] 2003 Act s.90(1)(c). For waiver of community burdens, see above, para.15–07. For an
example, see *Fleeman v Lyon*, 2009 G.W.D. 32-539.

[7] Particularly due to s.53 of the 2003 Act: see above, paras 13–14 to 13–16.

essentially administrative process rather than "real" litigation. And it has two key advantages over other methods of removing title conditions.[8]

In the first place, a variation or discharge by the Tribunal has universal effect. On registration it clears the title.[9] Thus the problems of large numbers of enforcers, or their identification, cease to matter. And, in a change from the previous law, it does not even matter if, on a proper view of the law, the condition had already ceased to exist: the Lands Tribunal will discharge it anyway—will kill the already dead.[10] Alternatively, the Tribunal can be asked to pronounce on the validity of a real burden—a new jurisdiction—although experience so far shows that this option is rarely chosen.[11]

In the second place, there is the benefit of certainty. A person who proceeds in any other way does so with an element of risk. If he ignores a real burden, he runs the risk that it is still alive and that neighbours will reach for interdict. If he seeks a minute of waiver, he runs the risk that he has failed to identify the correct enforcers and so get the correct signatures. But with the Lands Tribunal there is only the risk of failure in the application—and that risk, as we shall see shortly, is a relatively small one. Assuming that the application is successful, the burden is varied or discharged for all time.

Prospects of success

16–03   Because the jurisdiction is essentially discretionary, within the limits of certain statutory criteria,[12] the outcome of a Tribunal application can sometimes be difficult to predict. More often than not, however, applications are unopposed, in which case they are granted without further inquiry if they relate to real burdens (but not to servitudes or other title conditions).[13] And even in opposed cases, around three quarters of applications are successful,[14] with expenses generally following success.[15] A cumulative table of all opposed applications that have been heard under the 2003 Act, with a summary of the facts and the result, is published on an annual basis and gives a good idea of how a future application is likely to fare.[16] Although Tribunal decisions are not usually reported, most are available on the Tribunal's website.[17] In the end, however, as the Tribunal has often emphasised,[18] each case turns on its facts and on the

---

[8] For other methods of discharging real burdens and servitudes, see above, paras 13–22 to 13–25 and 13–29.

[9] 2003 Act s.104(2).

[10] 2003 Act s.90(1)(a) allows the Lands Tribunal to discharge "a title condition (or purported title condition)".

[11] 2003 Act s.90(1)(a)(ii). This extends to rules of the DMS but not to servitudes. Examples are *Halladale (Shaftesbury) Ltd*, Unreported June 20, 2005 Lands Tribunal; *Clarke v Grantham*, 2009 G.W.D. 38-645.

[12] Set out in the 2003 Act s.100. See further below, paras 16–7 to 16–12.

[13] 2003 Act s.97. But this does not extent to facility burdens, service burdens, and burdens in sheltered housing developments.

[14] That is the figures for real burdens as of the end of 2010. The success rate for applications in respect of servitudes is even higher.

[15] See para.16–05.

[16] The table appears in Pt V of the annual volumes on conveyancing produced by the present writers. At the time of writing, the most recent appeared in Reid and Gretton, *Conveyancing 2010*, pp.189–95.

[17] *http://www.lands-tribunal-scotland.org.uk/records.html*. They are also summarised and commented on in the annual conveyancing volumes by the present writers.

[18] See e.g. *Ord v Mashford*, 2006 S.L.T. (Sh. Ct) 15 at 20D–E; *Graham v Lee*, Unreported June 18, 2009 at para.26.

impression made on the Tribunal by a visit to the site.[19] And where an application is successful, there remains the possibility, admittedly uncommon in practice, that an order for payment of compensation will be made.[20]

Procedure

Any person who is subject to a title condition is able to apply for its variation 16–04 or discharge.[21] For negative burdens, this means not only the burdened owner but also any tenant or a person having use of the property.[22] In the case of community burdens, the owners of at least one quarter of the units are entitled to make an application for global variation or discharge, i.e. variation or discharge as regards the whole community.[23] Standard applications are made on form TC90(1)(a).[24]

On receipt of an application, the Tribunal must intimate it to various parties, notably the benefited owner or owners (or the holder of the burden, in the case of a personal real burden).[25] Intimation must also be made to the burdened owner if he or she is not the applicant. The Tribunal may intimate to other parties, for example tenants, if it thinks fit.[26] The parties to whom intimation is made must be given at least 21 days to make representations.[27] Any party wishing to do so must give a written statement of the facts and contentions upon which it is intended to rely.[28] A fee of £25 is payable.[29]

What happens next depends on whether the application is opposed (i.e. representations are made) or unopposed. If the application is unopposed, and it relates to real burdens, the Tribunal must (with minor exceptions) grant it without further inquiry.[30] If it is opposed, or if it does not relate to real burdens, the Tribunal makes a site visit and there is then usually a hearing—although the case can also be disposed of on the basis of written submissions if the parties agree.[31] In reaching a decision the Tribunal must apply the statutory criteria set out in s.100 of the 2003 Act, and discussed below.[32]

If the application relates to real burdens and is unopposed, the process will be swift—about two months from start to finish—and the result sure. It will

---

[19] A good example of the crucial part which a site visit can play is *Faeley v Clark*, 2006 G.W.D. 28-626.

[20] For compensation, see below, paras 16–13 to 16–15.

[21] 2003 Act s.90(1)(a)(i).

[22] This is because such a person is subject to the burden: see above, para.13–13. A "negative burden" is one which consists of an obligation to refrain from doing something: see above, para.13–01.

[23] 2003 Act s.91. So far this has been little used, but see *Fenwick v National Trust for Scotland*, 2009 G.W.D. 32-538.

[24] Lands Tribunal for Scotland Rules 2003 (SSI 2003/452) Sch.2. The equivalent form for applications in respect of DMS rules is DMS 22(1)(a): see Lands Tribunal for Scotland Amendment Rules 2009 (SSI 2009/259) r.8.

[25] 2003 Act s.93(1).

[26] 2003 Act s.93(3).

[27] 2003 Act s.94(a)(ii).

[28] 2003 Act s.96(1).

[29] Item 23 in Sch.2 to the Lands Tribunal for Scotland Rules 1971 (SI 1971/218), as inserted by the Lands Tribunal for Scotland Amendment (Fees) Rules 2004 (SSI 2004/480).

[30] 2003 Act s.97. The exceptions are for facility burdens, service burdens, and burdens in sheltered or retirement housing developments.

[31] As happened for example in *Graham v Parker*, 2007 GWD 30-524.

[32] See below, paras 16–7 to 16–12.

also be quite cheap: a fee of £238[33] plus advertising and other expenses (and of course legal fees). So at the outset it is important to consider whether an application is likely to meet with opposition. An opposed application tends to take from four to six months, and there is a fee of £155 for each day that the Tribunal sits.[34] On the other hand, assuming that the application is successful, it should be possible to get some of this back by way of an order for expenses against the unsuccessful objector, as discussed in the next section.

Expenses

16–05   Although, like any court, the Tribunal has a discretion in relation to expenses, it is directed by the legislation to "have regard, in particular, to the extent to which the application, or any opposition to it, is successful".[35] The Tribunal has set out its approach to expenses in a number of cases.[36] No expenses are normally due for the period before the objector makes representations, including for the costs of legal research and drawing up the application. But thereafter expenses should follow success, meaning that an applicant who is only partially successful—because, for example, he altered his proposal in response to opposition,[37] or he was granted a variation when he asked for a complete discharge—will only receive part of his expenses.[38] As it is common for applications only to be granted to the extent needed to allow the applicant to carry out his proposed project, "applicants would be well advised to consider carefully exactly how much to ask for in applications".[39] Another reason for a reduction in expenses is where there has been an element of fault in the conduct of the case, for example a failure to seek agreement with the objectors,[40] or a poorly drawn application which does not give proper notice of the case. An applicant who is unsuccessful is liable for the expenses of the objectors even although the application was reasonable in itself and was conducted in a reasonable way.[41]

The position of objectors

16–06   Thus far we have examined the position of a person seeking to have a title condition varied or discharged. But what of the neighbours who want to stop

---

[33] This comprises an application fee of £150 and a further fee of £88 for making the order. See items 17 and 21 in Sch.2 to the Lands Tribunal for Scotland Rules 1971, as amended in particular by the Lands Tribunal for Scotland Amendment (Fees) Rules 2003 (SSI 2003/521); and the Lands Tribunal for Scotland Amendment (Fees) Rules 2004 (SSI 2004/480).

[34] See item 20 in Sch.2 to the Lands Tribunal for Scotland Rules 1971, as amended by the Lands Tribunal for Scotland Amendment (Fees) Rules 2003 and the Lands Tribunal for Scotland Amendment (Fees) Rules 2004.

[35] 2003 Act s.103(1). Under the previous practice, expenses were not usually awarded against an objector even where the objection failed.

[36] *Donnelly and Regan v Mullen*, Unreported September 1, 2006 Lands Tribunal; *West Coast Property Developments Ltd v Clarke*, 2007 G.W.D. 29-511. See also Wright, in Robert Rennie (ed.), *The Promised Land: Property Law Reform* (2008), paras 7–50 to 7–54. A party litigant is entitled to expenses for the preparation of the case: see *Hamilton v Robertson*, Unreported May 14, 2008 Lands Tribunal.

[37] *Anderson v McKinnon*, Unreported August 20, 2008 Lands Tribunal.

[38] e.g. *Lawrie v Mashford*, 2008 G.W.D. 16-289.

[39] *West Coast Property Developments Ltd v Clarke*, 2007 G.W.D. 29-511. See also *Smith v Prior*, 2007 G.W.D. 30-523.

[40] e.g. *Kirkwood v Thomson*, Unreported April 24, 2008 Lands Tribunal.

[41] *Scott v Teasdale*, Unreported April 19, 2010 Lands Tribunal.

the proposed alteration or development in its tracks? In all likelihood they have already objected to planning permission, without success. Now they want to use private law where public law has failed. Naturally, the advice given to a client in this position will depend both on the nature of the condition and on the development or other use which is being proposed by the applicant. All too often, however, the best advice will be to give up. On the evidence of the cases so far, opposition is usually unsuccessful, and will attract significant liability in respect of expenses. In those circumstances only a determined client—and one, preferably, with deep pockets—will fight to preserve his or her amenity.[42]

THE STATUTORY FACTORS

Section 100

In reaching a decision in an opposed application, the Tribunal is required to 16–07 decide whether it is reasonable to grant the application, having regard to the factors set out in s.100.[43] These factors are:

"(a) any change in circumstances since the title condition was created (including, without prejudice to that generality, any change in the character of the benefited property, of the burdened property or of the neighbourhood of the properties);

(b) the extent to which the condition—
  (i) confers benefit on the benefited property; or
  (ii) where there is no benefited property, confers benefit on the public;

(c) the extent to which the condition impedes enjoyment of the burdened property;

(d) if the condition is an obligation to do something, how—
  (i) practicable; or
  (ii) costly,
it is to comply with the condition;

(e) the length of time which has elapsed since the condition was created;

(f) the purpose of the title condition;

(g) whether in relation to the burdened property there is the consent, or deemed consent, of a planning authority, or the consent of some other regulatory authority, for a use which the condition prevents;

(h) whether the owner of the burdened property is willing to pay compensation;

(i) if the application is under section 90(1)(b)(ii) of this Act [application for renewal of a burden which would otherwise be extinguished by compulsory purchase], the purpose for which the land is being acquired by the person proposing to register the conveyance; and

(j) any other factor which the Lands Tribunal considers to be material."

---

[42] As one of the Tribunal members, John Wright QC, observes (in Robert Rennie (ed.), *The Promised Land: Property Law Reform* (2008), para.7–54), the rule as to expenses may be "discouraging the defence of the reasonably defensible. Benefited proprietors, sometimes with the benefit of legal advice but perhaps sometimes also on the basis of general information about the expenses position given out by the tribunal, appear quite often to be taking 'cold feet' and either not opposing or withdrawing opposition, particularly when an expensive hearing looms".

[43] 2003 Act s.98.

Obviously, all factors are not of equal importance. Factor (i), for example, is confined to cases of compulsory purchase. The rather puzzling factor (h) seems to be disregarded in practice. Factor (d) is confined to affirmative burdens, which are rarely the subject of Lands Tribunal applications.[44] Factor (j) has not so far proved to be of importance. Nor is the order in the statute of significance. In fact the Tribunal usually begins its consideration with factor (f).

Factor (f): purpose of condition

16–08 The reason for having factor (f) at all is not entirely clear.[45] All the other factors contain an implied question, the answer to which points either in favour of discharge or against it. So for example, if the condition which is the subject of the application impedes development (factor (c)), or if planning permission has been granted (factor (g)), these answers support the granting of the application. But if the condition confers significant benefit (factor (b)), that is an answer which favours refusal. Factor (f) is of a different kind. Uniquely, it cannot stand alone, for no particular conclusion can be drawn from identifying the purpose of the condition. As a result, factor (f) can only be used *in conjunction* with some other factor. So far the Tribunal's approach has been to use it in conjunction with factor (a)—and sometimes, and more controversially, in conjunction with factor (b).[46]

In fact, the "purpose" of most burdens is usually found to be rather general and anodyne—typically to preserve the amenity of the group of properties which it burdens.[47] With one exception, which we will come to, not much can be learned from that.

Factor (a): change in circumstances

16–09 After factor (f) the Tribunal tends to consider whether any change of circumstances has occurred which might disturb the initial purpose of the condition and, perhaps, even defeat it entirely (factor (a)). In *West Coast Property Developments Ltd v Clarke*,[48] for example, changes of circumstances (the flatting of all the houses in the terrace in question and the building of mews houses) were found to be decisive in favour of granting the application.[49] But this is untypical. The experience so far is that factor (a) is usually of secondary importance.

Factor (b): extent of benefit to benefited property

16–10 Instead the crucial factors will be factors (b) and (c). They are intended to be used together. Most conditions will *both* confer benefit on the benefited

---

[44] An example is *Kennedy v Abbey Lane Properties*, Unreported March 29, 2010 Lands Tribunal.

[45] It was absent from the original list produced by the Scottish Law Commission. According to John Wright (in Robert Rennie (ed.), *The Promised Land: Property Law Reform* (2008), para. 7–22), its presence acknowledges the fact that, in the years before 2003, the Tribunal had begun to give weight to purpose, where it could be discerned, so that its omission might have suggested a change in approach.

[46] See below, para.16–10.

[47] See e.g. *Smith v Elrick*, 2007 G.W.D. 29-515.

[48] *West Coast Property Developments Ltd v Clarke*, 2007 G.W.D. 29-511.

[49] Another example is *Patterson v Drouet*, Unreported January 20, 2011 Lands Tribunal, in which maintenance burdens were apportioned by reference to rateable value figures which had not changed since 1989 and so did not take into account the change in use of the applicant's property from commercial to residential. And see also *Perth and Kinross Council v Chapman*, Unreported August 13, 2009 Lands Tribunal.

property and *also* impede use of the burdened, so that the question becomes whether the benefit is of greater value than the impediment.[50]

Benefit is rarely considered in the abstract, for in practice the applicant usually has in mind a particular project, typically the extension of an existing building or the erection of a new one, which is prevented by the burden. And as the benefit to the proprietor of the benefited property is the chance to stop the project, the Tribunal's task is to evaluate that benefit by considering the project's likely impact. Often one or both sides will lead expert evidence, but the Tribunal will make up its own mind particularly in the light of a site visit. All new building, of course, involves the initial inconvenience of the construction phase, but it has been said by the Inner House that "if the long-term user is acceptable it will usually be difficult to deny its allowance on the basis of short-term construction disturbance".[51]

In some early cases, the Tribunal chose to read factor (b) narrowly, in the light of its purpose (i.e. factor (f)). Benefit consistent with that purpose was accepted and evaluated, but benefit of a different kind was rejected as irrelevant for the purposes of factor (b). So for example where a burden was imposed to preserve only *general* amenity and over-development, it was of little consequence, on this approach, that the new building proposed by the applicant would have the highly particular effect of restricting the light in the objecting neighbour's sitting room. The burden's purpose was not to protect a neighbour's light.[52] This approach, however, caused difficulties for burdens of feudal origin, for where burdens were originally imposed by a superior—and in particular by an absentee superior—it was easy to conclude that their purpose was general and public and not specific and private. At any rate they were not for the benefit of immediate neighbours. The 2003 Act then seemed to pull in two different directions. On the one hand, it took care to ensure the survival of the burdens by transferring enforcement rights from superiors to neighbours[53]; but on the other hand—at least on the approach under discussion—it made such burdens easy to remove because, in an application to the Tribunal, the neighbours were unable to show any relevant benefit. Perhaps because of this, the Tribunal seems now to accept that a burden may confer relevant benefit even if that benefit was not within the purpose for which the burden was originally imposed. So in *Brown v Richardson*,[54] for example, the Tribunal agreed "that there may be benefit to the benefited proprietor even although that was not the original purpose".[55] But such benefit will still carry less weight than in a case where this was the original purpose of the burden.[56]

Finally, the Tribunal may try to assess the effectiveness of the burden as a whole. A burden which, while preventing the applicants' particular

---

[50] e.g. in *Gallagher v Wood*, 2007 G.W.D. 37-647, the Tribunal described its task as coming down "substantially, to balancing burden and benefit" (para.37).

[51] *McPherson v Mackie* [2007] CSIH 7; 2007 S.C.L.R. 351 at para.16, per Lord Eassie. For a discussion, see Robbie, (2008) Edin. L.R. 114.

[52] *Daly v Bryce*, 2006 G.W.D. 25-565. See also *Church of Scotland General Trustees v McLaren*, 2006 S.L.T. (Sh. Ct) 27, and, a surprisingly recent example, *Tower Hotel (Troon) Ltd v McCann*, Unreported March 4, 2010 Lands Tribunal.

[53] 2003 Act ss.52–56. See above, paras 13–14 to 13–16.

[54] *Brown v Richardson*, 2007 G.W.D. 28-490.

[55] See also *Smith v Prior*, 2007 G.W.D. 30-523.

[56] See *Scott v Teasdale*, Unreported December 22, 2009 Lands Tribunal, especially at para.43; *Corry v Maclachlan*, Unreported July 9, 2010 Lands Tribunal.

development, would not prevent other developments which would be more harmful still, is likely to be varied or discharged as being of little real benefit.[57]

Factor (c): extent to which enjoyment of burdened property impeded

16–11   Against factor (b) there must be balanced factor (c).[58] If, as typically, the burden restricts alterations and building, the Tribunal tends to view such restrictions as a serious impediment which can be justified only if, under factor (b), the proposed alterations or building would have a major impact on the benefited property. The following comments are typical:

> "The applicants' motives for extending are not of importance. They are exercising a normal wish to enjoy their property by extending their house. It would be a considerable hardship to them if they were unable to do so."[59]

> "Looking at the particular situation here, we consider that the respondents are proposing an extension and improvement of their property of an essentially normal and reasonable type, in line with modern living. We can in this day and age readily accept that a possible alternative of buying a larger property of comparable location and attractiveness would be expensive in comparison."[60]

Although further arguments are not usually necessary, it is possible to identify two which are likely to strengthen factor (c). The first is the degree of need for the project proposed by the applicant, or at least for *some* building project. In *J&L Leisure Ltd v Shaw*[61] the applicant's properties were derelict and urgently in need of replacement. In *Daly v Bryce*[62] the applicant's house, a 1960s bungalow, was outmoded and said to be in need of major refurbishment or replacement.[63]

The second is the absence of alternative uses for the property, at least for as long as the condition stands unmodified. In *J&L Leisure Ltd v Shaw*, where the property was in a conservation area, the Tribunal accepted that the "single storey housing [allowed under the condition] firstly might not be approved by the planners and secondly would be uneconomic".[64] In *Wilson v McNamee*[65] it was not easy to find a tenant for a hall which could only be used "for religious purposes". By contrast, one of the reasons for refusing the application in *Faeley v Clark*[66] was that the benefited proprietors had given consent in the past to

---

[57] *Ord v Mashford*, 2006 S.L.T. (Lands Tr) 15 at 25B; *Smith v Elrick*, 2007 G.W.D. 29-515; *Blackman v Best*, 2008 G.W.D. 11-214; *Hooper v Sinclair*, Unreported September 11, 2008 Lands Tribunal.

[58] Initially, the Tribunal had been inclined not to give factor (c) much weight, on the basis that the burden was voluntarily assumed by the applicant and was reflected in the price paid. See *Ord v Mashford*, 2006 S.L.T. (Lands Tr) 15 at 25L. But that rather unrealistic analysis has not prevailed.

[59] *Anderson v McKinnon*, 2007 G.W.D. 29-513.

[60] *Brown v Richardson*, 2007 G.W.D. 28-490.

[61] *J&L Leisure Ltd v Shaw*, 2007 G.W.D. 28-489.

[62] *Daly v Bryce*, 2006 G.W.D. 25-565.

[63] Conversely, if the applicant's house has already been modernised, and could in any event be extended in a less intrusive manner, this will argue against allowing the application. See *Corry v Maclachlan*, Unreported July 9, 2010 Lands Tribunal.

[64] *J&L Leisure Ltd v Shaw*, 2007 G.W.D. 28-489.

[65] *Wilson v McNamee*, Unreported September 16, 2007.

[66] *Faeley v Clark*, 2006 G.W.D. 28-626.

new buildings which were, from their point of view, less objectionable than what was now proposed, and might be expected to do so again in the future.

A third factor was initially treated by the Tribunal as pointing the other way. This was where the proposed development was being pursued only for commercial gain. In *West Coast Property Developments Ltd v Clarke*, for example, the Tribunal accepted, as a factor unhelpful to the applicant, that "this may simply be a speculative development with a view to realising profit".[67] However, in *McPherson v Mackie*,[68] the Inner House took issue with the Tribunal's attitude, at first instance, to the "potential windfall development value" which would accrue to the applicants if the condition were discharged and as a result they were able to demolish their house and sell the site as an access road to a proposed new development. "[I]n its characterisation of the development as 'windfall', with the possible moral judgment implied in the selection of that adjective, the Tribunal may have fallen into error."[69] The Tribunal's current position is to disregard questions of motive.[70]

Although most of the cases have concerned real burdens, the Tribunal's overall approach is much the same when it comes to servitudes. So where, as on a number of occasions, the application is for re-routing a servitude of way in order to allow some building project to proceed, the application is almost always granted, on the basis that "the purpose of the condition will continue to be fulfilled and there will be no real benefit to the benefited proprietor to set against the detriment to the burdened proprietor if the original route is maintained with the result of preventing reasonable development".[71]

As already mentioned, the Tribunal reaches its decision largely by weighing factor (b) against factor (c). If factor (b) is very strong—if, in other words, the applicant's building project will be seriously detrimental to the objector's property—the application will be refused.[72] But a lesser degree of prejudice is unlikely to block the application. Indeed, the very fact that the Act provides for compensation in respect of "substantial loss and disadvantage" shows that it was contemplated that applications could be granted even where to do so would be to have a material impact on the benefited owner.[73] Given the way in which factors (b) and (c) are currently interpreted, it seems likely that most applications will continue to succeed.

Factor (e): age of the condition

The only other factor which need be mentioned is factor (e). If a burden is   16–12
more than 100 years old, the burdened proprietor can secure its discharge by

---

[67] *West Coast Property Developments Ltd v Clarke*, 2007 G.W.D. 29-511. See also *Daly v Bryce*, 2006 G.W.D. 25-565: "this is not a case in which . . . the proposal to demolish and replace with two houses was motivated only by financial profit".

[68] *McPherson v Mackie* [2007] CSIH 7; 2007 S.C.L.R. 351.

[69] *McPherson v Mackie* [2007] CSIH 7; 2007 S.C.L.R. 351 at para.23.

[70] *Anderson v McKinnon*, 2007 G.W.D. 29-513; *Verrico v Tomlinson*, 2008 S.L.T. (Lands Tr) 2 at para.22.

[71] *Gibb v Kerr*, 2009 G.W.D. 38-646 at para.17. See also *Parkin v Kennedy*, Unreported March 23, 2010 at para.31. Other examples are: *George Wimpey East Scotland Ltd v Fleming*, 2006 S.L.T. (Lands Tr) 27 and 59; *Graham v Parker*, 2007 G.W.D. 30-524; *MacNab v McDowall*, Unreported October 24, 2007; *Jensen v Tyler*, 2008 S.L.T. (Lands Tr) 39.

[72] *Faeley v Clark*, 2006 G.W.D. 28-626; *Cocozza v Rutherford*, 2008 S.L.T. (Sh. Ct) 6.

[73] *J&L Leisure Ltd v Shaw*, 2007 G.W.D. 28-489; *G v A*, Unreported November 29, 2009 Lands Tribunal. But compensation will not always be enough to make up for the effect of the applicant's proposed innovation: see *Scott v Teasdale*, Unreported December 22, 2009 Lands Tribunal.

the execution, intimation and registration of a notice of termination. This is the so-called "sunset rule".[74] But if a burden is elderly but less than 100 years old, this is a factor which argues for its discharge in a normal application to the Lands Tribunal. In *Smith v Prior*,[75] the Tribunal had this to say about a restriction on building which had been imposed in 1934:

> "[T]o the extent that rights of control may produce sterility, there must come a time when, however attractive to its immediate neighbours, that should be at last relaxed. Holding the applicants to a prohibition on extension more than 70 years after it was imposed would seem to us to require quite strong justification."

Other cases, however, have tended to play down the significance of age, especially if the purpose of the burden can still be fulfilled.[76]

Youthfulness, of course, points the other way: the Tribunal would be reluctant to discharge a burden which was imposed only last year.[77] Most burdens, however, are neither very new nor very old, and in such cases factor (e) is likely to be of little importance.

Compensation

Two heads

16-13 Sometimes the Lands Tribunal is only willing to grant an application for variation or discharge on the basis that the applicant pays compensation to an objector or objectors. The applicant then has a choice between agreeing to pay the compensation fixed by the Tribunal or having the application refused.[78] The basis of compensation is unchanged from the former legislation.[79] Normally, compensation is payable only where "substantial" loss or disadvantage has followed on from the variation or discharge. An alternative head for compensation—to make up for any reduction in consideration in the original grant caused by the imposition of the condition—is hard to make out, and in any case is tied to a historical figure the value of which is not adjusted for inflation. As it is seldom encountered in practice, it will not be discussed further here.[80]

"Substantial loss or disadvantage"

16-14 "Substantial loss or disadvantage" is measured by reference to the decline in the value of the benefited property as a result of the development which is now

---

[74] See above, para.13–24.

[75] *Smith v Prior*, 2007 G.W.D. 30-523.

[76] *Ord v Mashford*, 2006 S.L.T. (Lands Tr) 15 at 25L. And see Wright, in Robert Rennie (ed.), *The Promised Land: Property Law Reform* (2008), paras 7–29 and 7–30.

[77] *Cattanach v Vine-Hall*, Unreported October 3, 2007 Lands Tribunal.

[78] Title Conditions (Scotland) Act 2003 s.90(9).

[79] 2003 Act s.90(7). The former law was s.1(4) of the Conveyancing and Feudal Reform (Scotland) Act 1970. For a discussion and much useful material, see Sir Crispin Agnew of Lochnaw, *Variation and Discharge of Land Obligations* (1999), Ch.7.

[80] See *Cumbernauld Development Corp v County Properties and Developments Ltd*, 1996 S.L.T. 1106; and, most recently, *Faeley v Douall*, Unreported November 19, 2010, Lands Tribunal.

to be allowed on the burdened.[81] But in assessing this amount account will be taken of other possible developments which might have gone ahead without any breach of the title condition.[82] In other words, the correct basis of claim is the difference between the value of the property with and without the benefit of the title condition. In practice expert evidence will usually be needed, and will usually be contested. It is well settled that no compensation is payable in respect of the loss of the possibility of extracting payment for minutes of waiver.[83]

In many cases the development, once completed, will have little or no effect on the value of the benefited property; yet during the construction period there may be considerable inconvenience, and indeed a temporary loss of value as represented by rental income. In principle, compensation is due even for such temporary loss, but in practice the sums involved will often be too small to qualify as "substantial".[84]

Problems of causation

Causation can raise difficult issues. One is the question of whether, if the title condition prevented a particular development, the compensation for its discharge should be computed by reference to the loss caused by the whole development. In other words, is the development caused by the discharge? Sometimes the causal connection may seem rather frail. In *George Wimpey East Scotland Ltd v Fleming*,[85] the Lands Tribunal allowed the variation of a servitude of way so that an access road was re-routed. As a result, the applicants were able to build 115 houses on their land. The objectors, who owned neighbouring houses, claimed compensation. In the Tribunal's view, however, compensation could not be measured by the loss caused by the 115 new houses. Rather, the only direct consequence of the variation was the, rather minor, re-routing of the access road, and for that no compensation was due. As the Tribunal noted, however, "[t]he situation in relation to discharge, for example, of a building restriction might be different: as soon as the building commences, all the works . . . might be a consequence of the discharge".[86]

Causation also raises a second issue, on which there is as yet no authority. In practice, applications for variation and discharge are often accompanied by a parallel application for planning permission. Does the order in which these consents are obtained affect the measure of compensation which the Tribunal is likely to order? If planning permission is obtained first, it becomes easy to argue that the eventual development takes place "in consequence of the discharge" of the title condition. But if the discharge comes first, the argument is harder to make. For the discharge, of itself, has no immediate consequences. Nothing is built on the land for the time being, and nothing can be built without planning permission. At the time when the Tribunal is asked to rule on

16–15

---

[81] For an unsuccessful attempt to claim on the basis of cost of cure, see *G v A*, Unreported February 10, 2010 Lands Tribunal.

[82] *Esplin v Higgitt*, 2008 G.W.D. 28-439.

[83] See Sir Crispin Agnew of Lochnaw, *Variation and Discharge of Land Obligations* (1999), paras 7–18 to 7–21 and the authorities there cited.

[84] *George Wimpey East Scotland Ltd v Fleming*, 2006 S.L.T. (Lands Tr) 59.

[85] *George Wimpey East Scotland Ltd v Fleming*, 2006 S.L.T. (Lands Tr) 59. And see also *West Coast Properties Ltd v Clark*, 2007 G.W.D. 29-511.

[86] *George Wimpey East Scotland Ltd v Fleming*, 2006 S.L.T. (Lands Tr) 59 at 64F.

compensation it cannot know whether planning permission will be granted or not, or, if granted, on what terms. The causal connection between discharge and potential development is thus fairly weak. Of course, in practice developers will often wish to obtain planning permission first—and indeed they are more likely to succeed before the Lands Tribunal if they do so.[87] Nonetheless, a developer who is anxious to reduce liability for compensation might be sensible to delay the planning application.

---

[87] This is partly because one of the statutory factors which favours an application before the Tribunal is that "there is the consent, or deemed consent, of a planning authority, or the consent of some other regulatory authority, for a use which the condition prevents" (2003 Act s.100(g)), and partly because an application is more likely to be rejected if the proposed project is still up in the air (*Hamilton v Robertson*, 2008 S.L.T. (Lands Tr) 25).

Chapter 17

EXECUTION OF DEEDS

Execution on or after August 1, 1995

The law of execution of deeds was recast by the Requirements of Writing   17–01
(Scotland) Act 1995, which applies to all documents executed on or after
August 1, 1995. To a substantial extent, however, the 1995 Act follows the
previous law, and many cases decided under that law continue to be of
relevance. The 1995 Act was itself amended in 2006 to allow the electronic
deeds used under automated registration of title to land ("ARTL").[1]

A summary account of the old law will be found at the end of this chapter.
But for the most part we consider only the law introduced by the 1995 Act.[2]

Subscribed writings and probative writings

By s.2 of the 1995 Act a deed is valid if it is subscribed by the granter. Nothing   17–02
further is needed. But for conveyancers this will rarely be enough. If a deed is
to be registered in the GRS or the Books of Council and Session or the sheriff
court books it requires to be "probative".[3] In practice the same rule is also
applied to deeds presented to the Land Register. A probative deed is one which,
from its appearance, is presumed to be validly executed. Under the 1995 Act
there are two routes to probativity, set out in ss.3 and 4. One is to supplement
the signature of the granter with a witnesss—or some equivalent of a witness.
The other is to apply to the court for a judicial docquet, endorsed on the deed,
to the effect that the deed was subscribed by the granter. In practice docquets
are used almost exclusively for wills,[4] and they will not be considered further
here.[5]

The relationship between validity and probativity is not always understood.
A formally valid deed is one which has been properly executed. This means
that it has been subscribed by the granter. A probative deed is one which is

---

[1] Automated Registration of Title to Land (Electronic Communications) (Scotland) Order 2006
(SSI 2006/491).

[2] For accounts of the 1995 Act see Kenneth G.C. Reid, *The Requirements of Writing (Scotland)
Act 1995* (1995); Robert Rennie and D.J. Cusine, *The Requirements of Writing* (1995); Currie on
Confirmation of Executors, 8th edn by Eilidh M. Scobbie (1995), Ch.4; Robert Rennie and Stewart
Brymer, *Conveyancing in the Electronic Age* (2008), Ch.2. In addition much useful material may
be found in the Scottish Law Commission's Report on *Requirements of Writing* (Scot. Law Com.
No.112, 1988)

[3] Requirements of Writing (Scotland) Act 1995 s.6(1), (2). Some exceptions are set out in subs.
(3). The word "probative" had a range of meanings under the old law and is avoided in the 1995
Act, but it is too convenient to abandon.

[4] A will cannot be used as the basis of an application for confirmation of executors unless it is
probative. See Succession (Scotland) Act 1964 s.21A.

[5] For the procedure, see Act of Sederunt (Requirements of Writing) 1996 (SI 1996/1534).

presumed to have been subscribed by the granter and hence is presumed to be formally valid.[6] This presumption is of value. After a gap in time the authenticity of deeds can be difficult to prove. But if a deed is probative, no proof need be brought. Rather it is for a person disputing authenticity to prove that the execution was not properly conducted. In practice this means that probative deeds can be relied on. That is one reason why conveyancers use them. Of course even probative writs may sometimes fail. It is possible for a deed to be both probative and invalid. Probativity confers only a presumption of validity, and the presumption can be rebutted. If George forges the granter's signature and then adds his own as a witness, the deed is probative under s.3 of the 1995 Act. But it is also invalid, because the granter did not in fact sign. In practice, however, probative deeds are rarely challenged, and even more rarely with success.[7]

Making probative deeds

17–03   Two things are required to make a deed probative. First, the granter must have subscribed, or, rather, must seem to have subscribed. And secondly the subscription must be attested by a witness, or, rather, seem to have been so witnessed. Special rules, considered later, apply in the case of electronic documents, or where the granter is a company or other juristic person.

The granter subscribes

17–04   The sovereign superscribes, that is to say, signs at the top of deeds.[8] According to Stair this is because "Princes have not the time to peruse the whole body [of the deed], wherein there is much of formality".[9] Everyone else, being members of the more leisured classes, must "subscribe", defined in the 1995 Act as meaning to sign at the end of the last page, but excluding any annexation such as a plan or schedule.[10] With multiple granters there may not be enough room for all of the signatures, in which case it is permissible to sign on an additional page or pages provided at least one granter signs at the end of the deed proper.[11] A person who grants in more than one capacity—for example as both an executor and an individual—need sign only once.[12] In addition to subscription, a will or other testamentary writing requires to be signed at least once on every sheet,[13] and the practice is for the testator to sign at the foot of each page.

Normally a party must sign by forename or initial plus surname.[14] An abbreviated or familiar form of the forename is also acceptable. The surname must come last. Thus Margaret Agnes Brown (nee Black) could sign as "Margaret Brown" or "Peggy Brown" or "Agnes Brown" or "Maggie Brown" or "Nancy Brown" or "M Brown" or "A Brown" or "M A Brown". Alternatively she could use the surname of "Black". But she could not sign as "Brown M A"

---

[6] See below, para.17–12.
[7] For an example of a successful challenge, see *Nicholas v Interbrew Ltd* [2005] CSOH 158; 2006 G.W.D. 1-27.
[8] A rule preserved by s.13(1)(a) of the 1995 Act.
[9] Stair IV, xlii, 3.
[10] 1995 Act s.7(1). For plans and schedules, see below, para.17–08.
[11] 1995 Act s.7(3).
[12] 1995 Act s.7(4).
[13] 1995 Act s.3(2).
[14] 1995 Act s.7(2)(b).

(more an educational statement than a signature) or as "N Brown"[15] or "Brown" or "Margaret".[16] As an alternative, the 1995 Act also allows signature by the full name by which the granter is identified in the deed,[17] but this is uncommon in practice. There is no requirement that the signature be the granter's usual signature. Some people have a number of "usual" signatures as well as some which are distinctly unusual. The signature must, however, be legible, for probativity requires that the deed "bears" to have been subscribed by the granter.[18] It is prudent to warn clients of this in advance. A deed bearing an illegible signature will usually be formally valid, as having been subscribed by the granter,[19] but it will not be probative.

Once subscribed, a deed is already formally valid. Adding a witness adds nothing to validity.[20] But without a witness the deed is not probative.

The witness attests

Only one witness is needed. Even a deed with multiple granters can make do 17–05 with a single witness provided that all the granters sign at the same time. In that case the witness need sign only once.[21] But if the granters sign at different times a separate witness[22] is needed for each occasion.

Like the granter, the witness must be of normal legal capacity. This means that the witness must be 16 or over, and mentally capable of acting.[23] A witness can be a grantee of the deed (for example a beneficiary under a will) although this is usually inadvisable as running the risk of challenge on other grounds, such as undue influence. A witness cannot be one of the granters.[24]

The witness attests to two distinct things. The first is the identity of the granter. The witness is required to "know" the granter.[25] But the standard is not exacting, and it is sufficient if the witness has credible information at the time of the witnessing. Prior acquaintance is not required.[26] It is good practice to ask for some form of identification, such as a passport or driving licence.

Secondly, the witness attests to the fact of subscription. Usually this means watching as the granter signs, but the 1995 Act allows a granter who has already signed to acknowledge the signature to the witness.[27] Acknowledgment is normally by words, but in theory might also be nonverbal.[28] There is no need for the witness to read the deed. The attestation relates to execution and not to content.

---

[15] "N" is not "an initial of a forename", as required by s.7(2)(b), but an initial of a familiar form of a forename.

[16] However, "Margaret" would be sufficient on non-probative documents (e.g. informal wills), provided it could be shown that that was the usual method of signature or was intended as the signature. See s.7(2)(c).

[17] 1995 Act s.7(2)(a).

[18] 1995 Act s.3(1)(a).

[19] 1995 Act s.2. And see e.g. *Stirling Stuart v Stirling Crawfurd's Trustees* (1885) 12 R. 610.

[20] Compare here the old law where (except in the case of holograph deeds) a deed was not formally valid until it had been witnessed.

[21] 1995 Act s.7(5). And see also s.3(6).

[22] Who could, in theory, be the same person.

[23] 1995 Act s.3(4)(c)(ii) and (iii).

[24] 1995 Act s.3(4)(b).

[25] 1995 Act s.3(4)(c)(i).

[26] 1995 Act s.3(5). There is continuity here with the old law, for which see *Walker v Adamson* (1716) Mor. 16896; and *Brock v Brock*, 1908 S.C. 964.

[27] 1995 Act s.3(7).

[28] *Cumming v Skeoch's Trustees* (1879) 6 R. 963; *MacDougall v MacDougall's Exrs*, 1994 S.L.T. 1178; *Lindsay v Milne*, 1995 S.L.T. 487; *McLure v McLure's Exr*, 1997 S.L.T. 127.

The witness must then sign.[29] Although the 1995 Act does not say so, the practice is to sign at the end, and by convention the granter signs on the right-hand side of the page and the witness on the left. The rules about methods of signing are the same as for granters.[30] The signature must occur immediately after the event which is witnessed, as "one continuous process".[31] This is to avoid possible substitution of documents: a witness who signs at once can have no doubts that the correct deed is being signed. Even a short time gap might be treated as fatal.[32] In cases where the signature is acknowledged by the granter, the relevant event is acknowledgment and not the initial signature. Thus a witness can sign 20 years after the granter, so long as the signature follows on immediately from the granter's acknowledgment.

Finally, the witness must be designed, by name and address.[33] Usually the full name is given, although this is more than the 1995 Act requires. The name must be given even in a case where it is clear from the signature itself. A business address is sufficient, and is common in practice. At one time occupations were given,[34] but this is not required by the 1995 Act and the practice is dying out. The designation can be added at any time before the deed is founded on in legal proceedings or registered for preservation in the Books of Council and Session or in sheriff court books.[35] Usually it appears in the testing clause, which is added within a few days of execution.

Sanctions for breach of the witnessing rules

17–06   Since probativity is concerned only with the appearance of a document, it may be asked what sanction exists for breaches of these various requirements, for instance that the witness should know the grantor.

After all, even if the witness did not know the granter, the deed is still both probative and—as a witness is not needed for formal validity—valid. If, however, there is a court action and it emerges that there has been a material breach (e.g. that the witness did not know the granter) then the deed loses the benefit of the presumption that it was subscribed by the granter.[36] In other words it becomes improbative, thus easing the task of a challenger.[37] Two other possible sanctions must be mentioned. One is that the solicitor who condones a breach may be guilty of professional misconduct, and the other is that the witness may be guilty of a criminal offence.

Testing clause

17–07   As its name suggests, a testing clause narrates the details of the attestation. Strictly, a testing clause is not required, except in the highly ususual case where

---

[29] 1995 Act s.3(1)(b). Compare s.3(1)(a) which requires that the deed is "subscribed" by the granter.
[30] 1995 Act s.7(5). See above, para.17–04.
[31] 1995 Act s.3(4)(e); and see s.3(6) for cases of multiple granters.
[32] Since the result of invalid attestation was invalid execution, the old law was more forgiving than the current law seems likely to be. See e.g. *Thomson v Clarkson's Trustees* (1892) 20 R. 59 (gap of 45 minutes allowed).
[33] 1995 Act s.3(1)(b).
[34] Not always accurately. In *Braithwaite v Bank of Scotland*, 1999 S.L.T. 25 a witness gave his occupation, as a joke, as "consultant gynaecologist".
[35] 1995 Act s.3(3)(a).
[36] 1995 Act s.3(4).
[37] See below, para.17–13.

there are alterations which need to be declared.[38] But in practice one is almost always used, and it contains the designation of the witness, and the date and place of execution.

Since the testing clause contains details of execution, it cannot be finalised until after the deed has been signed. The traditional practice is to finish the deed with the first words of the testing clause ("IN WITNESS WHEREOF"), and then to ensure that the granter and witness leave a suitable gap above their signatures for the testing clause to be added later.[39] But quite apart from the awkwardness of asking clients to sign a deed containing a gap, this method is open to the risk of new material being added, without the client's knowledge, after execution has taken place. Its diminishing popularity today, however, is due less to fear of fraud than to the virtual disappearance of the typewriters used for the testing clause. Today it is just as common for deeds to be printed with an outline testing clause, but with blanks for the date and place of execution and the name and address of the witness, which can be completed (in ink) after execution.

In the case of a disposition, the deed is prepared by the buyers' solicitors but executed by the sellers. Once the final version (the "engrossment") is ready, it is sent to the sellers' solicitor, along with a signing schedule.[40] After it is signed, it is retained by the sellers' solicitor until settlement, when it is given to the buyers' solicitor. It is only then that the testing clause is completed, by the buyers' solicitor, after which the deed is ready for registration.

Schedules and plans

Usually schedules and plans are signed by the granter, but this is a formal requirement only for annexations which contain a visual or verbal description of land.[41] Under the Act, plans and other visual representations must be signed on each page (if there is more than one), while a schedule containing a verbal description need be signed only on the last page. The requirement is for signature and not subscription. The witness need not sign and in practice does not usually do so. Indeed an annexation can be signed at a different time from the deed proper, provided only that it is signed prior to litigation or registration (including registration in the Land Register or the GRS).[42] But that would be unusual. 17–08

Two further steps are required if the annexation is to be treated as part of the deed.[43] First, the annexation must be referred to in the deed itself (e.g. "which subjects are hatched and delineated in red on the plan annexed and subscribed as relative hereto"). And secondly, the annexation must contain some kind of identifying tag, to link up with the reference in the deed. In the Keeper's view, this should normally mention the parties to the deed and (preferably) the date:

---

[38] For alterations see below, para.17–09.

[39] One might ask why the testing clause is not simply added after the signatures. Originally, the reason was to meet the requirement of the Subscription of Deeds Act 1681 that the designations of witnesses be "in the body of the deed". But while this requirement disappeared as long ago as 1874, the practice has simply continued.

[40] A form on which the date and place of signing and the designation of the witness are to be filled in. Its only purpose is to enable the testing clause to be completed, after which it can be torn up.

[41] 1995 Act s.8(1), (2).

[42] 1995 Act s.8(5).

[43] 1995 Act s.8(1), (2).

for example "This is the plan referred to in the foregoing Disposition by Elizabeth Anne Mackie in favour of James Murray dated August 11, 2011".[44]

There is no requirement that an annexation be physically attached to the deed, whether by stapling or otherwise, but this may often be good practice if the two are not to become separated.

Alterations

17–09   Occasionally a deed is altered after typing or printing. Usually this involves either (1) the deletion of words, whether by erasure or by scoring out, or (2) the addition of words, whether by writing over words previously erased or by interlineation or by marginal addition (i.e. additional words written in the margin of the deed).[45] Until the 1980s alterations were quite common. Now, with computers in almost universal use, they are rare, although not unknown.

There is no objection to alterations provided that they were made before the granter signs. They are then part of the deed as signed by the granter. No special steps need be taken.[46] By contrast, an alteration made after execution is not part of the deed and has no legal effect unless it is separately executed.[47] An obvious difficulty is dating alterations. A person reading a deed a year or two after execution can see the alteration but has no ready means of discovering when it was made. In probative deeds the problem is solved by means of a presumption. If the deed or (in practice) the testing clause contains a declaration that the alteration was made before subscription, the declaration is presumed to be true and the alteration is treated as part of the deed.[48] The presumption can of course be rebutted, but in practice contrary evidence may be hard to come by.[49]

Avoiding mistakes

17–10   Things can go wrong in the execution of deeds. For instance, the granter might sign in the wrong place or in the wrong way, or the witness might not know the granter or might sign before the granter rather than after. The best way of avoiding mistakes is for the solicitor to supervise the whole process.[50] Where this cannot be done, the client must be sent clear instructions written in a simple and non-technical style. In practice this is often done by a pre-printed schedule of signing particulars, which the client is asked to complete with details of the place and date of signing and the name and address of the witness.

Identifying a deed as probative

17–11   Often solicitors have to look at deeds which they had no part in executing. An obvious example is in examination of a GRS title on the purchase of land. In such cases the solicitor will be concerned to check that the deed is probative.

---

[44] See (1995) 40 J.L.S.S. 405.
[45] 1995 Act s.12(1) (definition of "alteration").
[46] Under the old law it was sometimes the practice to sign marginal additions, typically with the forename of the granter on one side and the surname on the other. But this is not required under the 1995 Act.
[47] 1995 Act s.5(1).
[48] 1995 Act s.5(4), (5).
[49] By s.5(3) all relevant evidence may be used for this purpose, whether written or oral.
[50] *Lindsay v Milne*, 1995 S.L.T. 487 at 488H, per Lord Prosser.

Fortunately, that is easily determined. Probativity is about what appears to have happened rather than about what actually happened. A deed is probative if it appears to have been validly subscribed and witnessed. More precisely, s.3(1) of the 1995 Act provides that a deed is probative ("presumed to have been subscribed by that granter") if four conditions are satisfied. These are (1) that the deed bears to have been subscribed by the granter; (2) that it bears to have been signed by a witness; (3) that it bears to state the name and address of the witness; and (4) negatively, that nothing in the deed indicates that it was not so subscribed and witnessed.

One presumption plus four

If a deed is probative, it is presumed to have been subscribed by the granter, 17–12 and hence (under s.2 of the 1995 Act) to be formally valid.[51] That is the main presumption created by probativity, and its main value. But, depending on the circumstances, subsidiary presumptions may also operate.[52] (1) If the deed gives the date of subscription, the deed is presumed to have been subscribed on that date. (2) If the deed gives the place of subscription, the deed is presumed to have been subscribed at that place.[53] In practice testing clauses invariably give both the date and place of execution, although the place is usually no more specific than the name of the town or city. (3) If the deed includes an annexation with a visual or verbal description of land (for example, a plan), and the annexation bears to have been signed by the granter, the annexation is presumed to have been so signed.[54] (4) Finally, as already mentioned, any statement in the deed or testing clause that an alteration was made before subscription is presumed to be true, and the alteration is presumed to form part of the deed.[55]

The presumptions are concerned solely with the formalities of execution. There is no presumption that the granter had title, or was mentally capable of making the grant, or, more generally, that the deed is legally effective. A deed may fail for reasons which have nothing to do with execution.

Disputing authenticity

A person wishing to challenge the authenticity of a probative deed has a choice 17–13 of approach. One possibility is to attack the deed directly by seeking to prove that the granter did not subscribe. If this can be done the deed is shown to be invalid. The other possibility is to attack the deed indirectly by proving merely that the attestation by the witness was not properly conducted.[56] In that case the deed is not shown to be invalid, but equally it is no longer presumed to be valid.[57] In other words, the deed ceases to be probative, so that a person seeking to found on it must then bring positive proof of its authenticity. After an interval of time that may be an impossible task. Since a deed is not probative in the first place unless it appears to be properly attested, it follows that an attack on the

---

[51] 1995 Act s.3(1).

[52] They are, however, contingent on the main presumption—except in the case of testamentary documents—on which see s.3(10).

[53] 1995 Act s.3(8).

[54] 1995 Act s.8(3), read in conjunction with s.3(1).

[55] 1995 Act s.5(4), (5).

[56] The fact that the onus of proof lies with the challenger shows, in effect, the existence of a further presumption that the deed was properly attested.

[57] 1995 Act s.3(4).

attestation process must depend on factors which are not patent from the deed itself. Section 3(4) of the 1995 Act gives an exhaustive list of such factors. They include: forgery of the witness's signature; non-age and mental incapacity; not knowing the granter; and failure to see the granter sign or acknowledge the signature, and failure to sign immediately thereafter.

Powers of attorney

17–14   A person can authorise someone to sign a deed on his behalf. This is just an application of the law of agency. Common examples are where a person is going to be out of the country for some time, or where a person has become physically or mentally frail.[58] Within the ARTL system digital signatures are made by solicitors on behalf of their clients.[59]

The usual way of authorising another person to sign is by executing a deed known as a power of attorney,[60] although companies and other juristic persons often proceed with less formality, and there is nothing in the 1995 Act which requires writing for the constitution of agency.[61] Where a power of attorney is used, it is normally registered for safekeeping in the Books of Council and Session. A power of attorney executed before April 2, 2001 is unaffected by the subsequent mental incapacity of the principal,[62] but powers granted since that date lapse on incapacity unless they were constituted as continuing powers of attorney under Pt 2 of the Adults with Incapacity (Scotland) Act 2000.[63] In order to qualify as a continuing power of attorney within the Act the deed must (i) state that the power is intended to be a continuing power, (ii) incorporate a certificate in prescribed form[64] by a solicitor, practising advocate or registered medical practitioner to the effect that the principal understands the nature and extent of the power and is not acting under undue influence or other vitiating factor, and (iii) be registered with the Public Guardian.[65]

Powers of attorney are restrictively construed, at least by conveyancers.[66] The agent has power to do only such things as the deed clearly envisages, and where a deed is signed under a power of attorney, the power of attorney must be examined to establish that the agent was acting lawfully. Where a conveyancing deed is executed under a power of attorney, this power should have been expressly conferred. A person holding a power of attorney cannot normally donate the property, since to do so would be contrary to the duty to act in the interests of the principal.

---

[58] Not too mentally frail, for an incapax cannot do any juridical act, and thus cannot grant a mandate or agency.

[59] See above, para.8–23.

[60] This is the English term, which has now come into general use in Scotland. "Mandate" is used for authority to sign within the ARTL system. The traditional term is "factory and commission". For styles see Halliday, paras 13–12 to 13–21.

[61] See in particular s.1(1), and see also *Dodds v Southern Pacific Personal Loans Ltd* [2007] CSOH 93; 2007 G.W.D. 21-352.

[62] Adults with Incapacity (Scotland) Act 2000 Sch.4, para.4, Previously, only powers of attorney granted on or after January 1, 1991 had this privilege: see Law Reform (Miscellaneous Provisions) (Scotland) Act 1990 s.71 (repealed by the 2000 Act Sch.6).

[63] Adults with Incapacity (Scotland) Act 2000 s.18. For further details, see Adrian Ward, *Adult Incapacity* (2003), Ch.6.

[64] For which see the Adults with Incapacity (Certificates in Relation to Powers of Attorney) (Scotland) Regulations 2008 (SSI 2008/56).

[65] Adults with Incapacity (Scotland) Act 2000 ss.15 and 19.

[66] Halliday, para.13–03.

The *Encyclopaedia of Scottish Legal Styles*[67] gives two different methods of drawing up a deed which is to be signed by an attorney. One is to have the deed run in the name of the attorney. ("I, AB, attorney of CD, conform to Power of Attorney in my favour, etc."). In that case the testing clause runs "IN WITNESS WHEREOF these presents are subscribed by me as attorney foresaid". The other method is not to mention the attorney in the deed (which runs in the name of the principal) but to say in the testing clause "IN WITNESS WHEREOF these presents are subscribed by me the said CD per my attorney AB (design) acting under Power of Attorney, etc". In both cases the deed is subscribed by the attorney, in the attorney's own name.[68]

Granter mentally incapable

A continuing power of attorney survives supervening mental incapacity, as just 17–15 seen, and the disposition or other deed can be granted by the attorney on behalf of the *incapax*. In the absence of a continuing power it is necessary to apply to the sheriff court for an intervention order or guardianship order under Pt 6 of the Adults with Incapacity (Scotland) Act 2000.[69] This replaces the former procedure of seeking the appointment of a curator bonis.[70] The applicant is required to give a conveyancing description of the property (including the title number if the property is registered in the Land Register), and the sheriff's interlocutor must itself be registered in the Land Register or the GRS.[71] Once appointed, an authorised person (intervenor) or guardian is in the position of an agent, and the disposition or other deed is drawn up and executed in the manner already described in relation to attorneys. Property used as the principal's house cannot be sold without the further consent of the Public Guardian.[72]

Granter blind or unable to write

A granter who is blind could choose to sign the deed himself or herself, or 17–16 grant a power of attorney giving authority to sign to someone else.[73] A granter who is not blind but merely unable to write could in theory give oral authority to an attorney,[74] although this invites problems of proof.[75] In practice both categories of granter are likely to use the special procedure set out in s.9 of the 1995 Act. This allows the giving of oral authority to sign, but only to a restricted class of persons—solicitors with practising certificates, advocates, justices of

---

[67] *Encyclopaedia of Scottish Legal Styles*, Vol.4, p.166.

[68] 1995 Act s.12(2). There is thus no need, as sometimes happened under the old law, for the attorney to sign in both names ("CD per his attorney AB"). In *Dodd v Southern Pacific Personal Loans Ltd* [2007] CSOH 93; 2007 G.W.D. 21-352 it was held sufficient for the attorney to sign only the principal's name, but this overlooks s.7(2) of the 1995 Act.

[69] See Adrian Ward, *Adult Incapacity* (2003), Ch.10, and for the conveyancing aspects Reid and Gretton, *Conveyancing 2002*, pp.100–11 (A.J.M. Steven and Alan Barr).

[70] Which is no longer competent: see Adults with Incapacity (Scotland) Act 2000 s.80.

[71] Adults with Incapacity (Scotland) Act 2000 ss.56 (intervention order) and 61 (guardianship order).

[72] Adults with Incapacity (Scotland) Act 2000 s.53(6) (authorised person) and Sch.2 para.6(1) (guardian).

[73] 1995 Act s.9(7).

[74] The 1995 Act neither asserts nor denies that oral authority is competent. But the general rule under the Act is that writing is required only in the cases set out in s.1(2). Powers of attorney are not listed.

[75] Alternatively such a person could sign by mark, which is sufficient for improbative deeds. See s.7(2)(c).

the peace, sheriff clerks, licensed conveyancers (for dispositions and standard securities) and licensed executry practitioners (for testamentary documents).[76] The idea is that those mentioned can be trusted to follow the instructions of the person in question and not to take advantage of the opportunity for fraud. Under the old law, execution by this method was known as notarial execution,[77] but notaries are no longer listed by name in the legislation,[78] except in relation to execution taking place outside Scotland. In practice, the signatories under the s.9 procedure are almost always solicitors.

Although the s.9 procedure can be used for deeds of all kinds, the typical case is the execution of a will on behalf of an old and frail testator.[79] A deed executed under s.9 can be either probative or improbative, but here we are concerned only with the former.[80] The procedure, which must be strictly adhered to, is as follows:

(i)   The granter, solicitor and witness[81] assemble.

(ii)   The granter declares that he or she is blind or unable to write.[82]

(iii) There is no requirement that this statement be true, and no duty on the solicitor to investigate its truth.

(iv)   The solicitor reads the document to the granter.[83] If there is a plan or equivalent, the solicitor must describe it—in some cases a challenging task.[84] Both steps can be dispensed with by the granter, even in cases of blindness.

(v)   The granter authorises the solicitor to subscribe.[85] This may be in words, or merely implied from the circumstances.[86]

(vi)   The solicitor subscribes.[87] In the case of a will a signature is also required on every sheet.[88]

(vii) The witness signs.[89] In signing, the witness attests to steps (3) to (5).[90] The actual subscription must have been observed, and it is not sufficient for the signature merely to be acknowledged.

(vii) The testing clause is added. It (or the deed proper) must contain a statement that the deed was read (or as the case may be, not read), and that the granter gave the solicitor authority to sign.[91]

---

[76] 1995 Act s.9(6); Public Appointments and Public Bodies etc. (Scotland) Act 2003 s.14(3). Outside Scotland the facility is extended to notaries public and any other person with official authority to execute documents on behalf of persons who are blind or unable to write.

[77] And indeed often still is.

[78] This is because the category is widened from notaries to all solicitors with practising certificates.

[79] Of course the person must be *capax*. Wills are often made by the dying, who may no longer be physically capable of writing.

[80] For improbative deeds (i.e. deeds formally valid under s.2), see s.9(1), (2).

[81] 1995 Act s.3(4)(dd). All references to s.3 in the context of this procedure are references to that section as amended by Sch.3.

[82] 1995 Act s.9(1).

[83] 1995 Act s.9(1).

[84] 1995 Act s.9(5).

[85] 1995 Act s.9(1).

[86] 1995 Act s.12(1) (definition of "authorised").

[87] 1995 Act s.9(1).

[88] 1995 Act s.3(2).

[89] 1995 Act s.3(1).

[90] 1995 Act s.3(4)(d), (dd).

[91] 1995 Act s.3(1).

Under the pre-1995 law, stages (i) to (vi) are required to be carried out as one continuous process,[92] and while this rule is not repeated by the 1995 Act (except in relation to the witness signing immediately after the solicitor),[93] a cautious view would be that the continuity requirement of the former law continues to apply. The final stage (the testing clause) can presumably be completed at any time.

A deed which bears to be executed in the manner just described is probative, i.e. is presumed to have been validly executed[94] on behalf of the granter.[95]

A solicitor who executes a deed under s.9 must not take benefit from it, and the rule is extended to close relatives (spouse or children). This means that in the case of a will, for example, the solicitor must not be included among the beneficiaries. Any purported conferral of benefit, direct or indirect, is invalid, but the deed is otherwise unaffected.[96]

Electronic deeds

Only deeds used within the ARTL system—currently dispositions, standard securities, discharges, and assignations of leases—can be in electronic form.[97] An electronic deed is authenticated by the digital signature of the granter, or in practice of the granter's solicitor acting under a written mandate.[98] A deed which appears to be so authenticated is probative, and a witness is not needed.[99] Further details can be found above in Ch.8.[100]   17–17

Companies

Juristic persons cannot hold a pen and so are the subject of a series of special rules in the 1995 Act. So far as companies are concerned, the relevant provisions apply to all companies incorporated under the Companies Acts, whether in Scotland or in England and Wales, in any case where the applicable law is the law of Scotland.[101] This covers all deeds which create real rights over Scottish land, even where the granter is an English company. The rules are straightforward. The company has a choice. Like a natural person, it can decide to use a witness. In that case the deed must be subscribed by a person representing the company—a director, the secretary, or an authorised person—and attested by a witness.[102] The usual rules of attestation, described earlier, apply. Alternatively the deed can be subscribed by two representatives of the company, without a witness. This means subscription by (a) two directors, or   17–18

---

[92] e.g. *Hynd's Trustee v Hynd's Trustees*, 1955 S.C. (HL) 1.

[93] 1995 Act s.3(4)(e).

[94] 1995 Act s.3(1).

[95] 1995 Act s.3(4)(dd). The effect of this provision seems to be to create a presumption that the solicitor signed with the authority of the granter. It is, however, troublesome that the presumption mentioned at the end of subs.(4) goes further than the presumption mentioned at the end of subs.(1).

[96] 1995 Act s.9(4). Under the previous law the conferral of benefit invalidated the entire deed.

[97] 1995 Act s.1(2A), (2B).

[98] 1995 Act s.2A.

[99] 1995 Act s.3A.

[100] See above, para.8–23.

[101] 1995 Act s.12(1) (definition of "company").

[102] 1995 Act s.3(1). See below, para.28–03 for the tension between this provision and the rule of company law that the board of directors must act as a collective entity.

(b) a director and the company secretary, or (c) two authorised persons.[103] Mixed doubles are not permitted, so that a deed subscribed by a director and an authorised person would not be probative.[104] There is no requirement that the second representative sign on the same day as the first.

A deed executed in the manner described above is probative, i.e. it is presumed to be subscribed by the company. That at least is what the Act says.[105] But the presumption is promptly negatived by a further rule that the person signing is not presumed to be authorised to sign.[106] The net result of these two somewhat inconsistent provisions is probably that the deed is presumed to be signed by the person who bears to sign it, but no more than that; so that a person relying on the deed should check out the signatory's credentials. If the signatory purports to be a director or the secretary, the position is easily verified by a search of the company file. If the signatory purports to be an authorised person, it will be necessary to see evidence of authority, for example a power of attorney or board minute.[107]

Less is required for improbative deeds, i.e. for deeds which are merely formally valid under s.2 of the 1995 Act. A deed granted by a company is formally valid if it is subscribed by a director or the secretary or an authorised person.[108]

Limited liability partnerships

17–19　The rules for limited liability partnerships ("LLP") follow those for companies.[109] Thus an LLP executes deeds through the signature of a member; and the deed is probative as well as merely valid if the signature is witnessed or the deed is signed (without a witness) by two members. But there is no presumption that a person bearing to sign as a member of an LLP was such a member, and the position requires to be verified.

Receivers, administrators and liquidators

17–20　Receivers, administrators, and liquidators are authorised by statute to execute deeds on behalf of the company.[110] It follows that a deed by a company in receivership, administration or liquidation is formally valid if subscribed by, respectively, the receiver, administrator or liquidator,[111] and is probative if the subscription is attested by a witness.[112]

---

[103] 1995 Act s.3(1A) as substituted by Sch.2 para.3(5).

[104] Unless either (i) one could be regarded as a witness to the signature of the other; or (ii) a director can be regarded as an authorised person. But while not probative, such a deed would be formally valid under s.2 and Sch.3 para.3(1).

[105] 1995 Act s.3(1A) as substituted by Sch.2 para.3(5).

[106] 1995 Act s.3(1C) as substituted by Sch.2 para.3(5).

[107] Sometimes there may be nothing in writing. The 1995 Act s.12(1) defines "authorised" to mean expressly or impliedly authorised. The definition also makes clear that the authority can be given generally, or in relation to a particular deed.

[108] 1995 Act Sch.3 para.3(1). For the tension between this provision and the rules of company law as to the power of directors, see below, para.28–03.

[109] 1995 Act Sch.2 para.3A.

[110] Insolvency Act 1986 Sch.1 para.9 (administrators), Sch.2 para.9 (receivers), Sch.4 para.7 (liquidators). These provisions are expressly saved by Sch.2 para.3(2) of the 1995 Act.

[111] 1995 Act s.2.

[112] 1995 Act s.3(1).

Partnerships

Partnerships execute deeds through the signature of a partner or some other 17–21
person authorised for this purpose.[113] Signatories can use either their own
name or the name of the firm.[114] As usual under the 1995 Act, bare subscription
is enough for formal validity, but probativity requires attestation by a witness.[115]
By contrast with the position for companies and LLPs, in a probative deed the
authority of the signatory is presumed.[116]

Local authorities

Local authorities execute deeds through the signature of an employee author- 17–22
ised for this purpose (a so-called "proper officer").[117] The deed is probative if
either the subscription is witnessed, or the deed is sealed with the common seal
of the authority.[118] The authority of the signatory is presumed.[119] A deed which
is subscribed without a witness or seal is formally valid but not probative.[120]

Other bodies corporate

Among the many other juristic persons, not yet mentioned, are building socie- 17–23
ties, industrial and provident societies, and universities. A small number of
these have their own rules of execution contained in the applicable statute or
statutory instrument. But in all other cases[121] execution is governed by para.5
of Sch.2 to the 1995 Act. This provides for subscription by a person representing the body corporate—either a member of the governing body (i.e. a
director or equivalent), or the secretary, or an authorised person.[122] As usual,
bare subscription achieves formal validity but not probativity.[123] For probativity there must also be attestation by a witness, or sealing with the common
seal.[124] If sealing is used, it must be carried out on the same day as the signatory signed, and by a person with authority to do so.[125] Authority to sign is not
presumed and should be investigated wherever possible.[126]

Foreign companies

Paragraph 5 of Sch.2 to the 1995 Act also applies to foreign companies. It 17–24
should be noted that Scots international private law provides that deeds relating
to immoveable property in Scotland must be executed as required by Scots law
rather than the law of the place of incorporation or the law of the place of

---

[113] 1995 Act Sch.2 para.2(1).
[114] 1995 Act Sch.2 para.2(2).
[115] 1995 Act ss.2 and 3.
[116] The presumption conferred by s.3(1) is that the deed is presumed to be subscribed by "that granter" (i.e. the partnership).
[117] 1995 Act Sch.2 para.4(1). For the definition of "proper officer", see s.12(1).
[118] 1995 Act s.3(1) (as amended, for local authorities, by Sch.2 para.4(5)).
[119] 1995 Act Sch.2 para.4(2). Unusually, the presumption applies even to improbative deeds.
[120] 1995 Act s.2.
[121] 1995 Act Sch.2 para.5(1), (2).
[122] 1995 Act Sch.2 para.5(2).
[123] 1995 Act s.2.
[124] 1995 Act s.3(1) (as amended, for bodies corporate, by Sch.2 para.5(5)).
[125] 1995 Act s.3(4)(h) as substituted by Sch.2 para.5(6).
[126] 1995 Act s.3(1B) as substituted by Sch.2 para.5(5).

execution.[127] It seems to be the case that execution in terms of the 1995 Act is not only necessary but is also sufficient, so that the deed will be validly executed even if the foreign law would impose a stricter standard.[128]

With foreign companies there are practical difficulties in verifying that those who sign for the company are indeed authorised to do so. A solution commonly adopted is to obtain a letter from a law firm in that country confirming that the deed has been properly executed.[129]

Excessive informality

17–25 It is possible for law to be too simple. If it is too easy to execute deeds, there is a danger that people will undertake obligations either unintentionally or with insufficient reflection. The 1995 Act requires no more than a signature at the end of the document. In some cases this may seem too low a threshold. The risk of unintentional obligations greatly exercised solicitors at the time when the 1995 Act was passed. Like other people, solicitors sign their letters; and this gave rise to the fear that letters which were intended to do no more than state a negotiating position would be treated as having formal, contractual effect. Some solicitors reacted by adding at the end of all letters an express statement that no contractual effect was intended (which must often have puzzled their clients). In fact the fear is largely misplaced. The rule is not that all subscribed documents are contractual in effect. Rather it is that contracts in relation to land must be subscribed.[130] Most letters could not conceivably be read as imposing contractual obligations. A docquet of denial is necessary only in the small number of cases where there is genuine danger of misinterpretation.

A more serious criticism is the opportunity for fraud. In many countries, deeds of a certain class require to be executed in front of a notary, who is regarded as a state official. In Scotland deeds have always been executed privately. For a person determined on fraud, the rules in the 1995 Act do not form much of an obstacle. The possibilities here are numerous. The granter's signature could be forged.[131] Or the granter could be persuaded to sign by misrepresentation,[132] or by force and fear,[133] or by the application of undue influence.[134] Another approach would be to allow the granter to sign normally, but then to alter what has been signed. Since the granter only signs at the end (except in the case of probative wills), it would be possible to substitute some of the earlier pages. If the document is too short to have earlier pages, it would

---

[127] Erskine III, ii, 40. For a full discussion see A.E. Anton and P.R. Beaumont, *Private International Law*, 2nd edn (1990), Ch.24.

[128] See also Companies Act 2006 s.48 (as substituted by the Overseas Companies (Execution of Documents and Registration of Charges) Regulations 2009 (SI 2009/1917) reg.5), which provides that references in any enactment to a document executed by a company by affixing its common seal includes, in relation to an overseas company signing under Scots law, execution in accordance with the Requirements of Writing (Scotland) Act 1995.

[129] Such a letter is likely to be needed for other purposes, including to confirm that the company was duly incorporated, that it has not been dissolved, that it is not in some form of bankruptcy process, and generally that it has full right and power to grant the deed in question. For a style, see below, para.28–12.

[130] 1995 Act s.1(2)(a)(i).

[131] *Kaur v Singh*, 1999 S.C. 180.

[132] As often argued in the so-called "cautionary wife" cases such as *Smith v Bank of Scotland*, 1997 S.C. (HL) 111.

[133] *Russo v Hardey*, 2000 G.W.D. 27-1049.

[134] *MacGilvary v Gilmartin*, 1986 S.L.T. 89.

still be possible to add text into the space reserved for the testing clause, or to make alterations elsewhere in the deed which are then declared in the testing clause (falsely) to have been added before subscription. There are, of course, some protections. The requirement that a witness must "know" the granter is at least a modest hindrance to forgery (except, of course, where the witness is also the forger). And after execution, deeds are usually handled by solicitors, who are in general trustworthy and can be relied on not to tamper. But the opportunities for fraud remain, and there is evidence that its incidence is increasing.

There are, of course, arguments the other way. A system which depends on execution in front of notaries is likely to be slow and expensive. The Scottish system is fast and cheap. These are important advantages, particularly in the commercial world.[135] Whether these advantages outweigh the drawbacks is a matter on which opinions may differ.

Execution before August 1, 1995

The 1995 Act applies to deeds executed on or after August, 1, 1995. But in the course of conveyancing it is often necessary to read and evaluate deeds executed before that date. The relevant rules may be summarised briefly.[136]   17–26

The normal method of executing a deed was by subscription of the granter and of two witnesses.[137] Such a deed was both formally valid and also probative. At one time the granter was also required to sign each separate sheet,[138] but this rule was abandoned with effect from November 29, 1970, except in the case of wills.[139] The rules for witnessing were broadly the same as they are under the 1995 Act. There were special rules for companies and other juristic persons.[140]

In general, a deed was not valid without witnesses. Hence an error in attestation was fatal to the deed.[141] But if the deed was in the handwriting of the granter (i.e. "holograph"), or if the signature was preceded by the words "adopted as holograph" in the granter's hand, the deed was formally valid although not probative. The "adopted as holograph" formula was used by solicitors for missives of sale and letters of obligation and its withdrawal is still resented by

---

[135] This is hardly a new thought. In his important work on *Testing of Deeds*, written in 1795, Robert Bell wrote that (pp.3–4) "although we may be forced to acknowledge, that a greater degree of security exists in some of these regulations [on notarial execution in other countries] than our own law admits of, we shall find that they are incumbered with unwieldy forms, and that the publication on which principally their security depended, must have unfitted them for many of the transactions of business; while . . . our own law joins to a sufficient degree of security, a facility and ease in the execution of our deeds, admirably fitted for the purposes of a rich and commercial people".

[136] For a fuller account, see Ch.15 of the first edition of this book.

[137] Subscription of Deeds Act 1681.

[138] Deeds Act 1696.

[139] Conveyancing and Feudal Reform (Scotland) Act 1970 s.44. Even in the case of wills, a failure to sign on each sheet could be cured by a petition under s.39 of the Convyeancing (Scotland) Act 1874, as an informality of execution.

[140] The rules for companies were in flux between 1990 and 1995. A table showing the rules at different times can be found at para.14–17 of the third edition of this book.

[141] For example, in *Williamson v Williamson*, 1997 S.C. 94 a will was denied effect because one of the witnesses had absent-mindedly signed using the surname of the testator instead of his own surname. Under the 1995 Act the will would have been perfectly valid, as having been subscribed by the testator.

some. Holograph documents tended to be home-made wills. Conveyancing deeds, then as now, were always attested.

Affidavits and other notarial documents[142]

17–27   An affidavit (also called a deposition) is a declaration made in writing and subscribed by the deponent, and the truth of which is sworn (or affirmed) by the deponent to a notary (or other person authorised by law to "receive" affidavits), the notary also signing. In receiving the affidavit the notary is acting as a public official. The law assumes that he will act conscientiously.

Affidavits are not covered by the 1995 Act, but are subject to common law. Witnessing is not necessary, though it is not uncommon. As far as Scots law is concerned, the notary need not use his or her seal, but if the affidavit is needed in a foreign matter the seal should always be used. If the affidavit consists of more than one sheet, it is probably only necessary to sign the last, but it is prudent for both notary and deponent to sign every sheet, especially if the affidavit is needed in a foreign matter. Again, if the affidavit is for foreign use the designation of the deponent should be fuller than is customary in Scots law: for instance, the date of birth should be stated.

The notary is professionally bound to be satisfied as to the identity of the deponent, and this duty must be taken seriously, because this lies at the very heart of the notarial system. It is good practice, especially if the affidavit is for foreign use, to append a docquet stating in what manner the notary was satisfied on this matter.[143] The notary is also under a professional duty to be satisfied that the deponent understands the document, which may give rise to problems if there are linguistic difficulties. It is indispensable that the notary should administer an oath or affirmation, for failure to do so renders the affidavit void.[144] There is no fixed form, but "I [swear by Almighty God] [solemnly and sincerely affirm] that to the best of my knowledge and belief the contents of this affidavit are true" is an appropriate style. The usual practice is for the deponent to stand and raise the right hand.[145]

A typical affidavit would begin: "At Dundee on the tenth day of November in the year two thousand and eleven compeared[146] Mungo Park of 41 St Mary's Road Milnathort in the County of Kinross who being solemnly sworn and examined[147] hereby depones . . ." and would end "all which is truth as the deponent shall answer to God".

Scots law does not make much use of notaries, apart from affidavits, though Scottish notaries will find themselves asked to notarise all sorts of things for foreign use. However, one Scottish document which does need notarisation and which must be mentioned here is the deed of renunciation of the occupancy rights of a non-entitled spouse or civil partner.[148]

---

[142] For more detail see (1997) 42 J.L.S.S. 50.

[143] e.g. "I satisfied myself as to the identity of the deponent by examination of her Spanish passport number 987654321".

[144] *Blair v North British and Mercantile Insurance Co* (1889) 16 R. 325.

[145] Some notaries ask the deponent to hold a Bible in the left.

[146] i.e. appeared.

[147] Meaning that the notary has checked that the deponent understands the meaning of the affidavit.

[148] See above, para.10–09.

CHAPTER 18

STAMP DUTY LAND TAX

Introduction

Most conveyancing transactions are subject to stamp duty land tax ("SDLT"), 18–01
which replaced stamp duty on December 1, 2003.[1] Stamp duty, long-established
if little admired, was a tax on deeds. If there was no deed, no tax was due. Further,
stamp duty could not be sued for directly, and its collection depended largely on
the rule that a deed not properly stamped would not be accepted for registration
in the Land Register or GRS. This meant that if registration was not needed a
deed might not be stamped, and even in the case of registrable deeds, such as
dispositions, purchasers occasionally preferred the risks of non-registration to
the cost of stamp duty. This benign regime is now at an end.[2] SDLT is a tax on
transactions and not on deeds. And while, as before, registration requires
evidence of payment, the tax is due whether registration takes place or not.
Indeed, even if no disposition is ever delivered, SDLT is due on missives alone
once possession is taken or the price substantially paid.[3]

Which transactions?

In principle SDLT is payable on any *land transaction*, that is to say, on the 18–02
acquisition of a *chargeable interest*.[4] "Acquisition" extends to initial creation,
transfer, variation and extinction, and the person so acquiring, in this extended
sense, is referred to in the legislation as the "purchaser".[5] So a tenant is a
purchaser, or the grantee of a minute of waiver of a real burden. A "chargeable
interest" is either (i) a right or power in or over land or, more mysteriously, (ii)
the benefit of an obligation, restriction or condition affecting (i).[6] The typical
chargeable interest is a real right in land, such as ownership, lease, real burden
or servitude. The limitation to land will be noted: no SDLT is payable in
relation to the sale of goods or the assignation of a life policy.

    Even for land there are exceptions. Rights in security, such as standard secu-
rities and floating charges, are exempt.[7] So are donations.[8] Thus if Mrs Smith
makes a present of a house to her husband, no SDLT is payable. The same is
true if the conveyance is by Mrs Smith's executor, in implement of Mrs Smith's

---

[1] See generally Finance Act 2003 Pt 4, as amended.
[2] For stamp duty, see Ch.15 of the second edition of this book.
[3] Finance Act 2003 s.44. If a disposition is eventually delivered, it is then a separate land
transaction, but the SDLT already paid is set off against any SDLT now due: see s.44(8).
[4] Finance Act 2003 s.43(1).
[5] Finance Act 2003 s.43(3), (4).
[6] Finance Act 2003 s.48(1).
[7] Finance Act 2003 s.48(2)(a).
[8] Finance Act 2003 Sch.3 para.1.

will. For the same reason SDLT is not due on deeds of assumption of trustees or on gratuitous declarations of trust. Further, even if the transaction is not an outright donation, nothing is due unless the consideration reaches the applicable threshold, currently £125,000 in the case of residential property.[9] As a result, some standard transactions are likely to escape payment, including grants of servitude, deeds of conditions, minutes of waiver, and variations of leases. Other exemptions are more esoteric. They include purchases by charities, and certain transactions in connection with divorce.[10] Even if no tax is due, however, it may still be necessary to make a return to HMRC.[11]

In practice, SDLT is payable mainly in two cases. One is the purchase of land, or of a lease over land. The other is the grant of new lease. Thus, although, strictly, SDLT is not deeds-based, payment is typically prompted by dispositions, by leases, and by assignations of leases. In addition, SDLT is payable in respect of involuntary transactions including acquisitions by statute, by common law, and by court order,[12] but only in the unusual case of consideration being paid.

Like stamp duty before it, SDLT is payable by the purchaser.[13] Clients may be unaware of this, or be aware of it but underestimate the amount which will be due. It is important that they are told at the start that the funds to be made available at settlement must include provision for SDLT. Even after such advice some clients resentfully regard SDLT as something charged by "the lawyers" and as such practically indistinguishable from fees.

Rates

18–03　Except in the case of the grant of leases, discussed later,[14] SDLT is based on the price paid by the purchaser ("chargeable consideration"), rounded down to the nearest £1.[15] For payments in kind, the relevant figure is the market value of the consideration.[16] As with all taxes, the rates change from time to time, and in recent years there were some reductions, often temporary in nature, due to a combination of political expediency and a desire to stimulate the housing market during a period of recession. A slightly reduced rate applies to residential property in so-called disadvantaged areas,[17] and, in what seems likely to be a temporary concession, no SDLT is payable by first-time buyers of residential property where the consideration does not exceed £250,000.[18] In Scotland, disadvantaged areas are identified by postcode.[19]

At the time of writing the normal rates are:

---

[9] Strictly this is not an exemption but a case where the relevant rate is, currently, 0 per cent.

[10] Respectively Finance Act 2003 s.68 Sch.8 and Sch.3 para.3.

[11] See below, para.18–11.

[12] Finance Act 2003 s.43(2).

[13] Finance Act 2003 s.85. While this was true as a matter of practice under stamp duty, it is formally so under SDLT.

[14] See below, para.18–10. Special rules are necessary only because the consideration involves rent. The assignation of a lease, however, follows the normal rules.

[15] Finance Act 2003 s.55 Sch.4 para.1.

[16] Finance Act 2003 Sch.4 para.7. For other cases, see Sch.4 generally.

[17] Finance Act 2003 Sch.6 para.5. It was, however, indicated in the 2011 budget that this is scheduled for abolition in a future year, following consultation.

[18] Finance Act 2003 s.57AA. The buyer must intend to occupy the the property as his or her only or main residence. If there is more than one buyer, all must be buying a house for the first time.

[19] The legislation has adopted the list of disadvantaged areas already made for the purposes of stamp duty by the Stamp Duty (Disadvantaged Areas) Regulations 2001 (SI 2001/3747). See Finance Act 2003 Sch.6 para.2. The complete list is given in Reid and Gretton, *Conveyancing* (2001), pp.41–43.

Consideration	Rate
Not more than £125,000 (residential property except in disadvantaged areas) or £150,000 (other property)	0%
From £125,001 (residential property) or £150,001 (other property) to £250,000	1%
From £250,001 to £500,000	3%
From £500,001 to £1,000,000	4%
More than £1,000,000	5% (residential property) or 4% (other property)

It will be seen that, at both the lowest and the highest rate, residential property is treated less favourably than other property. "Residential property" means a house and its garden, including houses in the process of construction.[20] Where any of the land is not residential, the whole transaction is classified as non-residential and benefits from the lower rate.[21] The same is true of a transaction comprising the sale of six or more separate houses.[22]

It would be natural to suppose that the first £125,000 (or £150,000) of the price will be charged at zero, the next slice at 1 per cent, and so on, rather in the way that the income tax band rates are applied, so that if a house were sold at £150,000 the duty would be (0 per cent × £125,000) + (1 per cent × £25,000) = £250. That would be reasonable, but it is not the law.[23] If a house is sold for £120,000 the duty is zero. If a house is sold for £200,000, the duty is £2,000. If a house is sold for £245,000, the duty is £2,450. If a house is sold for £255,000 the duty is £7,650. Thus, a 4 per cent increase in price (from £245,000 to £255,000) results in a 212 per cent increase in the tax payable. Hence, when a property is near one of the band boundaries, the exact price can assume considerable significance.[24]

Value added tax

In cases where value added tax ("VAT") is payable on the price, the price is 18–04 grossed up for SDLT purposes to include the VAT.[25] There is thus a tax on a tax. VAT may be payable in two main types of case. One is the sale of new,[26] non-domestic property. The other is the sale (or lease) of older non-domestic property, but only if the seller (or lessor) has waived exemption from VAT. Where exemption is waived only after settlement,[27] SDLT is not payable on the

---

[20] Finance Act 2003 s.116(1). Some special rules, e.g. for student halls of residence, are given in s.116(2), (3).

[21] Finance Act 2003 s.55(2).

[22] Finance Act 2003 s.116(7).

[23] Except for the SDLT due on rent under leases, for which see below, para.18–10.

[24] All taxes result in distortions of the economic activities which they feed on, and SDLT is certainly no exception. Keeping SDLT to a minimum can be a major issue in commercial transactions. A sale of land for £5 million is impossible unless £200,000 can be found to pay HMRC.

[25] Finance Act 2003 Sch.4 para.2.

[26] Meaning not more than three years old.

[27] i.e. the "effective date of the transaction", discussed below in para.18–12.

resulting VAT.[28] Although VAT is an important issue, it is essentially a matter for commercial conveyancing, and so will not be further dealt with here.

Linked transactions

18–05 Parties might seek to avoid SDLT by packaging a large transaction into a series of small ones, the price for each part being less than one of the threshold figures. This obvious evasion is prevented by the idea of linked transactions. Where transactions are linked, they are treated as a single transaction, and SDLT is paid on the total price.[29] Transactions are "linked" in the required sense "if they form part of a single scheme, arrangement or series of transactions between the same vendor and purchaser or, in either case, persons connected with them".[30] So if Alan sells Barbara a house for £200,000, SDLT cannot be avoided by having (for instance) four separate dispositions of one quarter *pro indiviso* shares, each with a price of £50,000. And given the wide definition of connected persons,[31] the same is true if some of the sales involve spouses, siblings or in-laws rather than Alan and Barbara themselves.

Sale of house with contents

18–06 Where a house or other building is sold together with moveable items such as carpets, the moveables are not part of the price for SDLT purposes.[32] Therefore, only that part of the price applicable to the heritage should be given as the price in the disposition. Missives often provide how the total price in a sale should be apportioned as between heritage and moveables, and the legislation requires that such apportionment be "on a just and reasonable basis".[33] Nonetheless the temptation may be to overstate the value of the moveables, so that SDLT is reduced or even (if the figure can be brought below £125,000) eliminated. This temptation should be resisted. A contract which falsely apportions price as between heritage and moveables might be unenforceable as contrary to public policy.[34] At any rate it is probably professional misconduct on the part of the solicitor,[35] there are specific penalties for assisting in the preparation or delivery of an incorrect return,[36] and the fraudulent evasion of SDLT is an offence punishable by up to seven years' imprisonment.[37] Whilst, however, a false apportionment is unacceptable, "no man in this country is under the smallest obligation, moral or other, so to arrange his legal relations to his business or to his property as to enable the Inland Revenue to put the largest possible shovel into his stores".[38] Drawing the line between a false, and a merely generous, estimate of the value of the moveables can be difficult, both morally and legally.

---

[28] Finance Act 2003 Sch.4 para.2.

[29] Finance Act 2003 s.55(4).

[30] Finance Act 2003 s.108(1).

[31] Finance Act 2003 s.108(1) incorporates the definition in the Corporation Tax Act 2010 s.1122.

[32] See above, para.18–02.

[33] Finance Act 2003 Sch.4 para.4(1).

[34] *Saunders v Edwards* [1987] 2 All E.R. 651, especially at 665, per Nicholls L.J.

[35] *Saunders v Edwards* [1987] 2 All E.R. 651, especially at 665, per Nicholls L.J.

[36] Finance Act 2003 s.96.

[37] Finance Act 2003 s.95.

[38] The immortal words of Lord President Clyde in *Ayrshire Pullman Motor Services v Commissioners of Inland Revenue* (1929) 14 T.C. 754.

Sale of a business

In commercial cases, different types of property may be sold in the course of 18–07
the same transaction, for example, land, goodwill, receivables, stock in trade,
and so on. SDLT is payable only in respect of land,[39] although HMRC will
generally treat much of the value of goodwill as attributable to the land with
which it is sold.

Options

The grant of an option to buy land is itself a land transaction separate from its 18–08
ultimate exercise.[40] So if A Ltd has an option to purchase land from B Ltd for
£1 million, and if the option itself carried a price of £200,000, the result is two
separate land transactions: the grant of the option, and the eventual disposition
by B Ltd to A Ltd. The fact that the option is taxable prevents avoidance
of SDLT by ascribing to the option a price which is really part of the price for
the land.

Excambions

Where Alan and Beth agree to excamb (i.e. exchange) land this can be effected 18–09
either by two separate dispositions, or by a single deed (known as a contract of
excambion) in which Alan conveys to Beth and Beth conveys to Alan.
Whichever method is chosen, SDLT is payable on the value of each property.[41]
For instance, if Alan dispones to Beth a property worth £270,000, and Beth
dispones to Alan a property worth £240,000 plus £30,000 in cash, SDLT will
be payable on the first transaction at 3 per cent and on the second transaction
at 1 per cent. This unfavourable outcome is modified where a person buys a
new house from a house-building company and pays partly by the exchange of
his existing house. No SDLT is then payable on the conveyance of the existing
house.[42]

Leases

Leases are taxed both on the rent and on any premium paid for the grant of the 18–10
lease. The position of the premium is straightforward. SDLT is paid at the rates
already described[43] except that, where the annual rent exceeds £1,000, the 0 per
cent band is replaced by 1 per cent in the case of non-residential property.[44]

Rent is, by its nature, more difficult to tax. Stamp duty was payable on the
annual rent but on a scale which rose with the duration of the lease. SDLT
applies a uniform scale, but to the total rent payable during the lease, discounted
at 3.5 per cent a year in respect of future payments.[45] This is known as the net
present value of rent. Rent reviews are disregarded if five or more years from
the start of the lease unless they produce an "abnormal" increase.[46] There is a

---

[39] See above, para.18–02.

[40] Finance Act 2003 s.46. The same rule applies to pre-emptions reserved by the seller, although in practice there will either be no consideration or one too small to attract SDLT.

[41] Finance Act 2003 s.47 Sch.4 para.5(3).

[42] Finance Act 2003 s.58A Sch.6A para.1. There are some qualifications.

[43] See above, para.18–03.

[44] Finance Act 2003 Sch.5 para.9A.

[45] Finance Act 2003 Sch.5 paras 2, 3, and 8.

[46] Finance Act 2003 Sch.17A paras 7(3) and 14.

threshold, for the net present value, of £125,000 for residential property and £150,000 for land which is not wholly residential.[47] If the net present value is below the threshold no SDLT is payable. If it is above the threshold, SDLT is payable at 1 per cent but only to the extent that the threshold is exceeded.[48] So for example if the net present value of the rent for a shop is £250,000, the SDLT due is £1,000 (1 per cent of £100,000).

In practice, a lease often takes the form of missives of let, which may or may not ultimately be followed by a formal lease. If possession is taken and rent paid on the basis of missives, SDLT is payable as if it were a formal lease. A subsequent grant of a lease might be a notifiable transaction[49] but no further tax would be due.[50]

Notifiable transactions

18–11   A key distinction is between those transactions which must be notified to HMRC and those which need not. It would be natural, but mistaken, to suppose that this is the same as the distinction between transactions which attract tax and transactions which do not. Admittedly no SDLT is due in respect of transactions where notification is not required, but by no means all transactions which are notifiable will involve the payment of tax. This is a trap for the unwary. It should not be assumed that because no tax is due, no return need be made to the HMRC, and a penalty will be levied for failure to make a return when one is needed.[51]

The transactions which are notifiable are:[52]

(i)   the transfer of ownership or of a lease for a consideration of £40,000 or more;

(ii)   the grant of a lease for seven years or more at premium of £40,000 or more or for an annual rent of £1,000 or more;

(iii) and any other transaction, including a lease of less than seven years, if SDLT is due, or would be due but for a relief (as opposed to an exemption).

Thus all dispositions must be notified other than those in implement of a gift or for a consideration of less than £40,000. The position is the same for assignations of leases. A new lease must always be notified if for seven years or more and either the premium is at least £40,000 or the annual rent at least £1,000. Otherwise notification is necessary only where SDLT is due or would be due but for a relief (such as disadvantaged areas relief, mentioned above). In practice the consideration for most other transactions will fall below even the lowest threshold for tax (currently £125,000) and so will not be notifiable. Common examples will include deeds of trust, minutes of waiver, deeds of conditions, deeds of servitude, and deeds of assumption and conveyance of

---

[47] For the meaning of residential property in this context, see above, para.18–03.

[48] Finance Act 2003 Sch.5 para.2. This use of the threshold is in contrast to that which applies in sales: see above, para.18–03.

[49] For notifiable transactions, see below, para.18–11.

[50] Finance Act 2003 s.44.

[51] Finance Act 2003 Sch.10 paras 3–5.

[52] Finance Act 2003 ss.77, 77A.

trustees. And of course no notification is required in respect of deeds, such as standard securities, which are wholly exempt from SDLT.[53]

Land transaction returns

A transaction which is notifiable is notified by sending to HMRC a land trans-   18–12
action return, followed by payment of any tax that is due.[54] Both must be done
within 30 days of the "effective date of the transaction", normally the date on
which the transaction is settled.[55] The obligation rests on the purchaser, lessee,
or other grantee of the deed.[56] If two people are buying together—a husband
and wife, for example—each is liable jointly and severally.[57] There are penalties for late notification and interest is due in the event of late payment.[58]

Although land transaction returns can be submitted on paper, this is slow
and will delay registration of the deed, perhaps beyond the 14 days allowed by
the letter of obligation.[59] The normal practice, therefore, is to submit returns
online. Speed is not the only advantage, for only questions relevant to the
transaction type appear on the screen, and inappropriate answers are detected,
giving an opportunity to provide corrections. Online submission is acknowledged by a receipt, usually within a few minutes, and, all being well, this
includes the official certificate (SDLT5) which is needed for registration in the
Land Register, GRS, or Books of Council and Session.[60] It also gives the
Unique Transaction Reference Number ("UTRN") which is used as the reference for payment. In ARTL transactions, the relevant form is completed within
the ARTL system and payment is collected by the Keeper on behalf of HMRC.[61]

The purchaser or other grantee must approve the land transaction return.
Paper returns include a declaration that they are correct and complete to the
best of the grantee's knowledge.[62] In the case of electronic returns, the grantee
signs a separate declaration (which is not submitted to HMRC) on the basis of
a draft of the return. If there is more than one grantee, each must sign,[63]
although in the case of trustees the signature of a single trustee is sufficient.[64]

When SDLT was first introduced, there were often considerable delays in
obtaining the SDLT certificate and hence in registering the deed. This created
particular problems for Scotland where, unlike in England and Wales, a
purchaser of land is vulnerable to the insolvency of the seller during the period
between payment of the price and registration of the disposition or other
deed.[65] The longer the delay in registration, the greater the vulnerability. The
problem has largely been solved by the online filing of returns, first introduced

---

[53] See above, para.18–02.
[54] Finance Act 2003 ss.76(1), (3), 86(1).
[55] Finance Act 2003 ss.119 and 121 (meaning of "completion").
[56] "Purchaser" is given an extended meaning by Finance Act 2003 s.43(4).
[57] Finance Act 2003 s.103.
[58] Finance Act 2003 ss.87 and Sch.10 paras 3–5; Finance Act 2009 s.106 Sch.55.
[59] For that reason the 14-day period was extended to 21 days for a number of years but, with the success of online submission of returns, it reverted to 14 days on November 1, 2010.
[60] Finance Act 2003 s.79. No certificate is needed for the registration of deeds in respect of which a land transaction return is not required, although until 2008 the grantee had to produce a "self-certificate" to that effect.
[61] See above, para.8–23.
[62] Finance Act 2003 Sch.10 para.1(1)(c).
[63] Finance Act 2003 s.103(4).
[64] Finance Act 2003 Sch.16 para.6.
[65] See *Burnett's Trustee v Grainger*, 2004 S.C. (HL) 19. See above, para.11–29.

in 2005, but in difficult cases—principally corporate transactions where the letter of obligation does not extend to the charges register and company file, or cases in which a return was filed online but no certificate was produced due to a system problem—HMRC allows personal presentation of the return at the Stamp Office in Edinburgh. This must be done within two working days of the effective date of the transaction. A handwritten SDLT certificate is then issued.[66]

---

[66] Reid and Gretton, *Conveyancing 2003*, pp.148–49 and *Conveyancing 2005*, pp.48–50.

CHAPTER 19

WARRANDICE AND POST-SETTLEMENT CLAIMS

Introduction

This chapter deals with claims which may arise after settlement of a transac-   19–01
tion has taken place. The subject has three aspects. The first is whether, after
settlement, the missives can to any extent still be founded on as a basis for a
claim. The second aspect, which relates only to defects and limitations in the
title, is whether a claim can be made under the warrandice clause in the disposition. The third aspect is whether it may be possible to have the disposition, or
other deed, judicially rectified. The third aspect is considered in the next
chapter.

CLAIMS UNDER MISSIVES

The continuing enforceability of missives

At common law the disposition superseded the missives, which could there-   19–02
fore no longer be relied upon or enforced after settlement.[1] Highly inconvenient in practice, this rule was subject to exceptions the precise scope of which
was never properly determined. Latterly it was routinely circumvented by an
express clause in the disposition,[2] known as a non-supersession clause, to the
effect that the missives were not after all superseded. Such a clause was made
unnecessary by s.2 of the Contract (Scotland) Act 1997, which provides that
"where a deed is executed in implement . . . of a contract, an unimplemented,
or otherwise unfulfilled, term of the contract shall not be taken to be superseded by virtue only of that execution or of the delivery and acceptance of the
deed". Thus the default rule is now that the missives are *not* superseded by
delivery of the disposition.

Problems may still arise. Suppose, for instance, that the extent of the property as identified in the missives is different from that identified in the disposition. If a mistake was made in drawing up the disposition, this can be rectified
under s.8 of the Law Reform (Miscellaneous Provisions) (Scotland) Act 1985.[3]
But sometimes there is no mistake and the disposition does indeed represent
the final intentions of the parties. In cases such as this the 1997 Act should not

---

[1] This topic has been much written about. A summary can be found in para.16–02 of the third
edition of this book. The leading, and notorious, case was *Winston v Patrick*, 1980 S.C. 246.

[2] At first the clause was put in the missives, but it later came to be held, in some cases at least,
that if missives were truly superseded, then they could not be consulted to see whether they
contained a clause providing that they should not be superseded. Thus the clause had to go in the
disposition itself.

[3] See below, Ch.20.

be construed as meaning that the missives prevail over the disposition. In a practical sense the 1997 Act deals chiefly not with such cases, but with collateral obligations, such as those concerning moveables, the physical condition of the property, and local authority consents.

Supersession clauses

19–03 Now that missives survive the disposition, it is normal for that survival to be made subject to a time limit. Thus the non-supersession clause of former years, designed to keep the missives alive, has come to be replaced by a supersession clause, designed to ensure their early demise.[4] The clause, which appears in the missives,[5] is in terms such as the following:

> "The missives of sale may not be founded upon[6] after a period of two years from the date of entry hereunder[7] except in so far as they are founded on in any court proceedings which have commenced within that period."[8]

Such clauses are a normal feature of standard missives such as the Combined Standard Clauses.[9] The two-year period is a compromise. Sellers would, in most cases, like to be free of the missives as soon as they receive the money, while buyers usually want time to find out whether the sellers' obligations have been properly implemented.[10] This two-year period seems in most cases to be satisfactory, but sometimes it turns out to be too short. This is particularly likely to happen if there is a missive clause dealing with a question which could take some time to resolve. For instance, it may be that the sellers had agreed to pay for certain remedial construction work. It is notorious that building work often takes longer than expected. In such cases the buyers' solicitors should seek to negotiate a longer period, and, if this proves impossible, must ensure that the two-year period does not slide by without the appropriate action being taken. *Hamilton v Rodwell*[11] is an illustration of how things can go wrong. Here the seller was bound to pay for certain repairs, and part of the price was put on joint deposit receipt, which would be payable to the seller

---

[4] The lawfulness of supersession clauses is recognised by s.2(2) of the Contract (Scotland) Act 1997.

[5] Today there is no reason, other than habit, for repeating the clause in the disposition.

[6] Or "shall cease to be enforceable". For the term "enforceable" in this context see *Smith v Lindsay & Kirk*, 1998 S.L.T. 1096, reversed 2000 S.C. 200. See further Reid and Gretton, *Conveyancing 1999*, p.41.

[7] Does this mean contractual date of entry or actual date of entry? See para.3–23(5). If the clause fails to specify when the clock starts to tick, it may be invalid: compare *Lonergan v W&P Food Service Ltd*, 2002 S.L.T. 908 with *Aziz v Whannel* [2010] CSOH 136; 2010 G.W.D. 33-682 at para.24, per Lord Glennie.

[8] In *Henderson v Marasa*, Unreported December 1, 2005 Glasgow Sheriff Court (summarised in Reid and Gretton, *Conveyancing 2006*, p.7), the supersession clause did not stipulate for continuing validity in the event of judicial enforcement, but missives were nonetheless allowed to be enforced by a court action begun within the prescribed period.

[9] See Combined Standard Clauses (2009) cl.22.

[10] Since most obligations in missives are the sellers', the continued enforceability of missives is chiefly for the benefit of the buyers. But in some cases they can be for the benefit of the sellers, though more often in commercial sales than domestic ones.

[11] *Hamilton v Rodwell*, 1998 S.C.L.R. 418; *Hamilton v Rodwell (No.2)*, 1999 G.W.D. 35-1706. See Reid and Gretton, *Conveyancing 1999*, p.4.

once he had done so. The seller never did pay for the repairs, and the purchasers had to. They accordingly claimed the sum in the D/R. But by this time the two-year period had elapsed and the missives were unenforceable. It was held that the purchasers had no right to the money.[12]

Finally, it should be noted that a supersession clause cannot be attacked on the ground that it is an attempt to contract out of the law of prescription.[13]

WARRANDICE CLAIMS UNDER THE DISPOSITION[14]

Introduction

Warrandice is a guarantee, expressed or implied, of good and unencumbered title. In dispositions there are three degrees of warrandice,[15] which are, in ascending order, simple, fact and deed, and absolute. The higher includes the lower, so that if a claim could be made under simple warrandice, it could also be made under fact and deed warrandice, and if a claim could be made under fact and deed warrandice, it could also be made under absolute warrandice. 19–04

Simple warrandice

Simple warrandice is a guarantee that the granter will do nothing subsequently to prejudice the title of the grantee. The content of this guarantee is minimal, for in most cases there is nothing that a granter could do to incur liability. If Ann dispones to Beth with simple warrandice, Ann can thereafter do nothing to affect the title, because Ann is no longer owner. Simple warrandice would however cover the following case. Ann grants a disposition to Beth on Monday, and fraudulently grants another disposition of the same property to Chris on Tuesday. Chris completes his title by registration on Wednesday. Assuming that Chris has acted in good faith, Beth has no remedy against Chris. But Beth can claim from Ann on the footing of warrandice, even simple warrandice. 19–05

Fact and deed warrandice

Fact and deed warrandice is a guarantee that the granter will do and has done nothing which could prejudice the title of the grantee. It thus covers what simple warrandice covers, but also covers past acts by the granter as well. Take the previous example and suppose that Beth had completed title first. Would Chris then have a claim against Ann? Not under simple warrandice, because the disposition by Ann to Beth was, at the time when Ann granted warrandice to Chris, not a future act but a past one. But if the warrandice by Ann to Chris was fact and deed warrandice, Chris would have a claim against Ann. 19–06

---

[12] But where this left the money is obscure, since one could equally argue that, since the missives had expired, the seller had no right to it either. For another illustration see *Albatown Ltd v Credential Group Ltd*, 2001 G.W.D. 27-1102, discussed in Reid and Gretton, *Conveyancing 2001*, p.63.

[13] Thus, it was held for non-supersession clauses, and the same logic seems to apply to supersession clauses. See *Ferguson v McIntyre*, 1993 S.L.T. 1269.

[14] The fullest account is Reid, in D.J. Cusine (ed.), *Scots Conveyancing Miscellany: Essays in Honour of Professor J. M. Halliday* (1987). See also Reid, *Property*, paras 701–719.

[15] In addition there is warrandice *debitum subesse* which is implied in onerous assignations of debt. This is a guarantee that at the date of the assignation the debt is payable to the cedent.

Absolute warrandice

19–07   Absolute warrandice guarantees the grantee against defects and limitations in
the title whether caused by the granter or not. Thus, suppose that Ann dispones
to Beth a farm, with absolute warrandice. It later turns out that title to one area
of ground is bad, this area actually being part of the title of the neighbouring
farm, though in terms of possession being part of the first farm. The reason for
this is that the previous owner—Ann's predecessor—had sold several hectares
to the neighbour, including the area in question, but that due to the wrong posi-
tioning of a fence the area remained in the possession of the first farm. Ann is
liable to Beth in warrandice. She would not have been liable if she had granted
to Beth only simple, or fact and deed, warrandice, because the defect did not
arise from her own act.

Wording of warrandice clause

19–08   In practice, the warrandice is always expressed in the conveyance, usually as
the final clause before the testing clause. The forms are: "I grant simple warrandice"; "I grant warrandice from my own facts and deeds"; "I grant warrandice". The last of these means absolute warrandice.[16]

Which type of warrandice?

19–09   If there is no warrandice clause, the law will imply one. In outline, the rule is
that simple warrandice is implied in conveyances by way of gift, and absolute
warrandice is implied in sales. But implied warrandice is overridden by express
warrandice. Thus, if a disposition by way of sale grants simple warrandice
only, the implication of absolute warrandice is excluded.

In sales by trustees or executors the practice is to grant fact and deed warrandice personally, and to bind the trust (or executry) estate in absolute warrandice. The practice in sales by heritable creditors is similar. The creditor grants
fact and deed warrandice personally and binds the debtor (the former owner)
in absolute warrandice.[17]

Missives do not usually make provision about warrandice. The grantee is in
that case entitled to the type of warrandice which is implied or is normally
granted in transactions of that type. If there is anything dubious about the title,
or part of it,[18] a decision needs to be made at missives stage about what sort of
warrandice should be granted, and this will simply mirror what the missives
themselves provide about good and marketable title.[19] Sometimes a property
with a doubtful title is sold for full value: in such cases the warrandice should
normally be absolute. But if the queries about the title mean that the parties
have bargained for a significantly below-market price, then the warrandice
should normally be fact and deed warrandice only, for in this latter case it is the
buyer who is assuming the risk. Sometimes absolute warrandice is granted
unthinkingly even if the missives provide that title is to be taken as it stands.

---

[16] Titles to Land Consolidation (Scotland) Act 1868 s.8.
[17] It is arguable that a purchaser should ask for absolute warrandice from the selling creditor: see
below, para.22–36.
[18] For it is perfectly competent to grant absolute warrandice for part of the property disponed
and lesser warrandice for some other part.
[19] As to which see above, Ch.6.

Remedies under warrandice

Warrandice is enforced by a claim for damages. If the defect in title is such that   19–10
the disponee loses the property entirely, the quantum of damages is the market
value of the property. If the defect is a lesser one, the quantum is the diminu-
tion in market value. Thus, suppose that Ann dispones a house to Beth, and it
then emerges that the garden ground is burdened by a servitude of way in
favour of a neighbouring property. In a warrandice claim, the court will hear
evidence as to what the market value would have been if the servitude had not
existed, and as to the actual market value subject to the servitude. The difference is then the measure of Beth's loss and of Ann's liability to Beth.[20] Probably
no claim can be entertained for solatium.[21]

Guarantee of good title: the need for eviction

Warrandice is generally said to be a guarantee that the title is (i) good and (ii)   19–11
unencumbered, and this is true as far as it goes. But no liability under warrandice can arise in respect of the first of these guarantees unless and until there
has been eviction.[22] Normally eviction means judicial eviction, that is to say, a
decree by which a better right is established by a third party.[23] But, as Viscount
Stair recognised, there can be eviction even without a court decree if the challenger's claim is based on an "unquestionable ground" which could not
sensibly be resisted.[24] This, however, is a high standard. Presumably a defect
so obvious that the Keeper grants rectification would qualify. But there is no
eviction if the challenger's title is affected by doubt,[25] still less if, as happened
in one case, the challenger has no current title but merely the prospect of
acquiring one in the future.[26] What unites both types of eviction—the judicial
and the extra-judicial—is the requirement of a challenge by a person with a
better title. In the absence of such a challenge there can be no warrandice claim
even if the title is obviously bad. So if a buyer, having paid the price and
accepted the disposition, is then refused registration by the Keeper, there is no
eviction and so no claim in warrandice.[27]

Guarantee of unencumbered title

Eviction is not needed for the guarantee of unencumbered title. A claim arises   19–12
in respect of any encumbrance which was unknown to the purchaser at the time

---

[20] *Welsh v Russell* (1894) 21 R. 769; *MacPherson v Williams* [2008] CSOH 25; 2008 G.W.D.
6-110.

[21] *Palmer v Beck*, 1993 S.L.T. 485, per Lord Kirkwood at 492.

[22] The word "eviction" is perhaps misleading, and it must accordingly be borne in mind that it
has a special meaning in the context of the law of warrandice. The word has been used in this
special sense for time immemorial.

[23] *Clark v Lindale Homes Ltd*, 1994 S.C. 210, one of the most important cases on the law
of warrandice. See also *Palmer v Beck*, 1993 S.L.T. 485. If the action is settled without decree,
there is still eviction provided that there was no good defence: *Watson v Swift's JF*, 1986
S.L.T. 217.

[24] Stair, II, iii, 46.

[25] *Holms v Ashford Estates Ltd* [2009] CSIH 28; 2009 S.L.T. 389. See Reid and Gretton,
Conveyancing 2009, pp.180–83.

[26] *Morris v Rae* [2011] CSIH 30; 2011 G.W.D. 13-305.

[27] Although there will be a claim under the good-and-marketable title obligation in the missives
if the missives are still in force: see para.below, para.19–13.

when warrandice was granted.[28] The last point requires emphasis. Thus, if land is subject to a servitude in favour of a neighbour, and the grantees were aware of this, they cannot subsequently sue the granters under warrandice. If they were unhappy with the position, they should have raised the point before settlement.[29] This is one of the reasons why a disposition tries to list all the burdens which affect the land, so as to make absolutely clear what the grantees are acquiring. Of course, for Land Register titles an encumbrance which is not shown on the Register has thereby ceased to exist unless, like a servitude, it is an overriding interest.[30]

Leases are treated differently from other encumbrances, and appear not to give rise to a warrandice claim.[31] However, where it is intended to convey property with vacant possession, it is standard practice to state this fact expressly in the deed,[32] so that in such a case the existence of a lease would give rise to a claim.

Concurrent claim under missives

19–13 The requirement of eviction can be circumvented by making a claim under the missives. Missives normally contain a guarantee of title, and insofar as the missives survive settlement,[33] this guarantee will also presumably survive. Hence, if the buyers discover, after settlement, that their title is not good and marketable, the sellers will normally be liable in terms of the missives. Eviction is not required.[34] For as long as they remain in force, therefore, missives are likely to provide a more attractive basis of claim. But as and when the missives have been superseded, which in most cases will be after two years, any claim will have to be based on the warrandice only.[35]

Transmission of warrandice

19–14 Suppose that Ann sells land to Beth, and Beth later sells to Chris. A defect in title then emerges. Chris can sue Beth under the warrandice which Beth granted to him. But he may not wish to do this. Perhaps Beth is bankrupt, or has disappeared. Can Chris claim from Ann? The answer is that he can, because the clause of assignation of writs which will normally have been part of the disposition by Beth to Chris[36] operates as an assignation to Chris of Beth's warrandice rights against Ann.[37]

---

[28] The relevant date is delivery of the disposition.

[29] Thus Roman law: D.19,1,1,1. But in earlier Roman law it was otherwise: *Orata v Gratidianus*, (91 B.C.) Cicero, *De Officiis* 3, 67. For discussion see Rodger, in P.G. Stein and A.D.E. Lewis (eds), *Studies in Justinian's Institutes* (1983).

[30] Land Registration (Scotland) Act s.3(1)(a). For overriding interests, see s.28(1).

[31] *Lothian and Border Farmers Ltd v McCutchion*, 1952 S.L.T. 450. The correctness of this decision is, however, not wholly free from doubt, although it has stood for 60 years.

[32] This is done in the entry clause: "with entry and vacant possession" (or "actual occupation"). The entry clause is discussed further above in para.11–19.

[33] Discussed at the beginning of the chapter.

[34] Reid, *Property*, paras 707 and 710.

[35] For discussion of this question see Steven, 1998 S.L.T. (News) 283.

[36] This clause is now implied: Land Registration (Scotland) Act 1979 s.16. See above, para.11–16.

[37] Stair, II, iii, 46. If, however, Chris sues Beth, then it appears that Beth can sue Ann. See *Christie v Cameron* (1898) 25 R. 824; *Cobham v Minter*, 1986 S.L.T. 336.

This, however, is subject to certain qualifications. Ann can be liable to Chris only to the extent that she would have been liable to Beth if Beth had not sold to Chris: *assignatus utitur jure auctoris*. Thus, if Ann had granted only simple warrandice to Beth, she would be unlikely to be liable to Chris. Or if the defect was caused by Beth's act, or by diligence by Beth's creditors, Ann cannot be liable to Chris.[38] Moreover, Ann's liability may be barred by negative prescription.

---

[38] Warrandice (even if absolute) does not extend to future acts by a successor in title.

CHAPTER 20

JUDICIAL RECTIFICATION OF DOCUMENTS

Wrong words or no words

20–01 Drafting being an imperfect art, deeds sometimes contain mistakes. For instance, words may have been missed out, or included without good reason, or the wrong words may have been used, or words which are unclear.[1] Often this is no more than a clerical error. Something went wrong in the typing, or the dictating, and the error is not picked up until it is too late. Less commonly there has been a failure to understand what the client actually wants. Where this happens it is usually because the solicitor has not received, or insisted upon, adequate instructions. For example, the client may have failed to mention the informal agreement reached with the seller (or buyer) over a glass of prosecco, with the result that the missives fail to include (or exclude) that elusive lock-up garage in the centre of town.

In general the best way to sort out a mistake is to produce a new version of the document. Missives can be amended, or a fresh disposition executed and registered. But this is not always possible. Too much time may have passed, so that the original parties are dead, or untraceable. Or, more seriously, the mistake may have grown into a dispute, for it is likely to benefit one party at the expense of the other. Recipients of windfall benefits are not always willing to relinquish them, and may seek to argue that the deed was what they had intended all along.[2] Indeed the dispute may be genuine enough, for parties in negotiation can quite easily be unclear on what precisely was agreed.[3]

Errors which cannot be rectified by agreement can sometimes be rectified judicially. By s.8 of the Law Reform (Miscellaneous Provisions) (Scotland) Act 1985 a power is conferred on the court to rectify documents which fail to express accurately the parties' intentions.[4] There is concurrent jurisdiction in the Court of Session and sheriff court.[5] In practice it is for the applicant to suggest the changes which are required, although further changes may be put

---

[1] There is a growing tendency to use rectification as a means of resolving ambiguity or uncertainty of language—quite often by a party which loses the argument on interpretation. See e.g. *Howgate Shopping Centre Ltd v Catercraft Services Ltd*, 2004 S.L.T. 231.

[2] e.g. *Cruickshank Botanic Gardens Trustees v Jamieson*, 2001 G.W.D. 19-735.

[3] e.g. *Rehman v Ahmad*, 1993 S.L.T. 741.

[4] This provision implemented the Scottish Law Commission's Report on *Rectification of Contractual and Other Documents* (Scot. Law Com. No.79, 1983). See generally William W. McBryde, *The Law of Contract in Scotland*, 3rd edn (2007), paras 8–102 to 8–108; Reid, (2009) 103 Prop. L.B. 1 and (2010) 104 Prop. L.B. 1.

[5] Law Reform (Miscellaneous Provisions) (Scotland) Act 1985 s.8(9). For the procedure, see Lord Macphail, *Sheriff Court Practice*, 3rd edn by T. Welsh et al. (2006), paras 24.12–24.14. See also Rules of the Court of Session 1994 Ch.73.

forward by the court.[6] In recent years applications for rectification have become more common as their value has come to be recognised.

Three types of case

The key provision is s.8(1), which is in the following terms: 20–02

> "Subject to section 9 of this Act, where the court is satisfied, on an application made to it, that
>
> (a) a document intended to express or to give effect to an agreement fails to express accurately the common intention of the parties to the agreement at the date when it was made; or
> (b) a document intended to create, transfer, vary or renounce a right, not being a document falling within paragraph (a) above, fails to express accurately the intention of the grantor of the document at the date when it was executed,
>
> it may order the document to be rectified in any manner that it may specify in order to give effect to that intention."

From this it will be seen that an application for rectification may be made in respect of:

(i) Documents intended to "express" an agreement, e.g. written contracts such as missives.
(ii) Documents intended to "give effect" to an agreement, i.e. to implement agreements, such as dispositions in implement of missives of sale.
(iii) Documents (not falling within (i) and (ii)) intended to create, transfer, vary or renounce a right.[7] Into this class fall documents which are not merely unilateral in form[8] but are unilateral in substance, such as dispositions by way of gift.

Type (i)

The three types are listed in ascending order of chance of success. Applications 20–03 in respect of type (i) documents frequently fail.[9] The reasons are not hard to find. For an application to succeed it is necessary to show that the document fails to "express" an agreement. But often there was no clear agreement prior to the document itself. Type (i) documents are usually contracts (such as missives of sale) which are the product of negotiation. Relatively speaking, it is uncommon for parties to reach a clear informal agreement first which is later reduced to writing. Much more commonly, the parties are negotiating up to the

---

[6] *Renyana-Stahl Anstalt v MacGregor*, 2001 S.L.T. 1247 at para.46, per Lord Macfadyen.
[7] 1985 Act s.8(1).
[8] Most conveyancing deeds are unilateral in form.
[9] *Shaw v William Grant (Minerals) Ltd*, 1989 S.L.T. 121; *Angus v Bryden*, 1992 S.L.T. 884; *Rehman v Ahmad*, 1993 S.L.T. 741; *Belhaven Brewery Co v Swift*, 1996 S.L.T. (Sh. Ct) 127; *Bovis Construction (Scotland) Ltd v Glantyre Engineering Ltd*, 1997 G.W.D. 32-1609; *Baird v Drumpellier & Mount Vernon Estates Ltd (No.2)*, 2002 G.W.D. 12-427. But not always: see e.g. *City Wall Properties (Scotland) Ltd v Pearl Assurance Plc* [2005] CSOH 137; *Brown v Rysaffe Trustee Co Ltd* [2011] CSOH 26; 2011 G.W.D. 10-234.

last moment, so that underlying agreement is achieved at the same moment as the signature of the document itself. That is not in itself an objection to the application of s.8.[10] But in practice it may then be difficult to show that the written text is wrong. That, after all, is the text which the parties signed up to, and anything before then is vulnerable to being dismissed as a mere negotiating position, abandoned by the time of the final text.[11] In the particular case of residential missives there may be little in the way of prior communication between the parties to found on. Of course, obvious errors will be rectified. For example, if missives mis-transcribe "31 High Street" as "13 High Street", the mistake is easily demonstrated, and unlikely to be controversial.[12] But if a mistake, or alleged mistake, suits one party but not the other (for example, an offer to purchase for £271,000 instead of £217,000, as intended), the prospects for rectification are less good.[13]

Type (ii)

20–04 Type (ii) documents "give effect" to an earlier agreement, written or oral. Most deeds used in day-to-day conveyancing fall into this category. Thus a disposition gives effect to missives of sale, or a standard security to the loan agreement with the bank or building society. The parties to the agreement must be same as those to the deed.[14] For the application to succeed it is necessary to show that the document "fails to express accurately the common intention of the parties to the agreement at the date when it was made".[15] Common intention is probably to be viewed objectively,[16] and is not the less compelling for being based on ignorance of a material fact.[17]

If the prior agreement was in writing, it will usually be obvious whether an error has been made. For example, if missives are concluded for the sale of property X, and the disposition conveys property Y as well, it is reasonable to conclude that property Y was added in error and that the deed should

---

[10] *Rehman v Ahmad*, 1993 S.L.T. 741 at 751I–L and 753B, per Lord Penrose; *Macdonald Estates Plc v Regenesis (2005) Dunfermline Ltd* [2007] CSOH 123; 2007 S.L.T. 791 at paras 159 and 160, per Lord Reed; *Brown v Rysaffe Trustee Co Ltd* [2011] CSOH 26; 2011 G.W.D. 10-234 at para.34, per Lord Glennie.

[11] But of course it depends on the facts and circumstances. In *Brown v Rysaffe Trustee Co Ltd* [2011] CSOH 26; 2011 G.W.D. 10-234, Lord Glennie said that (para.34): "There must be agreement—mere knowledge of what the other party wants to achieve will not do. But their agreement as to what it was meant to achieve can be discerned by looking at the document itself and all the surrounding circumstances, including any other contractual or other arrangement to which they may have intended to adhere; and including . . . the negotiations, if any, between the parties leading to the drafting and execution of the document and any expression of intent by one party to the other."

[12] But uncontroversial mistakes can be corrected consensually and do not require an application to the court.

[13] *Bovis Construction (Scotland) Ltd v Glantyre Engineering Ltd*, 1997 G.W.D. 32-1609. If, however, the mistake was known to the other party at the time of the offer, the doctrine of unfair advantage may provide a remedy. See *Angus v Bryden*, 1992 S.L.T. 884, and above, para.3–16.

[14] *Delikes Ltd v Scottish & Newcastle Plc*, 2000 S.L.T. (Sh. Ct) 67; *Macdonald Estates Plc v Regenesis (2005) Dunfermline Ltd* [2007] CSOH 123; 2007 S.L.T. 791 at para.177, per Lord Reed. But this may be subject to qualifications: see Reid and Gretton, *Conveyancing 2000*, pp.119–20.

[15] Law Reform (Miscellaneous Provisions) (Scotland) Act 1985 s.8(1)(a).

[16] But the law cannot be said to be settled. For a review of the authorities, see *Macdonald Estates Plc v Regenesis (2005) Dunfermline Ltd* [2007] CSOH 123; 2007 S.L.T. 791 at paras 161–65, per Lord Reed; Webster, 2012 J.R. (forthcoming).

[17] *Co-operative Wholesale Society Ltd v Ravenseft Properties Ltd*, 2003 S.C.L.R. 509.

be rectified.[18] Conversely, if the disposition is consistent with the missives, rectification is unlikely to succeed, for there is no better evidence of the parties' intentions than the written document in which they were expressed.[19] In theory it would be possible to argue that the written contract was itself inaccurate and should be rectified, but this turns a type (ii) case into a type (i) case, with often predictable results.[20] A different approach is to argue for a change of mind since the date of the contract.[21] This is made more difficult by s.8, which focuses on intention as at the date of the contract.[22] To accommodate changes of mind it would be necessary to argue that the deed was intended to give effect, not to the written contract in its original form, but to the contract as varied by some later and informal agreement.[23]

If the earlier agreement is not in writing, there may be difficulties in proving its terms, and rectification will be correspondingly harder to achieve. As with type (i) cases, it will not always be possible to separate out the agreement from the written deed which followed.[24]

Type (iii)

While in cases of the first two types it is necessary to show that the written 20–05 document departs from the common intention of the parties at the time of the underlying agreement, in type (iii) cases there is no underlying agreement and hence no common intention. A type (iii) deed is unilateral, and made without reference to a previous agreement. Examples might include an unheralded gift of land, made by disposition, or an *inter vivos* deed of trust.[25] Under s.8(1)(b) the concern is with the intention of the granter alone, and an application succeeds if it can be shown that the deed does not give effect to the granter's intention as at the date when it was executed. In theory it ought to be easier to show the intention of one person than of two. If the granter is also the person applying for rectification, there may be no one who can contradict his or her assertion that the deed was blundered. But a court might not always be convinced.[26] The Scottish Law Commission took a cautious view:

> "In the case of unilateral writings proof of the granter's intention will be inherently more difficult, for he is less likely to have communicated with any other party. It may therefore be difficult to establish what his true

---

[18] *Oliver v Gaughan*, 1990 G.W.D. 22-1247. See also *Aberdeen Rubber Ltd v Knowles & Sons (Fruiterers) Ltd*, 1995 S.C. (HL) 8.

[19] *Howgate Shopping Centre Ltd v Catercraft Services Ltd*, 2004 S.L.T. 231. Sometimes, though, the document itself is unclear, as in *McClymont v McCubbin*, 1995 S.L.T. 1248.

[20] *Angus v Bryden*, 1992 S.L.T. 884; *Baird v Drumpellier & Mount Vernon Estates Ltd (No.2)*, 2002 G.W.D. 12-427; *Moncrieff v McIntosh*, Unreported August 8, 2007 Forfar Sheriff Court.

[21] *Renyana-Stahl Anstalt v MacGregor*, 2001 S.L.T. 1247.

[22] Scot. Law Com. No.79, para.3.5. The relevant part of s.8(1) provides that the court must be satisfied that "a document intended to . . . give effect to an agreement fails to express accurately the common intention of the parties to the agreement at the date when it was made". "It" here refers to the agreement and not to the document: documents are not "made".

[23] *George Thompson Services Ltd v Moore*, 1993 S.L.T. 634.

[24] *Huewind Ltd v Clydesdale Bank Plc*, 1996 S.L.T. 369; *Royal Bank of Scotland v Shanks*, 1998 S.L.T. 355.

[25] *Hudson v St. John*, 1977 S.C. 255.

[26] For a discussion of the type of evidence that might be admissible, see *McEwan's Exrs v Arnot*, Unreported February 11, 2005 Perth Sheriff Court, discussed in Reid and Gretton, *Conveyancing 2005*, pp.132–34.

intention was and to what extent this has been misrepresented in writing. Moreover, a court would not be satisfied that a document was defectively expressed purely on the basis of an assertion that the writing was not what the granter had intended."[27]

Certainly a donor would not be able to withdraw a gift under the guise of rectification.

The boundary between types (ii) and (iii) is not easily drawn. Initially the courts took a broad view of type (iii). In one of the early leading cases, Lord President Hope gave the distinction as being between unilateral and bilateral documents. All unilateral documents came within type (iii).[28] But the view now taken—surely correctly—is that a type (iii) deed is one which does not implement a previous agreement.[29] The grantee must have had no prior entitlement to the grant. This means that most unilateral deeds are classified as type (ii) documents, and that type (iii) cases will be rare.

Which documents?

20–06 Section 8 applies to all documents other than those of a testamentary nature.[30] It is no objection that the document has been recorded in the GRS, or formed the basis of registration of a title in the Land Register.[31] There seem no reason why documents executed before the provision came into force should not qualify.[32] Perhaps surprisingly, there is no requirement that the document effects, or records, a juridical act.[33] The person seeking rectification need not have been a party to the document,[34] so that for example an owner of land could apply for rectification in respect of an earlier deed in the titles.

Mistakes in one document can lead to mistakes in another, and for that reason the court is empowered to order the rectification of any other document which is defectively expressed by reason of the defect in the original document.[35] A typical example would be an error in the description in a disposition which was then carried forward into a standard security.[36]

Which mistakes?

20–07 In principle, s.8 applies to all mistakes, both of commission and omission. The mistakes may touch fundamentals. For example, s.8 has been used to change

---

[27] Scot. Law Com. No.79, para.3.8.

[28] *Bank of Scotland v Graham's Trustee*, 1992 S.C. 79 at 86, per Lord President Hope: "The document with which we are concerned is a unilateral deed, not an agreement, so the relevant provision for present purposes is para.(b)". (The report in Session Cases mistakenly refers to "para.(a)".)

[29] *Royal Bank of Scotland v Shanks*, 1998 S.L.T. 355.

[30] Law Reform (Miscellaneous Provisions) (Scotland) Act 1985 s.8(6).

[31] 1985 Act s.8(5).

[32] The provision came into force on December 30, 1985: see s.60(2)(d). The deed rectified in *Bank of Scotland v Graham's Tr*, 1992 S.C. 79 was executed and recorded prior to that date, although the point was not raised.

[33] At least in type (ii) cases. This seems to mean that if Alan contracts with Barbara to write a sonnet but actually writes a limerick, Barbara can ask the court to rectify the verse.

[34] *Delikes Ltd v Scottish & Newcastle Plc*, 2000 S.L.T. (Sh. Ct) 67 at 70, per Sheriff Principal C.G.B. Nicholson QC.

[35] 1985 Act s.8(3).

[36] Scot. Law Com. No.79, para.5.1.

the description of the property being conveyed or over which rights are being created.[37] Words can be added, deleted, and substituted. Furthermore, s.8 is not confined to errors in expression but extends also to errors in expectation—to cases where the words themselves were correct but the result thereby achieved was wrong and contrary to the parties' intentions. In the leading case a bank's letter of consent was rectified on the basis that, while the words were those which the parties intended to use, their legal effect was not what was intended.[38] If pressed too far, this runs the risk of being a charter for incompetent conveyancing, rescuing even the wildest errors and misapprehensions on the part of the draftsman.

In fact there are important limitations. Only the actual terms of the deed may be rectified. Section 8 cannot be used to cure defects of execution, such as the absence of a signature, or a signature by the wrong person[39]; nor can it be used to change the parties to a deed.[40] Further, the court is not bound to grant rectification. Section 8(1) says "may" and not "shall".[41] In the exercise of this discretion regard will be had to various factors[42] including the extent of the changes proposed. It has been said that:

> "Rectification of a deed is one thing, but wholesale alteration of contractual terms is another which may go beyond the power conferred by the statute."[43]

Similarly, the court has warned that:

> "The more extensive the amendments proposed by a party, the more questionable may become the exercise of even a wide discretionary power in particular circumstances ... There is a qualification inherent in most if not all general discretionary powers that they require to be exercised within reasonable limits."[44]

The way in which this qualification will be applied remains to be seen. But it may be assumed that the extent of alterations will be measured by legal effect rather than by number of words.[45]

---

[37] *Oliver v Gaughan*, 1990 G.W.D. 22-1247; *Beneficial Bank Plc v Wardle*, 1996 G.W.D. 30-1825.

[38] *Bank of Ireland v Bass Brewers Ltd*, 2000 G.W.D. 20-786; 2000 G.W.D. 28-1077, discussed in Reid and Gretton, *Conveyancing* 2000, pp.118–19. The court having allowed a proof, rectification was later awarded as of consent. For a case where the court was less disposed to help, see *Co-operative Wholesale Society Ltd v Ravenseft Properties Ltd*, 2003 S.C.L.R. 509.

[39] *Bank of Scotland v Graham's Trustee*, 1992 S.C. 79 at 88, per Lord President Hope. In that case the problem of the granters having signed once rather than (as was demanded by the structure of the deed) twice was solved by rectifying the standard security so that only one signature was required. But if there had been no signature at all, the deed could not have been rescued.

[40] *Bank of Scotland v Brunswick Developments (1987) Ltd (No.2)*, 1999 S.C. (HL) 53.

[41] *Bank of Scotland v Brunswick Developments (1987) Ltd (No.2)*, 1997 S.C. 226 at 231D, per Lord President Rodger.

[42] In the case of a deed of conditions, for example, the good and harmonious governance of the community to which it relates: see *Sheltered Housing Management Ltd v Cairns*, 2003 S.L.T. 578 at paras 17 et seq., per Lord Nimmo Smith.

[43] *Huewind Ltd v Clydesdale Bank Plc*, 1996 S.L.T. 369 at 375D, per Lord Justice-Clerk Ross.

[44] *Norwich Union Life Insurance Society v Tanap Investments VK Ltd*, 1999 S.L.T. 204 at 211F–G, per Lord Penrose.

[45] *Norwich Union Life Insurance Society v Tanap Investments VK Ltd*, 1999 S.L.T. 204 at 211L–212A, per Lord Penrose.

A striking feature is the way in which s.8 has been used for mistakes which are mere conveyancing blunders. In one case the box marked "THE PROPRIETOR" in a standard security had been left blank, so that the security ostensibly had no granter, though in fact the owner had executed the deed. The omission was repaired by rectification.[46] In another, also involving a standard security, the property was insufficiently described. Again the missing details were able to be added.[47] This is rectification as the conveyancer's friend: for mistakes in conveyancing, s.8 provides a final line of defence.

Standard of proof

20–08 The court must, as usual, be satisfied on a balance of probabilities,[48] and may have regard to all evidence, whether written or oral.[49] Missives of sale can be consulted even after expiry due to a supersession clause.[50] In practice there may be a reluctance to overturn a written document on the basis of prior communings which were expressed orally, to say nothing of the difficulty of proving such communings.

Protection of third parties

20–09 Documents may affect more than the immediate parties, particularly in the case of deeds which create real rights. A person in this position could defend the application on the merits if it is brought to his or her attention.[51] More importantly, s.9 of the 1985 Act excludes rectification altogether if it would adversely affect, to a material extent, a person who relied on the document in its unrectified form (or on an entry on the Land Register made on the basis of such a document). Reliance involves acting or refraining to act, and must have been reasonable and without knowledge, actual or constructive, of the mistake. It is not reasonable to rely on a deed if the mistake is obvious.[52]

Thus suppose Anne, by mistake, conveys too much land to Brian. Brian registers his title in the Land Register. Two years later Brian grants a standard security to the Caledonian Bank. The Bank relies on the entry on the Land Register. Anne then seeks rectification, both of the disposition and of the standard security.[53] Rectification should succeed as to the disposition but not as to the standard security.[54] By contrast, an unsecured creditor does not usually lend in reliance on the register and would not be protected against

---

[46] *Bank of Scotland v Graham's Trustee*, 1992 S.C. 79.

[47] *Beneficial Bank Plc v Wardle*, 1996 G.W.D. 30-1825. As these cases suggest, it is easier to add words which are not there than to substitute words which were included in error. For erroneous words may confer a windfall benefit which leads to rectification being opposed. Perhaps the only completely safe conveyancing deed is a blank sheet of paper subscribed by the granter.

[48] *Rehman v Ahmad*, 1993 S.L.T. 741. And see Scot. Law Com. No.79, paras 4.3–4.6.

[49] 1985 Act s.8(2).

[50] *Renyana-Stahl Anstalt v MacGregor*, 2001 S.L.T. 1247.

[51] *Norwich Union Life Insurance Society v Tanap Investments VK Ltd (No.2)*, 2000 S.C. 515.

[52] *Co-operative Wholesale Society Ltd v Ravenseft Properties Ltd*, 2001 G.W.D. 24-904; 2002 S.C.L.R. 644.

[53] Rectification of the Land Register would also be required, for which see below, para.20–11.

[54] So that this plot of land will revert to Anne, but burdened by the security. It might be argued that the security too should be rectified, since if that led to rectification of the Register under the 1979 Act, the Bank would be protected by indemnity. But in that case the Keeper would be prejudiced.

rectification.[55] Not all examples are so straightforward, however. In practice, indeed, a case under s.9 is not easily made out. Thus before a third party can be said to have relied on a document, he or she must be shown to have been familiar with the very term which is now the subject of rectification.[56] And even if such close familiarity can be demonstrated, there is the further hurdle of showing that the act (or refraining from acting) was properly attributable to the term now to be rectified and not to some other cause.[57]

A practical difficulty is that the court may not always know about third parties. Where real rights are concerned a search of the register should be undertaken. In Land Register cases the court can require the Keeper to list those persons who have been given details of the relevant title sheet.[58] But some people will fall through the net, if only because not all real rights are registered. Here the 1985 Act makes special provision. A third party who was unaware of the application for rectification but later finds out can apply to the Court of Session within two years. But no application may be made later than five years after the original order. The court has power either to reduce the rectifying order or to require the original applicant to pay compensation.[59]

Effect of the order

A rectification order, in a conveyancing matter, will generally change the real 20–10 rights in a property. When does that change take effect? In other words, when does the order have real effect? It would be natural to suppose that this took place with effect from the date of registration in the property register. But in fact the provisions of the 1985 Act are complex and in some respects puzzling. The following is an attempt to explain them.

Entering the Land Register[60]

If the property is in the Land Register, the order does not have immediate real 20–11 effect. Real effect requires registration. Rectifying a deed achieves nothing of itself, for title flows from the Register and not from the deed.[61] Thus, in order to be effective, rectification of the deed must be followed by rectification of the Register itself.[62] One kind of rectification is thus followed by another. Contrary to the usual rule, the Land Register may be rectified even where this is to the

---

[55] The same applies to a trustee in sequestration or liquidator, as the representative of the ordinary unsecured creditors. See *Bank of Scotland v Graham's Trustee*, 1992 S.C. 79.

[56] *Shetland Housing Management Ltd v Cairns*, 2003 S.L.T. 578.

[57] *Jones v Wood* [2005] CSIH 31; 2005 S.L.T. 655. See Reid and Gretton, *Conveyancing 2005*, pp.134–38.

[58] Law Reform (Miscellaneous Provisions) (Scotland) Act 1985 s.9(6). How much use this will be is unclear. Often the only parties who will have requested details will be law firms, credit reference agencies, and search firms, all of whom will normally be acting for others.

[59] 1985 Act s.9(7), (8).

[60] For discussion and proposals for reform, see Scottish Law Commission, Report on *Land Registration* (Scot. Law Com. No.222, 2010), Pt 29.

[61] See above, para.8–07.

[62] As with reductions, it may be taken that the effect of rectification of a deed requires to enter the Register by rectification and not by registration. See *Short's Trustee v Keeper of the Registers of Scotland*, 1996 S.C. (HL) 14.

prejudice of a proprietor in possession.[63] No indemnity is payable.[64] But *bona fide* proprietors will often have been able to prevent the initial rectification of the deed, on principles already discussed.[65]

Entering the GRS

20–12 For property in the GRS, the order has real effect immediately, even without recording. But there is an incentive to record,[66] in that an unrecorded order cannot be pled against a third party who, in good faith and for value, acquires right to the land after rectification but before its recording.[67] This has the odd result that the rectified deed is deemed to have one text in a question with that third party but a different text in a question with everyone else, including those who inspected the Register prior to rectification.[68]

Retroactivity

20–13 The order has real effect when made (GRS) or when registered (Land Register), but the 1985 Act provides that the date when the real effect comes about is not the date when it begins to operate. The order is retroactive in effect, so that after the order takes real effect the document is deemed always to have been written in its rectified form.[69] But the court has power to modify this rule to take account of the position of third parties acting in reliance on the unrectified document.[70]

Retroactivity may make sense for personal rights, but it hardly does so for real rights. A deed recorded in the GRS is deemed always to have been recorded in its rectified version[71]; and an entry on the Land Register rectified in response to the rectification of the underlying deed is deemed always to have been so rectified.[72] The results are scarcely satisfactory. Suppose that in 2007 Alice conveys Whitemains and Blackmains to Bruce. Bruce registers his title in the Land Register. In 2011 both the disposition and the Register are rectified to exclude Whitemains, and Alice is entered on the Register as owner. Who owned Whitemains in 2009? The answer depends on the date of the question. In 2009 the answer to the question is Bruce. In 2011, following rectification, it is Alice. So it is correct to say that Bruce, not Alice, owned the property in 2009, and it is equally correct to say that Alice, not Bruce, owned the property in 2009: a historical fact changes according to when it is asserted.

---

[63] Land Registration (Scotland) Act 1979 s.9(3)(b). This includes a proprietor who acquires in good faith after the rectification of the deed but before the rectification of the Register. There is thus no equivalent in the Land Register of s.46(2) of the Conveyancing (Scotland) Act 1924. (Notwithstanding s.29(2) of the 1979 Act, the *Short's Trustee* litigation took for granted that s.46 did not apply to the Land Register.)

[64] 1979 Act s.12(3)(p).

[65] See above, para.20–09.

[66] What is recorded is the extract decree.

[67] Conveyancing (Scotland) Act 1924 Act s.46(1). By contrast with s.9(1)–(3) of the 1985 Act, there is no requirement of prejudicial reliance.

[68] This latter point arises from the fact that—unlike reduction (on which s.46(2) is modelled)—rectification operates retrospectively. So it is better to buy immediately after rectification than immediately before. But a person who buys immediately before may sometimes be able to have the rectification set aside under s.9(7) of the 1985 Act.

[69] Law Reform (Miscellaneous Provisions) (Scotland) Act 1985 s.8(4).

[70] 1985 Act s.9(4), (5).

[71] 1985 Act s.8(5).

[72] Land Registration (Scotland) Act 1979 s.9(3A).

If the rectification were to be reduced, to accommodate the interests of third parties, the answer in 2013 might once again be Bruce.[73] But the question has not changed, only the answer. The Land Register, it appears, has not been telling the truth. In property law it is awkward to rewrite history in this way. For example, obligations are quite often imposed on the "owner" of property, whether by statute,[74] or common law,[75] or by real burdens. Can Bruce, forced to perform such an obligation in 2009, demand compensation from Alice in 2011, and if so under what principle?

The position is worse if Bruce has granted subordinate real rights, particularly if they were unregistered and so not known to the court at the time of the application for rectification. For example, in 2008 Bruce might have granted a 15-year lease of Whitemains to Cara. In 2011, following rectification, this would cease to be a real right, retrospectively, as having been granted *a non domino*. In theory Cara would have until 2016 to have the initial rectification reduced, and her right restored.[76] But since Alice is a proprietor in possession, and in good faith, it is not clear that such a reduction could be given effect to on the Register.[77]

Reduction

Depending on the circumstances, reduction can sometimes be used as an alter- 20–14 native to rectification. For example, if in error a disposition conveys too much land, the disposition could be adjusted by means of a partial reduction.[78] Reduction is not, in general, retroactive in effect. A difficulty with reduction is that there is no special provision allowing rectification of the Land Register against a proprietor in possession, and some reductions will fall at this hurdle.[79]

---

[73] Under 1985 Act s.9(7). This assumes, possibly incorrectly, that the reduction is itself retrospective in effect. Further, for reasons explained below, it is not clear that such a reduction could ever get on the Register.

[74] e.g. Building (Scotland) Act 2003 ss.28–30.

[75] e.g. the common interest obligation of maintenance in respect of boundary walls.

[76] 1985 Act s.9(7), (8). However, as mentioned earlier it is not clear that a reduction would operate retrospectively. If not, the lease would still have been granted *a non domino* and its validity would now depend on the law of accretion.

[77] Section 9(3)(b) of the 1979 Act applies only to a rectification "consequential on the making of an order under" s.8. It is far from clear that a reduction of a s.8 order under s.9 is "consequential" in the sense of the provision.

[78] *Aberdeen Rubber Ltd v Knowles & Sons (Fruiterers) Ltd*, 1995 S.C. (HL) 8.

[79] *Short's Trustee v Keeper of the Registers of Scotland*, 1996 S.C. (HL) 14. But s.9(3)(a)(iii) of the 1979 Act (fraud or carelessness) may sometimes apply.

CHAPTER 21

HOME LOANS

INTRODUCTION

Mortgages

21–01 First, the word "mortgage". This is the English term, but of course it is widely used in Scotland, though not in legal language.[1] The Scottish equivalent is "heritable security". There is nowadays only one type of heritable security, the standard security. The term "home loan" is also quite common and is sometimes used in this book. Of course, a standard security can be over any heritable property, and not just residential property.

The client says that "the First National Bank of Pitlochry gave me a mortgage". The opposite is true. The debtor grants the security to the lender, in exchange for a loan.[2] And clients sometimes seem to think of a mortgage as an asset. It is an asset, but of the lender. For the debtor it means debt. The misconception is one that financial institutions do little to dispel.[3]

"Which type of mortgage is suited to your needs?" asks the advertisement. The truth is that there is only one type of "mortgage", namely the standard security. What is variable is not the "mortgage" but the terms of the loan contract that the security relates to. The question should be: "Which loan terms suit your needs?"

There are numerous lenders, and most offer a range of contract packages. Moreover, those packages change over time. Still, some basic issues remain fairly constant. Because what varies is the loan contract, not the security, much of this chapter is in fact as applicable to unsecured as to secured loans.

Secured loans are most commonly given to assist the borrower to buy the property that the loan is to be secured over, so that the buyer/borrower grants the security at the same time as acquiring the property. But it also happens that a security is granted over a property that the borrower already owns. This can happen for two main reasons: either the owner wants to borrow money, using the property as security, or the owner is "remortgaging", i.e. using the new loan to pay off an existing one.

---

[1] An exception is the Mortgage Rights (Scotland) Act 2001. There are also ship mortgages and aircraft mortgages.

[2] Thus in England, it is the debtor who is the mortgagor and the creditor who is the mortgagee.

[3] The way that financial institutions use language is often astonishing. A typical example: "Mortgages sold under the C&G and Lloyds TSB brands are a partnership between Cheltenham & Gloucester plc and Lloyds TSB Bank plc". (*http://www.lloydstsb.com/mortgages.asp?WT.mc_id=43000000134527169&WT.srch=1*) The mortgages are *sold*? The mortgages are a *partnership*? Welcome, O Earthlings, to Planet Zlbiamg. Even the FSA, which is supposed to promote financial transparency, speaks of "mortgage sales".

This chapter is concerned with the home loan market and the home loan packages available. Almost all of this chapter would be equally applicable on the southern side of the Border. The next chapter gives some account of the law and practice of heritable security, where Scotland and England diverge substantially.

One secured loan or more?

The normal practice is to obtain all the finance for house purchase from a 21–02 single lender. This is worth mentioning because in some other countries it is common to obtain a cocktail of loans from different lenders, each lender taking security and the whole package making up the total amount needed. However, owners may, after having bought, take out another secured loan with a different lender: such loans are commonly called "second mortgages".

When a house is sold, the modern practice is for the sellers to redeem the existing secured loan (from the proceeds of sale) and for the buyers to arrange their own loan. It is in theory possible for the buyers to take over the existing secured loan (a fact that would be reflected in the price paid) and to obtain a top-up loan as required. This was common in the nineteenth century, but today is almost unknown. In some countries, in contrast, it is the norm.

Drawdown

We mention this simply as a bit of terminology. A loan is said to be "drawn 21–03 down" by the borrower. This is another way of saying that the lender pays the loan money over to the borrower, or to the borrower's law firm, which then passes it on. Sometimes a loan is available only until a particular day, which failing the loan will not happen at all. This is a "drawdown deadline". Some loans are drawn down in "tranches". This, though common for commercial loans, is rare for home loans, where single-tranche drawdown is the norm. But tranched drawdown is sometimes used in "lifetime mortgages".[4]

Seller finance

Occasionally purchase finance is provided by the seller. The good way to do 21–04 this is for the property to be disponed to the buyer, with a simultaneous standard security granted by the buyer back to the seller, securing the unpaid balance of price. The bad way to do it is for ownership to remain with the seller until the whole price has been paid, years later. That used to be quite common, especially in the west of Scotland, but is today happily almost unknown. If the buyer failed to pay an instalment, unpleasant consequences could follow.[5] And when and if the last payment was finally made, often nobody remembered about the need for a disposition.

THE MARKET

The lenders

Once upon a time, house purchase loans were often obtained privately, some- 21–05 times by the solicitor putting two clients in touch with each other, one with

---

[4] See below, para.21–45.
[5] *Reid v Campbell*, 1958 S.L.T. (Sh. Ct) 45.

money to lend, and the other with a house to buy, though, of course, institutional lending was also common. Nowadays, private lending is rare. Until the 1980s the main providers of home loans were the building societies. Now other financial institutions have a large share of the market. There have been two main reasons for the change. The first is that historically the commercial banks seldom made home loans, mainly because they disliked long-term loans. In the 1980s that attitude changed. The second reason is the Building Societies Act 1986 enabled building societies to "demutualise", i.e. to convert into commercial banks, and many did so.[6] Thus the home loan market today involves both building societies (those that did not demutualise after 1986) and banks.

Building societies

21–06 Unlike the commercial banks, building societies are non-profit cooperatives. They are juristic persons, i.e. corporations, whose members are (subject to some qualifications) their depositors and borrowers. Thus, clients who have a home loan with a building society are members, and so, for instance, can vote at general meetings. It follows that a building society has no interest in exploiting its borrowers. Building societies claim that, because of their structure, they can offer loans on better terms than the commercial banks, and independent surveys confirm that this is true, though the difference is not a big one. Building societies were once restricted to lending only for house purchase and only on first-ranked security. These rules have been relaxed to some extent but home loan finance remains their core business.

Mortgage brokers

21–07 Mortgage brokers, also called mortgage intermediaries, arrange loans, especially for those whose creditworthiness may be uncertain. Brokers are normally paid a commission for new business by the lenders, and, if they arrange a life assurance policy, by the life assurance company. They may also charge a fee of several hundred pounds to their customer.

The CML

21–08 The Council of Mortgage Lenders ("CML") is a trade association whose membership includes almost all UK mortgage lenders. It publishes a *Lenders' Handbook for Scotland*,[7] Pt I of which sets out standard terms on which all the CML lenders have agreed, and Pt II the terms of individual lenders. All conveyancers need to be familiar with the CML *Handbook*. In most cases when property is bought there is a secured loan, and what the lender requires is just as important as what the buyer requires. If the customer defaults and the lender takes a loss,[8] the lender is likely to check to see if there was any failure on the part of the law firm to comply with the requirements of the CML *Handbook*, and, if so, may claim damages.

---

[6] None of them maintained their independence, all being eventually taken over.

[7] This used to be a print publication but is now digital. The CML website is *http://www.cml.org. uk/*. It contains much of interest to the conveyancer. The CML has four versions of its handbook, for England & Wales, Isle of Man, Northern Ireland and Scotland.

[8] Usually the lender will be repaid by the borrower. Even if that does not happen, the lender may recover in full from selling the property. But sometimes the lender ends up out of pocket, and that is when its eyes turn to the law firm that acted for it.

Some figures

Since the beginning of the financial crisis in 2007/2008 the number of new   21–09
home loans being made has fallen. In the first quarter of 2007 the total number
for the United Kingdom was 581,800. Three years later, in the first quarter of
2010, the figure was 216,700.[9]

Home loans can be put into four classes, namely (i) "first-time buyers", (ii)
"home movers", (iii) "remortgagers" and (iv) others, such as loans for home
improvement. Here are the figures for the first quarters of 2007 and 2010
respectively for the United Kingdom. The decline of the remortgage market is
striking.

	2007/Q1	2010/Q1
First-time buyers	95,208	50,275
Home movers	186,953	86,467
Remortgagers	281,392	77,591
Others	22,146	9,218

Home loans can also be classified according to the proportion they bear to the
value of the property. Here are the figures for the first quarters of 2007 and
2010 respectively. The decline in high LTV[10] loans is striking.

	2007/Q1	2010/Q1
Up to 30%	81,700	31,200
30% to 50%	87,300	35,700
50% to 75%	162,600	88,000
75% to 85%	88,400	38,000
85% to 90%	72,500	17,400
90% to 95%	54,900	5,000
Over 95%	26,400	400

Regulation

The home loan financial sector was once unregulated. Since 2004 the sector is   21–10
under statutory regulation by the Financial Services Authority ("FSA")[11] acting
under powers conferred by the Financial Services and Markets Act 2000.[12] The
FSA has rule-making powers which are the basis of the *Mortgages and Home*

---

[9] FSA figures. See "Mortgages Product Sales Data (PSD) Tables 2005–2010" at *http://www.
fsa.gov.uk/Pages/Doing/Regulated/Returns/psd/publications/index.shtml*. This is also the source
of the figures given below. For CML figures see *http://www.cml.org.uk/cml/publications/
annreport*.

[10] Loan to value, i.e. the amount of the loan expressed as a percentage of the value of the
property.

[11] *http://www.fsa.gov.uk/*.

[12] Financial Services and Markets Act 2000 (Regulated Activities) Order (SI 2001/544), as
amended.

Finance: Conduct of Business Sourcebook ("MCOB"). The Financial Ombudsman Service ("FOS") has powers of intervention.[13] Law firms involved in advising on home loans must either have "mainstream" authorisation from the FSA or be subject to the Law Society of Scotland's "incidental investment regime".[14]

THE CAPITAL SIDE OF THE LOAN

Introduction

21–11   A borrower must repay the loan. The borrower must also pay (not repay) the interest on it.[15] The loan itself is often called the "capital" or the "principal", to distinguish it from the interest. The capital/interest distinction is not a complete one. Both payment obligations are contractual. Both are secured by the standard security. And arrears of interest are added to capital. Still, the distinction is there. In this section we look at capital.

Term loans and on-demand loans

21–12   A loan may be (i) an on-demand loan; or (ii) a term loan. Which it is depends, obviously, on what the loan contract says. In the former, the creditor can demand repayment at any time, and equally the debtor can choose to repay at any time. An on-demand loan may in fact last for years, with interest being paid.[16] But that does not alter the fact that it is an on-demand loan and thus could be wound up by either party at any time. A term loan is a loan for a term, e.g. 20 years. The borrower has the use of the money for the defined period and cannot be required to repay it until then, though interest will be due.[17] Repayment may, according to what has been agreed, be either as a lump sum at the end of the term, or as instalments over the years. In the former case the capital of the loan remains unchanged through the life of the loan. In the latter the capital declines over time, to vanishing point.

Early repayment

21–13   The debtor in a term loan presumptively has no right to pay off the loan early, though this is subject to agreement to the contrary. Quite often the loan contract will provide that, although the borrower is entitled to repay early, in that event an "early repayment charge"—also called a "redemption penalty"—is due. These charges may be substantial and clients should be aware of them before agreeing to the loan. They tend to be used most commonly where a special loan deal is being offered that is particularly beneficial to the borrower in the first year or two. Such deals would be unworkable if the borrower could simply

---

[13] Its authority is conferred by the FSA.

[14] See Cullen, (2004) 49 J.L.S.S. April/44.

[15] Zero-interest loans are of course perfectly lawful, and are occasionally encountered, for example where one family member lends to another. For Islamic finance, see below, para.21–46.

[16] A common example is the overdraft. Overdrafts are (normally) on-demand loans, but may last for years.

[17] In theory the interest could all be left to accumulate, and then be paid in a single lump sum, together with the capital of the loan. But this is rare except where the term is very short—which it almost never is in residential secured lending.

remortgage with a new lender as soon as the initial period came to an end. Early repayment charges thus make possible deals that would otherwise be impossible.

Closing administration charge (exit charge)

It is common for there to be a payment due when the loan is fully repaid and 21–14 the debtor wishes a discharge to be registered. This goes by various names, such as a closing administration charge, redemption charge or exit charge. It used to be, in most cases, a reasonable figure of a few tens of pounds, covering the administrative costs of granting a deed of discharge. But nowadays the exit fee is often several hundred pounds. It is not unknown for lenders to make this charge without any right to do so. Any such right has to be based in the loan contract.

The term: how long?

The "term", i.e. the length of time the loan is to run, is negotiable.[18] A common 21–15 period is 25 years. Some lenders will go as far as 40 years. More than that is almost unknown. A lender may be reluctant to agree to a term running beyond the borrower's retirement age. Most loans are repaid much sooner than the term, because the property is sold. The average lifespan of a home loan is about seven years.

Acceleration

Loan agreements—secured or unsecured—almost always have an acceleration 21–16 clause whereby the lender is entitled to demand repayment in full, ahead of term, if there is an "event of default". Usually failure to pay an instalment is not an immediate event of default, but becomes one if the default continues for a defined period, such as one month or two months.

Paradoxically, there is sometimes also a clause tucked away saying that in any case the whole loan is repayable on demand irrespective of any default. We say "paradoxically" because an on-demand loan, as it would then be, needs no acceleration clause: indeed the two things contradict each other. Loans are either repayable on demand, or they are not. They cannot be both.

INTEREST

Market interest rates

Interest rates are a matter for agreement. In principle, market forces operate so 21–17 that lenders that demand too much will lose customers. Naturally, rates vary according to risk. A secured loan will generally be at a lower interest rate than an unsecured loan. There exists a widespread idea that the Bank of England sets rates. That is not true in law but is to some degree true in practice. Nobody is legally bound to have any regard to the Bank of England rate[19] but its influence

---

[18] And can sometimes be renegotiated later, e.g. if the borrower gets into financial difficulties. A lengthened term can mean reduced monthly payments.

[19] Except by means of contract. See below, para.21–20 for "base rate trackers".

in the market is great. Hence changes will in practice usually cause changes in home loan rates.

Timing of payments

21–18   Traditionally, payments were made twice a year, at Whitsunday and Martinmas. Nowadays they are almost invariably made on a monthly basis.

Fixed interest rate

21–19   Once upon a time the usual practice for loans, whether secured or unsecured, was that the interest rate was fixed at the outset and could not change, other than by mutual agreement. This made sense when market interest rates were fairly stable. It also made sense—and still makes sense—if the loan is an on-demand one, for either party can bail out at any time. It also made sense— and still makes sense—if the loan is a term loan but for a short term, such as three or six months. But if the term is a long one, and if market rates are, as they are nowadays, unstable, a fixed rate is problematic. It may soon be above or below the market rate. If market rates fall, borrowers will finds themselves paying an objectionably high interest rate.[20] Conversely if market rates rise the lender will find itself stuck with a poor investment. Still, fixed-rate long-term loans are possible, though they make sense only if the borrower has no right to pay off early, or has that right only on paying an early repayment charge. For example, to take an example from outside the world of conveyancing, long-term fixed-interest bond issues are common. But in the home loan market the modern practice is that interest rates fixed for the whole term are rare. What lenders will, however, offer, is a rate that is fixed for a certain number of years.

Variable interest rate

21–20   If the rate is a variable one, how is it determined? The reasonable approach would be to refer to some independently determined rate. This is common in commercial loans, where the rate is often tied to LIBOR.[21] Until recently it was rare for home loans. The commonest arrangement—and still very common—is that the contract allows the lender to choose the rate. The lender can do this at any time and simply writes to borrowers to notify changes. This is a remarkable arrangement: in what other kind of debt can creditors unilaterally vary the terms? Each lender has its own "standard variable rate" ("SVR"), but because of market forces these tend to be similar. Recently the "base rate tracker" has come into use. Here the interest rate is a floating one, and it is tied to the Bank of England base rate, being defined as a certain margin above that rate.

Timing of rate changes

21–21   A change of rate sometimes comes into effect the month after it is announced. In other cases there is an annual adjustment, although the rate chargeable is

---

[20] The borrower in this situation would wish to repay the loan and replace it by a loan at the current market rates, i.e. a lower rate. But the loan is a term loan and what is sauce for the goose is sauce for the gander. The loan contract may have no early-repayment option or have an early-repayment option coupled with an early repayment charge.

[21] London Inter-Bank Offered Rate. This is the constantly changing rate at which banks lend to and borrow from each other on the London Money Market. A commercial loan might thus be set at, for instance, LIBOR + 2.

normally adjusted whenever the general rate changes. For example, suppose that the rate is adjusted annually in April, and that in October a lender cuts its rate from 8 per cent to 7 per cent. The borrowers continue to pay at the old rate until the following April. During the interval they are thus overpaying, and this is taken into account at the annual adjustment.

Some types of deal as to interest rate

Often the interest is simply the lender's SVR. But there are numerous variants 21–22 available. One has already been mentioned—the rate that is fixed for the lifetime of the loan—but this is rare. Another is the rate that is fixed for an agreed period, such as, say, three years, after which it reverts to the SVR. Sometimes there is a variable rate but with a maximum (a "cap"). Sometimes there is both a maximum and a minimum—a "cap and collar". Quite common is the discount loan in which the rate is a certain number of points below the SVR for an agreed period. During this period the rate varies as the SVR varies, but always with the discount. The "reversion rate" is that rate that will apply after any fixed or discount period has elapsed.

There is the low-start or deferred-interest system under which the rate payable for the first so many months (e.g. 24 or 36) is both fixed and below the market rate. The low fixed-rate means the rate payable not the rate chargeable. The unpaid balance (chargeable but not payable) is added on to the capital. So after the grace period, not only do the borrowers start to pay full rate, but also their total indebtedness will have increased. So after the grace period, they will be paying, to the end of the loan, more than they would have done if they had opted for a more conventional loan.

Some lenders may offer a lower rate on a large loan. Higher rates are likely to be charged if the borrower has a poor credit record, or if the amount borrowed is a high proportion (e.g. 90 per cent) of the value of the property, for in such cases the risk is higher. Of course, if the property is genuinely worth more than the loan, then in principle the risk is zero. But as all bankers know, when security is enforced, it is remarkable how often it fetches less than the original valuation.

When comparing interest rates it is important to look at the annual percentage rate ("APR") as calculated in terms of the Consumer Credit Act 1974. The APR is a standardised way of calculating an interest rate, designed to make comparison easy.

REPAYMENT MORTGAGES AND INTEREST-ONLY MORTGAGES

Introduction

The market speaks of "mortgages" as being either "repayment mortgages" or 21–23 "interest-only mortgages". Both terms are misleading. Apart from the fact that what is being talked about is not the mortgage (the security) but the loan, all loans are repayment loans, because, obviously, loans have to be repaid, and no loan is interest-only, for the same reason. What these terms refer to is a difference in the way in which the capital is repaid. In a "repayment mortgage" the capital is paid off in instalments (normally monthly) over the term of the loan—20 years for example. Thus the capital gradually declines. Interest is paid on the declining capital debt. Thus if the loan is for 20 years, and if the contract requires repayment of part of the capital each month, then there are 20 × 12 = 240 term dates. This is also known as the "capital-and-interest" method, or the "amortisation" method. By contrast, in an "interest-only mortgage" no repayments of capital are made during the term, but only interest. The capital debt thus remains unchanged and is paid off in a single payment at the expiry of the term.

In a repayment mortgage, if the capital instalments were all of equal amounts, the effect would be that, over the years, less and less interest would be due (because of the declining amount of the capital), so that the total amount payable each month would fall off over time. This way of doing things is unusual in home loans, being unpopular with borrowers, especially because the earning power of the debtor is likely to be lower in the earlier years of the loan than in the later years. Hence long ago a system was devised whereby the monthly payments are kept constant (subject only to interest rate variations) during the whole lifetime of the loan. To this we now turn.

Repayment mortgages

21–24   In a repayment mortgage, the borrower pays to the lender, normally on a monthly basis, a sum that has within it two elements, namely (i) the interest due and (ii) part of the capital. The amount of the latter is calculated so that the whole capital will have been repaid by the end of the term. The monthly payment stays constant throughout the term, apart from any changes which may result from alterations to the interest rate, but the slice of that constant payment that represents capital repayment waxes, while the interest slice wanes. To begin with, nearly all of the monthly payment is interest. As the years go by, more and more of the capital is paid off, and so the total annual interest bill gradually falls. As it falls, more and more of the monthly payment is available for paying off the capital. Near the end of the life of the loan, nearly all the monthly payment is of capital. The monthly payment is mathematically calculated to ensure that the loan will be fully paid off at exactly the term. Each year the lender sends the borrower a statement showing how much capital has been repaid.

This method has, historically, been the most popular way of structuring home loan contracts. It is not difficult to understand, and the borrower has the assurance that the payments will, if kept up, guarantee the repayment of the whole loan by the end of the term. There is also the comfort of seeing, in the annual statement, the capital of the loan falling year by year, with the speed increasing as the years pass.

Interest-only mortgages

21–25   The other method is to pay nothing but interest during the term, thus keeping the capital constant. The capital is then paid off in a lump sum at the end of the term. These are occasionally called "bullet" loans or "balloon" loans but currently the normal term is "interest-only". To ensure that there will be money to repay the whole loan at term, the borrower will enter into some kind of savings scheme (known as the "repayment vehicle") which, all being well, will generate enough money. Some lenders require the borrower to do this. Others merely recommend it. A borrower who opts for an interest-only loan and does not set up a repayment vehicle thereby obtains the cheapest form of home loan, but runs the risk that when the Day of Reckoning comes, not enough money is available to pay off the loan.

Repayment vehicles

One type of repayment vehicle is the endowment mortgage, in which the 21–26
savings vehicle is a life assurance policy. A variant on the endowment mortgage is the unit-linked endowment. The life office invests in a unitised fund
and the maturity value is the value of the units at maturity.[22] These have a
higher risk/reward ratio than conventional endowments. If the investments do
well, the customer does better than in a conventional endowment, and vice
versa. The ISA[23] mortgage is another riskier repayment vehicle, but with tax
advantages. In a pension[24] mortgage the repayment vehicle is a personal
pension scheme which matures at retirement age (which will be the same date
as the term of the loan). Part of the pension will be commuted into a lump sum
which pays off the loan. The rest of the pension remains to give a regular
income. There is no assignation to the lender, since pension funds are non-
assignable. The attraction of the pension mortgage is that pension schemes
receive favourable tax treatment. Disadvantages are that the system may
compel retirement at the agreed time, and that there is no surrender value.
Pension mortgages are available only to the self-employed.

Flexible mortgages, offset mortgages, and current account mortgages

In the flexible mortgage the borrowers have a degree of flexibility as to how 21–27
much they pay in any given month. If they are feeling well off they can pay a
larger sum, while if times are hard they can pay less. In an offset mortgage the
rate is charged on the net balance, taking into account any credit balance on
another account, such as a current account. A current account mortgage is
similar: here the home loan is in essence an overdraft on the current account.
This too can benefit the borrower. Most people prefer, however, to keep their
home loans separate from their other bank accounts.

LIFE ASSURANCE

Introduction

Life assurance[25] is standard in connection with home loans. The borrower 21–28
usually wishes to be sure that in the event of death there will be a fund to pay
off the loan. People often have more than one life assurance policy, and one of
them may be linked to the home loan.

Types of life assurance

There are many different sorts of life assurance available. But the basics are as 21–29
follows:

(1) *Term assurance.* If the life assured dies within the next 15 years (or
whatever period is agreed) the life office will pay the sum assured.

---

[22] As with low-cost, with-profit endowment, there is a life assurance element whereby if the
borrower dies, the life office guarantees as a minimum to pay off the loan.

[23] Individual Savings Accounts. The predecessor of the ISA was the PEP (Personal Equity Plan)
and thus there exist some PEP mortgages though no new ones can be created.

[24] Or PPP (Personal Pension Plan).

[25] "Insurance" is the general term but for life the usual word is "assurance".

But if he or she dies even one day later, nothing is payable. This is cheaper, in terms of premiums, than the following two types, for the simple reason that in most cases the life office never has to pay out. An even cheaper variant is the reducing term assurance, in which the sum assured declines as the years pass, to zero at the end of the term.[26]

(2) *Whole-of-life assurance.* A whole-of-life policy matures on death, whenever that is. This is more expensive in terms of premiums because no one is immortal, and so the life office has to pay out one day.

(3) *Endowment assurance.* An endowment policy matures on the death of the life assured, but if the assured is still alive at a stated date (the 65th birthday for instance), the policy matures anyway. This is, in premium terms, the most expensive form of assurance. The life office is bound to pay some day, and at all events not later than the stated date. Endowment policies have now become unpopular and some companies have stopped offering them. But historically they have been of huge importance and there are many millions still in existence.

In the first two types (term assurance and whole-of-life assurance) the sum payable on death is generally a pre-determined sum stated in the policy itself. But in the third (endowment assurance) this is not usually the case.[27] There are two main types of endowment policy where the sum payable is not fixed but flexible. In the traditional "with-profits" endowment, the policy states a fixed sum which is the minimum which will be paid. But over the years "bonuses" are added to the policy, the amount of which will depend on the investment success of the life office. When the policy matures, the sum payable will normally be well in excess of the guaranteed minimum. These endowment policies have long been a popular way of combining life assurance with savings. A popular variant is the "low-cost with-profits" endowment. Here the minimum sum payable at the maturity date is less than the minimum sum payable at death. However, the policy holder hopes that the bonuses to be added over the years will more than make up the difference. These are only the basic types. In practice, there is a myriad of different endowment options. One variant which is worth mentioning is the low-start, low-cost, with-profits endowment, where the monthly payments to the life office are in the early years lower than they would otherwise be, and higher in the later years.

Functionally, endowment policies are a mixture of life assurance and savings. As savings, they are likely to perform better, in the longer term, than deposits, while avoiding the potential for extreme volatility that affects direct equity investment. However, they are opaque products. Policy holders are likely to know little about how the funds are invested or how the successive bonuses are determined.

The level of premium depends on various factors, including the age and health and sex of the life assured. Alex, aged 40, a heavy drinker, smoker and drug abuser, who works as a mercenary in central Africa, will not get such favourable terms as Tom, a healthy 21-year-old who avoids all drugs and hazardous activities, such as sexual intercourse, except under medical supervision.

---

[26] Such policies are widely used as "mortgage protection policies". See later.

[27] If it is, the endowment policy is a "without profits" policy. These are rare.

The life assured and the policy holder

The "life assured" is the person on whose death the policy becomes payable. 21–30
The "policy holder" is the person to whom, or to whose representatives, the
money is payable on maturity. In the first instance this is usually the same
person as the life assured, but need not be. Thus, a woman might take out a
policy on her husband's life: he would be the life assured but she would be the
policy holder.[28]

Joint life policies

Joint policies are possible, and sometimes are used by couples. There are two 21–31
main types: those payable on the first death to the survivor, and those payable
on the first death to the estate of the first to die. Joint policies payable on the
second death are possible but rare. It is (to coin a phrase) strange but true that
life offices themselves get muddled about these different types of joint policy.
Indeed it is sometimes difficult to determine from the policy documents themselves which kind of joint policy it is. So if clients take out a joint policy this
point should be clarified.

Assignation

A life policy is normally assignable, which is to say that the holder can transfer 21–32
it to someone else, by reason of sale or otherwise. The "insurable interest"
restrictions apply only for the creation of a policy. Once created, a policy can
be assigned to someone who has no insurable interest. The assignee then
becomes the policy holder, and if the policy matures will be the person paid by
the life office. Every assignation requires intimation to the life office.[29]

Realisation

Life policies normally acquire a capital value as time goes on. For instance, if 21–33
there is an endowment policy with a maturity value of £50,000, which will
mature next year when the life assured is 65, the present value of the policy is
of a similar figure. Thus the life office would be prepared to pay a large sum to
be freed of its liability to pay the money next year. This—the sum a life office
is prepared to pay to be freed of its obligations—is called the "surrender value".
In practice, however, the surrender values which are offered by the life offices
are not generous, and a better price can usually be obtained by selling the
policy. There is market for life policies.

Life assurance and home loans

Life assurance interacts with residential conveyancing in two ways. The first is 21–34
that the lender is likely to recommend, and may insist, that the borrower takes
out what is called a mortgage protection policy, or mortgage payment protection insurance ("MPPI"). This is "term" life assurance where the term is the
life of the mortgage and the maturity value is the loan. The policy is often of

---

[28] A familiar example from commerce is "key person insurance" whereby a business takes out
insurance on the life of a key employee, typically a director. But the person taking out the policy
must have an "insurable interest". One spouse has an insurable interest in the life of the other, and
a business has an insurable interest in the life of an employee.
[29] For assignation, see below, para.23–05.

the reducing type, so that at any stage the amount covered by the policy will be the current amount of capital due, which, if the capital-and-interest method is used, is a steadily declining figure.[30] The idea is that if the borrower dies during the life of the loan, there will be a fund out of which the loan can be paid off. The one case where the lender will not recommend, or insist on, a mortgage protection policy is where the home loan is of the endowment type, since that has inbuilt life assurance. To that we now turn.

Endowment mortgages

21–35 In an "endowment mortgage" the borrower takes out an endowment policy with a life office and a loan with the lender. The maturity period of the policy is the same as the term of the loan. Thus, if the borrower dies during the term, the policy matures and pays off the loan. If the borrower survives to term, the policy matures at exactly the right moment to pay off the loan. Unless it is a non-profit endowment (which is rare) there will usually be bonuses as well, so that after the loan has been paid off there will, with luck, be a surplus. During the life of the loan the borrower pays the lender interest only. The borrower thus has two monthly payments to make, one to the lender, of interest, and the other to the life office, of premiums.

At one time the life policy was invariably assigned to the lender, but nowadays most lenders do not require assignation, though there is usually a contractual right to demand an assignation. If the policy is assigned it works as additional security. This is because in the event of default on the loan the lender could surrender the policy to the life office, or auction it, though this seldom happens as in practice the lender simply sells the house.[31] If the borrower dies, the whole maturity value of an assigned policy is paid by the life office to the lender because the latter is the holder, even if the amount involved is greater than the debt. The lender then deducts the amount of the loan and pays the balance to the executor or whoever is entitled to the reversion to the policy.[32] Usually, of course, the borrower does survive to the age of 65 or whenever, and the life office pays any free balance to the borrower.

If the life policy is a low-cost, with-profits endowment, the minimum sum guaranteed to be payable on death is not less than the capital of the debt. But, unlike a conventional endowment, the sum payable at maturity at the end of the term is not so guaranteed. The borrower simply hopes that the accumulated bonuses will be enough to pay off the loan at that stage, and, even better, will deliver a surplus.

Endowment and capital-and-interest mortgages compared

21–36 Most existing home loans are either endowment or capital-and-interest, although not many new home loans are of the endowment type. How do they compare with each other in practice? With the endowment method, the monthly

---

[30] However, level term assurance is also often used. This would mean that if, for example, the borrower died 15 years into a 25-year mortgage, there would be a surplus left after repaying the loan.

[31] But if the sale of the house does not meet the debt, the life policy becomes important.

[32] Questions of great difficulty, and of great practical importance, can arise as to who is deemed to have paid off the loan. The first to die? The survivor? Both, equally? See Gretton, (1987) 32 J.L.S.S. 303 and (1988) 33 J.L.S.S. 141, but the subject awaits a full study. See also *Christie's Exr v Armstrong*, 1996 S.L.T. 948.

payment to the lender is smaller than it would be with the capital-and-interest method, but this does not mean that the endowment method is cheaper, because there are the assurance premiums to take into account too. But as against this the person with a capital-and-interest loan must also pay premiums on a mortgage protection policy, though because this is term assurance only the premiums will be fairly low.

Endowment mortgages can be less flexible than capital-and-interest mortgages in a number of respects. Early repayment of an endowment mortgage may be harder because capital has not declined. To release the capital value of the endowment policy, sale or surrender is required, which can be complicated and which may not realise a fair value.[33] Changing the term of the loan is harder with the endowment method because it normally involves renegotiating the life policy. Again, whereas it is usually easy to convert from capital-and-interest to endowment, the converse is more difficult, both for practical reasons and because if an endowment policy is surrendered, a loss usually results. So once into the endowment system, the borrower tends to be locked in. Again, the investment element in an endowment mortgage is inflexible in that the borrower is tied to a single company for the period of the loan.

Endowment mortgages peaked in the late 1980s when about 80 per cent of all new home loans took this form. During the 1990s their popularity waned and today it is uncommon for new home loans to be structured in this way. The reason lies in the fact that the returns on the endowment policies proved in general to be considerably lower than expected. In a majority of cases it turned out that the eventual maturity value was unlikely to be enough to pay off the loan. In many cases it turned out that the policies had been mis-sold, and the FSA required that borrowers be paid compensation.[34]

MISCELLANEOUS

Foreign currency mortgages

A foreign currency mortgage is one denominated in a foreign currency such as Euros or Japanese yen or Swiss francs. In other words, though the house is in Scotland the loan is in a foreign currency, and must be repaid in that currency. No law compels people to transact in sterling. Foreign currency loans are attractive when sterling interest rates are higher than interest rates in the foreign currency in question. Because of the possibility that sterling might depreciate against the other currency, thereby increasing the debt in sterling terms, foreign currency loans are risky and only for the financially sophisticated.   21–37

Indexed mortgages

An indexed mortgage is one where the capital is index-linked, so that the total debt varies over time according to the value of the property. They are rare.   21–38

---

[33] Early repayment in order to sell the existing house and to buy another, of the same or greater value, presents no difficulty in an endowment mortgage, for the policy can be used to finance the new mortgage. However, problems may arise if the owner wishes to sell but not to buy another house, or wishes to buy another house but of a lower value.

[34] For more on endowment mortgages, see paras 18–25 to 18–28 of the 3rd edition of this book.

Shared ownership and shared equity mortgages

21–39 Shared ownership and shared equity mortgages are similar. They tend to be found in special schemes with some public-sector involvement. In what is usually called a "shared ownership mortgage", the borrowers and lenders are co-owners of the house. The borrowers have a loan only in respect of their share. The contract provides for the transfer of the other share to them in slices, until they own it all.[35] The price payable for each slice is fixed by an index or by arbitration. The idea is to help those who could not afford to take a secured loan over the whole property. Such arrangements are uncommon. Deals of this sort can sometimes be set up with a housing association. The buyers pay the association rent for the slice not (yet) owned by them. A variant of this idea is where the sellers sell only a 50 per cent (or whatever) share, with the other 50 per cent to be bought by the buyers after (say) five years, or sooner at their option, at a value to be fixed by an independent valuer. The buyers need initially to get a loan only to cover the 50 per cent.

The term "shared equity mortgage" tends to be used for an arrangement on the following lines. The buyer is the sole owner. The lender advances whatever part of the purchase price is needed. But no interest is payable. Instead, when the property is sold, a percentage of the sale price is payable to the lender, and this obligation is secured to the lender by a standard security over the property.

Non-purchase home loans

21–40 This chapter deals with loans for house purchase. But a person may already own a house and wish to use it as security for a loan for some other purpose, such as improvements.

Buy-to-let loans

21–41 At one time, loans to enable a person to buy a house to let it out were almost unknown. Banks were not interested in long-term lending. Building societies would lend only to owner-occupiers. Moreover, in addition to the absence of a supply of funds, there was little demand, since the Rent Acts meant that rent levels were kept at a below-market rate. Investing in rented property was only for those with a death wish. In recent years, however, there has been a marked increase in buy-to-let loans.

Remortgages

21–42 A remortgage is where a new home loan is taken out and the proceeds used to pay off the old one. Perhaps the borrowers prefer the terms of the new loan. Or perhaps they wish to borrow more, but the existing lender will not agree. The motive must be strong because of the costs involved. These are: (i) re-survey fee, (ii) an administrative charge by the new lender and (iii) legal expenses. There may also be an early repayment fee due to the outgoing lender. Once remortgaging was rare. It became common in the 1990s, especially because lenders were competing for business. Since the credit crunch it has become less common.[36] The borrower generally seeks to keep costs down by not using a law firm.

---

[35] This is sometimes called "staircasing".
[36] See above, para.21–09.

Further advances

A further advance is where the borrower borrows more money from the same 21–43
lender, for example for home improvements. Lenders are usually willing to
make a further advance for this purpose so long as there is sufficient equity.[37]
Likewise a further advance is usually obtainable to pay for a large but unexpected repair, since the lender has an interest in ensuring the good condition of
the property. Because the original standard security will almost invariably
have been for all sums due and to become due, it automatically covers the
new advance.[38] Lenders will usually wish to know the purpose for which
the further advance is sought, and will often impose restrictions, especially in
the case of building societies.

Second mortgages

A second mortgage is where there is a further secured loan which, for whatever 21–44
reason, is not from the existing lender. There are some institutions which
specialise in these. As a postponed heritable security, it ranks second. A notice
of second charge should be sent to the first lender under s.13 of the Conveyancing
and Feudal Reform (Scotland) Act 1970.[39]

Equity release mortgages (lifetime mortgages)

People who have reached the age of, say, 70 will normally have paid off the 21–45
home loan and retired. But the pension may not be good. Why live in semi-
poverty while sitting on a valuable asset which, when they die, will merely
enrich their heirs? Why not release some of the equity and spend it while still
alive? This is the reasoning behind what are called "equity release mortgages",
"home income mortgages", or "lifetime mortgages". The way these work is
that the elderly person borrows,[40] and secures the debt on the house. Interest
only is payable.[41] The proceeds of the loan are typically used to buy an annuity.
Part of the income from the annuity is used to pay the interest on the loan. The
rest is free extra income. When the person dies, the capital is repaid. The net
effect is that the value of the estate at death is less than it would otherwise have
been. The money has, instead, been spent by the owner while still alive.
Insurance companies offer annuities, and some have pre-packaged equity
release schemes. Because the cost of an annuity depends on life expectancy at
commencement, these schemes make sense only for older people. The amount
of the loan is typically about 25 per cent of the value of the property. Thus most
of the value is still available to the heirs.

There are many variants on the market. One variant, sometimes called a
"home reversion", is actually not in the form of a loan at all. In this, there is a
sale and lease-back. The company thus becomes legal owner, and the elderly
person becomes tenant, at a nominal rent of say £5 per annum, the lease lasting
to death. Sometimes the owner sells only a share of the property, e.g. 50 per
cent. The price paid by the reversionary company will not be the current market

---

[37] Equity in this context means market value of the property minus secured debt.
[38] Subject to s.13 of the Conveyancing and Feudal Reform (Scotland) Act 1970.
[39] See below, para.22–26.
[40] This can be a lump sum. But borrowing in tranches is also possible, and such an arrangement
is sometimes called a drawdown mortgage.
[41] Unless it is a roll-up mortgage, in which interest is not paid but is accumulated with capital.

price, but a discounted figure, to reflect the fact that the company does not recover its investment until the death of the plan-holder.

Such schemes can be a good way of rescuing an elderly person from unnecessary poverty. But they can have drawbacks too. In the first place, if the person dies soon after the scheme is set up, the annuity company makes a large profit, the heirs suffer a large loss, and the elderly person gets little benefit. This, of course, is a risk inherent in any annuity deal. Naturally, it can work the other way round too, as with any annuity: if the person lives to 110, the annuity company suffers a large loss, and the elderly person can die happy in the knowledge of having done what was probably the best business deal of his or her life. Secondly, the estate is less than it would otherwise be. Whether this matters or not depends on the circumstances. If the elderly person has no spouse or children, this may be no problem. But if the person wants to leave a good estate to his or her heirs, this scheme may be inappropriate. Finally, the interest rate on the loan may be variable whereas the annuity is normally fixed. This is fine if interest rates fall, but can be a disaster if they rise. There have been many people who entered into an equity release deal and later came to regret it. The modern, and wise, trend is therefore for the interest to be a fixed rate.

Equity release schemes have often come in for criticism. Whilst they can be valuable, they need careful consideration. The money released may diminish welfare benefits.[42] There may be tax consequences. And of course the estate will in due course be smaller than it would otherwise have been.

Islamic mortgages

21–46   Islam does not forbid loans, nor does it forbid security for loans. But it does forbid loans bearing interest (*riba*). As those with money are generally unwilling to advance it except for a return, loans are normally out of the question, from a commercial point of view, if Islamic law (*Sharia*) is to be observed. But various devices have been developed which in functional terms are similar to loans bearing interest: what is key for religious purposes is the ostensible form of the arrangement. A mortgage that complies with *Sharia* is sometimes called a "*Halal* mortgage", but more usually an "Islamic mortgage". The term "*Sharia*-compliant mortgage" is also encountered. The three main types of Islamic mortgage are (i) *murabaha*, (ii) *ijara* and (iii) *musharaka*.[43]

In the *murabaha* mortgage, X wishes to buy a house. X's bank in fact buys it. The bank then immediately sells it to X, with the price payable by instalments over a certain number of years. The price is higher than the price the bank has paid. The difference in these two prices is calculated so as to be the same as interest. Thus a bank under this arrangement gets the same return on its money as it would in a conventional loan with interest. When the title will be conveyed to X depends on the agreement, but it is typically at the outset. The bank's right to the price is secured by a security over the property.

In the *ijara* mortgage, the set-up is very similar to hire purchase. The bank buys the property and rents it to X. At the end of the term a final lump sum is paid and at that stage the title is conveyed to X.

---

[42] Many elderly people fail to claim all the benefits to which they are entitled.
[43] These (including "Sharia") are Arabic terms, and their transliteration varies.

The *musharaka* mortgage is a mix of the first two, and has some similarity to the shared ownership and shared equity arrangements described above.[44] X and the bank are co-owners, with X gradually buying out the bank's share over the term of the mortgage. Details vary. Because of the inconvenience of frequent partial dispositions, title is sometimes vested in one or other of the parties, in trust.

Islamic mortgages are rare in Scotland.[45] They are not free from difficulty. Some Islamic mortgages may be invalidated by s.9 of the Conveyancing and Feudal Reform (Scotland) Act 1970, which prohibits arrangements that vest ownership in a lender for the purpose of securing an obligation. Some Islamic mortgages make the functional owner a tenant of the bank, the term being for more than 20 years, thus running up against the rule against leases that are structured to have a term of over 20 years.[46] Another difficulty is the absence of debtor-protection rules, especially for *ijara* and *musharaka*. This is because the debtor-protection rules all presuppose that a standard security is being used.[47] Finally, if title is vested in the bank there is the problem of what happens if the bank becomes insolvent.

How Much Can be Borrowed?

Amount borrowable: the two criteria

Here only ordinary house purchase loans are dealt with. Two factors determine 21–47 how much can be borrowed: the borrower's financial status, and the value of the property. But exactly how these factors will be applied varies from lender to lender, and also varies from one year to another. So what follows is only a general picture.

As for the financial status of the borrower, traditionally lenders focus on the annual income,[48] and then multiply that by a set figure, such as 3.5. Often there are joint borrowers (e.g. husband and wife) both with incomes, and then the second income is brought in, according to the formula used by the particular lender, for example counting the second income as one unit. Thus, for example, if the larger income is £50,000 and the smaller is £30,000, the maximum loan would be $(3.5 \times £50,000) + (£30,000) = £205,000$. Another approach is to lend a figure based on the combined income, e.g. 2.5 times the combined income. Extra income, such as overtime, may be included or excluded, or included at a reduced weighting, according to the policy of the lender. Recently there has been a tendency towards a more sophisticated, "mortgage affordability" approach, which brings in additional factors such as the number of dependants. Whatever approach is adopted, the lender is likely to ask questions about credit history. It may also carry out a credit search against the applicant with one of the three credit reference agencies.[49] Obviously, a problematic credit record

---

[44] See above, para.21–39.
[45] Not much has been written about them, but see Burnside, (2005) 50 J.L.S.S. Dec./58; and Burnside, (2009) 54 J.L.S.S. Aug./56.
[46] Land Tenure Reform (Scotland) Act 1974 s.8.
[47] For provisions concerned with debtor protection, see below, para.22–08.
[48] Deductions for tax, national insurance, etc. being ignored.
[49] Call Credit Plc, Equifax Plc, and Experian Plc.

may result in the loan being refused, or offered on terms less favourable to the borrower.

The other factor determining the amount borrowable is the value of the property. Once again, practice varies. Before the credit crunch some lenders were offering loans up to 100 per cent of value or even more. This, coupled with a widespread failure to check that borrowers could afford the loan, is widely regarded as having been one of the causes of the economic crisis. Since the credit crunch it has been difficult to borrow more than about 75 per cent of the value of the property. This percentage figure is called the "loan to value" figure (LTV). It is calculated, not on the purchase price, but on the valuation obtained by the lender from its surveyor. The valuation figure may be lower than the final purchase price, since a lender's surveyor may take a cautious approach. This point is important since it is often not appreciated by clients. Thus, if a 75 per cent loan is available, and the property is valued at £200,000, but bought for £220,000, the loan will be £150,000, not £165,000.

There are thus two maximum figures, one based on status and the other on value. Which applies? The answer normal answer is: whichever is the lower. Thus, suppose that the couple in our earlier example wish to buy a house which the surveyor values at £250,000. And suppose that the lender is prepared to lend 80 per cent of valuation, i.e. £200,000. The status-based maximum was £205,000. So the lender will lend up to £200,000. If the house is in fact bought for £250,000, the clients will have to find £50,000 out of their own pockets, plus the expenses involved in house purchase.

Since the credit crunch, lenders have tended to be more restrictive on both on the status side and on the property-value side, with the result that mortgage lending has fallen very substantially. From the point of view of potential borrowers, it is now much harder to obtain a house purchase loan than it used to be.

Evidence of income: self-certified loans

21–48 Lenders generally seek confirmation of income, either by being authorised to contact the salaries department of the borrower's employer, or by asking to see wages slips.

Non-status loans, also called self-certified loans, are where the lender relies on the borrower's own statement of his or her financial circumstances. They are typically used for self-employed borrowers where sufficient audited accounts are not available. In a non-status loan the maximum borrowable is typically lower than it would be for other customers. In addition, some lenders offer non-status loans (usually remortgages) to people who are or have been in financial difficulties, often at high rates of interest.[50] Such people are tempted because their financial problems undermine their credit status, thus making conventional borrowing harder.

High-LTV advances

21–49 "LTV", as already mentioned, means the loan as a percentage of property value. In high-LTV cases, lenders may insist that a guarantee be obtained from

---

[50] The advertisement may say "CCJs welcome". A CCJ (county court judgment) is roughly the equivalent in England of a sheriff court decree, the point being that such lenders are prepared to lend to people with a dubious credit record.

an insurance company. This is called a mortgage indemnity guarantee ("MIG"). The reason is that high percentage loans involve a greater risk to the lenders, for if there is default there is a greater danger that the forced sale of the property will not recoup the whole loan. About 80 per cent of enforcement cases involve home loans where the original LTV was 90 per cent or over.[51] For the MIG there is a one-off premium, sometimes called a "higher lending charge", payable by the borrowers. The cost depends on the circumstances, but can be expensive, and typically well over £1,000. Clients should be warned in advance. If there is default and the insurers have to pay, the insurer is subrogated and so can sue the borrower. Thus, the insurance policy is for the benefit of lenders, and not borrowers.[52] As an alternative, or in addition, in high-LTV cases the lenders may charge a higher interest rate.

The devious borrower

Some borrowers try to obtain a larger loan by questionable means. In self-certified loans, borrowers often overstate their income. A loan intended for commercial purposes (e.g. buy-to-let) may be presented as a loan for an ordinary home purchase. A buyer may attempt to get the lender to think that the property is worth more than it is so as too boost the amount of the loan.[53] The wise solicitor will have nothing to do with such ploys. 21–50

FEES

Entry chares

Setting up a home loan generally involves the payment of fees or charges. Sometimes these can be added to the loan itself, which is just as well, because they are often high—cumulatively they can run into the thousands of pounds—and have tended to become higher in recent years. (i) If a mortgage broker is used, there can be a brokerage or "intermediary" charge. (ii) Some lenders charge a "reservation" or "application" or "product" or "booking" charge when the application is made. (iii) Most lenders charge a "completion" or "arrangement" charge when the loan is actually made. (iv) Some lenders make a charge for the simple act of handing the money to the borrower. (v) There is also the conveyancing fee for the standard security. But in most home-loan cases the same law firm acts for both borrower and lender, and this fact keeps the fee down. In high-LTV cases, there will also usually be (vi) the "higher lending charge" discussed above.[54] These are in addition to the fees that buyers of heritable property will be paying anyway, loan or no loan, notably the valuation fee, the conveyancing fee, and the land registration fee. 21–51

---

[51] Emma McCallum and Ewen McCaig, *Mortgage Arrears and Repossessions in Scotland* (2002), p.52.

[52] Borrowers can buy insurance to protect themselves against unemployment. But such policies tend to be expensive.

[53] Such questionable methods seem to be used openly. For instance, in the January 2004 issue (p.47) of *Mortgage Advisor* it was suggested that the borrower use what is called the "inflated purchase price" method, in which the price reported to the lender and the price actually paid are different.

[54] See above, para.21–49.

Exit charges

21–52 An administration charge is payable for discharging a standard security, and an early-redemption charge is payable in some deals if the debtor wishes to pay the loan off early.

Unfairness

21–53 Unfairness is to some extent controlled by public law through the FSA, and through the Consumer Credit Act 1974. In private law there are the Unfair Terms in Consumer Contracts Regulations 1999. As for variable interest rates, there is English authority to suggest an implied term requiring the lender not to act wholly unreasonably in setting the rate.[55] Unethical conduct, however, continues to exist. Finally, in principle building societies, lacking shareholders who must be fed with profits, should be less likely to act unfairly than banks.

---

[55] *Paragon Finance Plc v Nash* [2002] 2 All E.R. 248.

CHAPTER 22

HERITABLE SECURITY

INTRODUCTION

Types of heritable security

Over time there have been various forms of heritable security. Three of them, the bond and disposition in security, the bond of cash credit and disposition in security, and the *ex facie* absolute disposition, were abolished by the Conveyancing and Feudal Reform (Scotland) Act 1970,[1] though the abolition was prospective, so that such securities granted before the Act continued to exist until discharge. A fourth form, the pecuniary real burden, lingered on, seldom used, until abolished by the Title Conditions (Scotland) Act 2003.[2] The 1970 Act created a new form, the standard security. This was a development of the old forms, with a new name. Much of the old law applies equally to standard securities. Since a standard security is a species of the genus, which is heritable security, a standard security can be, and often is, called a heritable security, and a standard security holder is often called a heritable creditor.

The standard security is a true or "proper" security, meaning that it is a subordinate real right. The real right of ownership remains with the debtor. Thus when a standard security is granted, there are two real rights in the same property: ownership and security.

The role of the law firm: advising the lending clients

The law firm may be acting for the lender, or for the borrower. In residential cases, it is usual, to keep expenses down, for the law firm to act for both, in which case it is important to keep firmly in mind the fact that there are two clients to both of whom duties are owed.[3]

We begin with the law firm's role when acting for the lender.[4] The lending client will in most cases be a professional money-lender, such as a bank, which presumably knows its own business, and which generally dictates the terms of the documents used, so that the role of the solicitor is mainly the technical one of ensuring that a valid security is constituted. There will be a letter of instruction from the lender that must be checked to see what the lender requires. In most cases the lender will be a member of the Council of Mortgage Lenders ("CML")[5] and if so the terms of the CML *Lenders' Handbook for Scotland*

22–01

22–02

---

[1] Conveyancing and Feudal Reform (Scotland) Act 1970 s.9(4).
[2] Title Conditions (Scotland) Act 2003 s.117.
[3] See above, para.1–10.
[4] See also above, para.2–21.
[5] For the CML, see above, para.21–08.

must be complied with. It must always be borne in mind that if there is eventual default, and the lender finds itself unable to recover in full, it will, as a matter of course, see whether there is any possibility of making a claim from the law firm that acted for it.

The role of the law firm: advising the borrowing clients

22–03   The law firm must check the documentation on behalf of the clients, and bring to their attention anything significant, especially anything that they might one day blame the law firm for not telling them. For instance, it is a good idea to draw to the borrowers' attention the fact that letting the property is not allowed without the lender's consent.[6] These duties of explanation are owed to the borrowing clients but also to the lending client.[7] Evidence that such advice has been given should be preserved.

Spouses and similar cases

22–04   If one person grants a deed, such as a standard security, for the benefit of another person, there is a danger that the decision to do so was not a free and informed one. For this reason the parties should be separately advised.[8] The classic example is where husband and wife are co-owners and wish to grant a standard security to secure the husband's business borrowings. The same law firm should not act for both parties, and the law firm acting for the wife should take care to explain the meaning and effect of what she is signing, and to verify, as far as it is possible to do so, that her consent is genuine and based on a true understanding of the risks. If this does not happen, she may be able to rescind.[9] The advice should be given in writing as well as in person.

Where there are joint borrowers, care must be taken if one borrower signs as agent of the other, because of the obvious danger of fraud. Indeed, CML lenders will not accept such a deed.[10] Moreover even where the standard security bears to be signed by both parties, experience shows that there is a risk that one signature may be forged: the cautious law agent will look carefully at both signatures. Of course, such forgeries can, and do, occur in other deeds, such as dispositions, but they are particularly common in the case of standard securities. It is difficult to sell a house, with a forged signature, without one's partner finding out about it, but it is rather easier to raise a secured loan with a forged signature.

Pro forma deeds

22–05   Most lenders use their own forms of standard security, so for the solicitor it is a question of filling in the blanks. In the case of an automated registration of

---

[6] Conveyancing and Feudal Reform (Scotland) Act 1970 Sch.3 Standard Condition 6.

[7] "You should explain to each borrower (and any other person signing or executing a document) his responsibilities and liabilities under the" mortgage conditions: CML *Lenders' Handbook for Scotland*, para.11.2.1.

[8] For a discussion of the issues surrounding "cautionary wives", see above, para.1–11.

[9] *Smith v Bank of Scotland* 1997 S.C. (HL) 111 is the leading case but has been limited by later decisions, especially *Royal Bank of Scotland Plc v Wilson,* 2004 S.C. 153. See further Eden, (2003) 7 Edin. L.R. 107, and Reid and Gretton, *Conveyancing 2003* (2004), p.73.

[10] CML *Lenders' Handbook for Scotland*, para.5.12.1.

title to land ("ARTL") transaction, this is done on a virtual deed.[11] *Pro forma* deeds generally make reference to what used to be called the "schedule of variations" but nowadays is usually called the "mortgage conditions", which is a deed that the lender will have registered in the Books of Council and Session. This deed is a standard-form loan contract and also operates as a variation of the standard conditions in the 1970 Act (discussed below).[12] The borrower is thus presented with a contract of adhesion: take it or leave it. There is virtually no possibility of negotiation of terms.[13]

Procedure

The lender will write to the law firm that is to act for it, which in residential 22–06 conveyancing is usually the borrowers' law firm. This package contains various bits and pieces. One is the letter of instruction itself. Next, there is a report on title, also called a certificate of title, with blanks to be filled in. After examining the title, the law firm completes the report and returns it to the lender.[14] Next, there is the standard security with blanks. The standard security is pre-printed in the lenders' preferred form. Thus, solicitors seldom have to draft complete standard securities themselves. The standard security is usually in duplicate, one copy being used as a draft and the other as the final version. With some lenders the styles can be downloaded from their website and completed on a computer. Next, there will be a copy of the lender's mortgage conditions. Then, in the case of a building society, there is a copy of the Rules of the Society. This is important because the borrowers will normally become members, with voting rights, etc. and so it should be passed on to the borrowers. Lastly, there will be a Schedule of Writs. This is a bit of paper, mainly blank, on which will eventually be entered a list of all the title deeds, and which will be sent to the lenders with the deeds after completion of the transaction. A copy should be retained, so that the file will show what deeds are held by the lenders. Sometimes, depending on the circumstances, other documentation may also be needed. For instance, the lenders might require a guarantee from a third party. In the case of an endowment mortgage, the lender may ask for an assignation, and in that case there will be a pre-printed assignation of the life policy, with blanks, once again in duplicate.

The engrossed standard security is sent to the borrowers for execution.[15] Execution by the lender is not necessary. A few days before settlement the certificate of title is sent to the lenders.[16] This states that the title is good—if it *is* good. "You should not submit your certificate of title unless it is unqualified or we have authorised you in writing to proceed notwithstanding any issues you have raised with us."[17] Payment of the loan is requested at the same time. The lender remits the money to the law firm, not directly to the borrowers. This is done by bank transfer. Now settlement can take place. If, after requisitioning

---

[11] For ARTL transactions, see above, para.8–23.

[12] See below, para.22–13.

[13] That is to say, in ordinary home loans. This book does not deal, except incidentally, with commercial conveyancing.

[14] The report must be handled with care because it may contain all sorts of unreasonable warranties.

[15] In ARTL transactions the solicitor executes by electronic signature on the client's behalf.

[16] See generally the CML *Lenders' Handbook for Scotland*, para.10.

[17] CML *Lenders' Handbook for Scotland*, para.10.1.

the funds, a significant problem crops up, the law firm must notify the lender. If there is a delay in settlement for more than a few days the lender will want the money back again for the period until settlement does take place.

After settlement the standard security must be sent off for registration without delay.[18] If the borrower is a company, the security must also be registered in the Companies Register.[19] If there is an assignation of a life policy, the intimation must be sent to the life office.[20]

Personal search and company search

22–07 In a typical conveyancing transaction the personal search covers both the buyers and the sellers.[21] Usually, if a problem arises it is because there is something in the search affecting the sellers, but the buyers' solicitors need to check the search against their own clients as well as against the sellers. The reason is that they have to make sure that the lender gets a good security. It occasionally emerges that a buyer is an undischarged bankrupt, and has failed to disclose this fact to the law firm.[22] For the same reason, if the borrower is a company, a company search will be needed.

Should a fresh personal search be made for a further advance? There is some uncertainty as to whether a supervening inhibition could affect a further advance,[23] but at all events if there is an inhibition the agent for the lender will wish to know that fact. And, obviously, if the borrower has been sequestrated, or granted a trust deed, the further advance will be refused. Similar remarks apply to the company search when there is a further advance. However, in practice lenders usually make further advances without the involvement of solicitors, and so searches are seldom made.

The multiple sources of rights and duties

22–08 In a loan secured by standard security it can be surprisingly difficult to determine what the rights and duties of the parties are. Those rights and duties in the typical case will have no fewer than six sources, and sometimes more. (i) The first is the loan contract. In a home loan this is usually contained in an offer of loan made by the bank and accepted by the borrower. (ii) The second is the standard security. (iii) The third is Pt II of the Conveyancing and Feudal Reform (Scotland) Act 1970. (iv) The fourth is Sch.3 to that Act. Though this is part of the Act, it was designed to function as a sort of standard-form contract, known as the standard conditions. (v) The fifth is the schedule of variations, or mortgage conditions, which most lenders use. (vi) The sixth source is represented by the various debtor-protection provisions. The main one is the Home Owner and Debtor Protection (Scotland) Act 2010, but others, such as the Consumer Credit Act 1974, may be applicable as well, according to circumstances. Thus even quite simple questions about the rights and duties of the parties can be difficult to answer, especially since these six sources can easily fail to dovetail with each other.

---

[18] In ARTL cases this happens online.
[19] See below, para.28–05.
[20] See also below, para.23–05.
[21] For personal searches, see above, paras 9–15 et seq.
[22] See e.g. *Halifax Plc v Gorman's Trustee*, 2000 S.L.T. 1409. See further below, para.29–02.
[23] See G.L. Gretton, *Law of Inhibition and Adjudication*, 2nd edn (1996), Ch.9.

DOCUMENTATION

The loan and the security

A standard security secures a loan. Unlike most other rights, a security has no 22–09
independent existence: it exists only in relation to another right, the secured
obligation. In traditional language, it is an accessory right.[24] The obligation can
exist without the security but the security cannot exist without an actual or at
least potential obligation. For example, in *Albatown Ltd v Credential Group
Ltd*[25] the transaction settled with payment of only part of the price, and the
buyer gave the seller a standard security to secure the balance. But the missives
had a standard two-year supersession clause. The two years passed with the
balance being paid. It was held that, with the extinction of the obligation to
pay, the security was likewise extinguished.

Although there must be an obligation, present or future, to be secured, it
does not have to be that of the granter of the security. It is possible for Jack to
grant a security for the debt of Jill. In that case, Jack has no personal liability.
Suppose that Jill's debt is £200,000 and Jack's property is worth £180,000. If
Jill defaults and the creditor forces the sale of the house, Jack will lose his
house, but he will not be liable for the shortfall of £20,000. This sort of arrangement is sometimes called third-party security. This should not be confused
with a similar state of affairs, where a third party grants a cautionary obligation
(guarantee) and then grants a standard security to secure that obligation. For
instance, in the example suppose that Jack had guaranteed Jill's debt and had
granted a security for that guarantee. In that case Jack would be personally
liable (contingently on Jill's default) for up to £200,000. In this latter case the
security granted by Jack secures his own obligation (the cautionary obligation)[26]
whereas in the first example the security secured an obligation of Jill's.[27]

A standard security can secure a specific debt of a definite amount, such as
a loan of £100,000. Or it can secure a specific overdraft account, where the
overdraft may rise and fall and rise again, so that what is secured is a fluctuating amount. Or it can secure "all sums due and to become due" by the debtor
to the creditor. This third possibility is the commonest. It is convenient because
it means that any further advance will automatically be covered by the security.
Without this system, lenders would be more reluctant to make a further
advance, or would have to insist on a new standard security, which would be
slow and expensive.

Often a Form A security (see below) will state the loan as a fixed sum, but
later have a clause stating that the security is to be good not only for the loan
but for all sums. Alternatively, a Form A security may not state the amount of
the loan at all, but merely have words obliging the grantor to pay to the grantee
all sums, for which obligation the security is granted.

Although convenient, "all sums" clauses can cause problems. Suppose that
Ishbel has a home loan with a bank and also has a current account with the
same bank. The current account is in overdraft. The standard security will

---

[24] See generally Steven, (2009) 13 Edin. L.R. 387.

[25] *Albatown Ltd v Credential Group Ltd*, 2001 G.W.D. 27-1102. See Reid and Gretton,
Conveyancing 2001, p.91.

[26] Of course, the cautionary obligation itself secures Jill's obligation.

[27] cf. *Bank of Scotland v Forman*, Unreported July 25, 2005, Peterhead Sheriff Court, discussed
Reid and Gretton, *Conveyancing 2005*, pp.116–18.

secure both the home loan account and the current account, and indeed any other sums she may owe. If she wishes to sell, the bank could refuse to discharge the security except against repayment of everything that is owed. Ishbel may not realise this. When she discusses the sale with her law firm, it should check not only the home loan account but also ask if other debts exist.

The wording of the standard security ought to say in an unambiguous and transparent way what obligations are secured. In practice it is not always unambiguous and even if it is, it is not always transparent.[28] This sort of verbal opacity is common[29]:

> "We ... and ... spouses ... (hereinafter referred to as 'the Obligant') hereby undertake to pay to The Royal Caledonian Bank plc (hereinafter referred to as 'the Bank', which expression includes its successors and assignees whomsoever) on demand all sums of principal, interest and charges which are now and which may at any time hereafter become due to the Bank by the Obligant whether solely or jointly with any other person, corporation, firm or other body and whether as principal or surety;[30] declaring that ... in the event of the foregoing personal obligation being granted by more than one person the expression 'the Obligant' means all such persons together and/or any one or more of them; and in all cases the obligations hereby undertaken by the Obligant shall bind all person(s) included in the expression 'the Obligant' and his, her or their executors and representatives whomsoever all jointly and severally without the necessity of discussing them in their order."[31]

Forms A and B

22–10 The 1970 Act[32] says that the security deed[33] can include the secured obligation, or it can merely identify that obligation, which itself is to be found outwith the security deed. A standard security containing the secured obligation is a form A security, while a standard security which refers to but does not contain the secured obligation is called a form B security. Both forms are given in Sch.2 to the Act, and either can be used.[34] In the case of home loans form A is the norm, while in commercial cases form B is the norm. The meaning and effect of form A are defined in s.10 of the 1970 Act. Form A is not perfectly drafted, but strict compliance with this and the other styles is not necessary.[35]

---

[28] See for example *Hambros Bank v Lloyds Bank*, 1999 S.L.T. 49; *Hambros Bank v Lloyds Bank (No.2)*, 1999 S.L.T. 649; *Norwich Union Life Insurance Society v Tanap Investments VK Ltd*, 1998 S.L.T. 623; 1999 S.L.T. 204; 2000 S.C. 515; *Royal Bank of Scotland v Shanks*, 1998 S.L.T. 355; *Hewit v Williamson*, 1998 S.C.L.R. 601.

[29] Taken from *Royal Bank of Scotland Plc v Wilson* [2010] UKSC 50; 2010 S.L.T. 1227.

[30] Curiously the technical term of English law is chosen rather than the technical term of Scots law ("cautioner") or the term most likely to be understood by those without legal training ("guarantor").

[31] These final words exclude the *beneficium discussionis*. But the *beneficium discussionis* never applies anyway, unless it is contracted for: Mercantile Law Amendment (Scotland) Act 1856 s.8.

[32] Conveyancing and Feudal Reform (Scotland) Act 1970 ss.9 and 10 Sch.2.

[33] The term "standard security" is used to mean both the deed and the subordinate real right created by the ensuing registration.

[34] The distinction between form A and form B is pointless, and an example of the 1970 Act's fussiness about inessentials.

[35] Halliday, para.52–31.

Interest rate

Form A requires the interest rate to be stated. As true fixed-interest loans are 22–11 rare, this creates a problem. The old practice was to state the rate in force at the time the security was entered into, adding that it was variable. Nowadays the usual practice is not to state the initial rate, but merely that the rate is variable. It is generally accepted that this is sufficient compliance with form A. Details about interest will then be given in the mortgage conditions, referred to in the security itself.[36]

Description

As with other deeds, the property must be identified by title number (or, if still 22–12 in the GRS, by a suitable conveyancing description). The rules are the same as for dispositions.[37] If a standard security is being granted over property which is being split off at the same time, there is a problem in that the description of the property has not yet been registered. In that case the split-off plan should be done in duplicate, one for the disposition and one for the standard security.[38]

The standard conditions

Schedule 3 to the 1970 Act sets out the "standard conditions" which, except 22–13 insofar as varied, apply to every standard security. The idea is to provide a ready-made contract. These conditions can be varied, and usually are. Most institutional lenders have their "mortgage conditions", long and tedious but important. These variations can be embodied in the standard security itself, but the normal practice is to register them in the Books of Council and Session. Each standard security simply refers to the registered deed, and this reference is part of the pre-printed style. Although the standard conditions were intended as a ready-made contract, the 1970 Act fails to keep consistently to this idea. Thus some parts of the standard conditions are in fact mandatory requirements that the parties cannot vary.[39] Indeed, the relationship between the body of the Act and the standard conditions is often a difficult one.

It has been mentioned above that the terms of a secured loan are often obscure because of the multiple sources of the rights and obligations of the parties.[40] An example is the basic question of whether the loan is an on-demand loan or whether it is a term loan, repayable over, say, 20 years.[41] Often the parties have agreed a term loan, yet the mortgage conditions may say that all loans are on-demand loans.[42] And if a form A standard security is used, that creates a presumption that the loan is an on-demand one.[43] The result is confusion. However, in most cases neither the lender nor the borrower will actually look at the mortgage conditions unless the latter gets into financial difficulties.

---

[36] See further D.J. Cusine and Robert Rennie, *Standard Securities*, 2nd edn (2002), para.3.32.
[37] As to which see above, Ch.12.
[38] *Registration of Title Practice Book* ("ROTPB"), paras 6.70 and 8.47.
[39] Conveyancing and Feudal Reform (Scotland) Act 1970 s.11.
[40] See above, para.22–08.
[41] For the distinction, see above, para.21–12.
[42] Indeed sometimes it will say in different places that it is an on-demand loan and that it is a term loan.
[43] 1970 Act s.10.

Another clause common in the mortgage conditions says that the borrower may neither transfer ownership nor grant any second security, unless with the lender's consent. This clause is arguably pointless. A standard security, being a real right, would be unaffected by any such transaction anyway. It is true that, if the borrower breaks this condition, and if the loan is a term loan, the lender could in theory accelerate the loan.[44] But if the borrower is keeping up the monthly payments, it is difficult to see why the lender would wish to do that, while if the borrower is not keeping up, then the lender could accelerate anyway.

Transfers subject to security

22–14 In the absence of the sort of clause just mentioned, a borrower is free to transfer ownership without the lender's consent. This is uncommon in practice since the main reason for transfer is sale and a buyer will normally insist on an unencumbered title. Such arrangements, when they happen, are generally family transactions. An example would be where the husband owns the house (or a half share of the house), and there is a separation agreement under which he is to transfer the house (or his share of it) to his wife.

If property is transferred subject to a security, neither personal liability nor real liability is affected. Personal liability for the loan remains with the borrower. Real liability stays with the property. Thus, in the event of default, the house could be sold even though it is in new ownership; but the new owner is not personally liable for the loan.[45]

If it is desired to transfer ownership to another person, keeping the loan and security in place, and for the outgoing owner to be freed of liability and for the incoming owner to take on liability, there are two possibilities. The first is for the disponer and disponee to agree that the latter will pay the loan, and that if for any reason the disponer is made to pay it, the disponee will indemnify the disponer. This is good as far as it goes but, since the lender has not agreed to the arrangement, the disponer is still liable, and so still at risk. If, for instance, the disponee later became bankrupt, the disponer would end up paying the debt. A more satisfactory method, therefore, is to obtain the lender's agreement. This can be done by discharging the old loan and security and putting in place a new secured loan. Another method that achieves the same substantive result is to have a bond of corroboration and discharge.[46] This is a tripartite deed, signed by the old owner, the new owner, and the lender. "Corroboration" means that the new owner is accepting personal liability under the loan contract. "Discharge" means that the lender is discharging the old owner of any personal liability. In addition, of course, there must be the disposition.

An example of a slightly different arrangement is where Eve owns a house, subject to a standard security, and marries Adam, and the couple agree on common ownership. A simple disposition of a half share will achieve this, though if the standard security has a prohibition on transfer then the consent of the lender will be required. But even then the result would be that, while ownership was shared, Eve alone would be the debtor. Hence it is usual in such

---

[44] For acceleration, see above, para.21–16.

[45] Subject to the Conveyancing (Scotland) Act 1874 s.47 and the Conveyancing (Scotland) Act 1924 s.15.

[46] Such a deed is classifiable as a "deed of variation" within the meaning of s.16 of the 1970 Act.

a case to have a deed of variation of the standard security whereby Adam assumes joint and several liability for the loan.

Joint borrowers

Often there are two borrowers, such as husband and wife. What normally 22–15 happens in such a case is that they have joint and several (solidary) liability for the loan, and that each one-half *pro indiviso* share is burdened with the whole loan. Sometimes they make future joint borrowings from the same lender. Assuming that the standard security contains, as it usually does, an "all sums due and to become due" clause, then the future loans will be on the same footing as the original one.

Problems can arise where future loans are made to only one of the parties. For example, Jack and Jill are co-owners and grant a standard security for a joint loan. Some years later Jack borrows money from the same lender. The loan is made to him alone. Will this loan be covered by the standard security? If so, does it affect only Jack's *pro indiviso* share or does it affect Jill's too? Is she personally liable for it? The answers depend on the facts of each case. Some banks use styles that expressly provide that any debt, incurred at any time, owed to the bank by either party burdens the whole property, and that each party is personally liable for it, even though the debt may be incurred without her consent or even knowledge.[47] Whether the use of such clauses in consumer transactions is ethical is open to debate. Possibly they might be challenged under the Unfair Terms in Consumer Contracts Regulations 1999.[48] A majority of institutional lenders use styles that are less clear and that may cover only joint debts. For instance, they provide that the deed covers debts due by "the borrower", a term that is defined as meaning Jack and Jill. Although such deeds almost always have a clause declaring liability to be joint and several, it is arguable that that clause does not extend the class of debts that is covered, but merely states the nature of the liability for those debts, and that only debts that are due by both are covered.[49] It is unsatisfactory that such a cloud of uncertainty and potential unfairness should exist, quite unnecessarily, as to everyday deeds. In practice there is seldom much chance of persuading the lender to change the wording, but the clients should be told of the possible implications.

This sort of problem used to be rare. Until the 1980s building societies provided most of the lending for house purchase and improvement, and did not normally lend for other purposes. The chance that Jack might later borrow from the building society without Jill's knowledge was thus slight. But in the 1980s building societies started to offer the sort of facilities formerly offered only by banks while banks started to offer home loans.

Problems can arise on the death of one party, especially where the loan is paid off by the maturing proceeds of an assigned life policy. Thus in *Christie v Armstrong*,[50] Ms Armstrong and Mr Christie bought a house in common with a survivorship destination. They had a joint loan secured on the house, and also an assigned policy over Mr Christie's life. Soon after the house had been bought, Mr Christie died, intestate, and the proceeds were, naturally, paid by

---

[47] For an example see *Royal Bank of Scotland Plc v Wilson*, 2009 S.L.T. 729; 2010 S.L.T. 1227.
[48] SI 1999/2083.
[49] See Reid and Gretton, *Conveyancing 2003*, p.79.
[50] *Christie v Armstrong*, 1996 S.C. 295.

the life office to the lender. The loan was thus extinguished, and Ms Armstrong was now sole owner, by virtue of the destination. Mr Christie's daughter was confirmed as her father's executor. Ms Christie argued that the whole loan had been repaid out of her father's estate (the policy) and that therefore Ms Armstrong should pay back to the estate one half. She sued Ms Armstrong. The argument was sustained in principle, but it was also held that proof was neces- sary to ascertain the intentions of the deceased[51] since it might have been his intention that there should be no right of relief in the circumstances which emerged.

Although the specific facts of *Christie* will not arise often, the points at issue are potentially relevant in a variety of cases. One unusual feature of *Christie* was that the life policy was only over one party's life. More common is the joint policy. Suppose that the whole policy matures on the first death and (being an assigned policy) immediately pays off the loan. Who has paid it off? Presumably that depends on to whom, or to whose estate, the proceeds would have been payable, had the policy not been assigned. Some joint policies are payable to the estate of the first to die, while others are payable to the survi- vor.[52] Which way the policy is written thus can make a large difference.

Finally, it often happens that one of the borrowers pays the whole of each monthly payment to the lender, or at least more than half of it. Later they become estranged. The overpayer may later (after the relationship has gone bad) claim a right of relief against the underpayer. This is the same issue as in *Christie* though arising in a different way. The underpaying party will claim that there was an unwritten understanding that relief would not be claimed. The overpayer is likely to deny this. The wise course is to have a pre-purchase agreement on such matters, but this seldom happens.[53]

Occupancy rights

22–16 Standard securities may require documentation in respect of occupancy rights. The documentation will be a renunciation or a consent, or a declaration, as appropriate.[54]

Standard securities over long leases

22–17 Long leases (over 20 years) are registrable,[55] and standard securities can be granted over them.[56] Few residential properties are held on leases of substan- tial duration, and indeed since 1974 it has been effectively impossible to create long leases of residential property.[57] But a small number of older properties are held on leasehold title. Until the 2000 Act there was no limit on long leases of commercial property, but a maximum duration of 175 years has now been imposed.[58] As with the 1974 Act this provision is not retrospective. At the time

---

[51] How those intentions were to be ascertained is not so easy to see.
[52] See above, para.21–31.
[53] See also above, para.10–18.
[54] See above, Ch.10.
[55] Registration of Leases (Scotland) Act 1857 s.1; Land Registration (Scotland) Act 1979 s.2(1) (a)(i).
[56] Conveyancing and Feudal Reform (Scotland) Act 1970 s.9(2), (8)(b).
[57] Land Tenure Reform (Scotland) Act 1974 Pt II.
[58] Abolition of Feudal Tenure etc. (Scotland) Act 2000 s.67.

of preparing this edition the Scottish Government was considering legislation to convert ultra-long leases into outright ownership.[59]

The lender's solicitors must check the terms of the lease, on such matters as ish, onerous conditions,[60] irritancy, need for landlord's consent to transactions, and rent.[61] If the security is being granted simultaneously with the grant of the lease, the validity of the landlord's title must be verified. But if the lease already exists, and the leasehold title sheet contains no exclusion of indemnity, that is normally sufficient, though the real burdens should be noted and considered. Prescription may have resolved any defect that there may have been in the landlord's title at the time when the lease was granted, either by curing that defect, or by fortifying the lease itself. But if the lease was granted only recently the validity of the landlord's title must be verified.

Tenants

Sometimes owners wish to let to tenants. In that case the lender must approve.[62] 22–18
But in practice this is often ignored. A tenancy given without the heritable creditor's consent is voidable at the instance of the heritable creditor.[63]

Property insurance

Standard condition 5 requires the debtor to insure the property. Most lenders 22–19
will offer the borrower a choice of, say, six insurance companies. The level required is normally reinstatement value rather than market value. Most policies have an automatic annual increase linked to inflation. Some lenders pay the premiums themselves and charge the borrower, while others leave it to the borrower to make the payments. Sometimes the policy is in the joint names of the lender and the owner, sometimes in the name of the lender, sometimes in the name of the borrower, and sometimes in the name of the borrower with the name of the lender endorsed on the policy. All these raise difficult theoretical questions as to the respective interests in the policy of the two parties, and also as to insurable interest. The lender is not concerned with contents insurance.

VARIATION, ASSIGNATION, RESTRICTION, AND DISCHARGE

Variation

By "variation" is here meant, not the variations of the standard conditions, 22–20
which are stated in the original security itself,[64] but subsequent variations, made after the security has already been registered. The subject is covered in s.16 of the 1970 Act. This states that variation is not appropriate where discharge, or restriction, or assignation would be appropriate. Where the term

---

[59] Based on the Scottish Law Commission's Report on *Conversion of Long Leases* (Scot. Law Com. No.204, 2006).

[60] Though bearing in mind that leasehold casualties were abolished by the Leasehold Casualties (Scotland) Act 2001.

[61] The latter is usually nominal for residential long leases.

[62] Conveyancing and Feudal Reform (Scotland) Act 1970 Sch.3 standard condition 6.

[63] *Trade Development Bank v Warriner and Mason (Scotland) Ltd*, 1980 S.C. 74. The law in this area is complex. For the case where the tenant has an assured tenancy, see Housing (Scotland) Act 2010 s.152.

[64] For which see above, para.22–13.

to be varied is contained in the original standard security as registered, the variation must itself be registered, but if the term to be varied is itself not registered, the variation need not be registered. So for example, in a form B security, a variation of a term in the (unregistered) loan contract would not have to be registered. An unregistered variation would still be binding contractually as between the parties. Presumably, therefore, the sanction for non-registration is that third parties would not be affected. But it is not easy to think of an illustrative example, especially as s.16(4) provides that even a registered variation does not affect real rights acquired by third parties prior to the variation.[65]

Such matters as further advances and changes in interest rate can be handled by a deed of variation, but in practice are not so handled. As to the first, virtually all standard securities are for "all sums due or to become due", and as for the second, there is normally a provision for a floating interest rate, whereby changes are made informally.[66] Hence, deeds of variation are rare. Sometimes a deed of variation is used when a couple split up, and one of them takes on the whole property and also the loan. It is also sometimes used when a single owner marries and the spouse, as well as taking a half-share of the title, also becomes jointly liable for the loan.

Assignation

22–21 Assignations (transfers) of standard securities are dealt with in s.14 of the 1970 Act.[67] The assignation must be registered. Once that is done, the assignee is substituted for the original creditor in all the rights, both personal and real. The rule *assignatus utitur jure auctoris* applies, as it does in assignations of any type, so that any defence which the debtors could have pled against the cedents (assignors) can equally be pled against the assignees. Thus, suppose that the price paid by the assignees is based on the assumption that a certain amount is still due under the security, and that assumption turns out to be false, and that the true sum is lower. In that case the debtors cannot be liable for more than the true amount, even though the assignees were in good faith.[68] Assignation is simple enough in the case of a fixed-sum standard security, but such securities are rare. If the standard security is for all sums, difficult problems can arise.[69]

It is quite common for lenders to sell a mortgage portfolio, such as £40,000,000 worth of mortgages. The sellers (the original creditors) are paid an agreed price, and the buyers take over the rights under the mortgages. Quite often the individual standard securities are not assigned, for reasons of convenience and to save expense. In that case, the sellers remain the heritable creditors, and the sale does not affect the borrowers. Indeed, they may not even know that a sale has taken place. Thus, for instance, they keep up payments to the same party, who then passes on such payments to the buyers. In other words, the sale is simply a contractual arrangement between the two financial institutions. This is called sale by "sub-participation".

---

[65] If this is in fact the true meaning of that subsection.

[66] See above, para.21–20.

[67] For assignation in general, see below, Ch.23.

[68] In which case, the assignee will normally have a claim against the cedent in warrandice.

[69] See e.g. *Watson v Bogue*, 1998 S.L.T. (Sh. Ct) 125; 1998 S.C.L.R. 512; *Sanderson's Trustees v Ambion Scotland Ltd*, 1994 S.L.T. 645; D.J. Cusine and Robert Rennie, *Standard Securities*, 2nd edn (2002), Ch.6; Gretton, 1994 S.L.T. (News) 207.

There can be no question of an assignation by the *debtor*. The debtor can transfer ownership of the property, of course, but that transfer is by disposition not assignation.[70] As for liability under the loan, that cannot be transferred, except with the creditor's consent.

Restriction

A restriction[71] is a discharge by the creditor, but limited to part of the property. 22–22 An example would be where Nestor sells a slice of garden to his neighbour, Hypatia. She would insist on a deed of restriction from his heritable creditor. A creditor is not normally obliged to grant such a deed, and so Nestor will have to be persuasive. But sometimes a creditor agrees in advance to grant restrictions. For example, a company buys a site and plans to build 40 houses, which will be sold one by one. The company has to borrow to carry out the development, and the loan is secured over the site. As each house is finished it is sold, but each buyer will insist on an unencumbered title. So the bank will grant a restriction for that house. This will have been envisaged in the builder/bank original contract. The contract will provide, for example that, in return for the deed, the bank must be paid 75 per cent of the sale price, thereby ensuring that as the extent of the security is reduced, so the outstanding loan is reduced also.

Restriction can be effected by a separate deed of restriction, duly registered. It is more common, however, for the lender to execute the disposition as a consenter to the effect of restricting the security.[72]

Discharge: in general

Discharges are regulated by s.17 of the 1970 Act. On complete repayment the 22–23 lender must grant a discharge to the borrower, which is then registered. The expense of this falls on the borrower. The statutory style[73] is imperfect. It requires that the discharge state that it is "in consideration of £ . . . being the whole amount secured by the standard security aftermentioned". But it can be difficult to know what sum to fill in. For example, a company grants a standard security for its current account, which is sometimes in credit and sometimes overdrawn. Ten years later the company decides to change its bank, at a time when the account happens to be in credit. A discharge is required. What sum can be filled in? There never was a principal sum. There was, instead, just an account with thousands of credit and debit entries. Another case where the statutory style is inappropriate is where the lender agrees to discharge the security without full repayment of the loan.[74] It is hard to see, in any case, why a clause of this sort is required. At common law it is not necessary to state the reason or cause of granting. In practice, deeds often depart considerably from the statutory style, and indeed there can be little doubt that a discharge which wholly omitted the consideration clause would be valid. But it is wise to adhere to the official style as nearly as is reasonably possible.

---

[70] Only incorporeals are transferred by assignation.

[71] Regulated by the Conveyancing and Feudal Reform (Scotland) Act 1970 s.15.

[72] See above, para.11–09. The 1970 Act makes no provision for effecting a restriction in this way, but there can be no question of its validity, under the common law of heritable security. The Act is not a code, but has to be supplemented frequently by the common law.

[73] 1970 Act Sch.4 form F.

[74] This would be unusual, but it can happen, for instance where there is a commercial loan secured over several properties.

Usually, the security being discharged is an all-sums security. Here, a peculiarity of the official style must be noted, namely that the all-sums aspect not only must be mentioned, but in fact affects the wording of the discharge at two separate places. In the following the words which are italicised must be inserted for the discharge of an all-sums security: "in consideration of . . . [75] *being the whole amount secured by the standard security aftermentioned* paid by . . . hereby discharge a standard security *for all sums due or to become due*".

The discharge is normally a separate deed. But it can alternatively be endorsed on the original standard security, and some standard securities have a pre-printed form of discharge at the end. Another possibility is that the discharge can be incorporated as part of a disposition. Thus, if A wants to dispone to B, and the plan is to discharge a standard security which X has, X could execute the disposition as well as A, as consenter, to the effect of discharging the security.[76]

Section 18 provides for the case where the lender fails to grant a discharge. This, again, is inadequately drafted, for various reasons, including the fact that it assumes that repayment of the loan is being offered at the same time. This is the same mistake as before: by the time the discharge is wanted there may be no outstanding loan.

A standard security, like any security, is an accessory right.[77] Hence, once the debt is gone, it secures nothing, and so is implicitly discharged.[78] Therefore, the deed of discharge is simply evidential. The (ex-) debtor wishes it to be granted as evidence that the property is now unencumbered. However, this is true in an unqualified way only of fixed-sum standard securities. By contrast, suppose that a standard security is granted for an overdraft. Over the years the account is sometimes in debit and sometimes in credit. It must not be supposed that the moment the debit balance disappears, the security is discharged. Therefore, in the case of all-sums standard securities, the discharge is more than merely evidential.

Discharge: separate debts

22–24 It would be natural to suppose that, if the clients pay the lenders the amount outstanding on the home loan, plus any exit charges,[79] the lenders will discharge the security. In most cases that would be right. But sometimes clients owe money to the same lenders under another contract. For instance, they might have a home loan and also an overdraft, or a business loan, and the standard security will in practice be so devised as to secure the overdraft as well as the home loan.[80] Hence, if the creditor is offered the amount due under the home loan, it can still refuse to discharge the security so long as the overdraft remains in existence. Indeed, a creditor is normally entitled to refuse to discharge a security in cases of contingent liability on a guarantee.[81] Often, in cases like

---

[75] In a residential standard security there is inserted here the loan figure stated in the original security deed.

[76] As with restriction, the 1970 Act does not expressly authorise this, but once again there can be no doubt of its competency under the common law.

[77] See above, para.22–09.

[78] *Cameron v Williamson* (1895) 22 R. 393.

[79] For which see above, para.21–52.

[80] Because the standard security will cover all sums due by that debtor to the creditor.

[81] For instance, Smith is director and chief shareholder of Smith Ltd. Smith Ltd has an overdraft with the bank, for which Smith has—as is usual in such cases—given the bank a guarantee.

this, the amounts due under the other contract are not large, and either they can be paid off, or the lender can be persuaded to discharge the security anyway.[82] Ideally, one should therefore (i) ask the clients whether they have any other debts to the lender, apart from the home loan, or any guarantees, and (ii) when asking the lender for a redemption statement, ask it to confirm that there are no liabilities other than the home loan.

Death

If the debtor dies, in most cases the loan will be paid off. There is usually a   22–25
source of funds for this, since in most cases a debtor will have taken out life assurance which will at least cover the amount of the loan.[83] In the unlikely event that this does not happen, whoever takes over the property (the spouse, or a legatee, etc.) must undertake, as a condition of taking the property, to pay off the loan. For the purposes of succession, the debt is deemed a burden on the heritable estate, and thus does not, for example, diminish *jus relictae*. However, if the debt is secured not only by the standard security but also by an assignation in security of a life policy, the debt is, for succession purposes, notionally ascribed both to the land and to the policy.[84]

The death of the creditor is much less usual, because the creditor is seldom a natural person. If he or she is, then the security and the loan which it secures simply forms part of the estate to be administered by the executor and transferred to a beneficiary, or sold. The debt (which, from the creditor's viewpoint, is an asset) is deemed heritable in the succession to the creditor's estate.[85]

MULTIPLE SECURITIES

Ranking

Only certain aspects of the complex subject of ranking[86] can be dealt with   22–26
here. Ranking is partly dealt with by the 1970 Act itself and partly by the common law.

The most important fact about a standard security is that it is a real right, and, like most other real rights, will obey the rule *prior tempore potior jure*.[87] So the first to be registered ranks first. Thus, if Adam holds a first-registered standard security for a loan of £50,000, and Barbara has a second-registered security for a loan of £25,000, and there is default and the house is sold for £60,000, after deduction of expenses, Adam takes £50,000 and Barbara takes the balance of £10,000. If, however, the two securities had been registered at the same time they would have ranked *pari passu*,[88] with the result that Adam would have received £40,000 and Barbara £20,000. Creditors are free to enter

---

[82] Though it will usually insist that any loan on a new house is with them as well.

[83] See above, para.21–34.

[84] *Graham v Graham* (1898) 5 S.L.T. 319; Gretton, (1987) 32 J.L.S.S. 303 and (1988) 33 J.L.S.S. 141. The area is one of great difficulty.

[85] Subject to s.117 of the Titles to Land Consolidation (Scotland) Act 1868.

[86] See Halliday, paras 57–27 to 57–42; D.J. Cusine and Robert Rennie, *Standard Securities*, 2nd edn (2002), Ch.7.

[87] Earlier by time, stronger by right.

[88] i.e. equally.

into a ranking agreement, the meaning of which is self-explanatory. Such agreements, though common in commercial cases, are rare in residential ones.

Account must also be taken of s.13 of the 1970 Act. If Adam's security is for all sums, a potential problem exists. For after the second security is granted, Adam might lend further sums, which would have the effect of eating up the equity[89] on which Barbara had relied. So common law developed a rule[90] whereby if Adam knew that a second security had been granted, any further advance by him could not prejudice the second security. The substance of this common law rule is given statutory force by s.13. Only voluntary further advances by Adam are so affected. Thus, interest accumulating is unaffected. And if the further advance had already been contracted for, it is unaffected.[91] The knowledge of Adam of the existence of the second security is a matter of actual knowledge. No formal notification procedure is laid down. But the practice is for Barbara, or her solicitor, to send what is sometimes called a "notice of second charge" to Adam. If her solicitor fails to do this that may constitute negligence. The exact meaning of s.13 is controversial. The main issue is this: if the first creditor, after receiving notice, does make a further advance, is that advance secured but postponed or is it unsecured? It is difficult to see any clear answer.[92]

Preparing postponed securities

22–27   Schedule 2 note 5 to the 1970 Act says that "where the security subjects are burdened by any other standard security . . . which ranks prior to the standard security which is being granted" the new standard security should refer to the fact twice, the second time being in the warrandice clause. The purpose of this provision is unclear. If the property is already burdened then the earlier security ranks first anyway.

It sometimes happens that an owner is granting two securities at the same time, to Sue and to Tom, and that the mutual intention of the three parties is that Sue's security should have priority. That can be achieved by good timing: ensuring that Sue's security is registered first, even if only by one day. But things can go wrong: if Sue delays registration, one can hardly expect Tom to wait for her. Hence the situation sometimes arises in which Tom's security is registered first, but is worded in conformity with Sch.2 note 5 to the 1970 Act. In that case the law is probably that Tom's security ranks first until Sue's is registered, and then Sue's ranks first and Tom's second.[93] But the law is not free from difficulty.[94]

---

[89] Meaning, in this context, market value minus secured debt.

[90] *Union Bank v National Bank* (1886) 14 R. (HL) 1.

[91] This would be rare in domestic cases. But commercial loans are often drawn down in tranches.

[92] See Gretton, (1980) 25 J.L.S.S 275; Halliday, (1981) 26 J.L.S.S. 26; Gretton, (1981) 26 J.L.S.S. 280.

[93] The qualification of the warrandice clause in itself probably does not have this effect. See *Leslie v McIndoe's Trustees* (1824) 3 S. 48. The court in *Trade Development Bank v Crittall Windows*, 1983 S.L.T. 510 disagreed with *Leslie*, but, contrary to what is said in the headnote, did not overrule it.

[94] For discussion see D.J. Cusine and Robert Rennie, *Standard Securities*, 2nd edn (2002), para.7.04. See also ROTPB, para.6.74.

DEFAULT

Acceleration

If the loan secured is an on-demand loan,[95] the lender can insist on repayment at   22–28
any time, though s.19 of the 1970 Act provides that the first step towards
enforcing its rights under the security itself is to serve a calling-up notice. If the
loan is a term loan, the contract, if properly drafted, will have an acceleration
clause. This is a clause, standard in all term-loan contracts, secured or unsecured,
whereby if the debtor defaults in a defined way (such as being in arrears for more
than 21 days on any instalment) the lender may, at its option, convert the loan
into an on-demand loan and call for repayment of the whole debt at once. For
obvious reasons, no acceleration clause is needed in an on-demand loan.

Occasionally term loans have no acceleration clause. This might cause problems. Take this example. Dorothea lends Barnaby £50,000, and the loan
contract says that it is repayable in two equal instalments, the first after two
years and the second after four. The contract is silent as to acceleration. A
standard security is granted for the loan. After the two years no payment is
made. Dorothea enforces by sale. How much can she take from the sale?
£50,000? Or just £25,000? The argument for the latter is that at the time of the
sale only £25,000 was due and resting owing. Section 27 of the 1970 Act,
which deals with what is to happen to the sale proceeds, simply says that the
lender is paid "the whole amount due under the standard security", which in
this context is ambiguous. The matter seems never to have been tested in court,
and it seems that there has been no discussion in the literature either. In
practice, it is generally assumed that where a term loan is secured by standard
security, a right of acceleration is implied, so that in our example Dorothea
could take the whole £50,000. And there is also an argument that common law
implies a right of acceleration in every loan contract for any breach which
amounts to a material or repudiatory breach.

Arrears

Arrears can arise for all sorts of reasons. The main ones are marital breakdown   22–29
and loss of employment.[96] In practice, solicitors are not often called on to
advise a borrower who is in arrears, since such people do not usually turn to
their lawyer. Often a debt counsellor can give the best advice. Home loan
arrears do not exist in isolation from the rest of the clients' affairs. The solution
may be a change of lifestyle. The following is limited to ways of cutting the
mortgage payments.

The clients should contact the lenders. Most lenders are reluctant to take
enforcement action at an early stage. Such action involves administrative costs
and is never good publicity. So, although creditors may not say so in so many
words, they are usually prepared to put up with some arrears on a temporary
basis. The theory is that they will be more understanding if the borrowers get
in touch with them to explain their problems. Debtors who are in financial
trouble are naturally reluctant to contact their creditors, but it is often wise to
do so. This may delay enforcement action, and in some cases a deal can be

---

[95] For on-demand and term loans, see above, para.21–12.
[96] See Emma McCallum and Ewen McCaig, *Mortgage Arrears and Repossessions in Scotland*
(2002).

struck. Moreover, under the Home Owner and Debtor Protection (Scotland) Act 2010 certain "pre-action requirements" are imposed on lenders before a "residential standard security" can be enforced. One of these is that "the creditor must make reasonable efforts to agree with the debtor proposals in respect of future payments".[97] What this means in practice is open to argument.

If the financial problems are likely to be temporary, some sort of renegotiation of the loan may be advisable and possible. The lenders may agree to a payment holiday or a period of reduced payments. But it must be borne in mind that during this time interest will continue to accumulate. Another idea is for payments to be put on an interest-only basis for several months. But this is possible only for capital-and-interest loans, as in others the monthly payments to the creditors are already interest-only. However, sometimes it is possible to arrange for an endowment policy to be put on ice for a period. But even for capital-and-interest loans this idea is often not of much use, since in the early years, when the problems are most likely to arise, most of the monthly payment is interest anyway. A common tactic for cases where the problems are likely to be temporary is to switch to a new loan, either with the same lender or a different one. A difficulty here is that a history of arrears may already have damaged the borrower's credit-rating. Yet another possibility is extending the term of the loan, which will result in reduced monthly payments. If the problems are not short-term, the best advice may be to cut the mortgage payments by selling the house and buying a cheaper one, with a smaller loan. This advice is too seldom given. But here too there may be a problem, which is that the sale price may be insufficient to pay off the secured debt—in other words, the problem of negative equity.

In some cases the social security system will help, though there is always a substantial period in which no assistance is available, and the system is much less generous than it used to be.[98] The clients should contact the local social security office.

One other possibility is a mortgage-to-rent scheme. Here a housing association buys the property and lets it back to the sellers. The clients thus avoid having to flit. Moreover, there may be substantial benefits in terms of social security payments, because whereas public assistance for paying a mortgage is difficult to get, rent will often be paid through housing benefit.

If the worst comes to the worst and the borrowers are put out on the street by the lenders, they will normally qualify to be rehoused by the local authority under the homelessness legislation.[99] If this looks like happening, the debtors should get in touch with the local housing department without delay, though the housing department should already have been alerted by the lenders.[100]

Negative equity

22–30 The "equity" in a property is the market value minus the secured debt. Thus if the property is worth £350,000 and there is a loan of £200,000 secured by standard security, the equity is £150,000. If the secured debt is greater than the

---

[97] Home Owner and Debtor Protection (Scotland) Act 2010 s.4(3).

[98] The rules are to be found in the massive Income Support (General) Regulations 1987 (SI 1987/1967). See generally N.J. Wikeley and A.I. Ogus, *Law of Social Security*, 5th edn (2002).

[99] Currently contained in the Housing (Scotland) Act 1987 Pt II.

[100] Conveyancing and Feudal Reform (Scotland) Act 1970 s.19B; Homelessness etc. (Scotland) Act 2003 s.11.

market value, the property is said to have negative equity. This can happen where a loan at a high percentage of the value is followed by a market slump. Or it can happen intentionally: there is no rule of law saying that a secured loan has to be less than the value of the collateral. Negative equity is a problem for both lenders and borrowers. It is a problem for the lenders because, if the borrowers default, sale of the property will not pay off the debt. It is a problem for the borrowers because it will be difficult to sell the house and buy a new one, because the sale will not generate enough money to pay off the existing loan. However, some lenders are prepared to allow negative equity to be transferred. For instance, Isadora buys a house for £200,000 with a £175,000 loan. Property values then fall. By agreement with the lender, Isadora sells it two years later for £150,000 and buys another house for £125,000. Assuming that she pays the expenses, she can repay £25,000 of the loan and now has a property worth £125,000 with a secured loan of £150,000. The lenders are at risk, but were at risk anyway.

Borrowers sometimes ask if they can walk away from a home loan, that is to say, hand the keys to the lender and give up the property and thereby be freed of the debt.[101] The answer is that such an action does not free the borrower of the debt. A borrower is personally liable for any shortfall suffered by the lender after a sale. In practice, however, lenders may not seek to recover the shortfall. But even then the borrower is likely to be listed with the credit reference agencies as a bad risk.

In practice, sales often fail to recoup what is due.[102] The reasons are complex. One reason is that defaults are commonest with high-LTV (loan to value) loans. In the second place, most defaults are in the early years of the loan, by which time market values may not have risen much, if at all. A third reason is that the accumulated unpaid interest has to be added to the debt, and the interest is compound interest. A fourth is that the enforcement process is expensive, and the expenses are paid first out of the proceeds. A fifth is that the borrowers, in financial difficulties, may not have maintained the property adequately, with loss of value as a result. A sixth is that the property will be marketed without furnishings, something which tends to make a property less attractive to buyers.

ENFORCEMENT[103]

Introduction

The term "repossession" is sometimes used, but it is inaccurate. Since   22–31
the lender never had possession in the first place, the question of *regaining* possession cannot arise. Even *possession* is not in itself the objective, except incidentally, to assist the sale of the property.

Standard securities are enforced only in a small minority of cases. But enforcement, though unpleasant, is sometimes necessary. Without the possibility of enforcement, the system would not work, for it would mean that home loan

---

[101] This question is asked only where there is negative equity. No rational person would wish to walk away from a property which had positive equity.

[102] Emma McCallum and Ewen McCaig, *Mortgage Arrears and Repossessions in Scotland* (2002), p.54.

[103] See generally Mark Higgins, *The Enforcement of Heritable Securities* (2010) (though this appeared before *Royal Bank of Scotland Plc v Wilson* [2010] UKSC 50; 2010 S.L.T. 1227).

finance would be unsecured finance, and commercial lenders could not contemplate lending substantial sums to consumers for long periods with no security. Without a system of heritable security, either home ownership would be limited to the small minority of families that could buy cash down—something many people would regard as socially undesirable—or some system functionally similar would have to be developed.

The law about enforcement is complex. Some of that complexity is unavoidable, but the law is more complex than it needs to be, and the enforcement provisions of the 1970 Act are not easy to understand. Since the previous edition of this book, there have been two major developments. In *Royal Bank of Scotland Plc v Wilson*[104] the Supreme Court held that the traditional interpretation of the 1970 Act, whereby a creditor has a choice of three roads to sale, namely (a) calling up, (b) notice of default, and (c) a s.24 warrant, was wrong. And the Home Owner and Debtor Protection (Scotland) Act 2010 made important pro-debtor changes to enforcement in the case of residential property.

The three roads to sale

22–32 In *Wilson* the Supreme Court held that, where the creditor seeks to enforce because the debtor has defaulted on the loan, a calling-up notice is necessary.[105] Since in practice that covers virtually all cases, the result is that in virtually all cases a calling-up notice is needed. Had it not been for the Home Owner and Debtor Protection (Scotland) Act 2010, the other two roads to sale—notice of default and s.24 warrants—would have become overgrown, traversed only by the rare rambler and landscape archaeologist. But the 2010 Act says that in residential cases a s.24 warrant is generally needed. The 2010 Act does not affect the *Wilson* decision, so that the position now is (i) that in non-residential cases a calling-up notice is needed and (ii) that in residential cases *both* a calling-up notice and (at least usually) a s.24 warrant are needed. In other words, in residential cases two roads must be taken for the one journey. But road (b), the notice of default, does now seem destined for almost complete disappearance.[106]

Calling up

22–33 The calling-up process is covered by s.19 of the 1970 Act. The creditor serves a calling-up notice, demanding repayment of the whole debt within two months.[107] If the two-month period expires without payment, the power of sale emerges automatically, except in residential cases, where a s.24 warrant (discussed below) is necessary in addition. The procedure is in principle extrajudicial. But in non-residential cases it is common for creditors to follow it up by an action of declarator that the right to sell has emerged. It is obviously prudent to do so, and moreover if the debtors refuse to give up possession a court action is needed anyway.

---

[104] *Royal Bank of Scotland Plc v Wilson* [2010] UKSC 50; 2010 S.L.T. 1227.

[105] On *Wilson* see Gretton, (2011) 15 Edin. L.R. 251.

[106] It was not much used anyway, even before 2010.

[107] It is important to observe the formalities in order to secure evidence that the notice has been served. On this see C. Waelde (ed.), *Professor McDonald's Conveyancing Opinions* (1998), p.169.

A calling-up notice is not relevant to the question of *when* payment becomes due. That is a matter for the loan contract.

> *Example (i)*. A standard security secures an on-demand loan. The creditor can demand the money immediately, and does not have to wait two months, though enforcing the standard security requires a notice, plus two months.

> *Example (ii)*. A standard security secures a term loan which matures in two years' time. The creditor cannot demand repayment now. So a calling-up notice served today would be invalid. But if there is default, thereby triggering acceleration, the lender could demand immediate repayment, and accordingly a calling-up notice would be valid.

In other words, the validity of a calling-up notice presupposes the maturity of the obligation.

The s.24 warrant

Section 24 of the 1970 Act is a special provision whereby the creditor can ask the court for power to sell. As a result of the *Wilson* decision,[108] in non-residential cases it is virtually never used, but in residential cases it is normally[109] required in addition to a calling-up notice.[110]

22–34

Residential property

In the 1970 Act as originally passed, no distinction was drawn between residential and other types of property. The Mortgage Rights (Scotland) Act 2001 changed that, and further changes were made by the Home Owner and Debtor Protection (Scotland) Act 2010, which repealed most of the 2001 Act. The idea is that in residential cases the court should have some discretion as to whether the creditor should be able to enforce. "Residential" has a broad meaning. Thus a farm would normally count, because on most farms there is a farmhouse. And "residential" does not mean that the property is the debtor's residence. So if a landlord grants a security, and the lender wishes to enforce, the property is "residential".

22–35

If a property is residential, the creditor must satisfy the court as to certain "pre-action requirements".[111] Further, as already mentioned, a s.24 warrant is needed, unless the debtor waives the requirement. This is to ensure that the sheriff has the chance to exercise discretion in favour of the debtor,[112] for the court is not to grant a warrant unless "it is reasonable in the circumstances of the case to do so".[113] The factors to be taken into account by the court are:

---

[108] *Royal Bank of Scotland Plc v Wilson*, 2010 S.L.T. 1227.

[109] "Normally" because the debtor can waive this requirement: see Conveyancing and Feudal Reform (Scotland) Act 1970 s.23A.

[110] 1970 Act s.20(2A).

[111] 1970 Act s.24A. One, as already mentioned (para.22–29), is to make reasonable efforts to make an agreement with the debtor in respect of future payments.

[112] Discretion was introduced by the Mortgage Rights (Scotland) Act 2001, but under that Act the initiative rested with the debtor, who had to apply to the court. Thus whereas the former system was opt-in, the current system is opt-out.

[113] 1970 Act s.24(5)(b).

"(a)   the nature of and reasons for the default;
 (b)   the ability of the debtor to fulfil within a reasonable time the
        obligations under the standard security in respect of which the
        debtor is in default;
 (c)   any action taken by the creditor to assist the debtor to fulfil those
        obligations;
 (d)   where appropriate, participation by the debtor in a debt payment
        programme approved under Part 1 of the Debt Arrangement and
        Attachment (Scotland) Act 2002; and
 (e)   the ability of the debtor and any other person residing at the security
        subjects to secure reasonable alternative accommodation."[114]

Finally, an "entitled resident" can seek to persuade the court to exercise discretion against sale.[115]

The sale

22–36   Although not required by law, the creditor will wish to get the debtors out of
the property, for otherwise the property is hardly marketable. Often the debtors
flit of their own accord, but if they do not, an order for ejection under s.5 of
the Heritable Securities (Scotland) Act 1894 is needed.

Once the power of sale has emerged and possession has been obtained, the
property can be sold. Sometimes this is done by an in-house solicitor for the
creditor, and sometimes by an outside firm. The marketing happens in the same
way as for any other property. Roups[116] are rare except as a last resort to shift
property that has not sold in the more conventional way. If there is more than
one security, it is possible for the postponed creditors to sell.[117]

Section 25 of the 1970 Act imposes a duty to advertise and a duty to get the
best price "that can reasonably be obtained".[118] These duties come to much the
same thing. If the creditors advertise properly then they should get the fair
market price, while conversely a fair market price is unlikely to be achieved
without proper advertising. The earlier law[119] contained detailed provisions as
to advertisement in relation to bonds and dispositions in security, but these
were not repeated in the 1970 Act. In practice, however, the old rules are often
followed, at least in spirit, to avoid any dispute about the sufficiency of the
advertising.[120]

If the debt is more than the value of the property, the creditor's own self-
interest will mean that a high price is sought. But if the debt is less than the
property's value, the incentive structure changes. A creditor that fails to obtain
the best price reasonably obtainable is liable in damages,[121] the quantum being

---

[114] 1970 Act s.24(7).

[115] 1970 Act s.24B. For the definition of "entitled resident" see s.24C.

[116] i.e. auctions.

[117] If both wish to sell the law is not certain, but see *Skipton Building Society v Wain*, 1986
S.L.T. 96.

[118] Which is not necessarily the same as the best price: see *Kensington Mortgage Co v Robertson*,
2004 S.C.L.R. 312.

[119] Conveyancing (Scotland) Act 1924 s.28.

[120] cf. Halliday, para.54–43. See also D.J. Cusine (ed.), *The Conveyancing Opinions of Professor
J. M. Halliday* (1992), p.314.

[121] *Royal Bank of Scotland v Johnston*, 1987 G.W.D. 1-5; *Wilson v Dunbar Bank Plc*, 2008
S.C. 457.

the difference between the actual price and the price that should have been obtained. The fact that a sale has not been properly conducted is not in itself a basis for damages.[122] In practice the burden of proof in damages actions of this sort is a fairly high one.[123] A creditor who delegates to professionals may in some circumstances be liable for their negligence.[124] It has been held that the debtor cannot interdict sale.[125]

Missives are concluded in the usual way. Usually no moveables will be included, since the creditor normally has no right to sell them. However, some lenders include in their standard conditions a right to sell any moveables in the premises. In that case they will be selling not as security holders but as agents. Selling creditors are reluctant to guarantee anything in the missives (e.g. about the physical condition of the property) and logically this should lower the price slightly.

The disposition is granted by the creditor.[126] The debtor's signature is not required, which is just as well, for in most cases it would not be made forthcoming. The practice is for the selling creditor to grant fact and deed warrandice personally and to bind the debtor in absolute warrandice. The debtor's warrandice will normally be worthless, because a debtor who could meet a warrandice claim would have been able to pay the lender in the first place. On one view, since the buyers are paying full market price they should be given full (absolute) warrandice from the seller, i.e. the heritable creditor.[127]

The normal Land Register reports should be obtained against the property and the sellers and also against the debtors though it is unlikely that any entry in the Personal Register could affect the sale. Thus, an inhibition against the debtors after the security was created but before the sale is irrelevant.[128] Documentation in respect of occupancy rights may be needed in respect of the debtor (if a natural person), but not in respect of the selling creditor, and should have been obtained at the time the security was granted.[129]

The risk of future challenge

Might the buyers find their title open to challenge by the former owner on the 22–37 ground of some irregularity in the sale? There are few definite answers here. There is a statutory provision in s.41 (as amended) of the Conveyancing (Scotland) Act 1924[130] which says, in broad terms, that a buyer will be protected by good faith. But the precise meaning of the section is arguable. Registration forms 1 and 2 ask whether the procedures necessary for the proper exercise of

---

[122] *Newport Farm Ltd v Damesh Holdings Ltd* [2003] All E.R. (D.) 114, a New Zealand case, is instructive.

[123] *Dick v Clydesdale Bank*, 1991 S.C. 365. For a case where a claim for damages failed, see *Davidson v Clydesdale Bank*, 2002 S.L.T. 1088. Generally on the duty to obtain the best price reasonably obtainable, see D.J. Cusine and Robert Rennie, *Standard Securities*, 2nd edn (2002), para.8.40.

[124] *Bisset v Standard Property Investment Plc*, 1999 G.W.D. 26-1253 on which see Reid and Gretton, *Conveyancing 1999*, pp.52–54; *Wilson v Dunbar Bank Plc*, 2008 S.C. 457.

[125] *Associated Relays v Turnbeam*, 1988 S.C.L.R. 220; *Gordaviran Ltd v Clydesdale Bank*, 1994 S.C.L.R. 248. The soundness of the decisions is not beyond dispute.

[126] For a style see Halliday, para.54–47.

[127] For warrandice, see above, paras 19–04 et seq.

[128] *Newcastle Building Society v White*, 1987 S.L.T. (Sh. Ct) 81; G.L. Gretton, *Law of Inhibition and Adjudication*, 2nd edn (1996), Ch.9.

[129] See above, para.10–14.

[130] As applied by s.32 of the Conveyancing and Feudal Reform (Scotland) Act 1970.

the power of sale have been complied with. If the applicant ticks the "yes" box, and does so negligently or fraudulently, then the possibility arises of rectification of the Register, though such rectification would have to be preceded by reduction of the disposition in the applicant's favour. The Keeper normally relies on what the applicant says in this connection, without further checks.[131]

In a residential case the buyer will expect to see the s.24 decree. If the selling creditor says that the debtors waived their rights,[132] this needs to be checked carefully, for the conditions for a valid waiver are not easy to satisfy. In a non-residential case a buyer would usually expect to see decree of declarator. If either type of decree is available, then in principle the buyer should be safe, for if the court has said that there is power of sale, there is power of sale. Nevertheless it would be usual to require sight of the calling-up notice. The buyer will wish to see evidence of advertisement in any event, because the fact that a creditor has power of sale does not mean that the exercise of the power is lawful.

A theoretical point

22–38   It is sometimes wrongly supposed that ownership is vested in the creditor. A standard security is indeed a real right, but a subordinate real right, not a real right of ownership. It is the debtor who has the real right of ownership. Another mistake is to suppose that, whilst the debtor is owner unless and until default, when default happens, or (in another version of the mistake) when the debtor is deprived of possession, the creditor become owner. This is not correct. The debtor remains the owner until the moment when ownership passes to the buyer, which happens when the disposition to the buyer is registered. Unless there is a decree of foreclosure,[133] which is very rare, the creditor never becomes owner.

When is the right of redemption cut off?

22–39   Up to what point do the debtors still have the right to pay off the debt and so save the property? This question seldom matters, for if the debtors could pay, why have they not paid earlier? But very occasionally debtors acquire funds at the eleventh hour. Section 23(3) of the 1970 Act says that, under the notice of default procedure, the debtors have the right to redeem right up to the moment when missives of sale are concluded. This is sensible, but no parallel provision exists for the other two roads to sale. A guess would be that the same rule would apply, since it is the only reasonable rule. However, it may be that in such a case the debtors would have to serve a notice of redemption.[134]

What happens to the proceeds of sale?

22–40   The distribution of the proceeds of sale is governed by s.27 of the 1970 Act. The creditor holds the proceeds in trust, first for payment of the expenses of

---

[131] ROTPB, para.6.73.

[132] Under 1970 Act s.23A.

[133] 1970 Act s.28. In some countries "foreclosure" means the enforcement of a security. In Scots law it has the much narrower meaning given by s.28.

[134] See *Forbes v Armstrong*, 1993 S.C.L.R. 204.

sale, secondly for payment of any prior secured debt, thirdly for payment of its own secured debt and any other secured debt having an equal ranking, fourthly for payment of any postponed secured debt, and fifthly, for payment to the debtor.[135] Payment at any of these levels can be made only to the extent that there are funds remaining from the previous levels. Suppose that the property is sold for £300,000, and there are four secured creditors, A, B, C and D. And suppose that the ranking is A first, then B and C *pari passu* (equally), and then D in last place (*ultimo loco*). A is owed £200,000, B is owed £150,000, C is owed £50,000, and D is owed £200,000. The result is that A receives £200,000, B receives £75,000, C receives £25,000, and D receives nothing. A few words of explanation. A is paid in full, leaving £100,000. This is shared by B and C equally. Since B was owed three times what C was owed, B receives three times what C receives. There is nothing left for D. The three creditors who have not been paid in full can still pursue the debtor for the shortfall.

In *Halifax Building Society v Smith*,[136] Sheriff Principal Caplan said: "Professor Halliday in his commentary on the Act . . . suggests that the tabulation in section 27 represents one of the better characteristics of modern draftsmanship. If this is so the terms thereof seem nevertheless to have sown a considerable amount of doubt and confusion". In complex cases the creditors will not want to take the risk of distributing the fund themselves, but will instead raise a multiplepoinding, so that the court can decide who gets what. In some cases, especially if there are arrestments, multiplepoinding may be unavoidable.

Diligence[137]

Sometimes another creditor of the debtor has inhibited before the sale, but this will not normally affect the secured creditor's power of sale.[138] Sometimes another creditor will seek to arrest in the hands of the selling creditor. This is because upon sale, if a surplus emerges, the debtor-creditor relationship is reversed, and the (ex-) debtor becomes a creditor and the (ex-)creditor a debtor. Thus, suppose Adam has a loan from a bank, with £40,000 outstanding, and there is default, and the bank sells. And suppose that after deduction of expenses the bank holds a surplus of £50,000. Adam is no longer the bank's debtor for £40,000 but its creditor for £10,000, and this is an asset which is arrestable by his other creditors. The arrestment must be in the hands of the selling creditor, not the selling creditor's solicitors.[139] The arrestment must be laid on, at latest, before distribution has taken place. There is some uncertainty as to how early the arrestment can take place, but it has been held that it is competent as soon as the selling creditor has taken possession, i.e. well before missives of sale will have been concluded, let alone the price received.[140]

22–41

---

[135] This text is a rough paraphrase of the statutory wording.

[136] *Halifax Building Society v Smith*, 1985 S.L.T. (Sh. Ct) 25.

[137] See G. Maher and D.J. Cusine, *Law and Practice of Diligence* (1990); G.L. Gretton, *Law of Inhibition and Adjudication*, 2nd edn (1996); and *Stair Memorial Encyclopaedia*, Vol.8.

[138] *Newcastle Building Society v White*, 1987 S.L.T. (Sh. Ct) 81; G. L. Gretton, *Law of Inhibition and Adjudication*, 2nd edn (1996), Ch.9.

[139] *Lord Advocate v Bank of India*, 1991 S.C.L.R. 320.

[140] *Abbey National Building Society v Barclays Bank Plc*, 1990 S.C.L.R. 639. It is open to argument whether this decision is correct. *Royal Bank of Scotland v Law*, 1996 S.L.T. 83 proceeded on somewhat different facts but the two decisions are not easy to reconcile.

Disburdenment

22–42   Section 26 of the 1970 Act provides that, on sale, the property is disburdened
automatically of the security and of any postponed or *pari passu* security. Prior
securities are not automatically discharged, but this is really just a theoretical
point. For one thing, if there is more than one security, the sale is normally by
the first-ranked creditor anyway. Moreover, if the sale were by a postponed
creditor, the proceeds would have to be paid in the first instance to the first
creditor in terms of s.27, so that security would be discharged by payment. The
rule is "pay up, discharge down", and the "paying up" will normally result in
"discharging up" too.

CHAPTER 23

ASSIGNATIONS

Introduction

Assignation is the transfer of incorporeal property. For instance, debts, intel- 23–01
lectual property rights and insurance policies are transferred by assignation.
Some types of assignation are subject to special rules. Thus, there are special
rules on the assignation of standard securities.[1] There are also special rules on
the assignation of intellectual property rights,[2] of leases,[3] of company shares,[4]
and of company bonds (i.e. debentures and loan stock).[5] This chapter does not
deal with these special types of assignation, but with the general law.

Rights assignable, not obligations

Only rights are assignable, not obligations. This is common sense. If obliga- 23–02
tions could be assigned, then a person could borrow money and at once assign
the obligation to repay, choosing, say, a tramp as an assignee. The substitution
of a new obligant is delegation, not assignation, and needs the creditor's
consent.[6] By contrast, rights can be assigned without the debtor's consent.[7] An
assignation of contractual rights will not normally mean that the assignee
undertakes the cedent's contractual obligations.[8]

---

[1] See above, para.22–21.

[2] Hector L. MacQueen, "Intellectual Property", in *The Laws of Scotland: Stair Memorial Encyclopaedia*, Vol.18 (1993), paras 811, 1006, 1197, 1227, 1248.

[3] See Halliday, Ch.46.

[4] Stock Transfer Act 1963, and, for "dematerialised" shares the Uncertificated Securities Regulations 2001 (SI 2001/3755).

[5] These are subject to the same legislation as company shares. The word "assignation" is not used for the transfer of shares and bonds.

[6] There are one or two exceptions. One is that the contract may itself permit delegation. Another exists in the law of leases: an assignation of a lease not only works as an assignation of the cedent's rights but also as a delegation of the cedent's obligations.

[7] Again, there are some exceptions. In particular, the original contract between debtor and cedent may expressly or implicitly exclude assignation: see e.g. *James Scott Ltd v Apollo Engineering Ltd*, 2000 S.L.T. 1262.

[8] See e.g. *Alex Lawrie Factors Ltd v Mitchell Engineering Ltd*, 2002 S.L.T (Sh. Ct) 93.

General law of assignation[9]

23–03   Assignation involves three steps, namely (i) the contract to assign, (ii) the deed of assignation, which must be delivered, and (iii) the intimation, i.e. the notification to the debtor in the obligation.[10] The relationship between them is similar to the relationship, in the sale of heritable property, between (i) missives, (ii) delivered disposition, and (iii) registration. With both assignations and dispositions, the right being transferred remains in the granter's patrimony until the grantee has completed title, whether by intimation or by registration.

Often steps (i) and (ii) are in the same document. Sometimes the document contains only (i), in which case the whole thing fails as an actual assignation. An example is *Bank of Scotland Cashflow Finance v Heritage International Transport Ltd*,[11] where the agreement merely said "you . . . shall . . . transfer the title of the debt to us by delivering to us such form of assignation as we may specify".

A statutory style of assignation is given in the Transmission of Moveable Property (Scotland) Act 1862.[12] This is optional, but in practice the statutory style tends to be followed, more or less. In fact, the common law is very lenient as to style: almost anything goes.[13] Indeed, the Requirements of Writing (Scotland) Act 1995 does not even require assignations to be in writing.[14]

The question of how intimation is made is a complex one. At common law it had to be done in a formal manner, and it was not sufficient that the debtor knew of the assignation. Case law has, however, wobbled on this point, and the current position is open to debate.[15] An optional method is set out in the 1862 Act, and in practice is generally used. This provides for intimation by recorded delivery post. A copy of the assignation must be attached[16]; nowadays, this can be a photocopy.[17] The intimation need not be probative and in practice normally is not. The intimation is made by the assignee (or by the assignee's solicitors).[18]

---

[9] This chapter cannot give a full account of this complex area of law. See Ross G. Anderson, *Assignation* (2008); Halliday, Ch.8; William W. McBryde, *The Law of Contract in Scotland*, 3rd edn (2007), Ch.12; Reid, *Property*, paras 652–662; Nienaber and Gretton, in R. Zimmermann, D. Visser and K. Reid (eds), *Mixed Legal Systems in Comparative Perspective: Property and Obligations in Scotland and South Africa* (2004), pp.787–818. For the history of assignation, see Luig, in K. Reid and R. Zimmermann (eds), *A History of Private Law in Scotland* (2000), Vol.1, pp.399–419. For possible reform, see Scottish Law Commission, Discussion Paper on *Moveable Transactions* (Scot. Law Com. D.P. No.151, 2011).

[10] In the assignation of real rights, intimation is replaced by registration or possession: see Reid, *Property*, para.657.

[11] *Bank of Scotland Cashflow Finance v Heritage International Transport Ltd*, 2003 S.L.T. (Sh. Ct) 107.

[12] See Halliday, paras 8–07 to 8–11 for examples based on this statute.

[13] See e.g. *Laurie v Ogilvy*, February 6, 1810 F.C.; *Carter v McIntosh* (1862) 24 D. 925; *Brownlee v Robb*, 1907 S.C. 1302.

[14] Requirements of Writing (Scotland) Act 1995 s.11(3)(a).

[15] To what extent informal intimation is valid is "one of the long slow burning questions in the law": William W. McBryde, *The Law of Contract in Scotland*, 3rd edn (2007), para.12–93. *Christie Owen & Davies Plc v Campbell*, 2009 S.C. 436 supports the "anything goes" view. For discussion, see Anderson, (2009) 13 Edin. L.R. 484.

[16] Like the common law of intimation, this presupposes that there has been a written assignation. So there is a puzzle as to why the 1995 Act does not require assignations to be in writing.

[17] The 1862 Act says that the copy must be "certified as correct" but it does not say how or by whom. In practice, intimations are usually by the assignee's solicitors, who do the certification.

[18] According to *Libertas-Kommerz GmbH v Johnston*, 1978 S.L.T. 222 it can be by the cedent.

The 1862 Act does not give a style of intimation, and the style used in practice is much the same as for intimations of assignations of life policies, for which see below.[19] Because of the importance of intimation, evidence of it is desirable. The usual course is to ask the debtor to acknowledge receipt of the intimation.

The right assigned passes at the time of intimation.[20] Thus, suppose that Mary gives Peter a personal bond for £10,000, and Peter assigns this to Anne on Monday. Anne intimates to Mary on Wednesday. But on the previous day, Henry, a creditor of Peter, arrests in Mary's hands. At the date of the arrestment the bond still belongs to Peter, and so the arrestment attaches it, and thus prevails over the right of Anne.

The debtor (Mary) can plead against the assignee (Anne) any defences that she could have pled against the cedent (Peter). The rule is *assignatus utitur jure auctoris*.[21] For instance, if Mary repays Peter £4,000, and he then assigns the bond to Anne, the latter taking it in good faith and believing the whole £10,000 is due, Anne can claim only £6,000 from Mary. Or Jack takes out life assurance, representing himself as drinking little, but in fact is an extreme alcoholic. He assigns the policy to Jill. The policy was voidable by the life office against Jack, and so is voidable against Jill, notwithstanding her good faith.[22]

In many cases it is preferable to embody a debt obligation not in a personal bond but in a negotiable instrument, such as a promissory note or a bill of exchange. The main reasons are that intimation of transfer is not necessary, and that the *assignatus utitur* rule does not apply. Thus, in the first example, if Mary had given Peter not a personal bond but a promissory note, Anne's right would prevail over Henry's. And in the second example, if this had been a promissory note, Anne would be unaffected by Peter's fraud, assuming that she was in good faith.[23]

General law of assignation in security

As well as being assigned outright, incorporeal property can be assigned in security (*cessio in securitatem debiti*). The idea is that the assignee holds the property as a security for a debt owed by the cedent. If the debt is repaid, the assignee will assign the property back to the cedent: this is called "retrocession". If the debt is not repaid, the assignee realises the property.

23–04

Thus suppose, in the previous example, that Peter assigns the bond to Anne as a security for a debt owed by him to her. If he defaults, Anne can enforce the bond against Mary. Or Anne could sell the bond. An assignation in security makes the assignee the legal holder of the incorporeal property, and the cedent is divested.[24] Thus, suppose that the bond provides for repayment by instalments. Mary would pay these instalments to Anne, not to Peter, for as long as Anne continued to be the legal holder of the bond. Of course the assignee in such a case is under a duty to account to the cedent for moneys received, for

---

[19] See below, para.23–05.

[20] Stair, III, i, 6.

[21] The assignee takes the right of his or her author.

[22] The facts of *Scottish Widows v Buist* (1877) 4 R. 1076.

[23] Because she would be a holder in due course: Bills of Exchange Act 1882 ss.29 and 38(2).

[24] Contrast, e.g. a standard security, where, despite the security, the debtor remains legally the owner of the property. Although Peter is divested of his right against Mary, he has a right against Anne in respect of the bond.

the assignee cannot recover more than is owed by the cedent. Thus, if a bond for £10,000 were assigned in security of a debt for £7,000, and the assignee is paid the £10,000 by the debtor in the bond, the assignee must return the excess of £3,000 to the cedent.

An assignation in security can be either in the form of an outright assignation (i.e. an *ex facie* absolute assignation plus a separate document setting forth that it is truly only an assignation in security),[25] or an assignation expressly in security.[26] The latter seems more common in practice, at least for life policies. The form of an assignation in security is similar to that of an outright assignation.

Life policies

23–05   Like other rights, life policies can be assigned either absolutely or in security. Such assignations used to be common, but now are uncommon, partly because endowment home loans have become uncommon and partly because, even where there is one, the lender will often not insist on an assignation.[27] Though it is uncertain whether the Policies of Assurance Act 1867 applies in Scotland,[28] the style of assignation in that Act tends to be used.[29] The Act does not give a style of intimation.[30] The usual practice is to send the intimation in duplicate, asking the life office to return one copy with an acknowledgment of receipt on it. The Act requires the life office to issue written acknowledgment of receipt of intimation, on payment of a fee of 25 pence.[31]

When the loan is paid off the policy is retroceded, i.e. re-assigned. The retrocession must be intimated in the same way as the original assignation. Usually the home loan is paid off not on maturity, but on a sale, and in that case the sellers may be using the same policy as a security for their next secured loan. So the retrocession may have to be followed immediately by a new assignation. This is done even where the same lender is involved in both the old and the new home loan. Thus, suppose that Rachel has an endowment home loan with Bank X. Her life policy is with LifeCo, and this policy has been assigned to Bank X as a security for the loan. She sells her house and buys another. This too is to be financed with an endowment home loan with Bank X. When she sells the first house she repays the existing loan. The standard security is discharged by Bank X, and Bank X also retrocedes the life policy to Rachel, with intimation to LifeCo. In respect of the new house there may immediately follow a new assignation by Rachel to Bank X, with a new intimation to LifeCo (plus a new standard security by Rachel to Bank X over the new house). All this must be done in the right order.[32]

---

[25] See Halliday, para.8–78 for an example.

[26] See Halliday, paras 8–76 and 8–77 for examples.

[27] See above, para.21–35.

[28] See Scottish Law Commission, Discussion Paper on *Moveable Transactions* (Scot. Law Com. D.P. No.151, 2011), para.4.67.

[29] For an example based on this style see Halliday, para.8–31.

[30] For styles see Halliday, para.8–35. See also D.J. Cusine and R. Rennie, *Standard Securities*, 2nd edn (2002), paras 2.09 and 3.36.

[31] This figure, having been rendered trivial by inflation, is nowadays not charged.

[32] In principle, there is no reason why it should be done this way. If the lender remains the same it seems safe to leave the policy in its original assigned state, provided that the original assignation covers all debts, present and future, due by Rachel to Bank X. But the practice is to retrocede and then reassign.

Implications of divestiture

Where incorporeal property is assigned in security, the assignee becomes the   23–06
holder of the property, as already mentioned. This can be a significant point in
a number of contexts. Two will be mentioned here. In the first place, suppose
that Rachel dies while the home loan is still outstanding. In that case the policy
matures. LifeCo owe the whole maturity value, bonuses and all, to Bank X.
This is so even if, as will normally be the case, the total maturity value is
greater than the home loan debt due to Bank X. Thus, suppose that the policy's
maturity value is £80,000 and the debt due by Rachel to Bank X is £55,000.
LifeCo will pay the whole £80,000 to Bank X, because Bank X is the holder of
the policy. Bank X will pay itself what it is owed out of the proceeds. The
surplus value (£25,000) is then owed by it to Rachel's executor, assuming that
the latter has confirmation.[33] Thus, although the surplus value belongs to
Rachel's estate, it is not owed to the estate by LifeCo. LifeCo owes nothing to
Rachel's estate, because although Rachel was the "life assured", she was not,
at the time of her death, the holder of the policy.

The second point concerns postponed securities. Rachel (whom we will now
suppose to have recovered from her life-threatening illness) is not the policy
holder. She only has a reversionary right. But her reversionary right itself has
a value, namely, the surplus value over and above the home loan debt. She
might wish to assign this reversionary right to Steve, and she may wish to do
this either outright or in security. To whom should intimation be made? Not to
LifeCo. The reason is that Rachel is not assigning the policy, but her reversionary right, which is a personal right against Bank X. So intimation should
be made to Bank X.[34] Assignations of reversionary rights are uncommon but
not unknown. The effect is to vest the reversion in Steve. For example, suppose
that Rachel assigns to Bank X, and later assigns the reversion to Steve in
security of a debt due by her to Steve. Rachel then succumbs to the grim reaper.
The policy has a final maturity value of £80,000. The home loan debt is
£55,000. The debt due by Rachel to Steve is £20,000. What happens is
as follows. LifeCo pays £80,000 to Bank X. LifeCo is now out of the
picture. Bank X takes £55,000. The surplus of £25,000 it pays over to the
holder of the reversion, Steve. Bank X is now out of the picture. Steve takes
£20,000. Steve then pays over the value of the sub-reversionary right, namely
£5,000, to Rachel's executor. Everyone is now happy, including, we hope,
Rachel.

Personal bond

An assignation in security is a security for a debt, and so there should be a   23–07
document (such as a personal bond) setting forth the terms of the loan contract.
This can be done as part of the assignation itself,[35] but usually the loan contract
will be in another document, such as a personal bond or a form A standard
security.[36] In that case the assignation should simply refer to that other
document.

---

[33] Assuming that the reversionary right to the policy was still vested in Rachel at her death.
[34] *Ayton v Romanes* (1895) 3 S.L.T. 203.
[35] See e.g. Halliday, paras 8–76 and 8–77.
[36] For form A standard securities, see above, para.22–10.

Enforcement clause

23–08 If Rachel lives and keeps up her payments to Bank X, the question of enforcement does not arise. Nor does it arise if Rachel dies, for in that case the maturity value is paid direct to the creditor. The question of enforcement arises if Rachel, while alive, defaults on her repayments to Bank X. In that case Bank X will, in all probability, not seek to enforce its security over the policy, but will enforce the standard security over the house, by sale. This will normally pay off the debt, and the policy can then be retroceded. But Bank X wishes to have the possibility of enforcement against the policy, for otherwise it would not have insisted on the assignation in the first place. This would be important if, for instance, the market value of the house proved to be smaller than the debt due, which occasionally happens. A security over a life policy can be enforced in two ways, namely surrender and sale. In a surrender, the policy holder (Bank X) renounces the policy, and in exchange the life office (LifeCo) makes a payment, called the surrender value. In a sale, the policy is auctioned. Someone will buy it as an investment, taking the benefit when, eventually, Rachel dies.

The right to enforce by surrender or sale is implied in an assignation, but in most cases these rights are also conferred expressly.[37] Obviously, enforcement cannot happen unless the borrowers default on the loan, but normally one would wish to ensure that the right to sell or surrender the policy did not emerge instantly upon default. Otherwise borrowers might be one day late in making the monthly payment and find that the next day, without telling them, the lenders had sold the policy. A warning period, such as seven days, is thus sometimes written in. In practice, however, assignations are often silent on the matter, but the risk is small, because lenders are seldom in a hurry to sell or surrender a life policy.

Mandates

23–09 The term "mandate" has a number of meanings. In conveyancing practice it often means an instruction by a client (Alan) to his solicitor (Genius & Co) to pay, out of moneys belonging to Alan which come into Genius & Co's hands, to a creditor of Alan. For example, suppose that Alan is buying a house and there is a delay in obtaining his home loan, which is to come from Bank X, which specialises in mortgage lending. Alan arranges bridging finance with his ordinary bank (Bank Y). As a condition of this, Bank Y has Alan sign a "mandate", which is a letter signed by Alan and addressed to Genius & Co, requiring the latter to pay to Bank Y the proceeds of the loan as and when this money is received by Genius & Co.[38] This gives Bank Y a certain degree of assurance that the loan will be repaid. Or the bank may obtain a mandate for the payment of the proceeds of the sale of the old house. The mandate will be expressed to be irrevocable without the consent of Bank Y. Sometimes the bank will ask the law firm to confirm that it will honour the mandate, but in general this request should be resisted, since it comes close to being a cautionary obligation on behalf of the client.

---

[37] It will often be found that these provisions are written into the mortgage conditions referred to in the standard security (for which see above, para.22–13). The assignation of the policy then simply has a short clause referring to those conditions.

[38] Bank X will make over the loan moneys not directly to Alan but to Alan's solicitors.

An obvious question is whether such mandates amount to an assignation of the future proceeds of the bank loan or of the sale. The question can arise in a number of circumstances. One example would be where another creditor of Alan serves an arrestment on Genius & Co, thereby attaching funds held for Alan. The answer is far from clear.[39] To avoid the difficulty, some banks use a document which is in the form of an assignation,[40] rather than a mandate. If a mandate has been used, and a problem arises as to its effect (e.g. where there has been an arrestment), the solicitor should refuse to release any money except on the basis of an agreed settlement between all interested parties. If such agreement cannot be arrived at, a multiplepoinding may be unavoidable.

---

[39] The subject is complex. See, for instance, *National Commercial Bank v Millar's Trustee*, 1964 S.L.T. (Notes) 57; and *Hernandez-Cimorra v Hernandez-Cimorra*, 1992 S.C.L.R. 611. For discussion see Gretton, (1994) 39 J.L.S.S. 175.

[40] In particular, using the words "do hereby assign".

CHAPTER 24

UNREGISTERED HOLDERS

Overview

24–01 An unregistered holder is someone who holds a valid conveyance and so has the power to acquire ownership by registration, but who has not, thus far at least, taken that step. The first part of this chapter explores the status and powers of an unregistered holder. This part is relevant regardless of whether the property is in the Land Register or still in the General Register of Sasines ("GRS"), although there are some differences as between the two registers. The second part deals with clauses of deduction of title, which continue to be where the title is still in the GRS, but not where it is in the Land Register.

THE UNREGISTERED HOLDER: STATUS AND POWERS

What is an unregistered holder?

24–02 Delivery of a conveyance does not transfer to the grantee the real right of ownership. For that the further step of registration is necessary.[1] By registration, "title" is said to be "completed", and, conversely, a person who could register but has not yet registered is said to have an "uncompleted title". Traditionally, such a person was known as an "uninfeft proprietor", but this term, never satisfactory,[2] became obsolete with the abolition of the feudal system although it is still sometimes used. The replacement coined by the Title Conditions (Scotland) Act 2003 is "unregistered holder".[3]

The status of being an unregistered holder is usually short-lived. If Jack buys 4 Privet Drive from Jill, the disposition would normally be registered within a few days. Nevertheless there can be cases where someone chooses not to complete title, at least in the short or medium term.

An unregistered holder is someone who is not the owner but who has the *power* to become owner, without the need for anyone else to co-operate (apart, of course, from the Keeper). An unregistered holder is someone who could become proprietor by taking a taxi to the offices of Registers of Scotland. We stress the word "power" because a mere personal right is not enough. If Morag

---

[1] Abolition of Feudal Tenure etc. (Scotland) Act 2000 s.4.

[2] For an "uninfeft proprietor" is not a proprietor. A proprietor has the real right of ownership. An unregistered holder has no real right.

[3] Title Conditions (Scotland) Act 2003 s.128(1) Sch.14 para.7(3)(a), substituting "unregistered holder" for "uninfeft proprietor" in s.3(6) of the Land Registration (Scotland) Act 1979. See above, para.11–07.

concludes missives to buy Blackmains from Jamie, she has the *right* to become owner, though she will have to pay the price first. But that is simply a personal right against Jamie. If she knocked at the Keeper's door clutching the missives she would be sent away. But as and when she has in her hand the disposition, bearing Jamie's signature, she has a power to complete title, and can do so whenever she chooses.

We have explained the concept by the most important example, that of a person who is an unregistered holder in relation to ownership of the land itself. But it is also possible to be an unregistered holder in respect of some types of subordinate real right, such as a registered lease.[4] The law is the same in these cases, and so for simplicity this chapter refers only to the main type of case.

An unregistered holder may be the immediate grantee of the proprietor, as Jack is in relation to Jill. But as will be seen, sometimes that is not so. There can develop chains of unregistered holders.

What is a general conveyance?

To understand the law of unregistered holders, it is necessary to know the distinction between special and general conveyances. A special conveyance is one that conveys a particular property that is identified in the deed. The disposition of 4 Privet Drive that Jill grants to Jack is a special disposition. A general conveyance contains no description of the property. It may seem surprising that a conveyance of land should lack a description, but it can happen. For example: 24–03

   (i)   Testament (will). ("I leave all my property to . . .").
   (ii) Trust deed for behoof of creditors. This is a general conveyance by the debtor of his or her assets to a trustee, the creditors being the beneficiaries.[5]
  (iii) Act and warrant in a sequestration. This is an interlocutor conveying the debtor's assets to the trustee in sequestration.[6]
  (iv) Deed of assumption and conveyance in favour of new trustees.[7]
   (v) Decree appointing a trustee or a judicial factor.[8]
  (vi) Legislation transferring land to a public body. For instance, when local government reorganisation took place in 1996, land was transferred by statute from the old councils to the new.[9] The latter, however, did not become owners merely by virtue of the statutory vesting: that vesting had the effect of a delivered, but not yet registered, disposition.

How does an unregistered holder complete title?

How does an unregistered holder complete title? Obviously, the answer is registration. But there are complications. If the conveyance is a general 24–04

---

[4] Another reason why "uninfeft proprietor" was a poor term even before feudal abolition.
[5] See below, para.29–04.
[6] See below, para.29–02.
[7] See below, para.25–17.
[8] Conveyancing Amendment (Scotland) Act 1938 s.1. The property law aspects of judicial factories are difficult. See Scottish Law Commission, Discussion Paper on *Judicial Factors* (Scot. Law Com. D.P. No.146, 2010), Pt 4.
[9] Local Government (Scotland) Act 1994 s.15; Local Authorities (Property Transfer) (Scotland) Order 1995 (SI 1995/2499).

conveyance, the property is going to have to be identified. In the Land Register, that is done on the application form. Suppose that Constantine is sequestrated. The act and warrant in favour of his trustee, Shona, is a general conveyance. Constantine owns a house. Shona completes an application form that gives the title number of the house and submits the form, plus the act and warrant, to the Keeper. The Keeper will then register her as owner (in her capacity as trustee). If the title is still in the GRS, what happens is that a new deed is drawn up, called a notice of title (discussed below).

If, on the other hand, the conveyance is a special conveyance, then matters are simpler. Registration in the Land Register or recording in the GRS goes ahead in the normal way, as where Jack registers the Jill/Jack disposition. But certain types of special conveyance are generally regarded as not being recordable in the GRS. An example is a confirmation to an executor, even though confirmations specify any and all heritable property. In such cases a notice of title is used. The question of which types of special conveyance are not recordable rests to some extent on the custom of conveyancers, and there is no case law.

Notices of title

24–05   Notices of title are used in the GRS but not in the Land Register.[10] The notice narrates that the last recorded title and the midcouple[11] (for instance, the confirmation, or the act and warrant) were examined by the solicitor named in the notice, and that the grantee "has right as proprietor" to the property in question, which is then fully described. The notice also contains a clause of deduction of title.[12] A statutory form of deed is provided and must be followed as closely as possible.[13] The notice of title is executed, not by the unregistered holder, but by the solicitor. The notice of title is the successor to the notarial instrument, examples of which can sometimes be seen in older titles.[14]

The risks of being an unregistered holder

24–06   Since an unregistered holder has no real right, there are risks. In particular the unregistered holder is at risk that the owner becomes insolvent or makes a competing grant. Thus in *Mitchells v Fergusson*,[15] William Donald owned a house in Ayr and sold it to Agnes Carsan. She paid and took possession and the disposition was delivered but she did not complete title. Thereafter creditors of Donald used diligence (adjudication). It was held that the diligence was effective since the house was still owned by Donald. Another leading case is *Burnett's Trustee v Grainger*.[16] Carlene Burnett owned a house in Peterculter. She sold it to Mr and Mrs Burnett. They paid and took possession and the disposition was delivered but they did not complete title. Later the seller was sequestrated and her trustee, Mr Reid, completed title. It was held that the

---

[10] Though their use for the Land Register as well has been recommended: Scottish Law Commission, Report on *Land Registration* (Scot. Law Com. No.222, 2010), Pt 15.

[11] For midcouples, see below, para.24–09.

[12] For deduction of title, see below, paras 24–11 et seq.

[13] Conveyancing (Scotland) Act 1924 s.4 Sch.B. The normal form is form 1 of Sch.B.

[14] 1924 Act s.6.

[15] *Mitchells v Fergusson* (1781) Mor. 10296. For a full account of this case see (2001) 5 Edin. L.R. 73.

[16] *Burnett's Trustee v Grainger*, 2004 S.C. (HL) 19.

property was now owned by the trustee, leaving the Burnetts with a damages claim against the seller (worth little) and a negligence claim against their law firm (for not having registered the disposition). Note that, immediately after the sequestration, there were two separate unregistered holders, (i) Mr and Mrs Burnett and (ii) Mr Reid. In this situation, whoever completed title first would prevail. Such a situation is called "the race to the Register". Finally, as well as insolvency, an unregistered holder also runs the risk that the owner will convey to someone else (or grant a subordinate real right to someone else). So the unregistered holder's position is precarious.

Reasons for not completing title

Usually a grantee wishes to complete title as quickly as possible. But there can 24–07 be exceptions, which tend to arise with general conveyances. In the first place, there may be little risk of supervening insolvency, or of a second grant of the same property. In the second place, registration may in the circumstances be troublesome and expensive. Since the property is not identified in the deed, it will have to be identified of new for the purposes of registration. In some cases that is a difficult and unwelcome task. Registration may also be expensive, particularly if the conveyance encompasses a number of different properties— as with a statutory general transfer of property from a public authority to a successor public authority. Finally, the unregistered holder can do certain juridical acts without first completing title, so that the benefit of registration may seem out of proportion to the trouble and the cost. In particular, the unregistered holder is able to sell the property and to grant a valid disposition, a subject to which we now turn.

Juridical acts by unregistered holders

Even without registration, the grantee of a conveyance can perform certain 24–08 juridical acts in relation to the property. This is a matter of statutory concession, for as far as the common law is concerned, the grantee is not owner, so any grant is *a non domino*. Only a limited range of acts is possible. The holder can:

- dispone[17];
- grant a standard security[18];
- create real burdens[19];
- if the right held is a lease, assign the lease or renounce it[20]; and
- if the right held is a standard security, assign, restrict, vary or discharge the security.[21]

---

[17] Conveyancing (Scotland) Act 1924 s.3.
[18] Conveyancing and Feudal Reform (Scotland) Act 1970 s.12. Subsection (2) says that the "the title of the grantee shall, for the purposes of the rights and obligations between the grantor and the grantee thereof and those deriving right from them, *but for no other purpose*" be as good as a normal standard security. From a lender's standpoint this is unsatisfactory and such standard securities are seldom seen in practice. By contrast, other deeds validly granted by unregistered holders are valid for *all* purposes.
[19] Title Conditions (Scotland) Act 2003 ss.4(2)(b), 123(1).
[20] 1924 Act s.24.
[21] 1924 Act s.3, applied by the 1970 Act s.32; 1970 Act Sch.4 note 1.

But other acts leading to the creation of real rights are not within the statutory concessions. For example, an unregistered holder could not grant a lease with real effect.[22] Nor, probably, could a deed of servitude be validly granted.[23]

What are midcouples?

24–09   To have the status of unregistered holder, a person must be "linked" by one or more "midcouples" (also called "links in title") to the registered holder. A midcouple must be a conveyance. Thus suppose that Lorna, proprietor of Blackmains, is sequestrated, and an act and warrant is issued in favour of her trustee in sequestration, Michael. Michael sells to Norman, and grants a disposition to him, without first having completed title. Pause the DVD at the moment before the Michael/Norman disposition is handed over. Lorna is owner. Michael is the unregistered holder. The midcouple is the act and warrant. Wind the DVD forward by 60 seconds. The disposition has just been handed over. Now Norman is the unregistered holder, and there are two midcouples, the act and warrant (in favour of Michael) and the disposition (in favour of Norman).

There may be several midcouples. Suppose that Lorna, when she was sequestrated, was not proprietor of Blackmains but only the unregistered holder. The registered owner was her uncle Aeneas, who died two years ago, leaving her the property. Her uncle's executor (Achilles) obtained confirmation and, without first completing title,[24] granted Lorna a docket transfer.[25] Lorna took possession, but never completed title. Thus title still appears in the name of Aeneas.[26] When Michael delivers the disposition to Norman, the midcouples that link Norman and Aeneas are: (i) the Aeneas/Achilles confirmation, (ii) the Achilles/Lorna docket, (iii) the Lorna/Michael act and warrant and (iv) the Michael/Norman disposition.

The statutory definition of "midcouple", which is not free from difficulty, is:

> "Any statute, conveyance, deed, instrument, decree or other writing whereby a right to land or to any real right in land is vested in or transmitted to any person . . . or any minute of a meeting at which any person is appointed to any place or office, if such appointment involves a right to land or to a real right in land . . ."[27]

Preservation of midcouples

24–10   If the midcouple is a deed,[28] such as deed of assumption and conveyance, or a docket transfer, it is good practice to register the midcouple in the Books of

---

[22] In itself a lease is a contract and an unregistered holder can enter into such a contract. But the contractual counterparty's right would lack real effect.

[23] But the law here is not wholly settled. For discussion see D.J. Cusine and R.R.M. Paisley, *Servitudes and Rights of Way* (1998), para.4–08. A servitude could, however, be granted or reserved within a disposition.

[24] A confirmed executor can complete title. But this is uncommon.

[25] See below, para.25–07.

[26] We put it this way to avoid the question of who is the owner, since Aeneas is dead. One of the authors takes the view that death does not extinguish personality, and that accordingly rights can still belong to a dead person.

[27] Conveyancing (Scotland) Act 1924 s.5.

[28] As opposed to a decree, which is already preserved in the register of the court in question. A confirmation is a decree.

Council and Session, as a convenient means of ensuring that it does not become lost. That is important, for ultimately the validity of the title rests upon the midcouple.

DEDUCTION OF TITLE

First registrations

In a first registration,[29] if the applicant does not have a disposition direct from 24–11
the existing owner, not only must the disposition be backed up by the necessary midcouples, as where the property is already in the Land Register, but it must contain a clause of deduction of title. Such a clause simply lists the midcouples, using a style laid down in the Conveyancing (Scotland) Act 1924. This begins by detailing the last recorded title, and then lists the conveyance or series of conveyances by which the present person has acquired right to the property. Thus suppose that Michelle buys property in 1994 and is sequestrated in 2010. Her title is in the GRS. The trustee in sequestration, Nigella, wishes to sell without first completing title. She grants a disposition to the buyer, Oliver. The disposition must contain a clause along these lines:[30]

> "Which subjects were last vested in the said[31] Michele Morag MacLeod whose title thereto is recorded in the said Division of the General Register of Sasines on the fourth day of September in the year nineteen hundred and ninety-four[32] and from whom I acquired right by the said[33] act and warrant in my favour."

It will be observed that the statutory style of deduction has three parts: (i) identification of person with the existing GRS title; (ii) date of that title; and (iii) the midcouple or midcouples. More is said about clauses of deduction of title at the end of this chapter.

Title continuing in the GRS

In most cases, either the property is already in the Land Register or the present 24–12
transaction will switch the property into that Register. But in a few types of case the property is still in the GRS and will remain there for the time being. An example would be where Roberta owns a house, her title being in the GRS, and dies. Her executor is Sally. Roberta's will leaves the house to Timothy. Sally dispones to Timothy. This disposition will be recorded in the GRS. It will need a clause of deduction of title, deducing title through the confirmation in Sally's favour. The system is precisely the same as in first registrations except that the midcouple (in the example given, the confirmation) is not sent to the Keeper.

---

[29] That is to say, where a property is being transferred from the GRS to the Land Register.

[30] 1924 Act s.3, Sch.A form 1.

[31] The person with the last recorded title must be designed, but she may have been designed earlier in the deed, in which case a simple reference is sufficient.

[32] Or simply "which subjects were last vested in the said Michele Morag MacLeod as aforesaid" if the information has already been given in an earlier part of the same deed.

[33] The midcouple must be specified fully, but here this has been done earlier in the same deed.

Some cases where the clause is not required

24-13 A clause of deduction of title is unnecessary where the granter already has a completed title. For instance, suppose that Penelope and Quintus buy a house with a survivorship clause in the title, and the title is in the GRS. Quintus then dies. Under the law of survivorship destinations, Penelope is deemed to have a completed title in the whole property the moment that Quintus dies.[34] Hence when she comes to dispone, it is not necessary for the disposition to contain a clause of deduction of title. The disposition should simply mention, in the narrative clause, the survivorship clause and the fact of Quintus's death. Next, a trustee in sequestration did not have to deduce title under the old law.[35] But the rule appears to be different for post-1985 sequestrations.[36] Liquidators and receivers do not need to deduce title since dispositions by them are considered to be dispositions by the company itself.[37] Thirdly, where a standard security holder sells, no deduction is required. Rather than being a conveyance to the creditor, a standard security confers a conditional power on the creditor to convey to someone else.

Errors in deductions

24-14 It is not uncommon to find an error in a clause of deduction of title in a deed recorded in the GRS. In general, such an error will be fatal, in the sense that the deed will fail to give a valid title. But the problem can usually be solved.[38] Suppose that Ulrica owns a property that is still in the GRS. She dies. Her confirmed executor is Vernon. Vernon does not complete title but dispones to Walter, to whom Ulrica bequeathed the property. The disposition is recorded in the GRS. It fails to include a clause of deduction of title, or perhaps it contains one but it is bungled. Despite the recorded deed, Walter is not the owner. His title is void. However, the disposition is still valid as a midcouple, because it is a conveyance. Walter could thus complete title by recording a notice of title with a clause deducing title though (a) the confirmation and (b) the disposition. This could be done even at one remove. Thus suppose that Walter were to die without having recorded the notice of title. His executor, Xerxes, is confirmed and dispones to Yvonne, to whom Walter bequeathed the property. This disposition could include a clause of deduction of title deducing through (a) Vernon's confirmation to Ulrica's estate, (b) the disposition by Vernon to Walter, and (c) Xerxes's confirmation to Walter's estate. There is no limit to the number of midcouples that may be used.

The problem of errors in the clause of deduction does not arise once a property has been transferred to the Land Register, because no such clause is required. But it is still necessary that the right midcouples should exist. If they do not, then the Land Register is inaccurate.

---

[34] See below, para.26–06.

[35] Bankruptcy (Scotland) Act 1913.

[36] Bankruptcy (Scotland) Act 1985. The reason is that s.100 of the Bankruptcy (Scotland) Act 1913 provided that a disposition by the trustee in sequestration took effect as if it had been granted by the bankrupt with the consent of the trustee. So if Jack owned land and was sequestrated, a disposition by his trustee was deemed to be a disposition by someone with a completed title, and so deduction was not required. The 1985 Act seems to contain no equivalent provision.

[37] Of course if the company itself is an unregistered holder, then deduction would be needed.

[38] Possibly this point was overlooked in *Haberstich v McCormick*, 1975 S.L.T. 181, though the facts of that case are not quite clear.

The word "vest"

The term "vest" is an ambiguous one. In the Conveyancing (Scotland) Act **24–15**
1924 it is used to signify a completed title. Thus, when a deduction of title
clause says that the subjects were "last vested in" someone it means that the
last completed title was in that person. But the word is sometimes also used in
a broader sense. Thus, in the law of succession, "vesting" is used to mean the
acquisition of an indefeasible beneficial right.[39] Again, sequestration "vests"
the estate of the bankrupt in the trustee, but this of itself gives the trustee a real
right only for certain types of property, not including heritage.[40]

Some examples of deduction clauses

Here are some examples of clauses of deduction of title. Actual clauses are **24–16**
needed only where the property is still in the GRS, but the underlying principles as to midcouples are equally applicable where the property is in the Land
Register.

(a) Anne owns property. She dies. Boris is confirmed as executor. Clare is
the beneficiary. Boris can, without completing title in his own name, dispone
to Clare, deducing title through the confirmation:

> "Which subjects were last vested in the said Anne . . . whose title thereto
> is recorded in . . . on . . . and from whom I acquired right as executor
> foresaid by said confirmation in my favour."[41]

(b) The same, but instead of disponing to Clare, Boris grants to Clare a
docket transfer.[42] The result of this is that Clare is unregistered holder.[43] Clare
could thereafter complete title by recording a notice of title, deducing title
through the confirmation in favour of Boris and the docket in favour of herself.
Or she could, without completing title herself, dispone to someone else,
deducing title in the same way.

(c) As (b). But Clare does not complete title. Clare dies. David is confirmed
as Clare's executor.[44] David could record a notice of title, or dispone, deducing
through (i) Boris's confirmation to Anne, (ii) the docket to Clare, and (iii)
David's confirmation to Clare's estate:

> "Which subjects were last vested in Anne [*design*] whose title thereto was
> recorded in . . . on . . . and from whom I acquired right as executor fore-
> said by (one) confirmation in favour of Boris as executor of the said Anne
> issued by the Commissariot of . . . at . . . on . . . (two) docket endorsed on
> a certificate of the last-mentioned confirmation by the said Boris in favour
> of the said Clare dated . . . and (three) said confirmation in my favour as
> executor of the said Clare dated as aforesaid."

---

[39] For discussion, see Gretton, (1986) 31 J.L.S.S. 148; Maher, (1986) 31 J.L.S.S. 396; Gordon,
(1987) 32 J.L.S.S. 218; Patrick, (1988) 33 J.L.S.S. 98; and Styles, (1989) 34 J.L.S.S. 338.

[40] Bankruptcy (Scotland) Act 1985 s.31. See below, para.29–02.

[41] In such a case the narrative clause will already have designed Anne and specified the
confirmation.

[42] Succession (Scotland) Act 1964 s.15(2).

[43] Because the docket will not be recorded.

[44] This may seem a complex case, but is quite common in practice.

(d) Alfred, Brenda and Chris are trustees with a completed title. Alfred resigns and Brenda dies. Chris executes a deed of assumption and conveyance appointing Donna and Elaine as new trustees.[45] This deed could be recorded in the GRS,[46] but let us suppose that it is not recorded. The three trustees (Chris, Donna and Elaine) can complete title by notice of title deducing through the deed of assumption and conveyance. The clause would run on the following lines:

> "Which subjects were last vested in the said Alfred . . . and Brenda . . . and Chris . . . as trustees foresaid whose title thereto was recorded in . . . on . . . and from whom, following the resignation of the said Alfred . . . by minute of resignation dated . . . and registered in the Books of Council and Session on . . . and also following the death of the said Brenda . . . on . . ., the said Chris . . . and Donna . . . and Elaine . . . acquired right as trustees foresaid by deed of assumption and conveyance by the said Chris . . . as trustee foresaid in favour of the said Chris . . . and Donna . . . and Elaine . . . as trustees foresaid dated . . . and registered in the Books of Council and Session on . . ."

As this example shows, the practice is that in a deed of assumption and conveyance, the granter is one of the grantees.

(e) Alan and Beth own a property in common, with no survivorship clause. Alan dies and Beth confirms as Alan's executor. She does not complete title. Beth is also the legatee of Alan's half share. Beth as executor dockets that half share to herself as an individual. Beth then sells the whole property. The deduction, which is needed only in respect of *Alan's* half share, would run:

> "Which subjects were last vested to the extent of a one half *pro indiviso* share in the late Alan [*design*][47] whose title thereto is recorded in . . . on . . . and from whom I acquired right by (primo) confirmation in my favour as executor of the said Alan . . . issued by the Commissariot of . . . at . . . on . . . [48] and (secundo) docket endorsed on a certificate of said confirmation by me as executor foresaid in favour of myself as an individual dated . . ."

(f) Suppose in the last example that Beth is sequestrated after she had granted the docket to herself, and that Cornelius, her trustee in sequestration, dispones to Darius. Here the two halves of the property will need separate deductions:

> "Which subjects were last vested to the extent of a one half *pro indiviso* share in the late Alan . . . [*design*] whose title thereto is recorded in . . . on . . . and from whom I as trustee in sequestration foresaid acquired right by (one) confirmation in favour of the said Beth . . . as executor of the said Alan . . . issued by the Commissariot of . . . at . . . on . . . (two) docket endorsed on a certificate of said confirmation by the said Beth . . . as

---

[45] See below, para.25–17.

[46] If it has a proper conveyancing description of the heritable property in the trust.

[47] No designation is needed if Alan has been designed earlier in the deed, in which case the wording is "in the said Alan".

[48] Or "said confirmation" if, as is likely, it has already been specified earlier in the deed.

executor in favour of herself as an individual dated . . . and (three) the said act and warrant in favour of myself as trustee in sequestration foresaid, and which subjects were last vested to the extent of the other one half *pro indiviso* share in the said Beth . . . whose title thereto is recorded in . . . on . . . and from whom I as trustee in sequestration foresaid acquired right by said act and warrant."

CHAPTER 25

TRUSTS AND EXECUTRIES

Introduction

25–01 When someone dies, the body, the soul and the property pass on. The body is buried or cremated. The fate of the soul is not a matter for the law. As for the deceased's property, two questions arise. The main one is: who gets what? This is the province of the law of succession, and of inheritance tax. But there is also the question of how who gets what, or in other words how the successors are to obtain title. Every death thus involves a conveyancing problem of getting rights out of the dead and into the living.

The law before 1964

25–02 Before the Succession (Scotland) Act 1964 there were two separate systems, according to whether moveable or heritable property was involved. For moveables, the process (subject to minor qualifications) was that the executor obtained confirmation from the sheriff, acting as commissary. Confirmation is a type of decree. This procedure was used in both testate and intestate cases. This is still the law. But the executor had, as such, no right to administer the heritage. The administration of the heritage itself could happen in two ways. In the first place, if the deceased was intestate, the heritage passed to the heir.[1] The law, in ascertaining the heir, preferred males to females and, subject to certain exceptions, the elder to the younger: the system thus displayed two mortal sins of modern theology, namely sexism and ageism. If there were children, the heir was the eldest son. If there were only daughters, the daughters were co-heirs, under the name heir-portioners. In the absence of issue, the heir would be a collateral heir, such as a brother, for always males were preferred to females. The procedure was that the heir petitioned the sheriff for a decree of service.[2] This decree then operated as a conveyance in his favour. Alternatively, he could complete title by the *clare constat* procedure, which involved application to the feudal superior. Both of these procedures were abolished by the 1964 Act, though they remained competent in respect of pre-Act deaths.

In the second place, if the deceased was testate, the heritable property would pass to whoever was entitled to it under the will. There are, in theory, two types of will or testament, namely the will or testament strictly so

---

[1] The full title was heir-at-law or heir-of-line, the two terms being synonymous. The heir's right could be subject to a liferent in favour of the relict, under the doctrine of terce (in favour of a widow) and courtesy (in favour of a widower).

[2] There were two types of service, special and general. Special service was appropriate for property in which the deceased had a completed title, and general service for other property. For service before the 19th century reforms, see Erskine, III, viii, 59.

called, and the trust disposition and settlement. In the former, the legacies are made direct to the legatees, while in the latter everything is conveyed to trustees (who in practice would be the same as the executors for the moveables), with the legatees having the status simply of beneficiaries under a trust.[3] After reforms in the nineteenth century, if there was a will (in the narrow sense) then either the legatee or the executor could deduce title through it. (If the executor did so, he would, of course, then convey to the legatee.) But if there was a trust disposition and settlement only the trustee could complete title.[4]

The pre-1964 law, which has just been stated in only the briefest fashion, is important not only by way of background to the modern law, but also because knowledge of it can still be relevant in current practice. The pre-1964 law still applies to pre-1964 deaths. Consequently, if the last recorded title to land is in the name of someone who died before the 1964 Act, it is necessary to employ the pre-1964 law to make up title. It might be thought that this never happens nowadays, but in fact such cases still occasionally crop up.

The law since 1964

The 1964 Act made radical changes, both as to who gets what and as to the mechanics of transfer. On the latter point, it extended the confirmation procedure to cover heritage as well as moveables. That made the service procedure redundant and accordingly it was abolished, though it remains competent for pre-1964 intestate deaths.[5] Hence, in intestate cases, title to land is now obtained through confirmation. For testate cases the situation is rather more complex, for there is a choice. Title can be taken in such cases either through confirmation or through the will. 25–03

Title through the will

After the 1964 Act was passed, there was some uncertainty as to whether only the confirmation was a valid midcouple, or whether the will (if there was one) was also a valid midcouple.[6] In practice there is usually a confirmation, and if there is, that is in practice used. But occasionally there is a will but no confirmation. To resolve the doubts, the Law Society of Scotland submitted a memorial to the Professors of Conveyancing, and the views which they expressed have been universally accepted.[7] They held that an executor can indeed take 25–04

---

[3] In a trust disposition and settlement typical wording would be: "I . . . assign dispone and convey to my said trustees my whole means and estate heritable and moveable real and personal wherever situated which shall belong to me at the time of my death . . . but these presents are granted in trust only for the following purposes . . . (Tertio) to convey and make over to . . . my house at 17 Carey Gilson Street Kirkcudbright". A will in the narrow sense simply says: "I bequeath to . . . my house at 17 Carey Gilson Street Kirkcudbright . . . and I appoint . . . as my executor".

[4] See, generally, ss.19 and 20 of the Titles to Land Consolidation (Scotland) Act 1868 and s.46 of the Conveyancing (Scotland) Act 1874. For full discussion see John Burns, *Conveyancing Practice*, 4th edn (1957, by Farquhar MacRitchie); and John Burns, *Handbook of Conveyancing*, 4th edn (1932). The 19th century reforms thus extended the role of the executor to heritage in testate cases.

[5] Titles to Land Consolidation (Scotland) Act 1868 s.26A.

[6] For midcouples, see above, para.24–09.

[7] See (1965) 10 J.L.S.S. 153; and (1966) 11 J.L.S.S. 84.

title through a will,[8] but they were divided as to the position of a legatee. Because the law on the latter point is uncertain, a legatee almost never attempts to use a will as a midcouple.[9]

One drawback that can arise in General Register of Sasines ("GRS") conveyancing where an executor deduces title through the will is that the protections afforded by s.17 of the 1964 Act[10] do not apply. However, the general view is that this drawback is not so serious as to justify an objection to a title which involves deduction through the will.

Confirmation

25–05 The general law and practice of confirmation falls outside the scope of this book,[11] but because of the importance of confirmation as a conveyancing document something needs to be said about it here. Four general points should be noted.

In the first place, confirmation is a conveyance, from the deceased to the executor. It is a judicial conveyance, and may be compared in this respect with the act and warrant in a sequestration.[12] However, unlike an act and warrant, it is a special conveyance,[13] in that it lists the various items of the estate of the deceased. Arguably, therefore, if the property is still in the GRS, it should be possible for the confirmation to be recorded directly so as to make the executor owner (in trust).[14] But this is never done in practice, and since in conveyancing settled practice tends to mature into settled law, it may be that a confirmation could not be so recorded. If an executor wishes to complete title to GRS property, a notice of title is used, deducing title through the confirmation.[15] The issue does not arise for property in the Land Register, as in that case the confirmation itself is sufficient to authorise registration.[16]

Secondly, an executor is a species of trustee under the Trusts (Scotland) Acts 1921 and 1961,[17] and also, to certain extent, at common law. This is important, because it means that the general body of trust law, or at least most of it, applies to executors. For example, where an executor dies without having completed the administration of the estate, the rules of lapsed trusts can be applied.[18] Or again, a purchaser from an executor has the protection afforded to any purchaser from a trustee under s.2 of the Trusts (Scotland) Act 1961.[19] Again, the persons beneficially entitled to succeed, whether as legatees, or by legal rights, or prior rights, or as heirs *ab intestato*, are in the position of beneficiaries of a trust, the

---

[8] And so a fortiori title can be deduced by a trustee through a trust disposition and settlement. The Professors added that "we strongly recommend that the confirmation should be used in preference to the will as a link in title".

[9] However, it seems that the Keeper is in some cases prepared to accept deeds by legatees where there is no confirmation: *Registration of Title Practice Book* ("ROTPB"), para.5.33.

[10] See below, para.25–14.

[11] See James Currie, *The Confirmation of Executors in Scotland*, 8th edn (1995, by Eilidh M. Scobie).

[12] For which see below, para.29–02.

[13] For special and general conveyances, see above, para.24–03.

[14] As was observed by Professor A.J. McDonald at (1965) 10 J.L.S.S. 71 at 72.

[15] For notices of title, see above, para.24–05.

[16] Land Registration (Scotland) Act 1979 Act s.3(6).

[17] Trusts (Scotland) Acts 1921 and 1961 s.2. Originally this was true only of executors nominate, but s.20 of the 1964 Act extended the 1921 Act to executors dative.

[18] For which see below, para.25–11.

[19] For which see below, para.25–13.

executor being the trustee. It is common for wills to declare that the executor is to be a trustee, but this would seem to be superfluous, at least under modern law.

Thirdly, what is required is "such a description as will be sufficient to identify the property or interest therein".[20] In practice a postal address is regarded as sufficient compliance. But obviously it makes sense to insert the title number, or, if the property is still in the GRS, a full conveyancing description. Unfortunately, executry practitioners sometimes fail to look at the land certificate, or at the GRS deeds.

Fourthly, once confirmation has been issued, the sheriff clerk will issue, if asked, not only the confirmation itself but also one or more "certificates of confirmation".[21] A certificate is a briefer document which refers to a single item of estate, and states that that item has been included in the confirmation. The point is that the executor will want to keep the confirmation itself, while the person taking the land—either a beneficiary or a purchaser—will also want it as a midcouple. The problem is solved by the certificate of confirmation, which is delivered to the grantee.

The confirmation as a link in title: registration

A confirmation does not of itself transfer title to the executor. It is a conveyance of land and, like any conveyance, gives no real right of itself: completion of title by registration—in the Land Register or the GRS as appropriate—is necessary for a real right to be obtained. 25–06

For the former, the executor simply applies on a form 2, enclosing the confirmation or a certificate of confirmation. If the property is still in the GRS, completing title will not trigger a first registration. The executor must expede and record a notice of title deducing title through the confirmation.[22]

Although the executor can complete title in this way, it is uncommon to do so without special reason, such as that the administration of the estate is likely to be prolonged. More usually the executor conveys to the buyer or beneficiary without having first completed title.

Transfer to a beneficiary without prior completion of title

There are two ways in which an executor can convey property to a beneficiary without first having completed title. The simplest is just to grant a disposition, the confirmation being the midcouple. The alternative is the docket procedure given by s.15 of the Succession (Scotland) Act 1964.[23] What happens is that the executor endorses on the certificate of confirmation (or on the confirmation itself, though that is rare in practice) a docket nominating the beneficiary as the person entitled to the property in question. The docketed certificate is then normally registered in the Books of Council and Session, though that is not a requirement of law. 25–07

The docket of itself does not give the beneficiary a real right, because a real right requires registration in the Land Register or GRS. The docket can be used

---

[20] Act of Sederunt (SI 1966/593).

[21] These are regulated by Act of Sederunt (SI 1971/1164).

[22] See above, para.24–05.

[23] The style is given in Sch.1 to the Succession (Scotland) Act 1964. Because of the wording of the style, it is uncertain whether it could be used where property is to be conveyed in implement of a deed of family arrangement. In practice a simple disposition should be used.

as a basis for registration in the Land Register but probably cannot be directly recorded in the GRS.[24] If the property is still in the GRS, the beneficiary prepares and records, in the GRS, a notice of title, with a clause of deduction of title listing as midcouples (a) the confirmation and (b) the docket.[25]

Alternatively, the beneficiary could hold the property indefinitely on the basis of the docket, without ever completing title. Eventually the beneficiary could then sell and dispone to a third party.[26] But while this is a common practice for beneficiaries, it poses certain risks,[27] and in our view title should always be completed immediately.

A docket can be in favour of the executor as an individual, and this is quite common, for the executor is often a beneficiary and sometimes the sole beneficiary. In that case, the wording on the docket is simply that the executor does hereby nominate herself or himself, and so forth.

The docket procedure is puzzling. It is a deed that conveys property. But the law already provides such a deed, namely the disposition. A disposition is no harder to draft than a docket. Indeed, of the two the docket is the more problematic, for if the nomination is not worded correctly the docket is probably invalid,[28] whereas the validity of a disposition does not depend on its narrative clause. Moreover, if the property is in the GRS the use of the docket means that two deeds (docket and notice of title) are needed for the beneficiary to complete title instead of just one (disposition). Why the 1964 Act introduced the docket is a mystery,[29] as is its use in practice. The latter is perhaps explained by departmentalisation in law firms. Those who do wills, trusts and executries do not do dispositions (which are the business of conveyancers), but they do do dockets.

Disposition to a buyer without prior completion of title

25–08 There are various reasons why the executor may sell the property, instead of transferring it to a beneficiary. Where this happens the docket procedure is not available, and an ordinary disposition must be used. If the title is still in the GRS, the deed must contain a clause of deduction of title.

Leases

25–09 This book does not generally deal with leases. However, if a lease is involved one complication deserves mention. The executors may have to assign the lease to the appropriate beneficiary within one year, failing which the lease is vulnerable to termination by the landlord.[30]

---

[24] The point is an open one, but such direct recording is never attempted in practice.

[25] See above, para.24–16(b).

[26] If the property is still in the GRS, the disposition should deduce title through (a) the confirmation; and (b) the docket. See above, para.24–16(b).

[27] See above, para.24–06.

[28] Authority on this issue is absent.

[29] Did the draftsperson think that a docket would confer a real right?

[30] Succession (Scotland) Act 1964 s.16. See further Angus McAllister, *Scottish Law of Leases*, 3rd edn (2002), Ch.8; M.C. Meston, *The Succession (Scotland) Act 1964*, 5th edn (2002); Reid and Gretton, *Conveyancing 2000*, pp.63–66. Significant cases are *Lord Rotherwick's Trustees v Hope*, 1975 S.L.T. 187; *Gifford v Buchanan*, 1983 S.L.T. 613; *Sproat v South West Services (Galloway) Ltd*, 2000 G.W.D. 37-1416; *McGrath v Nelson* [2010] CSOH 149; 2011 S.L.T. 107. For the liability of a solicitor for overlooking s.16, see *Paul v Ogilvie*, 2001 S.L.T. 171.

Where the deceased did not have a completed title

Sometimes the deceased did not have a completed title. Here is an example. 25–10
Alan owns a house and dies intestate. Beth, his widow, is entitled to the house
under prior rights. She is also the executrix dative. She confirms to her late
husband's estate, and executes a docket transfer in her own favour, but does not
complete title. Some years later she dies. Her will leaves the house to her niece
Christine, whom she also nominates as her executrix. Christine confirms to her
aunt's estate. The last person with a completed title was Alan. Christine can
validly dispone (to herself as beneficiary, or to a purchaser). She is linked to
the last completed title by an unbroken chain of valid midcouples, namely: (a)
Beth's confirmation to Alan's estate; (b) the docket transfer in favour of Beth;
and (c) Christine's confirmation to Beth's estate. If the property is still in the
GRS these midcouples will have to be listed in the clause of deduction of
title.[31]

Lapsed trusts

Now consider a variation on the above case. Suppose that although Beth 25–11
confirmed to her late husband's estate, and although she was entitled to the
house by virtue of prior rights, she did nothing to transfer the property to
herself as an individual. Here there is a problem. Beth had a succession right.
Christine can confirm to that right, i.e. to Beth's right in Alan's estate. But the
title is still stuck in Alan's executry, for there has been no transfer out of his
executry. In other words, there is a "lapsed trust".

A trust is said to lapse where (1) there is still trust property undistributed
but (2) there are no acting trustees, usually because all the trustees are dead.
That is what has happened here. There are various ways of unscrambling
a lapsed trust.[32] Those mentioned below are applicable to all types of
trust, including executries, except for the third, which is applicable only
to executries.

In the first place, where the beneficial right is absolutely vested and no
further trust administration is required with respect to that property, the beneficiary can apply to the court for an order authorising him or her to complete
title.[33] But this procedure is rare.

In the second place, anyone with an interest can petition the court for the
appointment of a new trustee.[34] The petition will itself suggest to the court a
suitable person to act. The decree then operates as a midcouple in favour of the
person appointed. Such petitions are quite common.

In the third place, where the executor has died, a new executor can be
appointed to the estate. In the example, this would mean someone else
becoming executor to Alan. That person could then dispone to the ultimate
beneficiary of Beth's estate, the disposition incorporating the consent of Beth's

---

[31] See above, para.24–16(c).

[32] The following is a list of the main ones. There are some others, such as the appointment of a
judicial factor.

[33] Trusts (Scotland) Act 1921 Act s.24. The decree is then a midcouple.

[34] 1921 Act s.22. Curiously, this section does not in fact mention the death of the sole trustee (or
all trustees) as a ground of petition. But the section has always been construed as covering such
cases, and indeed is seldom used for any other purpose. See W.A. Wilson and A.G.M. Duncan,
Trusts, Trustees and Executors, 2nd edn (1995), Ch.21.

executor.[35] A new executor appointed in this way is called an executor *ad non executa*, i.e. an executor appointed to an estate that had not been "executed" by the original executor.[36]

The fourth method, often used in practice, is the procedure set out in s.6 of the Executors (Scotland) Act 1900. Under this procedure, the executor (Christine) of the executor (Beth) can confirm to the unexecuted estate. This will involve confirming to the house twice in the same inventory. In the main body of the inventory, Christine would confirm to Beth's succession right to Alan's estate. Then, in an appendix to the inventory, Christine would enter the house itself. Confirmation issued in such terms operates as a midcouple in favour of Christine. She can then dispone (to herself, if she inherits from her aunt) the midcouples being (i) Beth's confirmation to Alan's estate and (ii) her own confirmation to her aunt's estate. One qualification to be noted is that this procedure is competent only where no further acts of administration are required in the trust or executry which has lapsed. In other words, it is available only where the only thing needed is to convey the property to the person beneficially entitled. This, however, is usually the case.

Lapsed trusts are a nuisance. So where it is anticipated that a trust will continue for some time, it is wise to have more than one trustee. In ongoing trusts there may, of course, be additional reasons for having more than one trustee, for difficult decisions may need to be taken, and two or three heads will be wiser than one.

In the example, it would not have been sufficient for Christine merely to confirm to her aunt's succession right to Alan's estate. Of course, such confirmation is necessary, for what may be called the internal purposes of Beth's executry, or in other words such aspects as beneficial succession to Beth, and tax liabilities for her estate. But such confirmation would be ineffectual for conveyancing purposes. The reason is that the entry in Christine's confirmation to Beth's estate concerns only Beth's beneficial right to the house, and title cannot be deduced through a mere beneficial right.[37] Hence the necessity of confirming to the title itself in an appendix under s.6 of the Executors (Scotland) Act 1900, or adopting some other means of rescuing title from the lapsed trust.

Destinations

25–12   Destinations are the subject of Ch.26, but a few words are appropriate here. If there is a survivorship destination in the title there is no need for confirmation in respect of that property, on the first death, because the survivor is deemed automatically the owner of the whole. Of course, on the second death there will have to be confirmation to the property. More strictly, there will have to be confirmation on the last death, for one can have a survivorship destination among three or more people, such as three sisters. Where, after the first death,

---

[35] In such a case, of course, it would be for Beth's executor to determine the person to whom the property should be conveyed. Alan's new executor would then simply follow that request. Alternatively Beth's executor could request Alan's new executor to convey to her, in her capacity as Beth's executor. The position would be the same if a new trustee to Alan's estate had been appointed under s.22 of the 1921 Act.

[36] The process is a common law one, subject to the Executors (Scotland) Act 1900 s.7.

[37] But only through a conveyance: see above, para.24–09. Once more the point is made that in the case of registered property no clause of deduction is needed (Land Registration (Scotland) Act 1979 Act s.15) but nevertheless precisely the same midcouples are required as in the case of GRS property.

the survivor dispones, no deduction of title is necessary because deduction of title is required only where the title of the granter is not complete. The fact of the earlier death is stated in the narrative clause.

A quite separate issue under the same heading of destinations is whether, in an *inter vivos* disposition in favour of trustees, it is necessary to add a survivorship destination. Though it is common to do so, it is unnecessary and indeed in principle inappropriate. Trust ownership is joint ownership. Each trustee does not have a share of the property. There is thus no question of such a non-existent share passing, on the death of one trustee, to the other trustees. A trustee who dies simply drops out of the picture. That death does not enlarge the rights of the other trustees. The title is a single one, under joint administration.[38]

Buying from an executor or trustee

In a purchase from an executor or trustee, it is not necessary to verify that there   25–13 is a power of sale, because in such cases s.2 of the Trusts (Scotland) Act 1961 protects the buyer. Good faith is not required. In other words, if an executor or trustee sells in breach of trust, the beneficiaries must pursue their remedy against the delinquent trustee, not against the purchaser.[39] Such cases are, however, rare, partly because breach of trust is rare and partly because in most cases trustees have an implied power of sale.[40]

A (perhaps rather remote) danger not covered by s.2 of the 1961 Act concerns statutory occupancy rights. Thus suppose that Petra occupies property as beneficiary of a trust, and is married to Peter. The trustees decide to sell the property. Peter may have occupancy rights.[41]

Lastly, a purchaser from a confirmed executor is protected, if in good faith, against the unlikely event of the subsequent reduction of the confirmation.[42]

The question of searches in the Personal Register against trustees and executors is discussed elsewhere.[43]

Buying from a beneficiary

Suppose that an executor or trustee has conveyed to a beneficiary, and the   25–14 beneficiary comes to sell within the period of positive prescription, and the property is still in the GRS.[44] Is it necessary for the buyer to check that the executor or trustee conveyed to the right person? In other words, does the buyer need to check the terms of the will or deed of trust? In the case of a beneficiary who has taken title from a confirmed executor, s.17 of the Succession (Scotland) Act 1964 protects those acquiring in good faith from that beneficiary.[45] Here, as so often, it is arguable what counts as good faith.

---

[38] See below, para.25–16.

[39] For a discussion of this whole area, see Scottish Law Commission, Discussion Paper on *Liability of Trustees to Third Parties* (Scot. Law Com. D.P. No.138, 2008), paras 2.25–2.38.

[40] Trusts (Scotland) Act 1921 s.4. In the unlikely event that they do not have it, they can usually acquire it from the court: 1921 Act s.5.

[41] See above, para.10–13.

[42] Succession (Scotland) Act 1964 s.17.

[43] See above, para.9–22.

[44] The issue here discussed is less likely to be relevant if the property is in the Land Register.

[45] That is to say, protected against the possibility that the beneficiary's title was reducible because the executor should have conveyed to someone else, or because the confirmation itself was reducible.

Some conveyancers would take the view that the will would have to be checked in order to be in good faith.

Section 17 applies only where the beneficiary took title from a confirmed executor. In other cases where a purchase is from a beneficiary, the buyer has no statutory protection. Thus, suppose that there is an *inter vivos* trust, and the trustees convey part of the estate, a house, to Alan. Alan then concludes missives to sell to Brenda. If the trustees should not have conveyed to Alan, the disposition to him will be voidable. But, if Brenda is in good faith, she will be protected at common law.[46] Hence the position is in fact effectively the same as under s.17 of the 1964 Act.[47]

Land Register protection

25–15 The two preceding paragraphs looked at the buyer's position under general law. Assuming that the title is in the Land Register, there will normally be a further layer of protection, but it should be borne in mind that titles in the Land Register can be undermined by "fraud or carelessness".[48]

Joint property

25–16 Where there is more than one trustee, or executor, they hold as joint owners, not owners in common.[49] Indeed, trust ownership appears to be the only case where joint ownership is possible for heritable property. Joint owners, unlike owners in common, do not have identifiable shares. If there are two owners in common, each has a half share, if three, a third, and so on, i.e. they have aliquot shares.[50] But nothing like that is the case for trustees. If there are two trustees and they assume a third, it would be wrong to suppose that the "share" of the first two fell from a half to a third. It is because the title is joint that, when one trustee dies, there is no "share" to pass to his or her estate. Instead, the surviving trustees carry on as before, owners of the whole. The position is the same if one trustee resigns.

Assumption

25–17 Trustees, including executors nominate (but not executors dative),[51] can normally assume new trustees.[52] This is rare in executries, but common in long-running trusts. It is done by a deed of assumption and conveyance.[53] This can take the form of a special conveyance, but is more usually done as a general conveyance, i.e. as a conveyance of the whole trust estate without specification of any particular property. If some of the existing trustees are to continue, the practice is to convey to themselves and to the new trustee or trustees, so that the granters will also be among the grantees. The new trustee or trustees adds

---

[46] At common law, voidability does not transmit against a disponee who gives value and is in good faith: see Reid, *Property*, para.692.

[47] Indeed, s.17 is to that extent merely declaratory of the common law.

[48] Land Registration (Scotland) Act 1979 ss.9(3)(a)(iii), s.12(3)(n). See above, para.8–16.

[49] The term *pro indiviso* ownership applies to both cases. For the differences between common and joint property, see Reid, *Property*, paras 17 et seq.

[50] Unless some other, unequal, division has been expressly provided for.

[51] Succession (Scotland) Act 1964 s.20, proviso. Though incompetent, the attempt is occasionally made.

[52] Trusts (Scotland) Act 1921 s.3.

[53] See s.21 of and Sch.B to the 1921 Act for the statutory style.

a docket at the foot accepting office. The deed is, as a matter of good practice, registered in the Books of Council and Session. It is wise to complete title in the name of the new body of trustees,[54] but this is not always done. The deed of assumption is a midcouple.[55]

Resignation

A trustee can normally resign, unless he or she is the sole trustee.[56] A sole trustee who wishes to resign must assume a new trustee first. A minute of resignation[57] by a trustee should, as a matter of good practice, be registered in the Books of Council and Session. The resignation must be intimated to the other trustees. The effect of resignation is to divest the resigning trustee.[58] That this can be achieved without conveying is due to the fact that the co-ownership of trustees is not ownership in common but joint ownership.

25–18

Execution of deeds by trustees

The practice is to ensure that conveyancing deeds are signed by all the trustees, including any whose title is completed by registration. But it is unclear whether this is legally necessary or whether majority execution is sufficient. Section 7 of the 1921 Act may perhaps mean that a majority is sufficient, but its terms are obscure.[59]

25–19

Warrandice by trustees

In a disposition to a beneficiary the practice is for the trustees or executors to grant fact and deed warrandice only. If the disposition is to a purchaser the practice is to grant fact and deed warrandice and to bind the trust estate in absolute warrandice.[60]

25–20

Charitable and religious trusts

Special rules apply to many religious and educational trusts.[61] The core idea is that of automatic completion of title. In other words, as, over the years, the trustees change, so each new set of trustees is deemed to have a completed title, the title of the original trustees continuing, by a fiction, in favour of their successors. Hence, as and when the present trustees grant a deed, they do so

25–21

---

[54] If the property is still in the GRS this will require a notice of title.

[55] See above, para.24–09.

[56] Trusts (Scotland) Act 1921 s.3. There are various exceptions stated in the section. Note also that an executor dative cannot resign: Succession (Scotland) Act 1964 s.20.

[57] 1921 Act s.19 and Sch.A.

[58] 1921 Act s.20.

[59] The proper construction of s.7 is uncertain. It is limited to dispositions to non-beneficiaries who are acting in good faith. It is unclear what presuppositions were being made as to the existing state of the law. In *Harland Engineering Co v Stark's Trustees*, 1913 2 S.L.T. 448; 1914 2 S.L.T. 292 it was held in the Outer House that a majority suffices. The case was reclaimed on a question of expenses, and in the Inner House some doubt was expressed as to whether the substantive decision had been correct. The law was thus obscure, and s.7 made it more so. See further Scottish Law Commission, Discussion Paper on *Liability of Trustees to Third Parties* (Scot. Law Com. D.P. No.138, 2008), paras 2.39–2.53.

[60] See above, paras 19–06 and 19–09.

[61] Titles to Land Consolidation (Scotland) Act 1868 s.26. For discussion see Halliday, para.39–18, and D.J. Cusine (ed.), *Conveyancing Opinions of Professor J.M. Halliday* (1985), no. 153. The precise meaning of s.26 is by no means clear.

from the position of persons having a completed title. This idea is more significant for properties still in the GRS, for it means that no clause of deduction of
title is needed. Similar rules apply where there is an *ex officio* trustee.[62]

In practice, the terms of the original trust often impose restrictions on the
trustees, limiting their power to sell the land. The zealous landowner who, in
1877, gave the land and money in trust for the building of a chapel for the
Congregation of the Auchnashuggle Free Reformed United Presbyterian New
Covenant Church of Scotland wanted to make sure that the building would
never be used for any other purpose. The present congregation (the last left in
Scotland) has decided to merge with the Church of Scotland, and wants to sell
the chapel. Can this be done? The question, which is one of some difficulty, is
a problem for the sellers and not for the purchaser, who will be protected by s.2
of the Trusts (Scotland) Act 1961.[63]

Liferents[64]

25–22 Viewed from the perspective of property law, there are two quite different
types of liferent. In the true or "proper" liferent, both liferenter and fiar have
real rights. The fiar has the real right of ownership, burdened by the subordinate real right of liferent. The fiar can sell, but naturally the buyer will obtain
the same right, which is to say ownership encumbered by the liferent. There
are no trustees. But proper liferents are uncommon. In practice, they seldom
exist except as a result of a home-made will.[65] More common is the "trust"
liferent, also called the "improper" liferent or "beneficiary" liferent. Here there
is just one real right, namely the real right of ownership of the trustees. The
rights of the liferenter and the fiar are beneficial rights under the trust. When
the beneficial liferenter dies, the trustees dispone to the beneficial fiar. Before
this happens, the latter can sell the beneficial right. But as with the sale of any
beneficial right under a trust, the sale is given effect to not by disposition but
by assignation, for what is being conveyed is incorporeal property, a personal
right against the trustees.

It sometimes happens that the liferenter no longer wishes to live in the lifer-
ented property. He or she may wish to move to a smaller house, or a house in a
different place, or move in with relatives, or to a nursing home. A well-drafted
will or other deed of trust will have anticipated this possibility by allowing the
trustees to sell, and providing that the proceeds of sale (whether invested, or
used to buy another house) will be subject to the same division of rights
between the beneficial liferenter and the beneficial fiar. If the deed is silent the
same thing can still happen if both parties agree. But it may be that the beneficial fiar is awkward. Or it may be that the beneficial fee is unvested. Or it may
be that the beneficial liferenter has become *incapax*. In such cases there can be
doubts as to whether the trustees have an implied power of sale. If necessary,

---

[62] Conveyancing (Scotland) Act 1874 s.45. The meaning of this term may not be free from
difficulty.

[63] See above, para.25–13.

[64] See generally, W.J. Dobie, *Manual of the Law of Liferent and Fee in Scotland* (1941); G.L.
Gretton and A.J.M. Steven, *Property Trusts and Succession* (2009), Ch.21.

[65] In such a case, to give effect to the proper liferent in conveyancing terms, the executor would
grant a disposition "to A in liferent and to B in fee" and title sheet in the Land Register would
reflect this.

the consent of the court may be sought.[66] In most cases, however, a power of sale will exist.[67] At all events, the problem is the concern only of the trustees, not of the purchaser.[68]

A worked example

Jack died in 1992, owner of a house. He left a trust disposition and settlement 25–23 directing his trustees to hold for his widow Mary in liferent and his daughter Kate in fee. The trustees completed title. Mary lived in the house until her death in 1997. Thereafter Kate lived in the house. But the trustees never got round to granting a disposition to Kate. Kate died in 2011. She left a trust disposition and settlement giving the house to her son Paul. Paul, however, does not wish to keep the house. He concludes missives to sell the house to Tom. How should the disposition to Tom be drafted?

In the first place, Paul, the seller, cannot dispone. He is not owner, nor is he linked to the recorded or registered title by any midcouples. Nor can Kate's trustees dispone. It is indeed true that where there is a trust the title is usually vested in the trustees, with the beneficiary having a personal right. But here the right vested in Kate's trustees is itself a personal right only. There are thus, so to speak, two levels of personal right. Kate's trustees cannot dispone because they are not the owners and, like Paul, are not linked to the recorded or registered title by any midcouples. The current completed title is that of Jack's trustees, and only they can grant the disposition. They hold for Kate, and since her death, for her trustees. They must therefore dispone to the person selected by Kate's trustees. The latter in turn must obtain a conveyance either to Paul himself or to Paul's nominee, i.e. Tom. In other words, Paul tells Kate's trustees to convey to Tom, and Kate's trustees then tell Jack's trustees to convey to Tom. The disposition is thus granted by Jack's trustees, and bears the consent of Kate's trustees and of Paul.[69] The real seller, Paul, is thus in conveyancing terms merely a consenter. If the title is in the GRS no clause of deduction of title is called for since the granters hold a completed title.[70] The narrative clause will refer to Jack's trust disposition and settlement and its terms, to Mary's death, to Kate's death, to Kate's trust disposition and settlement and its terms, to the confirmation in favour of Kate's trustees, and to the sale by Paul to Tom.

Would it have made any difference if Jack's trustees had never completed title? The answer is, very little. The last completed title would in that case be Jack's. Neither Paul nor Kate's trustees would be in a position to deduce title, because they would have no midcouples linking them to that last title. Kate's trustees have confirmed to her beneficial right to Jack's estate, and title cannot be deduced through a mere beneficial right. The disposition would be granted by Jack's trustees in the same terms as above. The only difference is that, in a GRS case, there would be a clause deducing title through the confirmation in favour of Jack's trustees.

---

[66] Under s.5 of the Trusts (Scotland) Act 1921 or s.1 of the Trusts (Scotland) Act 1961.
[67] *Mauchline, Petitioner*, 1992 S.L.T. 421.
[68] Who is protected by the Trusts (Scotland) Act 1961 s.2 (for which see above, para.25–13).
[69] For the effect of such consents, see above, para.11–09.
[70] If the title is in the Land Register such clauses are not needed anyway.

CHAPTER 26

DESTINATIONS

Overview

26–01 The first part of this chapter looks at the nature of destinations, the way they are created, and their effects. The second part deals with evacuation, which is say the ways in which destinations may cease to be operative. The third and last part considers the position of a buyer.

DESTINATIONS: NATURE, CREATION AND CONSEQUENCES

Introduction

26–02 There are two types of destinations. One is the destination-over, found in testaments and deeds of trust of various sorts. For instance, Horatia's will might say that her house is to go to Tara, whom failing to Yvonne. Thus, if Tara dies before Horatia, but Yvonne survives Horatia, then Yvonne takes the house.[1] The other sort of destination is the special destination, found in conveyances of heritable property.[2] The only common form in modern practice is the survivorship special destination. Thus, Ann and Brian Bell[3] take title to a house in the form "to the said Brian Bell and the said Ann Minto or Bell equally between them and to the survivor of them". This means that each takes a one half *pro indiviso* share, but each half share is subject to a destination in favour of the other. If Ann dies first, her share passes to Brian, and vice versa.[4] Thus the destination is shorthand for "half to Ann whom failing to Brian and the other half to Brian whom failing to Ann".

The reason why both devices share the name "destination" is that in both cases a deed that gives right to property makes provision for what is to happen to that property in the event of the death of the grantee. Destination-overs themselves divide into (i) the conditional institution and (ii) the substitution.[5]

---

[1] If a legatee predeceases, the legacy lapses, i.e. becomes void. A destination-over thus has the effect of preventing such lapse. There are also certain other principles of succession law which can prevent lapse, notably the *conditio si institutus sine liberis decesserit*.

[2] Special destinations in moveable property can, in theory, exist in certain types of case, but are almost unknown in practice. A destination-over can be of moveables just as much as of heritage.

[3] Usually one is dealing with spouses but survivorship destinations are competent in all types of case, such as cohabitants, civil partners and siblings.

[4] Men's average lifespans being shorter than women's, survivorship clauses operate more in favour of women than of men.

[5] For some history see Gretton, in Kenneth G.C. Reid, Marius J. de Waal and Reinhard Zimmermann (eds), *Exploring the Law of Succession* (2007) Ch.9. A special form of substitution was the tailzie (entail). The Entail Amendment Act 1848 made tailzies breakable. The Entail (Scotland) Act 1914 forbade new tailzies. The survivors were abolished by the Abolition of Feudal Tenure etc. (Scotland) Act 2000 s.50.

Conditional institutions

In conditional institution, the first grantee of the property is the "institute". The 26–03
person who is to take the property in the event of the institute's death is the
"conditional institute". The conditional institute can take the property only if
the institute has died before the date of vesting. Thus, suppose that Horatia's
will leaves a house to Tara whom failing to Yvonne and that this is by way of
conditional institution. Tara dies before Horatia. When Horatia dies Yvonne is
still alive. Yvonne takes the property as legatee. However, suppose that Tara
dies one day after the testator. In that case the legacy vested in Tara. On Tara's
death the property does not pass to Yvonne but forms part of Tara's estate.[6] In
that case, Yvonne's contingent right is said to "fly off".

Suppose, however, that Tara did not die. She would then receive a disposition from Horatia's executor. The disposition would simply be in favour of her,
Tara, not in favour of "Tara whom failing Yvonne", even though that was the
wording of the will. For Yvonne's right has flown off by the fact of Tara's
survival of the date of the vesting.[7]

Substitutions

In a substitution, Tara is again called the institute but Yvonne is called the 26–04
substitute. Substitution includes the effects of conditional institution, but additional effects as well. Thus, suppose that Horatia's will leaves her house to Tara
whom failing Yvonne, and Tara predeceases the testator, but Yvonne survives.
Then the house goes to Yvonne, just as in conditional institution. Or again, if
Tara survived but Yvonne predeceased, the effect is the same as in conditional
institution, namely that the property passes to Tara.

The difference between the two types of destination-over emerges where
both Tara *and* Yvonne survive the date of vesting. Suppose (to take the earlier
example) that Tara dies the day after the testator. Since we are now dealing
with a substitution and not a conditional institution, the legacy, although it had
vested in Tara, passes to Yvonne on Tara's death. The testator's executor must
convey to Yvonne, not to Tara's executor. Suppose, however, that Tara does not
so die. In that case she will receive a disposition from the testator's executor.
The form of the disposition should be to "Tara whom failing Yvonne". In other
words, where a destination-over in a will or deed of trust is a substitution, the
conveyance that gives effect to it should copy out the terms of the destination,
thereby converting the destination-over into a special destination.[8] But this
will be true only where both Tara and Yvonne survive the date of vesting. If
either predeceases, the conveyance will incorporate no special destination.

---

[6] Strictly what forms part of Tara's estate is a personal right against the testator's executor to
insist upon a transfer of the property. Since Tara will not have had time to take a conveyance, the
testator's executor will convey to Tara's executor, who will in turn convey to whoever is entitled
to the property in Tara's succession. (That person might be Yvonne, of course, but probably is not.)
Or, more simply, the conveyance could be direct by the testator's executor to the latter person, the
conveyance incorporating the consent of Tara's executor.

[7] In most wills the date of vesting is the date of the testator's death. But sometimes it is postponed, and the same applies to many *inter vivos* trusts.

[8] A special destination is itself a substitution. (It could never be a conditional institution,
because by the very nature of the case the institute is alive on vesting.) Hence there are two sorts
of substitution: a substitution in a testament and a substitution in a conveyance.

Again, suppose a will leaves a house to "Peter and Robert and the survivor". If this is a substitution, the executor must convey "to Peter and Robert and the survivor of them".[9] If, however, the destination-over in the will is a conditional institution, the executor simply conveys "to Peter and Robert".[10]

Where a special destination has to be used in a conveyance to a beneficiary, it is preferable that this be done in a disposition rather than a docket.[11] But a special destination in a docket transfer would probably be valid.

Identifying which is which

26–05   In a testament or deed of trust the property may be given simply to "A whom failing B" or to "A and B and the survivor". How is it possible to tell whether this is a conditional institution or a substitution? In the first place, the deed may make it clear which is intended, and a well-drafted deed will do so. If conditional institution is intended (and this is the most common case), this is typically done by saying: "To Tara whom failing *by her predecease* to Yvonne". This makes it clear that Yvonne is to take if and only if Tara predeceases Horatia. If the will or deed of trust does not make the intention clear, the common law supplies certain rules as to presumed intention.[12] These are as follows. (1) If the property in question is moveable, conditional institution is to be presumed. (2) If the property in question is heritable, substitution is to be presumed. (3) If the property is a mix of moveables and heritage, conditional institution is to be presumed.[13]

Special survivorship destinations to purchasers

26–06   Special destinations inserted in conveyances that implement the provisions of wills or trusts are not common. The vast majority of special destinations are contained in conveyances to purchasers and are inserted at the request of the purchasers. Such destinations can be of various types. Much the commonest is the ordinary survivorship destination. Here, two (or more) persons buy a house in common, the title being granted, at their request, to them both and the survivor of them. The usual case is spouses, but sometimes cohabitants do this, and it can also be found in other cases. It is possible to have more than two parties involved. For instance, three sisters might buy a house with the disposition to "A and B and C equally between them and to the survivors and survivor of them". That would give each a one third *pro indiviso* share in common ownership. If B then died, half of her share[14] would pass to A and the other half of her share to C, thus leaving A and C with a half of the whole. If C then died her half share of the whole would pass to A, who would thus then be the sole owner.

In many cases when two or more people buy a property a survivorship destination is inserted.[15] However, that should never be done without the express instructions of the clients. The reason is that the substantive effect of a

---

[9] Unless both Peter and Robert otherwise request.

[10] Unless Peter and Robert positively request a survivorship destination to be inserted.

[11] i.e. a docket transfer under s.15(2) of the Succession (Scotland) Act 1964: see above, para.25–07.

[12] The case law is of enormous bulk, but the following three rules are a fairly accurate summary.

[13] For example a legacy of a house and its contents. And a legacy of residue will often be mixed.

[14] A sixth of the whole.

[15] See Nichols, (1990) 35 J.L.S.S. 189.

survivorship destination is that of a legacy of the share of the property. Thus, if Kate and Luke buy a house with a survivorship destination, the substantive effect is that Luke is making a legacy to Kate of his half share, and vice versa. This requires instructions from the clients. Indeed, the need for instructions is especially strong because, as will be explained below, in most cases the effect of the destination cannot be defeated by a later will: whereas a legacy is revocable, a quasi-legacy by means of a survivorship destination is usually irrevocable.[16] Suppose that Kate and Luke become estranged. Kate makes a will leaving her half share to her sister. Soon afterwards, she dies. The legacy is likely to be ineffective, so that the half share will pass to Luke under the destination. The point must be explained to the clients, and their informed wishes ascertained. It should be borne in mind, and explained to the clients, that if each party wishes his or her share to pass, on death, to the survivor, this can also be secured by each party making a will to that effect. This presents little practical difficulty since it is common for people to make wills, or new wills, when buying a house.

An argument often heard in favour of the use of survivorship destinations is that on the first death the share passes to the survivor automatically, without need for confirmation or conveyance.[17] This can be useful. But confirmation is usually needed anyway, in which case the fact of automatic completion of title confers little benefit. It should also be said that special destinations often raise difficult issues of law and have often resulted in litigation.[18]

Power of evacuation: express provision

Usually dispositions that create destinations are silent as to whether there is or is not power to bring the destination to an end by *mortis causa* evacuation. In that case, certain presumptions apply.[19] But the wisdom of this silence seems questionable. It makes more sense to ask the clients what they want, and to provide accordingly. An evacuation clause is simple to draft. After the destination something on these lines is added: "But declaring that the said grantees and each of them shall have full right and power" (or "no right or power") "to evacuate the foregoing destination".[20] If there is such a clause and if it forbids evacuation, the traditional practice is to ensure that the deed is executed by the grantees as well as by the granter. But this is probably not strictly necessary, for by acceptance of the disposition a grantee is deemed to accept its terms.

26–07

Terminology

The distinction between conditional institution and substitution has been explained above. In a special destination, the second party can only be a substitute, not a conditional institute, for the institute cannot already be dead. Thus, if property is disponed to Ann and Brian and the survivor, Ann is institute for a one-half share, and Brian is the substitute for that share, and, for the other half share, Brian is the institute and Ann is the substitute. Another term for a substitute in a special destination is "heir of provision". This means a person who

26–08

---

[16] See below, paras 26–13 to 26–22.
[17] See below, para.26–09.
[18] See, for instance, Lord Cooper's remarks in *Hay's Trustee v Hay's Trustees*, 1951 S.C. 329.
[19] See below, para.26–16.
[20] It is also possible to provide that one party has, and the other has not, the power to evacuate.

inherits not by the general law of succession but by a special provision[21] in the title to some property. A "clause of return" is a special destination where the substitute (or heir of provision) is the granter of the conveyance which creates the destination. Thus, if Fred dispones to Gina whom failing to Fred himself, that is a clause of return. Or suppose a wife, owning a house, dispones it to herself and her husband equally and to the survivor. Then the destination attached to her resulting half share would be an ordinary special destination, but the destination attaching to her husband's half share would be a clause of return.

Where husband and wife (or siblings or others) acquire property together, their title is said to be *pro indiviso*[22] whether or not there is a survivorship destination and whether or not any survivorship destination that has been used is or is not capable of evacuation.[23] Further, the use of a survivorship destination, even one not capable of evacuation, does not convert the ownership from ownership in common to joint ownership.[24] The only case of joint ownership of immoveable property is ownership by trustees.[25]

Completion of title

26–09 When the institute in a special destination dies, the property passes to the substitute, unless the destination has been evacuated. But how does the substitute complete title? The answer depends on whether the special destination is (i) a survivorship one, or (ii) some other type.

If, as is almost always the case in modern practice, the destination is a survivorship destination, the substitute is deemed to have a completed title automatically by simple fact of the death of the institute.[26] Thus, suppose that two people buy a house, and take title "to and in favour of the said Ian Dewar Macdonald and Shona Beatrice Brodie or Macdonald equally between them and to the survivor of them". Ian then dies, the property still being owned by the two of them. Shona obtains a completed title in the whole property when Ian's heart ceases to beat. No conveyance to her of his half share is needed: his death itself operates as a registered conveyance. This is one of the rare cases when ownership of heritable property can pass from one person to another without a registered conveyance. The doctrine was introduced by *Bisset v Walker*.[27] The decision was wrong. But false legal doctrines, once settled and accepted, can become true doctrines, and the doctrine of automatic completion of title[28] is now, and has long been, settled and accepted as good law.

In the rare cases of other types of special destination, the rule is different. Thus, suppose that property is disponed to "Tara whom failing to Yvonne". Tara completes title and later dies. Yvonne takes the property, of course, but

---

[21] *Provisio hominis*, or, in the ablative, *provisione hominis*.

[22] i.e. undivided.

[23] For evacuation, see below, paras 26–13 et seq.

[24] *Munro v Munro*, 1972 S.L.T. (Sh. Ct) 6 held the contrary, but is incorrect. See e.g. *Steele v Caldwell*, 1979 S.L.T. 228.

[25] On joint property see Reid, *Property*, para.34.

[26] Unless the destination has been evacuated, for which see below.

[27] *Bisset v Walker*, November 26, 1799 F.C.

[28] The standard expression in practice is "automatic infeftment", but strictly speaking the term "infeftment" should not be used since feudal abolition.

she does not automatically acquire a completed title. A conveyance to her by Tara's executor is required, and Tara's executor has no choice but to grant it.[29]

Conveyance by the survivor

Suppose that title is taken by Jack and Jill with a survivorship destination, and Jack dies, so that Jill automatically acquires a completed title to his share. She now has a completed title to the whole. She sells. If the property is still in the GRS, Halliday[30] says that the disposition by Jill should contain a clause of deduction of title in respect of the half share formerly owned by her husband, the midcouple being the fact of Jack's death. Although a conveyance in such terms would be valid, in fact no clause of deduction of title is required. The reason is that a clause of deduction is needed (if the property is in the GRS) only where the granter does not have a completed title.   26–10

However, where Halliday's style is not used, it is wise, though not strictly necessary, to make reference in the disposition to Jack's death, in order to show how it is that Jill has a completed title to the whole. This can be done in the narrative clause. That clause will narrate that title was taken by such-and-such a disposition to Jack and Jill and the survivor, and that Jack died on such-and-such a date without having evacuated the said destination, etc.[31]

Destinations and leases

A destination in a lease[32] is subject to different rules from a destination in a disposition or feu disposition, the reason being that the landlord, as well as the substitute, is presumed to have an interest, by virtue of the doctrine of *delectus personae*. But destinations in assignations of leases are probably subject to the ordinary rules, though the point is uncertain.[33]   26–11

Destinations and liability

Suppose that when Jack dies, he is insolvent, and that his estate is then seques- trated. Does Jill keep Jack's share free from the claims of the creditors? Or can Jack's trustee in sequestration demand either that she return the share or pay its value? This question has caused considerable controversy. The better view is that Jill is liable for its value.[34]   26–12

EVACUATION

Introduction

A destination is "evacuated" when something happens to deprive it of its effect. Evacuation may be (i) *mortis causa*, by death of the substitute, or by death of   26–13

---

[29] Succession (Scotland) Act 1964 Act s.18(2). Note the words in that section: "if such convey-ance is necessary". In most cases no such conveyance is necessary because in most cases the destination is a survivorship destination so there is automatic completion of title. Before the 1964 Act, Yvonne would have completed title by a special process called service as heir of provision.

[30] Halliday, para.37–60.

[31] For the narrative clause, see above, paras 11–06 to 11–09.

[32] The destination clause in a lease is sometimes also called the alienation clause.

[33] See Gretton, 1982 S.L.T. (News) 213 for full discussion.

[34] *Fleming's Trustee v Fleming*, 2000 S.C. 206. For discussion see Reid and Gretton, *Conveyancing 1999*, pp. 64–66.

institute, bequeathing the property to a person other than the substitute (heir of provision); (ii) *inter vivos*, where something happens to extinguish the destination while all those concerning are still alive.

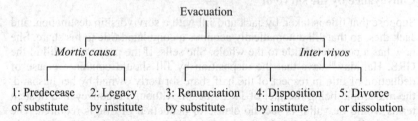

Evacuation

Mortis causa — *Inter vivos*

1: Predecease of substitute   2: Legacy by institute   3: Renunciation by substitute   4: Disposition by institute   5: Divorce or dissolution

Case 1: Evacuation by predecease of substitute

26–14   A special destination becomes null where the substitute (heir of provision) dies before the institute. Thus, suppose that property is disponed to Tara whom failing to Yvonne, and Yvonne then dies. The destination is evacuated by Yvonne's death, and if Tara were to die the next day the property would simply be part of her estate, so that Yvonne's representatives would have no rights. Or again, suppose that a husband and wife own their house in common with a survivorship destination. The husband dies. His share passes to his widow. She then dies. The destination attached to her original half share of the house became void when her husband died. So the whole house becomes part of her estate. Her husband's representatives have no rights.

Case 2: Legacy by institute

26–15   This type of evacuation raises complex issues. The first question is whether there is power to evacuate. If there is no power, the legacy will fail to take effect. The second question is whether, if there is power, the power has been validly exercised.

Is there power to evacuate *mortis causa*?

26–16   If the deed containing the destination has an expression provision about power to evacuate *mortis causa*, that settles the matter. If not, then certain default rules apply. (1) The power to evacuate is presumptively excluded (i) in marriage contracts, (ii) in clauses of return, and (iii) where the parties both contributed to the price. There is also (iv) a further possible case, namely where the destination arose out of a testament or trust.[35] (2) In other cases there is power to evacuate.

Rule (1) (iii) is particularly important in practice. The leading decision is *Perrett's Trustees v Perrett*.[36] This case, and later cases that elaborated the doctrine,[37] hold that, where there is a survivorship destination, and both parties

---

[35] See *Massy v Scott's Trustees* (1872) 11 M. 173; *Robertson v Hay-Boyd*, 1928 S.C. (HL) 8, per Lord Dunedin; Lord McLaren, *Wills and Succession*, 3rd edn (1894), pp.629–30; R. Candlish Henderson, *The Principles of Vesting in the Law of Succession*, 2nd edn (1938), p.328.

[36] *Perrett's Trustees v Perrett*, 1909 S.C. 522. The case is arguably wrong. But it became settled law and cannot now be questioned: see *Shand's Trs v Shand's Trustees*, 1966 S.C. 178.

[37] *Renouf's Trustees v Haining*, 1919 S.C. 497; *Taylor's Exrs v Brunton*, 1939 S.C. 444; *Brown's Trustee v Brown*, 1943 S.C. 488; *Hay's Trustee v Hay's Trustees*, 1951 S.C. 329. For a review, see Morton, 1984 S.L.T. (News) 133.

contributed to the price for the property,[38] there is a presumed agreement that neither can evacuate. If, however, only one party paid the price, there is a presumed agreement that that party can evacuate but that the other party cannot. In determining whether both parties have contributed to the price, the narrative clause of the deed is conclusive.[39] This is a practical point to be watched. Some conveyancers tend, in cases of a purchase by husband and wife, to declare in the narrative clause that both have paid the price, and they do this as words of style without checking the true facts. If in truth it was, say, the wife who paid the whole price, the narrative clause will destroy the power of evacuation she would otherwise have had.

Waiving the bar to evacuation

If there is no power to evacuate, or, in other words, if there is a bar to evacuation, 26–17 the substitute may waive that bar, i.e. agree to authorise the institute to evacuate. Such a waiver leaves the destination intact, merely converting an unevacuable destination into an evacuable destination. Such waivers are not often seen in practice: usually if co-owners have an unevacuable destination in the title and are unhappy with it, they will extinguish the destination altogether.

If, however, the half-way house is indeed desired (i.e. to keep the destination but to convert it from being unevacuable, to evacuable), this can be done by a (probative) deed, which does not have to be registered, though registration in the Books of Council and Session would be good practice. Even better would be a new conveyance which would have a clause expressly authorising evacuation. Thus, if Jack and Jill are co-owners with a survivorship destination which is unevacuable, they could dispone to themselves with a clause authorising evacuation. The practical benefit of this method is that the waiver of the bar to evacuation will not be overlooked at a later stage.

Exercise of power to evacuate *mortis causa*

Evacuation is by legacy to someone other than the substitute. If there is 26–18 no power to evacuate, a legacy will, of course, be ineffective. But even if power exists, the legacy will still be ineffective unless the wording meets the requirements set out in s.30 of the Succession (Scotland) Act 1964, namely that "it contains a specific reference to the destination and a declared intention on the part of the testator to evacuate it".[40] It is quite common to see legacies of property that is subject to a special destination that do not comply with s.30.

Case 3: Voluntary discharge of destination (renunciation by substitute)

The substitute may renounce the destination.[41] The best way to do this is in a 26–19 registered deed. For instance, Jack and Jill co-own a house with a survivorship

---

[38] Equal contribution is not necessary.

[39] *Gordon-Rodgers v Thomson's Exrs*, 1988 S.C. 145. But it is not conclusive if both parties so agree: *Hay's Trustee v Hay's Trustees*, 1951 S.C. 329. There exists a logical difficulty: how can the effect of a destination *at death* depend on what is or is not *subsequently* conceded?

[40] See *Stirling's Trustees*, 1977 S.L.T. 229; *Marshall v Marshall's Exr*, 1987 S.L.T. 49; *Gordon-Rodgers v Thomson's Exrs*, 1988 S.C. 145.

[41] We are not aware of express authority, but the competency of renunciation is clear on principle. This was also the *ius commune* rule: see Voet, *Commentarius ad Pandectas*, 36.1.65,

destination. They wish to continue as co-owners, but with the destination removed. They can simply dispone to themselves, omitting any destination (i.e. case 4 below). But in practice a simple renunciation, not in a registered deed,[42] is sometimes used. Whilst this is valid in a substantive sense, there is a difficulty. Suppose Jack dies. It may be—the law is uncertain—that automatic completion of title would still operate in Jill's favour, the position then being that Jill would be under an obligation to convey to the executor. If this is the law,[43] this would obviously be an inconvenient outcome.[44]

Case 4: Evacuation by *inter vivos* disposition

26–20 Evacuation *inter vivos* means some act, other than a will, which defeats a special destination. Voluntary discharge (see above) is thus a sort of *inter vivos* evacuation. But a special destination can also be evacuated by a conveyance. Thus, suppose that property is disponed to Tara whom failing Yvonne. If Tara subsequently dispones the property to Zenon, then Yvonne's contingent right is defeated. For a special destination can operate only where the institute still owns the property at the date of her death. Thus, a person who owns property, or a share of property, that is subject to a destination, can defeat that destination by alienating the property (or share therein) *inter vivos*, and this is true even if there is no power of *mortis causa* evacuation.

There is some older authority[45] suggesting that evacuation can be effected only by onerous *inter vivos* alienation (typically sale), and not by gratuitous *inter vivos* alienation (donation or gift). But the clear trend of the modern authorities is that it does not matter whether the alienation is onerous or not.[46] Thus, if Jack and Jill hold their house subject to a survivorship destination, and if Jack gratuitously dispones his half share to his brother, and then dies, a modern court would almost certainly hold that Jill had no rights in that half share.

Under Case 4 there are three sub-cases. (i) There is a disposition to a third party, as in the example just given. (ii) Brad and Jennifer co-own a house with a survivorship destination. They are separating, and it has been agreed that Jennifer is to have the house. They join together in disponing the whole property, with her as the sole disponee. It is done this way, rather than a disposition by Brad alone, just of his half share, because of the "*Raeburn* trap", discussed below. (iii) Fred and Ginger co-own a house with a survivorship destination. They are not separating, and neither is transferring a share to the other. Nevertheless, each wants that share to form part of his or her own estate in the event of death, and not necessarily to pass to the survivor. Accordingly they join in disponing the property to themselves, the disposition omitting any destination.

Following the decision in *Board of Management of Aberdeen College v Youngson*,[47] there was concern about whether Case 4 really works in sub-cases

---

[42] That is to say, not in the Land Register (or GRS). It might well be registered in the Books of Council and Session.

[43] Which it seems to be. See *Redfern's Exrs v Redfern*, 1996 S.L.T. 900, though there may be scope for debate as to the meaning of the decision.

[44] The potential problem would not exist in the case of destinations not of the survivorship type, for the doctrine of automatic completion of title does not extend to such destinations.

[45] See e.g. *Grahame v Ewen's Trustees* (1824) 2 S. 612 (NE 522); *Gillon's Trustees v Gillon* (1890) 17 R. 435; *Macdonald v Hall* (1893) 20 R. (HL) 88.

[46] *Steele v Caldwell*, 1979 S.L.T. 228; *Smith v Macintosh*, 1989 S.L.T. 148.

[47] *Board of Management of Aberdeen College v Youngson* [2005] CSOH 31; 2005 S.C. 335. See above, para.7–25.

(ii) and (iii). In sub-case (iii), the same parties (Fred and Ginger) are granters and grantees—as the Youngsons were in *Aberdeen College*. In sub-case (ii), where Brad and Jennifer dispone to Jennifer, Jennifer is, to the extent of a half share, disponing to herself. And it is *that* half share that is the main concern, for the worry would be that, if Jennifer dies, her original share might be subject to an unevacuated destination.[48] In short, in both cases the dispositions are not dispositions wholly in favour of third parties, and so their effectiveness might perhaps be questioned in the light of the *Aberdeen College* decision. For instance, the Lord Ordinary in that case says that "a deed or conveyance whereby a person purports to sell to himself does not involve any transfer nor any delivery. Without some independent third party or separate *persona*, it is no transaction at all".[49]

In fact, dispositions of types (ii) and (iii) are effective to evacuate the destination from the title. It is true that in sub-case (ii) no right of ownership is being transferred, because the grantees are already the owners. But all the parties having right are joining in altering the terms of the title.[50] Nevertheless, as matter of prudence, it seems sensible to include a clause of renunciation in the disposition—whether sub-case (ii) or (iii). A possible clause is the following:

> "And considering that hitherto we have held the said subjects as *pro indiviso* heritable proprietors under the special destination aftermentioned, and further considering that our intention is that the said special destination be wholly renounced, revoked and evacuated, as if it had never been constituted, therefore we each of us, with mutual consent, do hereby renounce, revoke and evacuate, as from the date of these presents, the survivorship destination contained in [*specify deed and details of registration*] . . ."

In practice, the disposition of type (iii) often contains a narrative clause about the intention to evacuate. That is good, but narrative is not quite the same as a *de praesenti* declaration, and so we would still suggest the use of the words of renunciation. As for dispositions of type (ii), it is not usual for the narrative to say anything about evacuation, so the addition of words of *de praesenti* renunciation is even more desirable. But all this is simply an insurance policy: it seems to us that the traditional practice is effective anyway.

The *Raeburn* trap

There exists a trap into which the unwary solicitor may fall.[51] It happens typically as follows. Adam and Eve own a house in common with a survivorship   26–21

---

[48] The *Raeburn* trap.

[49] *Board of Management of Aberdeen College v Youngson* [2005] CSOH 31; 2005 S.C. 335 at para.12.

[50] Likewise an owner can dispone to himself or herself for the purpose of *creating* a destination: see David Brand, Andrew Steven and Scott Wortley (eds), *Professor McDonald's Conveyancing Manual*, 7th edn (2004), para.12.7.

[51] First drawn to attention by an article by "GL" at 1977 S.L.T. (News) 197 and later by Johnstone, 1985 S.L.T. (News) 18. The trap's existence was confirmed by *Gardner's Exrs v Raeburn*, 1996 S.L.T. 745. For a case concerning separation agreements, in which *Gardner's Exrs* was distinguished, see *Lavery v Lavery*, 2008 Fam. L.R. 46, discussed Reid and Gretton, *Conveyancing 2008*, p.116.

destination. Adam goes off on the razzle-dazzle leaving Eve to cope with the house and the children. She sees her lawyer, he sees his lawyer, and it is agreed that he will make over his half share of the house to her. The court department of the wife's law firm send over a note to the conveyancing department asking them to draw up a conveyance. A conveyance of the half share is accordingly prepared and Adam signs it. It is registered. Eve is now owner of the whole house. A year or two later she dies. Her original half share is still subject to an unevacuated destination in favour of that scum-of-the-earth, Adam. So it passes to him. This is, one would imagine, not what had been intended when the settlement between the parties was reached.[52] From a practical point of view, the problem arises because the deal has been put together in the respective court departments of the firms, who have passed the conveyancing to the conveyancing department for implementation, without proper discussion.

If the problem comes to light while Eve is still alive and still owns the property,[53] what can be done? Adam could be approached to assist in putting matters right, by a deed renouncing the destination. Or she could dispone the property to a nominee, free of the destination.[54]

The whole problem can and should be avoided. The correct practice is for the disposition to be a disposition of the whole property, not merely Adam's half share. The disposition is granted by both Adam and Eve, with Eve as the sole disponee. This, on being registered, will wash the destination out of the title.[55]

The significance of the *Raeburn* trap has been much lessened by the rule, discussed below, that divorce evacuates any survivorship destination between the divorcing parties.

Case 5: Evacuation by divorce or dissolution

26–22 If there is a survivorship destination between spouses or civil partners, divorce or dissolution evacuates the destination.[56] This rule cannot benefit a couple who live together as if they were married, and who later part: to receive the benefits of divorce it is necessary first to get married. Nor can the rule benefit spouses who separate but who have not (yet) divorced. Of course, separation may be exactly the moment when one party, or both, wishes to make a will leaving his or her share to someone else. Yet if that person dies before the divorce, the legacy is likely to be ineffective because most destinations are non-evacuable.

THE BUYER'S POSITION

Verifying non-evacuation

26–23 Suppose that Jack and Jill take title with a survivorship destination. Jack dies. If Jill sells, how can the buyers, and the Keeper, be sure that Jack's share did

---

[52] One might seek to argue that Adam has conveyed to Eve all rights he has, and therefore he cannot retain his claim under the destination. The difficulty is that by the terms of the disposition he conveys only such rights as he has in the half share being transferred. The destination in his favour relates to the *other* half share.

[53] She can, of course, sell the property and if she does so Adam's contingent rights will fly off.

[54] i.e. Case 4 above. This may cause practical problems (but not insuperable ones) if there is a heritable security.

[55] Case 4(ii) above.

[56] Family Law (Scotland) Act 2006 s.19; Civil Partnership Act 2004 s.124A. The legislation allows the destination to opt out of the rule, but such opt-outs are unknown in practice.

indeed pass to her? That depends on establishing a negative fact, namely non-evacuation, and that can be awkward to do. They can verify from the public registers that Jack did not alienate his share *inter vivos*. They can verify the existence of the survivorship destination, and they can verify Jack's death by asking for the death certificate. But how can they be sure that Jack did not evacuate the destination by will?[57] In most cases, it is true, the destination will not have been capable of evacuation *mortis causa*, and this fact can normally be ascertained from the deed which created it. Even there, however, there is the possibility that Jill had by unregistered deed authorised Jack to evacuate, and that he did so. And Jill might have renounced her rights.[58]

The risk is fairly small. It has been suggested by Burns that when buying from someone in Jill's position "a purchaser has no duty of inquiry", which presumably means that, in a case of latent evacuation a purchaser, would be protected by good faith.[59] Whether this is correct, however, must be speculative. The Keeper expects to see either (i) written confirmation from the applicant's law firm or (ii) an affidavit from the seller that the destination was not evacuated.[60] It is difficult to see how the law firm could give the assurance under (i) unless it already had obtained (ii).

Where evacuation is by divorce or dissolution,[61] there is a statutory rule protecting good faith buyers.[62] Thus suppose Jack and Jill are spouses, and own a house with a survivorship destination. They divorce. The destination is thereby evacuated. Later Jack dies. Since the destination is no longer in force, his half share passes to his estate, not to Jill. But suppose that Jill nevertheless purports to sell the whole house to Cosmo. In that case, if Cosmo is in good faith, he obtains a good title to the whole property (in which case Jill would no doubt be liable to pay the value of Jack's half share to Jack's executors). This type of case presupposes that Jack's executors (or their successors) have not already completed title to Jack's share, for if they had done so that fact would be apparent on the face of the Land Register (or GRS) and so Cosmo could hardly be in good faith.

Verifying evacuation

Verifying evacuation is usually easier than verifying non-evacuation. But 26–24
nevertheless there may be difficult questions as to whether the power to evacuate existed, and the Keeper's policy in such cases is to "take a cautious approach".[63]

---

[57] Case 2 (above, paras 26–15 to 26–18).
[58] Case 3 (above, para.26–19).
[59] John Burns, *Conveyancing Practice*, 4th edn (1957), p.259.
[60] *Registration of Title Practice Book* ("ROTPB"), para.6.17.
[61] Case 5 (above, para.26–22).
[62] Family Law (Scotland) Act 2006 s.19(3); Civil Partnership Act 2004 s.124A(3).
[63] ROTPB, para.6.17.

CHAPTER 27

PARTNERSHIPS

Introduction

27–01 This chapter deals with ordinary partnerships[1] and limited partnerships,[2] but not with limited liability partnerships.[3]

The firm itself normally has no title

27–02 A partnership has its own separate juristic personality, distinct from its partners.[4] But this personality is more restricted than that of other juristic persons. Until relatively recently, a partnership, unlike a corporation, could not itself own land directly. Title had to be held by trustees for the firm. Whilst this restriction has been removed,[5] practice has not changed. It is more or less unknown in practice for title to immoveable property to be taken in the name of the firm itself. This chapter deals, therefore, with the normal case.

In theory it does not matter who the trustees for a firm are. They need not even be partners. The practice, however, is to appoint as the trustees some or all of the partners. If the number of partners is large, it may be unwise to make all of them trustees, for simple reasons of convenience. Being a trustee confers no real advantage on a partner. The economic interest in the firm rests on the fact of being a partner and not on the fact of being a trustee.[6]

The three levels of right

27–03 Where a partnership has immoveable property, there are three levels of right. (i) At the top level there is the title of the partners, or some of them, as trustees for the firm. Partnership title is thus merely a trust title, part of the general law of trusts. This is the master key for understanding the law. (ii) A trust must have a beneficiary, which in this case is the firm itself, as a separate juristic person. The firm thus comes in at the second level. The partners themselves are not the beneficiaries of this trust. (iii) The partners come in at the third level. They hold rights, not in the firm's property, but in the firm. Their rights are rather

---

[1] Under the Partnership Act 1890.

[2] Under the Limited Partnership Act 1907.

[3] For which see below, para.28–13.

[4] The Partnership Act 1890 ss.1 and 4(2) announces that it will use the term "partnership" to mean the *relationship* between the partners and the word "firm" to mean the separate juristic *person*. However, the rest of the Act often ignores this terminological distinction.

[5] Abolition of Feudal Tenure etc. (Scotland) Act 2000 s.70.

[6] However, in some firms, the heritable property is not partnership property at all, but is owned by one or two partners in their own interest, and merely made available to the firm.

like the rights of the members of a company.[7] A partner who is also a trustee thus appears at both the first and the third level.

The deed of trust will in the typical case be the disposition to the partners as trustees, declaring that the property is vested in the disponees in trust. The trust is a "bare trust", which is to say that the trust purposes are simply to hold for the benefit of a single beneficiary (the firm) and to dispose of the property at the direction of that beneficiary.

A trust presupposes a beneficiary. The question of whether the beneficiary of this trust is (a) the firm or (b) the partners of the firm is sometimes not properly focused.[8] Dispositions to firms sometimes state that the disponees are to hold in trust for the firm, and sometimes that they are to hold in trust both for the firm and for the partners present and future thereof. It seems open to question whether this latter style is correct. The accepted view, both traditional and modern, is that the beneficiary of the trust is the firm. To make both the firm and the partners the beneficiaries is to depart from this simple conception and may produce odd results. Thus, suppose that Mr Ant and Ms Bee take title in trust for the firm of Messrs Ant & Bee and for the partners present and future thereof. Such a clause appears to say that there are, at least at this stage, three beneficiaries, namely Messrs Ant & Bee, Mr Ant and Ms Bee. Does this mean that the beneficial right is divided into thirds? That seems to be the meaning, but it cannot be the real intention. The point might seem merely theoretical, but it could become a live one in some cases of insolvency. In addition, is it really intended that, for example, a so-called salaried partner should have a beneficial right which is ostensibly equal to that of the senior partner? On the contrary, it is the partnership agreement, and variations to it made from time to time, which does and should determine the rights and interests of the several partners.[9] Thus, the better practice is simply for the disposition to declare that the disponees hold in trust for the firm.

Of course, there is a sense in which the firm's property is held for the benefit of the partners, in the same sense as it is true to say that company property is held for the benefit of the shareholders. But a company does not hold its property in trust for the shareholders, and they are not beneficiaries in the legal sense of that term. Likewise partners, though in a functional or economic sense they may be the "owners" of the land of the firm, are not beneficiaries. The beneficiary is the firm. The role of the partners is to own the beneficiary.

Heritable property brought in by one partner

Sometmes an incoming partner brings in heritable property. This may happen either where a new partner joins an existing firm, or, more commonly, where a sole trader takes in partners and contributes the heritable property. A familiar example is where a farmer, owning his own land, takes his sons into partnership with him. In such a case the original disposition of the land cannot itself be the deed of trust. Ideally, the partnership deed should identify the land as property of the firm, and in that event the partnership deed will be the deed of trust. Sometimes the partnership deed is silent on the point, and disputes can

27–04

---

[7] Shareholders hold shares in the company, not in the company's property: see Gretton, 1987 J.R. 163.

[8] For instance J. Bennett Miller, *Law of Partnership in Scotland*, 2nd edn (by Gordon H. Brough, 1994), p.401 seems to say both that the trust is for the firm and that it is for the partners. It is difficult to see how both could be true.

[9] See Halliday, para.11–09.

then arise as to whether the land is property of the firm or not (that is, a dispute as to whether the partner with a completed title holds for himself or holds as trustee for the firm). An alternative approach would be for the incoming partner to dispone to himself and the other partners, with the disposition declaring the trust, but in the typical case this is hardly worth the effort.

Deeds granted by a firm

27–05 A disposition or other deed by a firm should not be granted simply by the firm itself, because the firm itself is not the owner.[10] The deed must be granted by the trustees. Whether all trustees with a completed title must sign, or a majority is sufficient, is a difficult and unresolved question.[11] The prudent approach is to have all sign.

Need the firm itself be a party?

27–06 The trustees with a completed title may not account for all of the current partners. If not, is it necessary that the other partners be party to the deed? It is good practice for this to be done[12] but it is not strictly necessary.[13] The partners hold as trustees for the firm, and s.2 of the Trusts (Scotland) Act 1961 enacts (in effect) that where trustees sell trust property, the purchaser's title shall not be challengeable on the ground that the sale was in breach of trust. Thus, even if the sale was without the firm's consent, a purchaser will have a good title.[14] This rule also applies to the grant of standard securities, though not to gratuitous deeds. Despite the modern rule, the pre-1961 practice of taking all current partners into the deed has continued, and this is sensible, if only to put the matter beyond dispute as between the partners themselves. Occasionally in dispositions the firm itself, as well as all the partners, is a consenter, though this is hardly necessary. In standard securities, however, the lender will usually require the personal bond element to be entered into by the firm as well as by all the partners,[15] and it is often found that the lender will expect the firm itself to be a co-granter of the security element as well.[16]

Outgoing and incoming partners

27–07 Suppose that firm X buys property, the title being taken in the name of Adam, Brenda, Charles, David and Erica, the partners at the time, as trustees for the firm. Later Adam, Brenda and Charles retire. If the firm then sells the property, can the disposition be granted by David and Erica on their own, or do the retired partners have to be brought in? The answer is the latter. Adam, Brenda and Charles are no longer partners, but they are still trustees, and hold the property as such. There is no rule of law to the effect that the trustees for a firm and its partners must be the same. It is possible to be a partner without being a trustee,

---

[10] In theory it might be but this is never the case in practice.

[11] See above, para.25–19.

[12] See Halliday, para.37–53.

[13] See Halliday, para.2–157. Banks often insist that it is done where they are the grantees of a standard security by a firm.

[14] See above, para.25–13.

[15] If the firm is personally bound, then the partners will be as well. But lenders nevertheless like all the partners to sign.

[16] If (see below) the standard security has to be signed by a former partner, the deed should be so drafted as to make it clear that that person incurs no personal liability.

and conversely a trustee without being a partner. So the fact that these persons have retired as partners has no effect on their continuing status as trustees with a completed title. They should therefore sign the deed, or resign as trustees.[17]

Just as an outgoing partner with a completed title as trustee does not cease to hold that title merely by ceasing to be a partner, so likewise an incoming partner does not become a trustee merely by becoming a partner. To become a trustee it is necessary to be assumed as such.

Resignation of trustees

It may be inconvenient to get hold of a retired partner. So the simplest way of avoiding the problem is to have outgoing partners execute a minute of resignation. By this is not meant resignation as a partner, though that will be required as well, but resignation as a trustee. This can be signed at the time as resigning as a partner. The deed should conform to s.19 of the Trusts (Scotland) Act 1921. The Act prescribes a style in Sch.A, but this often requires a certain amount of modification in partnership cases.[18] The resignation extinguishes the title of the resigning trustee,[19] trust property being held jointly rather than in common.[20] A sole trustee cannot resign. 27–08

Assumption of trustees

Resignations may excessively thin out the number of trustees with a completed title, and accordingly it may be wise from time to time to have additional partners assumed as trustees.[21] It may be convenient to modify the statutory style of deed of assumption so as to convert it into a conveyance of the specified property, from the existing trustees to themselves (unless they are at the same time resigning) and the new trustees.[22] 27–09

Dissolution

Dissolution of a partnership has no direct effect on the title, which continues to be held by the trustees. The beneficial right in the trust may pass to one partner or to a group of partners, but that is a separate issue. If the property is not to be sold, a disposition will be needed in favour of those beneficially entitled. In a typical case there will be a minute of dissolution which will regulate the matter. However, if the minute of dissolution directs that the property is to pass to a successor firm, the title could be left as it is. For, in that case, the minute of dissolution operates to assign the beneficial right to the new firm, and all that is needed is for that to be intimated to the trustees. 27–10

Does an outgoing partner need to dispone?

Even if an outgoing partner has a completed title, as trustee, it would be mistaken to grant a disposition of any particular share in the property to the 27–11

---

[17] See C. Waelde (ed.), *Professor McDonald's Conveyancing Opinions* (1998), p.16.
[18] For example, the deed of trust referred to in the style is usually the original disposition to the firm. On resignation as a trustee, see generally above, para.25–18.
[19] Trusts (Scotland) Act 1921 s.20.
[20] See above, para.25–16.
[21] 1921 Act s.21 and Sch.B. See generally above, para.25–17. To assume someone as a partner is not, in itself, to assume that person as a trustee of partnership property.
[22] This is authorised by the statutory style.

remaining or incoming partners. Title is held as joint property, not as common property, and there is no share which can be separately dealt with.[23] Although the departing partner may be handing over his or her share in the firm, that has nothing to do with the title. Hence, the only thing the outgoing partner should do is to resign as trustee at the same time as resigning as partner.

Incapacity, death, or sequestration of partners

27–12 Incapacity will normally entail ceasing to be a partner, but it does not terminate ownership. Moreover, if a guardian has been appointed, the guardian has no power to deal with trust estate. Since an *incapax* trustee cannot execute a deed of resignation, it may be necessary to have the trustee removed by the court.[24]

Death or sequestration of a partner can bring about the dissolution of the firm[25] but in practice partnership deeds commonly provide that the firm shall continue notwithstanding these events. The death of a partner extinguishes any title to heritable property. This is because trustee property is owned jointly and not in common. So any partner who has died can be left out of account entirely, though a copy of the death certificate should be put up with the titles, and the death should be narrated in the next deed. For the case where the death is of the sole, or sole surviving, partner with a completed title, see below.[26]

The sequestration of a trustee has no effect on the trust property[27] or on the bankrupt's status as trustee.[28] The bankrupt thus continues as trustee, though not usually as partner, and so will have to be one of the granters of any future deed affecting title. The trustee in sequestration has no right or title to the firm's property but only to the bankrupt partner's share in the partnership. The same is true, *mutatis mutandis*, of the case where a partner grants a trust deed for behoof of creditors.

Lapsed trust

27–13 If the sole trustee, or sole surviving trustee, dies, the result is a lapsed trust. This can be sorted out in the ordinary way, such as by a petition for new trustees under s.22 of the Trusts (Scotland) Act 1921 Act or (in most, though not all, cases) by procedure under s.6 of the Executors (Scotland) Act 1900.[29] Since a firm can itself now own heritable property,[30] s.24 of the 1921 Act could also be used, but in practice the vesting of title in the firm is usually regarded as undesirable.

Contracting out

27–14 It has been said above that an outgoing partner does not cease to be a trustee, unless he or she resigns as such, and likewise that an incoming partner does not become a trustee, unless assumed as such. Could these rules be contracted out

---

[23] See above, para.25–16.
[24] Under s.23 of the Trusts (Scotland) Act 1921.
[25] Partnership Act 1890 s.33.
[26] See below, para.27–13.
[27] Bankruptcy (Scotland) Act 1985 s.33.
[28] Though a bankrupt cannot be a trustee of a charitable trust: Charities and Trustee Investment (Scotland) Act 2005 2005 s.69.
[29] See above, para.25–11; Halliday, para.37–32.
[30] Abolition of Feudal Tenure etc. (Scotland) Act 2000 s.70.

of? In other words, could it be provided that every resigning partner (or partner becoming insane) should automatically cease to be a trustee, and that every incoming partner automatically be deemed to be assumed as trustee? These are difficult questions. One possibility might be for every partner for the time being to be treated as a trustee *ex officio*. Indeed, if this could be done it would not even be necessary for future partners to complete title or deduce title, because of the provisions of s.45 of the Conveyancing (Scotland) Act 1874. But all this seems speculative and risky.

Might there be a consensual provision that an outgoing partner would automatically cease to be a trustee? In principle this might seem unobjectionable, but again it cannot be recommended in practice. There seems to be no authority for such a device. Moreover, s.19 of the Trusts (Scotland) Act 1921 presupposes that any resignation by a trustee will be a resignation *de praesenti* whereas the suggested idea would involve a resignation *de futuro*.[31]

Bankruptcy of firm

A partnership may be sequestrated as such, either with or without the seques- 27–15
tration of its individual partners.[32] The firm's trustee in sequestration probably cannot grant a disposition of its heritable property; rather the disposition must be granted by the trustees for the firm. This seems unsatisfactory in a practical sense, especially if the trustees are themselves bankrupt, as is likely to be the case. It might be argued, on the other side, that s.31 of the Bankruptcy (Scotland) Act 1985 vests the property in the trustee. But what is vested? Vesting is *tantum et tale* and what the firm had was not title but only a beneficial right.[33] Again, it might be argued that the sequestration of the firm dissolves it and so each partner is deemed to have a share. But this is probably not an accurate way of stating the position.[34] In addition, even if true it would take us no further because title would still be stuck inside a trust; all that would have changed would have been the identity of the beneficiary.

Where a firm is sequestrated, it often happens that the partners are also sequestrated, or grant trust deeds, and it commonly happens that the insolvency practitioner who is trustee of the firm is also trustee for the partners. Will this fact be of assistance? Probably not. For a bankruptcy trustee has no right to deal with property which is vested in the bankrupt only in trust.[35] The result may seem absurd: an insolvency practitioner who is trustee for the bankrupt firm and also for all the bankrupt partners is nevertheless unable to grant a disposition of the firm's property. And no doubt for that reason the firm's trustee in sequestration does sometimes grant the disposition,[36] without getting the trustee-partners to sign. Yet, if the argument outlined above is correct, this procedure is improper. The practical advice is that the disposition should be signed, not only by the firm's trustee in sequestration, but also by those trustees

---

[31] Which is probably, but not certainly, competent.

[32] Bankruptcy (Scotland) Act 1985 s.6.

[33] If Ms Smith is a beneficiary under her aunt's trust, and is sequestrated, no one would suggest that the title held by the aunt's trustees could pass to Ms Smith's trustee in sequestration.

[34] There is authority that a sequestrated firm still exists as a juristic *persona*, the effect of sequestration being to dissolve the contract rather than the personality: see *Stewart & Macdonald v Brown* (1898) 25 R. 1042. But see also *Balmer v HM Advocate*, 2008 S.L.T. 799.

[35] See above, para.27–12.

[36] In a GRS case, deducing title through the act and warrant.

with a completed title, even if themselves bankrupt. This may be unsatisfactory from the practical point of view, but in the absence of any clear provision on the point in the legislation, and in the apparent absence of authority, it seems the wise approach. The trustees with a completed title would be under an obligation to co-operate.[37]

---

[37] See further William W. McBryde, *Bankruptcy*, 2nd edn (1995), paras 9.62–9.65.

CHAPTER 28

COMPANIES AND LIMITED LIABILITY PARTNERSHIPS

Introduction

This chapter deals with companies and, briefly, with limited liability partner- 28–01
ships. The last of these is included in this chapter because, despite its name, it
is more like a company than a partnership.

Scottish companies are registered at the Companies Office in Edinburgh.
English and Welsh companies are registered at the Companies Office at
Cardiff. In law these are separate. But for most administrative purposes they
function as a single entity, and indeed Edinburgh is now called a mere "regional
office", a description as unsound in law as true in substance. There is a single
website,[1] which does not reveal that it is the website of two separate
registrars.

In this chapter we speak of the "Companies Register". The term is wrong but
convenient. The legislation nowhere names the register. Each company has its
own file, now held in digital form.[2] The legislation does name a "Register of
Charges" in respect of security rights,[3] suggesting that there is a single
"Register of Charges", used by all companies, rather than—as is the case—a
separate "Register of Charges" for each company. So there are, confusingly,
countless "Registers of Charges" but no "Companies Register". Solicitors
often request the searchers to search in the "Register of Charges", but that is
insufficient because such a search will not disclose important information,
such as liquidation, that is kept in *another* part of the company file. In practice,
however, searchers will normally report back if there has been, for example, a
liquidation, even though not expressly so asked, because they are aware of the
irrationality of the official terminology.

Intra vires and *ultra vires*

The *ultra vires* doctrine has been abolished as far as its *external* effect is 28–02
concerned: "The validity of an act done by a company shall not be called into
question on the ground of lack of capacity by reason of anything in the company's constitution".[4] So those dealing with a company need not concern themselves with the question of whether the company is acting within its powers.
Good or bad faith is irrelevant. But the doctrine still applies *internally*. The
directors must not breach the company's constitution.

---

[1] *http://www.companieshouse.gov.uk*.
[2] Originally they were kept in paper form, later in microfiche, and since 2002 digitally.
[3] Companies Act 2006 s.885.
[4] Companies Act 2006 s.39. The change dates back to the Companies Act 1989.

Whilst the external aspect of the doctrine has been abolished, there remain some qualifications. Three in particular are worth noting. The first is that the abolition applies only to companies. Most other juristic persons are still subject to the common law rules about *ultra vires*.[5] The second is that charitable companies were excepted from the abolition, so that the external aspect of the *ultra vires* rule still applies to them.[6] The third is that any "substantial property transaction" between a company and one of its directors needs the approval of the company in general meeting,[7] which failing it is voidable.[8] This requirement, to which there are certain qualifications,[9] is sometimes overlooked.[10]

Powers of directors and the exercise of those powers

28–03 The directors act for the company. But they do not have that power individually. Company law sees the directors as a collective entity, namely the board. The board is the "organ" by which the company acts.[11] An individual director can act for the company only insofar as power has been conferred—which, of course, is common in practice.[12]

Tension exists between the rules of company law, which have just been outlined, and the rules about execution of deeds in the Requirements of Writing (Scotland) Act 1995.[13] Schedule 2 para.3(1) of the 1995 Act says that "where the granter of a document is a company, the document is signed by the company if it is signed on its behalf by a director, or by the secretary . . . or by a person authorised to sign . . .". Suppose that an offer is made to a company to buy some land. The board of directors meets. By a five-to-one majority, the vote is not to accept. The dissident director signs a letter of acceptance on behalf of the company. Is there a contract of sale?[14] Company law says no, but the 1995 Act seems to say yes. In practice the counterparty (the buyer in the example) may insist on seeing a certified copy of a board resolution, especially in higher-value transactions. The law may perhaps be that *decisions* must be made by the board (or by a person duly authorised by the board), but that the *implementation* of the decision can be by a single signature. That would lead to the conclusion that in the example there is no contract. However it is far from certain that this is indeed the law.[15]

---

[5] For a striking example, see *Piggins & Rix Ltd v Montrose Port Authority*, 1995 S.L.T. 418.

[6] Companies Act 1989 s.112. For English companies see s.42.

[7] Companies Act 2006 s.190 and following.

[8] Companies Act 2006 s.195.

[9] See generally ss.190–196.

[10] See e.g. *Micro Leisure Ltd v County Properties & Developments Ltd*, 1999 S.C. 501.

[11] The other organ is the general meeting, considered as an entity rather than as an event.

[12] Thus a "managing" director has general powers. An individual director can also bind the company if he or she has ostensible authority: see e.g. *Freeman & Lockyer v Buckhurst Park Properties* [1964] 1 All E.R. 630.

[13] A similar issue can in principle arise in partnership law: see the Law Commission and Scottish Law Commission, Report on *Partnership Law* (Scot. Law Com. No.192, 2003), paras 9.88, 9.93 and 9.97.

[14] The tension between company law and the 1995 Act becomes even greater if the acceptance was signed by the company secretary. In the eyes of company law the role of company secretaries is administrative.

[15] The discussion in the text has focussed on validity rather than probativity. Conveyancing deeds by companies will in practice be probative. For execution of deeds by companies, see above, para.17–18.

It can happen that while an act is within the powers of the company, the directors exceed their powers as laid down in the company's constitution. Here again, however, the legislation will, in general, protect a third party: "In favour of a person dealing with a company in good faith, the power of the directors to bind the company, or authorise others to do so, is deemed to be free of any limitation under the company's constitution".[16] Though the protection requires good faith, a person "is not to be regarded as acting in bad faith by reason only of his knowing that an act is beyond the powers of the directors under the company's constitution",[17] a provision which leaves one wondering whether "good faith" could ever be absent.

Designing the company

Juristic persons, like natural persons, must be designed in conveyancing deeds.[18] Traditionally, companies were designed by name and registered office. Whilst legally sufficient, during the 1990s this came to be regarded as less than best practice, which is to include the registration number as well. The main reason for this is that companies can change their names fairly easily,[19] and can even assume names previously held by other companies. It is even possible for companies to swap names, and this does sometimes happen, especially between connected companies.[20] Since such companies typically share the same registered office, the risks of confusion are obvious. Thus the fact that property is registered in the Land Register as having been bought by Zykkzyn Ltd of 1 Aristotle Square, Leeds LS44 MUG and is now being offered for sale by Zykkzyn Ltd of 1 Aristotle Square, Leeds LS44 MUG proves nothing. By contrast, a company registration number is a birthmark.

When acting for a company it is important to get the name right, in two senses. In the first place, the name must be the precise name of a registered company. This is obvious, but companies themselves sometimes get their own names wrong, for instance on their printed stationery. In the second place, a single economic enterprise often comprises several different companies, often with similar names and the same registered office. The human beings involved are sometimes vague as to which company is buying, taking a lease, etc. and indeed often do not realise that the matter has any significance. So when a local businessman says that he wants "his company" to buy some land, it should be realised that there may be several companies and the right one must be identified. Likewise when there are instructions to buy land for the "Stair & Erskine Group".

The traditional view is that a more exacting standard has to be applied to company names than to the names of natural persons, so that even very minor errors may be fatal. In an Opinion which has become well-known, Professor Halliday stated that the mere omission of an apostrophe in the name of the disponing company was fatal.[21] Nowadays the attitude of the courts in non-conveyancing matters is that an error in company designation is not fatal so

28–04

---

[16] Companies Act 2006 s.40(1).

[17] Companies Act 2006 s.40(2)(b)(iii).

[18] See above, para.11–06.

[19] And can also change the registered office.

[20] See *FJ Neale (Glasgow) Ltd v Vickery*, 1973 S.L.T. (Sh. Ct) 88. It is unsatisfactory that the law allows this sort of thing.

[21] D.J. Cusine (ed.), *The Conveyancing Opinions of Professor J. M. Halliday* (1992), p.265. And see C. Waelde (ed.), *Professor McDonald's Conveyancing Opinions* (1998), p.14.

long as nobody has been misled.[22] But the reported cases involve only immediate parties, whereas in conveyancing the class of parties who might now or later be misled is indefinitely large, and incapable of being fully ascertained. The law seems to us unsettled.

Registration of charges[23]

28–05 When a company grants a standard security it must be registered not only in the Land Register, or General Register of Sasines ("GRS"), but also in the Companies Register.[24] The latter must happen within "21 days beginning with the day after the day on which the charge is created".[25] Since a standard security ("charge") is created on registration in the Land Register (or GRS), the 21 days begin to run on the day after the registration. Failure to register in the Companies Register will cause the security to become ineffective,[26] though the debt secured remains a valid debt. Registration out of time is possible but only with the authority of the court.[27] If this happens, then the sequence is: (i) the security becomes effective on registration in the Land Register; (ii) after 21 days it becomes ineffective; (iii) if later registered on the authority of the court it becomes effective again. This authority is not always granted, and, when it is granted, is generally subject to conditions. If a law firm realises that it has failed to make timeous registration it should, in the typical case, petition the court immediately. Failure to register is a common error, and amounts to negligence. Of course if the company remains solvent, there lender will suffer no loss anyway.

When the Keeper registers a standard security in the Land Register, its validity can be guaranteed only if it is duly registered in the Companies Register. Hence the certificate issued by the Registrar of Companies[28] confirming due registration should be exhibited to the Keeper. Without it the Keeper would exclude indemnity for the security in respect of the possibility of its non-registration in the Companies Register. Of course, the certificate cannot be produced at the time of registration in the Land Register, because registration in the Companies Register happens after registration in the Land Register. But the gap should be only a matter of days.

Buying from a company: the search

28–06 When taking a deed from a company it is necessary to make sure that the company is duly incorporated and is not in insolvency. The main dangers are: (i) striking off,[29] (ii) liquidation, (iii) receivership, and (iv) administration. All these can be checked by a search in the company file at the Companies Office,

---

[22] See for example *Ben Cleuch Estates Ltd v Scottish Enterprise*, 2008 S.C. 252; and *AWD Chase De Vere Wealth Management Ltd v Melville Street Properties Ltd* [2009] CSOH 150; 2010 S.C.L.R. 521.

[23] For details see Gretton, (2002) 6 Edin. L.R. 146.

[24] Companies Act 2006 s.878. But see below, para.28–14.

[25] Companies Act 2006 s.886(1)(a).

[26] Companies Act 2006 s.889. In fact the section says that the security is "void . . . against (a) the liquidator . . . (b) an administrator . . . and (c) any creditor . . .". The meaning is obscure.

[27] 2006 Act s.888(2).

[28] 2006 Act s.885.

[29] 2006 Act s.1000.

which can be obtained through independent searchers or online.[30] A company search is also needed if the property is in the GRS and a company has held title during the prescriptive progress. Company searches are available in both interim and final form, so that the interim report can be seen on the eve of settlement and the final report a few weeks later.

Length of search

The usual practice is to ask for a search against the selling company beginning 28–07
from the date of the company's incorporation, or October 27, 1961, whichever is the later,[31] and ending 22 days after the registration of the disposition. This period is calculated to ensure that anything which has happened before the registration of the disposition will have had time to enter the company file. If the company being searched against is not the current seller, but a previous owner, it is necessary only to search up to 22 days after the date when the disposition granted by that company was registered.

What is being searched for?

Standard securities will be disclosed by the Companies Search, but they will in 28–08
any case be known from the form 10 or 12 report. Floating charges will also be disclosed, but they, in principle, should not matter to a buyer since they do not prevent the company from selling, and such sale will automatically discharge the floating charge in relation to the subjects sold. This is one of the key differences between a standard security and a floating charge: a standard security is a real right and thus attaches to the property, even if ownership changes, but a floating charge is not a real right unless and until it crystallises. However, there are two dangers for a buyer. The first is that floating charges often have a clause forbidding the company from selling its immoveable property without the chargeholder's consent. No one knows whether such a clause could prejudice a buyer's title,[32] but equally no one would wish to take the risk of it. The second danger is that the charge might have attached (crystallised) by liquidation or receivership,[33] a subject to which we will shortly return.

The memorandum for search should thus seek information about registered charges, liquidation, receivership, and also about administration. It should further inquire whether the company has been struck off.[34] Lastly, it is common to ask the searchers to report the names of the registered directors and secretary. This is to enable the buyer to be sure that the disposition is signed by persons authorised to sign it.[35] However, this step is not usually taken where the company is large and well-known.

---

[30] The Keeper does not provide company searches.

[31] October 27, 1961 is the date when charges first became registrable.

[32] *Trade Development Bank v Warriner & Mason (Scotland) Ltd*, 1980 S.C. 74 could be used to argue that a buyer would be affected, but the argument is not conclusive. The subject is difficult. It might be argued that a prohibition on alienation is ineffective as repugnant to the essence of a floating charge.

[33] Companies Act 1985 s.463; Insolvency Act 1986 s.53.

[34] Under s.1000 of the Companies Act 2006. This is common.

[35] Companies must register the names of the current directors and secretary: Companies Act 2006 ss.167 and 276. There is an argument that a purchaser in good faith would be protected if the signatories of the disposition were not properly appointed, but the issue is complex and a search on the point is a sensible precaution.

Certificate of non-crystallisation

28–09 As already mentioned, a floating charge is automatically discharged on a sale of property, provided that it has not already attached (crystallised).[36] This is because a floating charge can affect only that which belongs to the debtor company. The effect of attachment is to convert the floating charge into a "fixed" charge, which is a real right, so that the company can no longer alienate property free of the charge. The buyer should ask for[37] a certificate from the chargeholder certifying that the charge has not attached, and also that it will not be made to attach for a stated period, such as 21 days from the date of the certificate.[38] This is called a "certificate of non-crystallisation". Since it is common in a floating charge to have a clause forbidding sale of immoveable property without the consent of the chargeholder, it is advisable for the certificate to contain such a consent as well. Banks are often prepared to go further and grant a certificate which actually releases the property being sold from the ambit of the floating charge. This is slightly preferable, because, unlike a classic certificate of non-crystallisation, it is not fettered by a time limit, so that if there is a delay in settling the transaction, there is no need to go back to the bank for a fresh certificate.

The problems in this area (from the standpoint of a buyer from a company) have been considerably lessened by the decision of the House of Lords in *Sharp v Thomson*,[39] holding that when a selling company delivers the disposition, the property is deemed to be released from the ambit of the floating charge.

Letter of obligation and certificate of solvency

28–10 Although a selling company's law firm will grant a standard letter of obligation in the usual way, this will not normally cover the company search, for the final company search might contain an entry, such as liquidation, which did not show up on the interim report and so was undetectable by the law firm.[40] Where possible, therefore, the practice is to require some or all of the directors to grant what is sometimes called a "certificate of solvency", guaranteeing that the company is not insolvent and will not become so prior to the registration of the grantee's title.[41]

Lending to a company on standard security

28–11 Although a floating charge will not, subject to some qualifications, concern a purchaser from a company, it will usually concern someone taking a standard security. This is because floating charges usually have a clause whereby future standard securities are postponed to the floating charge.[42] It is, therefore,

---

[36] The two terms mean the same. The first is Scottish, and the second English, but the English term is widely used.

[37] And stipulate for in the missives.

[38] For an example, see John H. Sinclair and Euan Sinclair, *Handbook of Conveyancing Practice in Scotland*, 5th edn (2006), p.175.

[39] *Sharp v Thomson*, 1997 S.C. (HL) 66.

[40] For letters of obligation, see above, para.9–25.

[41] For an example, see John H. Sinclair and Euan Sinclair, *Handbook of Conveyancing Practice in Scotland*, 5th edn (2006), p.174.

[42] Companies Act 1985 s.464(1) (prospectively replaced by s.40 of the Bankruptcy and Diligence (Scotland) Act 2007).

particularly important for the lender to ascertain whether any prior floating charge has been granted, and if so, on what terms. Since a floating charge can be registered up to 21 days after its creation there exists a potential blind period.[43]

Foreign companies

The company may not be Scottish but incorporated elsewhere, such as in England, France, Liechtenstein, the Isle of Man, or the Cayman Islands.[44] How can one be sure that it is not dissolved or being dissolved or otherwise unable to give good title? And how can one know whether the persons signing the disposition are authorised to do so on behalf of the company? If the company is from outside the United Kingdom, it is advisable to see an "opinion letter" letter from a law firm in the country concerned,[45] certifying that the company is duly incorporated, and so forth. Since styles for such letters are difficult to find, we offer the following, which is for a secured loan, but which may be adapted according to circumstances: 28–12

"So far as we are aware, having made due enquiry:

(i) The borrower is a corporation with full juristic personality, and is duly incorporated, duly organised, validly existing and in good standing under the laws of Ruritania. Its corporate existence is not limited in time.

(ii) The execution, delivery and performance by the borrower of the [loan agreement] [personal bond] [other] and standard security are within the borrower's corporate powers, have been duly authorised by all necessary corporate action and they do not contravene (a) the constitution of the borrower (whether in the form of memorandum and articles of association, charter, bye-laws corporate statutes or otherwise) or (b) any legislative provision (whether statute, regulation, enactment or otherwise) or rule of law in force under the laws of Ruritania.

(iii) No authorisation or approval (including exchange control approval) or other action by, and no notice to, or filing or registration with, any governmental, administrative or other public agency, authority or court is required under the laws of Ruritania, except for [*specify*] which have been duly obtained or made and are in full force and effect.

(iv) Any decree obtained in the Scottish courts by the lender against the borrower in relation to said [loan agreement] [personal bond] [other] and standard security would be accorded full faith and credit under the laws of Ruritania.

(v) The persons signing the [loan agreement] [personal bond] [other] and standard security namely [*specify*] are duly authorised to do so on behalf of the borrower under the laws of Ruritania.

---

[43] See *AIB Finance v Bank of Scotland*, 1993 S.C. 588. When Pt 2 of the Bankruptcy and Diligence etc. (Scotland) Act 2007 comes into force, there will be a more rational system, namely that a floating charge will come into existence on registration, and not, as under current law, before registration.

[44] For the Keeper's views, see Beveridge, (2008) 53 J.L.S.S. Nov./17.

[45] Or from the foreign company's Scottish solicitors, if they are prepared to do so.

(vi) No insolvency proceedings have been opened against the borrower in the courts of Ruritania, or in any public agency or authority with power to open insolvency proceedings, and no other orders have been issued by any Ruritanian court or public agency or authority which could prejudice the effectiveness of the [loan agreement] [personal bond] [other] and standard security."[46]

Obtaining such a letter will increase costs, but that is because a foreign company has decided to involve itself in Scottish heritable property. The costs will be borne by the company itself.

The question of how a foreign company should execute a deed is discussed elsewhere.[47]

Limited liability partnerships

28–13 Limited liability partnerships ("LLPs") have full juristic personality, and are more akin to companies than to ordinary partnerships or limited partnerships.[48] Like companies, they come into being by registration.[49] Like companies, they have a registered office and a registered number, and so should be designed in deeds by name, number and registered office. If they acquire heritable property, they do so in their own name, like companies. The *ultra vires* doctrine does not apply.[50] Unlike companies, but like ordinary partnerships, each member acts on behalf of the firm. Thus in LLPs there is nothing that precisely corresponds to the board of directors of a company. Even if the partner exceeds his or her authority, the firm is bound, unless the counterparty was in bad faith.[51] LLPs can grant security rights, including standard securities and floating charges,[52] in the same way as companies, and the rules about registration of charges apply to LLPs as they do to companies.

The future

28–14 Two pieces of legislation already on the statute book but not yet activated are worth noting. One is Pt 2 of the Bankruptcy and Diligence etc. (Scotland) Act 2007, which, when brought into force, will repeal and replace the current legislation on floating charges. Under the Act, floating charges will come into existence on registration, a great improvement on the current rule, and registration itself will be in a new register, the Register of Floating Charges. The other piece of legislation is s.893 of the Companies Act 2006. This enables the Secretary of State to make an order whereby, once a security right has been created by registration (e.g. a standard security by registration in the Land Register), no *separate* registration in the Companies Register will be

---

[46] There is no such thing as a perfect style, and no doubt this style would be susceptible of improvement.

[47] See above, para.17–24.

[48] "The law relating to partnerships does not apply to a limited liability partnership": Limited Liability Partnerships Act 2000 s.1(5).

[49] The LLPs Register is kept by the Registrar of Companies.

[50] "A limited liability partnership has unlimited capacity": Limited Liability Partnerships Act 2000 s.1(3).

[51] Limited Liability Partnerships Act 2000 s.6.

[52] Limited Liability Partnerships (Scotland) Regulations 2001 (SSI 2001/128).

necessary. Instead, the registrar of the first register (here, the Keeper) would notify the Registrar of Companies, who would then note the security in the latter register. The net effect would be that the information would still be obtainable from two sources (Land Register and Companies Register) but that, as far as the creditor is concerned, only one registration would be needed.

CHAPTER 29

INSOLVENCY

Introduction

29–01 This chapter deals mainly with purchases from an insolvent estate. Purchases from a heritable creditor are dealt with elsewhere.[1] The subject is complex and we give only an outline.[2] Five forms of insolvency are considered, namely (i) sequestration, (ii) trust deeds for behoof of creditors, (iii) liquidation, (iv) receivership and (v) administration.

Sequestration

29–02 Sequestration can be applied for by the debtor or by a creditor. In either case a notice is registered in the Personal Register.[3] Unless the petition is by the debtor, the entry is a "warrant to cite", which means only that the petition has been presented, not that sequestration has happened or will happen, or, to use the technical term, "be awarded".[4] Thus the entry may mean that there has been a sequestration, or it may mean only that there has been an application for sequestration. In either case the entry has the effect of an inhibition.[5]

If the award is by the court, it is called the "act and warrant", if by the accountant in bankruptcy, the "determination"; but in either case it is a conveyance to the trustee (who in some cases will be the Accountant in Bankruptcy) of the bankrupt's assets. It is a general conveyance, which is to say that no property is individually identified.[6] The effect is to vest all the debtor's property in the trustee, but, as far as heritable property is concerned, this is like a disposition which has been delivered but not registered: the trustee is not owner but merely an unregistered holder.[7] As such, the trustee can sell without first completing title, although it is open to the trustee to complete title, and this is commoner than it once was.[8] If the property is still in the GRS, this

---

[1] See above, paras 22–36 and 22–37.

[2] For insolvency law generally, see William W. McBryde, *Bankruptcy*, 2nd edn (1995); Donna McKenzie Skene, *Insolvency Law in Scotland* (1999); J.B. St Clair and J.E. Drummond Young, *Law of Corporate Insolvency in Scotland*, 3rd edn (2004); J.H. Greene and I.M. Fletcher, *Law and Practice of Receivership in Scotland*, 3rd edn (2005).

[3] Bankruptcy (Scotland) Act 1985 s.14. The Personal Register is the Register of Inhibitions and Adjudications, which will be re-named the Register of Inhibitions once ss.79 and 80 of the Bankruptcy and Diligence etc. (Scotland) Act 2007 (abolishing adjudication for debt) come into force.

[4] The interlocutor granting the petition is delightfully called the award of sequestration. Congratulations, Jimmy, you're bust.

[5] Bankruptcy (Scotland) Act 1985 s.14(2).

[6] See above, para.24–03.

[7] See above, paras 24–02 to 24–04.

[8] The benefits (for the creditors) are strikingly illustrated by *Burnett's Tr v Grainger* [2004] UKHL 8; 2004 S.C. (HL) 19. See also above, para.24–06.

means recording a notice of title, deducing title through the act and warrant, or the determination, as the midcouple.[9]

Everything acquired by the bankrupt after sequestration also passes to the trustee. But eventually—normally after one year—the bankrupt is discharged,[10] which means that anything acquired thereafter may be kept, even though the debts have not been paid in full. The discharge of the bankrupt does not, however, mean that any assets which the trustee has not realised return to the ex-bankrupt. Unless they have been "abandoned" by the trustee, unrealised assets remain subject to the sequestration. Thus the trustee can sell them even after the bankrupt's discharge. However, if there is unrealised heritable property, and if the trustee has neither completed title nor renewed the statutory inhibition,[11] the bankrupt will be able to deal with such property again.[12] This state of affairs might seem unlikely to crop up in practice, but it sometimes does.

Occasionally an undischarged bankrupt acquires heritable property and grants a security over it. Although the law is unsettled, it seems likely that the security is invalid.[13] If so, then the general creditors take a windfall gain, because the acquired property falls under the sequestration.[14]

As well as acting as trustee in many cases, the Accountant in Bankruptcy also administers the Register of Insolvencies and generally oversees the bankruptcy system.[15] The Register of Insolvencies, which is available online, has more information about sequestrations, and trust deeds, than does the Personal Register.

Buying from a trustee in sequestration

The key document in a sequestration is the act and warrant, or the determination, vesting the estate in the trustee. Accordingly, the buyer must see this, and the Keeper too will require to see it.[16] It constitutes the midcouple for conveyancing purposes.[17] Unless the trustee is the Accountant in Bankruptcy, it is good practice for the buyer to require evidence that the trustee is a qualified insolvency practitioner.[18] It is likewise prudent to ensure that there has been due registration in the Personal Register.[19] Any outstanding heritable security must be discharged. This can be done either by an ordinary discharge or by the

29–03

---

[9] See above, para.24–05.

[10] Bankruptcy (Scotland) Act 1985 s.54.

[11] Bankruptcy (Scotland) Act 1985 s.14(4). The renewal must be registered timeously: *Roy's Trustee, Noter*, 2000 S.L.T. (Sh. Ct) 77; *Tewnion's Trustee, Noter*, 2000 S.L.T. (Sh. Ct) 37. For discussion see Reid and Gretton, *Conveyancing 2000*, pp.101–03. Whilst there is a deadline for the registration of a s.14 renewal, there is no deadline for the alternative, which is to complete title.

[12] This rule has two separate statutory bases: Conveyancing (Scotland) Act 1924 s.44, and Bankruptcy (Scotland) Act 1985 s.39A. The precise formulations in each case are not quite the same.

[13] See *Alliance & Leicester Building Society v Murray's Trustee*, 1994 S.C.L.R. 19; *Royal Bank of Scotland Plc v Lamb's Trustee*, 1998 S.C.L.R. 923; *Halifax Plc v Gorman's Trustee*, 2000 S.L.T. 1409. For discussion see Reid and Gretton, *Conveyancing 2000*, pp.98–101.

[14] Bankruptcy (Scotland) Act 1985 s.32.

[15] *http://www.aib.gov.uk/*.

[16] *Registration of Title Practice Book* ("ROTPB"), para.5.40.

[17] For midcouples, see above, para.24–09.

[18] Insolvency Act 1986 s.388.

[19] Under s.14 of the Bankruptcy (Scotland) Act 1985.

consent of the heritable creditor embodied in the disposition by the trustee.[20] However, inhibitions against the bankrupt need not be discharged.[21]

If the property is residential, there is the problem of s.40 of the Bankruptcy (Scotland) Act 1985, which provides that, where the property is a family home (as defined), the trustee must obtain certain consents before selling.[22] The section does not make it clear what happens if the trustee sells without such consents: the cautious purchaser must assume the worst.[23] There are practical problems here. What happens if the trustee has not obtained consents on the view that they are not needed? How can the purchaser be satisfied? How can the trustee show that the house was not a "family home"? There seems to be no neat solution. In practice a written assurance from the trustee should be acceptable, and is acceptable to the Keeper.[24]

Trust deeds for behoof of creditors

29–04 A trust deed for behoof of creditors is similar to sequestration but is voluntary and extrajudicial. The applicable legislation is the Protected Trust Deeds (Scotland) Regulations 2008 (as amended).[25] The deed that the debtor signs is a general conveyance to the trustee.[26] As in a sequestration, the beneficiaries of the trust are the creditors. As in a sequestration, the trustee can complete title or sell without having done so. A trust deed is said to be "protected" if certain procedures have successfully been gone through, meaning that the creditors cannot challenge it.[27] Protected status can be vetoed by a majority of creditors, counting by head, or by a third, counting by value.[28] A protected trust deed must appear in the Register of Insolvencies.[29] In practice, if a trust deed does not acquire protected status it is likely that there will be a sequestration.

If a trust deed excludes property, it could not, until 2010, acquire protected status. The position now is that a trust deed can be protected even if it excludes the family home.[30] The creditors can, of course, veto such a trust deed. But the house may have a security over it for a debt so large that there is little equity (perhaps none at all). If so, the general creditors have little interest in it, while the secured creditor can still if necessary enforce against the property. The practical point for a potential buyer is that the trustee under a trust deed may not have power to sell the house.

---

[20] In such a case either the trustee or the heritable creditor can sell. There is a procedure for determining which it is to be, but the purchaser is protected from any failure to go through that procedure properly: Bankruptcy (Scotland) Act 1985 s.39(7). If the heritable creditor sells, the disposition does not require the trustee's consent.

[21] Bankruptcy (Scotland) Act 1985 s.31(2); ROTPB, para.6.25. See also above, para.9–22.

[22] See generally William W. McBryde, *Bankruptcy*, 2nd edn (1995), paras 9–66 et seq. See also above, para.10–18.

[23] See William W. McBryde, *Bankruptcy*, 2nd edn (1995), para.9–79.

[24] ROTPB, para.5.42.

[25] SSI 2008/143, as amended by the Protected Trust Deeds (Scotland) Amendment Regulations (SSI 2010/298).

[26] See above, para.24–03.

[27] Protected Trust Deeds (Scotland) Regulations 2008 reg.11.

[28] Protected Trust Deeds (Scotland) Regulations 2008 reg.9.

[29] Protected Trust Deeds (Scotland) Regulations 2008 reg.10.

[30] Home Owner and Debtor Protection (Scotland) Act 2010 s.10 (amending s.5(4A) of the Bankruptcy (Scotland) Act 1985); Protected Trust Deeds (Scotland) Amendment Regulations (SSI 2010/298).

Buying from a trustee under a trust deed

The key document in a trust for behoof of creditors is the trust deed itself 29–05
which, as a general conveyance, is also a midcouple.[31] The deed must be
checked to ensure that heritable property is not excluded.[32] Unlike sequestrations, a trust deed is presumably a "dealing" which is potentially subject to the
occupancy rights of a non-entitled spouse or civil partner, with the result that
appropriate documentation may be required.[33] Lastly, a buyer may wish to
stipulate that the trust deed be a protected one. This is not necessary, but unprotected trust deeds can be awkward to deal with. Provided that it is so protected,
it is not necessary that any inhibitions against the bankrupt be discharged.[34]
However, any outstanding heritable security must be discharged. Evidence
should be obtained that the seller is a qualified insolvency practitioner.

Liquidation

Liquidation (also called winding up) is governed by the Insolvency Act 1986. 29–06
It is made subject to much of the law relating to sequestrations, which it therefore resembles in many but by no means all respects. Unlike sequestration,
liquidation is available for solvent as well as insolvent companies. Again,
whereas sequestration is always judicial, liquidation can be either judicial
("compulsory liquidation" or "winding up by the court") or extrajudicial
("voluntary liquidation"). The two divisions do not coincide: both solvent and
insolvent companies can go into either kind of liquidation. Another difference
is that whereas in sequestration there is a conveyance to the trustee (even if the
trustee may often choose not to complete title upon that conveyance), in liquidation there is no such conveyance.[35] What happens is that the liquidator
replaces the board of directors and in that way assumes control over the
company's assets. A company in liquidation still exists as a juristic person:
dissolution happens at the end of liquidation.

In a winding up by the court, an interim liquidator is appointed, like the
interim trustee in sequestration. In addition, there may be a provisional liquidator, who can be appointed to manage a company while a liquidation petition
is being considered by the court. Thus, the existence of a provisional liquidator
means that the company is not in liquidation, but that it soon may be. The fact
of liquidation appears in the Companies Register and in the Register of
Insolvencies,[36] but not in the Personal Register.

---

[31] For midcouples, see above, para.24–09.

[32] See the previous paragraph.

[33] See above, paras 10–05 et seq.

[34] See above, para.9–22.

[35] But see below, para.29–07 for cases where the company property is vested in the liquidator.

[36] Insolvency Act 1986 s.84(3) (winding-up resolutions); Insolvency Act 1986 s.130(1), read
with Scotland Act 1998 Sch.8 para.23(2), (3) (winding-up orders). In addition, the actual appointment of the liquidator must be registered in the Register of Insolvencies (Insolvency (Scotland)
Rules 1986 rr.4.18 and 4.19) and the Companies Register (Insolvency Act 1986 s.109). The registration provisions for company insolvency are primitive. Some recommendations for improvement
were made in the Scottish Law Commission's Report on *Sharp v Thomson* (Scot. Law Com.
No.208 (2007)) but the law remains in its unreformed state.

Buying from a liquidator

29–07 In a compulsory liquidation, the key document is the interlocutor ordering liquidation—the winding-up order. In a voluntary liquidation, the key document is the special resolution of the company. In either case the buyer must examine the document. The interlocutor or resolution should have been registered in the Companies Register. A winding-up order should also have been registered in the Register of Insolvencies. The liquidator's appointment should have been registered in the Companies Register and in the Register of Insolvencies. Evidence should be obtained as to the liquidator's status as an insolvency practitioner, as for sequestrations. Outstanding heritable securities must be discharged, for, as with sequestrations, a liquidator has no power to sell property free from security rights. The question of whether outstanding inhibitions need to be discharged has been subject to some uncertainty. The Bankruptcy and Diligence etc. Scotland Act 2007 amended the Insolvency Act 1986 to provide that the liquidator in a creditors' voluntary liquidation can sell free of an inhibition against the company.[37] There can be no doubt that the same is true of the liquidator in a compulsory liquidation. It is probable, by contrast, that the liquidator in a members' voluntary liquidation cannot sell free from inhibitions against the company.[38] If there is a floating charge, the charge-holder must consent to the sale, and if a receiver has been appointed under the charge, the receiver must consent.[39]

There is normally no vesting of the company's property in a liquidator. Approximately speaking, the liquidator simply replaces the board of directors. Hence, the disposition is from the company itself,[40] the liquidator simply signing on its behalf, though sometimes the liquidator is made a co-disponer or consenter. The deed should of course narrate the fact of liquidation, giving details of the winding-up order or resolution and appointment of the liquidator. There can be vesting in a liquidator, either under s.25 of the Titles to Land Consolidation (Scotland) Act 1868 or under s.145 of the Insolvency Act 1986, but in practice the use of these provisions is virtually unknown.

Receivership

29–08 Receivership is a means of enforcing a floating charge: no floating charge, no receivership. Floating charges created after September 15, 2003 cannot be enforced by receivership, except for certain specified categories.[41] So receivership is becoming rare, but will not vanish altogether. It is normally extrajudicial: the chargeholder executes an "instrument of appointment" which makes the charge attach (crystallise) and which appoints a receiver to run the company. Judicial receivership is competent but rare. The receiver displaces the board of directors for almost all purposes. When the charge attaches it becomes a real right in security, in favour of the chargeholder. But the chargeholder cannot deal with the property attached: that can be done only by the receiver. Thus,

---

[37] Insolvency Act 1986 s.166(1A).

[38] See further G.L. Gretton, *Law of Inhibition and Adjudication*, 2nd edn (1996), Ch.11; and ROTPB, para.6.26, both of which, however, pre-date the 2007 Act.

[39] In that case, consent by the chargeholder is not necessary. In cases where consent is required, it should be incorporated in the disposition.

[40] Halliday, para.4–05.

[41] Insolvency Act 1986 ss.72A to 72H.

there is a curious asymmetry[42]: the chargeholder has the real right of security but no power to do anything about it while the receiver has the power to enforce but no real right. A company may be simultaneously in liquidation and receivership: in that case the receiver normally has precedence over the liquidator.[43] Receivership does not appear in the Personal Register or Register of Insolvencies, but only in the Companies Register.[44]

One problem thrown up by *Sharp v Thomson*[45] is that in some cases the receiver's power of sale cannot be relied upon because, although the property still belongs to the company, it is subject to a delivered, though unregistered, disposition to a purchaser and so escapes the receivership. In practice the problem seems not to be a major one and the Keeper will normally register a purchase from a receiver without exclusion of indemnity.[46]

Buying from a receiver

In a receivership, there are two key documents, which must be seen and copies 29–09 of which should be kept. The first is the floating charge itself. This must be checked to see that it was properly executed, and that it covers the property now being sold. The standard phrase is "the whole property and undertaking" of the company, and this will cover all immoveable property. But there can be "limited asset floaters", for instance a charge restricted to the moveables. Such a charge would obviously be no basis for selling the heritage. It must also be verified that the charge was duly registered in the Register of Charges. The second key document is the instrument of appointment (or court order, though that would be rare). The buyers should verify that the instrument was validly executed,[47] that the appointee accepted the appointment,[48] and that the receivership was duly registered. They should also verify that the receiver is a qualified insolvency practitioner.

It sometimes happens that there is more than one receiver. In that case the purchaser should insist that both of them execute the disposition. However, if the company is simultaneously in receivership and in liquidation, it seems that there is no need to ask the liquidator to consent.[49] The deed runs in the name of the company, but narrating the details of the receivership, and the receiver signs on the company's behalf.[50]

A floating charge granted within two years of liquidation can be subject to challenge by the liquidator on the ground that it was granted to secure a pre-existing debt.[51] But there would appear to be no danger to a purchaser where there has been no liquidation at the time of the sale. The potential danger arises only where (i) there is a concurrent liquidation; (ii) the sale is by the receiver and not the liquidator; (iii) the liquidator does not consent; and (iv) the charge

---

[42] Much in the law of floating charges and receivership causes difficulty to the rational mind.
[43] *Manley, Ptr*, 1985 S.L.T. 42.
[44] Insolvency Act 1986 ss.53(1) and 54(3).
[45] *Sharp v Thomson*, 1997 S.C. (HL) 66. See further above, para.11–29.
[46] ROTPB, para.5.37.
[47] Insolvency Act 1986 s.53(1).
[48] Insolvency Act 1986 s.53(6)(a).
[49] J.H. Greene and I.M. Fletcher, *Law and Practice of Receivership in Scotland*, 3rd edn (2005), para.7.46.
[50] Halliday, para.4–07; J.H. Greene and I.M. Fletcher, *Law and Practice of Receivership in Scotland*, 3rd edn (2005), para.7–44.
[51] Insolvency Act 1986 s.245(2). In some types of case the challenge period is only one year.

was created within the period of challenge. Even in such cases the charge will usually be at least partly valid.[52] There seems to be no generally accepted good practice, but it is suggested that where (i), (ii) and (iv) apply, the receiver should be required to satisfy the purchaser, either by obtaining the liquidator's consent, or by giving an indemnity, or by providing a title insurance policy, or by producing evidence that the rule is inapplicable.

Whether outstanding heritable securities need to be discharged is a complex question, but in general the purchaser should insist on this, or on a court order enabling the receiver to sell free of them.[53] There is a parallel issue for inhibitions against the company.[54] An inhibition that precedes the creation of the charge must be discharged, or the receiver must obtain judicial authority to sell free of it.[55] An inhibition created at a later stage seems not to affect a receiver's power of sale.[56] However, the Keeper's practice is to exclude indemnity where the selling receiver has not obtained either a discharge of the inhibition or the authority of the court to sell free of it.[57]

Administration

29–10   Like liquidation and receivership, administration is a process for companies only. There is no vesting in the administrator, who takes control of the assets by taking control of the company itself. Administrations have become more common than formerly because most floating charges granted since 2003 cannot be enforced by receivership: in some respects, "administration is the new receivership". An administration is commenced by an "appointment" which may be by (a) the court, (b) the company, (c) the directors of the company or (d) a floating chargeholder.

Buying from an administrator

29–11   The key document is the appointment: this must be checked by the buyer, as should the administrator's status as an insolvency practitioner. The appointment should have been registered in both the Companies Register[58] and in the Personal Register.[59]

The disposition normally runs in the name of the company itself, narrating the appointment and with the administrator signing on its behalf.[60] Ordinarily there is no power to sell free of security rights (e.g. a standard security), except

---

[52] A floating charge is protected from challenge to the extent that it secures new money advanced after its creation. The rule in *Devaynes v Noble* (1816) 1 Merivale 529 (called *Clayton's Case*), adopted into Scots law by *Royal Bank v Christie* (1841) 2 Rob. 118, operates in favour of the chargeholder in such cases.

[53] Insolvency Act 1986 s.61.

[54] See G.L. Gretton, *Law of Inhibition and Adjudication*, 2nd edn (1996), Ch.11; J.H. Greene and I.M. Fletcher, *Law and Practice of Receivership in Scotland*, 3rd edn (2005), Ch.7.

[55] Insolvency Act 1986 s.61.

[56] See *Iona Hotels Ltd v Craig*, 1990 S.C. 330, an arrestment case, but the principle seems the same. The Insolvency Act 1986 s.61(1A) says that such an inhibition is not "effectual", but that seems to be merely in relation to the court's powers under s.61(1).

[57] ROTPB, para.6.23. See further *Armour & Mycroft, Ptrs*, 1983 S.L.T. 45; G.L. Gretton, *Law of Inhibition and Adjudication*, 2nd edn (1996), Ch.10; C. Waelde (ed.), *Professor McDonald's Conveyancing Opinions* (1998), p.176.

[58] Insolvency Act 1986 Sch.B1 para.46(4).

[59] Insolvency (Scotland) Rules 1986 (SI 1986/1915) r.2.19.

[60] Halliday, para.4–06.

with the consent of the creditor concerned, which would involve a discharge, either as a separate deed or within the disposition. However, the court can authorise a sale without consent,[61] and consent is never required in respect of floating charges.[62] Although the point is uncertain, an administrator probably cannot sell free of an undischarged inhibition.[63]

Warrandice, warranties and take-it-or-leave-it

Buyers from an insolvency practitioner will find that the sort of undertakings   29–12 and warranties that they could hope for in an ordinary purchase are difficult or impossible to obtain. The attitude of the seller is, understandably, take-it-or-leave-it. For instance, the usual practice is for absolute warrandice to be granted on behalf of the insolvent person or company and fact and deed warrandice on behalf of the insolvency practitioner.[64] The former is in practice of little value because the person is not worth suing. The latter is equally unlikely to be of value because if there is a title problem it will almost never be covered by fact and deed warrandice. Thus buyers from an insolvency practitioner, unlike ordinary purchasers, are effectively receiving no warrandice worth speaking about.

This is but one aspect of a general theme in insolvency conveyancing: the buyers must accept matters as they are, satisfy themselves, and absorb any risk there may be. As well as the warrandice issue, the seller will be reluctant to warrant the planning position or the building control position or that there is a good title to any moveables included in the sale, and so on. The qualified acceptance is thus likely to knock out many provisions which, in an ordinary case, the seller would be prepared to leave in, or merely to modify. On the whole the buyers must reconcile themselves to the situation, for the seller will usually not budge. But all this means that the buyers' solicitor needs to proceed with extra care, for there is unlikely to be any comeback against the seller if problems emerge.

A related point is that the right of the trustee, or liquidator, or receiver, or administrator, to sell the property will, subject to minor qualifications, be no better than that originally held by the insolvent person or company. So if Donald Debtor buys land, but his title is bad, his trustee in sequestration will, generally speaking, have no better right to sell the land than Donald had. Thus, in addition to the specialities applicable to the insolvency itself, the buyers' agent must make the usual examination of title.

Has the seller gone through the right hoops?

Some of the matters touched on in this chapter are requirements imposed by   29–13 legislation on the seller, of an administrative nature, and sanctioned typically by fines (e.g. registration of a liquidation in the Companies Register). Non-compliance will thus tend to affect the seller rather than the buyers. However, buyers often require evidence that these hoops have been duly gone

---

[61] Insolvency Act 1986 ss.15 and 16 and Sch.B1 para.71.

[62] Insolvency Act 1986 ss.15 and 16 and Sch.B1 para.70.

[63] The provisions of the Insolvency Act 1986 just mentioned probably cannot be construed as applying to inhibitions. See Halliday, para.2–142; G.L. Gretton, *Law of Inhibition and Adjudication*, 2nd edn (1996), Ch.11.

[64] For fact and deed warrandice, see above, para.19–06.

through, perhaps on the basis that there might possibly be situations in which they might have to defend their title on the basis of good faith.

Designation

29–14   The narrative clause of the disposition should narrate the insolvency and design the insolvency practitioner by reference to it, as well as in the ordinary manner. For instance, a disposition by a trustee in sequestration would typically run: "I . . . trustee in sequestration on the sequestrated estate of . . . conform to act and warrant . . . and as such trustee unregistered holder of . . . ".[65]

Buying from a non-Scottish insolvency practitioner

29–15   This chapter is confined to purchases from a Scottish insolvency practitioner, i.e. where the insolvency process is a Scottish one. From time to time a non-Scottish individual or company will have heritable property in Scotland and become formally insolvent under the laws of some other country. That other country is most commonly England, but other jurisdictions can be involved. The subject of "cross-border insolvency" is a complex one that cannot be entered into here, except to say that normally the foreign insolvency practitioner's power of sale will be recognised.[66]

---

[65] For narrative clauses, see above, paras 11–06 to 11–09.
[66] For the common law, see *Ayara v Coghill*, 1921 1 S.L.T. 321. The main legislative provisions are the Insolvency Act 1986 ss.72 and 426; the Insolvency Act 2000 s.14; and the Regulation on Insolvency Proceedings, (EC) No 1346/2000.

CHAPTER 30

NEW HOUSES, AND THE RIGHT TO BUY

NEW HOUSES[1]

Missives

For second-hand houses, the terms of missives are a matter for negotiation. But in the case of new houses, builders usually have a standard style, the terms of which are presented as being non-negotiable. Generally, it is in the form of an offer addressed to the builders to be signed personally by the prospective buyers.

Builders' missives have a reputation for unfairness and inflexibility. At their worst, they may amount to something like this: that the buyers will pay the price whenever the sellers ask for it, whether or not the house has defects, and whether or not the support works (roads, sewers, etc.) have been constructed. Often there is no proper description of the property being bought. The missives may absolve the sellers of the need to show clear searches or planning permission or building warrants or completion certificates. The missives may also reserve to the sellers the right unilaterally to alter the design of the house or the shape of the plot.[2] Reporting in 2003, the Housing Improvement Task Force concluded that such missives "leave the consumer in an unacceptably weak position, particularly if buyers are persuaded to sign the contract on the developer's premises, without having an opportunity to take legal advice first".[3]

Recently there have been signs of builders seeking, so to speak, to put their house in order, perhaps to head off possible legislative intervention. With effect from April 1, 2010 all builders who are registered with the National Housing-Building Council ("NHBC") or certain other organisations—in effect, most builders—have been subject to a Consumer Code for Home Builders, which deals with a range of subjects such as pre-purchase information, the reservation procedure, after-sales service, and complaints.[4] So far as missives are concerned, the Code states that the terms must be "clear and fair" and "comply with the Unfair Terms on Consumer Contracts Regulations 1999" (discussed below).[5] Builders must also advise buyers to appoint a "professional legal adviser" to

30–01

---

[1] See Allan, (1980) 25 J.L.S.S. 17; Brymer, (2002) 60 Prop. L.B. 1.

[2] See e.g. the contract in *Gray v Welsh* [2008] CSIH 11; 2008 G.W.D. 5-84.

[3] Housing Improvement Task Force, *Stewardship and Responsibility: A Policy Frame-work for Private Housing in Scotland* (2003), para.204. The Task Force recommended (paras 207–208) that the Scottish Executive review the subject, seeking a compromise between the interested parties but with the prospect of legislation if no agreement could be reached.

[4] See *http://www.consumercodeforhomebuilders.com/index.html*.

[5] Consumer Code for Home Builders (2010) r.3.1.

represent their interests.[6] The effect of these exhortations—for they are no more than that[7]—remains to be seen.

Assuming the buyer does not simply sign the contract on the spot but seeks legal advice, the solicitors can hardly but advise that the terms should be altered. The builders will resist, but if threatened with the loss of the sale will in practice often agree to changes. At all events, if unfair missives are entered into, the buyers' solicitors must inform their clients of the possible dangers, and do this in writing.

Often, the missives are not the first contract between the parties. It is common for buyers to pay a reservation fee of, say, £500, or even a deposit representing a first instalment of the purchase price.[8] For as long as a reservation agreement is in force, the Consumer Code says, the builder must not enter into a new reservation agreement or conclude missives with another customer for the same house.[9] But if the reservation period is short, this offers little in the way of protection to buyers.[10]

Unfair Terms in Consumer Contracts Regulations 1999

30–02   The Unfair Terms in Consumer Contracts Regulations 1999[11] have already been mentioned. They transpose an EU Directive from 1993.[12] But while it has always been clear that the Regulations apply to the sale and supply of moveable property—reg.6 refers to "goods"—there was doubt as to whether they also apply to land and to buildings on land. That doubt was removed for England by a decision of the Court of Appeal,[13] and it seems improbable that a Scottish court would reach a different conclusion.[14] If that is correct, then the Regulations could be used to strike down unfair terms in builders' missives.

The Regulations are restricted to contracts between a seller or supplier, acting for purposes related to his trade, business or profession, and a "consumer", defined as a natural person acting outside his trade, business or profession.[15] In consequence, the Regulations would not normally affect "ordinary" missives of sale, but they can apply to builders' missives unless the buyer is acting in the course of business or is a company or other juristic person. A term can be challenged as unfair only if it has not been "individually negotiated".[16] It is further provided that "a term shall always be regarded as not having been individually negotiated where it has been drafted in advance and the consumer has therefore not been able to influence the substance of the

---

[6] Consumer Code for Home Builders (2010) r.2.5.

[7] Though presumably NHBC could cancel the registration of the builder for non-compliance.

[8] Whilst deposits in commercial conveyancing are common, in residential conveyancing they are not. New houses are the exception.

[9] Consumer Code for Home Builders (2010) r.2.6. One might add that if the agreement did not have this effect, it would hardly deserve the name of "reservation".

[10] See *McDougall v Heritage Hotels Ltd* [2008] CSOH 54; 2008 S.L.T. 494, where the period was 14 days.

[11] Unfair Terms in Consumer Contracts Regulations 1999 (SI 1999/2083). See e.g. W.C.H. Ervine, *Consumer Law in Scotland*, 4th edn (2008).

[12] Council Directive 93/13/EEC [1993] O.J. L95/29.

[13] *R (Kahtun) v Newham BC* [2005] Q.B. 37.

[14] See also Case C-237/02 *Freiburger Kommunalbauten GmbH Baugesellschaft & Co KG v Hofstetter* [2004] E.C.R. I-03403, a decision of the European Court of Justice which takes for granted that Directive 93/13/EEC applies to land.

[15] SI 1999/2083 regs 3(1), 4(1).

[16] SI 1999/2083 reg.5(1).

term".[17] Where the buyers consult their solicitors on the terms before missives are concluded the builder might perhaps be able to argue that the terms are to be regarded as having been "individually negotiated". Such an argument will not be an easy one, however, for two reasons. In the first place, the burden of proof lies on the builder.[18] Secondly, the fact that *some* of the terms might be individually negotiated is unlikely to affect those which are not, for it is provided that "notwithstanding that a specific term or certain aspects of it in a contract has been individually negotiated, these Regulations shall apply to the rest of a contract if an overall assessment of it indicates that it is a pre-formulated standard contract".[19] In cases where the Regulations apply, the result is an important new set of rights for house buyers faced with standard-form contracts containing unpalatable terms.

The Regulations provide that a contractual term "shall not be binding on the consumer" if it is "unfair", that is to say, if "contrary to the requirement of good faith, it causes a significant imbalance in the parties' rights and obligations arising under the contract, to the detriment of the consumer".[20] Although authority is lacking, and much will depend on the wording of the contract in question, it is easy to see how terms commonly found in builders' missives might be vulnerable to challenge—for example, unreasonable provisions as to payment of the price and the running of interest, or provisions allowing the builder to change the design of the house or the shape of the plot, or to delay completion indefinitely and without financial penalty. There is, however, a specific exemption for adequacy of the price,[21] so that a consumer who has made what turns out to be a bad bargain cannot have the price struck down or altered as "unfair".

Disposition

Builders almost always use *pro forma* dispositions, and sometimes a copy of this is part of the missives. It will contain real burdens either directly or, much more commonly, by reference to a deed of conditions, and of course the clients must decide whether these burdens are acceptable. It is important to check the terms of the disposition carefully. There is a temptation to assume that the builders' solicitors have done a reasonable job. Surprisingly often this is not so. For instance, there may be errors in the description of the property, or the common parts, or amenity areas,[22] and so on. Sometimes the purchasers' solicitors point out some defect only to be met with the reply that the *pro forma* has already been examined by ten other firms without objection. They should not be intimidated by such a reply. If the defect is a real one, so much the worse for the other ten firms, and their clients.

A perennial problem with new houses is that the company prepares plans for the development, but the houses and their boundary fences and walls when built may not correspond exactly with the plans. The company will typically offer a disposition with a plan based on the design plan. This may look

30–03

---

[17] SI 1999/2083 reg.5(2).
[18] SI 1999/2083 reg.5(4).
[19] SI 1999/2083 reg.5(3).
[20] SI 1999/2083 regs 5(1), 8(1). For further guidance on the meaning of "unfair", see regs 5(5), 6(1) and Sch.2.
[21] SI 1999/2083 reg.6(2)(b).
[22] For problems in the description of amenity areas, see above, para.12–25.

beautiful and precise,[23] but it may not correspond to what is on the ground. The Keeper's practice is to delay issuing land certificates to purchasers until the development is complete, so as to minimise the danger of the sort of problems just described. This, however, is not wholly satisfactory for the earlier purchasers. Another implication is that a P16 Report cannot usually be obtained for the purchase of one of the earlier properties.[24]

Building faults and the NHBC

30–04 The builder's obligations are governed by the terms of the contract, read against the background of the common law, under which a builder is obliged to do work competently.[25] If faults emerge then the builder must (depending on the terms of the contract) pay damages. In most cases the builder will be a member of the NHBC,[26] which inspects houses in the course of construction and offers to purchasers a ten-year insurance policy, called Buildmark. The buyer does not pay a separate premium for this: the cost is borne by the builder and is thus in effect included in the overall price. The cover is more extensive for faults notified in the first two years than in the next eight: during the latter period only major faults are covered.[27] The NHBC also covers the risk that the builder might become insolvent before the house has been completed. The insurance is for the benefit of the owner for the time being. Thus if a builder builds a house and sells to Jack, and five years later Jack sells to Jill, the policy does not have to be assigned, though it should be handed over to Jill on settlement. Standard-form offers generally provide that if the house was built within the past ten years it must be covered by Buildmark or some equivalent scheme.[28]

Buildmark is the largest, but not the only, example of a new home warranty scheme, and it may be that the builder participates in some other acceptable scheme. If not, there should be certification from an independent expert.[29] A standard-form certificate can be found in the CML *Lenders' Handbook for Scotland*.[30]

Before settlement

30–05 New houses require various consents in public law.[31] The main ones are planning permission, and building warrant with completion certificate. These should be stipulated for in the missives and exhibited at or before settlement. If roads are not adopted, there should normally be a road bond.[32] Where the purchase is being financed by a loan, these and certain other checks are made

---

[23] Or it may not. Some plans offered by builders are extraordinarily sloppy. They may contain no measurements and no means of anchoring the plot to existing physical features.

[24] The Keeper runs a scheme called the Estate Plan Approval System. Where building companies participate in this the problems are much reduced. See para.12–07.

[25] *Owen v Fotheringham*, 1997 S.L.T. (Sh. Ct) 28.

[26] *http://www.nhbc.co.uk/*.

[27] But establishing liability can be fraught with difficulty: see *Cormack v National House Building Council*, 1998 S.L.T. 1051; and *Hughes v Barratt Urban Construction (Scotland) Ltd*, 2002 G.W.D. 12-353; 2003 G.W.D. 13-452. See also Deutsch, (2001) 41 Civ. P.B. 2.

[28] See e.g. Combined Standard Clauses (2009) cl.14.

[29] But the real value of such certificates may be limited.

[30] See paras 6.7.4–6.7.6. For the CML see above, para.21–05.

[31] See above, Ch.4.

[32] See above, para.4–25.

mandatory by the CML *Lenders' Handbook*.[33] So for example, before solicitors can send the certificate of title to the lender, they must obtain a cover note from the builder confirming that a final inspection has been carried out and that a new home warranty will be provided.[34] In addition, they must have received a completed copy of the CML Disclosure of Incentives Form from the seller's solicitors and must notify the lender if the missives provide for a cashback to the buyer or for part of the price to be satisfied by a non-cash incentive.[35] This follows concern that, in a slow market, the provision of incentives may mean that the real price for a house is considerably lower than the stated figure.[36]

PUBLIC SECTOR HOUSING: THE RIGHT-TO-BUY LEGISLATION

Introduction

One of the slogans of Thatcherism was "a property-owning democracy". Soon 30–06 after coming to power in 1979, the Conservatives introduced legislation to allow the tenants of council houses, and tenants renting from certain other types of landlord, compulsorily to purchase their houses or flats at below-market prices. The Scottish legislation was at first contained in the Tenants Rights etc. (Scotland) Act 1980 and is now in the Housing (Scotland) Act 1987, as amended, especially by the Housing (Scotland) Act 2001 and the Housing (Scotland) Act 2010. Judged by the number of sales, the legislation has been a considerable success. There was an initial rush to buy, as might be expected, but more than 20 years' later, in 2002/03, almost 19,000 houses were still being sold. Since then there has been a rapid decline in sales, partly due to the less favourable rules introduced by the 2001 Act. In the latest year for which figures are available (2009/10) only just over 2,000 sales were completed.[37] Nonetheless with around half a million houses having been sold altogether, the resulting depletion of the social housing stock is regarded as unsustainable. Accordingly, with effect from March 2, 2011, and subject to some exceptions, the 2010 Act brought the right to buy to an end for new tenants[38] and also for existing tenants taking on the lease of a house not previously let.[39] The right to buy, however, remains for existing tenants, except in certain "pressured areas" (discussed below) where it has been suspended.

Over the years the right-to-buy legislation has generated a large body of case law and the following is only an overview.[40] A broad distinction can be made between tenancies entered into before September 30, 2002 and those entered into after that date but before March 2, 2011. These are usually called, respectively, "preserved" and "modernised" tenancies.

---

[33] See e.g. paras 6.7.7 and 6.8.

[34] CML *Lenders' Handbook*, para.6.7.2.

[35] CML *Lenders' Handbook*, paras 6.4.1–6.4.4.

[36] The requirement met with a hostile reception from some solicitors. For the debate, see Reid and Gretton, *Conveyancing 2008*, pp.66–67.

[37] *http://www.scotland.gov.uk/Topics/Statistics/*.

[38] Including those returning to social housing after a break.

[39] Housing (Scotland) Act 1987 ss.61F and 61ZA.

[40] A valuable introduction is the Scottish Government's booklet, *Your Right to Buy your Home: A Guide for Scottish Secure Tenants* (2011).

The rules for preserved tenancies

30–07 Those eligible to buy are those who have held a tenacy from a local authority, or certain other public-sector landlords, since before September 30, 2002. Certain exceptions exist.[41] The amount of the discount—i.e. the amount by which the price is less than a fair market price—depends partly on whether the property is a flat or a house and partly on how long the applicant has been a tenant. For a flat the discount ranges from a minimum of 44 per cent to a maximum of 70 per cent. Two per cent is added for each year after an initial qualifying period of two years. For a house the discount ranges from 32 per cent to a maximum of 60 per cent, with 1 per cent being gained for each year. Thus a tenant of flat of 14 years' standing would get a discount of 68 per cent, and a tenant of a house of 20 years' standing would get a discount of 50 per cent.

The rules for modernised tenancies

30–08 For tenancies starting on or after September 30, 2002 (but before March 2, 2011) the rules are less favourable. The discount is the same regardless of whether the property is a flat or a house, but is lower than before. The minimum is 20 per cent and the maximum is 35 per cent, but the discount cannot exceed £15,000. The discount rises by 1 per cent for each year after the qualifying period of five years. Thus a tenant of six years' standing would get a discount of 21 per cent and a tenant of 19 years' standing would get a discount of 34 per cent, in each case, however, capped at a maximum discount of £15,000. Local authorities have power to designate areas as "pressured areas" for a maximum period of ten years.[42] The effect is to suspend the right to buy for modernised (but not preserved) tenancies. Extensive use has been made of this power, especially in the Highlands and in areas such as Aberdeenshire.

Procedure

30–09 The first step is to complete and submit the official "application to purchase" form.[43] The landlord will arrange for the property to be valued, at its own expense, and should then, within two months of receiving the application to purchase, make a formal offer to sell, at the valuation figure less the applicable discount. The tenant has two months after that to decide whether or not to accept. A tenant who considers that the landlord is not following the legislative requirements can take the matter to the Lands Tribunal.

The buyers' solicitors should carefully check the terms of the offer to sell.[44] They should ensure that the discount has been calculated correctly. They should ideally inspect the property, because there may be problems about shared amenity areas, access routes and so on. Council properties were not originally constructed with individual ownership in mind.

---

[41] For instance, some types of tied property, property specially adapted for the infirm, and so on. These exceptions have generated a great deal of litigation: see e.g. *Robb v Tayside Police Board*, 2009 S.L.T. (Lands Tr) 23.

[42] Housing (Scotland) Act 1987 ss.61B and 61C.

[43] 1987 Act ss.63–66. The form is prescribed in the Right to Purchase (Application Form) (Scotland) Order 2011 (SSI 2011/97).

[44] For disputes as to its terms, see e.g. *Ogg v Perth and Kinross Council*, 2005 Hous. L.R. 18.

Missives are concluded when the tenant sends to the landlord a "notice of acceptance" of the offer to sell.[45] Thereafter matters cease to be regulated by the legislation,[46] and so ordinary law and conveyancing practice apply. For instance, if the tenant dies after missives but before settlement, the tenant's rights pass to his or her executor.[47]

Clawback: repayment of discount

If the new owner "sells or otherwise disposes" of the property within three 30–10 years from the date of the notice of acceptance, the discount or part of it is repayable.[48] If this happens in the first year, the whole discount is repayable; if in the second year, the proportion falls to 66 per cent; if in the third year it falls to 33 per cent. After the expiry of the three-year period no discount is repayable. This contingent obligation to repay all or part of the discount is secured to the former landlord by a standard security, known as the discount standard security. The precise meaning of the provisions dealing with repayment of discount[49] has been the subject of some controversy.[50] The discount standard security ranks after a standard security securing a loan for the purchase price.[51]

Funding from a family member

It is quite common for a tenant—and especially an elderly tenant, who usually 30–11 qualifies for maximum discount—to exercise the right to buy at the suggestion of, and with finance provided by, a grown-up child, or other relative, or a friend (we will use the term "funder"). The arrangement is then commonly that when the tenant/purchaser dies, the property will pass to the funder. This can be done simply by a will, but the risk to the funder is that a will is revocable. Sometimes some form of contract is entered into, or a trust created in favour of the funder. The danger of such schemes is that if they are entered into within the three-year period they may amount to a "disposal", thereby triggering liability to repay the discount. "A disposal under section 72", it has been said, "need not involve a formal conveyance. It is sufficient that the former tenant puts it out of his power to deal with the house as owner".[52] Moreover, if liability is triggered, the full 100 per cent discount would be repayable because the "disposal" would typically be at the time of the purchase, and thus within the first 12 months after the exercise of the right to buy.[53]

It is difficult to be certain as to whether such schemes trigger liability, because the legislation does not define "disposal". However, in practice repayment may not be demanded simply because the ex-landlord is unaware of the arrangement. It is difficult to give reliable advice as to how to arrange matters

---

[45] If the landlord miscalculates the discount, the missives are void: see *McLaughlin v Thenew Housing Association Ltd*, 2007 Hous. L.R. 18.

[46] Apart from possible repayment of the discount.

[47] *Cooper's Exrs v City of Edinburgh DC*, 1991 S.C. (HL) 5.

[48] Housing (Scotland) Act 1987 s.72.

[49] Housing (Scotland) Act 1987 ss.72 and 73.

[50] *Jack's Exrs v Falkirk DC*, 1992 S.L.T. 5; *Clydebank DC v Keeper of the Registers*, 1994 S.L.T. (Lands Tr) 2; *McDonald's Tr v Aberdeen City Council*, 2000 S.C. 185.

[51] Housing (Scotland) Act 1987 s.72(5).

[52] *McDonald's Trustee v Aberdeen City Council*, 2000 S.C. 185 at 192H, per Lord Gill.

[53] Actually if the agreement is entered into before the right-to-buy missives have been concluded, then there is an argument (perhaps an absurd one), based on the wording of s.72, that it is not a qualifying disposal.

so as to avoid entirely the danger of triggering liability for discount. One safe method is simply to secure the finance by standard security, but that will not affect the question of who will take the property on death. Moreover, if the value of the house rises, the amount secured will no longer reflect the value of the house. Another possibility is to confer on the relative an option to buy (on the death of the tenant/purchaser) at a fixed sum (representing the original finance), which option can then be secured by standard security. Such an option would probably not be a "disposal" in itself, though it would become one at the date of its exercise, which, however, with any luck would be outwith the three-year period.

We cannot here give detailed analysis of this complex subject, but will conclude with two words of warning. The first is that such arrangements can be complex to draft and set up, not only because of the need to steer round the "disposal" rules, but also because of the need to regulate matters properly between the parties, for instance in relation to insurance, upkeep, the possibility that the tenant/purchaser might wish to move house, and so on.[54] The second warning is that in all such arrangements different solicitors must act for each party.

---

[54] For an instructive example, see *Hutchison v Graham's Exrx* [2006] CSOH 15; 2006 S.C.L.R. 587.

CONVEYANCING INDEX